Voices from the Catholic Worker

Voices from the Catholic Worker

Compiled and edited by *ROSALIE RIEGLE TROESTER*

 TEMPLE UNIVERSITY PRESS ✦ *Philadelphia*

Temple University Press, Philadelphia 19122
Copyright © 1993 by Temple University,
except interviews with Eileen Egan, which
are © Eileen Egan, and interviews with Michael
Harrington, which are © Stephanie Harrington
All rights reserved
Published 1993
Printed in the United States of America

The paper used in this publication meets the
minimum requirements of American National
Standard for Information Sciences—Permanence of Paper for Printed Library Materials,
ANSI Z39.48-1984 ∞

Library of Congress Cataloging-in-Publication Data
Voices from the Catholic Worker / compiled and
    edited by Rosalie Riegle Troester.
    p.   cm.
Includes bibliographical references and index.
ISBN 1-56639-058-3 (hard : alk. paper).—
ISBN 1-56639-059-1 (pbk. : alk. paper)
    1. Catholic Worker Movement.
    2. Day, Dorothy, 1891–1980.
    3. Oral history.
I. Troester, Rosalie Riegle.
BX810.C393V65   1993
267'.182—dc20   92-33411

For Frank Wolfarth Walsh,
who introduced me to Dorothy Day
and the Catholic Worker,
and in memory of Fr. John W. Troester,
who showed us love in action

You know, the Catholic Worker is not a liberal movement. It's a radical movement, and there's a sharp difference. Liberals say, "Hey! The homeless aren't being fed. Let's march on City Hall." Radicals say, "The homeless aren't being fed. Let's feed them."

—*Fr. Mike Baxter*

I don't see the Catholic Worker as having the remotest thing to do with being Catholic. I justify it on logical and rational terms. On terms having to do with the distribution of wealth. Having to do with environmentalism. Having to do with the elevation of human dignity. The Catholic Worker makes so much sense to me on all those levels that I don't see a religious justification as necessary.

—*David Stein*

I don't think Dorothy is the test of the Catholic Worker. She is simply there. But because she was there, for the rest of history, we have to not only think about the Gospel but think about the extraordinary and indigestible witness she gave to us. Dorothy helps to sharpen the edge of the Gospel, but the Catholic Worker isn't the movement of the followers of Dorothy Day. She's not the center point—the Gospel is.

—*Jim Forest*

Contents

Acknowledgments

THIS is a hard one: Do I list the people it's "impossible to thank" in order of importance or chronologically? I'll take the easy way out. First, the Saginaw peace community of the Vietnam time. We called it the Saginaw Valley Peace Watch, and it was through this group and through my friendship with Frank Walsh, then owner of the Old Town Bookstore, that I first read and then met Dorothy Day. There were two Catholic Worker houses in Saginaw during the sixties. St. Alexius House was started by Frank and others from Saginaw and Midland, including Bill and Mary Shepherd, whose daughter plays an important part in this book. Later, Jim and Schatzi Hanink started Thomas Merton House while Jim was teaching at Saginaw Valley College. Our current peace group continues in the same tradition of nonviolent resistance. Called the Home for Peace and Justice and animated by Dominican Sisters Ardeth Platte and Carol Gilbert, the Home has been an inspiration. To all these Saginaw friends, I owe the beginnings of this book.

Next would come Studs Terkel. When I first thought of doing an oral history of the Catholic Worker, I called Mr. Terkel and asked if he would teach me his trade. He asked a few questions, told me the book was a great idea, and politely said no. He said I wouldn't learn to do oral history by following another person around, that I should just plunge in and do it. He said if it worked, I'd know it. It did work. Another important literary influence is Robert Coles. His two books on the Worker and his commitment to illuminating the moral lessons in our lives have been an inspiration to me.

Phillip M. Runkel, curator of the Catholic Worker Archives at Marquette University in Milwaukee, has been my anchor since 1985. With unfailing courtesy and patience, Phil has responded to many requests for information, and I am honored that the tapes of *Voices from the Catholic Worker,* as well as all transcripts and related material, will be part of the rich repository of Catholic Worker research at Marquette. Whenever people tell me that the Catholic Worker has fragmented since Dorothy Day's death, I think of Phil Runkel and the cohesiveness and stability he provides.

Of course, all the Catholic Workers are deserving of special thanks. And here I include not only the 208 whom I interviewed but the other hundred or so who provided hospitality, interview leads, and, most of all, encouragement. This book

is theirs, not mine. Catholic Worker scholars William Miller, Harry Murray, and Pat Coy also gave me valuable lessons. I thank the CW photographers, too—Tina Sipula, Mary Farrell, Carolyn Prieb, and the other photographers whose works I retrieved from the archives. The narrators themselves fit me into their busy lives, often on scant notice, and were generous with their honesty, their insight, and their time. I thank the many people whose voices I couldn't fit into these pages, particularly the Cleveland CW community, Mike Kerwan of Washington, D.C., Mike and Nettie Cullen, whom I interviewed in Clonfert, Ireland, and Lorine Hewson of Garden City, Kansas, who traveled eight hours by train to meet me in Kansas City.

My colleagues at Saginaw Valley State University are also deserving of gratitude. Dr. Robert Yien and other members of the administration provided research support over a period of five years. This support, in the form of grants, released time, and a sabbatical, gave me time away from teaching to collect and edit the interviews and to write the book. I must also thank my colleagues in the College of Arts and Behavioral Sciences, especially historian Dr. Thomas Renna, for their understanding and support as I ventured into a new field. I received similar support, if not similar comprehension, from those in my own Department of English. Most of them couldn't understand why a teacher of writing and women's literature would go chasing all over the country with a tape recorder. Yet they were encouraging and always supportive, willingly picking up my departmental duties so I could finish the project.

Carol Shuler, transcriber par excellence, is a professional secretary in the best sense of the word, catching mistakes, going the extra mile, taking care of the details that slip by my disorganized mind. But more than that, for five years, she was the only one who really knew what I was doing and believed in it. As she typed the entire six thousand pages of original transcripts, the voices spoke to her, too, and we spent hours discussing the people and the ideas. I can never thank her enough for providing this community for me. She is not only my co-worker, she is my confidante and my friend.

Thanks, too, to my other friends—in the Saginaw community, in my alumnae community of St. Mary's College, and most surely within my family. I thank my "first husband," Edmund Meagher Troester, for his continued acceptance of an obsession he does not share, and our four daughters—Kathy, Maura, Ann, and Meg—for their cooperation and understanding. Maura also has been professionally helpful, reading portions of the interviews in the early stages and giving valuable suggestions as the manuscript neared completion. A drama critic in Chicago, Maura is a better writer than her mother and her ideas have made this a better book.

Thanks go, too, to Michael Ames, editor-in-chief at Temple University Press, for believing in this project, and to Deborah Stuart, production editor, Suzanne Schafer, copy editor, and Barbara Williams, book designer.

The old Beatles title "I Get By with a Little Help from My Friends" has been my motto for years, as I have always found grace in community rather than solitude. Creating this book has greatly expanded my community. So a final gift of gratitude goes to those I have forgotten to thank. You are all a part of who I am. All mistakes and misjudgments here are, of course, my own.

Introductory Notes

As my father would have said, the Catholic Worker stuck in my craw. I got my first taste in 1968 when I met Dorothy Day and some of the Workers at Thomas Merton House in Saginaw, Michigan. I didn't know how to cough it up, and I wouldn't swallow it, wouldn't make the adjustments necessary to actually *be* someone called a Catholic Worker. So I coated it with loved busyness, with going to school and teaching and raising daughters and making some mild mischief at the Pentagon. The Catholic Worker stayed in my throat, a sometimes uncomfortable irritant, for almost fifteen years.

One day I was playing around with some interviews I'd collected from my students. Trying to capture their personalities on paper, I wrote oral history portraits like the one Studs Terkel had drawn of Dorothy Day in *Hard Times*. Then it hit me: I could do this with the followers of Dorothy Day, could combine my interest in oral history with my interest in the Worker. Maybe I could even cough up a book and get this lump of Catholic Worker ideas out of my system once and for all. That was in 1980. Twelve years later, I've coughed up a book.

You know, a key to Aristotle's ethics is a sense that you learn by imitating others. That's what tradition is all about. Dorothy handed on tradition to us. She didn't start something incredibly revolutionary and new; deep down she and Peter Maurin and all the others knew that what they were hitting on was really very old. They were handing something on, they weren't starting anything. None of us are called to start a community; we're called to join one and to be faithful to one. That's what Dorothy did. She joined one and said, "Hey, I'm going to take it seriously!" —Fr. Mike Baxter

Voices from the Catholic Worker is about people who take this community and its values seriously. Because they do, my work as a collector of their experiences has been easy. Thanks to the foresight of Dorothy Day and Will Ready, Marquette University librarian, box after box of Catholic Worker writing—newsletters, correspondence, pictures, the iconography and hagiography of a movement—finds its way to the Catholic Worker Archives in Milwaukee. There, under the careful eye of archivist Phillip M. Runkel, it is catalogued and made accessible to scholars and other curious people. This archive, the ongoing record of a movement, provides cohesiveness in itself. So do the many newsletters that crisscross between the approximately 130 Catholic Worker houses of hospitality. So do the national gatherings that are held every few years.

I began my research by traveling to Milwaukee, reading in the archives and learning the bones of the movement. Supported by what I'd learned there and from scholars such as William Miller and Mel Piehl, I began the interviews, starting in 1986 with Saginaw friends and then moving out to Tom Cordaro and Fr. Tom Lumpkin at the first Saginaw Faith and Resistance Retreat. The last two interviews were with Chuck Matthei and Robert Ellsberg at the Sojourners Conference in Grand Rapids in August 1991. In between, I listened to over two hundred Catholic Workers. Some of them work quietly in the eddies of our cities; some are prominent in the small world of the Catholic Left. Some are committed, some are disillusioned (these were harder to locate), some are "pioneers," happy to pass on the tradition, and some are young people who need to hear the stories. Many are "lifers," as John Williams calls them, people who have chosen the Worker as a permanent vocation. I listened to feminists who have trouble with the Catholic Church, as I do, to priests who told me they find in the Worker a place to live honestly, to several "Catholic Worker kids," and to homosexuals who feel alienated even in Catholic Worker communities. Catholic, Protestant, Jewish, non-denominated. Young and old, male and female, married and single. Mostly white, articulate, educated, and middle class. I heard diverse and sometimes conflicting viewpoints, but also an underlying agreement. For a movement that purports to be independent and anarchistic, I found a surprising community between individuals and also a community between communities.

Robert Coles says self-disclosure is an American phenomenon.* (My daughter Maura thinks perhaps it's a disease.) Collecting the narratives was exciting because many Workers *do* value self-disclosure and are experienced in telling their stories. If a potential subject showed hesitation, I did not press, but few requests for interviews were refused and only one person decided not to be included in the book after speaking with me. When I had individual contacts, I'd write ahead, but even if I didn't, Workers were cooperative, often on short notice and at some inconvenience. One delightful subject answered my usual opening question: "How did you get to the Worker?" with one word—"Hitchhiked!" But for most, this single question erased the artificiality of the interview situation and started us off. The narrators truly would "confide their tales to a passing stranger," and their openness is a tribute to their sense of self-worth and of the worth in their lives. They take themselves seriously (sometimes too much so, I'm afraid, but then we all do). Mostly it's the ideas they take seriously, and you will find these ideas in the pages that follow.

* Robert Coles, *The Call of Stories: Teaching and the Moral Imagination.*

Catholic Workers know the legends of the movement—the scripture, if you will—and I found this knowing cohesive. Passages from Day's *The Long Loneliness* and aphorisms from Peter Maurin's "Easy Essays" are quoted with regularity. Catholic Worker jokes are also part of the legend, and you'll hear some of these in *Voices*, although not as many as I would have liked. When I travel to gatherings or Worker houses now, we laugh more, especially about my mechanical ineptness with even a simple tape recorder. We also chuckle at how circumstances and perceptions have changed since the interviews took place.

I came to the Catholic Worker not as a sociologist or an oral historian but as a student with a little knowledge about the Worker—all of it from reading—who wanted to know how the theory worked out in practice. Interview theorists might call me a participant observer, but I rarely had time to observe or participate. I'd blow in, sit down, listen deeply, and then leave. But I learned, as a student should, learned about the Catholic Worker movement itself and how cohesive it really is, but also about how language works as it changes from speech to the printed word, and about how the mind works and doesn't.

When I began the project, I thought if I just looked long enough and deep enough and at enough Workers, the truth would emerge and I'd be able to define the Catholic Worker. I planned to wrap the project up neatly in an epilogue titled "Toward a Definition." But Jay Dolan of Notre Dame's Center for the Study of American Catholicism was right. He has said that "trying to define the Catholic Worker is like trying to bottle morning fog." I couldn't do it. Perhaps no one can.

A very nice thing happened the last time I was in jail. Ronnie's mother was holding our baby and she was telling her, "Mommy's cooking dinner, and Grandad's watching TV, and I get to hold you. And Daddy's out making . . . no, I can't say that. Daddy's out . . ." And she couldn't think of a good description. She finally said, "Daddy's out feeding the poor." I like that description, that connection. I like it when the common categories don't fit. I get very nervous if what we're doing is so normal that it's easy to describe.
—Larry Purcell

What I do here is what I tell my writing students: "Show, don't tell." So there are many descriptions, not one, many truths, not *the* truth. These truths sometimes bump up against each other, and that, too, is mirrored in this book. What individual readers see, react to, and remember, will depend largely on what they bring to the reading. But I hope the truths in *Voices* bump up against the truths readers hold—challenge them, inspire them, worry them, and stick in their craw. I hope some readers will swallow the Catholic Worker and go to a Catholic Worker house or start their own.

I'm concerned about one group of readers: people who know some of the narrators personally. "That's not the Tina Sipula I know!" or "Surely, Jeff Dietrich never said *that!*" There's always a gap between how we create ourselves and how others see us. It was Chuck Trapkus of the Rock Island Catholic Worker who pointed out to me the difficulty in separating what we think about people from what they write. So those who know a speaker well may find it easy to see some words here as hypocritical or too idealistic. Like the rest of us, Catholic Workers rarely live up to their spoken intentions. These contradictions will be especially sharp in a community where someone has left "with blood on the floor," to use Chris Montesano's phrase.

I should say a word about the Catholic Worker's language. Because they read the newsletters and newspapers of the movement, and often the historical literature, most Catholic Workers speak their language well. Many readers won't.

> *When I first picked up the* Catholic Worker, *they had their own kind of "in" language. It struck me that you had to read other things before you could fully understand what they were saying. The paper was a part of something, not something that stood on its own. "Personalism" was a term and "culture" . . . and "cultivation." Used like code words. It was quirky.*
>
> —John Williams

If the code appears difficult, bear with it and let the meanings grow as they did for me. Even a seemingly simple concept like personalism needs many illustrations before we're really comfortable with it. Incidentally, it was nice to realize that the interview method itself illustrates a facet of personalism.

Methodology

My interview model was conversation, not survey, and no two interviews were alike. I asked people questions about their backgrounds, their motivations, and their goals, using Theodor Reik's listening theory to develop a dynamic with each narrator, trying to hear where he or she wanted the conversation to go. One of my techniques was to ask what questions they would ask themselves; if the rapport was good, we'd travel some interesting and previously unexplored territory. If a narrator indicated he or she felt uncomfortable about a question, I'd usually back off, or suggest that one of us turn off the tape.

There are several restricted tapes and some narrators shared secrets that will never be repeated. This is how it should be; I set out to learn, not to collect gossip. After I had completed the interviews and was editing the transcripts, I read Michael Frisch's work on sharing authority (or author-ity) with those I interviewed and realized that "our book" does just that.* The narrators are the authors of their own texts, and I have done the compiling and the editing. There's a contradiction here, though. On one hand, I shared authority by sending each narrator a copy of his or her edited transcript; on the other hand, I'm more selective than many oral historians, so my editing input is heavier than most. (This text includes about seven percent of the 6,600 transcribed pages.) And while I've frequently removed my original questions from the narrative, I am still present—in the questions I asked, in the selecting, the editing, and the arranging—more present than the actual number of my words reveals. In some chapters, I've combined conversations that occurred separately and have written transitions between speeches, creating mythical roundtable discussions. (If you want the unvarnished speech, go to the Marquette Archives and read the verbatim version of the tapes, or listen to the tapes themselves. There you'll get all the interruptions, the pauses and fresh starts, the tag ending tics that plague our spoken language.)

I think my approval technique eased some of these contradictions. As I edited each interview, I made preliminary decisions on what to include in the book and put the words in bold in the transcript. These transcripts were then sent to individual narrators with a letter asking them to check their words for accuracy and telling them they could make changes before signing the text as "approved" and sending it back to me.

The responses to these mailings ranged widely: almost everyone eventually returned his or her corrected transcript. A few didn't read them; some read and made a few corrections. Some made many emendations, clarifying ideas, finishing sentences, and so on. These changes were added to the archive copy of the transcript and to the appropriate section of the book. Some—I'm thinking particularly of Jonathan Kirkendall and Kathe McKenna here—added elaborate updates, and these, too, were included. Occasionally the changes contradicted what was said originally, and in such cases, I usually included both versions. Two narrators, understandably shy after years of being misquoted, asked to see the final selections for the book and I complied.

Organization

These interviews, like the Worker itself, have refused to fit into neat categories. History and work and person are intertwined, just as they are in life. In

---

* Michael Frisch, *Shared Authority*. After thinking about Frisch's ideas and talking to him, I changed the title page of the book to read "Compiled and edited by Rosalie Riegle Troester," instead of listing myself as author.

fact, Bob Chaps gave me a wonderful metaphor to describe this. He compared the Catholic Worker experience to a tapestry and said that when one looks at a tapestry from the back side, one sees another picture. Perhaps oral history also gives another picture, one with more loose threads and less design than conventional historical scholarship but also more texture and more input from the two "weavers," the narrator and the recorder.

Part One is history, not a comprehensive history of the movement, but the memories of several generations—the pioneers before World War II, the lonely voices from the fifties, and several voices from the sixties and seventies. Because I came to the Worker through the antiwar movement, my questions reflect this interest; thus pacifism and resistance to militarism may receive a disproportionate share of the narrative in all five parts. The first two chapters are followed by memories of Dorothy Day, Peter Maurin, and Ammon Hennacy, and then an interview with the late Michael Harrington, recorded when he was in remission from cancer. He died one year later. My brother-in-law, to whom this book is dedicated, died of leukemia a month after Mike and I talked; it was an emotional interview for both of us.

Part Two describes the work, and most of its chapters are arranged as roundtable discussions, that is, as constructed conversations among many participants rather than the rambling dialogue between two people that occurs during an actual interview. For these chapters, I've selected portions from many transcripts. Roundtables are a traditional CW way to engage in "clarification of thought," Peter Maurin's name for the intellectual work that was so much a part of his message. When I compiled these roundtables, I imagined them as occurring at a mythical national gathering, one modeled after the two I've attended and after the Midwest gatherings held every fall in Sugar Creek, Iowa. For identification, I've added the city where each narrator lives or the place or places where the primary Worker commitment occurred.

Part Two begins with beginnings, with how people come to the Worker (and sometimes to the Catholic Church), and continues with why they came—to provide hospitality, to start agrarian communities, to resist U.S. militarism, to combine work and scholarship. Because the Worker started in New York, the reflections of those who live, or have lived, in the "mother house" are also in this overview section.

Part Three is about living together. It includes a roundtable on the concept of community, a collection of interviews about how married couples with children are living as Workers, and narrations from five "Catholic Worker kids."

Part Four, "Doing the Work," shows how individual houses, and individual Workers, live a Catholic Worker life. Six communities are treated in individual chapters, not because the houses are more important than others, but because the interviews had strong internal coherence. In two more chapters, house descriptions and histories are grouped to show how different people work out Catholic Worker philosophy to fit their circumstances. One individual Worker and one family tell their stories as separate chapters.

Part Five mixes many voices, as Workers discuss the Catholic Worker as Catholic. Beginning with a roundtable on spirituality, this section continues with a discussion on relationships between Catholic Worker and Catholic Church, concluding with three moral issues that have caused conflict within both the Worker and the larger Christian community—abortion, homosexuality, and the role of women. Because abortion and homosexuality have not been widely discussed in actual sessions for clarification of thought, I compiled these chapters as excerpts from individual interviews, not as discussions.

For the past ten years, people have been saying that the Catholic Worker is flying apart as a movement. During the eighties, deep conflict within the New York community contributed to this sense of disintegration. In researching and writing this book, however, I found a much stronger and more cohesive movement than I expected. The conflicts have not disappeared, and in fact may appear to be spreading, as the number of houses grows as well as the diversity of those who use the Catholic Worker name. But Nina Polcyn Moore once told me: "With Dorothy gone, maybe from now on, all the people in the different houses will have to live with each other, grow with each other, suffer with each other, help each other out of confusions." I see the ongoing concern about who is or isn't a Catholic Worker as the com-unity Nina is talking about. One doesn't worry about one's Catholic Worker brothers and sisters without an underlying love. The concern with identity, the newsletters, the archives, the national gatherings—all these point to a unity that will endure. This book is organized to reflect that strength.

Dorothy Day told Robert Coles, "We write in response to what we care about, what we believe to be important, what we want to share with others."* I care about the Catholic Worker, care about the Workers. Recording the interviews gave me community without the reverse commitment of joining one, and for seven years, writing the book took up so much of my time that I didn't have to be doing the work. Or rather, the writing was the work. It is finished. The Worker remains in my throat.

* Robert Coles, *Dorothy Day: A Radical Devotion,* p. xi.

PART ONE

History

CHAPTER 1

In the Beginning Was . . .

There's such a sense of participating in this great adventure. Dorothy
was a part of the progressive, heroic struggle to make our nation
a better place and to keep alive the light of justice and liberty. She
lived in Greenwich Village and actually knew Eugene Debs and Emma
Goldman and Jack Reed. I get chills whenever I think that I'm part of
that. You know, too, it was wonderful to hear from Dorothy of the rich
tradition of brokenness and sinfulness and scandal that those of us in
the Catholic Worker come from. We're so far less than perfect, but
we're called by this incredible ideal.

—Jeff Dietrich

DOROTHY Day met Peter Maurin in 1932. She was a recent Roman Catholic
convert with strong ties to pacifism and the American Left. He was a French
peasant whose philosophy developed in the decentralist and personalist tradition
of Emmanuel Mournier and Nicolas Berdyaev. Both were writers. Out of that
meeting grew a newspaper called the *Catholic Worker.* And out of that newspaper
grew houses of hospitality that provided meals and often lodging to those made
homeless by the Great Depression. As Day was to write in her autobiography,
The Long Loneliness:

We were just sitting there talking when Peter Maurin came in. We were just
sitting there talking when lines of people began to form saying, "We need
bread." We could not say, "Go, be thou filled." If there were six small loaves
and a few fish, we had to divide them. There was always bread.

We were just sitting there talking and people moved in on us. Let those
who can take it, take it. Some moved out and that made room for more.
And somehow the walls expanded. We were just sitting there talking and
someone said, "Let's all go live on a farm." It was as casual as all that I often
think. It just came about. It just happened.

The idea of applying basic Christianity to social problems spread rapidly throughout the country. Emanating from the first houses on the Lower East Side of Man-

hattan, houses of hospitality opened in Buffalo, Cleveland, Detroit, South Bend, Chicago, Minneapolis, San Francisco, Los Angeles, and other cities. People also started Catholic Worker farms, which attempted—usually unsuccessfully—to live out Maurin's agrarian ideal.

Both Day and Maurin traveled indefatigably, visiting Catholic Worker houses and speaking at colleges and churches—wherever they could find audiences. These audiences diminished, however, as the clouds of World War II shadowed the country. Day's uncompromising pacifism was hard listening for a nation angered by the excesses of totalitarianism; the burgeoning war economy diminished the need for hospitality to the unemployed, and many Catholic Worker houses closed.

The issue of pacifism caused deep conflict within the movement, and by the end of the war only ten houses of hospitality remained. Day was saddened and shocked at the destruction of Hiroshima and Nagasaki and wrote forcefully against the jubilation reported by the secular press, urging instead that the United States "destroy the two billion dollars' worth of equipment, . . . destroy all the formulas, put on sackcloth and ashes, weep and repent."*

The fifties were a time of hanging on, with Day's influence muted and a rag-tag group of radicals resisting the civil defense drills and continuing to serve those afflicted by alcoholism and other chronic causes of poverty. However, as "elder statesman" Tom Cornell points out, it was the lonely forties and fifties that deepened Day's spirituality and gave her the strength to persevere throughout the sixties. The fifties also saw the emergence of Michael Harrington, the most famous CW alumnus, and Ammon Hennacy, one of the movement's most colorful anarchists.

It wasn't until Vietnam that the Catholic Worker began to grow again in numbers and influence, with individual Workers among the first and most forceful voices against the war. Several Catholic Workers were jailed for public draft card burnings; Workers Tom Lewis, Jim Forest, Michael Cullen, Larry Rosebaugh, Chuck Fullenkamp, Johnny Baranski, John Williams, and probably others were imprisoned for destroying draft files. And it was in the sixties that I discovered the Worker through my involvement with the Saginaw Valley Peace Watch and the two short-lived houses started in Saginaw during that decade.

During the seventies, Dorothy's heart condition restricted her travel, but she continued to lead the movement from her room at Maryhouse, a former music school in Manhattan purchased to provide housing for homeless women. When Day died in 1980, reporters asked *Catholic Worker* editor Peggy Scherer what

* Dorothy Day, "Atom Bomb," *Catholic Worker,* November 1945.

would happen. "We may have lost Dorothy, but we still have the Gospel," she replied. Torn by conflict and a continuing diversity, but united by common aims and means and armed with a radical reading of the Gospel, the movement continues.* Today, there are over 130 farms and houses of hospitality in the United States, Europe, and Australia, communities of Catholic Workers who follow the social and spiritual vision of Dorothy Day and Peter Maurin.

I think we tend not to understand or to value how social change happens. We don't hold up as examples the grassroots movements like the labor movement, the women's movement, the peace movement, the civil rights movement—all of which have obtained tremendously important victories in the short history of this nation. We don't teach that grassroots history. And because we don't teach it, we don't believe in it. We don't believe that kind of change is possible, but those movements teach us that it works, if we would but attend to them. One way to honor that history is to tell the stories. To tell them around a dinner table, tell them at home in the families, incorporate them into our family and individual lives.   —Pat Coy

This chapter presents some of these stories, told in roughly chronological order. Joe Zarrella was one of Dorothy Day's first recruits and is still one of the lights of the Catholic Worker movement, loved by both his contemporaries and the young people, remembered always for his humor, his honesty, and his insights. I interviewed Joe and his wife, Alice, at their home in Tell City, Indiana. His stories add to the myth, build the tradition.

Joe Zarrella: I wasn't particularly a good Catholic. In fact, I came from a typical Italian family where you were baptized and made your first communion and got married in the church, and that was about the extent of it. My friends were socialists and communists. Interested in social questions. I began to wonder what our church had to say about it and somebody gave me a copy of the *Catholic Worker.* Then on May Day in 1935, I decided to take the day off from work. Had an up-

---

* For comprehensive histories of the Catholic Worker movement, see the several books by Day herself; Mel Piehl, *Breaking Bread: The Catholic Worker and the Origin of Catholic Radicalism in America;* and William D. Miller, *A Harsh and Dreadful Love: Dorothy Day and the Catholic Worker Movement.* For additional material on Catholic Worker activism during the Vietnam War, see Francine du Plessix Gray, *Divine Disobedience: Profiles in Catholic Radicalism,* and Patricia McNeal, *Harder than War: Catholic Peacemaking in Twentieth-Century America,* as well as Anne Klejment's essay on the Catonsville Nine draft board raid and Catholic Worker pacifism in *A Revolution of the Heart: Essays on the Catholic Worker,* edited by Patrick Coy.

set stomach or something. On the way home, I suddenly decided to get off at Fourteenth Street for the May Day parade. What possessed me, to this day I will never know. But it was a fortunate decision. When I got down to Union Square, they were distributing the *Catholic Worker,* and I asked if I could help. That was the beginning—when the bug bit me—and I was captured. And it was exciting! Never a dull moment. [Pause] Always, always exciting.

I met Miss Day shortly after that and I was thinking about coming down and joining the Worker, but I was saying, "God! She's an old woman. How many more years does she have to go?" I was so young . . . so young, and I really idolized her. I lived at the Worker on Mott Street until Alice and I were married in June of 1942. And I have never considered us as leaving the Catholic Worker. We merely changed residence and moved to Tell City. Miss Day did not encourage married couples to live at the Worker.

Ro: Alice, how did you hear about the Catholic Worker?

Alice Zarrella: Well, I had the same ideas out here [in Tell City, Indiana] as they did in New York. And then I found the paper and I met Dorothy when she came out to St. Meinrad's Monastery which is just down the road from us. And then she . . . I have this rare distinction that she asked me to come to New York. She asked me, and Peter asked me.

Joe: That's the strange thing about the Worker. People come and nobody asks them.

Ro: Except for Alice.

Alice: I have it in a letter. Dorothy came and visited my family to show them that it was a respectable place.

Joe: In the very early days, we had very little money, you know. Always up to our eyeballs in debt to the neighbors. Thank God those Italians who took care of us were such loving people. On Monday morning, Gerry [Griffin] and I would go for the mail. We wouldn't have any money to start the week, but one of us would say, "Well, at least we'll get a dollar today from the Lautner girl." Every Monday we got a dollar from Alice. She'd be making six, seven dollars a week.

Alice: And when I had more, I'd send two.

Joe: So one day she showed up. Came into the office with her big hat.

Ro: A traveling hat?

Joe: Right.

Alice: No. I always wore a hat.

Joe: I said, "So that's Alice Lautner!" Well, you can put a lot of meaning in that. But anyway, that was the beginning of our relationship.

Ro: Alice, when Dorothy met you, did she sort of have the idea you two would get together?

Joe: Oh, no!

Alice: No. After I got there, I was not popular with Dorothy. And I . . . it didn't work out the way Miss Day thought it was going to. I did not become a satellite. The person who was closest to her was the most disrespectful, and that was Mary Johnson, who lived in the front apartment on Mott Street. They were a riot together. Mrs. Johnson was older than Dorothy even. They were great friends and loving enemies.

Ro: So Mrs. Johnson would talk back to her?

Alice: Oh, yeah.

Joe: Oh, my!

Ro: You would never, though, would you Joe?

Joe: Oh, no! [Joe and Alice both laugh.]

Alice: Never.

Joe: Oh, those were great times! Mrs. Johnson was a hit or miss cook; when she was good, she was excellent, but when she was bad . . . and so we had an agreement between us, particularly with gravy. Whoever got the gravy first would kind of give a little signal, you know, and we'd pass it by if necessary, so only one of us was affected by it. But they were really wonderful people, made our life very livable, and I don't know that Dorothy could have done some of the things she did without the Johnsons. Because they took care of [her daughter] Tamar.

Alice: They were like grandparents.

Joe: Mr. and Mrs. Johnson gave Tamar some stability and gave Miss Day some peace of mind. For any mother to live the life that Dorothy did—to have your daughter and to leave her, to . . . to be torn. She truly loved that child, and to have this tension, plus all the other people she was taking care of . . .

Alice: Mr. Johnson edited a magazine for the Propagation of the Faith. Fulton Sheen was his boss. They were not living off the Worker, and that's why they could [take care of us]. And whenever Miss Day had guests, we'd take them to the Johnsons'.

Joe: I remember this abbot from St. Meinrad's came to visit us and all these cockroaches were crawling around while we were having coffee. Now this abbot was a very prestigious person, and you could see him being *so* uncomfortable. I got the feeling I'd better move him out, so I took him upstairs to Mrs. Johnson's place. Continued the conversation in a more sanitary atmosphere.

You wonder why the health department didn't come down on us. We violated practically every health rule in the book. No hot water. Primitive cooking facilities. One toilet for a whole floor. No heat except for open fireplaces and a few kerosene heaters. Most of the time we dressed up to go to bed. No place to take a bath or anything like that.

And the bedbugs! One time it was so bad that we took the beds up on the roof, soaked the mattresses with kerosene, and blow-torched the bed frames and the springs. But they still came back. Peter seemed to be the only one who was immune. Well, finally, somebody complained to the health department. Not because of the health specifically, but they were trying to get rid of the bread line. So the health people came down, and they made us put in a sink where the bread line was because we were handling food without washing our hands or anything. Dorothy asked them why they investigated.

"Well, we got a letter. Somebody was complaining about you."

"Who was it?" They said it was anonymous.

"Do you answer all anonymous letters?"

"Yes."

And she said, "Well, you might be deluged then." [Laughter.] And she browbeat him. But you know, before those people left, they gave us a donation.

People would come, and they'd need a bed to sleep. Well, you can't turn somebody away. So you'd get up and give them your bed, and you'd sleep down in the office. For a while there, we were giving our bed away so often, we said, "To hell with it," you know, and just slept downstairs. If we had some money, we'd give them thirty, thirty-five cents, whatever it was to get a bed in a flophouse.

Alice: Imagine being able to sleep for thirty-five cents!

Ro: Alice, how did you feel about all the dirt and the bugs and all when you walked in with your big-brimmed hat?

Alice: Well, it didn't really bother me. I mean I was wanting that kind of life. Dorothy used to say that was the problem—that people romanticized the poverty. And I think you do, actually. But it wasn't [romantic]. It was a dirty, ugly life, but it didn't bother any of us. I mean it was really strange. I guess the ones it bothered didn't stay.

Joe: We came to accept it as a very natural kind of thing. We were a very happy-go-lucky bunch despite all those deprivations.

Alice: Mostly when Dorothy came home, she'd bring a car. Somebody was always giving her an old broken-down car, and we'd be thrilled to death because we'd have one for a few weeks. Then it would die because nobody ever gave her a good one.

Joe: Well, remember the station wagon? I called it "my prize." I wrote an article in the paper asking for a car, and I got one. From a very rich girl in East Hampton, Long Island. Oh, good gracious! Talk about sumptuous!

Ro: And she was getting the *Worker*?

Joe: Yeah. We used that wagon to pick up food all over the place. Especially bread. And places like Macy's . . . they used to have these demonstrations with vegetable-cutting machines. They'd put this stuff in a bucket, and we'd go over there and pick up the vegetables for our soup.

Ro: Did you do any union organizing?

Joe: At the time we came, labor was beginning to feel its oats and was organizing in the CIO, so we were on picket lines quite a bit. Dwight Larrowe and I went out to Pennsylvania when the Bethlehem steel strike was on. We drove that station wagon I got all around this big picket line. It reached around the whole city. Had coffee and bread and whatnot in the back, to give to the strikers. The seamen's strike was probably the biggest we were involved in.

Ro: Didn't you actually move down to the wharves?

Joe: Right. We set up a headquarters down there. That was pretty dangerous.

Ro: Did Dorothy go down?

Joe: I don't think so, no. The men went. It was pretty dangerous. You know those fellows with their little hooks trying to find somebody in the river and put a hook in his back. Yeah, it was a violent, violent strike.

I guess we were kind of protective of Miss Day, though, and didn't always let her know everything that was going on, especially when she was away. I know I used to write to her: "Even though we're broke, we're getting along." I never really told her of the troubles we had. And they were many. We were constantly on the verge of being closed down because of lack of money. Lots of times I'd go up to George Shuster at the *Commonweal,* the man who got Peter and Dorothy together, and borrow money from him. But Dorothy didn't know about all these things. When she came home, we didn't bother her.

Alice: When I came, we were gearing up for the Second World War through the Spanish Civil War. All the people didn't recognize it, but we were, and that's when conscientious objection became not just an idea, but a real reality. When conscription passed and they had to register, that's what I got involved with. The War Resisters League and Fellowship of Reconciliation—all the peace movements came out of the Spanish situation.

Joe: Franco was [considered] a saint by most of the people in the church, and so when we took a neutral position, we got hell from both sides, both from the loyalists and from the Franco men. Oh, Dorothy took a beating from her friends on that! We paid a terrible price in subscriptions for the pacifism. Up until World War II, a lot of people in the Catholic Worker movement were . . . maybe never really thought about it too seriously, but they could accept being against war. But when it came down to the actual thing, that was a *big* break. Like the whole Chicago group. It was a real trying time for the Worker.

    The letter Miss Day wrote and sent to all the houses was a very tough thing for her to do. But it was such an important principle, so basic to the very belief of the Catholic Worker that she couldn't allow people to run a house of hospitality and not be against the war. You know, either you were a Catholic Worker, and you believed in peace and conscientious objection as part of the Worker . . . It's not that you couldn't live at that house or anything like that, but you couldn't say "I'm a Catholic Worker" and be running a house and not believe in those things.

Alice: If it hadn't been for the Catholic Worker's stand on conscientious objection, I don't think such a classification would have been accepted [by the government]. I was involved with the Association of Catholic Conscientious Objectors. Arthur Sheehan was the head of it. And everybody would write in and be registered with us. We kept files. I don't know whatever happened to them.

Ro: Joe, didn't you go down to testify in Washington?

Joe: We testified against conscription. And to get the recognition that we could be conscientious objectors. Catholics had a tougher time than the other groups. The church didn't recognize conscientious objection, so we had no real basis for it. I did it by proving that I was against all forms of war.

Alice: All forms of violence.

Joe: Yeah. Well, I got my conscientious objector status and decided I wanted to be an ambulance driver. Because I felt [the soldiers] really believed in the justice of this war, and *they* were giving up their life for something they really believed in, so we should, in turn, be willing to sacrifice our life for what *we* believed. It also seemed a work of mercy and more in line with my whole idea of the Catholic Worker. The funny part was that when I was overseas, I had more respect as a conscientious objector than I did at home.

Alice: He was with the American Field Service.

Joe: Which was a volunteer organization. We paid our own way and bought all our equipment. We were considered civilians, and I wasn't under anybody's command.

Ro: Alice, did you come back to Indiana when Joe went with the American Field Service? What was it like to come back here?

Alice: Well, it was difficult because . . . The war years weren't very happy for anybody. And Joe wasn't really well received when he came here. And then he became a labor organizer and organized the factory that my father was superintendent of. So we were not very . . . it was real bad. We had some real difficult years in Tell City. But people have grown up now, you know, and they realize . . . until Joe organized the factory, there was no such thing as paid vacations or paid holidays or insurance, none of that. What is accepted today is enormous. Oh, they have no idea what unions did!

Joe: She's not telling you the whole story. The abhorrence . . .

Alice: Well, she can figure that out. You don't have to dramatize it. And I think the town has grown up now. Fifteen cents an hour! That's what some of our workers were making.

Joe: Labor has pressed its pants, as they used to say about the Communist Party. When people finally got the things they were fighting for, they became middle class and forgot about the struggle. As a result, they aren't progressive enough to think further than just the bread and butter.

Ro: Now did you work in the factory where Alice's dad was the supervisor?

Joe: Yes. I learned woodworking. I now have it as a hobby because of that.

Alice: He does it in his head. He has a Peter Maurin room in his head.

Joe: Well, all I can say is that I'm grateful I was touched by Dorothy Day and Peter Maurin. And you know what else? Being at the Catholic Worker I was spoiled. Because at the Catholic Worker I saw the *best*. The best minds in the world. It was exciting. I've never had a dull moment in my life since I came to the Catholic Worker.

Alice: I think you said that.

Ro: Hmmm. [Laughs.] Do you think there were more characters in those early days?

Joe: Oh, we had lots of characters!

Alice: Frankly, they all were characters.

People who spent time in New York not only took CW ideas to other parts of the country, as Alice and Joe did, but also selected strands of philosophy from which they developed special interests and activities. For example, Christian socialist John Cort's long-standing involvement in the labor movement had its origins at the Catholic Worker.

Ro: Do you know what, John? One day, while I was researching for the interviews, I learned that Dorothy was in Flint, in my hometown, the very month I was born, February 1937. Isn't that a coincidence? Do you remember that?

John Cort: Oh, yes! Yes. She climbed through the window and visited the sit-down strikers in the General Motors plant in Flint. The only woman allowed in the plant. Did a great piece of reporting on that visit to the sit-down strikers. And that showed, too, a certain inconsistency in her positions on pacifism. One [instance] was her words in defense of the Cuban revolution, and another was her remarks about those sit-down strikers. They were piling up weapons, mostly pipes that they found in the plant, in order to resist any attack that might be launched against them by the police. And she defended their obvious intention of resisting violently to the police. Kind of excused it. That report of the Flint sit-down strike was part of what inspired my interest in the labor movement. On February twenty-seventh of 1937, about a dozen of us sat around the kitchen table in the Catholic Worker and founded the Association of Catholic Trade Unionists (ACTU).

Ro: In some histories of American Catholicism, the Association of Catholic Trade Unionists is described as counteracting Communist influence in the trade unions, as sort of sanitizing the unions so that Catholics would be able to join them.

John: I suppose that's one way you could interpret the ACTU's activity. That organization has been the butt or the target of a lot of very bad PR, articles and books by people who tend to sympathize with the Stalinist line. And who call it a red-baiting, clerical fascist organization, whose only purpose in life was to thwart and defeat and counteract all these idealistic, wonderful trade unionists who were inspired by the Communist Party and by Marxism.

Ro: Well! [Laughs.] Now John, you were a Harvard graduate in French literature and history and you were dealing with people from completely different backgrounds. Were you accepted? Did they listen to you? Did they want you?

John: Well . . . [Laughs.]

Ro: Did you want *them?*

John: I wanted them. There was no question about that. I was completely committed and fascinated by the labor movement. Maybe living at the Worker with those nine guys off the Bowery . . . I remember Joe Hughes, a seaman who joined the Catholic Worker in the original seamen's strike. He and I were good friends. He was kind of alcoholic. There was a rumor that Dorothy, at one point, was considering marrying him. He wrote quite well, but he was, unfortunately, pretty addicted to the old sauce.

Ro: The Irish curse.

John: The Irish curse. He and I got along extremely well. Joe Hughes helped to baptize me, you might say, into the proletarian world. And I always got along fairly well. People thought I was gullible, naive, and sort of a religious fanatic.

Ro: Did you take advantage of that?

John: I probably suffered from it more than took advantage of it. I can remember vividly one early meeting in the ACTU headquarters around the corner on Canal Street. A Larry Delaney was there, a funny young Irishman from Time-Life. I was giving a sort of *ferverino*—very religious—and pointing to the crucifix on the wall and saying we should have more of that spirit. And Larry broke in, "There goes Cort raising that phony religious business again!"

Ro: What did the ACTU achieve?

John: It lasted for about thirty years, and at one time, it actually had fourteen chapters and over a hundred labor schools, most of them in New York and Detroit. It served, I think, as an inspiration—a motivation or a needle perhaps—for the Jesuits to found a lot of other labor schools all over the country. So there were hundreds of labor schools doing the kind of thing we were doing—training young trade unionists in public speaking, parliamentary law, labor history, negotiating procedures, grievance procedures—all that kind of thing. All that was valuable.

Also, if there has been some kind of idealism in the labor movement—and I think there has—an idealism sustained over the years, and some concern about racketeering and also a freeing of the labor movement from Communist leadership (and I make no apologies for that; I think it was a valuable thing to do), then the ACTU deserves some credit.

You know, Dorothy Day had a very significant and important influence for good on a great many people. At a critical time in the history of the United States, and of Catholicism, particularly. The Catholic Worker was founded in 1933—the depths of the depression. Twenty-five or thirty percent (nobody's quite certain) of employable citizens were unemployed, and there was a great deal of suffering. Hunger and worse. A lot of people—particularly young Catholics—were terribly concerned and wondering if there was any solution. Now I did not agree with their solutions. But certainly the basic thing they were doing, the works of mercy—feeding the hungry, clothing the naked, sheltering the shelterless— were the first immediate answer. If people are hungry, you have to feed them. I think that saved the faith of a lot of people.

Many of us who became interested didn't buy the whole thing: the agrarianism, the total pacifism, the anarchism or personalism (whatever you want to call it). But [the Catholic Worker] got me interested, for instance, in the cooperative movement, in the trade union movement. A lot of people were like that. Came to the Catholic Worker and didn't buy the whole schmeer but nevertheless got involved in various aspects of social justice and social action.

Young people came to New York from around the country, often returning to their hometowns to start houses of their own. These early houses were united by frequent visits from Dorothy Day and Peter Maurin and also by attendance at the retreats given by Fr. John J. Hugo. One of these visitors to New York was Justine L'Esperance, a young social worker from Marygrove College in Detroit. She later married Lou Murphy, founder of the first Detroit community. They raised their six children at St. Martha's House, probably the earliest house of hospitality for families.

Justine Murphy: I still remember seeing Mott Street. Talk about cultural impact! I think the average product of the Catholic school . . . you have sort of a one-dimensional approach to Catholic living. I know I certainly did as an eighteen-year-old. So meeting Dorothy, attending the discussion groups on Friday, all the rest of it . . . it was absolutely mind-boggling!

I suppose that particular summer was the thing that really most changed me and my life. Then the next year at Marygrove, I was taking a course in journalism, and one of my assignments was to come down to 1432 Bagley to visit the

St. Francis House and interview a Mr. Louis Murphy. (I had heard much about Mr. Louis Murphy in New York and had to confess to my embarrassment that I had never met the man. This they couldn't believe.) But anyhow that's when I was introduced to the ideas of hospitality, you know, on the local level.

Nina Polcyn Moore also came to New York from the Midwest.

Nina Polcyn Moore: There's a saying that St. Teresa saw this *T* written in heaven. Well, I saw this *CW* written in heaven. The *Catholic Worker* spoke to me. It was absolutely rich and I devoured every word. I thought, "I just can't stand it! I must go to New York, and I must see this place."

So I went. It was 1935. New York was such a busy place and so full of ferment and ideas. You could sit on the front stoop and . . . in just one day when I was there, Sigred Undset came and Father [Thomas] Judge, who founded a religious order, came, and Sister Peter Claver came, too. (Sister was the woman who gave Dorothy her first dollar, and she's still alive in Philadelphia.) It was a wonderful place to sit because it was a center of ideas and inspiration, a center of the richness of Catholic social thought. And a new kind of Catholicism, a new kind of personal responsibility and a new kind of outlook. We did things like picket the German counsel against Hitler. It takes a lot of courage to picket, no matter when or how or what.

You know, I've been thinking. I was born in 1914, just about the time World War I was started and there has been no peace ever, really. It's one war after another. It just seems . . . It's just unbelievable, isn't it? Wherever it is, it just keeps on and on, eating us all up. Eating up all the money that should go to the poor.

Nina came home from her time in New York and began the first Milwaukee Catholic Worker, Holy Family House. Florence Weinfurter, remembered by Marquette students as the manager of Cardijn's Bookstore, was one of those who joined her.

Florence Weinfurter: I don't regret the life I had. No, not a bit. I think I'd like to start this interview with how I came to participate in the Catholic Worker here in Milwaukee. I had read some things about Dorothy Day, so when I saw that there was going to be a Catholic Worker house of hospitality opened, I decided to go to that opening. I was a young working woman with the Wisconsin Electric Power Company at that time.

I went alone. Didn't know anybody. The priest who was blessing the house made it quite clear that he did not adhere to Dorothy's stand about war because he was a chaplain in the army. I was one of the very few people who came that day. I was, in the main, a little older than most of them. I enjoyed what the young people were saying and doing, and they insisted that I come again. I guess they latched on to me because there was nobody else.

Ro: How did the archbishop feel about you?

Florence: When the house was ready for opening, Nina and some of the young men were to go to the chancery, just to tell them that we were opening. And what the chancery said was, "We will tolerate you." They said it in Latin. Nina doesn't remember that, but *I* remember that. I recall it because she told me. Anyway, that was the kind of support we got.

Also, in the course of that time . . . now I'm not sure if this was after the house was closed or not, but I was still clerking at Wisconsin Electric Power Company, and one day a gentleman called on me. He flipped out his badge and he was from the House Un-American Activities Committee. He was, yes, and I got the job of answering his questions. He knew the names of the people [in the Milwaukee Catholic Worker], and I don't recall whether he also knew the places at which they worked. (Obviously he knew where *I* worked.) He asked me to evaluate all these individuals. Well, I told him, of course, that they were all wonderful people. And after a while, he left. When I had to tell Nina and Margaret Blaser, who was the other person here, we got a little paranoid. We thought people were tapping our telephones. That's what happens to you. They had to have spies. Otherwise they wouldn't have known so much.

You know, we had these strong friendships, and we were concerned about the underprivileged, and we had . . . There was a great measure of personal sacrifice to keep a house like that going. And also to spread the patterns that Dorothy was writing in the newspaper. In addition to our roundtable discussions, we were always reading. I never stopped that. Even to this day, I haven't. I am fairly critical.

Ro: Yes. Um . . . can you tell me a little more about that early house?

Florence: Well, let's see. I remember we had two houses. We sheltered the men who were lining up at that period when so many people were unemployed and unable to produce enough to eat. There was the first house, and then we moved to a street underneath a railroad track. Some murder had been committed there just before we moved in, but we didn't pay any attention to that little thing. Strangely enough, we were never stopped or bothered in any way, even though we would come home rather late at night on the streetcars.

We would have our meetings on Sunday afternoon, and we went to a cafeteria and bought ice cream cones, and then went to the upper level and conducted our meetings there. [Laughs.] There were others involved at that time, quite a lot of other people, but I don't remember all their names. Dave Host gave us lectures at Holy Family House. We were reading good writers, mostly European writers in translation, and discussing those things. And it was illuminating, of course, for me. We presented a play John Cogley wrote. He was from the Worker in Chicago, and I remember that I cooked the spaghetti. The play was to . . . to spread the word.

Most of the equipment came from the School Sisters of St. Francis. They'd also give us food and they'd give us their old coffee grounds. Different people contributed anonymously, Dean O'Sullivan (of Marquette's School of Journalism) among them. And Father Dietz, and there was a Mary White, also, who kept us going when we didn't have any money. We didn't know we were poverty-stricken, but I guess we were.

There was Larry Heaney, who was a friend of Nina's, who gave up all his belongings and his home and his money and took over the care of this new Catholic Worker house. He ran it until he married a girl who was a social worker. (I think her name was Ruth Ann.)

Ro: How did the Milwaukee house stand on pacifism?

Florence: I guess we were pacifists, more or less. We didn't know exactly what we were . . . how far we were going. We had doubts, you see, and I guess we . . . oh, yes . . . we went to Father Hugo to enlighten us about what stance we should or could take. You know, he was totally non-participating. Father Hugo was a stringent believer. The retreats were eight days. We weren't to speak during that period of time. There was much reading of the Scriptures, and much meditating, and much silence. That's about all I can tell you about it. Oh, and your clothing . . . you know, what you should wear and not wear.

And then along came war. (I'm telling this in a very, very condensed way.) Anyway, there was this big problem about who would be a CO [conscientious objector], and what stance they would take, and so on and so forth. Well, all the fellows either became COs, working only partially for the government and the Army, or became soldiers. It became evident that we couldn't control Holy Family House from the outside. So one day, we decided to send a telegram to Dorothy that we were closing up. Well, she didn't like it one little bit. But that was really all we could do at the time.

> Sr. Ruth Heaney, Larry Heaney's widow and now a Benedictine nun, remembers the early Milwaukee house and Fr. Hugo's retreats.

Sr. Ruth Heaney: It's been a rich life. I'm an old lady over seventy-five. And here I am still able to do all kinds of things. Well, Nina Polcyn and Larry were classmates down at St. Matthew's parish, and when Nina found a good thing, she introduced it to him. He was operating the Catholic Worker house in Milwaukee when I met him.

A year or so after I graduated from St. Mary's at Notre Dame, I went to Milwaukee to work at the St. Vincent de Paul Society. When you move to a new town, naturally the first thing you do is go to the Catholic Worker 'cause you have a home there. So I met Larry at Holy Family House, and we were married in Milwaukee. We had known each other about six months, I guess, and got married down at St. Matthew's where Larry had been baptized. A very simple ceremony.

Ro: How did your parents feel about this?

Sr. Ruth: My parents were hurt. I used to say a lot of Catholic Worker parents *do* suffer because they don't understand. You see, the first bishop of Salt Lake City, Bishop Duane Hunt, had grown up as a childhood friend of my mother. We often saw him through the years, and he got the scholarship for me to go to St. Mary's. I was just like his little girl. Well, this Bishop Hunt was under the impression that the Catholic Worker was a Communist front organization, and so he was hurt. And my parents were hurt. But there's always pain, you know, because people don't understand.

Ro: Can you remember anything else about that first Milwaukee house?

Sr. Ruth: Well, I can remember Larry telling me a curious story. It seems that the Salvation Army in Milwaukee had always cooperated with the cops by giving them the names of the men staying at their houses overnight. But Larry wouldn't do that at Holy Family.

He said to the police, "If you come to me with a description of a person who's accused of a crime, if you tell me what his name is and what he looks like, I'll tell you if he's here. But I'm not going to give you everybody's names. You don't go down to the hotels and ask for names and addresses. You only come here because they're poor, and the fact that they haven't got fifty-dollar bills in their pockets isn't a reason to have their names picked up by the cops."

Larry got a black lawyer, assuming that as a minority person he would sympathize with his ideas, but he didn't. However, Larry won in court—proved that it was his home, and that he didn't have to be limited by the state as to how many guests he could have, or tell the police who they were.

Ro: Neat! What did you do after the house closed?

Sr. Ruth: Well, we went to the farm in Easton, Pennsylvania, for a while, to Maryfarm. Then, as the war got going, Peter sent us up to Camp Simon, the CO camp, to try to indoctrinate the men who were there. You know, they were already halfway there because they'd registered as conscientious objectors. But it didn't work. It was run by the government, and there was no place for us in the system. Especially with a baby. We used to hang the diapers on a line around a wood cookstove.* [Laughs.]

Ro: What about the famous Father Hugo retreats?

Sr. Ruth: Oh, my! Father Hugo was a deeply spiritual man, but his asceticism . . . um . . . it was just non-Benedictine. It was not whole, and Peter had been so whole. I remember once Father Hugo said, "If you smoke, you love God just this much—the length of the cigarette—if you won't quit smoking for His sake." Some of the healthier ones among us . . . well, they either had sufficient education or enough spiritual insight to recognize that this was another kind of spirituality and not one they wanted to buy into. Yet Dorothy [Day] did. I didn't understand it at the time.

Dorothy Gauchat from Cleveland also remembers the retreats.

Dorothy Gauchat: Dorothy put out a call to all the Catholic Workers that she wanted them to come to make this retreat because she was. She herself was such a dynamic holy person. And she wanted all the Workers, you know, to really build their commitment on a strong . . . on a spiritual faith.

Ro: You know, people have said that Father Hugo was quite Jansenistic.

Dorothy: That unfortunately was the impression, I guess, in the way some people responded to his call to live Christianity. And that's totally untrue. If you really listened to Father Hugo, he was talking about the cross. It was John of the Cross. That's who he was following.

You know, he kept talking about the "sample" God has given us. By sample he meant beauty, food, cigarettes, all these good things. A lot of people got carried away on the cigarette thing, you know. This is how it came to me, and I was only a twenty-one-year-old kid. These are all good things, but they're only *samples* of God's goodness, and they have to be used as such. In other words, our life can't be directed towards wanting all of those things, towards satisfying our desires in all of those areas. In themselves, they are good. We can use them, you know, to reach the goal of really living the way Christ wanted us to live. Living the Sermon on the Mount. Not let those things get in the way. That's all.

At the retreat, we'd gather in the dining room, and these nuns made such

* For a history of this camp, see Gordon C. Zahn, *Another Part of the War: The Camp Simon Story.*

beautiful meals. But people would sit down and not eat that food. To sacrifice it. And I still can see [Father Hugo] at the table saying, "Hey! That's not the message. If somebody puts a good steak in front of you, you don't say you can't eat it. You eat it."

One of the quotations Dorothy left with me was, "You must receive as humbly as you give." So if somebody puts a steak in front of you, you thank God. On the other hand, if having steaks every day and having all the extras and niceties in your life is your consuming drive, then you're on the wrong track.

Notre Dame biologist Julian Pleasants also attended an early retreat.

Julian Pleasants: We started the house [in South Bend] in February of 1941, I think, and within a few months Dorothy was saying we had to make a retreat. Said if we didn't make this retreat, we'd fall by the wayside. She didn't say that we were out of the movement if we didn't go, but she said it was essential. And so . . . golly! I had just gotten out of the hospital, but we hitchhiked to that little place, to Oakmont, Pennsylvania. Now this, I suppose, was the first retreat. There was one in Easton later that summer, I believe. Both with Father John Hugo. We had an eight-day closed retreat. Very impressive.

The most important thing I got out of it was the necessity of daily meditation. We'd been going to daily Mass, but meditation seemed an awful thing to do when there was so much work to be done at the house. Father Hugo convinced me it was essential, though, and I think he was right. It wasn't meditation in the usual sense of contemplating something very abstract or spiritual. It was often just saying to myself, "How will I deal with what I have to do today?" "What would Jesus have done and what can be expected of somebody like me?"

I didn't agree with the giving up things at all. Father Hugo said that the best thing to do with good things was to give them up. And I just didn't think that was Dorothy's attitude at all. She didn't want to give them up, she wanted to give them *away.* It was a totally different approach. Dorothy liked her good literature, her good music, and she never really felt that obligated. I think she got out of the retreat only the notion that you had to be *ready* to give them up. She took what worked for her and hoped other people would take what worked for them.

Ro: Well, maybe she had a little larger vision than some of the people who listened to her. Now how did the South Bend house stand on pacifism during the war?

Julian: Well, I'm not sure we even knew about the letter that was so hard on the people who chose not to be pacifists. We hadn't really thought that it was an intregal part of what we were joining.

Ro: So it was never really an issue in the South Bend house?

Julian: No. We never espoused total pacifism. I signed up for noncombatant service. But the other fellow with me didn't even sign up for that. We'd get big bundles of the paper to distribute, and if it had something in it we didn't agree with, we just didn't send them out that month. The strange thing is that Dorothy rather put up with this. She never was hard on us. Years later I wrote a piece saying that I felt the Catholic Worker had so much to offer people who were only against particular wars, people who were not total pacifists. She printed that in the paper. You know, I kind of think she was unduly impressed by the fact that I was a scientist. She rather felt that I was one of the more scholarly members of the group. I don't know why.

Ro: Hmmm. What can you tell me about that first South Bend house?

Julian: Well, let's see. We had a big dining room and lots of bedrooms and a clothes room. We rented the twelve rooms on the floor above Mr. Kolupa's drugstore. He was Notre Dame's oldest living alumnus at one time, and had to endure many troubles because of us. A very patient, tolerant man to put up with us. We put seventy people up, with some of them on the floor because we had bed space for only thirty-two, but we didn't want to turn people away. If we had a little money, we'd take them to a boardinghouse down the street.

Our house was open during a transition period [in the U.S. economy], and we probably had a somewhat different clientele from the big city houses. Looking back on it, I see that we probably helped build the U.S. industrial war machine. A lot of people were being drawn to South Bend because of Bendix and Studebaker, even though we weren't at war yet in early 1941. But already we were supplying England, and there were ads all over the South, people told me, inviting people to come North. They'd stay with us until they got their first paycheck. And then as time went on, these people were out on their own, and we wound up with largely alcoholics.

Ro: How did you support the house?

Julian: In the beginning it was primarily Notre Dame professors who had heard Dorothy talk. After a time, Father John Cavanaugh got us food from the dining halls. But the war machine got geared up and the number of men coming to the house began to dwindle. We finally closed it in 1944.

Julian and his wife, Mary Jane, moved with other families to the outskirts of South Bend and raised their children, choosing a simple semi-agrarian lifestyle.

Mary Jane Pleasants: Oh, it was a very exciting time to be living! We always felt that. We were a part of the church, very strongly a part of the church, and doing many of the things that later were allowed [by Vatican II]. The para-liturgies we had for the family were very meaningful for us. We're not sure they were so meaningful for the children.

Julian: We felt we could handle anything. We had problems to lick, but we knew what to do. If you read the *Catholic Worker,* you heard about Dom Virgil Michel, you heard about the Christian Family Movement, you heard about the Rural Life Movement. The Catholic Worker put all these things together so each person could integrate it for himself. On our little plot of land outside of town, we thought we had the answers that would work, not just for us but for everybody. Decentralism wasn't abandoning a hopeless world. Why, we were the pioneers! Setting a pattern for a new way of living! As we got more into the idea that our farming would be part time, we saw this as a much more universal pattern. Only so many people could manage to be economically independent, but if you were going to use this kind of life to create a good neighborhood for rearing children and to have opportunities for meaningful work for the whole family, you didn't need lots of land and you didn't need to be an expert in innumerable things. We were pioneers in do-it-yourself. If you couldn't cure industrialism of its miserable alienating work, you could at least do some things yourself. You didn't have to choose between TV and industrial work. There was another alternative.

Mary Jane: We were never completely free of the system, though, and you always worked. We never managed to be self-sufficient as far as money was concerned.

Julian: We would have liked to be, but . . .

Mary Jane: We had a nice garden, and lots of animals when the kids were here, but it was never complete. It was a good place to raise children, though.

Julian: Dorothy thought it was a great idea. In her acceptance speech for the Laetare Medal in 1972, she commented that she was very proud that our little community had continued. You know, it wasn't a typical Catholic Worker farming community. It was an intentional community but not a commune. We never owned a single thing in common, but we sure shared our work and our time.

Ro: Catholic Worker farms have always been problematic, to say the least. Maybe it helped that you never called this a Catholic Worker farm.

Julian: Well, you can't blame the Catholic Worker farms. If they're going to bring people of all kinds of abilities and disabilities, and they're going to live it in a kind of anarchic fashion, why, they can't do any better than they did. Running a farm is very demanding. People would speak very poetically about following the cycles of life, but golly! You're *tyrannized* by the cycles of life! It's nothing sentimental at all. You have to do things when they have to be done or there's nothing at all. One day's delay could mean a whole year's production is lost.

That's another reason anarchism is not exactly compatible with farm life. It's a very regimented kind of life, but people can see why they're being regimented. We worked our kids pretty hard and nowadays there aren't many kids growing up who have that much chance to do meaningful work. I think they saw that it was necessary, though. We weren't doing it to impress them with obedience or discipline them in some way. We did it because it had to be done. We didn't have any money and we had to have food, so it was all useful work. We still think this way of living works well for families. We have lots of land out here that we don't really need, and you could have a cohesive neighborhood here.

Sr. Ruth Heaney also had ties to South Bend; she was graduated from St. Mary's College in 1937.

Sr. Ruth: After Larry and I were married in Milwaukee, we went immediately to Maryfarm near Easton, in eastern Pennsylvania. Oh, it was lovely! Our oldest child was born there, and I was very much in love. Larry was a wonderful man, and we'd been married two or three years before I kind of saw that he had any faults. (He said I had been unrealistic, but he really *was* wonderful.)

Oh, we were happy. That's all I can say. We were very, very happy, although I suppose there were people who smiled at the newlyweds, you know. We were able to go to Mass most mornings. In a chapel in the upper barn. You'd think it was Christmas. The hay was off to one side and there would be pigs, maybe, at the lower level, and we'd hear them shuffling about during Mass. We had dialogue Masses up there, way back then, in '40 and '41, maybe even dialogue homilies. It was wonderful! Virgil Michel would come to Maryfarm, and Peter would never say a word, for once. He said, "Dom Virgil Michel can teach me."

Dorothy came out a lot. She was such a strong and dominant lady. It was, after all, like we were on her turf, but I think everyone was rather inclined to be docile around her. I . . . I don't really have strong stories, strong memories of her. I think I saw her as interfering with my marriage a little bit, and I resented that. Telling Larry to do this or do that, you know, and he wouldn't have a chance to consult with me. He didn't entirely like it, either. By the second year, we had the baby. And I'm not sure . . . they always say it's unfair to judge someone by the insights of another period. Maybe we didn't have as much consciousness then that the governed need to be consulted a little more and that you delegate as much as possible.

Dorothy just didn't delegate. And of course she was a city girl who had no understanding of the farm, so we were left with the problem of how to interpret what she said or how to apply Peter's ideas. It was up to us to work it out.

Oh, I'm sure a lot of money was wasted [at Maryfarm] because there wasn't a clear-cut line of authority. John [Filligar] knew how to farm, but he didn't have the philosophy of the Catholic Worker. I'm sure it was just at sixes and sevens, and everybody had to be discouraged, no doubt. But those were the years when there was an attempt to have real community. Do the Buleys enter into your story? Mrs. Buley used to bake bread for us all. That was her contribution, and Mr. Buley was a big man and unintelligent, and they were very poor. They were like . . . like transients who somehow got settled there. Larry used to say that the father got his ego enhanced by being a troublemaker. Today, we would probably say he had a poor self-image. When you suffer from lack of self-esteem, you've got to get it somehow, and he would do it by being obstructionist. I used to tutor one of those little boys. It would take all day, you know, and he would learn to write his name, but the next day he would have forgotten it. Oh, my! There were serious problems in that family.

Once Dorothy came out, and things weren't going well. She wrote an article in the next issue of the paper and said Larry Heaney was the new manager of Maryfarm. And he hadn't been consulted. She hadn't talked to anybody about it, but that was the way she was. Very . . . she simply said how things were, and that was the way they were, you know. Anyway, Victor Smith, who was in the community, had been a Benedictine monk, and he immediately came and offered Larry obedience. That was his way, from having been a monk. Larry felt really bad about that.

> Later, the Heaneys purchased land in Starkenburg, Missouri, and moved there with Gertrude and Marty Paul. Sr. Ruth's children still own the land.

Sr. Ruth: It's a hill farm. Oh, it's a lovely farm for hill land. We have about twenty, twenty-five acres of level land, too, with a creek running through the place. I remember one day our oldest daughter . . . we had gone up on the hill to pick berries and she said, "Oh, Mom! Let's than God for such a beautiful farm." She was just a little kid.

The farm is right next to the shrine to our Lady of Sorrows, which was the first religious shrine west of the Mississippi River. Pilgrimages are still held out there—formal ones a couple times a year, and many informal ones. So it was a beautiful spot. We bought it because it was near the church, and there was a school, too. The O'Fallon Precious Blood Sisters taught there, and a musician from Maria Lach in Germany had influenced them, so we walked into another dialogue mass! In March of 1947, in that little rural parish. It was wonderful. That place was God's . . . He had a hand in our having that farm.

The pastor, Father Peter Minwegen, was a liturgist, so we had lovely, lovely, lovely ceremonies and Masses and para-liturgies. He had a hard time with the Catholic Worker ideas, though. He'd say, "Let somebody else take care of these people."

Larry would tell us, "Don't be pushing [Catholic Worker] ideas on these people." Of course, they could see what we were doing. I remember an eighteen-year-old boy came out to the farm. He had been in an orphanage, and the folks at the Chicago Catholic Worker sent him to us. And another fellow was a drinker. I remember taking his shoes one time, so he couldn't go into town to drink. I don't know if there was some lack of wisdom in taking these men or not. But I was careful; as soon as the girls got a little bit older, you know, we didn't do it anymore. But nobody else was doing it either, so there was that dilemma.

Larry died when our sixth baby was born. We were both in the hospital at the same time, I having the baby and he with pneumonia. It's funny. After Larry died, I just didn't have that utterly bereft feeling that people have. His physical presence wasn't there, but I just felt his love and support so strongly. All the time. I would feel his physical presence if I felt very desperate at night, or had trouble with one of the kids or . . . You know how things are in a family. I would feel his presence with me.

I stayed on the farm to raise the children. Didn't know a good alternative. I had six children with the oldest one not yet eight. Anyone's going to be poor with all these children, and I just felt it was easier to be poor on the farm, where you've got some control over things, than in the city. We had to carry water, and we didn't have electricity at first. It really was primitive. We rented the land out to other farmers, but we had a garden and a cow. Daisy. A wonderful Jersey cow. Our neighbors had a Holstein herd, and they didn't want their male calves, so I'd buy them. The calf would take half of Daisy and the family the other half, and we would have a veal calf to sell every six to eight weeks. We had a huge garden, and we . . . we managed.

And then the ideas . . . People lived simply and my kids—our kids—have acquired that feeling. None of them live elaborately now, and they don't keep up with the Joneses. They have modest tastes. I wouldn't say they really believe in subsistence [living] because your marriage makes a difference in that kind of thing, but they have absorbed a lot of the ideas and live simply.

For instance, we used to try to go into town only once a week. That requires planning, but you just don't want to use the gas if you don't have to and you don't want to put the . . . stuff in the air from the exhaust in the car. We've never used sprays. My son is farming it now, and he wouldn't dream of doing something non-ecological. Well, we've always had those ideas [because of] Peter's influence. My son-in-law said, "Most people are lucky to be five years ahead of their time. You people were twenty-five years ahead."

When we came out to the farm, we said there probably weren't fifty people in America who understood what we were doing. (There probably weren't twenty-five.) And I think my kids suffered from these ideas because there were so few of us. Now you scratch a young person, and they have some idea of community and rural living and simplicity and going barefoot. I know my oldest daughter really suffered over being different, but when she was about thirteen, she said, "Oh Mom! I used to wish you were like everybody else, and now I'm glad you're not. But I do wish we could have had a community."

They were lonely, and there wasn't really much of anybody to talk ideas with. Although the Catholic Workers from St. Louis came out every month or so. And our children would go in and spend a week's vacation in town with Anne and Bolen Carter. So they were exposed to more culture than the local community could provide. And then a friend gave me the Sunday *New York Times* for years.

We stayed on the farm till the children got through high school. We never knew whether that was a mistake or not. I don't know. Still don't. They didn't want to move, but now I know that children never want to move. I think now the children are kind of proud of being early generation Catholic Worker people. Oh, I was comfortable there. I was able to work hard and not mind and not be lonely. Think and pray and work. I'm okay doing that.

From the beginning, Catholic Workers in Chicago were different from those in other cities. Dr. Arthur Falls, one of the few blacks active in the movement, talks about his involvement with the first Chicago Catholic Worker at 1841 Taylor Street.*

Dr. Arthur Falls: When I was very young, of course, Negro Catholics were not considered part of the church. They were a "missionary problem." Nobody ever explained why we were a problem. When my mother took me to enroll in the school at Holy Angels, I was denied admission because I was a "problem." It's very interesting that some thirty years later, my son was barred from his parish school for the same reason. At Our Lady of Solace. (It was very little solace. My wife and I had many unfortunate experiences there.)

---

* For a history of the Worker in Chicago, see Frank Sicius's essay in Patrick Coy, ed., *A Revolution of the Heart: Essays on the Catholic Worker.*

At any rate, in spite of the fact that the first citizen of Chicago was DuSable, who was both colored and a Catholic, we were considered to be a missionary problem. [Laughs.] The role of the Catholic in Chicago at that time, in terms of the black community, was enemy. If you were a Catholic, you were an enemy. If you were an *Irish* Catholic, you were a deadly enemy. The archdiocese was divided up into these ethnic parishes—German Catholic, Irish Catholic, Italian Catholic—and people in these various parishes on Sunday would cross each other going to Mass and not speak to each other.

Ro: Can you remember how you first heard of the Catholic Worker?

Arthur: I think I saw something about it in the local Catholic paper. I wrote Dorothy, and she immediately appointed me Chicago editor of the *Catholic Worker.* Well, of course, the Catholic Worker believed in equality. So I said to Dorothy, "If that's true, why don't you demonstrate it in your masthead by having one colored person and one white shaking hands. And she immediately changed it.

Peter Maurin came to Chicago, and we had this very first meeting [at St. Patrick's on Adams Street]. It was fairly well attended. After Peter spoke and I called upon the group for discussion . . . I never will forget this: a middle-aged woman got up right in the middle of the church and said just because she was a Catholic didn't mean she had to "associate with niggers." And walked right out!

It's a very complex picture. The old saying: Damned if you did and damned if you didn't. The chancery office was very . . . they tried to break up the Catholic Worker. They called some of the . . . well, some of the white [members of the Worker here] and tried to get them to disassociate from us.

Ro: I . . . I'm ashamed of my church.

Arthur: Well, don't be. I was never ashamed of my church. I was ashamed of the activities of those in the church. Many, many times as a child and even as an adult, I was asked, "How can you stay in the church that represents everything that you're fighting?" My answer is that I also am the Catholic Church. And I'm fighting to bring into the church what we think should exist. The black people didn't call upon me, either. People said, "Yeah, Falls is a Catholic. But the things he says aren't what the Catholics are saying." So I was considered an anomaly. I'd bring other people, people who weren't Catholic, to the Catholic Worker meetings. I brought rabbis and ministers as well as priests. Social workers. Doctors. Lawyers. I had a regular postgraduate course by bringing these people in because a lot of the young Catholic people had never—believe it or not—had *never* talked to a non-Catholic. They'd gone to Catholic schools and they'd never sat down and talked to non-Catholics. One man said to me, "I understand you're going to give a program with some non-Catholics. Aren't you afraid you're going to lose your religion?" I told him my religion wasn't that fragile. As far as Negro Catholics were concerned, you couldn't participate in the Catholic Church, but you weren't supposed to participate with non-Catholics, either.

Ro: Didn't give you much room.

Arthur: We were out in limbo. My wife and I have been fighting . . . well, I'd been working in social activity for a long, long time. Even before we married. And the first opportunity that I had to really have Catholic participation was to open the Catholic Worker group here in Chicago.

To the anti-Communist, the word "worker" was the dangerous thing. We participated in union activity and everything else, and on the picket lines, the cops would say to the young people, "I'll teach you Catholicism at the end of my club!" Chicago didn't have any laws in terms of picketing, so the police could take whatever action they wanted.

There's one thing I always said at Catholic Worker meetings, but I've said it elsewhere, too. It's that if you're right, you don't always lose. So many people have taken the attitude that you can't win. And I keep saying that if you're right, you don't always lose.

Ed Marciniak, another early Chicago Catholic Worker, first became associated with the house on Blue Island Avenue in 1938.

Ed Marciniak: I remember when I stumbled upon the *Catholic Worker.* It was a revelation! I'd order four copies, and leave three of them on the Elevated. For me at that point, it brought into focus the liturgy, the church's interest in the labor movement, and that personal responsibility—the initiative of lay people. We were to be self-starters, not merely followers. That's what excited me, probably more than anything else—that personal responsibility part. People *personally* went into a house of hospitality. Not thirdhand. Not through an intermediary, but one-on-one.

In those early days, we'd have clarification of thought every month. The speaker would come in at three or four o'clock, and we'd talk and have sandwiches or something. We'd keep talking and talking. Maybe go out to a restaurant and talk some more. But anyway, people would ask us, "What did you learn?"

Well, we'd hem and haw. 'Cause the real reason we'd invited a speaker was so that we could educate him or her in the discussion period. That was true. It was a mutuality. And the speaker, I think, understood that. We wanted them to find out about the Catholic Worker. That's why we invited them. But we also wanted to hear what they had to say. A lot of ideas were floating around, and you'd try to grasp them. It was a fascinating period with all kinds of intellectual ferment about one thing or another. Just a mind-boggling experience! I met a great many priests. It was just amazing. They traveled down the road together with you.

You know, many of the issues that were raised by the Catholic Worker were picked up by other people. There was Friendship House, and the Catholic Interracial Council, and then a social action department of the U.S. Catholic Conference. The success of the movement is that something new—a pioneer way—is highlighted, made visible in some way, and picked up.

Ro: Do you think that's co-opting?

Ed: Oh, no! That's success. Its agenda was adopted and that's important to me. Dorothy understood that the cause was young and [needed to be heard]. Maybe that was her socialist as well as her Christian background. You wanted your stuff adopted. Embraced. Institutionalized. And it was.

Another voice from these Chicago pioneer days is Jim O'Gara, who later became editor of *Commonweal.* He and his wife, Joan, remember Chicago.

Jim O'Gara: In the early days in Chicago, the house was a fairly small place. (This was the house on Blue Island Avenue.) They crammed in about three hundred people on cold nights, sleeping side by side on the floor. Wrapped up in newspapers in the worst days. The city of Chicago cracked down on the house for that, said it was a fire hazard and unsanitary and so on. Which it was. But the alternative, sometimes, was being out on the street in zero weather. But anyway, they sent police and we had to reduce the number to about fifty. In my time, the war industries hadn't ended the depression yet. We were feeding, oh, about a thousand meals a day, and sleeping fifty people in the house. And of course giving out clothes and doing other things like that.

Ro: Could you talk a little bit about the women's house in Chicago, Joan?

Joan O'Gara: Well, it was a parish house, not a Catholic Worker house, located downtown, on State Street near the cathedral. I had a very slight connection with it in that I gave two evenings a week to stay overnight there. I guess they housed about thirty women. Antoinette de Roulet was basically in charge of it and she was a librarian, so she was gone all day, and a couple who had come into the house from the street took care of it. I don't remember too much. The women were mostly older, but I remember we had one young woman who was retarded and was everybody's pet. I also remember one night they brought a young woman in who had tried to kill herself by jumping into the Chicago River. They just left her with me, and I didn't know what to do. So we got her into bed, and I lay down next to her and stayed awake all night to make sure she didn't try to run out of the house and jump in the river again. I had no training at all. I just decided I was going to spend the two nights each week.

Jim: How young we were! I was, I think, twenty-one years old. It was a miracle that things didn't go badly. In addition to the corporal works of mercy, we published a tabloid-size paper which looked a great deal like the New York *Catholic Worker.* That began in June of 1938. Before my time, John Cogley was the editor, Ed Marciniak was the managing editor, and Al and Catherine Reser and Marty Paul were associate editors. By the time I came along, the masthead had been changed to say simply "published by the staff of the St. Joseph House of Hospitality."

Ro: Solves a lot of problems.

Jim: My recollection is that John Cogley and Ed Marciniak played the key roles on the paper. Ed wrote consistently good labor and social action articles. John wrote a very popular monthly column, among other things. Pulled more mail than anything we published.

Next to Dorothy, John Cogley was, I think, the most outstanding journalist the movement ever produced. And Dorothy Day was kind enough to say that many people would tell her that our Chicago paper was better than the New York paper, although I think that's subject to some debate.

I would say the Catholic Worker in Chicago had great Catholic support compared to some other places. We were pretty respectable, actually, in Catholic Chicago. In fact it went so far that the diocese listed us on the institutional diocesan telephone list. (Didn't give us any money, though.)

We had good attendance at lectures and so on, although not always as good as we would have liked. At one point, I remember we had a Benedictine come to lecture on mendicancy, and to tell you the truth, we'd forgotten he was coming, and I don't know that much advertising was done. Anyway, there was practically nobody there for the lecture. So we went upstairs in the house and persuaded the guys [staying there] to put together as many good clothes as they could assemble, go out the back door and come in the front. They were our audience.

Well, John and I came up with a ploy to solve the audience problem. We decided to make the lectures hard to come by. When we published the announcements, for instance, of a series on the liturgy by Father Gregory O'Brien, we wrote, "Attendance by reservation only." And we were *flooded* with applications! They were hanging from the rafters! [Laughter.]

Ro: Jim, can you talk about the split over the pacifist issue?

Jim: Well, in 1940, the pacifist issue became increasingly debated both inside and outside the movement. Early that year, a couple of Catholic Worker groups on the West Coast, I understand, refused to distribute the New York paper because they disagreed on the pacifist issue, something that I thought was an extremely foolish and ill-advised thing to do. That summer Dorothy sent a letter to all the houses saying that only pacifists should be heading Catholic Worker houses of hospitality. There were, as I remember, about forty or fifty houses and farms around the country at that time.

Now this letter, I would say, was a very untypical thing for Dorothy to do. The movement was completely unorganized. It didn't have rules and regulations. It didn't have authoritarian structure. But because of the burning of the paper on the West Coast, or the refusal to distribute it, Dorothy was upset and sent this letter, which, in turn, upset an awful lot of people.

The West Coast action brought the issue to a head. For instance, in Chicago John Cogley was the head of the house, and he was aided by Tom Sullivan. Neither one of them was a pacifist. So in line with Dorothy's letter, Tom Sullivan left the house. Left the Catholic Worker. And John Cogley said that he planned to do the same thing. (Of course, Tom Sullivan returned to the Catholic Worker after wartime service in the Air Corps and ended up running the house in New York for something like a record of ten years.) Ed Marciniak planned to register as a conscientious objector, but he was unable to move in and run the house.

For my part, I was not a pacifist, but at that point I leaned toward conscientious objection to war—to modern war. I felt pretty much at the time that the use of weapons in modern war couldn't be justified according to traditional rules of just war. This was a position that I was to change very drastically as Hitler moved across Europe and one country after another went down, and we learned more and more about the position of the Jews and so on. But even if I wasn't actually a pacifist, I certainly didn't want to see the house closed, so I said I'd move in and take over the house when John left. As it turned out, after I moved in, John decided to stay, and he and I ran the house together until I was drafted.

Later that summer, all of us attended a Catholic Worker retreat at the CW farm in Easton, given by Monsignor Paul Hanley Furfey. It was a disappointment in the sense that the pacifism position wasn't really thrashed out. It was discussed at one gathering, you know, sort of a solemn high gathering of all the Workers, but non-pacifists like John Cogley were strangely silent. They didn't do much arguing about the issue. Arthur Sheehan, as I remember, presented the case for the pacifist position, but there wasn't a tremendous amout of opposition. There simply was, I guess you'd say, a certain amount of silent dissent. And it should be noted that the non-pacifists were very much in the minority, although Tom

Sullivan will tell you that he never thought Peter Maurin was a pacifist. Pacifism it seems to me, was pretty much part and parcel of the movement, by and large, although it never became a big issue until the war in Europe became crucial.

.I would make a clear distinction between the Monsignor Furfey retreat and the Father Hugo type. There was a definite difference between the two. I think Father Hugo was more . . . I'm trying to think of a non-pejorative word. [Laughs.] 'Cause I was not in sympathy with Father Hugo's approach. Some of us felt that Father Hugo was more of a Jansenist.

Ro: Now did Dorothy continue to visit you, even though she knew how the Chicago house felt?

Jim: Oh, yeah. As far as I could see, Dorothy never let [the pacifism issue] interfere with her personal feelings at all. But I should be clear on this: The non-pacifist position of the Chicago Catholic Worker was probably not widely known. For instance, we never took this up in the Chicago *Catholic Worker.* We seemed to have reached some kind of a consensus that this was something for the family to discuss and not to have a big public issue about it. Not to split the movement, so to speak. I look back now and think we made a mistake in not making our differences more explicit 'cause I think it would have helped in what Peter called "clarification of thought." Many of the pacifists, I think, showed their confusion when they got into the CO camps and found that they didn't really belong there and ended up going into the service anyway.

In September of 1941, I got notice from the draft board. I told them that I would prefer medical service. Surprisingly, they gave me a classification as a conscientious objector. I told them there was a mistake, that I wasn't a conscientious objector. They said, "In that case, raise your right hand. You're in the Army."

Ro: Now did they think you were a CO because you were associated with the Worker?

Jim: Yes. They were under some pressure from Catholic figures who were telling them that they shouldn't cause the closing of this very valuable work. In fact when John Cogley's turn came, he had to come up with somebody who said that they'd keep the house open before the draft board would even take him. We decided at that point that probably the best thing was to stop publication of the paper and then the house closed down very quickly.

The end of World War II found the Catholic Worker movement diminished in both numbers and influence. Those who persevered, however, report that the fifties were times of deepening intellectual and spiritual commitment. Dorothy Day, Ammon Hennacy, and their friends were arrested several times for resisting "Operation Alert," the air raid drills concocted by the Federal Civil Defense Administration to allay citizens' fears of what was then called the atomic bomb. For an extended account of Day's imprisonment for this civil disobedience, see Judith Malina's story in Chapter 3. Tom Cornell, a former editor of the *Catholic Worker,* puts the action in context.

Tom Cornell: The resistance to the civil defense drills started with just that kind of casualness that Dorothy refers to in the postscript of *The Long Loneliness:* "We were just sitting there talking." But it turned out to be a big deal, finally. The last year, there were probably two thousand people out, one thousand in City Hall Park and another thousand at the various campuses around the city. It became clear that [the government] couldn't continue to keep these raids going without paying a political price, so they dropped the whole thing. John Kennedy was just beginning his presidency, and that had something to do with it, I believe. The previous administration, the Eisenhower administration, wanted to alert all the homeowners in the United States to the good job the administration had done preparing for nuclear attack. Wanted to get people to build fallout shelters. And everybody got a little yellow pamphlet which said: "Build a fallout shelter. In the unexpected event that our government's efforts prove unsuccessful, and there is a war, if you don't have a shelter, rip your front door off and put it on the side of your house and heap up some earth, and get under it and stay there for two weeks." John Kennedy wouldn't sign it, but Eisenhower probably would have. It was ludicrous beyond belief. That, I think, was one of the elements that scuttled civil defense.

But there was a concerted effort on the part of the peace communities to address civil defense as a danger. The Catholic Worker and the War Resisters League did it through nonviolent direct action, sitting down year after year after year, the War Resisters League's organizational ability at last bringing out large numbers of people who had been sensitized by SANE and the other left-liberal groups.

The *Catholic Worker* talks to the converted for the most part. SANE was doing outreach with education—buying spot ads on the TV and radio, big ads in the *New York Times.* A whole page with nothing but a cockroach in the middle. The headline read "The Survivor of World War III." Remember that one? The FOR [Fellowship of Reconciliation] was doing its own particular approach—somewhat more liberal, somewhat less threatening. FOR people would put signs up: "This house has no fallout shelter. Peace is our only security." I still see those signs twenty-five years later.

We weathered some other difficult tempests, too. It was a very, very difficult time, one of the real low points in the Catholic Worker history, when the 223 Chrystie Street house had been confiscated by the city. We rented the storefront at 175 Chrystie Street but couldn't house anybody there. Had to hire apartments around. Before that . . . 39 Spring Street was even worse. Long, long steep stairway to one big room that had to be the soup kitchen, the editorial office, reception area. One toilet, and it was filthy. Constantly filthy. You could have one person assigned to nothing else but cleanup, and you couldn't keep the place clean. It was depressing beyond belief. It looked as if the Catholic Worker might even die. The subscriptions hadn't gone up very much from the post–World War II low.

Ro: Grim time.

Tom: Money just wasn't coming in. The annual budget then was less than seventy thousand dollars for printing and all of it. Then the Ford Foundation offered a grant of sixty-five thousand. Money for a year's budget. Dorothy turned it down.

I said "Why, Dorothy?" Now, I wasn't defending the idea that we should have accepted it. I just wanted to hear *why* she turned it down.

She said, "I knew a guy who worked for Ford out in Detroit, worked on these concrete floors for many, many years. He got arthritis, and they wouldn't put a carpet on it. They wouldn't put a wood floor down."

I didn't believe it. I knew that Dorothy always gave the answer she felt like giving at the time. Ask her ten minutes later, and she'd give you another.

Ro: They could both be true.

Tom: Yeah. They could all be true. Then I figured Dorothy was a lot shrewder than she appeared to be. If she accepted sixty-five thousand dollars, she would feel constrained in conscience to tell people. If you've got a year's budget in the bank, why should nickel-and-dimers send . . . why should my father-in-law send his ten dollars every three months? And that's what you really need, a lot of people giving small sums of money. This way people feel an investment in the Worker, an identification.

The narratives here move to the sixties, when the Worker again became a mecca for young people caught up in the dissatisfaction with "the system." Here's Jim Forest, a former associate editor of the *Catholic Worker.*

Ro: Jim, let's talk about the sixties a bit, especially the crazy part. For instance, what was the "big stomp"?

Jim Forest: Hmmm . . . the "big stomp." That sounds like an Ed Sanders phrase. Ed was a peripheral character who was always hanging around the Catholic

Worker. And was the founding editor of the magazine mimeographed at the Catholic Worker (well, one or two issues, probably) called *Fuck You: A Magazine of the Arts*. That was the main occasion of the big stomp! People then were kind of amused by the idea of a Catholic mimeograph machine being used to publish this outrageous journal. I guess today it wouldn't be considered at all outrageous, but at the time it was pretty scandalous.

I was down at the Abbey of Gesthemane, staying with Thomas Merton. Called up the Catholic Worker. Dorothy picked up the telephone, which didn't often happen. And she was mad. You could hear that she was mad! She said, "Did you have anything to do with this?"

I didn't laugh.

"With what?"

"This, this, this, thing!"

When she told me . . . it wasn't easy for her to say the name of the publication, but she did. I could recall having heard people like Ed Sanders and Nelson Barr and Bob Kaye and Jean Morton and others talking about this. It was a kind of running gag, you know, that they were going to start this magazine. I never took it seriously. It was so outrageous. High school. But sometimes high school students actually do some of the things they joke about, and they did this. (This magazine, I'm told, sells for a quite a bit of money. Even libraries have bought it. If I had kept a copy, I could sell it for maybe five hundred or a thousand dollars.)

At the time, we were seeing the so-called sixties happening right up front. People who were important figures had some little connection with the Catholic Worker. Alan Ginsberg was reading poetry at the Catholic Worker the first night I came to visit. And Ed Sanders had his musical group, the Fugs. He liked doing things that were outrageous—just loved the word "fuck" and was always looking for a chance to use in it in one way or another.

I think Dorothy felt furious because these folks were using the poor. They were risking what the Catholic Worker was doing. They were compromising her tolerance and exploiting her hospitality. But, you know, I'm not sure that magazine was even printed at the Catholic Worker. We didn't have very much equipment and our mimeograph machine was so dreadful. They claimed it was, but more likely it was done on the War Resisters League mimeograph machine, which was better. I suspect that was just part of the bluff. But the cardinal wouldn't be interested in hearing arguments about whose mimeograph machine it was.

We didn't know. I don't think any of us knew how nip and tuck it had been sometimes with the chancery, and how hard it had been for Dorothy to keep the paper going as an up-front Catholic publication called the *Catholic Worker.* Not "Christian Worker" or "Jesus Says," but *Catholic Worker.* On the one hand, she had to find ways to convince the Catholic Church that this was a sincere, deeply rooted, obedient phenomenon, that it came out of discipleship, that it was authentic, and that it had a genuine place in the Catholic Church. Very difficult. And on the other hand, she didn't want to bother the volunteers with a lot of the struggles she had. Volunteers would come and go. It was largely carried on her shoulders.

She was very good with the young people. She really wanted to . . . she didn't want to blow her stack at us too much. She tried to work in a very gentle, story-telling, invitational way, by and large. But I think she felt used. And I think she *was* used, actually. There was a kind of decadent quality about what was going on. But it was the subculture in New York at the time. And at the Catholic Worker, the door didn't close very rapidly. It didn't throw people out, so people could find a niche there that they wouldn't find anyplace else. It was heartbreaking for her, later in her life, to see that there was very little reverence left in the Catholic Worker movement. A lot of the people coming to the Catholic Worker movement couldn't . . . wouldn't open themselves to her love of the church. They were there for . . . oh, God knows! Who knows what their motives were? But they thought things that were precious to her were ridiculous.

Ro: How many draft cards did you burn?

Jim: Well, I don't know. I mean we took out sacks and sacks of them from this building in Milwaukee, and we burned them.

Ro: No, not draft files. I mean your own cards.

Jim: I don't know if I ever burned my own draft card. I don't remember. I probably . . . yes, I did. There was a press conference, and I burned it, and it was in the newspapers and everything. I should remember that. It didn't seem to me very significant at the time, and it doesn't seem very significant to me now.

Tom Cornell would burn his just routinely. It was only once that it mattered to the government, and he went to prison for that. Most of the time, they just scoffed at it. But there was some member of Congress who was up in arms about it at one point. He was able to make it into a national issue and so, naturally, we rose to the bait. Enthusiastically! We were made for each other, that congressman and us. [Loud laughter.] He opened the door and we flew through.

Ro: I'm thinking that maybe . . . maybe there were rituals during the sixties that . . . things like burning draft cards might have taken the place of liturgy for people who couldn't pray publicly.

Jim: Well, I don't have a very romantic idea of most of the things we did. I . . . maybe later in my life I'll have a more positive attitude toward it. People were in a state of fierce alienation, and there was a kind of vandalism. We weren't interested in breaking windows or writing our names on the walls. That was not nearly important enough. We were furious at America. Rightly so. That fury was at the center of much that we did. And if we could do something outrageous, that was great!

But I think Dorothy's approach was centered on something else. And when it's gone, the Catholic Worker movement is dead. The Catholic Worker movement centers its radicalism in care for people. It constantly makes everything accountable to that experience—to what is happening to people. All people. The Catholic Worker has probably been saved by that centering. And all of us who are part of the Catholic Worker probably are saved by that.

Ro: She had trouble, I think, with the Milwaukee Fourteen and your involvement in it. And Michael Cullen's.

Jim: She did. Oh yes! But she never said, "To hell with you!" She had second . . . her first thoughts were quite different from her second thoughts. She expressed her first thoughts about [this kind of action] in a talk at the National Liturgical Conference in Washington, the summer or fall of 1968. I approved of the Baltimore Four [burning of the draft files].* These were my friends, and we needed to do something to support them and make what they had done more significant. I wish she'd had the second thoughts much sooner than she did, because then it would have been the Milwaukee Thirteen. I don't see this as some kind of new ceremony. I'm not happy with it as a ceremony. I'm a major critic of the Plowshares stuff.†

Ro: But yet you went to the meeting in the barn.

Jim: Which meeting in the barn?

Ro: Well, I'm remembering what I've read.

Jim: Oh yes, yes, yes. That's right. I went to that. Yes. We were all there. But Dorothy's opinion pushed me a lot. I was, of course, passionate to do something about the war in Vietnam and not just to be encouraging people to be draft resisters or conscientious objectors or whatever. What was going on in Vietnam was very real to me because I had a dear friend who was a Vietnamese Buddhist monk.‡ So I was very open to this, but it was Dorothy's enthusiasm. Then when

---

* The Catonsville Nine and the Baltimore Four were the first actions by the Catholic Left—or the ultraresistance, as it came to be called—that destroyed property.
† Plowshares actions are discussed in Chapter 9. They're seen by most scholars of peace studies as direct descendants of the ultraresistance during the Vietnam War.
‡ Jim worked at Fellowship of Reconciliation with the monk Thich Nhat Hanh.

she turned around and had a second thought, I was quite let down. By that time I was in jail.

[Thomas] Merton had the same feelings [as Dorothy did]. At the time, I was very annoyed by both of them. You know, once you've done something, you tend to become very annoyed with people who don't agree, especially if you admire them. Now I see that her criticism was well founded and quite right.

What we did was good. I'm not sorry I did it, but I wouldn't build any shrines over it. It was one cry of the heart at the time. It disturbs me, though, to see it become a kind of institution.

Tom Cornell remembers the Vietnam years at the New York house.

Ro: Now you were no longer editor of the newspaper after you married Monica, were you?

Tom: No, but I had lot to do with the political orientation of the Worker. Whenever there was a question about coalition with other groups, Dorothy would take my advice. I was close to the War Resisters League, on the staff of the FOR [Fellowship of Reconciliation] and a member of CNVA [the Committee for Non-Violent Action] before it dissolved. I was able to be an effective ambassador from the Worker to those folks. We did have some successes. The deflation of the civil defense movement. Then came the nuclear test ban treaty, the atmospheric treaty. That was a big success. And we haven't had any successes since, except for restraining the government to a degree in regard to the war in Vietnam.

We didn't end the war. It lasted twelve years. [Pauses.] And it was very, very frustrating. The longer it went on, the more desperate our young people became. Roger [LaPorte] burned himself to death in 1965.* Desperation there. By 1968, you found that people were questioning their commitment to nonviolence. We'd done everything. Petitioned en masse. Written letters. We had written articles. We'd had demonstrations, we had educated people, we had fasted and we had prayed. And it only got worse.

I was already older. The silent generation, as we were called. But more than anybody else of my generation, I knew people from the previous generations, not only in the secular movement, but in the Catholic Worker movement: Ade Bethune and Joe Zarrella and Bob Ludlow and Tom Sullivan. And the women. Pat Rusk, Eileen Fantino, Mary Ann McCoy, and . . . others. John Cort. People going back to the thirties. So I can be a kind of living link between the people of the fifties through the eighties and the people from the thirties and forties.

* Roger LaPorte was a young Catholic Worker who immolated himself in front of the U.S. Mission to the United Nations on November 9, 1965, in protest against the escalating U.S. involvement in the Vietnam War.

The sense of desperation that kids were experiencing in the sixties—you could see it in their rejection of institutional values. There was just this horrible anxiety. All the institutions of the Western world were under attack, from the university to the town hall to the church. And it wasn't rational.

Remember the Chicago draft board action? I remember one of the boys who was close to that. He was also apparently quite close to the heart of the Catholic Worker in Chicago at that time. Well, he held up a cup of coffee and a donut and said, "These are my body and blood." Meaning, "Hell! Let's take it *all* out of the church! The reality is just this—just the bread line and the resistance to the war." But that's just not true. There's the primacy of the spiritual. Peter used to say that: the primacy of the spiritual. With every change of consciousness, you have to ask yourself, "What does the primacy of the spiritual mean?" I think we felt we had an alternative that made some kind of sense. People were paying a price. David Miller and Jim Wilson and Terry Sullivan and Jack Cook and others were doing significant prison time. (I was no longer draft eligible.)

Ro: Then why did you keep burning your draft card?

Tom: Because I had to. Because television cameras were aiming at me. Because I know what a good picture is. It was a tremendously economical action, too. I may not have been draft eligible, but I was responsible legally for having that Goddamn card on my person. And well you remember what a tremendous impact those draft card burnings made! It was the biggest thing in the resistance movement up to that point.

The working press were on our side, basically. When the [first] draft card burning took place, the *Times* helped to choreograph it, told us when to have it and where, so it would hit the Sunday papers. And Sunday morning . . . God! We're on every front page! And television interviews and radio interviews and Merv Griffin . . . all that stuff!

And I was at a point where [the action] was indicated for me. I was publicly urging young men to acts of resistance, so I really had some kind of moral obligation to share that vulnerability. I shared it by burning the card. I was very lucky to get only six months. We expected what everybody else was getting—two and a half to three and a half years.

I wrote a statement upon burning the draft card, describing in some depth precisely how I perceived it at the time. (And since then, I haven't changed in the slightest, not in that regard.) *Commonweal* published that in a box opposite an editorial in which, for the first time, they took a position against the bombing of North Vietnam.

Ro: Um . . . hmmm. What do you feel best about from that period?

Tom: I think it's that I helped to keep the Catholic Worker movement centered in New York on an even keel during that time. Starting with Roger [LaPorte's] death. That was when I realized that things could really blow up.

Roger's death . . . it happened in November of '65. The telephone rang. Five-thirty in the morning. Bruce Porter from the *Post* was on the line. We were friends.

"I hate to wake you up. I have some terrible news." Yaugh! I figured I'd call Dorothy around eight-thirty. She'd already heard about it.

"What are we going to do?"

Chris [Kearns] just shooed all the reporters away. Let everybody know that if they talked to reporters, that would be against Dorothy's will, which is tantamount to saying good-bye. (We had no redress, no committees or any of that shit. If you're out, you're out.) But we realized we had to say something to the press. By about ten-thirty, I had something written. Read it to Dorothy and she said, "You can release that." They came with cameras and heavy equipment and all the cables they had to have then. It was just one interview after another all day long.

An elderly Quaker lady in Detroit had burned herself. What would have happened if we had a rash of suicides, of self-immolations? We make this moral judgement: "This is the wrong thing to do." How do we tell our constituencies—the younger and less stable people, or any people, any people at all—so no one else will do it? And still respect the sacrifice of Roger LaPorte? Very delicately, that's how. I was also very much concerned what the Catholic Worker was going to look like.

Well, that was '65. Sixty-eight was no easier. There was despair and frustration leading to ultimate acts. What if a Catholic Worker house blew up? I think it was . . . I pride myself on having participated with others in trying to talk sense to people. Trying to offer alternatives. The Tiger Cage project. The Meal of Reconciliation project. Fasting and prayer. Holding up [as models] the Buddhists in Vietnam. Addressing things that we could address. The political prisoner issue. And building the mass demonstrations. We were in on every single stage, in all of those demonstrations. One or another of us was on every single committee of the Mobilization from the time it was first conceptualized until it fell apart.

When the bishops wrote the letter on peace in '83, I was one of only three pacifist consultants. I think that the recognition that Dorothy was given in the Peace Pastoral was important. I don't think that would have happened if we hadn't kept a steady keel during the sixties. Despite the crazies.

You know, I asked Dorothy once . . . it seemed to me that there were a lot more of them around in the sixties than before. She said, "No, no, no, no. It's always the same." However, I remember people storming into her room: "You're a fake. You're a phony. When is the last time you peeled a carrot? All you do is go off flying around to see the fucking pope. Where are you going next? The world is burning down, and you're not even scraping a carrot." And toward the end of her life, she finally admitted that had been the hardest time. She wanted to deny it at the time, but she knew that things *could* blow up.

Bill Griffin was part of that younger generation but had a different approach.

Bill Griffin: I'd gone into the army after spending two years in Canada. My going had been very hard on my parents. The student movement had passed the more Gandhian phase, had become vicious. "Off the pig!" Now the war in Vietnam was a vicious, brutal, unjust war. The troubles [during] the Vietnam War were, in my estimation, almost a civil war in the United States. The assassinations in 1968. Washington was burning. I was at Georgetown studying languages, living around Dupont Circle. We went up on the roof of our building after the Martin Luther King murder in April and watched the city burn.

I was a draft dodger, I guess you'd say. You read back historically—in all the wars, a lot of Americans have gone to Canada. And [our] country [was] founded also by a lot of people who didn't want to serve in the German army, or the French army.

Ro: I've always heard that my ancestors came to get away from Bismarck's conscription.

Bill: Yes. A little-known part of American history is this resistance to a large standing army. It's only been part of our [policy] since the Second World War.

Anyway, it wasn't . . . it wasn't a very good time in Canada, so I came back and just sort of submitted to whatever would happen. I didn't have any kind of religious . . . you know, [I was in] the adolescent stage where you're giving up mechanical kinds of belief and you're trying to make your own more authentic kind. I went into the military. Met some very good people. There was a liberal side to the army, and they put me with that, with some nurses at Madigan General Hospital at Fort Lewis. At that time, in '72, there were many for drug detoxication. (A lot of drugs. Mostly pot, but also heroin, and I was able to keep above that because I was a little above the peer pressure.) But there were also a lot of amputees coming back for rehab.

I remember very vividly the '72 bombing of Hanoi. It was a period of trying to find something—anything—valid in American society. Then I came across the *Catholic Worker*. In a certain sense, that redeemed the honor of the country.

These people were resisting the war, but they hadn't become as violent as the people they were opposing. I remember a column of Dorothy's where she said she was very glad her grandson was returning from Vietnam safe and sound. (We heard later that he's had problems with Agent Orange.) But she could be very glad for his safety and then end up writing about this horrible, vicious war. So she could be part of American society and still be . . . love it and still criticize it.

Ro: Which hadn't been your experience up until then.

Bill: No. It was either love it unquestioningly or hate it unquestioningly. A very black-and-white kind of thinking. Thank God I didn't go to Vietnam! I know people who did do it decently, who didn't get involved in atrocities, didn't get involved with drugs, and tried to do the honorable service. But there is no question that there were many other people who were caught up in terrible things.

So I came across the *Catholic Worker* and said, "After I finish . . ." I came to the Catholic Worker in February of '74, to St. Joseph House. At that time the soup line was not that long, maybe a hundred people. The Bowery was an old men's ghetto. Old pensioners trying to make ends meet. Not much evidence of alcoholism, but when there was, it was striking. There wasn't that much drug abuse, except among the younger people. Vietnam veterans who were on the street and unable to reenter [society].

> **B**ill is now a registered nurse. He still lives in the Worker neighborhood and writes for the *Catholic Worker.* Several Catholic Workers were imprisoned for burning draft files during the Vietnam War. Perhaps most famous was Michael Cullen, founder of Casa Maria in Milwaukee, who was deported to Ireland for his spearheading of the Milwaukee Fourteen. Less well known is Tom Lewis, an artist and still a faithful Catholic Worker, who lived at Baltimore's Viva House Catholic Worker during part of the Vietnam era and is now affiliated with the Mustard Seed Catholic Worker in Worcester, Massachusetts.

Tom Lewis: Father Phil Berrigan and I both had a history of nonviolence through the civil rights movement. We realized that destroying a draft record would be a little different than sitting at a lunch counter, certainly. I would say we really struggled with it and really explored what that would mean. Particularly in the sense of responsibility, of knowing that perhaps others would [follow us]. We were aware that we were taking a step that was very threatening to us personally, as well as a . . . I wouldn't say a change as much as a . . . a continuance of what the Catholic Workers were doing by destroying draft cards. We spoke to many people in the peace community. We decided the way to support these young Catholic Workers who were going to prison for burning their draft cards was to destroy the draft files themselves.

As Dan Berrigan put it, 1-A files are actually death certificates. Do they have a right to even be considered property? There's a fundamental difference between violence to property and violence to people. And there's a fundamental misunderstanding when people associate the two as one. Any kind of violence against people is not nonviolent. But what about destroying a death certificate? So with prayer, with much discussion and discernment, we moved to do the first draft board witness in Baltimore.

The main draft office was actually across the street from my art studio, which made it very convenient. There were four of us, and we were called the Baltimore Four. Myself, Phil Berrigan (he was Father Philip Berrigan then), a United Church of Christ minister—Reverend Jim Mengel—and a young poet named David Eberhardt. So the four of us went in.

We had decided to pour our blood. That was another issue. What would we do to these files once we were inside? Would we burn them? We talked to a lawyer about it and he said, "Well, why don't you pour honey on them or something?" But Phil came up with that symbol, with blood.

Ro: I think someone has said it's not a very American symbol.

Tom: We certainly talked about it as being a Biblical symbol and certainly a healing symbol. And also a very sobering symbol of what in fact those 1-A files were.

Ro: How did you feel about that symbol as an artist?

Tom: Well, I personally liked the idea of fire. But I adjusted. One thing about these actions over the years—especially ones where there's a lot of risk involved like draft board witnesses, like Plowshare witness—a community develops, and we learn to kind of listen and adjust and trust. Rather than it being all one person's vision, it's a combination of everyone's. So we went in and poured the blood on the files and, expectedly, the government got very upset, and placed very serious charges on the four of us. And then, you know, began that legal process.

Ro: How did you feel walking in, knowing this was the first time? Weren't you just absolutely scared to death?

Tom: Well, you know, it's interesting. Fear is a healthy thing. When you proceed with a witness like this, my experience is that fear is replaced by a kind of . . . I would say it's a spirit of hope. That's the best way I can put it. And as a Catholic, I think that has something to do with divine help or intervention. We essentially did everything the best we could as human beings. All the planning was very carefully thought out. We contacted several press people ahead of time, people we could trust. We didn't tell them exactly what we were doing 'cause we were very careful not to exploit them for a potential conspiracy indictment. A support person gave them a packet of information which they would open after we went into the building. [After some initial confusion] 'cause a truck was blocking the view, we went right in to the files and poured our blood on them.

We didn't try to leave. We prepared the best we could as human beings and then basically left it in the Lord's hands. There's some kind of inner strength. I call it . . . I think it's spiritual.

Ro: It could also be adrenalin.

Tom: Well, I'm sure there are medical or psychological explanations for it, which is fine. When we did this action, we weren't thinking that many others would do anything like it. We were thinking primarily that it was morally the correct thing to do, and I think we made it possible for all of us to see that you can do more than stand on the sideline. I don't see us as heroes. If there were any heroes, I think they were the young Catholic Workers who were the first to burn their draft cards and go to prison. To be quite honest, they led the way. What they did was morally correct and we just caught up with them.

Well, we were taken to trial and of course were found guilty and had a sentencing date in May, a couple of months away. And we were out and continuing our work, and I was getting ready to go to jail. We were facing about twenty years. And then a short time before our sentencing date, Phil said to me, "Let's do it again."

My heart dropped. I realized it would mean still more jail time, and I was frightened. At the same time, there was something in me that knew it was the correct thing to do. I said, "Let's talk more about it." So we did—had some good talks about it. I felt on a political level that Phil would potentially be very isolated if he were the only person doing it again, so we agreed on this and proceeded to search for other people. People just emerged. The Melvilles, the two missionaries from Guatemala. Dan Berrigan, of course. So nine of us came together for what eventually was called the Catonsville Nine. I so much admired Phil's courage and honesty. He was really the first Catholic priest to do such a thing in this country. Really the first to be arrested. Certainly during the Vietnam era, there were no bishops that I recall . . . certainly no voices in the Catholic hierarchy that were saying anything against the war publicly. I personally felt it was important to have more priests involved.

We left for the Catonsville action in the middle of the day. In fact, we met at my mother's house in the suburbs. She had prepared a little ham for us. And I remember telling her (we still laugh about it) that, no, we wouldn't have lunch today. She knew something was happening, but of course didn't know what, so she certainly had to trust. Once again, we had the press in another place. They were there within minutes of the witness . . . of going into the Catonsville draft office and taking the files out in big trash containers and burning them on the parking lot.

Ro: So you got your symbol this time?

Tom: Yes. The various symbols emerged. Dan was concerned about fire because of the safety. Correctly so. We picked Catonsville partly because we were able to take the records outside and have a very open and a very safe place to burn them.

I also came up with the symbol of napalm. I had researched it in the military law library in Georgetown a week before, so I learned that there actually existed a way of making a kind of homemade napalm. That was also an indictment of the sickness of the military—that they would figure out how to make their own napalm in case they ran out of the professional stuff. So we made it the night before in a kind of ritual together, kind of a liturgy, and then used it to burn the 1-A files. Dan Berrigan said it was far better to burn those death certificates with napalm than burn the people in Vietnam.

Phil and I were to be sentenced on Friday from the Baltimore Four witness and we did Catonsville on Tuesday. Needless to say, they were quite upset, especially with Phil and I. We both received six-year sentences that Friday. The Catonsville trial came later. Phil and I were taken back and forth from jail to court in handcuffs.

And that's where I met Dorothy Day for the first time. I remember we were sitting up in front of the courtroom, and someone came up and said, "Look around, look around. Dorothy is here to see you." And there was this beautiful face, almost like it was surrounded by sunshine. White hair and great smiling face of Dorothy in the courtroom.

I was in jail from that time on. I've never personally spoken to Dorothy, other than seeing her in the court when she came to support us. And certainly to approve of us. It certainly is my understanding that she approved of what we did. In fact, she writes about Catonsville as being a liturgy and a very proven way.

I recall a very interesting letter from Thomas Merton. Dan had written to Merton prior to Catonsville, written that it was a witness that would involve destruction of property and what that meant. Merton is very clear in his reply. Raising questions about destruction of property and relating it to what the young political radicals were talking about—destroying buildings. Pointing out that there might be a person in that building, and we would be responsible for that person. And he, of course, ruled out any kind of destruction of property that might harm a person.

So, in a way, both Catonsville and Baltimore actually set the limits for the nonviolent peace movement about destruction of property. Being very clear about the type of property and the . . . the liturgy of what we did. We were quite clear about taking responsibility for the safety of everyone. Not like the red groups. We very clearly said no to "Burn, baby, burn!" and set very clear limits. Many in the general peace movement did not support Catonsville. They just couldn't understand the idea of a spiritual witness and the continuance of it to prison, couldn't understand the clear nonviolent statement and the personal responsibility of going to prison for many years.

Tom was initially sent to jail for six years, the highest sentence given to resisters at that time, although his sentence was later reduced to three years. Involved in the Catonsville and Baltimore trials were Willa Bickham and her husband, Brendan Walsh, who founded Viva House in Baltimore in 1968.

Willa Bickham: Tom Lewis was a very great influence on our life. In one of the front rooms, we have some huge etchings that he's done, like six feet by six feet. Four panels that portray the entire Catonsville Nine time and the Baltimore Four time. When he got out of prison, he came back to live with us.

Our first house guests [when we opened Viva House] were the Catonsville Nine folks. They were on the lam at that point because they hadn't surrendered. And we had lots and lots of visitors when the trial started. The theme for the support work during the trial was "Come to Agnew country!" It was the biggest antiwar demonstration ever held in Baltimore. Lots of activity. People came from all over the country and it was a real focus of attention for the antiwar movement.

Dorothy Day came down for the trial and stayed at the house a couple of nights. Then she took us aside and asked Brendan and me if our feelings would be hurt if she stayed at the local convent 'cause it was too noisy at the house. *So* many people! I mean we packed them in every room. I remember her coming over and doing dishes, though.

Even after the trial, the house was filled with folks who were working very hard against the war. We had no trouble at that time getting money or volunteers. There was a lot of enthusiasm. [Aptly enough, the Viva House newspaper is called *Enthusiasm.*] Anything people could do to end the war in Vietnam, they were willing to do. And they knew that we were involved in the works of mercy as well as resisting the works of war. We did a soup kitchen for, oh, about a hundred, a hundred fifty people a day every day.

Mary Jane and Julian Pleasants, from the "pioneer generation," speak of these days from South Bend, Indiana.

Mary Jane: The late sixties were horrible times for all of us, I think. We lost a lot of our earlier confidence. All the time I was growing up, I used to think the church and the state and I were all on the same side. But that really fell apart in the late sixties. We were disillusioned about the state and the church did not jump in to be a leader, in any sense. So we were discouraged both about the country and about the church. Our children faced having to go to a war that they didn't believe in. We lost a lot of enthusiasm, as did the whole country, and we felt things were out of control, in contrast to when our children were younger.

Julian: I think part of the reason we had been so optimistic earlier . . . we figured as Catholics we had the answers. In 1964 the pope had said he was going to reconsider birth control, and I thought that was fine because I believed birth control was a fine idea. I'm a biologist and I saw that you could easily overshoot . . . not the absolute capacity of the land but its ability at the present moment to take care of all these people. So I wrote a piece in an early book in favor of the use of contraceptives. Then in 1968 the pope went against everything his group had advised him to do. So '68 was a bad year for me.

I was a real admirer of Hubert Humphrey, but I was also very impressed with Eugene McCarthy, and the way the whole Democratic thing turned out that year was so destructive. Then I think that was the year that the Russians marched into Czechoslovakia. It had seemed that Czechoslovakia was showing "communism with a human face," and that was wiped out. So with everything in our own church and in our own country and in the world, why, it was a discouraging time. I don't think we can think that as Catholics we have the answers to things anymore.

Ro: So the young people today don't really have that certainty?

Julian: No, I don't think they do. And that's hard. That's very hard. Part of the optimism that carried the pioneers through this country was unwarranted—the Protestant ethic and manifest destiny. Subdue the land. They had a religious optimism which was unjustified. But it's a powerful force. It enables you to do things you couldn't otherwise do.

After the Vietnam War ended, many of the Catholic Worker houses adjusted to upheavals in their local communities. One could see Viva House in Baltimore as typical in this respect.

Willa: When we were doing straight shelter, it was twenty-four hours a day, seven days a week. So we tied ourselves up completely. It took three people full time just to help these families find places, get their lives in order, and all that kind of stuff. We had become like an agency of the city. I mean these social workers would call us night and day. The state hospital would actually dump people at our door. Their van would pull up and they'd . . . that was their discharge plan, you know. "Viva House." But they wouldn't contact us. They would just dump the person at the door, whether we had room or not.

Then in 1980, our neighborhood was declared an historic area, of all things. The poorest white neighborhood in Baltimore. We fought very hard against this historic designation. We went door to door. Had a funeral procession to bury the city council bill. We had meetings every night, and we lost.

The city council bill had nothing to do with historic preservation of the area. This is your inner-city slum. Substandard housing. The folks behind the preservation status were newcomers to the neighborhood who used historic preservation as a real estate gimmick. It had nothing to do with human needs. It was human greed. A good tax shelter introduced by our local senator. If it's declared historic and you do certain repair work, it could be written off your income tax [as] accelerated tax depreciation.

So it was just a real estate gimmick and indeed the properties started turning over *so* fast. I mean people were making money like crazy. A house would be bought and sold like four or five times in a year, each time jacking the price up and putting the poor people who lived there out of a home, of course. Nobody lived in the house, and the whole scheme had nothing at all to do with housing. Just real estate speculation and preying on the people who thought if the word "historic" was there, it must be a good thing for Baltimore.

There was one family involved in the majority of the speculation. Three sisters within this one family. We almost got sued because we put out a leaflet listing all their properties. They call it flipping. You know, you buy it like on Tuesday for ten thousand dollars and you sell it to an investor for twenty thousand on Wednesday. Real quick profit. So as a result, part of our neighborhood, the square around us called Union Square, has been gentrified. Property values went up out of sight completely, like four or five hundred percent. As we knew they would.

It really affects the fixed-income people, of course—the home owners. We knew the renters were going to get booted out, but the home owners were mostly old people on social security. They couldn't afford those high taxes. A lot of the neighborhood changed and housing was a real crunch. So that's when we began our shelter for women.

Gentrification has devastated our neighborhood, destroyed the entire community. Violence has increased and property crime. Nobody looks out for anybody, and we don't know each other any more. The gentry come without children, buy a "starter house," and sell it within a year or two. Children, you know, are great community builders. If you have a child, you go walking around the neighborhood and talk to everybody. So it's been very hard on the neighborhood. But we were here first, here since 1968. And we're not going to move.

We've certainly been the squeaky wheel in the city for making the homeless visible. We've done Christmas plays in front of city hall. "There is no room at the inn, Baltimore City, no place for the poor." After we decided to shut down the women's shelter, we made it perfectly clear that we knew the money for the poor was being diverted into the city's tourism. All the fancy sidewalks . . . uh, "street furniture," they call it. The Hyatt Hotel was built by Mr. Pritzger, who's one of the ten wealthiest families in our country. He even got federal subsidies, got grants to build the Hyatt Hotel.

To shut us up, they kept telling us about this trickle-down theory. "Just be patient, be patient. We'll have all this big tourist industry in the city, and the money will come trickling down to the poor. They will get some crumbs from the rich." Well, we haven't seen crumbs nor trickle yet.

Some houses, like Viva House, survived. Houses come and houses go, like the two houses in my town of Saginaw that opened and closed during the late sixties. Here's Daniel Marshall's sardonic capsule history of a Berkeley attempt, followed by a later closing in that supposedly most open of university communities.

Daniel Marshall: So we opened a Catholic Worker house in Berkeley. It was very exciting. The community movement, the hippie movement, was just starting. We decided to do away with rules and base the whole thing on spontaneity. And, of course, we wore ourselves out in about two days, and the whole thing flew apart in four months.

Daniel later went to Tivoli and then was helpful in beginning Arthur Sheehan House in Brooklyn with Jacques Travers. John Cooper describes a more recent Berkeley attempt.

John Cooper: In 1985, I had quite an abrupt feeling that I wanted to serve the poor. I tried doing it at various places. At the Food Project in Berkeley . . . they fired me. Hospitality House in the Tenderloin of San Francisco, St. Anthony's in San Francisco. Each of them went a day. I ended up at Martin's [Martin de Porres Soup Kitchen in San Francisco]. Terrific spirit there. After working there for several months, I realized I could save on transportation and do the same thing in Berkeley. So we set up here in People's Park, where the people are. Serving out of the back of a truck, at least for now.

Ro: Where were you before you came . . . before you got this call to serve the poor?

John: I was driving a cab in San Francisco.

Ro: You're not exactly a Milquetoast man. How do you see your personality affecting the Worker here?

John: Oh, badly on the whole. I am a starter of things, but I'm not a "keeper going" of things. I don't have that personality. I'm an initiator. I have the restlessness of temperament and the drive and ambition to get something started, but you need a different person to keep things going. You need someone who's gentler. But then that gentle person couldn't have started it.

In May 1989, this open letter was printed in the *Catholic Agitator,* the newspaper of the Los Angeles Catholic Worker:

> Dear Friends: We towed a building on to People's Park this morning and opened for breakfast as People's Cafe—the Berkeley Catholic Worker House of Hospitality. We'd like to explain our action and ask for your support and your prayers.
>
> We opened the house so the poor who wander the Southside streets can have a place in which they may be received with the respect they deserve as children of God. After our two-year search for premises and after being turned down in 28 locations, still the people have no house. We opened the house on People's Park because that is where the people are. . . . Please support us. . . . Raise your voices please on behalf of the poor who have no voice. And then come by and see our house—People's Cafe. And please pray for us that we may do God's work peacefully and with love.
>
> In God's Light,
>
> > *John Cooper, Michele Frazier, Trish Maniatis*
> > Berkeley Catholic Worker

The People's Cafe arrived twenty years after the People's Park riots that signaled the beginning of the Berkeley Free Speech Movement. "Twenty years later, the university still wants to build student dormitories, while others want the park left to the people who use it most—the homeless," wrote Bill Kenkelen of the *National Catholic Reporter.* Ten months later, during the night of March 10, 1990, the People's Cafe was removed from the park by California police dressed in riot gear.

Other Worker communities have had equally frustrating but ultimately more successful searches for housing. Barbara Blaine's story of St. Elizabeth's in Chicago shows how misunderstanding can hinder hospitality.

Barbara Blaine: It's a long story. There is no city more Catholic than Chicago. Huge physical plants. So many parishes! In 1986, two hundred parishes were slated to be closed in one year. Two hundred! And of course, tons of parish schools have already closed. It's a slap in the face to homeless persons to know that there's an empty building that belongs to the archdiocese. Just sitting there. And most of those empty buildings are heated, to keep the pipes from freezing.

We figured we were a group of homeless people. Let's see if we can get the archdiocese to let us use one of the empty convents. Well, we found out that the convents are not really all empty. Most of them have thirty bedrooms or so and three or four nuns rattling around in them.

Ro: Couldn't a few of them move together?

Barbara: Well, you'd think so. But they just don't do that. And each parish thinks to itself, kind of. There isn't even a mechanism to try to connect them. Each pastor is responsible for his own little kingdom or domain—his empire. It's his turf, and the other people can't get into it. The archdiocese has made a big effort over the past years to try to use buildings for good purposes. I have to give them credit for that. Catholic Charities has taken over a number of abandoned schools and convents and rectories and turned them into really creative things. And we finally were able to get this convent at St. Therese's for our Worker. But it took us a long time, an incredibly long time.

After a whole lot of negotiations and false hopes, they finally offered us a rectory on the South Side that we really didn't want. Well, I shouldn't say "we." Barbara didn't want it. I didn't want to move to the South Side. Most of the guests were white. The South Side is all black. It's like moving to a new city. And all our support was up on the North Side. So I figured we'd lose all our support and have to change our whole focus. And like reculturize ourselves. (I don't think that's a word, but you know what I mean.) Come into a whole new culture. I didn't want to do that lightly. We talked about it a lot. Then through all of this, we're trying to pray and discover what God wants of us. Does all this trouble maybe mean that we shouldn't even be having the house? Dorothy always said if it's meant to be, God blesses the work.

Ro: It's not always instant success, though.

Barbara: Well, we weren't talking about success. We were talking about survival. Finally, we had this sense that God was really calling us to the South Side after all. So we came down and met with the pastor and met with people in the parish. We were going to move into this rectory on June fifteenth.

On June first, a new pastor was assigned. And he said we couldn't move into the parish. So we didn't know what to do. Again. There was all kinds of turmoil with . . . I mean Gary [Olivero] and I weren't getting along. It was hot summertime with roaches all over the place, and everybody was kind of on each other's nerves. So we really seriously thought it was time to close the house.

Once again, though, the diocese finally came through, and offered us this place, which is also on the South Side. The people down here had really been burned by a white pastor, who caused an incredible amount of pain in this black parish. So the new pastor said we couldn't come unless the parish thought it was okay. Which was fine with us, of course.

Well, anyway, they had their parish meeting and decided to let the Catholic Worker use the building. Yea!!! We were pretty excited until we came down and saw the place. It was really, really *bad.* The building had been empty for eight years, and it hadn't been heated for the past five. So all the paint had peeled, and all the plaster had cracked. It was filthy. People had even left food upstairs, and it was really gross. But there were a lot of windows, and the building was solid. So we figured we'd put some elbow grease into it and make it livable. And we did.

The city of Los Angeles has, for some who don't live there (and maybe some who do) a sense of unreality, of being too big for belief. Even the Los Angeles Catholic Worker once fell prey to bigness. Catherine Morris and I talked about this in late 1987.

Catherine Morris: You know, I think we need some history here. Did Jeff [Catherine's husband] talk about spending several years working with the powers-that-be in the city? Well, I'll tell you . . . it was something!

One summer—it was 1974—we saw this article about L.A. having adopted the Philadelphia Plan for Skid Row. And there was a city council meeting about it, so I went. At the end of the meeting, you could stand up and say somethig if you wanted to. So I did, and all these people rushed over and wanted to talk to me, wanted to know where I was from and if [the L.A. Worker and Hospitality Kitchen] would be their "clients." The same thing happened at the next meeting. All these people wanted to get into this issue, but they had to have a client. And I was the only person expressing the opinion that was also their point of view.

The third week, I told Jeff I didn't want to go to those meetings anymore. "Why don't you go?" So he did. He latched onto these people. Hospitality Kitchen became the client of both Community Design Center and Legal Aid Foundation, and they all started working together.

So then, through this association, we did this really interesting thing. We went to the library and we looked up this Philadelphia Plan. We contacted Leonard Blumberg, the author, at Temple University, and he came out here. He'd been a CO [conscientious objector] during World War II, and he knew all about the Catholic Worker and so forth. And so he came and stayed with us. It turns out that the Philadelphia Plan had been a *complete* failure! And yet the city of Los Angeles was adopting it. So the Community Design Center, the Los Angeles Catholic Worker, the Legal Aid Foundation, and the Public Inebriate Program wrote up this study. It was like any study you'd see from the government. And then someone who worked with the council chambers put the reports on the city council tables. So when the council members walked in, they looked at it and started asking where it came from. And Jeff and Gary Squires were asked to come to the next meeting.

Well, it turns out that the council dropped the Philadelphia Plan and accepted their study. Jeff was put on the Skid Row Task Force of the Community Redevelopment Agency and became its chairman for a couple of years. Actually, he created the new plan for the redevelopment of the area. Spent countless hours on this project. We often had to cover for him at the soup kitchen, but he didn't just drop out. And these people, you know, these people in their suits and ties, would come and talk to him. He'd be stirring soup and he'd be talking to them.

The first phase of the plan he created was to have a development corporation. They adopted it, funded it, and set it up. And he chose the board of directors and became the chairman of the board for the first three years. He also continued going to the meetings of the Skid Row Task Force. And so he spent like five years on this. Many, many, many, many hours.

Actually this figured into the . . . uh . . . time of tension. Because finally we were saying that corporations and boards of directors didn't have a part in the Catholic Worker. That was turned around to Jeff. "Tell us how many boards of directors you're on." He was on eight or something like that. 'Cause they breed each other, you know.

And so he actually took a period of time, actually fasted for the whole of Advent—a water fast—trying to discern what he should do about this. At the end of that fast, he resigned from every board he was on. Now he doesn't engage in that kind of work at all. He used to be called upon all the time to go to meetings and speak about the "street side" of things. Definitely the Skid Row spokesperson. And at first it looked like the development corporation was really making a tremendous contribution to the row, but it really . . .

Ro: Do they ever?

Catherine: No. That's what he learned. The hard way. He said he'd much rather serve the soup himself and just get done what he could get done than pay someone fifty thousand dollars to go around talking to get Skid Row more money. So that was an interesting period, a very interesting period. It was very, very exhausting, too.

Then there was the big breakup, the trauma with the house, and we're still recovering from that. At one point I believe, we had nine projects in-house—Justice Bakery, Guadalupe Playground, the Nuestra Tienda (an at-cost store), Inner City Law Center. Let's see, I don't want to leave something out. We had the *Agitator,* Hospitality Kitchen, Hospitality Free Medical Clinic, Hennacy Hospitality House, Zedakah Hospitality House (which we just lost from the earthquake). It seems like I'm still leaving something out, and I can't think what it is.

We started projects in two ways. Either to meet a need that we noticed, or else someone expressed an interest in doing something, and then the community supported it by getting the project started. The Justice Bakery started, for example, in the back room of the kitchen. They'd work in the back room while we were working in the kitchen, and they'd do the baking after we finished. And that grew to baking *while* we were working in the kitchen, so it was really a zoo there for a couple of years.

The bakery hires people right off the street and immediately pays them a decent wage. Never deals with minimum wage at all. I can't quote the wages now, but the bakery is probably nearing ten years old and at the time they started, they were paying five dollars an hour. To people who maybe did nothing but put cookies in a bag, and had trouble doing that. I can remember some of the early bakery employees, and they were pretty handicapped.

So the bakery grew. Through Jeff's involvement in the Skid Row Development Corporation, they had the opportunity to move to their own building. It was still a Catholic Worker project, but it was incorporated, and that didn't stand with the CW idea of noninvolvement in the structure. But that really never caused any problem because the idea of the project was to create revenue for the employees. Tony [Trafecanty] worked as an unpaid manager and still does.

Let's see. The at-cost store ended because Larry and Carol, who ran it, were leaving the area. They were ready to turn the management of the store over to someone else in the community, but no one picked it up. It was a time when there were fewer and fewer families using the store, anyway, so it closed.

The playground was open for five years, I think. Then the hot project was the Law Center. As it grew and started really entering into court action and all, they needed more money, and they felt the need to hire people. Lawyers were donating their time. Clerical people were being hired. They incorporated. This pattern began, and we didn't meet it at that point, and question it, and weigh it against the philosophy of the Worker. So in effect we went along with them. But then as things seemed to be kind of snowballing, we challenged it, and that was the period of greatest tension in the community. People just didn't see eye to eye with the direction the community was taking. Jeff and I saw the period as a return to the roots. We had been going in directions away from the real simplicity of the Worker ideals. And it was not well received—the challenge that was presented.

I think the decision had to be made. The history of this particular Worker community, from its beginnings with Dan and Chris Delany, was that the community members worked full time with the community projects. We didn't have part-time jobs and, you know, help with paying the rent and those kinds of things. We worked full time at the Worker.

The changes I'm describing are how we see what happened, and how the analysis has come about after it all took place. At the time it was coming down, we just knew that a whole lot of people were really mad at us, and that it was very personally directed at Jeff and Catherine, and that we were seen as very authoritarian. But we just kept riding out the tide, the tide of people leaving. Finally, just six of us—Jeff, Catherine, Julia Occhiogrosso, Jonathan and Rio Parfrey, and Meredith Males—had been here from the onset of the struggle to the end. (Well, we were a little bigger than that. Some other folks were still with us.)

We asked a Sister of St. Joseph of Orange, Kathleen Schinhofen, to help us. She works with conflict resolution, and she was a tremendous help in sorting things out—naming things, and giving us a vocabulary, and explaining that what we were going through was similar to what happens in many religious orders. And she gave us diagrams to show us what was happening and really saw us through a change in structure. Helped us to set down our beliefs and values. Then there was the famous day in January of '86 when we went to our friend Mavis Cain's house and wrote our mission statement. In Kathleen's vocabulary, we were beginning a "refoundation."

I'm already looking at it from the other side, the side of reconciliation and how we do that. How do we come back together? Reconciliation is a process, but it's . . . it's also the will of God. Oddly enough in this time of difficulty, we would pick as our mission to start new houses. We said that in '86 we'd start a house in Las Vegas and in '87 we'd start a house in Orange County, in the belly of the beast. And so we have done that. It's a tremendous loss to L.A. to have Julia in Las Vegas and Rio and Jonathan and their children away from us in Orange County. But because their houses are going well and their ministry is strengthening, we feel that it was a good mission. But we mind not being with them. We mind not having them here.

I don't know about the future. For a while, we weren't sure there *was* a future for Los Angeles. But now we've got our heads turned towards the wind and have started feeling the wind again.

> *We have all known the long loneliness and we have learned that the only solution is love and that love comes with community. It all happened while we sat there talking, and it is still going on.*
>
> —Dorothy Day, postcript to *The Long Loneliness*

CHAPTER 2

The Word

The first time I ever heard of the Catholic Worker was when I saw the newspaper. It was in March or April of 1970. I was still in the Episcopal church, so I read it to see what "they" were doing—Catholics. They had their own kind of "in" language. It struck me that you had to read other things before you could fully understand what they were saying. It was a part of something, not something that stood on its own. "Personalism" was a term and "culture" and "cultivation." Used like code words. It was quirky.

Then when I was in prison [for burning draft records in San Jose], a friend tried to send me the *Catholic Worker,* and the prison wouldn't allow it in. We were able to get *Peacemaker Newsletter* and some other things, so I thought, "Wow! What's in this paper that's so threatening? I'm going to check this out!" So, of course, when I got out, I did.

—John Williams

Here's one thing we always do: When people make a contribution to the Denver Catholic Worker, we start sending them our newsletter. And oftentimes that ends the contribution because people begin to see our perspective.

—Sr. Anna Koop

T HE Catholic Worker was first a newspaper and even today, the distinctive Ade Bethune masthead and "penny a copy" slogan of the *Catholic Worker* define the movement for many people. Even though it's no longer the only periodical that speaks to the Christian Left, the newspaper continues to generate interest, particularly within the movement itself where it is sometimes seen as less provocative than when Day was editor. This chapter begins with the reminiscence of "pioneers," continues with memories of several of the editors through the years—Tom Cornell, Jim Forest, Pat Jordan, Peggy Scherer, Jane Sammon— and concludes with reflections from leaders in other houses with influential newspapers.*

* Readers wanting an analysis and history of the *Catholic Worker* should see the work of Nancy L. Roberts, especially her *Dorothy Day and the "Catholic Worker."*

Ade Bethune first came upon the Worker in late 1933.

Ade Bethune: Dorothy Weston gave me a kind of a tour of the place, and sent me home with copies of the paper. And all the way home on the "el," I read these things and I, ah . . . fires were being kindled. I also noticed that the paper was not terribly attractive looking, and I thought it could benefit from some more exciting black-and-white pictures. I had . . . I was acquainted with *New Masses,* and thought they had beautiful black-and-white pictures. I was aiming to do something like that for the Catholic paper, so I made four pictures and sent them down to the Catholic Worker. After a while I got a postcard back saying, "We love your drawings, and we will print them. Thank you, The editors." Oh, I was thrilled!

I wasn't terribly impressed by the masthead, though. Dorothy had got two little cuts from her printer. One showed a laborer with a maul and the other one had a pick-ax over his shoulder, and they occupied the two opposite corners of the top of the paper. Then an astute reader wrote to Dorothy: "You're really not doing right for all your emphasis on being interracial. Your two workers are white. Where is the black one?" So Dorothy got [a picture of a] black worker [from the printer]. It wasn't quite the same size as the other one, but now at least she had both black and white.*

In 1935, I was going to give Dorothy a surprise. Just rushing in where angels fear to tread, I made a new masthead. I brought the two workers together with a cross in the middle and Christ's arm over them. So there was a black worker and a white worker and they were being unified.

Dorothy was really pleased with the masthead, and it still exists, basically. Except that some . . . eight years ago, maybe, a movement started. The original masthead, which only lasted a very short time, had been racist. Now the one that we'd lived with for so long was sexist. There should be a woman in it. And people wrote to me with all kinds of complicated ideas that didn't read "woman," you know. It took me quite a while, but finally I decided to make the woman a mother and an agricultural worker. She has a baby on her back, and she's holding a basket of food—grain or nuts or whatever—that she has reaped. You know, a harvest. So now we have a new masthead.

Joe and Alice Zarrella speak of the early days of the newspaper.

Joe Zarrella: Oh, I remember something about Ade's pictures. Ade Bethune's pictures—at that time, they were very revolutionary, and some people thought

---

* The "astute reader" was Dr. Arthur Falls of Chicago, one of the few blacks active in the movement.

they were sacrilegious. Anyway, some woman complained about her "John the Baptist." You know, the wild hair and loin cloth and . . . Mr. Breen answered the phone. "Listen lady, if you were in the desert for forty days and forty nights, you'd look worse than that." Bang!

The paper was important. Yes, it was. We used to sell the paper every Sunday in front of a different church. We'd sell papers at Times Square or Union Square or whenever there were rallies. And then we'd leave them on the subway, too.

Getting the paper out was a really long process, see? Because in those days, we had to type up the mailing list every month. We had a subscription list of ninety thousand papers. (Well, some of it was bundles.) Even typing up twenty, thirty thousand names—that's a job. It took us all month. With these old second-hand manual typewriters. If there was nothing else going on, we sat down and typed until late in the night. People would come down and want to know what they could do. We'd grab a box like "Pennsylvania," and say, "Okay, you type this." People like Charlie O'Rourke would come down constantly—a faithful person— and change addresses for us and type the lists.

Alice Zarrella: You didn't type the labels singly. If you had real good fingers, you could type six months at a time, but that dumb carbon would slip, and then you'd have to do them again. There were those little perforated things that you had to line up, and I can remember my fingers used to really get tired.

Joe: And then when the paper was ready to go, we involved the whole house. Had everybody up and in the front office. Got them to fold the papers, put the stickers on, bundle them and put . . . We didn't have any addressograph machine, just plain gum-back labels, and this smelly rubber glue. And we used to get it mailed out in one day!

Years later the labels were run off on an addressograph, but still laboriously typed by hand. Then Jeannette Noel moved from Hubbardston, Massachusetts, to New York. Today she's queen of the computer file that holds all the addresses.

Jeannette Noel: I started very lightly. The whole file needed to be changed. Everything—all the thousands of addresses for the paper—was by state instead of by name. So if they moved from one state to another, there was no way you could find a card [for them] if they didn't give their old address. So first we took that file [by states] and put it alphabetically. In those days, you had to type the addresses on little stencils. When the address changes came in, there were like six different operations. I told Frank [Donovan] I could run the addressograph machine. (I was so desperate to do something, something that wasn't too tiring.)

So I started doing labels. And then they started talking computers. I didn't like computers. Yet I was fascinated. All the addresses are in there now.

Former editors of the *Catholic Worker* reflect on their time at the paper.

Tom Cornell: When I first came on in 1962, I asked Dorothy how to do it.

"Don't worry, the printers will teach you everything."

But it *is* something you have to learn by doing. Editing was easy because there was always plenty of copy. I never had to solicit a manuscript. At that time, a guy like [Thomas] Merton couldn't find anybody else to publish stuff on peace. He'd write under the name of Benedict Monk or some other equally translucent pseudonym. Then came the *National Catholic Reporter*. People can now get published and paid and get good circulation on top of it. The *Worker* is now competing in a bigger field.

Ro: What was it like being editor of the paper?

Tom: Wonderful! For the two years that I was editor, Dorothy was there very little of the time.

Ro: Did she ever disagree with your decisions?

Tom: Well, Dorothy and I *did* fight a lot, I guess. The first time she upbraided me was for the second issue I put out. It was October of '62, and I had three priests in one issue. "This is a layman's paper." (She didn't say "lay paper.") "This is a layman's movement. One priest is okay. Two is okay. Three is one too many!" She was not anticlerical. But she did have an idea that she got from Peter—and I think it's valid—that the priests should not be the leaders in the social area. Lay people should have the leadership; clergy should give support when they know it's right.

If I made a mistake—for instance, I let an anniversary of Peter Maurin's death go by without putting any "Easy Essays" in the paper—if I made a mistake, Dorothy was incensed. But whenever she called me down, she'd always make up for it. The next day, or very soon after, she'd either take me out to a restaurant or suggest that I go to a movie or something. To make up. Or she would make me a little meal, and invite me up to [her sister's]. Make a little chicken soup for me. It was a very mother-and-son relationship, really.

She was very modest. She didn't like . . . she would be in her bed clothes, and some seminarian or young priest would show up. Some fool would bring them right into her apartment while she was sitting there in her night clothes. That embarrassed her terribly. But she would entertain me in her night clothes.

Boy, I was tense, though. I was very thin. I weighed fifty pounds less than I do now. I just couldn't keep anything on my stomach in New York. The food was terrible, so I'd go to a Chinese restaurant and get a bowl of fried rice for sixty-five cents. If I had sixty-five cents. (We weren't even given five dollars a week like they are now.) So I'd go out on the street corners and sell the papers. The only editor in town who hawked his own paper on the street. "Read the *Catholic Worker!* But a penny a copy. Show your girl you're a big spender!" And in a couple of hours, I'd be able to go and get some fried rice.

Pat Jordan was managing editor in 1973 and 1974.

Pat Jordan: Dorothy was always very self-critical and very, very protective of the paper. Felt a responsibility for every word. Part of this, I think, was in terms of the archdiocese. She'd been called on the carpet for things printed in the paper and had taken the responsibility that she was the editor. We would have gone over the paper beforehand, but there were always mistakes. She would scrutinize it thoroughly and was usually very negative. She would work herself through that and then begin pointing out all the positive things, but her initial response was always, for herself, "We didn't do well enough." Very self-critical. Toward the end, she got more comfortable with us as editors, and began to say things like, "You can cut whatever you want. You can cut mine." But before that, there was this sort of back and forth.

What impressed us—and she'd stress it so often, too—was that her writing was her vocation. She was a journalist. This gave her a deep freedom even within the Catholic Worker. Something as involving as the Catholic Worker can just zap you of any freedom that you might have. You become burdened by it. But she always had her own ability as a writer to look to, and that gave her an independence from the Worker and even from the paper itself. This was, you know, a real strength for her. It replenished her.

I remember that the printers would always ask if Dorothy was coming. Because they just loved her. These were working men and their politics would tend toward the reactionary, but they just had the utmost admiration for Dorothy. "That woman can write!" The things she had written had really stood out to them. And how many galleys had they scanned in their lives? She was a remarkable writer. The proof of the pudding was that she could write for that kind of person—for the man in the street, as Peter Maurin would say. Some of the articles by other writers got very long-winded and theoretical.

One of the marvelous things about her travels . . . she kept meeting new people, and that brought new blood into the paper and also kept it much more practically oriented. We'd have somebody who was working with the woodcutters or somebody with the grape strike. Always we'd try to be very practical and personalist in that sense, showing what individuals or small groups of people were doing to create a better place. She often said we should be "proclaimers and acclaimers" rather than "denouncers." We shouldn't just be writing against the government. We should be talking about what was building up the Mystical Body, showing what people were doing, how they were throwing in their lot. So people all across the world could say, "Gee, look at these people! They just opened up their house to people, or they decided to create a small school for mothers who didn't have any place to leave their children when they were going to work." Often [Dorothy] would prefer to start the paper with articles like that and then move to the more theoretical things. She also loved to have letter columns because, once again, there was that human voice coming in.

Obviously different managing editors had different approaches to things. We would write her while she was traveling and tell her what was going in the paper. The Catholic Worker and what it meant was pretty new to me, and I was studying as I went along and reading Peter Maurin for the first time and that sort of thing. And yet having a lot of the decision making . . . at any rate, we'd try to understand what Dorothy's mind might be about a particular article.

There was a young Catholic Worker from Chicago when we were there. He went down, I think, with the Venceremos Brigade to Cuba. And when he came back, he wrote a piece on Cuba. He had gone down there as an advocate of nonviolence and when he had seen the revolution and how he felt it was being threatened by the United States, he wrote a piece that said basically it's all right for these people to defend themselves by force of arms. And we came up with what we thought was a clever title, "Up from Nonviolence." We put that on the front page. Well, Dorothy really never said anything critical to us about that. But she wrote in one of her columns how young people around the Catholic Worker were struggling with these very hard questions about violence and nonviolence. Well, some years later—or maybe it wasn't that long later—Gordon Zahn wrote a piece in *Commonweal* about how even the Catholic Worker was slipping from its adherence to nonviolence. This really wasn't the case. The case was that some editor had put on this title. Dorothy's way of dealing with this was to say, "These people are wrestling with real questions." She didn't come down on us and say we blew it. We really learned that we had to be more attentive to titles and even maybe the placing of a particular article because that was an obvious failure to understand what the Catholic Worker was about.

Jim Forest was on the masthead as associate editor from November 1961 to February 1962.

Jim Forest: The movement grew out of a journalist's head and her . . . her theory and practice of journalism was quite different from the norm. Even before the

Catholic Worker got its identity fairly well defined, even in the early issues, you see that Dorothy's journalistic slant is essentially a positive one. She wasn't trying to *depress* people into revolution. She's trying to *inspire* people to revolution, and it's a quite different method. She never ever used the columns of the paper to attack people, as far as I can remember.

Probably one of the good things about the *Catholic Worker,* both when I was there and now, is that they're not writing a self-portrait of the community. That was never Dorothy's idea, although maybe some people in the Catholic Worker movement would like it to be. When I was editing the paper, I found Dorothy's slant annoying, in a way. I felt we were perhaps giving people too idealistic a view of the community. But Dorothy had seen so much of the other.

She'd come from a family of journalists, grown up with this other idea of journalism, and had been involved in newspapers like the Socialist *Call.* Probably the Socialist newspapers were much closer to the Catholic Worker press than the mass media, but still they tended to print horror stories, like Dorothy's stories about living on two dollars a week. It was a revolution through fear and anger rather than through love.

Ro: Some people are saying now that the *Catholic Worker* is losing the stamp that Dorothy gave it, because she always applied religious principles to what was happening in the world. Applied them specifically. And the *Catholic Worker* is, to a large extent, ignoring both abortion and homosexuality, two of the most divisive issues of the day.

Jim: Yeah. I have wished that the *Catholic Worker* were more outspoken in its opposition to abortion. I have missed that. I suppose the reason is that there is division within the communities, and so they decide that the solution is not to speak about it. That deep division astonishes me with the deep affirmation of life the Catholic Worker has. God! I don't know what I'd do if I were in anybody's shoes at one of the houses now. Or if I was managing editor of the *Catholic Worker* in New York. It must be hell, really. It was very, very difficult when I was there. It must be even more difficult now.

Gary Donatelli was once on the masthead and now works at Bailey House, a hospice for homeless AIDS victims.

Gary Donatelli: One thing that I really fault the editors for is not writing about [the issue of homosexuality in the church]. But then, I don't know how influential the *Catholic Worker* is at this point in time. I know from visiting many other Catholic Worker houses that when you mention the New York paper, people just sort of shrug their shoulders. It's not the guiding light to many people. It does offer encouragement, but to many Catholic Workers, it's not like they're blazing trails.

Peggy Scherer was co-managing editor with various others from 1979 to 1986. In 1987 she joined Gary at Bailey House and now lives in Washington, D.C.

Peggy Scherer: There were always other people making editorial decisions the entire time I worked there. I was never the only editor. In the saga of the last years, I and a few other people pushed to get the masthead changed until it reflected a little bit more honestly who was making the decisions. As it does now. But yes, I was one of the people who made the decisions. If I made a decision, then I'd acknowledge it and stand up to it, or apologize and change it if I thought it was wrong. I think that's critical and just, for my own good as well as for the good of other people. Some of the hedging comes out of an idea of humility that is very unhealthy. False humility can damage not only the people who have the false sense of humility but also those who are subject to it.

Brian Terrell lived at the New York house and then the Davenport Worker before moving to Maloy, Iowa.

Brian Terrell: I think a lot of the problems [the New York] community has are around the newspaper. They take that paper so seriously that we'd almost be better off without it these days, it seems to me. You know, there are lots of good newspapers [in the movement], but I don't think anybody worries so much about what goes in [theirs] as they do in New York. They spend hours—weeks sometimes—on little phrases, on how things should be edited. There's a lot of community tension around that paper. And I think, too, they see it as *the* Catholic Worker, so they have a responsibility.

Jane Sammon has been on the masthead since May 1974.

Jane Sammon: I think many people think of a newspaper as having an opinion but not as encouraging a certain point of view. And that was sort of fundamental to the *Worker*—that it was trying to give certain points of view, and that it would be an organ of the Catholic Worker movement. Now that doesn't mean that everybody necessarily agrees with everything being said there, although I think there would certainly be something you'd want consonant with whatever that philosophy was about.

Ro: You know, there isn't very much humor in it.

Jane: Well, gracious! We wouldn't want to break out of something here, would we now? [Laughter.] Yeah, I would agree. At times it does seem terribly academic or serious.

Ro: Written humor seems so hard for me. So often the context is lost. Hey, I hope people [write you] about that editorial [calling the church not to be tax exempt] because that means they read it.

Jane: They might. They might. We have to rejoice in the letters that say things like, "Take your paper and shove it where the moon don't shine." We got a letter like that once. Worded just like that.

Ro: Oh, my God! [Laughter.] What about the word changes in the "Aims and Means"?* For instance, in the 1940 version, the one that's reprinted so often, Dorothy talks about "propaganda." "We're doing this to propagandize." The new "Aims" doesn't use that word 'cause the meaning has changed for readers today. Anyway, how do you decide when the "Aims and Means" is going to be revised or the words changed?

Jane: Well, I don't think they necessarily did this when the founding people were still living, but we like to hear a variety of people's thoughts on what might be pertinent to reword.

Ro: A change of vocabulary?

Jane: I think the attempt was not to change the vocabulary to the point that it wasn't recognizable, but to use vocabulary that might make sense to an audience for today.

Ro: I guess that shows the elasticity of the language.

Jane: Well, I think language *is* elastic. I also think it's seriously flawed and that a language of bureaucracy has been superimposed.

Ro: And we pick up so much of it up without realizing. You know, though, everybody has their own jargon. I think there's a Catholic Worker jargon, too.

Jane: Oh, yes!

Ro: It may be jargon to someone outside but not to someone inside. It's jargon if you don't know the total meaning—if you know just the "tip of the iceberg" meaning. To me, the word "personalism" is a good example. If you don't really

* Each May, the *Catholic Worker* editors print a column called "The Aims and Means of the Catholic Worker Movement." It is updated from time to time. The May 1992 version is reprinted in Appendix C.

know what that means, it can be just a word people throw around. If you really understand, it's a very good word for the whole concept. But some people use jargon to keep other people from knowing.

Jane: Oh yes. It's a . . . it *is* a weapon. Of course we can become quite elitist and esoteric in how we speak with each other.

Ro: Jargon can also keep us from really looking at what we're doing, maybe.

Jane: Yes, but I wouldn't call "personalism" a jargon word because it's a word we can define. We can ask what it means. To me, a word like "brainstorming" is jargon. When I hear words like "feedback," "dialogue," "networking" . . . The word "appropriate" drives me crazy. It's a weapon, and I find it very unpleasant. I hope that we don't get into any of that lingo. Those words keep us away from one another.

Most of the Catholic Worker houses across the country have their own periodicals. Some, such as the *Catholic Agitator* in Los Angeles, rival the original paper in influence. Jeff Dietrich serves as editor.

Jeff Dietrich: I jokingly refer to the *Catholic Agitator* as the *National Enquirer* of the Catholic Worker. Or even the *USA Today* of the movement. Modesty is not one of my formal traits, but I don't think of myself as having terribly profound ideas. I try to be in touch with the roots, the philosophical roots, but I don't read Kropotkin, or Eric Gill, so it doesn't . . . I'm sure the paper reflects me and the fact that I'm really touched by the movement.

From the very first, I wanted it to look different from the *Catholic Worker.* I felt people weren't going to read too much. If I got people to look at the pictures and read the headlines . . . I mean maybe that's being really kind of cynical, but I . . . I just think it's true. I didn't have any training in graphic arts, but I knew what I wanted it to look like—*Rolling Stone.* I always think of the newspaper as first and foremost to keep in contact with people. And then the other thing is, you develop the relationship and they send the bucks, okay?

Patty Burns of Philadelphia shows how easily and inexpensively a new paper can be started.

Ro: So here you are starting out with this really good-looking newsletter.

Patty Burns: Pretty good, huh?

Ro: Who has the layout skills? And where did you get the equipment?

Patty: Well, Angela [Jones] and Mark [White] had both worked on the *Agitator* while they were in L.A. so they basically knew everything. It was a whole new prospect doing something in Philadelphia, though. We not only didn't have the equipment, we didn't have any money, either. We bought a couple of sheets of pressed type and then Mark got them xeroxed and cut them out and pasted them onto the paper. No one who does layouts believes us, but we did. Quite amazing! And he did all the lines by hand, too. You can buy this tape stuff, but we couldn't afford it, so he did them all by hand and then put a piece of tape on them and cut them out. And Angela's really good as well. We just had the bare minimum of equipment—a layout book and a couple of other things. Basically it was just exacto-knife.

Scott Schaeffer-Duffy of St. Francis and St. Therese Catholic Worker in Worcester, Massachusetts, discusses the development of the Catholic Worker paper he edits.

Scott Schaeffer-Duffy: When we started the newspaper, we didn't want it to go just to people already pretty much convinced, so initially we didn't mail it, just distributed it, primarily on the street or on racks in about eight different grocery stores. At the peak, we were distributing seven thousand papers, [with] about four thousand through grocery stores.

Periodically, we have trouble with some of the stores. The managers may feel free periodicals clutter their place. I'm not exactly sure if it's politically motivated, but from time to time one of our racks gets destroyed or thrown away. But anyway, then we go to different college campuses and distribute them by hand to the students.

Initially, we really shied away from a mailing list because we know it's a lot of work. Especially addressing it by hand and that kind of thing. Also an expense. But now that we're a little down with people in the community, our circulation has gone down. We're not distributing as much by hand because we don't have the hands to do it, so we're mailing four hundred or so, and those have gone farther and farther away. But our main focus is not to address the Catholic Worker community, it's to address the community at large. And not just Catholics. Some of the articles are tailored to reach out to people who are not even Christians.

Ro: And you've had at least two humor . . .

Scott: Yeah. When we told the bishop we were going to have a newspaper—the bishop of Worcester, Bishop Harrington, who is a good friend and a strong supporter of the Worker—he said, "Well, I like that Catholic Worker paper in New York, but there are no funnies. No humor." So since we were coming out on April Fools Day, we did an insert—a spoof of the Worcester daily paper, which is quite conservative.

This year, we spoofed *Worcester Magazine,* which is kind of a yuppie journal.

We wrote as if it were written for the destitute poor. So an article would be on dumpstering. Instead of dining out, it's "soup kitchening," and that kind of thing. Had lots of fun with that.

Ro: What's "in" with the poor. [Laughter.] Now who does the writing?

Scott: Well, our community was five members—five solid members—when we began. We try as much as possible for every decision to be made in consensus, so we worked together, splitting everything up fairly equally . . . uh, initially. But we found as we went along that for some people, it was a real burden to try to write an article. It became clear that it's not just a matter of dividing it perfectly equally. So, for instance, one person decided to concentrate on doing more of our art. Also, we've been getting stuff submitted to us, which is nice. We had three poems in the last issue. One of them is by a published poet. The other two were by a street person here in Worcester, who's a really tough alcoholic and a very nice guy in a lot of ways. So we just ran them both together.

The paper is my pride and joy. I'd love to see it come out every month, and I'd love . . . frankly I'd like to see us print forty thousand copies and distribute [them] in every grocery store in Worcester. I'd love to see . . . if we have a working community of five or six people, when the paper comes out, three or four of us will hit the streets every day and distribute it by hand. When we go to Mass to sell our bread, we'll distribute five hundred copies at every church. We'll have it in the grocery stores, we'll have it on the street, we'll have it all over Worcester County.

Mary Kay Meyer of Shalom House in Kansas City, Kansas, has another perspective.

Mary Kay Meyer: When I first came, we got excited and said, "Let's get a news-letter out!" Now we're beginning to question ourselves. "But what can we say that isn't being said? And what can we say that justifies the trees?" I'm sick of paper. I'm sick of paper and I'm sick of ideas. People sitting around talkin' forever and readin' forever about ideas.

CHAPTER 3

Memories of Dorothy Day

She had an enormous capacity for close friendships. Really quite extraordinary. Each friendship was unique, and she had many, many of them—people who loved her, and people that she loved.

—Mary Lathrop

I had worked in state hospitals and TB hospitals, and I knew the misery. It's terrible to feel isolated. And I always felt, you know, that I was different, different and peculiar, and when I met Dorothy I felt, "No. I'm not different after all." I felt as if . . . "Well, yes. Now I belong to a group of people." I just felt as if I'd always known her. She just seemed so serene and so comfortable, and I felt comfortable, too. There was nothing very spectacular or dramatic about it—I just felt I'd met a kindred spirit.

—Dr. Margaret Magee

A LMOST everyone I interviewed talked about Dorothy, whether they knew her or not. Many did know her well, however, and I was able to talk to several of her closest friends. I myself met her only once, but the night she visited my town of Saginaw remains forever in memory. Dorothy was gracious but rather distant as she met the "peace people" who had assembled to greet her. She spent most of the night sitting at a separate table with a young black woman, listening to her story and talking earnestly with her. That's the picture that has stayed in my mind since 1968. Dorothy was one of those magnet personalities who drew people to her as much by her manner as by her mind.*

Included in this chapter are stories from the early days told by Joe and Alice

---

* To learn more about Dorothy Day (1891–1980), start with her autobiography, *The Long Loneliness,* and continue with her other books, which include material from her columns in the *Catholic Worker.* An excellent anthology of her works is Robert Ellsberg, ed., *By Little and By Little,* recently reprinted by Orbis Books as *Dorothy Day: Selected Writings.* William D. Miller has written the definitive biography, Jim Forest a readable *Love Is the Measure,* and Robert Coles a tribute based on extensive interviews at the end of her life, *Dorothy Day: A Radical Devotion.*

Zarrella, John Cort, and Ade Bethune. Judith Malina talks of the time she was imprisoned with Dorothy for resisting the civil defense air raid drills. Former *Commonweal* editor Jim O'Gara, Jim Forest, and Fr. Richard McSorley analyze her influence. Tom Cornell and Michael Harrington remember the fifties, and Catherine Morris, Chris and Dan Delany, Kathleen and Pat Jordan, Mary Lathrop, Brian Terrell, Terry Rogers, Jim Eder, Kathe McKenna, and Robert Ellsberg tell of more recent times. Bob Tavani concludes with a loving tribute to the last years of her life.

Joe Zarrella (New York City and Tell City, Indiana): Do you know? A wonderful thing about the time Alice and I were there—it was a formative age in my life, and Miss Day was growing, too. We watched her grow and we grew with her because she shared the things that became important to her. At one time she said, "You could have been my son." Oh, I . . . I always, always think of her.

Ro: How did you feel towards her?

Joe: Most people think I . . .

Alice Zarrella (New York City and Tell City, Indiana): He was in love with her.

Joe: Yeah. I really . . . you know, I really idolized her. Anything that she asked me to do, I did. And, you know, she was . . . your first great influences mean so much. I really *did* do anything that she wanted. I maybe didn't particularly like it, but I did it.

I'd try to make her life easier. When she'd come home, I'd meet her at the bus or at the train, and I'd always have her room ready and have some flowers for her. Once I saved some money and bought her a Victrola [and a record] of Wagner's *Tannhauser*. She loved Wagner, which was something very difficult to understand.

I loved to hear her laugh. When we'd be sitting around with just a few people, she was a very natural person and a wonderful storyteller. We'd learn about her life, and she'd talk to us about books and music. Those . . . those were the wonderful moments.

Alice: Dorothy was gone an awful lot. While Dorothy was gone, we all did this work. Then when Dorothy came back, everything had to stand still, you see, because we had to catch up with all the travels and everything.

You know, she didn't develop a very close relationship with the girls in the house, other than with Margie [Hughes]. Like Joe said, at first Dorothy seemed a lot older because of her position and her manner. While we all loved her and admired her, there wasn't really a closeness there. I think she was worried about us girls [with] all these men in the house. We didn't know it at the time, though. We were too stupid to be tempted. [Laughter.] We loved her, and it was kind of a reverence, I guess, but it was strange. I, myself, felt a lot closer to Peter. After we were married [and moved to Tell City,] and Dorothy'd come out to the house, we became closer, though. She'd always be knitting. She made bandages for lepers, and she always managed to leave one so that I had to finish it. I'd wash it and send it on. Can you remember that, Joe? I mean it was a huge bandage—yards and yards. The last time she came, she was driving the awfulest old car you ever saw!

Joe: A hideous car! And she drove it all the way from New York and then drove it back. I never worried so much in my life.

Alice: A two-seated convertible. The canvas top was just about gone. It was a racy looking car, though.

Joe: In its day.

Alice: Well, it was still racy looking, you know, and I think she delighted in driving it. But oh, she was a terrible driver!

Joe: Yeah, she sure was!

Ro: What about the sainthood business?*

Joe: You know, lots of people always quote that business about Dorothy saying, "Don't make me a saint; I don't want to be dismissed so easily." And I think—now this is a personal opinion—but I think the reason she said that was not that she was against canonization or saints. Dorothy was forever quoting the saints. She was saying that she didn't want to be considered a saint like people in those days considered them. The Berkeley Street statue, pietistic kind of person.

Dorothy was not a person who mingled easily with people, and when we had visitors, she didn't particularly care to come down and converse with them. Well, one day somebody went up to Miss Day. She said, "Miss Day. Do you have visions?"

Miss Day said, "Oh shit!"

---

* Since initiating the movement in 1983, the Claretian order has collected hundreds of letters supporting Dorothy Day's canonization, according to Linda Ashton of Claretian Publications. Fr. Henry Fehren has distributed 223,000 Dorothy Day prayer cards. Fr. Daniel Berrigan calls instead for a popular canonization, a sentiment echoed by several Catholic Workers I interviewed.

You know, that's the perfect response to that kind of a thing. I remember one time she was taking some people through the house. (I won't mention who they were because they were not only wealthy people but very well known.) This woman was really sincerely concerned about the poverty and she said, "What should we do about this, Miss Day?"

Dorothy said, "Let's blow it all up!"

Jane Sammon (New York City): Dorothy could laugh at herself. That's a great gift. You know, when I first met her in 1972, I didn't feel [she was older than I was]. Her voice didn't sound like the voice of a person her age, it just sounded very . . . nothing about her voice was vulnerable.

Ro: I just met her once, but I remember thinking that old people's personalities sometimes sort of fade away from their face. And hers seemed to be coming out more. It was like she was *more* rather than less as she got older. More concentrated, maybe.

Jane: Anyone can pick up one of her books, reach out to a page, and find her there. But the myths! For instance, someone said the other day that she never lived in a room by herself. We have to correct the midrash—the myths—that grow up around a person.

> *My favorite quote was Stanley Vishnewski's . . . "Once you get to know her, she's just like any other crabby old lady."*   —Betsy Keenan

> *Tom Cornell used to say Dorothy wanted to be an anarchist but only if she got to be the anarch.*   —Brian Terrell

Ade Bethune (New York City and Newport, Rhode Island): I remember I'd already received a card from the editors saying that they were going to use some of my drawings in the paper. Then I saw a notice that they could use clothes, so I started gathering old clothes, and one day I went down to the Catholic Worker with two bags of clothes.

I guess I must have looked petrified when I arrived, being so shy and not dressed to the hilt, I would say. A big tall woman who looked as though she had been carved with an ax, you know, strolled across the room. Heh! I was scared of her. But she said very kindly, "Are these your things? I'm awfully sorry we don't have any room, but we'll try to put you somewhere."

She thought I needed a room. Hospitality was being practiced on me! I said, "Well, I'm the girl who made the pictures."

"Oh, you are?" she said. "Sit right down." I thought Dorothy was very bossy at first. She sat me down on a pile of newspapers and sat herself on another pile.

Dorothy was interested in the stories of the saints. Real people doing the works of mercy. Not abstract personifications but real people. St. Vincent de Paul with the little babies that he gave homes to, and St. Martin de Porres taking care of the sick. So every month I studied the saints whose feast days were that month and made the pictures for the *Catholic Worker.*

Ro: Did you get over being afraid of Dorothy?

Ade: Oh, of course. You see, I was afraid of people in general. Somewhat anti-social. One of the great things I owe to Dorothy is that she taught me a love of people. Because that's what she had. She was able to see God in people.

You know another thing, something people don't understand sometimes: she desired good things. One time somebody said that my drawings were not . . . there was not enough bitterness or strength in them. Too namby-pamby, not critical enough. And so I said to Dorothy, "Should I do something about that? What do you want me to do?"

And Dorothy said, "Oh no! Please. We don't have enough good things in the world. I want *beautiful* things. I want vines and grapes and mothers. Good things!"

John Cort (New York City and Boston): Good things. Yeah. I first heard Dorothy speak in May of '36. Before she'd finished, I had decided to join the Catholic Worker. I was captured by her sense of humor. And by her laugh, which was rather infectious and attractive. I remember saying to myself, "This woman is getting a lot of fun out of life. And I'd like to get some of that for myself, so maybe I'd better try the same kind of life."

The Catholic Worker was then at 115 Mott Street—in Little Italy, just north of Chinatown. A slummy area, with old houses full of bedbugs and rats. Things got pretty sloppy and cruddy. The notion was that, according to personalism, or personal responsibility as it was called, you didn't tell people to do anything. You just set a good example, and hoped they'd profit from your good example and begin to do good things. But it didn't work too well. People were sleeping at all hours, and they weren't making their beds. They weren't sweeping up. So I decided I'd post some very simple rules. The first rule was "Everybody out of bed by nine o'clock." Two: "Everybody make their own bed." Three: "Everybody take turns sweeping up."

Well, my roommate (from whom I acquired a very sizable dose of tuberculosis) was a charming Irish alcoholic from the Bowery, John Griffin. He'd been there for some time and had absorbed more of the [theory] than the others, and he thought these rules were a violation of the sacred principles of personalism. So he appealed to Dorothy and Dorothy agreed with him and told me to take those rules down. So I did. And concluded that what we had there was a form of anarchist dictatorship. There wasn't any democratic, participatory decision making. Dorothy made all the decisions. She was the abbess, as we called her. She made the rules. Or took down the rules.

She was a strong-willed woman, and it's amazing with the philosophy that she had, that she was able to keep that movement going for so long and so successfully. It says something for personalism and personal responsibility. She was authoritarian, but she seemed to have a sense of when to let people go their own way and when to step in before things got just impossible. When she stepped in, she could step in with a lot of force. A lot of force.

Dorothy and I argued a good deal. She used to call me her wayward son. Which is kind of complimentary in one way because I was so argumentative and such a dissenter. But I remember her basically and most essentially as a woman of heroic virtue. Intellectual, not-so-sensible, romantic. Agrarianism and extreme pacifism and a little bit of anarchism—all floating up there in her head. She was a complex woman.

And yet she had a good deal of common sense. Her life became something of a mess, but she was able to learn from that and to decide that she had to straighten it out. I think she came to the Catholic Church partly as a result of tasting the dregs of human experience. But yet, as I say, she was able to straighten herself out. A lot of common sense there.

Michael Harrington (New York City): I'd been brought up in a very middle-class way. Taught that I was to stand up whenever a woman entered the room. So when I went to the Worker, I still had these very middle-class habits. One of the reasons why Dorothy and I got along quite well was that Dorothy liked that old-fashioned aspect of me. She loved the fact that I held the door open for her and pulled her chair out. It was sort of ridiculous in the dining room at the Catholic Worker where we had rats and roaches, but I would hold Dorothy's chair for her. Dorothy was very feminine, which was strange for a woman whose first arrest was as a feminist. In the period when she first came to New York, Dorothy led a liberated life, certainly. For a young girl, moving in with Forster, having a baby without benefit of clergy . . . yet there was this very feminine, very old-fashioned aspect.

At the Worker, people would give us books. I remember one time there was something by the psychiatrist Steckel on autoeroticism. I was interested in it, interested in just about everything at that point. At dinner, I said I was reading this very interesting book. Dorothy got terribly upset. "Michael! We do not even *talk* about such things!"

When Dorothy talked about her own girlhood in the Village, she made it sound much more innocent than it was, as it turns out. I mean you would have thought that Forster was the only man Dorothy ever had anything to do with, which was not the case. And of course we didn't know what we know now from the [William Miller] biography—that she had an abortion.

So Dorothy was very puritanical. I remember when Dwight Macdonald was interviewing Dorothy for the *New Yorker.* Like so many people, Dwight fell in love with Dorothy. Not in the passionate sense, but in admiration. So he did something which . . . if the magazine had known about it at the time, it would've blown a gasket! He gave Dorothy his manuscript before he turned it in. I was right there when Dorothy was sanitizing her life. Dwight had come across the quotation in Malcolm Cowley's book, *Exile's Return,* that said Dorothy could drink all the Italian gangsters under the table in the Sixth Avenue speakeasies. And to hear Dorothy tell it, when she was in these speakeasies, she was drinking sarsaparilla or something.

There used to be endless speculation at the Worker about her Village days. Who were her lovers? Did she have an affair with Eugene O'Neill? To this day, I don't have any idea whether . . . I mean to hear Dorothy talk, she and Eugene O'Neill were simply good friends. My impression of O'Neill was that if he were good friends with a woman, it tended to go beyond friendship. But we never knew. That was a very funny thing about Dorothy. For all of her radicalism politically, Dorothy had a profoundly conservative streak in her makeup. She was a very conservative Catholic, theologically. Had some real trouble, I think, with some of Vatican II.

For instance, here's a story: I arrived at the Worker shortly after Cardinal Spellman had sent McIntyre down to read the riot act. What was apparently bugging Spellman was that the paper was called the *Catholic Worker.* What he was angling for, and didn't get, was for her to drop the word "Catholic." He believed [the name] was an attempt to indicate that this was a *Catholic* position, and he didn't want anybody else speaking for the church. This was the famous occasion when McIntyre said to her, "What would you do if the cardinal told you to shut down the Catholic Worker?"

She said, "If our dear, sweet cardinal, who is the vicar of Christ in New York City, told me to shut down the Catholic Worker, I would close it down immediately." She was dead serious. That's what drove me crazy. Dorothy really did go around referring to Spellman as "our dear, sweet cardinal" and "the vicar of Christ."

I remember one time Dorothy shared a platform with Elizabeth Gurley Flynn, who was a leader of the Communist Party but also somebody Dorothy had known in the old days. Flynn was a Wobbly, and Dorothy, of course, was always pro-

Wobbly. Well, the *Brooklyn Tablet*, which at that point was really a fascist news-paper—racist, terrible—the *Tablet* raised hell because there was a papal ban against Catholics sharing platforms with Communists. Clearly it was directed to Italian politics, supporting the Christian Democrats in Italy. But the pope, being in control, decreed it for the whole church. The *Brooklyn Tablet* wanted to know how Dorothy Day dared share a platform with this atheistic, godless, communistic woman.

Dorothy came to me and said, "Michael, why did I do it?" That is to say, "Give me some reasons why I did it." I read the papal text and looked at this and looked at that and came up with some theory. But Dorothy really didn't care. She didn't have a theoretical mind. Dorothy did it because this was a radical friend from the past who was being persecuted. Dorothy responded as a human being.

Ro: Sure. Bob, would she talk to you about her relationship with Forster Batter-ham?*

Bob Tavani (New York City and Minnesota): Oh, yes! I remember she told me that she had to go down to collect the money from Forster [to pay for Tamar's school]. He wouldn't mail it. "He made me come down so he could see me. It killed me. And I'd look through the window and if the new mistress was there, I couldn't go in."

When that mistress was dying twenty or thirty years later, she called Dorothy. "Listen, I'm poor, and I have no place to go, and I'm dying." And Dorothy took her in, and brought her to the house on Staten Island. She had Forster there, reading the *Times* and looking out the window at the water, "like a Mormon with two wives."

You know, I think she loved Forster a lot, but she would've been bored out of her mind if she'd settled down with him. Unless she'd had ten kids or something, she would've been bored out of her tree. Forster wasn't the most interesting person in the world. He was probably good for just as long as she was with him. She would have been loyal, though, would have been faithful.

Ro: Didn't she take care of him for a while, too?

Bob: Oh yeah, several times when he was in the hospital. And she'd say very ironically (I mean she was no fool), "He only calls me when he's sick." But she also said, "You can't take back a piece of your heart once it's given. You can't."

Ro: Tom, what do you remember about her relationship with Forster Batterham?

---

* Dorothy was reluctant to write about Batterham, the father of her daughter Tamar; however, her close friends know that he remained in her heart.

Tom Cornell (New York City and Waterbury, Connecticut): Well, she wanted to avoid scandal. Very, very seldom saw him, although they were on the telephone often. (She really had to go after him to pay for Tamar's schooling.) I forget what year it was, maybe '64, when he first became ill with cancer of the rectum. A telephone call came to 175 Chrystie Street. She picked it up in the front office. Talked privately. Came out looking shaken.

"Tom, would you get me a cab? Forster is at St. Vincent's. He's got cancer." She came back about an hour later. She looked quite different. He wasn't in any straits. "They were all there. All those people from Greenwich Village from the twenties. You know what one of them said to me? 'If you'd only married Gene [O'Neill], he'd be alive today.' " She just went on and on and on.

Forster always had a woman. Once she saw him with one on the street. Dorothy said, "You should have seen her. Painted hussy! Red hair. Large breasts." Forster was embarrassing her by playing to this woman. [Her reaction] was also, it seemed to me, pretty girlish. It was part of her charm that she could lapse from grande dame to girl.

Forster was quite feeble at her funeral. They led him to the side altar [to see her]. Did he really know who this woman was? Did he have any idea of how profound her influence had been?

Ro: Yeah, I wonder. [Pause] This may be sort of a silly question, Tom, but what bugged you the most about Dorothy?

Tom: Her lack of appreciation for other people's humor. She had a sense of humor, but it was her own. Also, she made snap judgments. Sometimes I think she misjudged people. One aspect of Dorothy's personality that is very seldom alluded to is her jealousy. She was very jealous for the Catholic Worker. Dorothy's jealousy in regard to [direct action] was manifested in a conversation with Dan Berrigan. "You're taking our kids away. This is not our kind of activity, and you're taking our kids away." * If you went up to Frank and Maisie Sheed's for a Sunday afternoon, you were considered possibly disloyal. If you went up to the Baroness [Catherine] de Hueck's Friendship House too often, she'd say, "Where is your loyalty? Up in Harlem or down here?"

Her relationship with the baroness was something else! I remember when she was in Rome. We're at the Vatican right under the Bernini columns. Here comes this hefty woman. Approaches Dorothy very aggressively. (I didn't know who it was.)

---

* Tom here interprets this line differently than he did in an earlier interview with Anne Klejment. See her "War Resistance and Property Destruction" in Coy, *A Revolution of the Heart,* p. 287.

"Dorothy Day!" she bellows. "Dorothy Day! You're going to die!" And then she throws herself into Dorothy's bosom. It was the baroness. Well, Dorothy didn't want to hear about her death. She was struggling with her declining . . . her heart was giving her signs. And here's this woman saying . . . It wasn't what Dorothy wanted to hear. And she also didn't want to have the baroness throwing herself into her arms. She just stood there ramrod stiff. There was a rivalry there. Dorothy did not like the baroness's lapses into anti-Sovietism at all. She thought of the Russian church as a suffering church, the Russian people as a suffering people. And of course Tolstoy and Dostoyevsky were very important to her spirituality.

Dorothy was very humble. The [World War II] years and immediately after—that's really the important part of her life. The influence of Father Hugo was very, very deep. That very rigorous kind of spirituality. Her isolation during the war . . . See, immediately before the war she was a grande dame already. She was still fairly young, but she was invited to all kinds of conferences. Evelyn Waugh would take her out to lunch. Joe Kennedy, Jr., John Kennedy, Bobby Kennedy—they'd all stop by. Gene McCarthy, of course. People in the labor movement. Bishops from all over. She was Cardinal Cushing's guest whenever she went to his diocese.

I don't think Dorothy started with any intention of leading a movement. I think her confessors told her it was God's will, and that the authority upon her shoulders was devolving naturally. She didn't seek that authority, it came to her, and that's why she could exercise it so effectively.

After the war, there were very few houses, and only one-third of the [newspaper] circulation. She was no longer sought after. *America* didn't print her name for fifteen years. Friends of mine found that their vocations [to the priesthood] were questioned and even denied if their association with the Catholic Worker was any too enthusiastic. For instance, I got involved with the Worker when I was a freshman at Fairfield. Everybody there told me to stay away from Dorothy Day. "She's on a lunatic fringe." "A formal heretic." "A Jansenist." It must have seemed to her as if she was an outcast.

Ro: So she felt this isolation.

Tom: Yes, she did. It was something she had to deal with, and it was part of her spiritual growth. The growth during the war itself with the Hugo retreat, and then the . . . I think she really severely suffered the privations of the war. She felt very much what was happening to people in Europe—the suffering. She understood that the people who pay the price for war are always the most vulnerable ones.

So I think that was part of . . . she stopped smoking then. She stopped drinking. To the end of her life she drank very, very, very little. I only saw her drink one thimbleful of wine in all the years I knew her. She *was* addicted to coffee, though. She had been addicted to cigarettes, a very heavy smoker. And [she had been] a heavy drinker. Malcolm Cowley wrote in his memoirs that she could drink a stevedore under the table, and she fumed about that.

She had very masculine traits in some ways. Her leadership. Maybe it's arbitrary to assign that to the masculine. But I think . . . she felt like a woman to me, but she *did* have the kind of force, the power that you associate with an Avila.*

Jim Forest (New York City and Alkmaar, Holland): When I think of Dorothy, I think of her first and foremost as a woman at prayer. Dorothy was a praying person. If she was at the farm at Tivoli, there was a fairly good chance you'd find her in the chapel. Either there or at the table drinking coffee with visitors.

If she was in the chapel, she'd be by herself, even if other people were there. Those old knees and those thick, dark stockings and those bulky shoes. She'd be there for a long time. I'm sure it wasn't that comfortable for her to be on her knees at that point. I can remember—nosy, snooping-around person that I was and still am—going up to look into her missal or Bible or whatever she had left on the pew, looking through and seeing all these lists of people she was praying for. In that unmistakable italic-like handwriting.

Dorothy realized there was no time with God, only eternity. In fact, one of the most important parts of her intercession was praying for people who had committed suicide. She had a great deal of sympathy for them. Now probably that was partly connected to her apparent attempt at suicide when she was a young woman. And certainly few of us can say they haven't thought seriously about killing themselves. I certainly have. Dorothy was quite convinced that you could pray at any time for something that had happened in the past, and she was particularly concerned about praying for those people who had committed suicide. You couldn't reverse the fact that they were dead. You couldn't change history in that way, but you could perhaps change something about that person's death or something that happened in that person's thoughts. I'm not sure what she thought she was doing, but she knew that she could pray for them and that God's eternity is different than time.

You know, another interesting thing about her: people at the Worker would be very critical of the hierarchy, especially Cardinal Spellman, and I was not least among them. Dorothy could be very critical of him, too, but if anyone spoke

* St. Teresa of Avila, reformer of the Carmelite order and one of only two women saints to receive the title Doctor of the Church.

against him, she'd always stand up for him. And it wouldn't be in generalities. She told me once that Spellman had priests who didn't like to receive calls to go down to the Bowery to administer the last rites. He told the person answering the phone, "If any of those calls come through, give them to me personally." Dorothy knew things like that about people, and she would tell them to show their good side. She was quite different than most of us. If we decide we don't like somebody, we make it a kind of hobby to collect reasons not to like that person. We develop quite a number of reasons to justify our irritation. Dorothy had a lot of reasons to dislike Cardinal Spellman, but it was more her hobby to find out things to admire about him.

Oh! I remember once how startled I was to find, next to Dorothy's bed, a tiny little statue of Joan of Arc, wearing armor. She responded to my surprise: "Well, she wasn't canonized for being a soldier. She was canonized because she followed her conscience." Now Joan of Arc was dead before she was out of her teens. The more I think about it, the more I think Dorothy admired her armor as much as her conscience. She thought all of us should be willing to risk our lives, put our lives on the line, fight for what we think is right. She wasn't this analytical machine but she was consistent. And she wasn't embarrassed to admire a warrior saint.

Jim O'Gara (formerly Chicago, now Rockville Center, New York): In my experience, Dorothy was an extremely orthodox Catholic, not at all theologically a dissident. She certainly would not at all favor abortion. She would, I think, take a very dim view of homosexual behavior. She was not radical in the way that many people are in the church today.

Ro: But, for instance, her stands on labor were often at odds with at least the masses of the church.

Jim: I would say Dorothy was at odds with people who were not familiar with Catholic social thought. Dorothy was familiar with Catholic teaching on subjects like labor, poverty, things like that, in the way that most Catholics are not. Even today. She had read the things that most people don't bother to read, so she was for an orthodox position. She was for a papal position. So in that sense she was completely orthodox. She may have differed from the majority of American Catholics, but she was completely orthodox.

Brian Terrell (New York City and Maloy, Iowa): Well, except for some nostalgia that any old woman ought to have for things from the past that aren't anymore, I never noticed that Dorothy was conservative liturgically. During my first years in New York, we had a dining room Mass every Monday night. Right there on that metal table. And we were within ten minutes' walk of probably thirty Masses with silver goblets. Some priests would use the missal, some wouldn't. [Dan] Berrigan would come sometimes and he'd never wear vestments, but Dorothy wouldn't be upset.

Another thing I remember . . . Charlotte Rose, Dorothy's great-granddaughter, was baptized at Tivoli. The presiding minister at this affair was Archbishop Francis from Woodstock, New York, an Old Catholic archbishop. He came with one of his priests and did a great liturgy. It was just a lovely day all around. And this man was a schismatic, supposedly. According to the rules, we were all in mortal sin just for being there. And Dorothy welcomed him. Now that just doesn't fit her image as a "loyal daughter of the church," does it?

Judith Malina (New York City): I shared a cell with Dorothy [in 1957].* She asked to be put in the cell with me to protect me. (That was exceptional for her. She generally was quiet and humble in the prison situation. Quiet, although very firm. Oh, as firm as a rock!) You see, I was being set upon by some tough young women with clearly sexual implications. I was much tinier then than I am now, even, but I don't think it was so much that. I was young and was wearing a little white lace dress and my hair was long. One young woman asked in a loud way to have me put in her cell because she was interested in me. And Dorothy, seeing this as a danger to me, said in a voice . . . it was extraordinary. She merely spoke an irrefutable statement: "She belongs in my cell."

Now here's a kind of theologically interesting story. Dorothy had asked that I be put into her cell because of this aggressive woman. Shortly after that, this woman (let's call her Maria) was freed. And a few days after that, her picture was in the paper because she had tried to kill herself. She had gone back on heroin, and didn't want to face it, and had shot herself in the stomach. She was sent back to prison for possession of a gun and was in the prison hospital.

Dorothy immediately initiated prayers for her. And she said that she felt that she should not have interfered, that if I had been put in this woman's cell, it's perfectly possible that I might have helped this woman. (This was Dorothy's point of view. I'm not sure of it at all.) Dorothy felt this was a lesson in not interfering. She very much felt it was her fault and said she should have let me go into Maria's cell.

In political activism, there's a seeming contradiction. (Although in the saints, all seeming contradictions are resolved in love.) It's the seeming contradiction

---

* Malina's first published diary contains several moving passages about Dorothy (*The Diaries of Judith A. Malina, 1947–1957* [New York: Grove Press, 1984]). When I talked to her in 1987, I was able to glean details about the time she and Dorothy were jailed together for protesting the civil defense air raid drills.

between the activists who take the step—make the decision—and those who possess a certain quietism of allowing God to do the work. Of stepping aside and looking at the suffering and saying, "Where I can, I will prevent it. On the other hand, this is the way of the world."

Dorothy was an anarchist. My affinity to her was as an activist, anarchist comrade. My theater [the Living Theater] is about a hope that we can organize our lives in an anarchist way, in a more humane way. And I had in common with her this spirit. All the time we were in jail, she tried to teach me that anarchism is holiness, which I had never understood. I had thought there was much contradiction between anarchism and holiness. But now we come to the contradiction between activism and holiness and activism and anarchism.

Anarchism is activist. Dorothy walked out on the street to make that civil defense protest in order to make what anyone would call trouble. That is, she wanted people to notice the contradiction, so she sat out in the street in the sunlight. Saying, "This is my street and I'm not going to fall in a hole because I'm afraid my fellow man is going to kill me. I'm not going to support that structure."

This was an active decision, challenging the whole society. And also a tension-building decision. Everyone went underground for the civil defense drills, but Dorothy said, "I will not go." A very strong act of will, an act of will in which she contradicts what everybody wants her to do, including the church. It was a great privilege and marvel to be secluded with a woman like that, to come close to such a soul. A beautiful experience. But a contradiction, too, because it was also the most horrible place I'd ever been in. Surrounded with . . . with ugliness. Architectural ugliness and more. Nine hundred women, and I think eight hundred were prostitutes and about seven hundred were drug addicts. Whole layers of suffering and misery. So it was incredible to be exposed, at the same time, to both the highest that the human spirit is capable of and the most incredible expressions of suffering. Including a debasement of the natural poetry of the language.

Dorothy became very quickly a legend in the prison. There was a lot of press at the time and a picket line outside. Everybody was aware of it, and we were certainly celebrities of a sort inside the prison. Most of the guards were Catholic, and they came to her and had their Bibles blessed and their rosaries kissed. Priests came. And the wealthy came on pilgrimage. She was always sort of annoyed about this, at how people were outwardly . . . when she would hear, "Nineteen Philippine priests would like to see you," she would make an angry face. But then I'm sure she was absolutely heavenly when she confronted them, because she was . . . because she responded to any human being. She responded the same way to these terrified, struggling, suffering women in jail, these women who couldn't speak without uttering the Oedipal adjective, who felt themselves compelled to say as many negative things as they could.

There was unbelievable fear in the prison. Most of the women had that dreadful word "incorrigible" stamped on their record, which means that they had to go to jail for a certain period of time every year. They were in that field of repeated suffering . . . a wheel of suffering. Like their mothers and their grandmothers and their great-grandmothers, all without really steady men in the family. But a succession of women falling into prostitution or drugs, going through the same suffering and misery. And feeling really indicted by fate. Angry and victimized. Angry and struggling. Somehow Dorothy managed to bring a certain light.

Ro: Did you and Dorothy go through a strip search?

Judith: Oh, yes. It was extremely humiliating and the jokes that were made were unpleasant, but I have a tough skin. But Dorothy . . . Dorothy had been chaste for many, many years. When a chaste woman is poked like that and subjected to really thoughtless handling in which someone searches the inside of her body, without any consideration for the dignity of the person they're searching . . . Dorothy bled for several days after that and was in considerable pain. When it happened, I was standing in the outer part of the office and I heard her cry out in pain.

The two young women who searched us were not medical or paramedical people. They made obscene jokes during the whole procedure. I think Dorothy could forgive the obscene jokes. (She used to say she has a deaf ear which she turns on in such moments.) But it was really horrible to see the lack of dignity. Everybody who came into that prison was subjected to the same kind of treatment, probably on the basis that they were all rotten and deserved it.

And everyone's nerves are raw, if only because they can't go down to the drugstore and have a malted milk. Or because they can't call their brother or get to sleep on this metal plate which serves as a bed. The noise is terrible and the heat is . . . when I was in with Dorothy, we were in the middle of a heat wave.

It was unbelievably cramped in those narrow quarters. The Women's House of Detention was built to hold about three or four hundred people and there were nine hundred there. Dorothy and I were in a cell which was about four and a half feet wide with that tiny space taken up mostly by a bed that had another little metal bed that pulled out from under it. In which Dorothy slept, not I. Because you can't deal with a saint. You've got to take the more comfortable bed because she won't.

You can't say, "Look, you're older and more decrepit." Not to a saint. She wouldn't hear of it. This is one of the troubles with dealing with that kind of person.

Ro: What other troubles are there in dealing with saints? What other things were different about being with Dorothy?

Judith: Most of what was different was just better. The same as with other people, only better. I think the only difficulty one might point to is that a saint is, as it were, a living reproach. One wants to live up to the good example, but as my friend Steve Ben Israel says, "We've all been swimming in dirty water." If we all feel our own "dirty waterness," and we feel the world and its greed and its fears and its anger . . . when you confront someone who approaches these things from a higher level, you have to take their example and start to work very hard on yourself. I had to, as it were, try to become a saint myself. Dorothy was very careful about that, though. She was not sanctimonious. She was not irreproachable.

For instance, when we met the warden . . . the warden arranged a meeting with us in the most clumsy and unpleasant way—in the middle of the dining hall with the prisoners all standing around listening to us. And he told us immediately that he didn't regard us as being in the same class as the other prisoners. They are all hearing this. Now can you imagine!

Dorothy immediately . . . she was knitting something. She said to me right away, "Don't argue."

She didn't want to continue on that level, but I couldn't help myself. I argued with the man. I argue with everybody. And I try to make everybody understand what I think are some very basic fundamental principles. I do this all the time. I think you might have noticed it. [Laughs.] Identifying the ground on which we differ and then trying to unify it. That's my purpose. I'm a unifier. The more I talked, the more Dorothy muttered, "Don't answer him. Don't argue."

Later she talked to me about it, and I think in a way she's right. Although I have my character to deal with here. One has to know when to enter the arena and when to remain outside, when it's wise not to meddle, and when one must take an active step. I think she was peculiarly wise in this knowledge, in this sensitivity to what is useful to human suffering and what, in spite of our good intentions, can only increase it.

Oh, here's a strange tale. I don't know what would have happened if it had actually come to something. One day I was swabbing the cell. No, I wasn't swabbing the cell. You see, I try to make the lie come true even as I tell it now. Isn't that a strange psychological twist? I'll begin again.

It was unbelievably hot. There were just six little panes of glass for windows. There was a little screen behind them, but it was completely clogged. Just no air at all. Sweltering! In the middle of the window, there was one little pane which was clear glass, the only one we could look out of.

And I said, "Oh God, if only there was some air coming in!"

Dorothy made a little prayer to Vincent Ferrer whose story we were studying. (The same St. Vincent Ferrer who put all the Jews into synagogues and set fire to them. But he also had some noble aspects.) And she made up a little jingle. "St. Vincent Ferrer, give us some air." We were both sweating terribly and really suffering from the heat. It was unbelievable—close and damp and hot.

I said, "I'd like to break that little window!"

Dorothy said, "Go ahead! Break it! Break it!!"

And I took off my shoe, and tapped the pane with the heel, and it cracked. I thought surely this would mean the end. They would put me in seclusion, in the tank or whatever. I was absolutely terrified! I had broken a prison window.

Dorothy said, "What are you frightened of? I told you to do it."

"Look. You told me, but I did it."

"I'm going to say that I stirred you up to it."

"And I'll say that you had nothing to do with it. I broke it of my own free will!"

We argued about this question, and then it was decided . . . I don't remember if Dorothy suggested it or I did. It was decided (using the passive voice) that when I was swabbing the cell, I broke the window with the handle of the mop.

That was a lie born of fear, as all lies are. Fortunately we didn't have to use it. No one ever saw the broken window. But we lived in twenty-five days of fear. Every single time the guard walked by, we lived in fear of that broken window. My guess is that if we had been questioned, that neither Dorothy nor I would have talked about that ridiculous mop handle. I think we would have told the truth, in spite of this madness of deciding we were going to lie.

Ro: Do you know what that reminds me of? It just . . . it sounds almost girlish.

Judith: Our whole experience there . . . I must say that my relationship with Dorothy for those thirty days was like . . . was very girlish in just that sense. Somehow we were determined to have fun, too. In spite of the tragedy around us. In spite of the seriousness of our cause. Certainly, either of us was willing to break into highly serious rhetoric at any moment. She could do it on a high level, and I certainly could do it all the time. To a fault. But I think that there was a certain spirit of fun, a certain spirit of even joyousness that Dorothy exuded. Always did.

Ro: Did she ever tell stories about her pre-Worker life?

Judith: Oh, yes. Oh, yes! She talked about Mike Gold, Eugene O'Neill—all those stories. And we talked a lot about her marriage. She was very worried that she had given . . . that she had said she was not married because she didn't want to bring up this juvenile event. She also talked a lot about Forster. Forster came and picketed outside the prison, and that touched her tremendously.

We talked a lot about sexuality and a woman's life. We talked about children, all those things. Very deeply . . . very deeply. We also laughed a lot and giggled after lights out, telling funny stories. She would read me something from the *Lives of the Saints,* and I would read something from our [Jewish] liturgy, and we'd talk about holy things. Then after a while, we'd start telling funny stories and laughing a lot, too. It was wonderful that we had both.

I think she unified the concepts of idea and practice better than anyone . . . better than anyone. And her ideas were able to extend all the way. All the way to the pacifist idea, all the way to the anarchist idea. All the way to the poverty. Dorothy's human generosity could include the most pitiful person and the finest in the same embrace, and so I finally learned what she'd been trying to teach me, that anarchism is holiness. It's a holiness here and now which consists of treating each other as holy beings. No dividing into good ones and bad ones.

Fr. Richard McSorley (Washington, D.C.): Dorothy was always reliable for doing the best thing. Like at the Eucharistic Congress in Philadelphia in 1976. They had scheduled a military Mass as part of the Congress. And on Hiroshima Day, August the sixth. A committee of us went to see the priest who was running it, and he said he didn't know it was Hiroshima Day, which was even worse. We asked all the main speakers to say something, and the only one who did was Dorothy Day. She did it in her own unique way, however, without criticizing the archdiocese. She just said that this was the day which commemorated Hiroshima and that if we went to Mass on this day, we should certainly do it in repentance.

One other example that impressed me very much, especially because I'm a Jesuit priest, is when a reporter asked her, "What do you think about your Jesuit friends? They have very nice rooms and very nice food, and you're living with the poor and the outcast. Don't you think it would be better for them to live here with you or to live at least this style?"

And she said, "Well, I know that the spirit calls people in different ways. I don't know what the spirit of God tells other people, but I do know what the spirit of God calls me to, and I know that there are other people called to other things."

Well, the reporter was very insistent and asked the same question again, and she gave the same answer. Now I think that's a real sample of the Catholic Worker spirit. If she had said that the Jesuits are better off imitating her, she would be implicitly saying that "I'm better than . . ." Well, no doubt she *was* "better than." But she wasn't saying that, and she didn't think that. And that's the mark of all the saints. That they consider themselves the least of all. They not only genuinely feel that, they live it. They live it. She never pretended that she was more important than any one of the guests that she served.

I remember that I went up to see Dorothy Day about a year before she died. You know, a nationally known priest once said on a public platform that she was the single most influential Catholic of the last fifty years, that she had represented the church on every controversial issue, on the right side, the Gospel side. She's represented the church for racial justice, for economic justice for workers, for the right to form unions, for solidarity with the poor, and for peace opposing war. It was a Gospel influence. And an influence of prayer.

I saw her once in the chapel at Tivoli, saying the rosary by herself. Now that didn't impress me much at the time. But later on I remembered that she kept the devotion to the rosary while many Catholics just put it aside. She kept inviting people to join with her in that tradition and it lives on. It lives on. [Pause] She was very peaceful during our visit.

I asked her if there was any time that she had conflict with the diocese. And she said, "No, I don't recall any."

I said, "How about the time when you helped support the strike of the gravediggers, and the archbishop had the seminarians out digging the graves?" She just kind of parried that question. "Well, I was called into the chancery office once in New York, and I passed rows of desks. Finally, I got to this monsignor's desk and he stood up and he said, 'Thank you, Miss Day, for coming. Now would you please be seated.' And so we sat down and he said, 'We have some complaints in our office about what you're doing. But we know what you're doing. We don't need to be instructed by other people. We told them that we'd talk to you. Now we have, and that's enough.'" She smiled at us. "That was the way we got along with the archdiocese."

Terry Rogers (New York City): I lived on the third floor, and Dorothy did, too. I remember her as a very spontaneous person. If she was in the mood to talk, she'd holler out, "Guess who I just heard from?" Or "Sit down and listen to this symphony with me."

I remember we were all hot and crabby one day, and she comes in and says, "It's a beautiful day. Let's go up to the Cloisters." Like we didn't have anything else to do. "Thanks a lot, Dorothy! The guardian angels will look after the house."

She was so silly. I mean she was so, you know . . . sometimes she'd be enormously grim and sad and grieved and serious about stuff, but other times, she'd be just plain silly. Happy and very girlish and silly. Maybe that was because she didn't directly deal with the day-to-day workings of the house at that point.

Ro: Terry, what's your favorite Dorothy story?

Terry: My most favorite story about Dorothy? It was in the spring. A young runaway had been living in the house, and that had caused some difficulty. Dorothy had been away. She came back and presumably got a lot of complaints. (That always would happen. She'd come back and different factions in the house would say, "Oh, those other . . . you know, da, da, da.") Some of the older people felt some of the younger people were not being sensitive to their environment. Well, Dorothy and I had a fight, basically. She was really scolding me. I left. Got home late that night. It was dark and as I pulled back the curtain and walked into the alcove where my bed was, I was just *overcome* with this gorgeous fragrance of lilacs. Just overcome! I turned on the light, and there was this huge vase of lilacs on my bed, and this note from Dorothy. "Please forgive a crabby old woman."

You know, though, after I became one of the people who'd been kicked out of the Catholic Worker, I met other people who got kicked out.* And I learned Dorothy would make decisions like that—quickly and sort of unilaterally and nearly always very awkwardly. She wouldn't always sit down with the person and go through it. It would be just BOOM! People would be bitter. Dorothy did not have a lot of social poise in some circumstances. I think she was in many ways shy, in many ways ill at ease in certain kinds of situations. And the way she would use authority was often real ambivalent, I think.

Mary Lathrop (New York City): Well, I just very quickly became attached to her. I have to be honest. I have to tell you that it really was a mother-daughter relationship. She really was my mother. I suppose a psychologist would call it some sort of a bonding, or the social scientist would call the Catholic Worker a primary group. It partly has to do with the fact that my mother and I . . . it's all kind of sad stuff. Sometimes Dorothy would correct me when I'd say uncomplimentary things about my own mother. "Don't say that," she said, "because it hurts me. I am a mother, too."

In the last few years of her life, I used to take dinners to her 'cause she sometimes had trouble eating Catholic Worker food. I'd cook fish dinner for her, with a potato and a vegetable or something like that, and cover it up and take it to her.

* Terry told me the story this way: When she was traveling with her boyfriend, a young Catholic Worker from England, she received a postcard from Dorothy saying she was no longer welcome to live at the Worker. Terry never learned why. Although Dorothy eventually "made it up," as Terry said, there was no apology and the two were never again close.

And one time she said to me, "You're taking care of your old mother." "You're taking care of your old mother," she said. But she showed me a book once that was inscribed to her as "the mother of thousands." Thousands! So it's not just me.

She was a perfectly mature spiritual being. And somehow this kind of flowed out of her, and you could participate in it if you were in her presence. I remember in the kitchen one morning down at the beach house [on Staten Island]. It's right by the ocean, and the sun was glistening on the water and the little kitchen was very bright. There was a statue of the Virgin on the shelf. Dorothy was there with one or two other people. And it was just very pristine and right and happy.

Catherine Morris (Los Angeles): Well, my times with her were really exciting . . . yeah, pretty exciting. Like when we were in jail together. I'd never met her, you know, even though I'd written to her. This was the [United] Farm Workers strike in Fresno. Ninety of us rode on buses all night, rode down from San Francisco to the strike area. We'd been at a Jesuit conference and we kind of officiously presented ourselves. "We've come to spend the day with you."

And Chris Hartmire said, "We'd like you to get arrested with the farm workers. They're being held in jail, and we need some other folks to give support and clout to this."

And we said, "Oh, well, see we're just here for the day. We really didn't plan to spend the night."

So they talked back and forth and finally someone suggested saying Mass. So they had Mass. I don't know if you've ever been to a Farm Workers Mass, but they're pretty exciting. The vestments are always the union flag—red vestments with the white circle and the black eagle—and it's all rouser-dowser songs and all.

Well, the Mass ended and wham! Chris Hartmire jumps up again, and he says, "All right, now we have to get out to the strike lines. So those of you who stand with justice and are going to be arrested, come over here, and the rest of you come over here."

I was with another Sister of the Holy Child, and we looked at each other and she said, "Oh, shit!" So then we went over on the side to stand with justice and got whipped out in cars to the strike line. They told us to stand a foot apart. There we were! Not facing guns, but there were lead pipes and dogs on chains. Scary! Well, we weren't there very long before we were arrested. They hauled us all away in buses and put us in barracks on this farm. Pretty soon the next batch [of strikers] was being brought in. And there was Dorothy, sitting on her little fold-up camp chair.*

* The scene Catherine describes was captured by Bob Fitch's famous picture of Day flanked by two police officers and their weapons.

I don't know why I thought she'd know me, you know, but I go running out of the line and say, "Dorothy, I'm Catherine from the Los Angeles Catholic Worker." And she looks at me like, "Yes, dear." So I thought she wasn't taking it in, but I was pretty excited to see her anyway. Then later, she sent someone in to get me. And every day she'd come out with her little seat and send somebody in to get me and we'd talk.

But I wouldn't get to talk to her for very long 'cause all the other nuns would come roaring out to talk to her, too. A lot of other Holy Child Sisters ended up getting arrested, and Dorothy told me, "I can't believe the Holy Child Sisters are in jail with me! They're the sisters who put Tamar out of school."

We were there for thirteen days, I think. She ended up in the newspapers and all the growers' wives were coming to explain to her what good Catholics their husbands were and how she was misinformed and so on and so forth. So many people came to see her that it made her sick.

Jeff and I later went to see her at Tivoli.* I think it was in 1975. Anyway, we went east, to the farm, and she was just sitting around, you know. We'd sit with her for hours. She talked constantly—just told stories. She was pulling all kinds of skeletons out of the closet. We were amazed. "Whoa . . . Dorothy's saying this?" You know, all kinds of relationships, who ran off with who and all that kind of stuff. She was very reminiscent. We don't know if she was trying to convey some message to us through the stories or what, but she just seemed to feel like going over these things.

Ro: Hmmm . . . Maybe she just saw it as sharing with family. Or talking about her family, saying that somehow families go on. I think maybe if there is any sort of message in this, it's that all the scandals, all the rifts, all the dissent . . . you know, at the end, it doesn't matter so much. But maybe I'm reading too much into it. Maybe it was just a way to relive her life again.

Catherine: Yeah. She didn't seem . . . you know, it didn't seem to bother her. Some of the stuff she was telling was rather scandalous. We had wonderful times at Tivoli. It was so funny being there at the Peacemakers [Conference]. They were doing the cooking and some people were vegetarians and others were this and that, so every meal was really hysterical. With signs that said, "This has no meat" and "This has no onions" and "This has no milk" and so on.

Dorothy would wait for us, and we'd go in and eat at her table. One day, she was going on about all these signs, about how ridiculous it was to think so much about your gut, that you should just eat what's in front of you. And so then we

* Sr. Catherine left her order and married Catholic Worker Jeff Dietrich. Together they are the mainstays of the Los Angeles Catholic Worker.

got our food and sat down, and her first comment was, "I don't know why they don't take the peeling off the potatoes."

Chris Delany (Sacramento): You know, Dorothy lived with us for two weeks when we had the L.A. Worker, before Dan gave it to Jeff Dietrich. I was really nervous about her coming. I thought, "Oh God! She's like the Mother General, and she's going to come and check up on us and everything."

But I was just charmed. Dorothy was just an utterly human person. She'd sit at a table and tell stories. Kind of hold court. People would come from all over and talk to her. One interesting thing: I had this thing about murder mysteries. Just loved them. And I used to sneak them up to my room and read them like they were pornographic trash because I just . . . you know, everybody at the Worker was so intellectual. (Or pseudointellectual.) Well, it came out that she was a devotee, too.

Dan Delany (Sacramento): She bought you one, didn't she? A mystery by Josephine Tey. Yeah, I remember that time, too. You know, as the evening wore on, she'd complain that she was an old lady. (She was in her early seventies then and she walked with a cane.) At about eight o'clock, she started talking like that, and then about nine, she'd go upstairs. Anyway, she'd go to her room about nine o'clock, but her light never went out till midnight. Then in the morning, her light would go on about six, but she didn't come down until nine. So she was putting in three hours at night and three hours in the morning. By herself—doing her correspondence, praying, reading the Scripture—doing as she damn well pleased! And I thought, "Boy! No wonder she's a spiritual powerhouse!"

Jim Eder (Chicago): I met Dorothy when she was speaking at DePaul University. A couple of theologians were on the stage with her and it was kind of boring. But then she started talking in a real simple way. She looked genuinely dumpy, you know, like somebody's grandma, but I thought, "That lady knows what she's talking about." The clarity, that incredible clarity!

A couple people from the audience asked really silly questions, and I was really impressed because Dorothy thought these people were worthy of being listened to. Really treated the audience with dignity. There was one person with a speech impediment who wanted to know why the Catholic Worker didn't side with the IRA or something, and she was real patient. I would have thrown most of those people out on their ear if I'd been in charge, but she had respect for everybody.

You know, she never did remember what my name was, though. Once I helped her fix her lamp shade, so she always talked about me as "that nice man from Chicago who fixed my shade."

Kathe McKenna (Boston): I remember when she came to Boston to give a talk. And John and I were on the same program, you know, representing local people who were doing the work. The [Vietnam] war was escalating. It was taking its toll on people, and I think Dorothy recognized that people were just drowning in anger.

I was trembling in my boots. Here was the matriarch! Dorothy was certainly tough, although she'd been enormously supportive of everything we had done. (She always had a special place in her heart for people who were doing the work. Starting a house put you in a unique position in her eyes.) But John and I were not pacifists at the time. And we were going to talk about that, about our anger and our . . . even if she was there.

We were prepared for the worst because we knew that she tended to be rather adamant about pacifism. We did, in fact, share how we felt, and I remember when we broke loose and told the nuns. It was rather emotional. Intense. We were saying things they didn't expect. And Dorothy didn't expect it, either.

After it was all over, we were drinking coffee and Dorothy came up to us and said in her wonderfully stiff, warm way, "You must feel very strongly about what you believe." And she just smiled and left it at that.

Ro: Kathleen Jordan, what's your most valuable memory of Dorothy?

Kathleen Jordan (New York City and Staten Island): For me, I guess it was her emphasis on the primacy of the spiritual. Of course, lots of other people have said that, too, but she was able to integrate it. It wasn't a spiritualism that was removed from day-to-day life or from a sense of a radical Christian life. And then there was the blessing of having this little time with her out at Spanish Camp on Staten Island. With one baby and another on the way and spending afternoon after afternoon with this elderly woman on the beach. We miss her very much.

Pat Jordan (New York City and Staten Island): We so often think about Dorothy. Our son Justin just loves to go down and fish and catch eels and all. And I often think of Dorothy telling us about being right out in back of our cottage with her brother John in a boat full of eels and it tipping over. And she writes in *The Long Loneliness* about the fellow who did the beachcombing right below where we live. You know, I came from California where there were lovely beaches. When we came out here, I was quite disappointed because it's very rocky and . . . not Malibu at all. And I think it was through Dorothy . . . this also was an example of her teaching.

What I saw at first was the old tires, the refrigerator somebody had left down there, whatever it was. She taught me how to see the beauty in this beach. And in everything else. We'd be driving along and she'd see a stand of wild clover and she'd say, "Stop the car. That is wild clover! When I was a girl, my mother used to pick the wild clover and put it in pillowcases to make the house smell good." And she'd pick it and bring it back to the beach house. Even in her seventies!

All these gifts . . . well, obviously the gift of our own family. We came from different parts of the country and happened to meet at the Catholic Worker. And now we happen to know these children. It's thanks to Dorothy and the Catholic Worker that any of these good things happened in our lives.

And there was Dorothy's deep sense of beauty. When I was living in the house, I'd sometimes go up to her room on a Saturday and see her, maybe about something to do with the house or the paper. And I'd interrupt her during the opera time [while she was listening to the Metropolitan Opera on the radio]. I'd walk in and see her almost in ecstasy. That taught me a great deal about what prayer meant to her.

When we were getting married, she told us a number of times that beauty will save the world. "Remember what Dostoyevsky said: 'Beauty will save the world.'" We would see that in her. She didn't separate the natural and supernatural. It was . . . they were so close together.

Oh, I remember just little things. She kept a sense for femininity. She was a very beautiful person with a real reserve about her, almost Victorian. When we were at the Worker, there was . . . I remember a college student who came to spend the summer. She told us how she went up to see Dorothy one morning. Dorothy opened up her purse and took out some perfume or something and put it on a handkerchief and gave it to the young woman. "Just always remember that you're a woman." To make sure that even in a very poor situation, you remembered what a gift it was of who you were. And she was also saying to her, "You have to maintain your dignity in an environment that's pretty rough."

I remember once I was down at the front door of the Worker, working off my anxieties or something by cleaning. Sometimes we'd get loads of white shirts which nobody on the clothing line wanted because they'd get dirty so quickly. So we had scores of white shirts, and I was just about to rip up this perfectly fine white shirt [to use] as a rag for cleaning. Dorothy stopped me. She said, "You can't do that with that perfectly good shirt. Everything is sacramental." It stopped   me   short. That you really have to pay attention to everything.

Robert Ellsberg (New York City): Oh, yes. I met Dorothy pretty soon after I came. Of course, I was excited and very flattered when she acknowledged me and took an interest in me. She liked to hear stories, and she'd have this kind of girlish giggle, so it was fun to just amuse her. I developed a kind of irreverent sort of relationship with her, because that's what she responded to the best. She disliked people bowing and scraping.

Dorothy always fixed you in a slot, put a label on you in a way. And she was disoriented until she could do that. It might be somebody that you knew in common, [or] where you came from. If you were from Ireland or grew up in South Bend or something. It was very hard to find somebody who didn't share some kind of human experience. Having children. Liking a certain book or liking cats, or whatever it would be. So she could connect with anybody. She was very good at that. She'd think of you in a certain way and that could be unfortunate, I guess, if it wasn't the way you thought of yourself or something.

Bob: You know, I met her at Tivoli. The reason she started talking to me . . . it was kind of sad in a way. I mean here she was . . . she was walking through the house early one morning. Everybody else had gone apple picking, and she just grabbed me and said, "Come and talk to me." It was like saying she was lonely. (She knew I had shared a place with her granddaughter for a while, and she also knew I had been a Jesuit, so she probably figured I was somebody she could talk to.)

What I saw was this old woman who was tired, but who still had a mind sharp as a tack. She wanted somebody who wasn't going to drive her crazy. I had that much decency left to try not to burden her, so she knew that she could just tell me different things. And it was beautiful. I was eight months in her life. There were a lot of other people, but I got a piece. I got a choice piece.

And I . . . I say this with no desire to be humble or anything like that, but I really felt like the gifts of God . . . you know, people can pray for them and work for them, and He gives them to some people who don't even deserve them. I never asked for it. As a matter of fact, I hadn't even been a decent person. I'd been screwing around and living badly and taking drugs and doing whatever I felt like doing for myself. And God just chose me, you know. Or *she* just chose me. There were a lot of people who'd been much better people that she didn't choose for friends. Maybe she sensed a little of the same kind of spirit—reckless and headstrong and generous. Loving. The kind of person who would take a risk.

Old Eleanor, one of the guests at Maryhouse . . . (Eleanor was a class act. She was an editor at one point in her life and when the paper came out, she was the first one we gave it to. If Eleanor liked it, then we had a good issue.) Anyway, Eleanor said to me one time, she said, "Well, you were her type." And I thought to myself, "Could that possibly be true?" That wasn't a false modesty. I wasn't being, you know . . . I just never really, really understood that I could be something to her. And I think that that's why I could leave so easily, you know, and not even realize that it hurt her because I didn't . . . what would she want me for? I was probably just another burden. But she liked me, I guess. That's a nice thing to say about somebody who might be a saint someday.

One time I wrote . . . when I was first at the Worker, I was trying to understand it, and I wrote down what I called "twelve marks of the Catholic Worker." And I put them up on the wall to see how she'd respond, you know, and how other people in the community would respond. This was up at Tivoli. And she came to me and she said, "Not bad! But you forgot number one—freedom!" People forget that. The people who are proselytizing Catholics in the Catholic Worker—she would be aghast! She really *did* believe in freedom. And she was a free person herself. She knew what she believed and what she wanted for herself, and she told people, but I never had the impression that she was trying to manipulate me into something that I wasn't.

When I first met her, she said, "Don't tell me your problems." She was tired. She'd already had two heart attacks, you know, and really, she just wanted somebody who would listen. But she was going to give her half, too, because what she did . . . She could sense that I was really feeling shameful about my life after I came out of the Jesuits. She didn't talk to me about my life. You know what she did instead? She told me all the worst things she had done in *her* life. So that I would know. And she never said . . . but that was the intention. She didn't draw the moral, but let me think it through. And it worked perfectly. I thought to myself, "Jesus, if she did all those things . . . had an abortion . . ."

Ro: So she even talked to you about that.

Bob: Yeah. And she told me another fabulous story. She said when she was twenty-two, she was exhausted, so she married this sugar daddy, just to go to Europe to take a rest. "What I remember about Europe is falling asleep on a yacht off Capri and having a drink in the Eiffel Tower. When I got back, we were staying in the Hotel New Yorker. One morning I got up before he did and took all the jewelry he had given me and put it on the counter and went home to my mother."

The thing that amazed me about all that was the courage. Women didn't do that kind of stuff in those days. Most women wouldn't have the moxie to marry somebody just for a vacation. She needed a rest, and so she took one. She didn't think it was a good thing to do ultimately, but it was a tough thing, a gutsy thing.

She was normal. She just had that wholeness that many people in her generation had. That's what I loved—the fact that she was healthy. She took the healthiness that she had, and she tried a lot of different things. Got herself in trouble. And then had the humility to say, "Look I can't . . . I'm not doing good

with my life. So I'm going to go to a church and have them tell me what to do."
This was a headstrong woman, somebody who by nature liked to . . . but she
admitted that she'd come to a dead end.

"I can't handle my own life, and I'm going to look for wisdom someplace else.
I'm going to ask them." And she had this little nun teach her the catechism. A
donkey, and she was humble enough to listen to her and to learn it, to memorize
the catechism. To come into a church that ultimately she found a scandal, and to
stay and change it.

Dorothy was a big soul and I caught her at the end. I . . . I haven't finished
grieving; I probably never will. I . . . I don't mind crying for Dorothy. She was
so beautiful, you know. I mean just to see at the end how she . . . it sounds like
you're making up some kind of bullshit story about a saint. She got thin. Her skin
stretched. She was quite beautiful again. With a diaphanous quality. She prayed
every day, and she listened to the opera, and she jotted notes. This woman who
had written these wonderful columns was writing just this little trickle every
day. One sentence, two sentences—some little bit that she had read that day or
something from her past, or something about how much she loved the trees in
the city. Just this little trickle, but what a drop . . . what a distilled drop.

CHAPTER 4

Memories of Peter Maurin

Peter *lived* all of those ideals—he lived the poverty, he lived the prayer life, he lived the work.

—Alice Zarrella

Peter Maurin was a teacher. He stepped into a culture that was barely able to hear what he had to say and asked people to listen and to agree and to learn. The Catholic Worker movement now suffers from a lack of good and holy teachers.

—Ann O'Connor

T HE Workers I talked to didn't have nearly as many "Peter stories" as "Dorothy stories," both because he wasn't as personally accessible as she was and because he died over forty years ago.* Participants in this roundtable who remember Maurin include Sr. Ruth Heaney, Joe and Alice Zarrella, Jim O'Gara, John Cort, and Michael Harrington. Younger Workers Mike Garvey, Brian Terrell, Gary Donatelli, Chris Montesano, and Daniel Marshall tell how his life and work have influenced their lives.

Mike Garvey (South Bend, Indiana): How do you distinguish between coincidence in the secular world and miracle in our own? For instance, Peter Maurin was driving George Shuster crazy down at *Commonweal*. To get rid of him, Shuster sent him to Dorothy. Well, at that time in her life, with the goofiness that she was going through, Dorothy needed to run into somebody as nuts as Peter Maurin. And he probably really needed to run into somebody as crazy as Dorothy Day. So on one level, yeah, of course it was just a coincidence . . . looked at from another point of view, it's miraculous.

* Scholarship abounds, however, on this first of the Catholic Worker scholars (1877–1949). The Paulist Press published Marc Ellis, *Peter Maurin: Prophet in the Twentieth Century* in 1981, and Ellis also has an essay on Maurin, as does Geoffrey Gneuhs, in Coy, *A Revolution of the Heart*. Some of Maurin's "Easy Essays" have been reprinted by the Franciscan Herald Press in Chicago.

Joe Zarrella (New York City and Tell City, Indiana): Miraculous? Well, I guess so, but . . . I remember the first time I had Peter as a roommate. It was on Charles Street, before I'd really moved in, so I usually slept downstairs on a table. But one night I got a bed upstairs. No heat in the place, of course. I was in my underwear getting ready to go to bed and Peter walked in. Of course, he immediately started to talk, kept talking to me for about two hours. And I didn't have common sense to get underneath the covers! [Laughter.]

But Peter didn't make the impression on me, I mean he didn't have the *influence* on me that Dorothy did. I'd say Peter, at that particular time in my life, was too academic for me. (That doesn't say anything about Peter, it says more about me. I was only nineteen, twenty years old.) But Peter was just a wonderful person, I guess the most detached person I've ever met. Never even complained about the bedbugs in the place, and, of course, we had plenty. (I think he was immune to them, actually.) I don't ever remember him asking for anything. Ever. He didn't demand any attention. And I never once ever heard of him playing.

He was always either indoctrinating or educating. There was no fun, you know, no idle chatter with Peter. He never had any money, and yet he was always on the go. The only possessions he had were books, and even those he gave away freely. All you had to do was tell Peter you were interested in something, and [he'd say,] "I have a book for you."

Mike: Oh, that reminds me of a Notre Dame story. Seems Peter came out to South Bend and was lecturing everybody in sight. Willis Nutting of Notre Dame, a scholar who had followed Peter's advice and bought a farm out in the country with the Pleasants, was out there plowing his field by hand. And here's Peter, following him up one furrow and down another, all the time preaching to him about the dignity of manual labor. And reading from a book.

Joe: Oh, I remember another cute story about Peter. A girl from *Time* magazine came to interview Peter one day. She was very good-looking, so we all crowded into the office, not so much to hear Peter but to look at the girl. And Peter was sitting very close to this girl. Peter always made points either with his finger or with his hand. And here he was talking to this girl, and constantly grabbing her by the knee. Or pounding on her leg. I remember saying to myself, "My goodness! He's the only man who could get away with that!"

Ro: I guess! [Laughter.] Now you traveled with him, didn't you, Joe? Did you make the travel arrangements?

Joe: Yeah. And I made the arrangements for the speaking, arrangements at the schools or wherever we were going. Believe me, traveling with Peter was an experience! The first thing I had to get used to was being separated from my luggage. When we arrived in a bus station, he'd lock our suitcases in the lockers. Now that was okay for Peter because his suitcases only had books. Mine had clothes, and that made it very difficult to keep clean.

After about a month on the road with Peter, I said to him, "Peter, let's get a room with a bath." And Peter said, "Oh, I had an opportunity to get a bath in Pittsburgh." Peter was not a very fastidious person; he was in the realm of the intellect.

On the bus, he was always talking to me. But he really wasn't talking to *me,* he was talking to the people in the bus. Using me as a kind of conveyor. He spoke very loudly, so everybody could hear him. Lots of times we'd be sitting together, and he'd be thinking and meditating on another "Easy Essay," and he'd be gesticulating and moving his hands and mouthing these things. Sometimes I'd try to slink down. Didn't want people to think I was with him.

I was with Peter for two or three months. Philadelphia, Pittsburgh, Detroit and to Chicago . . . uh, Milwaukee, St. Louis. When we got to St. Louis, I was ready to come home. It was Christmastime, and I wanted to get home and celebrate Christmas with the family—the Catholic Worker family. I missed everybody, so I jumped the bus and came back home. Left Peter.

Dorothy was constantly telling all of us young turks about the importance of Peter, and that we didn't "respect" him enough. I don't think I would have come to the Worker if I had just met Peter. I might have been impressed with him. I might have been very respectful of his mind and his grasp of history and all those things, but he wouldn't have moved me. Now I'm not saying he didn't move some people. He made the one big convert and that was Dorothy.

Alice Zarrella (New York City and Tell City, Indiana): Peter became what he wanted everybody to be—a scholar and a worker. And he exemplified in his life what he expected from the rest of the people, but they didn't live up to his expectation.

Peter *lived* all of those ideals—he lived the poverty, he lived the prayer life, he lived the work. Really a Benedictine. *Ore et labore.* It was difficult, though, to talk to Peter because he had a very pronounced accent, and a lot of the people couldn't understand what he was saying. He lectured, really. He didn't talk.

Joe: But Peter respected. Peter was truly a listener. And he would never interrupt you. When you spoke, he listened. But you better get your words in because when he started, he'd go on for a long time. And so unless you had that kind of a mind, he wore you out. He'd give you the whole history of an idea, take you through the process. Maybe when he finished, you knew where he was trying to get to, but you'd wonder why he didn't say that right away.

Alice: He didn't speak the way he wrote. It was a real contradiction. When he talked, he reminded me of Karl Rahner, you know, who goes around the block forty times before he walks in the door. That was Peter.

Joe: He worked his "Easy Essays" constantly. A very thorough person. I'm sure they went through a refining process because you can't write that simply and precisely otherwise.

Alice: I remember that when Peter would read something he wanted to remember, he'd take the page and rip it out and throw it away, so he'd have to remember what was on it.

Joe: Here are some pictures of Peter that I took at Maryfarm. This one I like to call "Sermon on the Mount with Peter." [Passes photo to Rosalie.]

Ro: Oh, that's great! Everyone at the farm is clustered around him.

Joe: And he's gesticulating and sticking his finger up.

Alice: Mrs. [Lillian] Weis was there.

Ro: Pardon me?

Alice: Mrs. Weis, this lady who always took care of him. Brought him food.

Ro: Oh, *Weis!* God! I thought you said "his *wife."* [Laughter.]

Alice: She had a kind of crush on him, I think.

Ro: On Peter?

Joe: Oh yes! Oh my!

Michael Harrington (New York City): Peter Maurin . . . he died a year or two before I got there. You know, I never figured out whether anybody liked Peter. (That was my great project, which I never completed.) I always had my suspicions that Dorothy didn't like Peter much, either, but it was indelicate of me to ask, and I've always been a delicate person, so I didn't. Dorothy used to talk endlessly about him, but in very revealing terms. About how she met Peter and they decided to start the *Catholic Worker* and Peter just assumed that he'd write the entire newspaper. He was sort of taken aback when it turned out that Dorothy was actually a journalist of some substance, that it was not going to be just *his* paper. I think he thought it'd be wall-to-wall "Easy Essays." As Dorothy told the story, it was sort of, "Isn't that charming of Peter?" Well, it occurred to me that if you're a writer, it might not have been such a charming . . . you know, [his was] a rather arrogant assumption.

To this day, I don't know how people really felt about Peter. This endless talk about Peter. Dorothy would give whole lectures on Peter. It seemed to me she got very boring when she talked about Peter, and that also made me suspicious. I really feel that Dorothy was ambivalent, but since I never discussed it with anybody, I have no idea whether this is true or false.

John Cort (New York City): Hmmm . . . interesting. Oh, I remember meeting Peter the first night I came to the Worker. I was sleeping in a room with three or four . . . I don't know how many other men. Peter Maurin was in the bed next to me. Snoring, I remember. It was an extremely hot night in July. In the jungle of New York—Lower East Side, Little Italy. And I remember the bedbugs started biting, but I was so exulted that I didn't mind. It just seemed very dramatic. Melodramatic, even. And so I was able to survive that night. But I just barely survived Peter! Peter and I were not intellectually simpatico. And I might say that Dorothy and I weren't entirely intellectually simpatico either, because she sort of followed Peter. Strangely, because she was an ex-Communist and was wedded to the labor movement. Peter was anti-union, actually.

Ro: I'd think your education in French literature would have helped the two of you to get along.

John: Well, faith-wise, we agreed on a great deal.

Ro: But you didn't buy the medieval village . . .

John: I didn't buy that. It attracted me, but it just didn't make logical, rational sense in the modern world. I was caught and attracted by a sentence of Eric Gill. (*The Autobiography of Eric Gill* was sort of compulsory reading at the Worker. He said "men," but let's say "people" in deference to the feminists.) "People work best when they own and control their own tools and materials." Peter took that, of course, to imply that everybody should be craftsmen and work either on little farms in the green valley somewhere or do handicrafts or make their shoes by hand and their clothes and so on. Live in an agrarian handicraft economy or society. And I applied it to industrial society—to worker cooperatives. Producer cooperatives. Using sophisticated technology. I didn't buy agrarianism, which was Catholic Worker gospel. I also didn't buy the kind of anarchistic tendency that Dorothy and Peter shared, and I didn't buy total pacifism, either. So I was kind of a heretic at the Catholic Worker.

Jim O'Gara (formerly Chicago, now Rockville Center, New York): You know, a lot of things are said in Peter's name that Peter wouldn't particularly agree with. And a lot of things are attributed to him. For instance, I'm very dubious that he would claim the label of anarchist in any serious sense that anarchism could be defined. If he'd call himself an anarchist, I think it would only be in a very loose metaphorical sort of sense, not in any sense a political scientist would use.

And about his idea of being a scholar and a worker—I don't think scholar-worker and farmer-scholar are contradictory or anything. Fine for a farmer to be a scholar if he has that bent, or for a worker to be a scholar if he has that bent. But I don't . . . the point of Peter's farm program was that it proposed a solution to the social question: that's the crux of the matter. I don't consider it [a solution] in the long term. It may help a few people solve their immediate problems. But as a long-range solution to the problem of industrial capitalism, I don't think that's it.

Part of the problem with Peter, of course, was that he had a strong French accent. At first I could never tell what he was talking about. I remember one time when he was visiting us in Chicago, and Father [Martin] Carrabine had arranged for him to lecture to the students of St. Ignatius Jesuit High School. I asked one of the kids afterwards how he liked Peter's lecture. And he said, "Well, it was interesting. He sure was mad at that Smith fellow. Kept talking about that 'damn Smith.'" Finally I figured out what the kid meant. That's the way Peter pronounced Adam Smith—"a damn Smith."

Brian Terrell (New York City and Maloy, Iowa): I think today we need to look again into the revolutionary ideas Peter was talking about. What we're doing in Maloy, Iowa, in an area where everybody's packing up to leave, in an area that's losing its topsoil and poisoning its water, is only a gesture. But we hope to see life there improved and hope to make it so that someday soon, the young people who grow up there won't want to leave. There just isn't anything we can fix with our own efforts, and we can't fool ourselves anymore. It's in God's hands. I . . . I don't want to be a quietist, and we still have to do what . . . what we can do, but I think this is forcing us to look into deeper solutions, at Peter's solutions.

Ro: Oh, Brian! That sounds so pessimistic to me. Maybe if we just hear Peter's ideas again, hear them as they relate to our lives today, it will make a difference. You know, he always said, "The truth has to be restated every twenty years." Do you think you can do that from Maloy? Will you be able to convince people to come out to Iowa and become agrarian philosophers?

Gary Donatelli (New York City): I think times have changed too much. For example, when Peter was talking about hospitality, he was talking about hospitality for homeless people who could be workers. Today, that's . . . perhaps there are a lot of homeless people who could be working, but a lot of it's mental illness. And people who just don't have a place, particularly in this city. Now today, you're not going to take some folks in off the streets of New York and start talking to them about an agrarian revolution or a distributive economy. It's not going to make much sense to them. They're not going to be interested. And even if they could be interested in it, I'm not so sure it's what needs to be shared with people.

When we were in New York together, Brian, we didn't think very concretely or realistically. We had these sort of utopian ideas about decentralist economies and governments, and yet we wouldn't *say* we were utopian. Maybe part of the problem is we pretend to have an economic vision today, and I don't know that it applies to the world in the eighties and nineties. The Catholic Worker—and Peter's economics—are only dialectical with the thirties. There's no critique of our present economy, just rejection. It doesn't come to terms with it, doesn't wrestle with it. I think that's a weakness. If we're going to be anarchist, we need to be dialectical with the present. We're not scratching the surface.

Chris Montesano (Sheep Ranch, California): Well, I see a tremendous richness in the traditional theory of the Worker. Whenever Dorothy spoke, she'd always begin with talking about Peter Maurin's vision. The three questions: Why are things the way they are? How should things be? And how do we make a path from things as they are to things as they should be?

It took me years before I began to understand the breadth of the Worker vision, especially Peter's aspect . . . you know, the whole vision of returning to the land, what that meant. I think it was an incredibly prophetic vision, and it's only now beginning to see fruition. Because in some ways, unless you have . . . unless all of us in American society begin to change our lifestyle, our basic lifestyle . . . You can do all the resistance you want, but if you're not changing how you live . . . In other words, if you continue to live your life supported by the corporate structure of the United States . . . We're all in a stranglehold, including all of us at Sheep Ranch. We are not a free people. I think a tremendously important aspect of nonviolence is withdrawal, withdrawing your support from those things that are immoral. Simply living off donations, or using discarded produce—these [actions] are fine, but you're still living off the system as it exists.

That's what farms are trying to address. You withdraw from the corporate structure to begin to create new structures, a "new system in the shell of the old." All of this is in the Worker movement. Workers have talked about it for years . . . worker ownership of the means of production and distribution. That's what we're about with our candle craft.

Peter's concept of work comes out of a spiritual dimension. He didn't look at work as . . . in both the capitalist and the communist society, work is looked upon as something that's bought or sold. Labor is a commodity. But in Peter's vision, work is a *gift.* Given for the common good. And the reason why one works is to share gifts and talents, in common with others, to help create a better kind of society.

So that ties into craft and to worker ownership of the means of production and distribution. Trying to create structures that are more human. It's a whole world-wide problem now, the dehumanization of the workplace. The only way you can recapture the humanity is to have that spiritual dimension, to have work happen in that kind of a setting.

Daniel Marshall (Brooklyn): It's so good to hear that. So few people even dare to acknowledge they admire Peter Maurin. Lots of people feel Peter's writings are silly.

Ro: Because of the rhyming?

Daniel: That kind of thing. I think they also feel uncomfortable with the 1930s diction and the . . . the whole intellectual approach. The tendency to put things into formal principles and to quote Thomas Aquinas and to identify as a Catholic— all those things they're not sure that they agree with.

You know, there is no Catholic Worker party line. Is there a party line in Catholicism even? But that's what Peter was after. I think he was trying . . . I think he was saying there is a certain tradition, and he was out to present a synthesis of the tradition, but that the application was up to each person.

Sr. Ruth Heaney (Starkenburg, Missouri): My first encounter with the Catholic Worker was when I was a student at St. Mary's College in Notre Dame, Indiana. Peter was known as a kind of eccentric old man who went from university to university and had all these university friends. He spoke to the student body at St. Mary's. I knew that we'd heard a great man talk, and that I heard something different than my friends did. In the early days, Peter and Dorothy weren't yet disgraceful. You know, they were still accepted.

I think of Peter so strongly and poignantly every time I'm in New York. I see the subways and the poverty and feel so hopeless and helpless, and I think of how Peter evolved his ideas from the distress that he saw in the Bowery. Although I don't think he realized that if you want peace, [you have to] work for justice. And if you want justice, [you have to] work for peace, because the military takes too much of our money. I don't believe he knew that, and I also don't think he knew that maybe there wasn't going to be enough land to go around. We've just got too many people for everybody to have five acres and be independent.

Peter wanted to call the paper the "Christian Radical," you know.* He said "radical" refers to roots, and we need our roots. He didn't want to use the word "Catholic"; he wanted the word "Christian" because he already had an ecumenical sense, long before the ecumenical movement. And didn't want the Worker' limited to either labor or peace [because] he had a larger vision. Peter was the most integrated person you'd ever want to meet, you know, and my husband, Larry, just worshiped the ground he walked on.

Ro: Can you tell some stories about Peter? You and Larry seemed to know him better than anyone else did.

Sr. Ruth: Well, I *do* have a couple of funny Peter stories. When Peter would come to the different houses, he'd simply put himself at the hands of whoever was running the house, just do what he was asked to do. Well, he was visiting us in Milwaukee one time and had gone to morning Mass with Larry. After Mass, Larry looked over at Peter, and he was praying, so Larry prayed. And then he got out a rosary and Peter took out his rosary, too. And they stayed in that church for nearly an hour afterwards, with Peter waiting for Larry to decide what they should do, and Larry waiting for Peter to decide. Almost an hour before Larry made a move!

And I remember one of Peter's little jokes at the farm. If everybody would be lying out under a shade tree, Peter would say, "Well, back to the land doesn't mean literally."

I remember, too, one time when we were all in the kitchen, and I said something, and Peter said to me, "Oh, I'll send you on a speaking tour." And Ade [Bethune] said, "I thought you wanted people who had babies to stay home and take care of them." And Peter just laughed. Even if he thought I could speak well, he still wanted me at home.

Here's one story Larry used to tell. It seems that one Saturday afternoon Peter went to a professor's house with his broken English and all, and this professor's wife didn't know that he was her husband's houseguest. She thought he wanted to read the meter and told him where the basement was. Then when the professor wondered why Peter didn't come, his wife said, "Well, somebody did come, and I thought he wanted to read the meter, so I sent him to the basement." And there was Peter, down in the basement, sitting on an old box and writing an "Easy Essay." Just waiting. Taking what life offers.

* In *The Long Loneliness*, Day remembers Maurin's wanting to call the paper the "Catholic Radical."

Peter left the Worker at one time, you know. I remember Larry being distressed and saying that there were clearly some problems that Peter didn't want to articulate. He wouldn't have wanted to interfere with what Dorothy was doing, and yet he didn't exactly agree with it, so he just disappeared for a time. For almost a year, I guess. And she was advertising in the paper for him to contact them and come home. I think that was . . . well, there's always that problem. How do you deal with differences?

The last time we saw Peter was a beautiful time for Larry. This was before we left Milwaukee. Peter had come on what was his last journey, at least as far as I know. He was too tired to indoctrinate all the time, so he was just visiting up at our house, and he talked about himself a little bit. He played with the children, and . . . Larry just treasured that evening because Peter had really been his spiritual father. Larry was kind of considered a Catholic Worker saint, and he felt that Peter had been this source of . . . of all the good things that had come into his life—me and all the good things that had come. It was awfully good for Larry, I think, to have Peter. Oh, he loved Peter! I've always felt that Larry had been able to secure Peter's death. Peter had . . . had not been himself and had been deteriorating mentally and physically in his last years. We knew he was failing on his last visit with us, and I think Larry's prayer obtained Peter's release.

CHAPTER 5

Memories of Ammon Hennacy

Our friends would come to Notre Dame to hear Ammon. One of them was a gung-ho ex-marine. And Ammon . . . well, he was a gung-ho *anti*-marine.

—*Julian Pleasants*

Ammon never had anything. *Anything!* He lived on less than nothing because of his conscience. And the only thing he ever got out of it was the satisfaction . . . his ego. So let him have it. Let him have his ego.

—*Dorothy Day, as told to Utah Phillips*

Ammon Hennacy (1893–1970) was the most theatrical of Catholic Workers, famous for his aphorisms and his solitary picketing. While in jail for refusing to serve in the military during World War II, he became convinced of the truth of the Sermon on the Mount but appeared to remain anti-Catholic even during his brief time as a convert to the church. He spent most of the last twenty years of his life as a Catholic Worker, living wholeheartedly his "one-man revolution" and influencing many Workers throughout the country.*

In this roundtable, several Catholic Workers remember their contacts with him, including Mary Lathrop, who helped him to start a Catholic Worker house in Salt Lake City. The scholar Pat Coy reflects on Hennacy's influence and the chapter ends with the memories of a man who could be called his successor—the folksinger Utah Phillips.

Florence Weinfurter (Milwaukee): For a while, Ammon Hennacy was interested in us, in our Catholic Worker house here in Milwaukee. (He was a local then.) A very friendly individual, but firm in what he believed. Wouldn't eat anything that came from animals. One time later, he came back into town. He had walked forever, from La Crosse or wherever. I had dinner with him, and wouldn't you

---

* Those interested in reading more about this passionate anarchist should see Coy's essay in his anthology, *A Revolution of the Heart,* and also Hennacy's autobiographies.

know? I forgot he wasn't eating anything from the animals. I don't know what we had for him, but anyway, he wouldn't eat it. That's what I remember.

Pat Murray (Peninsula, Ohio): Ammon used to come stay with us [when we were in Chillicothe, Ohio]. Oh my, he was a hard man!

Mary Murray (Peninsula, Ohio): Oh, yeah. But interesting! I mean it was a real shot in the arm to have him with us in person.

Pat: We'd invite all our friends to come and hear Ammon talk. He had this speech about the Worker and about his own life. And if you came fifteen minutes late, he'd stop his talk and start all over again, right from the beginning. And if another person came, he'd start all over a third time. Of course, we'd scour the countryside to find the people to come hear him.

Mary: Well, we couldn't get that many people to come. Especially after the first time.

Pat: He used to call me a pipsqueak. And he wrote in his book about us. Said we were nice people but not very radical.

Fr. Bernie Gilgun (Hubbardston and Worcester, Massachusetts): When I first went down to New York to see Dorothy, she was out. Ammon was at his desk, and he received us. It was another priest and myself, and he made a great show of the fact that it had been so long since he'd seen two good priests together. Made a big point of saying that that's why he was able to give us so much time.

Oh, he absolutely capitvated me. I really loved Ammon. So that whenever he came to Worcester after that, I was always on the scene. And when it came time to name the house [in Hubbardston], it was . . . his autobiography had just come out—*The Book of Ammon.* So we named our house the House of Ammon. But he never visited there. He was pretty sick then, and he died within months.

Ro: But he knew about it, didn't he? I think he might like houses to be named after him.

Fr. Bernie: Oh, yes. He was . . . yes.

Julian Pleasants (South Bend, Indiana): Our friends would come to Notre Dame to hear Ammon. One of them was a gung-ho ex-marine. And Ammon . . . well, he was a gung-ho *anti*-marine. They were entranced by his personality. Even though he was all for pacifism and they were all for the military, he was their kind of guy. So he made a lot of contacts with people just by his brashness and his outspokenness. I think of him off and on because he always picked up trash along the roadside as he walked. He said he did it for the community in lieu of paying taxes. And I still do that.

Michael Harrington (New York City): Well, Ammon Hennacy drove me crazy! When Ammon was my roommate, I used to be very careful. When I'd first wake up, I wouldn't open my eyes. I'd just lie there and listen to see if Ammon was around. Because I knew that if he were, he'd be waiting. Just waiting.

He would say, "I knew a socialist in Ohio in 1911 who became a white slaver. I knew a socialist who used to beat blacks." I mean, he knew every horror story about socialists. Then he used to soapbox down in the Wall Street area, talk on behalf of Catholicism and anarchism. And he really threw people off. To put it mildly, [they were] not accustomed to having the two joined together.

People would ask him, "You're an anarchist. Now are you in favor of free love?"

And his answer was always, "Are you in favor of bought love?" Just totally irrelevant, with all these sort of anarchist sayings.

He became a Catholic only because he was in love with Dorothy. I think it had very little to do with the Holy Spirit and very much to do with the human love. I remember he would fast and picket on every anniversary of Hiroshima. And just take whatever it is you need so you don't kill yourself—water or some juice. Every year, he would fast longer. I was there the year he fasted more than forty days. And there was, I think, a little pride that he had now out-fasted Jesus. That Jesus had only done forty days and Ammon had done forty-three or something like that. Take that, God!

Mike Garvey (South Bend, Indiana): Stanley Vishnewski said, "Man cannot serve two masters, God and Ammon." I wonder if Ammon Hennacy is coming back into vogue.

Tom Cornell (New York City): Hmmm. Maybe. The War Resisters League liked Ammon. Ammon liked them to the degree he could like any other men. He didn't like men in general. Almost universally, he liked women but not men.

Mary Lathrop (New York City): Yes . . . yes. Ammon was in jail, in Sandstone Prison, when I came [to the Worker]. He came out a couple of months later. I immediately latched on to him, and we were picketing and fasting together, picketing up at the Civil Defense Office against air raid drills. And we did the City Hall Park protest. I cried because they wouldn't arrest me.

Ammon was very, very energetic, very . . . a great enthusiast, with a wonderful sense of humor. He was in great physical shape for his age. He was what I thought of as a leader and somebody I could . . . maybe a father figure or something. I was only twenty-six. He was forty years older than I was. Ammon kind of sneaked in there and started romancing me. I didn't want it, and I didn't like it, but I liked Ammon. (He kind of got me on the rebound . . . I had a crush on Charlie Butterworth, you see, at that point. And Charlie had this thing about chastity.)

The burden of freedom at the Catholic Worker is really total. You're totally responsible for your life and for your vision of what you as a person can do in the Catholic Worker. It's a really huge burden, I think, perhaps more than many young people are able to assume. I wasn't ready for infinite freedom. So anyhow, what happened was that Dorothy decided that I should go on a trip with her. All that time, I was driving poor Dorothy crazy. "Should I marry Ammon, or shouldn't I marry Ammon?" On and on and on and on. Poor Dorothy. She told me once, "You will get tired of that old flesh and start chasing after younger men."

Finally, I said to myself, "This has got to be decided once and for all." I can't remember whether I made the sign of the cross or not, but I opened the Bible and put my finger on . . . and I looked down at what was under my finger. "Woe, woe unto you that you should play the harlot and be his." Can you believe that? It's the truth! And that was the end of it. Not the end of my friendship with Ammon, but the end of that problem.

Later Ammon wanted me to go out West with him to start a house in Salt Lake City. And I just said, "No. No!" He kept after me. Finally I said, "Well, I'll go if you're perfectly aware that there's going to be nothing between us whatsoever, nothing at all. There will be fasting and picketing, and I'll help with the house and do what I can. There will be no shenanigans."

We rented a storefront, a very large place. I painted some murals. The house was called Joe Hill House, and Ammon wanted a twelve-by-fifteen-foot mural of Joe Hill being executed. I didn't want that, but I painted it anyway.

I lived in a hotel next door, and Ammon stayed at another hotel up the street, but we had . . . I finally decided to just flee. I told him my reputation was . . . was worth nothing. He said, "Well, what do you care? What do you care what people think?"

Pat Coy (St. Louis): I wrote my M.A. thesis on Hennacy, I guess because I became fascinated with his one-dimensionalism. He had a vision which he clung to tenaciously, and in some cases quite stupidly, I think, because he sacrificed some important values in terms of relationships and community. To hold on to his vision, he had to sacrifice certain things. Maybe even certain people. And yet at the same time, that [tenacity] is a great example for us today.

Ammon didn't . . . couldn't live well with people. Although it wasn't because he was selfish. Dorothy herself often said that Ammon was a reproach to the rest of us because he'd always give up his bed and always take the lowest place in that sense; however, he often put himself in the highest place in other senses. But he was certainly willing to live the life that he preached.

◆

Utah Phillips remembers Ammon Hennacy.

Ro: Why don't you start with you and Ammon in Utah? Or with Utah in Utah.

Utah Phillips (Salt Lake City): Well, I wasn't Utah then. Uh . . . some of this is a little difficult. Let's see. I got back from Korea, where I'd been a soldier for reasons completely unknown to me. Of course, I was there towards the end, but the situation was still pretty much the same—it was a combat zone. When I got back, I was so upset by what I'd seen and what I'd done—so enraged—that I just got on the trains. Rode for a while on the freight trains. Drunk most of the time. (I'm still a recovering alcoholic.) And I didn't know if I could ever live in the United States again.

I got back into Salt Lake and got a dumb job at Western Movie Supply. Part of my job was to mail packages. (This was around 1960.) Well, I saw this white-haired elderly gentleman walking around in front of the post office with a picket sign, some wild sign about tax refusal and Hiroshima. I didn't pay much attention to it, but it provoked my curiosity. I was attracted to what he was saying, and I noticed that he'd stop every now and then and sit down under a bush and drink some water. So one day I sat down with him. Well, I was late getting back to work. And then I was late getting back to work *a lot.*

He caught my anger and my rage, caught something about the way I'd talk what I'd seen and done in Korea, the way I'd talk about the general dilapidated appearance of reality. He detected this as anarchic, so I guess he looked at me as bein' a little further down his road than a lot of the people around him. So he began to . . . not to work on me, but to talk.

Ammon was a talker, a great talker. He outlined his plans for opening a house of hospitality, the Joe Hill House. I'd never heard of the Catholic Worker at that time. He was traveling with Mary Lathrop, who was a beautiful young woman. Oh, the rumors that flew around about them! Wonderful, delicious rumors that, of course, Ammon played to the hilt.

Ammon was a deeply passionate man. And that led to . . . Oh, how many misunderstandings about he and Dorothy Day! His great passion—physical passion—for her and her great spiritual passion for him. His was an animal passion, and hers was a very deep spiritual passion. They met in some ways and in other ways went past each other like ships passing in the night. But it was beautiful, just beautiful, that kind of relationship.

Mary Lathrop painted the mural on the Joe Hill House, the mural of the execution of Joe Hill. Above the firing squad, Mary had this massive boiling cloud with a crucified Christ emerging out of it. Well, Joe Hill was an atheist, and he would've hated that mural.

By that time, I'd been in the IWW [Industrial Workers of the World] for ten years or so. Joined the Wobblies in the early fifties, before I went to Korea. For macho reasons, mainly. "To inherit the mantle of their authenticity." I rejoined later on for more sensible reasons. Anarchial syndicalism is simply *right*. I've been in it now for almost thirty years . . . better than thirty years. Ammon had been a Wobbly, you know, just like Dorothy Day had been. Well, Ammon ran the Joe Hill House, and I slung soup there and listened to him talk and walked out my anger on an enormous picket line, an endless picket line.

He took everybody in. The police record shows night after night, at night court, "Sent to Joe Hill House." Instead of sending them to the drunk tank. 'Cause it saved the county some money. Look it up—it's right in their books.

So I was makin' soup at the Hill House. Ammon would push a grocery cart sixty blocks a day. He was strong. Inhumanly strong. And he'd bring back unlabeled cans that they couldn't sell because the labels had fallen off and nobody knew what was in 'em. Well, we didn't know, either. It could be cranberry sauce or brussels sprouts. Whatever it was, it went into the pot. So the stew changed—evolved—over the winter. And the old hands there, like sheep herders coming down from the mountains to winter in, they knew that the best part was at the bottom, caked up at the bottom. So they'd use a long-handled fork to dig that stuff out.

Other Catholic Workers would show up. Like Terry Sullivan from Denver. (He'd been with Liberation News Service in New York and had worked with Karl Meyer in Chicago.) There was Pat, an airline stewardess who came from the New York house. And Cajun—Murphy Dowouis—the Cajun who was Ammon's right-hand person. Cajun wound up having to leave the Joe Hill House to do time in Texas on a draft resistance bust. Well, you know, I fell into that community.

Ammon reached out and grabbed my alcoholism first. Said I had to stop drinking. So okay. He was just like AA, telling me an alcoholic recognizes his capacity for booze and fights against the next drink every day. Every minute.

Then he said, "Okay. Now we're going to deal with your capacity for violence, this rage you have. Let's treat it like booze. Pacifism isn't a catalogue of beliefs, that if you subscribe to it, you're a pacifist. It's an attitude just like AA." So he told me to recognize my capacity for violence and deal with it in every situation, every minute of every day.

He said, "A pacifist is something you are always *becoming.* You're never really completely there. You've got to give up violent thought, too, not just fists, guns, knives, clubs—overt violence. Nonviolence is going forth into the world completely disarmed. Disarmed of the weapons of privilege, the weapons of sexual privilege, the weapons of racial privilege, the weapons of economic privilege."

All of which, as a white man in mid-twentieth century America, I had grown up with. I had come . . . when I was a soldier in Korea, as GIs in a small Asian country, we were given the power to beat those privileges to death. To be sexually aggressive. To be physically aggressive, you know, violently aggressive. We were white men, and our commanders were saying that having GI babies in Korea would eventually improve the intelligence of the Korean population. That kind of stuff. An unlimited license, you know, for racism, sexism, and ripping off whatever wasn't nailed down. So Ammon said, "We're going to have to give up the weapons of privilege, see? And go forth into the world completely unarmed."

If there is a worthy life task, that's the one that I have set myself to. And that's why Ammon Hennacy continues to alter my life. Because that's a horrendous struggle. That's at the core of the anarchist struggle, of Ammon's struggle. To stay clean. And he changed many lives. Then it's up to us to go out and help other people to change their lives.

In carrying out this mission, our narrator changed his name to Utah Phillips and began singing folk songs professionally. He performed at the 1991 national Catholic Worker gathering in Boston.

I caught him earlier, in Ann Arbor, Michigan, where he was singing at the Unitarian Church.

Utah: Ammon was stubborn, egocentric . . . in fact, I raised the egocentrism with Dorothy when I met her in 1970. That was the year Ammon died, and I took Ammon's love. Anyway, I mentioned Ammon's self-centeredness as criticism of him. She said, "Ammon never had anything. *Anything!* He didn't ask for anything. He lived on less than nothing because of his conscience. And the only thing he ever got out of it was the satisfaction . . . his ego. So let him have it. Let him have his ego."

Ro: Some say Ammon became Catholic just because he loved Dorothy.

Utah: Good possibility. You can read that whole long explanation at the end of his *Autobiography of a Catholic Anarchist.* All you can do is take him at his word.

You could on everything else, so why not? He was a "Sermon on the Mount Christian" to begin with. And that's the core of it. That's the center of it. If you're not doing what's in the Sermon on the Mount, then your feet are on real shaky ground. So he was at the center. Didn't have all the rest of it.

But, you know, he began talking later on . . . I'd ask him about Dorothy after they'd had a real falling out. A little bitterly he used to say, "Oh, she's talking to the bishop too much." And one time he showed me the original manuscript to *One Man Revolution in America.* And Dorothy Day wasn't in it.

I said, "Ammon! Dorothy's not in the book."

And Ammon said, "Well, she's still alive. She could chicken out at any time. If you've got to have heroes, make sure they're dead so they can't blow it."

Which is stern, but really Ammon. I know she had a great affection for him. In fact, when I went to see her, she took an old book, a first edition of Peter Maurin's *The Green Revolution,* and wrote my name in it, and autographed it "To Ammon's friend." I cherish that gift.

Dorothy was moved by him, and I wish they could've gotten it together. I wish they could've gotten it together. No one could have lit any brighter candle than would have come out of that.

Ro: What do you remember about Ammon from the Joe Hill House? Was it all men?

Utah: It was pretty much all men. Yeah. Pretty much all men. I remember Ammon in front of Federal District Judge Ritter. (He never pled innocent or guilty when he was picked up for picketing illegally.) Judge Ritter would say, "What the hell is an anarchist?"

And Ammon would say, "An anarchist is anybody who don't need a cop to tell him what to do."

"But you broke the law."

And Ammon would say, "Oh judge! Your damn laws! The good people don't need them, and the bad people don't obey them."

"You think you can change the world that way?"

"Well, maybe not. But it damn sure can't change me!"

And then he talked . . . you know, on the Friday night meetings, he talked to the transients or whoever was there. Kids from college. There was one Mormon reporter used to come, Paul Swenson. Paul just loved Ammon. But Ammon would talk about Clarence Darrow or Eugene Debs, or Lucy Parsons—talk about people he had met, you know, and whom he really respected. And it was always the same rule: No heroes until they were dead. 'Cause they might chicken out.

I've seen him physically attacked and turn around and shake the person's hand.

Say to the man, "You're not as mean as you think you are." And people would come back, after they'd knocked him down, and they'd protect him. Even though they didn't agree with him.

Another thing that Ammon would do, maybe not often enough, but I've seen him do it . . . There was a little coffee shop around the corner from the post office. When we were picketing, we'd go in and take a break, go in and get warm. Somebody would follow us in, someone who'd been cautiously watching the picket line. You didn't know what was going to happen, but he'd challenge Ammon on his sign or his politics.

Instead of blurting out what he was there for, saying "These are my politics, take it or leave it," Ammon would . . . it seemed to me that he understood that people don't get asked questions very often. And people who aren't asked questions don't question.

Well, Ammon would ask a question. And that'd put the person off, sort of surprise them. And then he'd ask the next one. "What do you think about the war? Oh, you were in the Second World War? Where did you serve?" Things like that. This guy's being asked questions for maybe the first time in his life.

So you begin to divest. You begin to empty yourself out to the listening ear. Well, once you got all that stuff out, you know, there's a big empty space. Time to put it back. See? So every point that Ammon gave up . . . Good lesson. You give up a point. Give up your politics. Give away every point. Say, "Well, you may be right about that." Say, "I never thought about that. Gee . . ."

And then take every point back, once there's room to put it in. Just take time. Be patient about it. Instead of bleeding your politics and then playing cut and run. That just polarizes everything. I saw him do that kind of questioning, but I don't think it comes out in his writing.

Ro: No. In his writing, he has the floor.

Utah: Right. He had the floor but . . . and there *were* times, like in front of students or something like that, that he would provoke. Put it all out there to provoke.

Ro: What about the Friday nights? Which way would he use?

Utah: Well, it was more conversational. You could tell, in the last couple of years of Joe Hill House, that he wanted to get through the Friday nights as a kind of an obligation, so he could get to the music. Ammon liked to sing. I'd be there and Cajun'd be there, and we'd be making up songs about the Joe Hill House, you know, about things going on around us.

Ammon always got along better with the Mormons than he did with the Catholics. 'Cause he thought they'd been persecuted and still had the memory, so they were more giving and more outgoing, considering what he was trying to do, than the Catholic Church was. Those big picket lines—for peace, for civil rights, open housing—Ammon would digress over to the cathedral. Walk up to the parsonage, the vicarage . . . wherever the people live who run that place. Walk up the front steps with a list of questions and tack it to the front door. Like Luther.

Ro: He didn't call the Joe Hill House a Catholic Worker house, did he?

Utah: He called it St. Joseph House. It was Joe Hill House, St. Joseph's House of Hospitality. It was always very clear that it was a Catholic Worker house. On one window he had a phrase by John Dewey that I can't remember, and on the other window was a quote from Eugene Debs: "As long as there is a working class, I am in it . . . As long as there is a criminal . . . something, something . . . As long as there is a soul in prison, I am not free."

St. Joseph House was always open, and the front window was always getting broken out. He was sleeping people on the floor—stacked in there like cordwood. The house was right downtown at first, but then Ammon moved it further out, and finally out to the Roper Yards of the railroad. That was the last Joe Hill House Ammon had.

Ro: So he had three different places?

Utah: Yes. Because he wanted the transients—the people tramping on the freights. He didn't want the town drunks. After a while, he said, "This is a treadmill to oblivion. I'm just doing the police's work downtown." I don't know if that was a failing on his part, or if he thought it was, I just know that he didn't want to be downtown with the town drunks. He wanted to be with the travelin' people and with the Indians.

Ro: Do a lot of people still ride the rails?

Utah: You bet. Out in the West, in the good weather, you don't see empties without people in them. It's a little harder to find empties, though, with the rail box. The yards are a little tighter now. Well, in many places they're a *lot* tighter because of military loads and toxic wastes and nuclear stuff going through. And if there's ever an accident of course, they blame the tramps. Instead of worker error or bad equipment or faulty road bed, they always say it was some tramp throwin' out cigarette butts. Well, then the yard shuts down, you know, and a tramp can't get through anymore. But I know a lot of great old tramps who've been at it for years and years. (I'm still a grand duke in the hobo federation, Hobo Convention. I keep my hand in.)

Ro: Do you think those men, with their independence, maybe spoke to Ammon more than the down-and-outers of the town?

Utah: I think when you talk about Pierce and some of the big tramps, yeah, they had more to say to him. He had more to say to them. They were . . . tramps are conscientious malingerers. There's a class of people on the skids, people who've had broken minds from the time they were kids, and nobody's paid attention enough to see. So they just get on the road, running away from whatever it is that galled them. Of course, you take it with you, so you just keep on running. You got sick people. You got broken people. Broken by war, broken by having their jobs run out—a skill, a craft that's no longer needed. I'm talking about forty-five, fifty-year-old . . . there's no retraining, you know. What do you do?

But then there's another class of people who just can't stand to have a boss. Just can't . . . incapable of taking a master for more than a couple of days. They get up a roadstake washing dishes, chipping bricks, cleaning the bricks off, and then head down the road. See the country. Hard life. Dangerous. But there are some people who won't come indoors if you give them a ticket for a hotel. You know, you go to the jungle, they wouldn't come in even if the weather was bad.

They're just anarchic—unconsciously anarchist. They have nothing to do with the state. Unlike Ammon, they're not self-conscious. Ammon was a self-conscious anarchist. He decided. Figured out the words to go with the gut feeling, see? And then a way to put it in the world by talking and doing. To formalize it. But I don't think he was any different from ninety percent of the people who came to the house. Under the appropriate circumstances, many of them could've become Ammon Hennacy because they had that fear and hatred . . . fear and mistrust of the state. Fear and mistrust of authority.

I really wouldn't want to get too close to talking about Ammon's psychology of resisting the state. You know, the psychologists say, "Well, you're resisting authority. What happened in your childhood?" I don't want to pick it apart like that, and I think it's different for everybody. But I rather think you're right. I hadn't thought about that, that Ammon was drawn to the people who were still more whole people. The town drunks were *parts* of people. And he couldn't get anywhere talking to parts of people.

They sure needed the help, though. They needed the place to warm . . . you know, and anybody who could make it out there was sure more than welcome. It was a long walk. I guess Ammon also got tired of the windows downtown being broken out all the time. And of course the rules were "no cops" and "no booze." So it didn't matter if it was bloody murder, you never called the cops. You handled your own stuff.

Ro: You had to kick a lot of folks out, didn't you?

Utah: Yeah. Over and over again. So I guess it wears thin after a while. Especially when you're doing something for people, and they refuse to take responsibility. You know? So Ammon said, "Screw this! I'll go a little further down the street."

Gee, I remember the great Fred Thompson, a great Wobbly, an anarchial syndicalist of the first water. I remember we had a problem in the IWW. Some people who had joined it belonged to a neo-fascist organization. Wore Nazi uniforms, the whole bit. And I panicked. Called up Fred Thompson.

He said, "You know, under some conditions, a fascist is an anarchist driven mad. An anarchist will say, 'You've got to learn to do it yourself. You got to take control of your life. Become your own government. Don't let other people do it for you. Get together with people of like mind and do it yourselves.' And the people don't do it and don't do it and don't do it. And finally in despair the anarchist will say, 'Okay, damn it! You've had your chance. Now I'm going to do it for you. I'm going to ram it down your throat.'" Out of despair and frustration. He told me the greatest organizer the IWW ever had in New York, an Italian American, became Mussolini's right-hand man.

Ro: Scary!

Utah: Yeah. I don't know. I don't think Ammon ever was that extreme, but there might have been a little edge of that in there. But Ammon had such discipline. Such discipline. Do you know his rules for life? Ammon's prison rules? You never rat—Loyalty. You take a position and stick to it—Consistency. Because in prison if you change your position, they can jerk you around. Never hit a cop—because if one can't beat you up, two can. And then the other rule is: Never go into the slam with anything that you can't give up. Because if you've got something like an alcohol addiction or a caffeine or a nicotine addiction, they can take it away from you. These are his four prison rules to apply every place in your life.

You know, Ammon was spared. No vices. There wasn't anything that anybody could take away from him. It was probably just petulance over their seemingly deteriorating relationship, but Ammon always felt . . . The flaw he fastened onto in Dorothy was the little jar of instant coffee she always had in her purse. She couldn't get past the caffeine addiction. She'd given up smoking, but he thought that, in terms of doing time, coffee is what they'd eventually get her on.

Ro: Was he a bit holier than thou in all this? Scrupulous, maybe?

Utah: Oh, he'd tell you what he was going to do. He wouldn't tell *you* right or wrong. "This is what *I'm* going to do. Take it or leave it."

Sometimes, yeah, he'd say, "Why don't you do this?" He'd hold himself up as the be-all and end-all. He'd do that surgically, I felt, do it in cases where the provocation was really essential. You know, where you really had to have a bucket of cold water thrown in your face. In *my* face. And then you'd have to step back and look at it and get past the ego. Which is really getting past your own. Because this is a strong man talking to a strong man, okay? Get past the egos and say, "Yeah. That's right."

Ro: Well, it seems to me . . . I just know his writings, of course, but he did have this tremendously forceful personality.

Utah: No foolin'!

Ro: [Laughs.] So that ego would tend to be there, and people would perceive that he wanted to control, even though he may not have, really. Did you have any big fights with him? Any monumental arguments?

Utah: Let me think. No. Ammon was always . . . Ammon understood the condition that I was in, which was one of great fragility. I had another unsuccessful marriage when I got to Salt Lake, and this one created a child. I was politically involved in an unhealthy way . . . I mean going to meetings every night rather than paying attention. He wasn't there to hang me up. He was there to offer me tools to figure it out. It took me a long time, too. (I'm still doing it, you know.) But he was a model of gentleness and kindness and forthrightness. And unbearably honest.

And that shorthand. He talked in this shorthand that would just nail you to the wall. And then you had to choose. The tools for choosing were there at hand. And I . . . I admired him. I loved him a great deal. I realized that what he was doing was something that I'd like to do but probably can't, except in my own limited way. But at least I had that reference.

It's like growing up in the old world, the child of a craftsman. And then being able to go into the world after the craftsman is dead, not just armed with the skills and the tools inherited, but with a sensibility toward how matter is organized. Ammon was a spiritual father whom I loved as a father. And now I have his inheritance. It's for me to decide what I'll create in the world with it.

I remember the night I learned he had died. I was playing up in a little town in Vermont, and a call came in from Ethel Hale. (Supporter of Ammon's, a great woman in Salt Lake.) She told me Ammon had died. That he'd . . . when he was in the hospital dying, he'd told Ethel that if she ever found out where I was to tell me to "stay out of politics." So I have.

CHAPTER 6

The Ideals of One's Youth
Michael Harrington

> What would happen if men remained loyal to the ideals of their youth?
> —*Ignazio Silone,* Bread and Wine

HARRINGTON'S famous phrase of the fifties, "The Catholic Worker was as far left as I could go and still be in the church," continues to inspire young Workers forty years later. Both *The Other America* and his autobiography, *Long Distance Runner,* show how his "politics on the left wing of the possible" were influenced by the two years he spent with Dorothy Day and the Catholic Worker movement. In 1953, he left the Worker and the Roman Catholic Church and began his career as a writer and activist, defining himself as a democratic socialist and working in both traditional and alternative politics. He is most frequently remembered for *The Other America,* which inspired the Democratic administration's War on Poverty.

In 1984, Harrington learned that he had cancer and began the long fight, using all the weapons at his disposal: surgery, chemotherapy, continued work on implementing his ideals. I spent an afternoon with him in July 1988 when he was in remission. He died one year later.

Michael Harrington: I was nineteen when I graduated from Holy Cross, and I wanted to be a poet. My parents thought that wasn't the shrewdest career move they'd ever heard, so my father asked me if I'd go to law school for a year and at least give it a try. At that time I'd just fallen in love with a young woman at Wellesley. It's not a very long hitchhike from Yale to Wellesley, so I said, "Sure!" I got into Yale and, of course, broke up with her that fall.

Yale Law School was the most radical law school in the United States at the time. That's where I became a socialist. It didn't teach law, thank God! It taught courses in legal philosophy, and I enjoyed it enormously. But by my second semester, I'd already decided to quit. The day I knew I was going to quit was the day I got my grades. If you got two letters, one from the law school with your grades and the other from the *Yale Law Journal*, that meant you were in the top ten percent of the class. Well, I got the two letters. And my immediate reaction was, "Good. Now I can leave." See, I didn't want to leave as a failure. I wanted to know that I could do it if I wanted to, could be in the top ten percent at an elite law school. And I proved it to myself.

As a matter of fact, I worked my tail off that first semester. In part because I was an Irish Catholic from Holy Cross, and I wanted to show all of these Wasps from Yale—and from Harvard, Princeton, Amherst, and the like—that, by God, we're as good as they are! And as soon as I got the grades, and it turned out that I had done very, very well indeed, I stopped studying. Cut back to one hour a day and started going over to the library, which has easy chairs and poetry. Began to spend my time reading poetry and novels. Taking it easy. Of course, by this time I had a reputation among the faculty as being one of the bright students, so my grades hardly changed at all. That's the way things go.

Then I went to [the University of] Chicago. Chicago was the most exciting place intellectually that's ever been, before or since. I get lyric about Chicago. Chicago was Camelot and I actually was there. Chicago was just . . . it was un-believable! When I went to Chicago, I figured it'd be a snap. I was really going to bowl them over. I didn't do well at all my first quarter, though. Wound up fine, but it turned out I was competing with people who were every bit as good as [those at] Yale and a lot more sophisticated about literature than I was.

There was a great thing about Chicago: You were there for the enrichment of your spirit and your mind and if this coincided with a good grade, all right. But if ever there was a conflict, you opted for the spirit and against the grade. At Chicago, you had to put in for your grades in order to actually get them. They didn't automatically send them. To show their contempt for the whole grading process, some students never put in for them at all.

I remember once I had this very important final exam coming up. On my way home, I bought a novel by Joseph Conrad. *Victory.* I decided that before I sat down to study for this exam, I'd read a little bit. Well, I stayed up until four o'clock in the morning reading the novel. Never did study for the exam.

Chicago was a place where you could go for a beer and get into a long discussion of Marx versus Augustine. It was intellectually the most passionate place I've ever been. In some ways, the radical movement in New York had aspects of that. The people at the Worker were taking ideas and ideals very, very seriously.

Ro: How did you get to the Worker?

Michael: Well, in the fall of 1949, I decided to come to New York and be a poet. And in a sense (I don't want to exaggerate this point, but in a sense), the idea of modern art was an ideal. It meant turning away from money, turning away from . . . It was not what the son of a lawyer and a schoolteacher was supposed to do. So you could say there was a certain idealism already at work, although it took the form of a commitment to art, rather than a commitment to social change or to religion. But one afternoon when I was on the bus with a young woman, Peggy Brennan, we got into this typical conversation. You know, "What would you do if you had a million dollars?"

I found myself saying, "Well, I'd give it away." The next day I wrote a letter to the American Friends Service Committee, offering to volunteer. Immediately. The AFSC turned me down because I had no money. But then the war—the Korean War—broke out. I became a conscientious objector and went into the Army Medical Corps Reserve on the assumption I would soon be in Korea as a medic. But that didn't happen.

At that point, I was out of the church. I came back, though. Read my way back into the church, through reading books on the Index, a touch I've always loved.* And the minute I did that, I went down to the Catholic Worker.

The one thing I knew was that the Catholic Worker was as far left as you could go and still be in the Catholic Church. You see, I had come back to the church, not on a Jesuit basis but on a Pascalian, or Kierkegaardian, basis. Not with a sense that I could prove the truth of the church, not with a rationalist "it's-all-in-Thomas-Aquinas" Catholicism, but in a rather heterodox and existentialist way. So I lived with a tension, an ambiguity, for the entire two years I was at the Worker.

During that time, though, I used to try to go to Mass daily, and pretty much did. Many of us recited the hours privately, and then we had monastic compline together, so it would be typical for me to be in church, not once, but two or even three times during the course of the day. But in that entire period, I was carrying on a dialogue with myself. I finally came to the conclusion, "No. Much as I still admire this institution, much as I still love this institution, I don't believe in it." That knowledge came to me when I was riding a bus to give a talk at a Communion breakfast down in Pennsylvania.

I thought the decision would be terribly wrenching, that it would be a psychologically horrible moment for me. And instead it was just okay. I still don't quite understand it. I left the Worker when I left the church. It was rather hard to be at

---

* The *Index Liborum Prohibitorum* is a list of books that papal censors considered dangerous to the faith of Roman Catholics.

the Worker and not be a Catholic, so I took off. Remember, this was the Pius XII church. (I don't think I've written this story. I'm not sure. One of my friends thinks I've put down every thought I've ever had.) Anyway, Dorothy called me up, which was unusual. Asked me to go to lunch, which was super-unusual. She'd heard I had left the church, and she wanted to know why.

"Was it a woman?"

And I said, "No, Dorothy. It's theology."

And Dorothy sort of said, "Oh, I'm so happy to hear that."

Dorothy was a real Pius XII Catholic. Quite puritanical. Even though she drove Francis Spellman bananas with her politics, she shared that Spellman sense that the *real* sins were the sins of the flesh. And [my leaving the church] was only intellectual, something you could get over, whereas the sins of the flesh really grew on you.

Ro: Maybe that's because she was quite a passionate person herself.

Michael: I suspect so. Uh . . . one of my problems . . . it's sort of a strange dialectic. Very tortured, I guess. But the immediate issue that caused me to leave the church was the existence of the devil and hell. Particularly the notion that a finite human act, however monstrous, could be the cause of an infinite punishment. And my feeling was that it was all right if Adolf Hitler burned in hell for two, three, four, five thousand years, but there should be an end to it. And so I rejected hell, but was still trying to hold for God and heaven.

Then I said to myself, "But if there is no hell, and everybody's destined for heaven anyway, why was this earth created so miserably?" In a sense, there's a logic in the heaven-hell dichotomy because it says we were put on earth to freely choose which way to go. If I had decided I couldn't tolerate or believe in one of the options, then I had to reject the other one, too.

It was through that crazy dialectic that I came to the conclusion that I no longer believe in God. And I must say, even with the current cancer and having had to look at dying rather squarely in the face, I have not even been tempted to revise that. I don't particularly understand it. [Pause] It's very strange.

I *do* think about it from time to time. My cousin Peggy, who was a nun, came to New York in 1985, shortly before I was going to be operated on for my first cancer. I was very, very close to her, particularly as a small child. (I was an only child, and we were practically brother and sister. So close. I went to kindergarten early so I could go with her.) Anyway, I told her I hadn't changed my mind about God as a result of the possibility of death. "But if I'm wrong, and I wake up and there *is* a God, I will say to Him, 'Why did you mumble so?'"

I told her I wasn't afraid and she just said, "I don't see any reason you should be." I mean I'm really not. If there is a God, I'll find it puzzling, but maybe I can get some of the answers then. Death might be a very alienating experience for some people. It isn't for me. Even now, when it's not an academic question. You know, I believe that when I die, I die. And I hope that when I do, I don't linger around at it for a long time. The pain of it, I'm not . . . I would like to avoid.

My father just dropped dead. I've always thought that's the way to go. Came downstairs in the morning and put some water on the stove to boil. When my mother came down, he was dead, and the water hadn't even boiled off. It was [snap] just like that. It's hell on the survivors to have a person suddenly just disappear from the planet, but . . .

I don't know . . . in a paradoxical way, I regard myself as a religious person. I take it very seriously. I define religion as dealing with ultimate significance—with birth, with sex, with death. It's an attempt, I think, to explain a world which can be pretty cruel, pretty unfair. Unfair to you, unfair to people you love, et cetera.

Ro: Um . . . hmm. Well, if both religion and politics are guides to action, it's hard for me to see how you can be so expansive and willing to accept changes in the political guide and yet in the other guide, the religious guide, you frankly . . .

Michael: Well, there are two things. One: I've often wondered if I had been brought up in the church going into Vatican II, would I have left? I don't know. It certainly would have been different. But I was brought up in that rigid kind of Catholicism. All of my teachers drilled into me that if you messed with any one doctrine in this marvelously symmetric, integrated whole, the whole thing came tumbling down. You could not pick and choose.

Now . . . and I've thought about this since. This is the contrast you're talking about. It's very strange . . . I am not politically dogmatic. For instance, I never became a Marxist. And I never was a dogmatic Catholic Worker. There was a dimension, a scrupulous religious dimension, at the Worker. Dorothy took it very, very seriously. Jansenist. At times it became a denigration of material comfort, period. I remember very well saying to myself, at the time, that I . . . that nice things are nice things. Good food is good food, and good food is better than rotten food. We ate rotten food at the Worker. We bought the cheapest cuts of meat or begged for the meat the butchers were about to throw out. We usually ate stale bread. And I said to myself, "This is not good." If you didn't conform to this line, you know, [they said you] were not radical. The ultimate insult. You were holding back.

There was a standard Catholic Worker statement in my time: "What are you here for?" We were gung-ho. Dorothy was always talking about being fools for Christ. St. Simeon Stylites sitting on the pillar. A heavy dose of existentialism in Dorothy.

We used to talk about two St. Teresas, known around the house as the "big T" and the "little T." Lisieux and Avila. St. John of the Cross was very fashionable. We thought Cardinal Spellman wasn't a very good Catholic, that he was much too lax. And we also felt, you know, that the pope should give away the Vatican and that sort of stuff.

Remember that I was also considered the far right wing of the Catholic Worker. (Tom Sullivan, who voted Democratic, was the right wing.) I never became an absolute pacifist, even when I was there. I always used to maintain, essentially, the traditional Catholic teaching on the just war. That violence is sometimes justified and sometimes not, and one had to examine the case in terms of whether the cause was just, the means proportional to the end, et cetera. As far as I was concerned, up until Hiroshima, World War II was a just war.

I think Dorothy never understood how enormously influential she was. Once at a party, I said to Bill Buckley, "When the history of America and Catholicism in the 1950s is written, Francis Cardinal Spellman will be a footnote and Dorothy Day will be a chapter."

Bill said, "Very funny, Michael, very funny." But it's not far from wrong. When I was at the Worker in the early fifties—which was, in some ways, a low point in terms of influence for Dorothy, when she was least popular with anybody—we appeared at that point as a small band of nuts. Catholic puritans. Totally marginal radicals. And who would have predicted, at that point, that the bishops of the United States would write a pastoral letter on nuclear weapons and quote Dorothy Day? It turns out the Dorothy Day in 1952 was closer to what became the official position of the hierarchy than Spellman. Spellman is nowhere in there, 'cause he was simply a cold warrior.

I'm amazed, as I go around the country, how many Dorothy Day this, that, and the other things there are—Dorothy Day soup kitchens and Dorothy Day shelters. And there are a lot of people who know that I was at the Worker.

The Worker is . . . well, it's hard to say because the Worker was so many different things, so many different strands. Certainly, Dorothy kept a pacifist witness at a time when there was practically nobody else doing it. And that was very important. The anarchist theory isn't worth the powder to blow it to hell. The decentralism is important if you don't take it too literally—the message that there was an enormous danger in socialist and left-wing statism, that the Left had been much too uncritical of bureaucracy, much too impersonalist, much too authoritarian, much too [much in favor of] social engineering. Communitarianism. Decentralization. Personalism . . . I think if you don't get too literal-minded about them, they're profoundly true.

Dorothy's criticism of socialism was in terms of the notion of subsidiarity, the principle that, wherever possible, things should be done on the most decentralized and intra-personal level, should be done by the family, the neighborhood, the community, rather than the state. And I think most socialists now understand that.

Dorothy was basically not political at all. She *called* it anarchism, but what she wanted was for everybody to perform the works of mercy. To transform their lives in a Christian way. Dorothy was for community. She was for charity. She was for the works of mercy. That's what Dorothy cared about. And if everybody did that, you wouldn't need a welfare state. Where she was wrong is, don't hold your breath until everybody starts to lead that kind of a life. In the meantime, people are hungry and, by God, somebody has got to give them food stamps! And thank God they've got food stamps! It's better than nothing.

Even at the Worker, I was a bit of a heretic. Because I was . . . even though I would not go as far as to vote Democratic, I actually believed that political action could change things. I remember Dorothy was very upset when I joined the Socialist Party. Dorothy didn't vote and just couldn't understand why I'd embraced Holy Mother the State. I remember saying at the time—it was true then and it's true now—that I certainly rejected any kind of a centralized, bureaucratic socialism. And that no, I was not embracing Holy Mother the State, but that I *did* believe in political action.

I used to have big arguments with Dorothy where I said that if you really wanted to go back to organic farming to grow the food of the world, you'd better have some plan for the several billion people who are going to starve to death. Because without our current agricultural productivity, we can't begin to feed the world. We would have endless discussions about these things. About why there should be traffic lights, et cetera. That was something about the radical movement in general during that period: There was time to think. The one good consequence of Joe McCarthy was that we didn't have to spend our time organizing demonstrations. There were no left-wing mass movement of any kind— no antiwar movement, no anti-intervention in Central America movement.

Well, there were some exceptions. I remember I helped organize in the campaign for clemency for the Rosenbergs while I was at the Worker. Wrote the articles in the newspaper and did some of the communicating with people in Europe. But we . . . the difference between that period and, let's say, the period of the Vietnam War is enormous. During the Vietnam War, the Worker was a center for people seriously involved in mass mobilization, draft resistance, and all that sort of thing.

When I was at the Worker, the Korean War was on. We were opposed to it and in favor of some form of resistance, but there was no mass movement. We would regularly picket on behalf of the workers in Barcelona. Or go to May Day meetings at the Labor Temple where you would have the more reasonable Trotskyists and various anarchists like the Wobblies. But only a handful of people. The whole non-communist Left in New York City would fit into a pretty small auditorium at that stage of the game.

Ro: What things do you remember, uh . . . remember fondly, about your years at the Worker?

Michael: Well, I've always loved Gregorian chant. We considered the liturgical movement as part of getting back to the real purity of the faith, and there was sort of a split between singing the liturgy in the vernacular and restoring the purity of the Latin.

There was a church in St. Louis, on the North Side, which I loved. With a monsignor by the name of Martin Hellriegel, who had a big liturgical movement. And there, even the grade school kids knew how to chant. I used to go there whenever I could go to St. Louis.

Ro: What would you do when it got too crazy in New York?

Michael: Well, I'd go to the Newburgh farm. One time I went to the Staten Island farm for rest and recreation. Ha! Betty Dellinger, Dave Dellinger's wife, was about to give birth, and, in true Catholic Worker fashion, was going to do so at the Worker farm. I found it so nerve-racking . . . I was very much against that attitude on the part of the Worker. Had big arguments about it. My attitude was you can have a baby at home only if you live in a hospital. I got so nervous that I went back to Chrystie Street to relax.

And then I remember going away to a monastery to decide whether I should tell the Army Medical Corps Reserve to get lost. I didn't talk to anybody, just shut off for three days. Thought and prayed and decided to tell the Army to get lost.

Here's a crazy story. I eventually got my CO status and then had to take a regular army physical because now I had to do alternate service. All of a sudden, I'm told to get dressed and go home. The guy says, "Mister, we're putting you with the guys with no arms and no legs. You're 4-F!"

So I simply walked out. After this long period of thinking I might go to jail. I remember sitting down on a bench outside the Army Induction Center in downtown Manhattan and just laughing. Laughing. The whole thing was so absurd.

See, I have a condition which is endemic to the Missouri River Valley. It's called histoplasmosis. My lungs have all kinds of scar tissue, and it shows up on an X ray as advanced tuberculosis. In fact, [it looks like] I'm about one inch from the grave, but it was diagnosed for me in 1950, so it has obviously not been deadly. Anyway, I wrote the government a letter and told them they'd made a mistake, that [what they saw on the X ray] was not tuberculosis but histoplasmosis. And the government never answered. My theory is that there was a code on my medical form which said "xyz." It meant, "Hey, anybody out there! If there is any way you can flunk this nut . . ." And then when I wrote them a letter telling them why I should pass the physical, they just *knew* I was a clinical case.

One of my happiest periods at the Worker was when I was the night watchman. I forget how long it lasted, maybe six months. I would make a tour of the house every hour and press one of those security things to show that I'd been to a check station. It would take all of five minutes. I'd listen to good music and write poetry and read books. All night long.

I published five poems in *Poetry Chicago* when I was at the Worker, the only time I ever got published as a poet. But I kept on writing poetry for maybe three years after I left the Worker. Took it very seriously. Then two things happened. One, I got more and more involved with the socialist movement. Two, I came to the cold-blooded conclusion that I might have some *talent* for writing poetry but I certainly had no genius. The world did not need another simply talented poet.

I wrote a very 1940s, 1950s kind of controlled poetry. Would work sometimes for two weeks on a ten-line poem, spend two or three hours and maybe change one word. In terms of my later writing, I'm convinced that this concern with finding precisely the right word, that this tremendous discipline, built up a certain facility with words, a certain sensitivity. Whatever value my writing has as prose, I think, owes something to the discipline of trying to be a poet.

Ro: I can hear in your prose that you learned to sense rhythm, too. And another thing I like in your work is that there's this marriage of the personal and political. You're not afraid to let your voice show through, not afraid to carry on conversations with yourself in the writing. I didn't sense that in *Politics at God's Funeral,* though. Did you set out to write that as a straight academic . . .

Michael: See, there's always been a war in me. I view a lot of my work as translation, as making complex ideas more accessible to people. But I don't want simply to be a translator. I absolutely love scholarship—scholarship for the sake of scholarship, frankly. One side of me would like to write a book so obscure that nobody would ever read it who isn't as passionately concerned as I am with these issues.

Ro: But that's elitist, and that's something that you haven't been, it seems to me.

Michael: No, but I don't want to be only a translator, either. When I wrote my book, *Socialism,* which came out in 1972, my wife was really my salvation, because I probably discarded a third of it. My problem would be that I would do all this research, and be able to tell you what Karl Marx had for breakfast on March eighteenth in 1874 or something like that. And I'd say, "Well, as Marx was eating his blah blah . . ." It slows down the pace, and you want to make it move.

Ro: Umm . . . hmmm. What are you reading now?

Michael: In the morning the first thing I read, normally, is the American philosopher [Charles S.] Peirce. Nineteenth-century Harvard. More and more thought of as one of the earliest pragmatists, friend of William James, et cetera. So I'm reading him. Then I'm reading a book of philosophic discourses on modernism by Habermas, which I've got with me today. I read on the trains. I'm rereading *The Red and the Black* by Stendhal. Then I'm reading stuff for the book I'm working on.

Ro: Okay! Do you do any beach reading?

Michael: Oh, sure. I love spy novels like John le Carré. He's not really beach reading, though, because he's a fairly serious writer. I love le Carré novels and I reread them. They're political—fictionalized politics. In the hospital last time, I read *Bonfire of the Vanities.* When I go to the chemo, the first two days aren't bad but the last two days are. You see, there's no such thing as chemotherapy; instead there are dozens of chemotherapies, and the particular stuff that bothers me is platinum, which I get on the third day. That's why the third and the fourth day are like a . . . a monstrous hangover. I'm just listless. I can't read. I can't write. Can't even watch television very much. I just lie there and want time to pass.

And, you know, I've realized I'm now an IV drug user. I mean, I get two IVs each time I go in, so I've had fourteen by now. You want them to get the IV in on the first crack. At Einstein, the interns still do them. Some are good at it and some are not. One guy . . . it took him about three passes and that ain't fun.

Ro: Oh. It's . . . it's always a bad time when they're putting John's in.* [Pause] Let's get back to the Worker. What else do you remember about the house?

* My brother-in-law, Fr. John W. Troester, was undergoing chemotherapy for leukemia at the time of this interview. John died the next month, Michael one year later.

"The Lord's Supper," woodcut by Fritz Eichenberg.

Michael: Well, have you seen the Fritz Eichenberg thing of me? [Points to Eichenberg's "The Lord's Supper." This print hangs on the wall of almost every Catholic Worker house.] Eileen [Egan] said [the young man standing in the doorway] was me, and then I looked at it, and it certainly is. With the long nose and the magazine in my pocket. I was there.

Ro: Hm . . . hmmm. [Pause] Michael, were you coming in or going out?

✦

Michael: I developed a theory that the more radical a communitarian somebody was, the less able to live in community he was. The people nobody liked were the ones who always wanted to go whole-hog and share toothbrushes and all that kind of stuff. They had the most idealized visions of community. They'd imagine a perfect society in which everybody loved everybody, including them.

The Worker was not an unhappy place. There were tensions, though, and I think there were tensions about me. I started playing a fairly significant role very quickly. One of the reasons was that I got along very much with Dorothy. Another reason was that I spoke well. Tom [Sullivan] ran the house. Bob [Ludlow] ran the paper. I did all kinds of odd jobs, including a lot of writing for the paper. As time went on, I did a lot of speaking. Dorothy was wonderful. She'd get invitations, invitations sent to Dorothy Day, but she'd treat them as if they were invitations to the movement. And she would answer: "Thank you for the invitation. Michael Harrington will come." To someone who had never heard of Michael Harrington. I'm not sure how happy they were. Here they'd been trying to get this famous Catholic woman and instead they get a twenty-three-year-old you-know-who.

I remember one time I was speaking for the Worker at a Protestant church, and the local bishop got furious that a Catholic was speaking at a heretical church. Complained to Spellman or something like that. It was the good old days.

We had some really wonderful characters. There was a very nice guy, Hector Black. The last I heard he was living in a slum in Atlanta. He was a vegetarian. Wouldn't wear leather shoes or leather belts. Tried as far as possible to be totally consistent with an ethic of respect for all forms of life.

Ro: Were there many women in the house?

Michael: Yes, there were some. Remember, this was the Pius XII church. The attitude was that women should keep their heads covered and their mouths shut. We made a big thing out of that at the Worker. And a lot of sort of left-wing Catholics always insisted that if you addressed a man and wife, you always put the man's name first, because he was the Christ figure. He was the head of the house and she was the helpmate. There was a very explicit male chauvinism.

Now that was strange because we were living in a community where whenever we made a decision, we all had a completely democratic, anarchist discussion, and then Dorothy made up her mind. The place was run on a führer concept, and Dorothy was the führer. So you had a house totally dominated by a woman, but it was male chauvinist in its ideology.

Ro: What were the guests like, compared to today?

Michael: Oh, very different. Very different. I would say the Bowery was about ninety-five percent white. The Catholic Worker house was about that way, too. An occasional black. Most of the people in the house were Irish, Italian, or Polish. On the Bowery, you would never meet a Jew. I think this has now changed, but at that point alcoholism was simply not a problem with the Jews. In terms of social class, I roomed with a guy who had been an Associated Press writer, another guy who'd been a dentist. (There were two beds in my room, so I got whoever was the next person through the door.)

Most of the people in the house felt we were crazy because we didn't have to be there. "What in the hell are you doing in a miserable, no-good, rotten place like this?" And also, "What are you doing bothering with somebody like me?"

I remember John Derry . . . I'm sure he's long since dead. An old fashioned working-class Irish type. He and his wife lived there. I think they were the only couple. They were both alcoholics, and I remember telling him that alcoholism was a disease and not a sin. I had been reading a Belgian priest who wrote on Freud, wrote very ingeniously about the difference between an evil which is to be borne and an evil which you commit. I was explaining to John that alcoholism is an evil to be borne. And he said, "You're wrong, Michael. I'm a sinner and I'm going to go to hell for it."

We went out of our way not to proselytize anybody in the house, but the result was, although we claimed that we had personal relations with people, it was still a two-class society. There were those people who were there because they had to be, people whose lives had been overwhelmed by their problems. And there were those of us who were there out of some religious . . .

There was Smokey Joe, a Polish fellow, who'd periodically go off on a toot and usually break into somebody's house. But he was very nonviolent, and so the people would find this drunken guy sitting in front of their television set and call the cops and they'd bring him back. It was all first-name and that sort of stuff.

Ro: Did you go down to the Worker much after you left?

Michael: I've always . . . uh, very carefully gone back to give talks, including when Dorothy was alive and since Dorothy died.

Ro: A cordial relationship?

Michael: Oh, yes . . . yes, yes. When Dorothy was still alive, we'd go downstairs to the kitchen [in Maryhouse] and have coffee. Towards the end of her life, Dorothy would send word that she wanted to come down, but was just feeling too rotten.

At her funeral . . . it was the damnedest funeral I've ever seen. I went to the wake the night before, which was at the Worker, of course. She was in a wooden box, which I'm sure violated absolutely all the rules of New York. But nobody was going to tell the Worker not to do it.

I saw lots of people from my "class." (People were sort of grouped by when they were at the Worker.) It was announced that the funeral the next morning would be private, that only family could go to the funeral. A bunch of us were standing around, and we all said, "No way!" So the next morning about . . . oh, I would say about three hundred people showed up. And they didn't know what to do, so they finally said, "Well, we'll ask you to decide for yourself. Only those people who consider themselves part of the family should fall in behind the coffin." Whereupon, of course, everybody fell in.

I also loved the funeral 'cause the recessional was "A Mighty Fortress Is Our God." I thought, "Leave it to the Catholic Worker! Here is this woman who's going to be a Catholic saint, and the recessional is a hymn by Martin Luther!"

Ro: So you think she's going to be a saint?

Michael: Oh, sure! As a matter of fact, I'm sort of terrified that this pope—who is not my favorite pope, I must say—that he might figure out that she's a perfect saint from his point of view. Because she's a political and social radical and a totally conservative, orthodox, and obedient daughter of the church. It crossed my mind when I got my second cancer, and I thought it would wreck my ideological life, but if Dorothy wanted to cure my cancer . . . [Here the tape was turned off.]

Ro: One last question. *Bread and Wine* by Silone was one of Dorothy's favorite books. One of the great lines is: "What would happen if men remained loyal to the ideals of their youth?" Do you think you have, Mike?

Michael: Sure. When I was nine, I decided I wanted to be a writer. Well, I'm a writer. What I've become is not what . . . it's very different, yet did that impulse persist? Of course. When I was four and a half years old, in St. Rose's kindergarten, I used to not eat lunch so I could give my lunch money to save a baby for Jesus in China. And I'm totally convinced that what I'm doing to this very minute is out of that same impulse. If you had said to me then that it would be as a socialist and an atheist, I wouldn't have understood what you were talking about. And a little later I would have said that was absurd. But yes. I mean I . . . one of the things that I'm struck by are the continuities. They're extraordinary. It's almost as if my life has been a well-plotted story. Almost.

Singing Old Songs

Jim Eder: At Tivoli when we had these intimate community things, Stanley Vishnewski would sometimes sing old Catholic Worker songs. One was called "The First Street Blues."* (We make it "The Kenmore Street Blues" when we sing it around Chicago.) It's part of an operetta that was put on in the 1940s by folks who lived in New York. [Singing]

> *We stayed at First Street for a while, for a while.*
> *We did not know the Worker style, the Worker style.*
> *And now the beasties all abide on me.*
> *I would a bourgeois life were mine.*

> *While all our friends are having dates, having dates.*
> *We're discussing hourly rates, hourly rates.*
> *And though an intellectual life is fine,*
> *I would a bourgeois life were mine.*

> *Now this is strictly entre nous, entre nous.*
> *We only tell the two of you, two of you.*
> *And though the Workers say they're pacifist,*
> *They really all are communist.*

> *But after all that's said and done, said and done.*
> *It really was a lot of fun, lot of fun.*
> *And though we suffered like the damned in hell,*
> *We kind of miss that First Street smell.*

Stanley taught it to me, and I kind of spread it through the Midwest. You still hear it now and then. We did it at a [Sugar Creek] meeting a couple of years ago, and there was a young lady there from Green Bay, Wisconsin. She said, "Oh Jim,

---

* Unfortunately, I've been unable to identify either the composer of the song or her daughter.

that's just the greatest song. My mom was around the Catholic Worker [when she was younger], and I want to sing it for her. Can you write down the words?" So I did, and she went back to Green Bay and started singing this song to her mom.

She got a few bars out, and her mother said, "Where did you hear that? Where did you hear that?" She said, "I wrote that song."

PART TWO

The Work

CHAPTER 7

Coming and Becoming

Stories of Conversion

> Somebody asked me once if I felt I had a calling to the Worker, and I
> said, "It always sounds like you're hearing voices."
> — *Kassie Temple*

OFTEN my first interview question was, "How did you come to the Catholic Worker?" Here are some of the answers I heard.

Many folks come to the New York house from all over the country. Some stay, some leave, some start Catholic Worker communities near their birthplaces. Richard Cleaver, Gary Donatelli, and Brian Terrell were called "the altar boys" by their fellow Workers. They're still close friends but living different lifestyles. Richard is Secretary for Peace Education at the American Friends Service Committee in Ann Arbor, Michigan; Gary works at Bailey House, the first city-funded AIDS hospice for the homeless in New York City; Brian, his wife, Betsy Keenan, and their two children, Clara and Elijah, are part of the permanent Worker community at Strangers and Guests in far-off Maloy, Iowa.

Richard Cleaver: The last place in the world I wanted to go was New York. Because I knew, like every Iowa boy knows, that people die in New York within six weeks of arrival. It's just a dangerous place. Full of crazy people. But Ann Marie Fraser said, "You know, it looks to me like you'd really fit in well at the Catholic Worker. And here I wasn't even Catholic!*

"Why don't you try it out? It's a very informal place." (Little did I know how informal!) So against all of my better judgment, I said, "I'll go and show them I don't belong there." I arrived and within forty-eight hours, I realized that she

---

* Richard had begun the application process for the Episcopal priesthood. Ann Marie Fraser, editor of the *Catholic Worker* at the time, worked in the national office of the Episcopal Church, which coordinated the volunteer service requirement for priest candidates.

had been absolutely right. It was the *perfect* place for me. I had never felt quite so much at home before.

And do you want to hear another little different twist? Most folks who come here were brought up good, pious Catholics with their parents saying, "We understand your doing good works, but why do you have to get politics involved?" Well, I'd been brought up with all of these politics and very little formal religion. So my parents' attitude was sort of like, "Well, we understand why you're doing all this political stuff, but why do you have to mix it up with religion?"

Gary Donatelli: When I first came to the New York house, I was thrilled. It was like everything I wanted and then some. Squalor! Dirt! Poverty! Bedbugs! The works! There wasn't a clean sheet in the house. I got a heavy dose immediately. Stayed a good ten years. Lived in the house maybe about five years and then lived in the neighborhood another six, but was still directly involved in the house. You know, taking the house, the soup line, that sort of business.

Ro: Did you go after college?

Gary: I went to school in Detroit. To a small place called Duns Scotus College.

Ro: It's a Franciscan seminary.

Gary: Yeah. We got the *Catholic Worker* there. It sure sounded a whole lot better than what was going on with the Franciscans. A little more exciting, a little more honest about what it was doing. I [left Duns Scotus] and went to a little more school, at the University of Akron. That seemed even more pointless than the seminary. It was just a matter of time, of working up enough courage to tell my dad I was going to throw in the towel on college education. I used to say I got my degree at the urban branch of Peter Maurin's agronomic university.

Brian Terrell: I'm a native of Green Bay, Wisconsin. Came to the Catholic Worker in the fall of '75. I'd been a college student at St. Norbert's in De Pere, Wisconsin for a year and had just a very, very vague idea what the Catholic Worker movement might be.

I had been looking at several religious orders. They'd send me these glossy full-color brochures and information on how to begin a ten to fifteen-year process towards becoming a member of their institution. I had the feeling the religious orders were looking for the same kind of persons they already had. And those were the same kind of people the corporate world was looking for.

I thought the Worker might be different. Also, I'd never heard anyone say they were a Christian pacifist, but I was having ideas like that and the little bit that I knew about the Worker, I could . . . I felt like words were being put to things that I had inside. So I wrote to them and they answered with a few lines on the back of a card saying, "If you're interested in coming, just come on out." It was that simple.

Ro: What was it like walking into the New York house?

Brian: Well, after about twenty-four hours on a Greyhound bus and then coming into New York for the first time, I was pretty dazed. But I was really amazed at how welcoming everyone was. Some people say the New York Worker is very cold and everyone is rude. I've known people who've walked in the door intending to stay for a while and have decided they couldn't do it because of how . . . Later on, I was able to understand why.

There were times when people would come, and I would feel just terrible because I'd be so exhausted that I couldn't even *pretend* to be interested in them. Sometimes at the Worker, in New York especially, young people come to visit— college students or seminarians—with lots of idealism and lots of questions. A few of those are fine and can be a real joy, but sometimes you get them in bus-loads—twenty-five and thirty—over and over again, and you just get . . . you get tired of touring them around. I know sometimes I'd be painfully aware of how inhospitable I was if I'd just had to deal with too many people that day, too many needs. Fortunately, at the moment I arrived, people were able to give me a nice welcome. I do remember how depressing my first bowl of soup was, though.

A real healthy thing for me when I first came is that I suddenly had friends who were not my age—friends who were thirty and forty and seventy and eighty years old. That was a very nice thing for a nineteen-year-old kid.

Marc Ellis came to the New York Worker right after graduating from college. His chronicle of that experience, *A Year at the Catholic Worker,* was published in 1978 by Paulist Press. He now teaches theology at Mary-knoll Seminary in Ossining, New York, and calls for a Jewish theology of liberation.

Marc Ellis: I received a scholarship to Vanderbilt for my graduate school, but after reading [William] Miller's book, I decided to go to the Catholic Worker instead. I wanted to try to understand what it was like to live a committed life.

Being at the Catholic Worker was a very difficult experience for me. It was the first time in a Catholic atmosphere. I remember being afraid. It seemed uh . . . very quiet. I seemed to be very loud, although I was at that time, and still am, quite shy. But I wanted to know personally if the future of the Christian community was going to be different, or *could* be different, than the past. In relation to the Jewish community, too.

Ro: When I read your book, it sounded like you were lonely a lot of the time.

Marc: Yes. I was middle class. I had [hardly ever] seen suffering, except when we'd visit my grandparents in New York. I used to see . . . we referred to them as "beggars" on the street. Mostly World War II veterans. People on skateboards without legs. I had never met somebody who was really poor. We had a maid come in once a week. She was not well-to-do, obviously. We used to give her things, but they had food. And culture. I had never seen people without culture. Never seen destitute people. So that was one level of it. The second level of it was living there. I had never lived where people mumbled in their sleep . . . you know, all this stuff. The third level was I was a young Jewish boy in a Catholic environment, and it was the first cross-cultural experience I ever had. Yes, that time for me was very lonely. It was also one of the most—or maybe *the* most—important in my life.

Tom Cornell was editor of the *Catholic Worker* from 1962 to 1964.

Tom Cornell: I was born and brought up in Bridgeport [Connecticut]. Working-class town. Ethnic. Administered by the Socialist Party from 1932 to about 1954 or so. I was able to vote straight Socialist and win.

Ro: Was this your parents' orientation, too?

Tom: No. They were Democrats. I went to Fairfield Prep, and then Fairfield University. Eight years with the Jesuits. I was captured by the Worker from the start.

Ro: Hmmm. Was it a romantic or a rational capture?

Tom: Well, I suppose there was some emotional, maybe romantic, element to it. But I think more than that, I recognized upon reading *The Long Loneliness* that there was an authenticity that I did not find elsewhere, and that my faith was really endangered because of that lack.

The effects of original sin are universal. We all fail in some ways, and I am very, very grateful to the Jesuits for a lot of things. I just wonder, though, if I hadn't found the Worker at age nineteen, where would I have been at twenty-four? I sensed sometimes that the teachers of philosophy didn't understand what they were teaching, really didn't *understand.* In my youthful arrogance, I assumed . . . I believed that I understood better than they did. Even now, I think I may have been right.

I found an intellectual integrity at the Worker and a spiritual integrity and an evangelical integrity that I did not find anywhere else. This is what the church ought to be. Of course, I came upon the Worker during a golden age. Nineteen fifty-three. The McCarthy period. Deeply reactionary, but with a lot of unem-ployment. People like Mike Harrington, Eddie Egan, Marty Corbin. Bob Ludlow should be in that list. Norman Stein, Al Gullion—all males here. The women weren't . . . they were more doers. The guys were thinkers. They thought beau-tifully, and they spoke beautifully, and they wrote beautifully. The women *did* the things. That's all right. We have to remember what kind of age it was.

Kathleen Jordan, her husband, Pat, and their children lived in the Catho-lic Worker beach house at Spanish Camp on Staten Island when I inter-viewed them.

Kathleen Jordan: I remember reading in the autobiographies of C. S. Lewis and Eric Gill that they liked everything about the church except Christ. When I first went to the Catholic Worker, I liked everything about it except I didn't want to meet Dorothy Day. Because I had such antipathy toward the Roman Catholic Church, and I knew that to her it was "Mother Church." I just couldn't manage that at the time. I was . . . not so much estranged from faith but from the church as an institution.

Ro: Was it because of feminism?

Kathleen: Women's issues came a little bit later. It was much more the impa-tience of youth about hypocrisy. I was just thirsty, I think, for . . . for a movement like the Catholic Worker where people really were trying to integrate faith and action. It was just a great blessing to me, you know. But of course it doesn't take long until you see the foibles. It's a way, not an answer. It's a way. But I did feel much more of a clarity in terms of at least trying to live a Christian life, I guess.

Pat Jordan: Many of the people who came to the Worker were the highest ideal-ists, and when they found out that the Worker wasn't the kingdom of God, the resentments they had felt in other places turned on the Worker as well. Some people came with no religious orientation at all. Some people—and I'm sure this is still the case—don't have the foggiest idea what it's all about. They may be attracted to the social action. They may be attracted to the personalism. Or to the anarchism. There are all of these various things. As Dorothy often said to us, there are very few people who understand the whole picture. And we were fortunate, of course, to be there when she was. Over time you got more and more and more of a sense of what that whole picture was. We would be scratch-ing our heads: "Well, what does this mean? How does this fit in?" And she'd say, "Well, you know, I didn't understand Peter's whole thing for many years." That was always a big help to us.

She was a very good teacher. Of course, it wasn't like you had classes. But you'd sit for hours, you know, opening the mail and talking. She was just this wonderful conversationalist, so in that sense, she was a master teacher. We were searching and she would counsel us. Sometimes people would come and spend several weeks in the summer, and you had a sense that they understood the Catholic Worker better than people who'd been living there for years. In the way that they responded to people, the responsibility that they took.

Dorothy always called it a school. And she always stressed everybody's individual vocation. She would say to us, "You will know your vocation by the happiness that it brings you." No, "by the *joy* that it brings you." Happiness wasn't the word—joy was. She'd always talk about C. S. Lewis and *Surprised by Joy.* (It wasn't "Surprised by Happiness.") "You will know. You will know when it's right." And she often would say that the gold moves on and the dross remains.

Ro: I thought that was Stanley [Vishnewski's] line.

Pat: No, she would say that. She would say it about herself, say that she was the dross.

Kathleen: It was always rather sobering. Particularly when you were one of the ones still there.

Teka Childress is a member of the St. Louis Catholic Worker Community.

Teka Childress: My full name is Mary Kathleen Tekawitha, but I've been called Teka since I can remember. Tekawitha was a Mohawk who became a Christian very early on. My mother admired her.

Ro: One of the things I'm curious about is what in your childhood gave you this orientation. Why didn't you just move to the suburbs and shop in the malls?

Teka: Oh, my goodness, that's hard! I have no idea. Well, part of it is my parents loved me very much, and they had a great deal of faith. I think that was a priority, therefore, in my life . . . my relationship with God and my love of people. My parents were very active as well in the civil rights movement and both of them worked for ERA. They were active in their parish and both working for justice and also on social issues. I remember driving through this neighborhood when I was a kid and we . . . I always had a lot of exposure. Through my parents, I had some exposure to people who weren't well off and some exposure to people from different backgrounds. I think being loved by my parents is a . . . you know, it helps you want to reach out and love others, and then also just my experience with them being active in social justice issues.

I just fell into Karen House, though. I didn't know anything about the Catholic Worker, or not very much. My friend Virginia Druhe was one of the people who started the house. I told her, "Well, if you ever need any help, just call me." This was when they first opened. It was one of the first shelters for women in St. Louis, and the demand was just so great. They used to take sixty-five or seventy women and children. Really jammed packed. At one point, there were eighteen two-year-olds, I think. Just incredible! A real madhouse with crises all over.

Well, one day they called me and asked me to take house. I guess I was twenty at the time. Absolutely no idea what I was doing. One of the guests was a very responsible woman, though, and she really took house, and I helped her. That would be a more accurate description of what happened.

Amazingly enough, I loved it! I don't know why, but I did. It was very challenging. It was an extremely busy day, a long day, and I was hopping about all the time. But I came back, got to know the women, and basically, once I knew these people, I didn't want to live my life without them. I love living with the people here and love just the . . . the involvement of my life with theirs.

But I love it also because of the tradition of working for peace and justice in the Catholic Worker. That's always been my other interest. I still continue to work as an organizer a great deal. For instance, I'm very active right now opposing U.S. intervention in Central America. I do that and I live here.

Ro: Will you be going to Central America?

Teka: No, I'll probably stay here. See, I so much identify with the pettiness and selfishness and . . . and the being stuck that people experience in this society. You know, all the worrying about things that aren't important and being wrapped up in whether they have what they think they need. I'm not big on getting a lot of clothes and that sort of thing, but I have my petty little things that I worry about, like when I'm going to have a soda or something. There's so much I identify with in this culture that I think I'm a good person to invite conversion—of myself and other people.

So if I had chosen . . . I couldn't have found a better life. I'm not here on the way to somewhere. I . . . I just can't think of any place in the world I would rather be. This is really my home, a home I had never expected to find. At different times, guests have said, "I'm so glad you've let us come here." And I realize *I'm* so glad that someone let me come here, too. I never expected it. I wasn't necessarily looking for it. It's all grace.

Don Timmerman comes from a large, dirt-poor farm family and was ordained a Salvatorian priest in Tanzania. Interested in lay catechetical work and base communities, he found himself unable to work within the church there and returned to the United States, finally finding his way to Casa Maria in Milwaukee in 1973. He's still there.

Don Timmerman: One day I was on my way to Dubuque. And this rain started to come down like you wouldn't believe! Just sheets of rain! I said, "This is ridiculous! I'm never going to get to Dubuque. But I've got the whole day off. I know! I'll go to that place I've heard about—to Casa Maria." And now I see that this was God sending me the next thing I had to do.

So I came here to Casa, rang the doorbell several times. It wasn't working. Finally, I just walked in the door, walked over toys and kids. The house was just chaos! I asked one of the people who the manager was, or who ran the place, and she said she didn't know.

I said to myself, "Oh, my gosh!"

Somebody else came in and said, "I know! You're probably looking for Gene." After a long time, Gene Byrnes finally came down the steps, real slow, looking all dragged out. Burned out, exhausted. And he brought me up here where we are now [in the staff quarters on the third floor], set me down, and we just talked. Talked about the Catholic Worker movement. Talked about everything.

We must have talked three hours. By the end of the three hours, I had decided that this was what I wanted to do. With all my experience with poverty in Africa, I never realized there was poverty in the United States. Here I'd been a seminarian in the United States and hadn't realized there were poor people here. That's hard to believe, but it's true.

I just loved it at Casa. And after a while, I could quit teaching 'cause we got more people to move into the house. One of the people was Mike Trokan. I used to help him picket with the United Farm Workers. He came by for a visit and fell in love with one of the women who was working here. I remember he said, "I'd really like to join your community, but I don't know if I'm able to give up everything."

And I said, "Mike, you're not giving up a heck of a lot. You're probably just as poor as we are."

Robert Ellsberg was the youngest person to edit the *Catholic Worker.* He now is editor-in-chief at Maryknoll's Orbis Books, where he has been responsible for bringing the works of many of the liberation theologians to the United States.

Robert Ellsberg: I went to the Worker with a lot of idealism and a . . . a kind of yearning for moral purity. And out of a sense of too much compromise in my life, too much tendency to intellectualize. I think it's probably my habitual sin—to sit on the sidelines and take everything in and analyze and that sort of thing.

I'd grown up with a family very affected by the whole culture, the antiwar movement, and I was a very committed pacifist, a student of Gandhi. Raised as an Episcopalian, but I felt more that my community was the peace movement, and was fairly distant, uh . . . disillusioned with my church background.

I guess I still thought of myself as Christian, but in some way the church was not good enough for me. I felt called to make a supreme sacrifice, and I didn't feel the church challenged me to do that, so I'd not had very much to do with it, really. I went to the Catholic Worker because it seemed to me a Christianity on the front lines. The barricades. The Gospel in action.

I'd also had a basically middle-class upbringing—a stereotype, maybe, of the [typical] Catholic Worker as a middle-class kid working off his guilt or something. (My experience, actually, was that more people came from a Catholic working-class background when I was there.) And I was . . . felt I came from a more privileged background. And had, you know, this need to get my hands dirty.

A very important experience for me was just interacting with people very different from myself. We always believed that nonviolence is not all just going to jail and marching on picket lines and things, but just being able to sit down comfortably and converse with somebody who'd be completely invisible or even repulsive if they were sitting on the sidewalk on Fifth Avenue or something. And being able to have a relationship with that person. I tend to be introverted and not very outgoing, and that was the single most difficult thing for me—to get over that kind of shyness and discomfort. (Maybe I've slipped back into it.) People down in the Bowery were maybe hypersensitive to phoniness and do-gooderism if they felt you were using them to get over your own guilt or to be a saint or whatever. [They] could see through the phoniness and cut you down to size, and you get a lot of that crap knocked out of you.

I don't feel, uh . . . the same kind of call to complete consistency and purity as I did back then. Call it compromise or getting older or whatever, I don't know. But I recognize some parts of myself still in the nineteen-year-old who went there sixteen years ago. [I have] an affection for that person and a certain respect for that person, but I can also see that I wasn't nearly as pure then as I thought I was.

Ro: You were also nineteen.

Robert: I was also nineteen. But I was, you know, at least in the short term, fairly successful at the Worker. Mastered the language there and went pretty soon into a leadership role. Ended up the year [being] editor of the newspaper when I was twenty.

Ro: You're Dan Ellsberg's son?

Robert: Yes.

Ro: Was that . . . how would you say that made a difference? Or *did* it make a difference?

Robert: I think it had a lot to do with the motivation that brought me to the Worker.

Ro: You weren't leaving your parents to go to the Worker, in other words?

Robert: No, not really. But I think that I was . . . with the experience of his trial and everything, I developed from my father this urge to test myself. To see if I could give everything, sort of go to the limit. And I found other ways at the Catholic Worker . . . ways that were probably easier for me than they would've been for somebody else, when I think about it—courting arrest, going to jail, fasting in jail, non-cooperating, whatever it was. That sort of thing, which appeared very heroic to some people, was really much easier for me than it would have been to stick with the personal, uncongenial, difficult work of caring for people in the house. It was very difficult for me to sleep in a dormitory and have to . . . uh . . . get lice or wash up vomit or something like that. I'm not a . . . I have more of a fastidious streak in me.

But you know, there are different gifts, and people kind of . . . everybody found their own place in the Worker. There was that kind of freedom. Nobody handed out assignments or jobs, and that could be difficult. You arrive there and no one tells you what to do. I surely thought there'd be a kind of indoctrination or training program or something like that. A novice master or something to take you under her wing and tell you what to do. And there wasn't. You really just . . . you learned. Maybe by imitation to a certain extent, but who do you imitate exactly?

The only hierarchy at the Catholic Worker when I was there was determined by who had keys to the house and who didn't. It was sort of, "You've been here long enough. Why don't you start pulling your weight and take responsibility?"

There'd be somebody there sort of in charge of the house during the day and at night. We'd sign up on a roster at the beginning of the week and [take] assignments, so there'd be somebody to answer the phone, answer the door. [During] each of those [times], day or night, there were certain kinds of routines and responsibilities. At night you had to wash the floor, turn out the lights, wait for the bread to arrive for the next morning. In the morning there were different . . . there'd be somebody in charge of the soup line, and somebody would take over after that, and there was a kind of rhythm and routine of the day. I lived in the house for a year and was really just schooled by following the rhythm and routine of daily life.

[After a while,] I got a job as an orderly at a home for terminal cancer patients, at St. Rose's. That was congenial to me, working nights. And it was a gentle kind of hands-on work with people and the surroundings. I was the only person working on the floor, all night long. That was the most truly contemplative period of my life. I spent a lot of time [exploring the] contradictions in my life.

Ro: A retreat time?

Robert: It was in a way. I began reading all these French Catholic novels. And I came out of that period a Catholic. The major thing for me was that I went to the Catholic Worker, like I described before, with a kind of smugness about the Christian churches. The Catholic Worker was my church. And I kind of felt grateful [to be there] and a superiority . . . a . . . uh, smugness toward the rest of the institutional church and [all its] compromises. Of course, everyone talked about all our voluntary poverty and all that sort of thing. Well, I didn't have any financial needs or responsibilities while I was there. They were taken care of.

Ro: Comfortable.

Robert: Yeah. There's a very great danger of self-righteousness. Anyway, before I was received into the Catholic Church, I went up to Dorothy to tell her of my decision. I felt, in a way, this embarrassment about saying I was going to become a Catholic. It sounded so dramatic. Like I was going to become a monk or leave the world or something. Was this some dramatic gesture to call attention to myself? I was so sensitive about triumphalism that I almost didn't tell her at all.

We were chatting as usual. I said, "There's something I wanted to talk to you about."

"Yes?"

And I said something like, "Well, I've been thinking about . . . well, thinking about is not the right word, I've been . . ." I started stumbling along like this for . . . and she just sat there perplexed.

She finally said, "What is it?"

"I'm thinking of becoming a Catholic."

She was very quiet. I thought she didn't hear me or that she was going to say, "Well, why would you do that?" Instead, she finally asked, "Well, you're an Episcopalian, right?"

I said, "Yes."

"I always thought the Episcopalians were a little well-to-do."

Of course, she was pleased. She didn't act as if another sinner has been saved or something. There was something . . . you know, it seemed like an obvious thing to do, and I felt very great relief from that. I was glad she didn't make a big deal out of it. I went to see her again after the deed was done. She gave me a big hug and was just very . . . just very warm. I learned later that it probably meant more to her than she let on.

Dorothy had this feeling that the Worker was a kind of a school, that people would graduate and move on to all kinds of things. It wasn't that the whole world should be at the Catholic Worker, but that it was very important for people to have that experience, that formation or whatever, that they would take into other things. And it was . . . one thing I always liked about Dorothy [was that] she totally admired a Studs Terkel or a Dwight Macdonald or a Robert Coles . . . intellectuals or professionals, and her [favorite] writers, too, who managed to bring human values to their work. People who were faithful in some way. And they were not all Christian. She loved the respect for human beings that they brought to their writing. Which for her was compassion and a kind of . . . a loyalty to the human scale of things.

You didn't have to tip your hat to the Trinity. [It was] just a distinctive kind of sacramentality, a sense of the holiness of the everyday, a sense for community that's inclusive of the saints as well as all the rest of us. She would very much agree that not everybody live in a soup kitchen or a house of hospitality. We need editors, we need journalists, we need teachers. These are all potentially religious vocations, all opportunities to live the beatitudes, to be peacemakers. Ultimately, those were the kinds of things that brought me to the church, I guess.

I no longer felt I had to find a church that was worthy of me and of my exulted appreciation and interpretation of the Gospel. But that . . . I guess it was a conversion in the *real* sense, not in the sense of going from one church to another, but a kind of . . . um . . . just humility and experience of my own brokenness and need and sin and desire for forgiveness.

I interviewed Lynn Klein at the Denver Catholic Worker gathering in 1990. She and her fiancé, Bob Lassalle, had been traveling the country, talking to Catholic Worker couples about marriage and family. Here she talks about her faith journey.

Lynn Lassalle-Klein: My story is real different from Bob's. [Bob had come to the Catholic Worker after being in Jesuit seminary and working with Ailanthus Peace Community in Boston.] I never was a part . . . I never had anyone or any group with me on my journey. You know, I was always kind of flailing around. Had gone to the Dominican Republic in the early eighties when I was twenty-three. It was the first time I'd been in a third world country and really had any . . . developed any sort of friendships with someone who was "oppressed." And that really marked me.

But then I started taking this weird turn into computers. I got very involved . . . this was the work I was doing to put myself through school. And that became my community, these computer people. I moved out to California. Very hip crowd. Eccentric. I was really testing the waters of my faith. I had this idea that a Christian could "be anywhere and be at home" if you were in the right relationship to God. But I found that wasn't the way God was calling me.

The materialism of it was killing me. I remember buying a VCR. The VCR symbolized my . . . I was just consuming, consuming. Buying *stuff!* Things, ideas, fads! And also the . . . the constant "playing" that I think some middle-class people our age do. I look back now and I realize that it was a real desert time. I was caught in this thing, and it was killing me.

None of these computer friends of mine understood. I would get into these intellectual conversations about God. I remember at one point feeling like the conversation was killing the spirit, the Holy Spirit. It's kind of a strange thing to say, but I remember I felt beaten up. It was just a very empty, empty time. But I just kept saying yes. I [didn't] even know what the question was, but I knew I had the choice and I just kept saying yes. I'd pray, "Help me to get out of this because it's killing me and I'm caught."

Ro: Almost an addiction.

Lynn: Sort of. I think it was an addiction to security, not a material security, but just this "fun" way of life.

Ro: How did you have the guts to get out?

Lynn: Well, I started school at the Graduate Theological Union, and that was a real step back for me. I started to find a language for my experience. And I saw that the place where it made the most sense for me to be as a middle-class North American woman was [working with] Central American refugees or in AIDS ministry. I needed to move. I decided to do the Central American work, and I knew about the Worker. What I was looking for was a faith community, but it was very foreign to me. And this is when Bob and I met each other, too. One of the things I like about the Catholic Worker and what, actually, I really like about Bob is I can relate to this guy. Catholic Workers are just normal people, just a group of friends trying to live the Gospel together. It makes you feel like, "Yeah, I can do it, too."

Jim Levinson and I talked in the spacious living room at Noonday Farm, the CW farm attached to Boston's Haley House. Sun glinted in the windows, the sounds of children and lunch preparations came from the kitchen. Jim has a Ph.D. in economics. The "us" here includes his wife, Louise Cochran.

Jim Levinson: What led us to Haley House was in good part our experience overseas in low-income countries. Interestingly, when I was reading Dan Berrigan's play, "The Trial of The Catonsville Nine," I noticed that a good number of the nine had spent time in Latin America or Africa or Asia. It struck me first [only] as an interesting coincidence, and then I realized it wasn't a coincidence at all. Something happens to many people who work in these countries, something that makes them ripe for this kind of involvement.

Some people are able to build defense mechanisms around themselves—armor—so as not to feel anything when they're dealing with very poor people. But others of us are not so good at such defense mechanisms, and when we experience that kind of suffering, we're never quite the same again. I think that's what happened to Louise and myself.

I'd been working in some pretty fancy . . . doing some pretty fancy work, like university teaching and working for the U.S. State Department, both in Washington and overseas. I developed a hypothesis after . . . oh, almost eighteen years of this kind of work. (Economists always develop hypotheses.) And my hypothesis was that there is an inverse relationship between one's income, wealth, reputation, status, on the one hand, and how close one is to the problem on the other. So if one is feeding a hungry child, one is low caste. If you're training the person who's feeding the hungry child, you're a little higher on the totem pole. If you're administering the program, you're still a little higher. And if you're doing what I was doing, being part of a professional elite of university people—doing the consulting, writing the journal articles, and so forth—you're the top of the heap, the best paid. But you're also the most removed, and you never have to see a hungry child. Well, Louise and I reached the point of feeling that we really needed to be grounded, needed to be in touch with people in need.

Right out of college, I went to India for six years. Came back and did my graduate study, did university teaching from '72 to '76, then worked for two years in Bangladesh. It's very hard to live and work in Bangladesh. Its government really is remarkably callous towards its poor and suffering people. After we returned to the States, I continued to do consulting work although I was, at the same time, doing some music study in Boston.

Our last big trip was 1981. We went to the Philippines. And I was actually working for the Marcos government. It wasn't difficult to see what was going on. After a few days, we said to each other, "We're on the wrong side! We can't do this anymore." Something fundamental had to change. Interestingly, on that Philippines trip, we went into a used bookstore. As if by divine providence, there on the bookshelf was a 1971 copy of the *Holy Cross Quarterly* about the Berrigans. We were very ripe. We devoured it. Came back to the States.

Noah at this time was one year old, and we'd been thinking a lot about what it means to have a child, what it means in terms of our own interests and involvement. We had seen many people who were involved in issues relating to peace and justice who would have children and then basically build a moat around themselves and their children. Become concerned only with the material well-being of their children. We had one set of cousins who joined something called the Toy of the Month Club. And that became our shorthand for that particular kind of life. Our laughter at that time was nervous laughter, though, because the syndrome had its hooks in us as well.

Then we talked to Molly Rush. She has six kids and she told us that when she did the King of Prussia Plowshares Eight action, it was not *in spite of* her children but *on behalf of* her children. And that had a mesmerizing effect on us. That was the counterweight to the Toy of the Month Club.

Then Jonah House invited us to a Pentagon action on the Feast of the Holy Innocents. Now, Louise's father was a Presbyterian minister. I'm Jewish. Neither of us had ever heard of the Feast of the Holy Innocents, but there was something compelling about this invitation to the Pentagon.

A friend said, "You shouldn't go because when you come back, there'll be no one to talk to. So only go if you can find people to go with." We began calling around. And by chance, after a good number of calls, we heard of Haley House and the peace group called Ailanthus. (It's named after the Ailanthus tree that grows through the cracks in the cement, a tree that thrives in adversity.)

So we went over and drove down to Washington with them and had an incredible . . . as close as I've ever come to, and *will* ever come to, a real conversion experience. Right there on the steps of the Pentagon. It was quite extraordinary.

They were doing guerrilla theater. People were lying on the steps, covered with ashes and blood, as if they were nuclear victims. A young woman was singing about the child who never grew up because he or she was killed at Hiroshima. Then a van pulled up. The idea was that some number of us should go forward and put these bodies in the van. They hadn't figured out exactly who would do that, but somehow at that moment, I . . . I knew that was my part. I had Noah in the backpack. My older daughter, Mira, was holding one hand, and Louise was holding the other hand. Louise took the backpack, and I went forward. Went and picked up this body and got blood and ashes all over my newly cleaned coat.

And all of the pain that I had experienced in these other countries just . . . it all came gushing out, and I was just weeping inconsolably, holding onto this body. I put the body in the van, but I couldn't let go. People were saying, "Hey, come on. We've got other bodies." But I couldn't let go of this body.

Months later, I met the person who was the body. He had been a senior official at General Electric but could no longer work there and had joined up with Jonah House for this particular Feast of the Innocents. He had been to church in Philadelphia on Christmas, and the priest had said to him, "Take a piece of straw from the manger, put it in your shoe and do something that Jesus would have done." And he went to the Feast of the Holy Innocents at the Pentagon. The whole experience was awesome. Within six months, we had moved into Haley House.

Ro: Did you become Catholic?

Jim: No. But Louise did. Louise did. I have continued to be Jewish. We're an interfaith group [here at Noonday]. David and Bill are Protestant; Louise, Claire, and Lisa are Catholic; Mark Benjamin and I are Jewish. We have a very rich interfaith life which includes a Jewish sabbath home service every Friday night, and a Monday evening worship that is essentially Christian, although it's a sensitive worship. There are bits of Christian liturgical language that I as a Jew have trouble with, and people are sensitive to that. They've been willing to adapt it without watering down the service, and that feels real good. In fact, interestingly, with the kind of attention paid to . . . to things spiritual and the reinforcement that one gets in this kind of company for pursuing one's spiritual journey, I have been doing new and deeper things within Judaism. My grandfather had been a cantor and his ancestors back through the generations. And now I am a cantor, also.

With personality and paint, artist Jonathan Kirkendall has brightened Dorothy Day House in Washington, D.C. His parents are Baptist missionaries, and he grew up in the Middle East.

Jonathan Kirkendall: When I told my Baptist friends I had become Catholic, they all said, "Well, it's about time!"

Ro: What do your parents think?

Jonathan: They were devastated. They saw it as a real rejection, although it wasn't. So much has changed . . . they haven't lived in the States since 1963. I've discovered that so much of what is confusing between Catholicism and the faith of the Baptists is a matter of language. They're both talking about the same things, but they insist on using different words.

The Catholics say you make a response to God through the sacraments. The Baptists say you make a response to God and accept Jesus Christ as your Savior by asking every day what God's will is. The Catholics call it works, the Baptists call it responsibility. They're talking about the same thing.

My brothers and sisters thought that somehow I literally was keeping count of how many times I went to Mass and confession, and if I had enough points, then *maybe* I could get into heaven. They didn't understand that the whole thing is grace.

Ro: How do you relate to the institution?

Jonathan: Oh, barely! Dorothy Day was a traditionalist in many ways, and I like that. I find myself sort of a conservative Catholic. I mean, I actually say the rosary. (I can't quite figure out confession.) You know, a good friend of mine, from another Baptist missionary family, said, "You were *born* Catholic." But I had a horrible time joining the church. A Jesuit finally said to me, "Look, you can have problems with the institution, but I want you to know that no one has more problems with the institution than Catholic priests have. So come home."

When we met, Bob Imholt had recently joined a new community, the Tacoma Catholic Worker.

Bob Imholt: I'm amazed, from what I've read about her, that Dorothy Day came into the church. It's mysterious to me. And it's mysterious to me why I'm here, too. Other than the fact that there's just this wonderful extended community. That's what I said yes to. When people ask me if I'm Catholic, I really hesitate.

Ro: But you're Catholic Worker?

Bob: Yes, I am. I look at my twenties as kind of a religious purgatory, a spiritual purgatory. I spent thirteen years in the army, seven as an enlisted person. Went right out of high school. Officer Candidate School and all that routine and became a second lieutenant. I was into the steady paycheck and the career, and I had the attitude that all you had to do was work hard. You didn't have to necessarily be really smart, just had to work hard, and the American dream, so to speak, was attainable. I think the bulk of the folks I've been exposed to in the church [feel like that]. Not the St. Leo's community, though.

Ro: What's that?

Bob: That's a Jesuit parish here in Tacoma. Wonderful! Very proactive in a whole bunch of different stuff. We're all here in Hilltop, which is the . . . the heart of Tacoma. It's Tacoma's ghetto, I guess. That's where all the violence and . . . The Worker house is right in the middle of it. And it's a block from L'Arche, and the JVC [Jesuit Volunteer Corps] house is just a couple blocks away, so everybody belongs to St. Leo's. I'd say St. Leo's is far and away the poorest parish in the city in terms of finances, but it does, in my mind, far and away the most work. It's a pretty place.

Ro: Where did you meet these folks?

Bob: Well, there's a Jesuit priest in our community named Bill Bichsel. (Everybody calls him Bix.) Around about 1982, when the Trident submarines were first being moved into the Bangor submarine base, Bix was very active in the protest movement. Involved particularly in that protest.

And there is now a person in our community who was the commander of one of two sixty-person teams, [army teams] delegated to react to the civil disturbance created by Bix and others. I was that person. A newly commissioned second lieutenant. I was there. At that time, with my philosophy in life, I probably would have very gleefully arrested Bix and hauled him off to jail and felt quite self-righteous about it. (Bix did get arrested at that demonstration, as a matter of fact, and spent six months in jail.)

Ro: So how did you cross the line to the other side?

Bob: [Long sigh.] Boy, that's the question that . . . In my twenties . . . I went to probably ten or twelve different places looking for a spiritual home. Lutheran and Mormon and everything but Catholic, I think. Nothing felt like home. And so I got to the point where I said, "Okay, if God is out there, if there really is a God, and he or she really has something for me to do, then he or she will talk to me. And until that point in time, I'm going to just go on with my life."

And here I am. I feel almost like I'm being . . . I'm being pulled along in this. There's a tremendous amount of peace that comes with being where you know you're supposed to be.

Ro: Uh huh. Do some of your former . . . like your kids and maybe your former wife, do they think you've gone nutty?

Bob: Yeah. They don't understand. I don't know that I blame them. "Why don't you get a job and lead a normal life?" My response to that is pretty consistent. I tell them this is what I feel called to do. I don't know whether I'm ever going to have another job—another *real* job—again. The folks that we hang out with are the same folks that Christ was hanging out with, the folks that the rest of society thinks are a little off-center and moody and the nerds of the world, so to speak. Those are the people you can learn the most from.

When we talked, Linda Greenwald lived in Poulsbo, Washington, and provided a Catholic Worker presence in the Ground Zero community.

Ro: Linda, what about your family? You're quite far away from them, aren't you?

Linda Greenwald: Three thousand miles. It's no coincidence.

Ro: We could turn the tape off if you want.

Linda: No. My parents have grown in being able to understand the peace work, but they've never really accepted my going to jail from time to time. I think what's been the hardest for my parents is our lifestyle. I gave up new furniture and a car and all that stuff, and they see that as a criticism of the way they live, I guess. It's just real hard for them to accept. I'm real careful to support the good that they've been able to give from their lives, but they're real defensive. I try to explain that the values I have are values I got from them and the church, to a large degree, but no, everything is not roses with my family at all.

Chris Montesano is a member of the Catholic Worker community in Sheep Ranch, California.

Chris Montesano: I grew up in the Vietnam era, and all authority was null and void. For example, there was a period when I went through a real difficult time with my parents. Didn't recognize their gift. There were lots of things my parents didn't understand about pacifism, about the whole nuclear war issue, the Vietnam War. As I've grown older, I've realized they gave me a tremendous gift—a gift of love.

Another thing that's opened this awareness up is [my wife] Joan's involvement in the county mental health [system]. So many people grow up with violence in the home. And I know, for example, that my father was abused as a child by his father. His father used to grab them by the ear and pull them by the ear. Beat them with belts. Things like that.

Dan Berrigan said, "The violence stops here." In my father, the violence stopped with him. He told me he would never treat his children like his father treated him. That was a tremendous gift he gave me. My mother, too. Their loving was a tremendous gift, and in my rebellious years I couldn't see that.

Donna Domiziano lives at the Mustard Seed Catholic Worker in Worcester, Massachusetts.

Donna Domiziano: Well, actually, I came in backwards. I didn't come in as a Catholic Worker, I mean knowing about the Catholic Worker and then coming. I just fell in love with the street people. Just loved the soup kitchen work. I don't know why. There's just something special about working with the poor. They are very giving people themselves and I get a lot. I have fun, too.

It took me a long time to get here, though. One summer I came down with our youth kids from St. Joan of Arc Church and helped out. Painted the dining room and helped serve one meal a day. I really liked it, but I was scared—scared that

I was getting called to do it. So I dropped out. Didn't come near the place for around six years. That was one way not to . . . I really fought it for all those years.

Then gradually, I started coming again, and then came more and more. I quit teaching and was working for a family health agency. Then I was taking time off to come down here, or was calling in all the time. I finally said, "This is ridiculous! Just resign." But it took me all those years to come to be poor. It took me a long time. So I came to the Catholic Worker kind of backwards, but I like it anyway. Yeah.

Ro: What did your folks think?

Donna: Well, it wasn't nearly as dramatic for my parents as my going to Guatemala a couple years ago. If I'm happy, they're happy. My father sent me some money yesterday, so I called home to thank him for it. He laughed about it. He said, "If you come home for a couple of days, you know, I'll pay . . ." And then we laughed 'cause when I was teaching, if I took time out and went home, he'd want to give me money to make up for the salary I lost.

I said, "Don't forget now. Being poor is great. If I come home for a few days, I'm not losing any pay, remember?" And he laughed.

Ro: Do you miss the normal life?

Donna: No, because I didn't . . . when I finally came, I was ready. If I had done it when I wasn't ready, it might not have worked, and I might have missed it too much . . . missed the things.

Fr. Bernie Gilgun is another active member of the Mustard Seed.

Ro: Father Bernie, why did Dorothy and Peter's philosophy speak to you and not to your brother priests?

Fr. Bernie Gilgun: I was called to follow that life. The love of God was poured out into my heart. It was a gift from God to show me that life. It was my vocation. It wasn't theirs. And for His plan, it didn't need to be.

I'll tell you a great influence in my life, one that made it possible for me to follow that life in a way that others would not have been free to do, to follow the light as I was free to follow it. It was my family. I come from a large family. I was brought up with a grandmother and a couple of aunts living in the house with us. All holy, all truly saints. My mother and father were absolutely saints. All these aunts and grandmothers saints. And my brothers and sisters holy, too.

We're eight living still. We were ten born. There are eight of us, and we are in contact almost every day. We still live in the same city. In the same city. In my father's family, there were . . . my father's mother had ten children. My mother's mother had twelve children. All those children, those twenty-two—my aunts and uncles—and the ones they married are all buried in our cemetery in Woburn, Massachusetts. Beyond that, my mother and father, my two grandparents, all four great-grandparents . . . all buried in that same cemetery. On my father's side, three of his great-grandparents are Gilguns, if you could believe it. All the Gilguns of Ireland came to Woburn, and they're all my relatives. We had this great consciousness of family.

Without ever saying a word, my brothers and sisters were for me the touchstone of orthodoxy. If it played with them, with all of them, and there was great variety among them, but with all the one faith, then . . . So if I was saying something that didn't ring true, I'd have heard from some of them. As long as I didn't hear from them, I really wasn't . . . well, I was concerned, terribly concerned about what the bishop thought. The family and the bishop were my touchstones, yeah. That's why I was free. It was an extraordinary thing . . . an extraordinary thing. Beautiful brothers and sisters that I trusted.

Trusted that God was as good as His word. Trusted that the vision of the Gospel could be believed. Trust in God and the Sacred Heart of Jesus. Trust . . . trust. My mother and father had great trust in the Sacred Heart of Jesus. But my family was very significant. That can't be exaggerated enough. And they always knew. I've got eight aces in the hole. You know, when I was drinking compulsively—an alcoholic—none of my brothers and sisters ever quit on me. Never, never.

Patty Burns, once of California, was a founding member of Sister Peter Claver House in Philadelphia.

Ro: Patty, how do your parents feel about all this?

Patty Burns: My mother died a number of years ago. She would have been very supportive. My dad . . . my dad is supportive of me as a person. He probably doesn't think what I'm doing is such a good idea. I'm the youngest of seven, and I get the feeling that he just wishes I was settled so he wouldn't have to worry about me. He doesn't really understand, and he wouldn't encourage me to do it on its own merits, but because I want to do it, that's enough for him.

I don't always tell him everything because he's not going to agree, usually. He was a colonel in the Marine Corps and went to the Naval Academy, so he's . . . he's always telling me that the military paid for everything I've ever had. There's no denying that. I grew up in the suburbs and had everything I ever wanted because . . . He wouldn't have been able to go to college if he hadn't gone to the Naval Academy. What he doesn't understand is that people should be able to go to college even though they are not in the military. The military *did* do all kinds of good things in his life. He's very thankful and grateful to the military and the whole government because it provided him with a way out of his small town and provided for all of us. We have seven kids and we all went to college. It gave a lot of stability to his life. What I'd like to see is a whole new way of providing that for people.

The main thing about my childhood was not just having everything I wanted (although that was part of it) but also having people tell me every day, "You're great! Do whatever you want. You want to be a doctor? That's great. Go be a doctor. You can do anything you want!" I'll always have that. I'm always going to feel like I can do things. And that doesn't often come with poverty.

Claire Schaeffer-Duffy has also traveled far from the life she lived with her parents.

Claire Schaeffer-Duffy: We were married in Washington, at St. Patrick's Church. My parents were not happy about the wedding initially. It was a lot to ask of them because they aren't Catholic, and they had enormous concern over the way of life I was choosing. (Well, I shouldn't say enormous, but significant concern.) I think they felt that up until the marriage this life of . . . at the Catholic Worker in Washington, D.C., would be a passing thing. Then they met Scott and realized it wasn't. My father is a diplomat, so we had all kinds of people at our wedding. The whole gamut.

Ro: Did your father feel you were somehow challenging what he was doing or casting doubts on the way he'd chosen to live in the world?

Claire: Probably. I was a rather judgmental young person. Even now, you know. When you find a way that you think is right, you expect everyone else to . . . to adhere. And I think part of it also is the child really wants their parents' blessing, so when they don't give it, they kind of insist on it, whether the parents can authenticate that or not. And that puts a lot of pressure on the parents. That's part of a child's immaturity. I certainly wasn't making it easy for my father! But it's much more peaceful now.

Ro: Grandchildren tend to help, don't they? [Claire and Scott were expecting their second child when we talked.]

Claire: Yeah. They do.

Ro: So at the wedding you had these two worlds.

Claire: Oh, we had three or four different worlds. We had the people in the resistance community. We had friends of the family who were coming from diplomatic backgrounds—a very different set of politics. I had my friends from the women's community bakery where I worked. They were gay, and quite suspicious of marriage in general. And then we had some of the people who had lived at the [Catholic Worker] house. So it was really a cross section of humanity, but that's the way I think a wedding should be.

Ro: What was the reception like? Was it your mother's kind of reception?

Claire: No, it was not at all her kind of reception. My mother was very, very, very good, though. We didn't ask for gifts. We asked people to bring a dish, so everybody brought food and it was a big kind of potluck, but we also ordered fifteen large pizzas because my husband loves pizza. And that was brought in very ceremoniously by the pizza people down the street. And we had quite a bit of beer, and my mother provided wine. The cutlery was rented, so it was rather elegant cutlery for pizza and potluck. But that was good because I think paper plates are really so harmful for the environment. Everyone provided something. One friend helped me get the tablecloths from the Community for Creative Non-Violence. Another friend helped arrange the flowers for centerpieces, so everyone was giving something. Nothing was catered or done by outsiders.

Gayle Catinella was living at Chicago St. Francis House when we talked. After she and Dan McGuire married and started a family, they moved to Mary Farm, the former McGuire family farm in Nebraska.

Gayle Catinella: I wanted to quit talking about the problems of the world and *do* something. I was sick of conferences and meetings and hearing the same people saying the same thing every year, with nothing really happening. They would get really angry and say our government was a bunch of fascists and stuff and then go home and cook dinner and watch television. And I was also twenty-one and wanting to "find myself," you know.

I'd been working Soup Kitchen [at St. Thomas Church, just down the street] for about three years and at the shelter here in Uptown for several years, too. Really loved it here, and loved being with people who believed in simple living. At the time, I hated the Catholic Worker, though. I thought [St. Francis House] was just the most dingy, grimy, dirty, depressing place I've ever been in my life. So I didn't spend much time here. But I loved the people, the do-gooders who loved the people they served. They were really neat, and I wanted to serve the poor, too, because of their example.

So I decided to try it out. I spent the first night at St. Francis thinking, "Is that a roach I feel? Is a mouse going to run over me?" And there was one bathroom for all of us. One shower. Three toilets. But when I had lived at home, I had such a hard time that I thought, "I'll try it. I can do it for a summer. I lived in Central America. I can do this." By the end of the summer, I didn't want to leave. If you can survive two months here, you can . . . Some of the guests have been here a long time. They're really good people, but they're not easy.

The true reason that I'll stay with the Catholic Worker is that I just don't belong anywhere else. This is where the puzzle pieces of my life fit. And why, I have no idea. I can call it God's call and the fulfillment of God's gifts inside of me and all that, but that's too big of a mystery for me to try to work out myself. For some reason that I'll never understand, God put me here. I came as a guest, you know, and I experienced love and healing and total acceptance by people who I had nothing in common with. Who I would never choose as friends, to be quite blunt. I didn't come here because of Dorothy Day, because of any big ideals or anything. I came here because I was a broken person who needed a place to be. Just like everybody else who comes.

CHAPTER 8

Hospitality
A Roundtable Discussion

During the eleven years I have spent around the Catholic Worker here in Minneapolis and in New York and California, countless times I have been overwhelmed by a sense of futility, the grave feeling that we are all putting not just our fingers but our heads and hearts and maybe even our souls into this gaping hole in the dike that will simply never be filled. I have had hard dreams of the sad-eyed, angry, disaffected ones from all the cities of the earth flooding our doors until we run out of bread and kind words, and unkind words, too. Must we be caught, both we and our more disadvantaged brothers and sisters, in an endless cycle of bread and pain? Are we doomed to break our dreams with brokenness?

—*Bob Tavani,* Catholic Worker, *May 1984*

When I was on trial one time for civil disobedience, the prosecutor got a little pompous and said, "Well, what would you do if someone just came into your living room one day and sat down and wouldn't leave?"

And I laughed. I said, "That happens pretty often, really. We talk to them. We wait. Find out what they want and explain to them what we have."

—*Virginia Druhe*

You know, it used to drive Dorothy Day crazy when people would give that band-aid analogy. Part of it may have been because many of the people who were criticizing weren't themselves doing anything concrete for the poor. But also, there was just this incredible lack of faith—no faith that handing this person a piece of bread would have any eternal meaning.

—*Fr. Mike Baxter*

D URING the depression, the missions called it "a hot and a flop." Catholic Workers offer food and shelter, and something more—something of themselves. Hospitality is central to their purpose. But it's difficult to define in particular situations, especially when homelessness reaches crisis proportions. So how to say no. How to say yes, and to whom. Is the Catholic Worker style of hospitality confirming people in dependency? What does it mean to have power over people's lives? Is the gulf between "Worker" and "guest" always unbridgeable? These questions are the subject of some of the liveliest discussions in the movement.*

This roundtable includes a large number of people from across the country. I act as a kind of moderator and have occasionally written brief transitions to provide continuity. I've used pseudonyms for those who didn't identify themselves as Catholic Workers.

John Williams (Seattle): People would call, as they do in all houses. "Help!! This person needs a place to stay!" And we would be full.

"Well, can't you put them in your living room?"

"Why don't you put them in *your* living room?"

"Oh! Oh, no! We don't *do* that kind of thing!"

What I finally realized, past their own questioning of me to my questioning of myself, was that yes, I *could* put somebody in the living room, but what about the next call? The dining room? Then the bathroom and the closet? Sure, I could take in more people, but then I'm not really offering a home to anybody. I don't really do anything to assuage my guilt by taking in another ten families and hanging them on hooks. Because I'll still get another ten phone calls.

Fr. Richard McSorley (Washington, D.C.): I've seen so many conflicts. It's almost an in-built conflict in the Catholic Worker about how many [guests] you take into a house. One theory is that when a stranger comes to the door, it's Christ and you let him in. And the other theory is that if you're going to let Christ in, you don't want to have Christ sleep under the sink, and you don't want Christ to crowd out all the other Christs that are already in there.

Brian Terrell (Maloy, Iowa): I think in the controversy between quality and quantity of hospitality, it's the new people who are always going to be calling for quantity, who want to have people sleeping on the landings of the stairways.

In the CW, different people are doing different types of hospitality. What we were doing in Davenport was, for the most part, temporary hospitality. Welcom-

---

* For a recent treatment of the subject, see Catholic Worker and scholar Harry Murray's *Do Not Neglect Hospitality: The Catholic Worker and the Homeless.*

ing the stranger. That's a completely different thing from taking a few people into your home and [having] your home become their home. In temporary hospitality, it's still our home, and when you're a guest in somebody's home, you simply don't take the liberties you have in your own house.

Betsy Keenan (Maloy, Iowa): For instance, in Davenport I could read till late at night because I had my own room, but the lights in [the guests'] bedroom had to be out at ten because there were six people sleeping there.

Brian: People would often criticize us for having our own private bedrooms or for drinking beer in the community room. But people were staying with us temporarily and living in a more dormitory situation. And yeah, I wouldn't make that somebody's home for a long term. We tried to do that a few times, tried to mix the two kinds of hospitality, and it never really worked out. I don't think it would be healthy for someone to live in a dormitory for years on end.

Ro: But aren't people doing that now all over the place? How do you pick who gets the luxury hospitality? It seems to me you'd pick people who can get along with others, so you'd choose the least sick people. Which means you're not serving the least ones.

Betsy: Faces flash in my mind when you say that. Real cases.

Kassie Temple (New York City): Dorothy said that the one thing we can share is a lack of privacy, and I don't find that overwhelming personally. Having a room of one's own is a very recent notion of privacy and most of the world still doesn't have one.

Barbara Blaine (Chicago): Well, I'll tell you. We used to serve dinner to forty or fifty people in one of those tiny apartments at the old St. Elizabeth's. The kitchen was like six feet wide. Totally gross! I mean that's the only word to describe it. Absolute rule by roaches! Then after dinner we'd clean up and fold up all the chairs and the tables and roll out the beds. In the morning, it was just the opposite—cleaning up the beds and setting up the tables and getting breakfast ready. I think this is a continual struggle in the Catholic Worker—dealing with the boundaries between quality and quantity. There was no quality at that time, needless to say.

Bob Tavani (Minneapolis): I remember Dorothy talking to those people in Syracuse when they were giving unlimited hospitality. They were young people who were overgenerous, who didn't know how to set boundaries, and got themselves exhausted. The place was just a wreck. Like a city shelter. Dorothy said, "Do your share and do it well. And then agitate the rest of the community to do their share."

Jeff Dietrich (Los Angeles): Sometimes, I guess there *is* a sense of . . . you know, you're shoveling sand or rolling a Sisyphean rock up the hill and going back down and rolling it up again. Still, I just feel liberated when I get to the soup kitchen. "I'm so glad to see you. I'm so glad for your unsightliness. I'm so glad for your touching my life with your bizarreness and your unstructured chaos."

Catherine Morris (Los Angeles): Chaos is right! At our weekly house meeting, we had a hospitality review [on who was staying at Hennacy House]. Someone said, "I don't recognize the guy with the white hair, and who's the Oriental woman who's having a baby in a month and doesn't speak English?" And then two nights ago, I told a man he could sleep on the couch for a night. And he's still here.

It's like one of those questions about which child you would pick not to have. January of this year was horrendous! One drug addict after another. Everybody who came ripped off a TV and disappeared. And so we've been trying to be really careful, and what do we have in the house right now? Another drug addict! It's changed so much in the eighteen years of the community's life. Jeff said at the meeting that maybe we should just concentrate. "We do pretty good with crazy people." But we're greatly outnumbered by our guests in L.A., so they have to be a bit low-maintenance.

Fr. Jack Keehan (Chicago): Yeah. You can only take on so much. Interestingly enough, while I admire some people's sense of decency and loving and forgiveness and all that, I also think it's sometimes necessary to tell people, "Well, now you've come to the end of the line, my friend. I am pissed off at you, and you have to leave." And from my own experience I know you sometimes *do* have to intimidate them into leaving or they'll immediately try to intimidate you.

"Well, if you don't give me some money, I'm going to go out and rob somebody. I can rob one of these little old ladies."

"Get your ass out of here, you son of a bitch. If you could rob one of those old ladies, you would, and you wouldn't be wasting my time."

Kathe McKenna (Boston): When people come in to Haley House, we ask them to abide by a different set of rules. Sometimes they laugh at us. Sometimes they accept the challenge. But the key is that they recognize it's important to us, and they engage in it with us. They recognize there's a different way, in *our* behavior as well as *their* behavior. Because we're just as violent as they are. We're just violent in a different way, violent in control. I don't think that you can purport to believe in nonviolence and not live with violence. It's not an academic issue.

Someone has said that once you try to dominate another, you've already been violent. And we're trying to dominate all the time, trying to make guys over into something else. Consciously, subconsciously and every other way. We have to learn to check our violence just like they do.

Frank Walsh (Saginaw, Michigan): At St. Alexius House, it was really the folks you'd call "guests" who were into the rules. Usually some guy would surface and find himself in an administrative capacity. Checking people in and checking them out. A lot of guys who showed up were born dictators. [Laughs.] And if the breaks had been going right, they would have been police chiefs somewhere because they were very interested in policing other people. And we folks weren't strong on the policing aspect.

I remember Big Bill, who came from nowhere. Big Bill just had more personality than you could shake a stick at, and he could just do *anything*. He was kind of the heart and soul of the place there for a while. Until he just left with the money and [Jim] Gaertner's car. But we wanted there to be as much . . . well, all kinds of freedom, really. And some folks . . . there was always a struggle with rules.

Sometimes these rules would be drawn up and written down. Because, as I recall, it was part of the philosophy that the guests would make their own rules. And we had weekly meetings. Gripe sessions, really. People would always want somebody else kicked out. Somebody was smoking in the wrong place, or somebody was supposed to have brought a bottle in, those kinds of things.

Ro: Did your guests feel threatened by you folks?

Frank: No, I don't think so. I think we may have been intimidated by them.

Kathy Shuh-Ries (Milwaukee): Well, we have rules [at Casa Maria] and I don't think Dorothy would have liked 'em. (There's probably an awful lot Dorothy Day wouldn't have liked about the house.) The rules are more for staff survival. The staff changes so much, you know. If you're comfortable with the person doing their own wash and you don't mind teaching them how the machine works, that might be fine. Another Worker, who doesn't want to take the time to show them how to use it or doesn't like to fix it if it breaks, will feel more comfortable doing the wash herself. It's a matter of tolerance. And skill in communication, too.

Bob: Well, Dorothy would say you can't do everything. In a caring way, she was quite detached about it. A lot of people come to the Worker for their own emotional needs, and part of their emotional baggage is that sometimes they don't know how to draw boundaries. She drew boundaries very quickly, and she herself would bounce people. The typical young Catholic Worker today . . . they forbear, forbear, forbear. That's their own need. Dorothy was healthy. Dorothy had problems, but she never wondered who she was. She knew who she was right from the get-go. A lot of the people who come now are not in the same situation, and they're trying to find themselves by helping the poor. Sometimes they make mistakes, or what I think of as mistakes. Providing sloppy or mean-spirited hospitality.

Ro: Okay. But what about the people who spend so much time thinking about the quality of their hospitality? The people who are into the form, I guess. They . . . they're not into their heart.

Bob: Don't you think that's condescension? What they're thinking is, "I've got this and I'm giving it to them." They're not really accepting these people as their equals. As soon as you start making that division between giving and receiving, you're condescending.

John Cooper (Berkeley, California): You know, the fact is that one person is having to come to others for food because he doesn't have any money, because he doesn't have a job, because he drinks heavily. He has that right.

Another person is coming to us for food because there are emotional problems in her life and even though the state has given that person a monthly check, she spent the check on ridiculous living for a week and has no more left. I don't see how we're going to change that. That is the person's right. [In Berkeley] we just brought food out to People's Park for anyone who wanted to eat it. I'm not sure how you change the system, whatever the system is.

When you look at the system a little bit more closely, you find it's not so much a *system* at all—it's the interaction of myriad people with an established way of doing things. Each has their story and their own needs. Their own lives are part of the system. (I'm not putting this very well.) What I must do about this guy who is drunk all the time, what I must do about this person who is walking up and down the street screaming, what I must even do about this little teenybopper who has run away from home is . . . is to try to feed them with grace and dignity. To try. That's all . . . that's all.

Debbie McQuade (Los Angeles): You've gotta try, gotta keep going. This community is really my only experience of community other than the convent and families, you know, regular old families. I could say fifty million good things about it, but when you come in to visit, you might even get a hug and kiss, but then everybody turns around and does what they've been doing. Nobody shows you around much or asks you if you want a cup of coffee or says, "This is the community room. We're going to be busy for an hour, so why don't you sit here and read and then we'll come back and check in with you." Nobody says any of those logical things. You're just kind of left on your own. It doesn't make sense in terms of graciousness. And it doesn't feel right, at least for me.

Barbara: Well, it's hard to be so nicey-nicey if folks are mentally ill, though. You know, most Catholic Worker houses are filled with mentally ill people. And I think people *know* they have a problem. Even in that little old apartment in the old St. Elizabeth's, Gary Olivero made them feel accepted with their problem. So *they* had to be accepting to someone else. It wasn't always smooth and easy, but at least that was the goal, and Gary worked real hard to have that happen.

Now, of course, we've got much more room.* Women and children can stay all day, but the men have to go out between nine and five. And it's not because we expect the men to go out and find a job, or that men are supposed to be gone during the day. But we wanted women to feel safe and secure, and we wanted it to be a nice place for them. Men in the household . . . I mean, it's been our experience that when men stay in the house, they do nothing except sit around and make a mess, just sit there and smoke and drink coffee. They don't do anything to clean up.

On the other hand, some of the women we have . . . every one of the women who lives with us was a bag lady once. Every one of them. And we have seen transformations. The people now have been with us for a long time, and they have changed from being their obnoxious dirty kind of nasty selves and have become really domestic. Almost too much so. When they spend all day cleaning up a room, they don't want a man messing it up. So the men and the women fight, and we've found that it just makes sense to make the men leave during the day. Except for Ray [Matthews], of course.†

Ro: Barb, one day I noticed that when you wheeled Ray in to breakfast, you bent over and kissed the top of his head, just like you would your grandpa. That kind of gesture just isn't present in a shelter.

Barbara: Well, Ray is special, there's no denying that. In most places, there's a sense of wanting to keep a distance from homeless people, that somehow they're different from us. Something interesting along that line happens at St. E's now.

* St. Elizabeth's is now housed in the former St. Therese's convent on Chicago's South Side. A large building, almost too large. See Chapter 1 for this community's saga of finding a home.
† Ray Matthews lived to be over a hundred, spending the last twenty years of his life with the late Gary Olivero and the St. Elizabeth community. A pacifist and a vegetarian, he met Gary in Grand Rapids at a peace demonstration against the Vietnam War and moved with him to Chicago.

The people have been there so long that they don't look at themselves as home-less. I used to run the women's shelter in Uptown, and that's where most of the women here came from. They've been in a house now for a couple years, and so they've become really domesticated and they keep clean and some of them fix their hair. You know, they don't look like the normal street people. So volunteers who come sometimes don't have a sense of really helping a homeless person. They don't understand. [The men and women who live with us] have one foot in the door and one foot out the door. If we weren't there for them, most would be back on the street. They wouldn't be capable of getting themselves together and making it on their own.

Gayle Catinella (Chicago): Like my friend Miss Minnie. For a while, I roomed at St. Francis with one of the permanent guests, with Miss Minnie. Her health was failing rapidly, and we weren't quite ready to put her in a nursing home, so I thought it'd be better if I stayed in the same room. We had a very, very, good relationship—just hit it off. Miss Minnie was my friend. Finally she just couldn't walk up the stairs anymore, and it was just too much for her to be here.

We'd been trying to get her into a very good nursing home, and they said they didn't have any room, so we moved her to a place two blocks from here. It didn't have a very good reputation, but people could go to see her every day.

We figured if people visited her regularly, it would be ókay. But it wasn't. They didn't give her insulin, and she ended up with chronic bed sores. On Halloween she was rushed to the hospital, and they told us that she'd been terribly ne-glected. So now we're working with a group to help bring a lawsuit against the nursing home.

Miss Minnie finally got into the place we originally tried, and they were ex-cellent. But she was pretty much lost. She couldn't eat. She didn't talk. She had tubes everywhere. So I just had to wait for her to die. When you love someone so much, it's really difficult to rationalize anything. It's been really hard to figure out just where my personal responsibility lay. Should I have moved out of the house into an apartment and taken care of her? Or was it totally beyond my control and something that I should just trust that God is going to take care of? Obviously, she'd deteriorated, and that wasn't my fault. But we had done so much. I mean when I moved in, she lived out of two bags, slept sitting up in a chair every night with two coats on. She was thousands of dollars in debt and just a mess. And by the end of her stay here, she was . . . she had a nice wardrobe. She slept in a bed. Changed her clothes every day and had regular baths. No more lice in her hair. The renaissance of her life was just amazing. And then to have it all blown to hell!

St. Francis is our home. It's not a social service agency, it's a home, and we open up our home to people who are in need. We offer hospitality and no one really understands what that means. When you think of hospitality, you think of a Tupperware party, not a Catholic Worker. We don't claim to be social workers here. We claim to be people.

Kassie: At Maryhouse—and I imagine it's true of other houses as well—the so-called "guests" have lived here for years and are indeed the hostesses. The people who come because of Catholic Worker philosophy tend to spend shorter times. I remember somebody saying something to me once about Sandra being a "guest." I started to laugh.

"Sandra has lived here for twelve years, and you've lived here for about twelve days. And *you're* the host?"

Jeannette Noel (New York City): These [people are] so special to God and we're doing all this crap to them now. We are going to be looking up at them so high, you know. They're the ones who are going to get top shelving, not us. You know, sometimes I wish I was out there [on the street]. 'Cause our holiness and our trying to get close to God depends on the misery of the poor. And that seems so unfair to me. That puzzles me.

Kathy: Yeah. Some of them have been through *so* much! I remember we had this crew of women who stayed on the couch. One woman in particular wanted Don [Timmerman] to tuck her in every night. She also loved Leo [Kathy's former husband] because he'd buy her cigarettes. But every night her ritual was having Don tuck her in, and so Don would tuck her in. Eventually she got *so* sick! Had pneumonia and emphysema and she ended up in a nursing home. But she got lonesome for the house, which is hard to imagine 'cause it doesn't have all the creature comforts a nursing home would. But she tied her sheets together, slid down from her second-floor window, and showed up in her pajamas at the door with a twenty-five-dollar cab fare. She just stood there, looking so pathetic. "I was just so lonesome, I had to come back and see you."

Sometimes, though, we were so stretched out trying to meet all the needs that we lost track of the personalism . . . and that was illustrated to me once by a woman who came to the house. She was an older woman with very severe emphysema, so we were worried about her and trying to get her settled in an apartment and trying to get her set up with a doctor's appointment and everything. Suddenly, she just started crying and she said, "You know everyone is so willing to *do* everything for me. All I really want is someone to sit down with me and have a cup of coffee."

I think that's what Dorothy really meant about a harsh and dreadful love. It's real hard to sit down with someone who hasn't changed clothes for weeks or who . . . We had to cut one woman's clothes off because she had lived in them for so long. That's the real test—can you see the person who comes through that door and hear what they're saying?

The flip side of this is that any one of us could be that person. I think I really realized that three years ago when I went through a divorce. It was just excruciating and devastating emotionally. I realized then that I could be one of those people walking through the door. When you are on the staff, it's so easy to judge or to make decisions for people about their lives.

Ro: Have you ever really had any sort of scary things happen?

Kathy: Yes. We did have a bunch of guests once . . . . this was one of the things that helped us decide that we would stick with families. It's very, very hard working with someone who is very, very drunk. They don't remember what they say. They don't remember what they do. Oftentimes they get very violent.

The biggest trouble we would have was with couples. Usually with drug or alcohol problems. They had nothing to lose. They could survive being on the street. Once about two or three of these young couples ganged up together and decided they were going to take over the house. At that time, there were only two women in the house, and the men were gone all the time. But we would always . . . we would usually ask that one of the men be left behind because you need to confront people who are drunk in twos or threes. It doesn't matter if you're a male or a female, it's just easier in a group.

Well, these couples decided they were going to take over. They wrote on the walls, and they wrote on the sheets and they . . . We quick called a meeting and told them they had to leave. But before they left, they tried to rip off the food room. Tried to steal the bedding. They were leaving through both doors at the same time. It was really something!

Oh, and I remember another time! All of a sudden we had two men in the basement trying to rip off the food room. We had a person slashing their wrists on the second floor and we had someone else . . . oh, a sick child who needed to go to the hospital. Sometimes you get crises one on top of the other and they made us think, "Do we want this going on here? Is this a safe place? How much can we take? How much can this house take?" And so we have had to define in order to survive.

Ro: Some people say that the personalist philosophy actually encourages that kind of chaos.

Kathy: No, I don't think so. No, not at all. We have had guests who, for the first time in their life, are treated as human beings. We have had people who have come through the house and pulled their lives back together. One woman was very, very violent and very hostile when she came. After knowing us for a couple of years, first as a guest and then living close by, she came back one day. She had makeup on and she had done her hair, and she said, "You did so much for me. I want to start doing something for you." So she started cooking meals. The house becomes family.

Debbie: It is family. You know, I've got some aunts who are really strange ladies. My favorite one kind of lives in the soap operas. I've hardly ever watched a soap opera in my life, but I adore this woman. She's good and kind and wonderful, and what I'm saying is when Aunt Jennie is talking about her soap opera world, it would never occur to me to try to argue her out of it. To say it's a terrible value system or anything. This is my aunt. I just love her and I . . . to use a corny word, I kind of embrace that whole thing.

Anyway, that's the kind of attitude to have with the guests, so that you really like them as persons. Sometimes later you do things to help them, but what you need to do first is just *like* them and accept them. If they don't change or get their life together or allow you to be helpful, that's all right. You'll still like them. If they change, that's great, but if they don't, that's okay, too. That's the family thing. One of the fun things is when my children ask me if someone is a Worker or a guest.

First, you start really paying attention to people. For instance, I know that Sue is from a real difficult family background, and she's a very strong feminist because of it, and that she seems very hard and very cold. She used to be an alcoholic and gay and heavily into the bar scene, and now she's quit drinking and is really celibate. And from two packs a day, she hasn't smoked any for about a hundred days. So she's doing wonderfully.

This woman . . . I grew up in the sixties, so I used all the obscene words, you know, but now I'm a mother of seven kids, so I've put all that stuff behind me, and I don't particularly care to get back into it. And Sue . . . it's like she wants to give you this big test to see if you really like her. When I first came here . . . well, she's just a jerk to new people. Really nasty. I hated her at first. She used a lot of bad language in front of my kids, and it made me really uncomfortable. "Where's the fucking milk for the Goddamn dinner, you asshole!" That kind of thing. I was desperately trying to make friends with her, and she was just, you know . . . holding me off. Anyways, now I love her.

She kisses my kids good morning, and she tells me about how she was one of a dozen kids, and her dad beat all of them and none of them have maintained contact, and . . . and I've picked up on the affection she has for the people here. I mean she has a lot of difficulty sharing it, but she really does. She said last night, "I'm not like some of the people around here who have a family. The Catholic Worker is all the family I've got."

Sometimes it happens in the line at the Kitchen. A couple guys start joking, and we're all laughing and it's just . . . it's the feeling of all being in this together. What's that James Joyce line? "The Catholic Church is 'Here comes everybody!'" We'll be connected with somebody a lot older or a lot younger or connected with people who are broken in a way that we're not broken. You cross the barriers.

For example, Bob and my boys and I went to Magic Mountain [one day]. Now I shouldn't even have to pay to get in an amusement park. I mean I can't handle anything scarier than the merry-go-round. But Bob loves this stuff. He's not scared at all, so he could go on all the rides with my kids. Now Bob is kind of . . . I don't know what the word is . . . he's a little retarded, but I think it's emotional rather than an IQ thing. Something's the matter, but when we went to Magic Mountain, he knew more about it than me. (I was scared to death.) I could just turn to him as one person to another and say, "Gee, Bob, I'm really glad you're here. I don't know what I would have done without you." And I wasn't being phony. Somehow it got all scrabbled where we were just two adults, one who was competent—him—and one who was incompetent—me—taking these little kids to Magic Mountain.

John Mahoney (Washington, D.C.): Well, sometimes it's not a "magic mountain." I remember how we missed with Anatoly. Anatoly was in his fifties, maybe. A Russian Jewish immigrant who spoke very little English. Just a real saintly, quiet, beautiful man. If you looked into his eyes, you could see the face of Christ.

When we first arrived at [St. Francis House], one of the women in community would make cheese toast for breakfast—just a plain piece of bread with some cheese on it and toasted in the oven. Anatoly would take a piece and then very softly, very mildly—not using good words but very reverently—he would say, "Thank you very much for breakfast." In his broken English. He never missed a morning.

Because we had a lot of confusion going on in the beginning, we never picked up on a lot of things. Anatoly had mental illness, severe mental illness, and we hadn't picked up on it. And one day he jumped off a bridge.

Donna Domiziano (Worcester, Massachusetts): Oh, dear! Well, we've had our problems at the Mustard Seed, too. Last year the drugs were pretty bad, but thank goodness, a lot of the drug people moved on. For two reasons, okay? First, a lot of police started to come in and out. We said, "Fine. The Mustard Seed is open to anyone." And that meant police, also.

Some of the clients said, "How come they're coming in?"

I said, "Do I question you?"

"Well, no."

"Well, I don't question them. If you can come in, they can come in. If you're not doing anything, don't worry about it. And if you are, then worry. This is not a church sanctuary, and if they catch you with something on you, they can arrest you. Do you understand?"

"Sure, Donna! We don't have any."

And then I find my first bag of cocaine in the men's room. I used to do spot-checking because of the kids who come around. I was on the warpath. I didn't like playing policewoman. I really . . . it was a hard role, but it had to be done for the safety of people here. So when I found my first little bag of cocaine, I went on a royal Italian rampage. Yelling . . . I was *so* mad! I'm on the bench crying. One of the dealers said, "Just stop crying. I'm going to go out and talk to them. This isn't going to happen again."

He comes back. "Just stop crying. They're going to move on. It's not going to be here anymore. Just stop." And sure enough, they moved on. Out of respect for the place. Not only because they knew I was going to . . . I had to call the police for the cocaine. They knew it. That was an understood thing.

I miss some of them, though. They really were for the poor. A couple of them called from jail. I really do miss them, but they just can't start all that up again.

Now we have a big alcohol problem . . . well, we always have. I went on a rampage last week. I'm raking up the yard and I get down to the far corner and I see all these bottles. So I'm yelling, "I'm sick of it! We're going to put up gates!" When I get mad, I get mad.

But the next night, there wasn't one bottle on the ground. I can't tell you how good they've been since then. So it's developing . . . there's a lot of growth going on. I think things are really growing into a little community and family. Yes. I'm the mother yelling and screaming. I do. I can't help it sometimes. That's the way I feel about it, and they know it. They know they'll hear from me if they act up.

Charles Walzem (Washington, D.C.): The way I see it . . . sometimes it's very disheartening, but we don't force-feed these people. And this could be a shortcoming. Maybe the personalism can sometimes be a cause of their failure, particularly when they're mentally ill. They've been rejected by so many others in society. When they come to us, they have a different feeling of acceptance than they felt in the mental hospital maybe, and they sometimes think they can get off the medication. So maybe the acceptance, in a way, is causing them to get sick again. It's a rather involved question, and it varies from individual to individual. Some individuals are misdiagnosed and don't need that medication. For others, that quite simply isn't so. I would not care to think, even in my wildest nightmares, that their neglect in taking their medication and their follow-up treatment was because of our Catholic Worker so-called personalism. Because some of these people are very unbalanced.

Tom Cornell (Waterbury, Connecticut): We've always asked ourselves, "Are we really doing people a favor when we give them a bowl of soup? Are we perhaps enabling them to continue drinking? To continue malingering? To continue to avoid their responsibilities? Are we confirming them in vice instead of supporting them?"

Ro: Confirming them in dependency?

Tom: Yeah. The question isn't too burdensome to us because the people who come to the Catholic Worker are the most desperate, and our vocation, really, is to the least of these our brothers and sisters. The *least*. Go down to our soup kitchen. Look at the reformable ones. Small percentage. Most are too far gone with drugs, alcohol, and other causes of debility. Just too far gone.

Does the welfare system confirm people in dependency? Should we be enabling them in a positive way instead of enabling them only to continue to squander what little resources they have? The answer that occurs to me is that we need *massive* educational work and massive intervention for the young. I mean even positive intervention on the part of the state. As an anarchist, I'll say this. Let's start with getting sugar out of the diet, or at least lower in the diet. Even the poorest people I know will recognize that their children should not be allowed to eat all the candy they want. They don't know about hypoglycemia; it's too many syllables. But with some basic education, you can teach them to cut down the sugar, and they find that their kids act better.

Teaching women how to shop, how to cook. The enormous amount of waste that you see in the supermarket cart. A woman pays for this stuff with food stamps, and most of it is shit. Processed food full of poisons. She brings the stuff home to three or four kids in a three-room apartment with no central heating, just a space heater somewhere. And inevitably the television, usually with cable for which she's paying twelve dollars a month at least. And that television set is never turned off until everyone is asleep.

Ro: Education of mothers?

Tom: It's almost always females raising children, but you have to teach men how to be men, too. It's harder to grab them, though. The women are anchored to reality more firmly than men are. The product of the womb follows the womb. And I think that women have a better chance than men. Men seem to be almost ineducable until their late twenties. All this bravado and machismo from the Puerto Rican and black males—it's nothing but a cover-up for a felt insecurity in their masculinity.

It takes more than pollinating to be a father. A bee can pollinate. The men don't even take care of the women; the women take care of them. Here's this boy shouting, "What are you if you don't have a woman?" I go into his apartment. I see a double bed. The woman and the children are in the double bed, and he's on a little mattress in the corner. She calls him over whenever she wants to be serviced. He's a dog on a leash. She gives him money from her AFDC check so he can have a bone or two a day of marijuana. And that's being a man? He's a puppy dog! On a leash.

Ro: Then you're talking about massive early childhood intervention rather than absolutely removing children from their parents.

Tom: They have to be taken away from their mothers, in some circumstances. And in the cases where it's indicated, they shouldn't wait so long.

But the Worker does not spend a hell of a lot of energy addressing the question of what the government should do. We think about what *we* should do— we as individual Christians, as Catholics, as a community of Catholic Christians. It's obvious from the history of the Worker, from the reading, that we *do* make comments about the larger situation, but we don't get bogged down in electoral politics, or in power plays. Catholic Workers do direct service to the poor— the corporal works of mercy and the spiritual works of mercy, too. But I think we sometimes forget that among the spiritual works of mercy is to counsel the doubtful, instruct the ignorant, reprove the sinner.

Hospitality isn't just giving a person a cot underneath the eaves. If each family would take one person—one person!—and lavish enough TLC and time to bring that person along inch by inch . . .

Kathy: I never want Casa Maria to be there to change people. Sometimes we tend to have the social worker attitude: "I'm going to do all these wonderful things for you, and you will change. Just like magic you'll be a totally different person!" It just doesn't happen. I think the bottom line, whether you're a parent or a nurse or a spouse or an art teacher, is just loving that person and really respecting them for what they are, for *who* they are. Not to change them but just to love them.

To take a system that is not working well and to try to create a new system within the older is one kind of change. I think changing systems is good, but I don't think you change people by forcing beliefs or attitudes on them. I have a hard time sometimes, within the Catholic Worker, with people who are busy changing the world but can't be human beings to the people closest to them. But I guess, though, that's part of our human nature, too, one of the things that makes us fallible.

Dennis Coday (Kansas City, Missouri): All of us want to "fix it." We want to straighten out the world, rehabilitate all these alcoholics, take the people off the streets. We've all got the characteristics of codependency. You become so involved with the task to be completed that nothing else is in sight. This wonderful theology and spirituality that we tout in the newsletters and in the books is lost. And the *doing* closes you off to being really present to the people who are here, the guests and the volunteers. That's the core of it, you know, and to lose sight of that . . . if you lose that, then no matter how many people you're feeding, no matter how many diapers you're giving out, no matter how many marches you're going on, it just doesn't make sense anymore.

Margaret Quigley Garvey (South Bend, Indiana): Well, all this being active . . . I remember, Dan Berrigan gave a retreat at Notre Dame a few years ago, a silent retreat on the Book of Revelations. A lot of people said they wanted more lectures about how to be active. But maybe that was what the whole retreat was about—the *right* way to be active. We're already so crazy active, every one of us, that we need this solitude to reflect on what God really wants us to do as individuals.

We always had that at the Catholic Worker. I don't know. I laugh now and say [being at the Davenport Worker] was a piece of cake because if you were totally exhausted, the community could keep the house going and you could get away. And I think that's not the case in most houses now.

Ro: As a mother, I think it would be neat to have somebody "take house" once in a while without me telling them to do it. But what do you do, Kassie, when you need to get away from the house?

Kassie: The language of "getting away . . ." This is my home. It's . . . again, we can all glamorize our lives. I have a friend who has five children and she works and does most of the housework. Anyway, she was fascinated about the cooking for a hundred we do here, and she was asking, "Well, how do you do it? What kind of pots do you have?" Housewife talk.

And then she said, "How often do you cook?"

I said, "Oh, once a week." We burst out laughing. She cooks for seven three times a day, so that's twenty-one times seven a week. You ask if I ever get any respite. You know what the question means. People who have large families also know what it means, but the question wouldn't be put in the same way.

Gary Donatelli (New York City): Well, I enjoyed hospitality most of the time. (And I guess I was good at it.) But there were also times when I was on automatic. "Okay, it's time to be on the door. I'll go down and be Mister Hospitality." Personable. Kind. But when it became all automatic, when my heart wasn't there, that was an indication that I needed to hit the road. I needed something else, so that I could come back and do it well, not just do it.

Richard Cleaver (New York City): Remember? We used to talk about the Martha complex. [That's] when people start getting testy and snatching things out of other people's hands, asking people to do something and then doing it themselves—things like that. [They think] they're the only person doing any work. We'd say, "Ahhhh, a case of the Martha complex. Time to spend the weekend at Staten Island."

I do remember a wonderful story about this! I think it was Kathy Clarkson. We were all going down [to Washington]. They were having a big banquet at the White House for the initialing ceremony of the Panama Canal Treaty. (This would have been in the fall of '77, before Central America was the hot subject. A lot of the Latin American solidarity groups were Argentine exiles and Chilean exiles and so on who lived in New York.) The [Central American exiles] chartered a bus, and there was to be a little demonstration because all the dictators were going to be at this big banquet—Pinochet and all of those people in their big black limousines. And Dorothy said to Kathy, "Oh, you're looking a little peaked. Maybe you should get arrested and spend some time in jail. You need a rest." [Laughter.]

Mary Kay Meyer (Kansas City, Kansas): Washington! We have an inaugural that costs thirty million dollars. Thirty million dollars for twenty-five words! And last winter some of our men froze their feet. Simply because their shoes were so broken. I tend to look at life through our sock box, and our sock box is empty much of the time. And there are empty sock boxes at shelters all over the United States.

Ro: Now Mary Kay, you work with immigrant men who may be in the country illegally. What would you do if somebody from the immigration service came to you looking for them?

Mary Kay: I would say, "This is our home. Be gone."

Catherine: Well, it's kind of a home for our volunteers, too, the people who don't live with us but come down to help on a regular basis. We have people who've been coming for years and years and years. They're like family. You know, if Pat Carter is here, it's either a Monday or a Wednesday. Bob Koenig is at the kitchen twice a week, all through the winter. Dozens and dozens of people that we've known for years. And we affect them. We aren't making converts to our own lifestyle, but in talking to people . . . A couple of years ago Bob Koenig had never even been to a demonstration. And now he goes out to the Nevada Test Site with us. He goes across the line with us. Last time his wife went across, too.

We've watched people who think that serving the poor is just a beautiful thing and that's why they've come to work at the kitchen, watched them start making the connections that we talk about, and the connections that are visualized by the posters and the leaflets on the refrigerators. And when we close the kitchen to go to demonstrations, they start realizing that the arms race is the other side of the coin of poverty. Like one woman . . . she had worked with us all summer. Teaches history in a pretigious school. When she went back to the faculty meeting in September, they all went around in a circle and talked about their summers. This person had been to Tanzania and that person to Paris and this person had been here and there. She said, "Well, I've been working on Skid Row." She told us that afterwards they asked her more questions than anybody else.

Pat Carter just does it all. He's a retired pilot who raised nine kids and knows how to fix everything. There's always a sign for him slapped up on the refrigerator door. "Pat Carter, change the toilet seats" or "Fix the kitchen drain."

He tells us all the time, "I hope you realize how grateful I am that you've got this kitchen here." He just loves working. He's sixty going on forty-two, and retirement was a big blow to him. (His wife told us that for the first couple of years, he'd just mope around, until he found a second vocation here.) He doesn't see civil disobedience tóo much, but he'll drive us out to Las Vegas anytime. And he's definitely a Catholic Worker, too.

Larry Ray-Keil (Seattle): You should see some of the older volunteers we have. They're just . . . they think this is the greatest change that's ever happened in their lives. One woman has Alzheimer's. She forgets everything else in her life, but she'll get here. She does the bread wonderfully, slices and butters all of it.

Ro: That's interesting. This may be the one time when she really feels she's existing. What about the power relations between staff and guests?

Teka Childress (St. Louis): Because we run the house and the guests don't, we have power. There's no getting around it. I decide whether *they* stay here. They don't decide whether *I* stay here. There's no way that can be a relationship without some sort of power. Now I . . . what I strive to do is not to be arbitrary in how I exercise the power. Not do it because they made me mad or hurt my feelings or some such thing. There's no way [the relationships will be any different] unless we change and this becomes a house where everybody lives here permanently and guests have the responsibility of saying who stays and who doesn't. Unless it becomes completely their house, too, and then you can't do shelter anymore.

I realize the power, but I also realize I don't have the right not to exercise it. With the people we have who are mentally ill and absolutely unable or unwilling to make decisions, it would be less Christian and less loving to not exercise it. So I have to. That doesn't mean I feel very good about it, even still.

Jonathan Kirkendall (Washington, D.C.): We're right in the middle of our revolution at Dorothy Day House. We're trying to share this power around, trying to have everybody more involved, trying to break down as many barriers as we can between what were formerly known as "guests" and formerly known as "staff."

That's a model that institutional shelters work out of. Actually, I think we fell into it by default. We weren't trying to be a shelter, but people come here who have been in the system, and they would classify us as counselors or staff workers, and call us that, so we'd call ourselves that. For instance, we used to sit separately for meals, staff at some tables, families at some. Now we put the three tables together, and we all sit around one big table. The difficulty is balancing those of us who *want* to be here and those of us who *have* to be here. When people who have to be here have been with us for quite a while, we can't just go by the guidelines anymore. They enter our lives. We realized that we couldn't continue to follow the guidelines and apply them all equally, so we had a revolution.

Ro: How do these guidelines work out?

Jonathan: Well, the guidelines are basic to everyone, and we have the contract, which says how an individual will follow the guidelines. This contract is up for review once a month. People say, "During this one month, I will work on thus and such." I think it helps people order their lives. Now we're rethinking this. We don't know what it means yet. We're doing away with these general guidelines, and we want to walk more closely with people.

Our revolution meeting was the first meeting we'd ever had that wasn't just staff. Before we had it, we talked among the Catholic Workers. "What does it mean to be equal with your guests? What does it mean to be community with these people?" At the meeting, the guests talked about their disputes and their problems in living here. And we talked about our problems living here.

It was disorganized. All of the kids came—three infants, a six-year-old, a seven-year-old, an eight-year-old, an eleven-year-old. Chaos! The mothers have some very good ideas, though, and it was very exciting. For example, one of the complaints was that the guidelines give staff access to all the guest rooms, night or day. One woman said, "I feel like I'm living in somebody else's house." We're trying to erase that feeling.

But last weekend was very hard. Frankly, I think it was the hardest weekend I've ever had here. Linda had the relapse. We had to call Protective Services because we knew she was doing drugs and in a crack house, and we had to do something to help the children. We had to deal with them Saturday night and there was a drug bust across the street that night, too. Then we had to talk to the social worker about Linda. It was an awful weekend, just awful!

I went up later Sunday night to check on Linda's boys. The eight-year-old had crawled down from his bunk bed and snuggled into bed with his brother. And it just broke my heart to see them. These wonderful, normal kids. Uh . . . innocent—that's the word I want. Not naive, but innocent. Good kids, not little monsters.

And I just . . . I went to my room and wrote in my journal. I was just so angry that nothing was going right, that we had stepped out for this woman over and over again, and then she abandons her kids. I wrote, "Tonight I do not believe that God is on the side of the poor, but I know that I am. Jesus Christ, you are absolutely meaningless to me!"

I was really getting down. I have chronic pain from an injury and when I get anxious, the pain is just debilitating. I had to get out, so I went to a friend's house with a swimming pool. (Obviously on the other side of town.) I told her I didn't believe in God and His option for the poor. I just didn't understand what was going on. Now this is this middle-aged, very upper-middle-class woman. And she told me, "It's not that God doesn't have a place for the poor. Jesus put his ass on the cross for us. And told us, 'The least you can do is open up your heart to the poor.'"

And suddenly I realized that the reason I didn't see or feel God's presence was because I was in the middle of God's presence. I couldn't see God in all this because I was in the middle of God—walking with Linda, giving her one more chance. God wants us to walk with each other. There is no one else. And where I was became a very good place to be.

CHAPTER 9

Protest and Resistance

A Roundtable Discussion

Prison can be a sane place to be when times are insane.

—Tom Lewis

I remember once we saw a train stopped on a siding. It was coming from the [Rock Island] Arsenal. All these flatcars loaded down with howitzers. Bound for Thailand. Here they are shipping these things out right under our noses!

The train was stopped. And so the first thing we do is run and get some bedsheets and make up some banners and run out there and at least *label* the thing. Just as we're about to take a lunch break, and as a couple people have vowed to actually stand in front of the train when it begins to move, zip, it's gone. At a moment when there's only two of us holding a banner. We like run alongside the thing as best we can until it's out of sight. And we just felt so helpless and so stupid and so worthless and so inconsequential. Of all things and at all times! We . . . we should have been able to do something.

—Chuck Trapkus

Rachelle Linner has the best line: "In the olden days, we used to get plenary indulgences. Now we get prison sentences."

—Margaret Quigley Garvey

I celebrate Christmas even though Christ doesn't come. And Easter, even though a lot of the Resurrection I don't see. So I guess I do [resistance] as a spirituality and as a prayer. You know, Gandhi said about Smuts, the [apartheid] leader in South Africa: "He won't stop fighting because he has no more strength to fight, he'll stop fighting because he has no more *heart* to fight." Not to win out over them, but to win them over.

—Sr. Char Madigan

PROTEST and resistance—or "saying no" and "acting no," as Sojourners Community leader Jim Wallis would say—are important marks of the Catholic Worker movement. Workers point out that they are both protesting and resisting by living counterculturally in community and providing hospitality, but many feel the tension between providing this hospitality and speaking openly and forcefully against policies which make hospitality necessary. While the issues that interest Workers include environmental concerns, urban renewal, the oppression of marginalized people within the Roman Catholic Church, abortion, and the death penalty, most frequently addressed are the government's activities in third world nations and its expensive militarism with the resulting threat of nuclear war.

Protest normally consists of leafleting, marching peacefully with signs and banners which often carry the logo of the *Catholic Worker,* and conducting prayer vigils, including public stations of the cross on Good Friday and other paraliturgical services. Resistance or civil disobedience can range from "crossing the line," a simple trespass action, to the nonviolent property destruction known as Plowshares Disarmament Actions, with imagery taken from the biblical prophecy. Plowshares actions can result in long prison sentences, the length depending, it seems, more on the jurisdiction of the trial than on the nature of the action. Sites of both protest and resistance can be military bases, facilities that manufacture or store weapons, nuclear test sites, or government buildings, including local congressional offices. Many Catholic Workers resist the federal tax on long-distance telephone charges, a tax earmarked to pay for past wars; some also resist income taxes.

In the roundtable that follows, we see a diversity of viewpoints. (Because I've composed transitions to construct a group conversation from individual interviews, some of the speakers may sound here as if they're in greater disagreement with each other than is actually the case.) Four Workers talk about tax resistance—an anonymous narrator, Chuck Quilty, Karl Meyer, and Pat Coy. Then Sr. Anna Koop discusses why she chooses hospitality over resistance, and Jane Sammon, Brian Terrell, Steve Soucy, and Mary Aileen Schmeil ponder relationships between Workers and workers and think about communicating with people who don't see things the same way Workers do. Sue Frankel-Streit of Dorothy Day House in Washington, D.C., describes how that group chose a protest site, Willa Bickham of Baltimore's Viva House tells about an unusual resistance action at Johns Hopkins, Chuck Quilty describes his ongoing confrontations with the Rock Island Arsenal, and Chuck Trapkus reveals his sense of loneliness and isolation when the resistance community in Rock Island dwindled. Sr. Char Madigan of the Minneapolis St. Joseph House connects the strands of her life as a Catholic Worker. Tina Sipula, founder of Clare House in Bloomington, Illinois, points out the hierarchical thinking in looking at Plowshares actions as the pinnacle of resistance. Mary West, Jim Forest, and I discuss the relationships between fear and resistance, and Paul Magno, Marcia Timmel, Scott Schaeffer-Duffy, Fr. Tom Lumpkin, Jeff Dietrich, and Darla Bradley talk about life in prison. Finally, Tom Lewis discusses how contemporary Plowshares actions differ from the Vietnam-era draft board raids in which he participated.

Many Catholic Workers don't participate in the national income tax system, by living below the tax level, by not filing, or by taking extra deductions on their tax returns.

Anonymous: When I started reading the *Catholic Worker,* I started thinking about tax resistance. I moved back to Chicago in '73, and every single April fifteenth I thought about tax resistance, but something inside of me . . . I was just locked. There was always some reason. I'd feel like I had to be secure in a job so that I could keep paying on a lease or a car or something like that.

Well, in 1980, Archbishop Romero was assassinated. Just prior to his assassination, he had written an open letter to President Carter asking him not to send military aid to El Salvador, explaining how it was used against the people. And then about five days after he was killed, Carter sent 5.7 million dollars to the government of El Salvador for military credits.

I was so sickened by Archbishop Romero's death and so . . . uh, enlightened by his faithfulness in life that I just . . . the whole tax thing . . . there wasn't any question. There was no tension. I was totally released and freed. I said, "I'll never pay another nickel for military aid anyplace." I was working for Catholic Charities and I just submitted a form to personnel informing them that it was necessary that I change my federal tax status. I filled out the form the right way, and to this day, I don't pay taxes.

I've received twenty-three letters from the IRS since August of this year. It's frustrating. These letters don't even come from people. You don't even have a name to write to. They're just forms with return envelopes to Kansas City.

How do I feel? I feel really pretty peaceful about it. I'm not evading, I'm just saying I won't pay. I will not pay for a war. I live with my mother now, and she's almost eighty-seven years old. She really doesn't understand why I do this. She feels uneasy . . . she's had to accept registered mail from the IRS for me, and that's very nerve-racking to her. I'm sorry that I upset my mother like this, but I'm not going to put other mothers' or grandmothers' lives at risk by paying for war on other people. I would prefer to go to jail. And that would be the worst scenario for her, but it's not as bad as people getting killed.

I know many, many tax resisters. This neighborhood [Uptown in Chicago] is filled with them. So many of these young folks who've come to the neighborhood to work with the soup kitchen or the Catholic Worker—the whole scene here— many of them are tax resisters.

Karl Meyer (Chicago): You see, in 1969, I published an article in the *Catholic Worker* which explained exactly how to claim extra allowances on the W-4. I looked up the IRS regulations and the statutes and found out what the consequences would be and spelled all this out and also advocated that people put the tax refusal money into alternative funds in order to do good things with it.

When we started this W-4 method, we were striking at the foundation of the IRS tax collection system. The IRS had never been bothered very much about tax refusers because they were only a handful of self-employed people whose income probably wasn't very high anyway. Not worth going after. But now this W-4 method made tax refusal accessible to people who worked for wages and salaries. And suddenly tax resisters were springing up all around the country! It was also taken up by the Libertarian protest movement.

The IRS thought, "We'll nip this in the bud. We'll put some people in jail and strike the fear of God in them." Or fear of the IRS. Well, making martyrs really works: more people just hear about it. But they tried. Within a period of a couple years, they indicted maybe a dozen people for W-4. I got the most time because I was the inventor or leader of it. I got one year maximum on two counts to be served consecutively. Served nine months.

Since that time, though, the IRS knows there's nothing they can do to me. They can't put me in jail without a trial, and they don't want to give that type of public relations to the idea. They think they can intimidate you. But once they find you can't be intimidated . . . and they know they can't collect, so I'm invulnerable to them.

Let me sing you a song. I wrote a duet some years ago called "Some Enchanted Tax Men." It's between agent Roy Suzuki of the IRS and his boss when he gets back to the IRS office to report on his day of collecting. I hope I remember it. [Coughs.] Okay, this is how it goes:

> *Some enchanted evening*
> *You may meet a stranger.*
> *You may meet a stranger*
> *Across a crowded room.*
> *He'll pull out his badge*
> *And ask for your wage.*

And it goes on like that. Then later he says,

Who would believe it?
Who would say it's so?
I found him at [the book store]. I collected dough.
(His boss says) Oh, Suzuki, how did you know?
Now that you found him, never let him go.
Don't get sentimental. Remember he's your foe.
Now that you found him, never let him go.

And there's more, between Suzuki and his boss. I used to sing it on tax day. Anyway, once when I was leafleting in front of the IRS building, I saw a man standing nearby, listening to me and watching. He asked for a copy of [my handout]. And then another one. Then I recognized him. Roy Suzuki! He wanted a copy of the paper that had the song about him.

Chuck Quilty (Rock Island, Illinois): You know, I've been a tax resister for over twenty years now. Started with telephone tax resistance around '68. Then I suppose, in a sense, the fact that I didn't have any income . . . income tax resistance started then, too. I still consider going below the poverty level or having no income as probably the best form of [tax resistance].

I think I stopped withholding for somewhere between six and eight years. Right at the height of the Vietnam War. But towards the end of that war, evidently the problem was becoming so severe that they were getting concerned about it, so they decided to pick some select political examples. I was the one in the Midwest chosen to be sacrificed upon the altar. And that was quite an experience! That was the first real serious prison sentence I was looking at. I ended up getting six years probation, three years on each count but served concurrently, so I spent a total of three years on probation, which is not a big deal.

Ro: Didn't they try to take your house?

Chuck: Yeah, they did that a few years ago. Tried to seize this house. We framed the seizure notice. [Laughs.] Seriously, I think we have to hang those symbols out and let people know where we stand. The bit about the house was pure harassment anyway. I think they were after eight hundred dollars.

Once something they were investigating me for was thrown into automatic collection erroneously. I contacted the IRS lawyers in Chicago and told them, "You guys made a mistake. This was thrown into collection; I should be in audit." They said, "Yeah, you're right, but we can't do anything about it now. We can't stop our system." So they came after me and levied my check at the time. For three months straight. Didn't leave me a thing to eat, which was illegal. Anyway, the other year *did* end up in audit. My wife and I were both called in, the only time in the whole twenty years. Judy was very nervous about it. I'd had contacts with all the agents and gone through the trials with them and everything, so I told her to relax and enjoy it.

"Just let me do the talking. We're really going to have a good time." (I was hoping it would come out that way, anyway.) We walked in, and this guy announced right off the bat that they had dropped the criminal fraud charges, but he was charging me with civil fraud. The penalty would be half the taxes that I owed. I started laughing at him. "I'll write my own brief to Chicago and beat you out of that so fast you won't know what hit you!" (Afterwards, I did write a one-page letter as a brief and never heard another thing about it.)

Anyway, in the course of the conversation that day, we got to talking about resistance and Vietnam and the whole bit. I got this guy so nervous, he got up and bumped into a chair and looked down at it and said, "Excuse me." So Judy *did* end up laughing!

If you ever want to find out how to take on the government, pretend you're not afraid. Even if you have to fake it. Because they don't know how to deal with people who aren't intimidated.

Oh, I've got another funny resistance story for you. Gary Eklund was the first Iowa resister to the [reinstated] draft [registration], and his name was turned over for prosecution. A bunch of us got together and decided we'd support him, but we didn't have enough money to take out a full-page ad. So we decided to buy this little itsy-bitsy ad on the back of the paper and see if anybody picked up on it. The ad announced that some eight of us would be showing up at the FBI office on Friday at such and such a time to turn ourselves in for aiding and abetting draft resisters. Sure enough, the press picked it up, so front page. Free.

Pat Coy (St. Louis): We still have a tax resistance group here in St. Louis. Some of us from the Worker were founders. We have an escrow account and an alternative fund. We have quite a bit of money in both, and we use the interest from those accounts for funding social change activities—giving no-interest loans and financing them. Some of us are still publicly resisting. We usually do one or two public actions a year, one around tax day and then one sometime in January or February. We have a public education forum of some sort, you know, to invite people into dialogue about the connections between military taxes and . . . and adherence to the Gospel, I guess.

You know, Martin Luther King used to talk about creating moments of tension. To consciously and pragmatically create a moment of tension where the truth could be spoken. Where falsehood would be stripped away because you would see more clearly the forces of evil and the forces of truth. And so what we'd try to do in our tax resistance was to use those moments when the IRS would confront us by trying to levy our salary. We'd do some publicity and use that moment to give resistant tax monies away publicly. For instance, at one time we created a five-hundred-dollar scholarship at St. Louis U. for black students in financial need. We used resisted federal tax monies. [This was] when the federal government was cutting back on student financial aid in order to fund Reagan's military buildup. We did that sort of thing year after year, giving money to different groups, calling press conferences on the days of levies or when people would be called into the IRS offices.

Ro: Some people see these tension-building but nonviolent acts as provocative and therefore against the spirit of pacifism. How do you answer people who say that?

Pat: Well, first of all, we have to ask about the nature of human relationships. I think we'd all agree that our relationships between each other—people to people, people to institutions, institutions to institutions—all three of those levels have inherently within them a certain degree of tension. It's always present and we know that, even in marriage, even in community life. Now, nonviolent actions create these moments of tension. King used to go around the country creating moments of tension merely by his presence in support of a particular group, like the garbage workers in Memphis or the open housing people in the Northern cities.

I don't think this is provocative in the sense that it provokes violence. It's provocative in the sense that it provokes the necessary condition, the possibility for people to deal with tension creatively. It creates the possibility for us to honestly look within ourselves to find our own violence. And also to name the violence that's always present in our relationships, even our relationships with institutions. It's usually destructive if it's covered up, just like it is in our personal relations.

Ro: In other words, pacifism does not just mean smoothing over tensions?

Pat: Right. Quite to the contrary. Pacifism has almost nothing to do with passivity, which is what it is often confused with. It has to do with courage, and it has to do with honesty. Honesty to the moment. It doesn't have to do with sitting back and not becoming involved but rather with the opposite—putting forth the truth and trying to be honest with ourselves in that process.

Ro: Let's talk about other forms of protest and resistance. Anna, Rocky Flats has been part of your focus from the beginning, hasn't it?

Sr. Anna Koop (Denver): Yes. The activity at Rocky Flats—in terms of a large campaign, the national rallies and such—started right when we were beginning the house.

Ro: Now your housemate, Jennifer Haines, spends so much time in jail, and you don't. Why not?

Anna: Well, I don't know. Maybe I'm chicken. I think it's because my calling is hospitality. Which is not to say that I don't ever feel moved. (I have been arrested a number of times.) The reason I've chosen not to spend long periods of time in jail is because I have really allowed myself to become an anchor at the house. And I'd need to know that somebody else was there who felt comfortable with providing that.

Jane Sammon (New York City): Well, Dorothy always emphasized that what we were supposed to be doing first and foremost were the corporal works of mercy. And out of that, other things might come. It wouldn't be like one as opposed to the other. And that yes, of course, you're going to make the connections, and you're going to take up a stand as she did with the . . . whether it was with the air raid drills in the fifties or anything else. But it wasn't going to become specialized. We're not just a soup kitchen. Or not just a resistance community. There's always the primacy of the spiritual and that's what motivates the life here. It isn't that everybody ever coming to the Worker is going to be going to Mass daily or that people are even going to take part in prayer, but we can't dismiss that as the foundation. And that will have to continue as well as other things for a place to be called a Catholic Worker house. Maybe all these other things we speak about are matters of personal pride that we're not even aware of, do you know? So that's the end of my sermon. [Laughs.]

Ro: Well, I hear so many people talk about being called to do civil disobedience. What if someone gets this "call?"

Jane: I think we can become very aware of our own need to protest a certain situation, become filled with that and maybe objectify the people who might be . . . whether they're [working] in [a weapons] plant, whether they're at the Riverside Research Institute, whether they're in the IRS building. I don't think destroying property, even if one says this property is illegal to be held by the government in the first place . . . I think at times [an action like this] just doesn't assume those who work there are human. Not intentionally, perhaps. I just think that one has to be very careful in trying to welcome someone else into one's point of view for the sake of conversion.

When we're younger, we get a little more seduced by our own rhetoric. At times that could become very alienating. There has to be a certain *posture* of nonviolence, it seems to me. To really learn to listen to another's point of view and respect what another is saying. I know I don't do that half the time. It's a conversion of heart. That doesn't mean you get a little membership card that says now you're truly nonviolent in the face of this person who is considered your adversary.

Also, the Worker offers people a chance to learn the value of manual labor. While you're here, if you *do* get a job, you get one that needs only a body, so that we avoid being seduced into thinking we use our mind but not our hands. The Worker has offered us this chance to redeem ourselves from the idea that we're so divided in the tasks we perform. If we become too entrenched in a world which doesn't show us the life of a working person, it might lead us into mere rhetoric. To be in the place of those who have to use their bodies as a commodity— maybe that sobers one into realizing how people can get caught up in work they can't bear doing, even if it is for the IRS, how work they do just for a paycheck becomes so . . . Does any of this make sense to you?

Brian Terrell (Maloy, Iowa): But have you ever read Hannah Arendt's *Eichmann in Jerusalem?* About the banality of evil. Eichmann wasn't an anti-Semite at all. He was just doing his job. Throughout his career, he gave money to Zionist organizations. Most of the people involved in "the final solution" weren't anti-Semites, just bureaucrats. Just . . . draftees. If the Holocaust had depended upon anti-Semites, it never would've happened. We don't have to worry about bad, evil people. We have to worry about people just doing their jobs.

Ro: People obeying orders.

Brian: Yeah. Even though people here might feel a little bit squeamish, they do it anyway. They're not under any great duress like the young soldiers I saw in Honduras; they're not going to be shot if they quit. For the most part, the people in the U.S. military feel like their bread is buttered by the government. Which it is. They're given a little piece of the action—just enough. They're being exploited, too, but they're given enough to identify with the system.

Lots of folks in the peace movement are always cautioning us to remember that the people on the other side believe in what they're doing just as much as you do, and that we always have to respect that. That's a lot of crap! I've hardly ever met anybody guarding a missile who really believes in their job. Usually they don't even know what they're guarding. "Hell, man, I'm just doin' my job!"

Betsy Keenan (Maloy, Iowa): Well, some of that is denial, too.

Brian: Yeah. But you don't hear the young men guarding the missile silos in Missouri say, "I'm here keeping my country free. This thing is defending us." They know better.

Ro: That seems to be just a media script. Okay, which do you think is the most dangerous, the zealots or the drones?

Brian: There aren't enough zealots. Again, if the Nazi Holocaust had depended upon anti-Semites . . .

Sue Frankel-Streit (Washington, D.C.): I don't know how you talk to them, though. In any way. Because I live in Washington, I see that the whole system is fatally flawed. How can somebody transform their hearts when they have to accept PAC money? Change is not going to come from the top, and we do a lot of protesting, but I feel we don't have a lot of concrete answers. Maybe we [have answers] about the way to live our own lives, but somehow things have to begin to change at another level.

Ro: But you're rejecting the political level.

Sue: Right. What am I saying besides "Give up all your money and live out of the dumpsters"? Everyone's not going to do that. [Sue and her husband Bill Streit later took part in a Plowshares action and served a term in prison.]

Ro: There are so many sites for protest in Washington, Sue. How do you pick which ones to focus on?

Sue: Of course, Catholic Workers aren't alone in all this; there're lots of other groups, some working like we do, such as the Sojourners Community, and others which are more strictly political. But we wanted a new focus a couple years ago, and we learned about the Naval Surface Warfare Center. It's out in the suburbs. Nice neighborhood, and very quiet and kind of low-key. Big golf course in the front. Just a sign that says, "Naval Surface Warfare Center." We sent for some information and got back this pamphlet saying—just bragging, really—how much this place is doing on SDI [Strategic Defense Initiative]. Trident, biological and chemical warfare, all this stuff. So that's started to be one of the places where we vigil and hand out leaflets.

Before that we went out to the Department of Energy. They plan and analyze the nuclear tests in Nevada. We found out that seventy percent of their budget actually goes for nuclear weapons. And this is the Department of *Energy!*

Mary Aileen Schmeil (Chicago): I agree with what you said earlier, Sue. The hardest part is learning how to talk to these people. Or to other people who don't agree with us and don't even understand the problem. It's trying to find the vocabulary and the language, not to change people's minds necessarily, but to at least express that this is a legitimate stance. I think the dialogue is essential, though, because it's in the Gospel dynamics that we have to . . . we can't just go off and become a separatist pacifist movement. It's important that we acknowledge the society we live in. We have to get our hands dirty, without selling out, you know. But there's a thin line. As Yeats said, "I can see nothing clearly. All is mystery."

Willa Bickham (Baltimore): Well, we all try to make some things pretty clear, I guess. For instance, Johns Hopkins gets more money from military research than any other university in the country. We call it Military U. It also happens to be the largest employer in Baltimore. It's the power—the power and the culture of our city, and the status, definitely. People on the board of trustees of Hopkins sit on the boards for the gas and electric companies and the banks and the newspapers. So it's a hard . . . we're really up against it fighting Hopkins.

In the demonstrations we've had out at their lab, when we've done civil disobedience, we often go up on the rooftop. It takes a little engineering. We bring our ladder and very easily get up on the roof, and then take the ladder out on a truck. They take you down in a cherry picker after the police arrest. It's a real naval operation. They lower you down with your police officer, one at a time. So the kids really like that, you know.

Our philosophy certainly is, "If it's not fun, don't do it." Anyone can get so enmeshed and entangled in the day-to-day trivia. Just get caught up in a whirlwind and so hyper about what you have to do for every poor person in the city that you lose sight of the forest. When you can't see that, you could spend your whole life putting on these band-aids and not get to the root of the problem. It's very hard for people to understand the fix between the military budget and the poor, and making that clear is part of our role as a Catholic Worker.

Steve Soucy (Chicago and Orland, Maine): Yeah, but I see it as harder for people to see than you think. My first real live demonstration was when I was visiting the L. A. Catholic Worker. We went to a Pledge of Resistance demonstration out at the Federal Building near UCLA. Kind of a mob scene. A lot of people and very few of us were involved in any of the planning. We were just given the signs and told to march and told how to behave. It felt real weird and uncomfortable, partly because I didn't really see what good it was doing. The big picture I could see. There was a necessity for it. You have to do something, but I didn't really have any opportunity to understand why somebody else disagreed with me or give them any opportunity [to see what we were saying], other than the leaflets.

There was no opportunity for them to understand us in a personal way because . . . and so it was very sterile, you know. There were some pretty heavy actions there, too. They were burying a coffin on the federal grounds, trying their best to get arrested.

Ro: Did they?

Steve: No. Well, I don't think so, or if they were, the charges were dropped. That was kind of new at the time, too. The tactics in California changed from heavy prosecution to no prosecution and trying to defuse it.

Ro: Did that work?

Steve: I don't know. If they're after getting people discouraged and giving up, I don't think that's happened. But I think it also took away a bit of a stage for some of the folks who are demonstrating to get attention.

Ro: Was it coordinated by the Catholic Worker house?

Steve: No, we just went to a big action that the Pledge people did.

Sr. Char Madigan (Minneapolis): On my bad days, you know, I think none of it makes any difference. And then on other days, I think there have been judges who have changed, and who used to put people in jail and now don't. I think there's a tide in this country with people beginning to see that corporate weapon building wasn't for patriotism, but for profit and greed. Our blowing the whistle on that corporate greed is beginning to be accepted. The courts are saying they can't do anything about it because Honeywell isn't on trial, but they're certainly no longer willing to put us in jail.

Ro: Why do you keep doing it?

Char: I celebrate Christmas even though Christ doesn't come. Or Easter, even though a lot of the Resurrection I don't see. So I guess I do it as a spirituality and as a prayer. You know, Gandhi said about Smuts, the [apartheid] leader in South Africa: "He won't stop fighting because he has no more strength to fight, he'll stop fighting because he has no more *heart* to fight." Not to win out over them, but to win them over.

It's a systemic thing. And so a lot of my work is not just standing at Honeywell but talking in the churches. I only talk if they'll let me talk about St. Joe's *and* the Honeywell project, and [make] the connection. But your question about why we keep doing it: perhaps we *are* using energy senselessly. We had hoped eight years ago that we would grow to be thousands and thousands resisting Honeywell, and we haven't. And yet many other peace movements have broken off from the Honeywell Project.

We really are mosquitos on an elephant. It's how you spend your energy. Is this band-aid at St. Joe's a good way to spend your energy? Is nonviolent resistance at Honeywell?

Mary West (Detroit): Our house has been real blessed inasmuch as it's always had people who have expected going to jail as both necessary and desirable. No one has ever been forced to do civil disobedience if they were in the house, and yet it's been kind of a common understanding that it was desirable and that there would be openness to people going to jail and taking time away from the house. So that's supported, and when people come into the house, they implicitly agree to shouldering the extra work if someone goes away.

We really struggle in our own hearts and in our own minds to make the connection between the work that we do at the soup kitchen and at the house, and the work that we do in jail. In some respects we're going to jail to protest the way poor people are treated. All these resources go into armaments, and so there is nothing, or next to nothing, going for poor people.

But you know, the poor people don't necessarily see it that way, though. They just know we're gone, and they think going to jail on trespass charges is absurd. One person asked me, "Why don't you go to jail for B and E? You know, do it for something worthwhile, not this trespass stuff!" So they don't necessarily see us as going to jail for them, and yet we've tried to make that a part of our analysis.

Ro: I was reading something today about protest as a form of empowerment. Could you talk about that?

Mary: Sure. I think there's an ongoing struggle throughout the history of believing people to determine and invest themselves in what the source of power really is. In the Old Testament, the people of Israel are always being tempted to idolatry. That's the big sin—idolatry. They wanted to believe in the idols of war and the idols of fertility and everything that the prevailing culture had to offer.

In our time, it isn't any different. There are idols of eroticism and idols of war in a proportion unimaginable to people in the Old Testament. The seductive power of that kind of idolatry is almost irresistible and the prevailing culture has, by and large, bought into it. And yet there seems to be kind of a remnant, a rag-tag group of people, who find their power in the transcendent, very personal God. To kind of stand against the prevailing culture and witness that power.

I don't think they're ever fooled for very long into thinking that the power is theirs. I don't think that's what protesting means, although it's often misinterpreted that way—that people are seen as being self-righteous and know-it-alls. I think a true witness of protest says that we're real powerless, basically, but that we have found the source of power in a God who loves and gives and is a God of justice and mercy. It works.

You've seen it work at Wurtsmith.* There's a movement of the Spirit. Now I'm not one who easily speaks in charismatic terms at all, and yet, my deepest experiences of the spirit of God have come through liturgies at Wurtsmith. Easter Sunday morning, the first time we went up there to Oscoda, was striking in that respect. We stood literally in the shadows of these bombers, and we were surrounded with machine guns, and we said a Eucharist there, and it was clear where the power was. It was clear to all of us that the power was in these simple elements that this motley group of people stood around, and that it wasn't in those arms at all. I think that when you confront that, when you make your . . . your little prayer in the face of what is symbolic of the powers of war, it's a real spiritual experience, a real transcendent, almost a mystical experience. Emotionally, you know, you're frightened and cold, and you're tired, and yet there's a real spiritual sense of the ultimate power of the Resurrection.

Ro: I think so many people, the people filled with anger and hate . . . at the bottom they're afraid. Maybe we all are. And maybe tapping into this power makes you not afraid.

Mary: Yeah. I think it does, or at least tells you that fear and anger aren't the last thing—aren't the ultimate thing—that there's something beyond that. None of us have denied that we're scared when we go out there. And we're scared about nuclear weapons, and we're scared about the tensions among the superpowers, and yet there's something about that kind of resurrection experience where you understand the power of life over death. That the life of God really has conquered death in an ultimate way.

Jim Forest (New York City): Well, yes, but what about the fear in the other guy? Thomas Merton said the root of war is fear. If that's true, then peace work has to have something to do with helping people overcome that fear. If you manage to reinforce the fear, no matter under what banner you're doing it, you're contributing to the problem of war. In this way, a significant number of peace movement activities probably do more harm than good.

People who see the structures of life collapsing around them . . . they're living in fear. They see everything coming apart at the seams. And then along come reli-

---

* Mary and I have been together in resistance actions at Wurtsmith Air Force Base in Oscoda, Michigan.

gious people, attacking what they see as the structures of society. That's scary to them, too. One of the things that's very often missing in a peace movement is a compassion for—a sense of sympathy for—those people who are frightened by Communism, frightened by change, frightened by AIDS, frightened by divorce rates, frightened by the possibility that their kids are going to end up gay. All the ten thousand things they're worried about . . .

Ro: And you're saying that an act of nonviolent civil resistance makes those people even more afraid.

Jim: It can. I think if there is a sympathy for people who are afraid and you can work from that, you can do some good things with an act of property destruction. It's not inevitably bad. But when it becomes . . . when you decorate it with all kinds of slogans like "This is an act of disarmament," I think that's just American hype. For me, disarmament is when a person who has a weapon puts it away. Gets rid of it. Melts it down.

If I steal your gun from you, that's not an act of disarmament because you want every bit as much to have that weapon in the future as you did in the past. Maybe more. So it's a question of how do we change? How do we become a converted people?

Ro: Maybe what Mary is saying is that the resistance, or the protest, is a way to get rid of our own fear. I'm speaking pretty personally here. I went to the Pentagon all by myself, as part of Jonah House's "Year of Atonement" . . . or "Year of Election," I guess they called it. But really to try to get over my own fear. I felt really vulnerable. Mrs. Middle Class. I'd never even been in the building, and God, it *is* scary! But part of the reason I did it . . . this may sound a little trite . . . but, for me it was meeting the beast. After I went there, I wasn't as afraid anymore. Maybe the people who beat on the silos in a Plowshares action, or do any other kind of protest or resistance, are doing it so they won't be so afraid. Like me.

Jim: Maybe. I don't know. I really don't. I don't want this to come across like some kind of a big attack on the people who do these things 'cause they're wonderful people. Spiritually very deep. And Dorothy felt that way about [the people in the Milwaukee Fourteen action I was involved in]. In the end, she didn't agree with what we had done, but she treasured us and supported us, wrote about us, published our things in the newspaper. [Pause] But she also made it clear that this was not her idea of the best way to bring about the change that we wanted.

Tina Sipula (Bloomington, Illinois): Hospitality comes first. If your cornerstone is going to jail and getting arrested and wearing that red badge of courage, I think you ought to get out. "If you haven't been to jail, you're nothing, and I just really can't talk to you." I feel it everywhere.

Ro: Even in the Worker?

Tina: Yeah. Even in the Worker. I can only speak for me, but I don't judge people who do *not* do it and people who *do* it. I can only think of what they're thinking in terms of Jesus, and I know they're thinking in those terms. How else could anybody go in and hammer a nose cone and take seventeen years in prison? God! *Think* about that! To know that they're going to get seventeen years.* I've spent many, many, many hours thinking about this. And I could do it some day. Today's not my day.

Ro: How will you know?

Tina: I don't know. I don't know. But some day it will come.

Ro: Umm . . . hmm. Chuck Quilty, I always think of you as a longtime Midwest resister. Could you tell us some of your stories about confronting the Rock Island Arsenal?

Chuck: Sure.[†] There was a lot of stuff that we didn't get arrested for—a blood spilling, praying inside the Arsenal at the flagpole, morning prayer services out at Fort Armstrong, stuff like that. That went on for a long time. The real crucial moment came when Brian Terrell and I walked in one December twenty-eighth.[‡] I forget what year—'79 or something like that. We had drawn blood here the night before. My son Danny was this little tyke then. (He was named after Phil and Dan Berrigan.) Lots of the Workers were here, and Danny came out to the kitchen just as my blood was being drawn. He said, "Geez, Dad, you throw some really weird parties!"

---

* Tina is referring here to Fr. Carl Kabat and Helen Woodson, who were sentenced to seventeen years for their Silo Pruning Hooks action in 1984. Helen remains in prison for that action.

† Chuck explains: "The Arsenal is an island in the middle of the Mississippi. Between Illinois and Iowa. It's now officially a federal reservation, [and includes] both Rock Island Arsenal and the headquarters for the United States Army Munitions and Chemical Command, which has three Arsenals under it—Rock Island, Picatinny, and Watervliet. (Possibly Huntsville, Alabama, too.) The U.S. Army Munitions and Chemical Command also runs Savannah Army Depot just north of the Quad Cities, by Palisades State Park. That's the only place in the country that has an army training school for people who handle chemical, nuclear, and biological warfare."

‡ December 28, the Feast of the Holy Innocents, commemorates King Herod's slaughter of the firstborn Jewish children in an attempt to kill Jesus.

We splashed blood all over the front of the administration building. That changed everything. The rules had been broken. We had crossed some line that made it very clear to them that we were dangerous. They refused to call it what it was. They *knew* it was blood, but they called it everything else under the sun. "A red substance." "Paint." Anyway, blood has this ability to soak into brick walls real quickly. When Brian and I were finally released later that day, the fire trucks were still washing down the walls. We've thrown blood over there since then, but usually just on the front lawn. Blood is too powerful to use every day.

At that point, we became dangerous. But it's clear that it's the ideas, not what we're doing. The guards just lost it that day. Brian and I sat down on the front sidewalk and everybody kept coming in—generals and all kinds of bigwigs. Two of them walked up with their guns out, pointed at Brian. "We have orders that you are to leave."

We said, "Okay. We'll probably be done about noon."

It was just meant to be a flippant remark; maybe it was too flippant. These guys whirled around and got on their radios and said, "We need a backup over here. Got two people resisting." Here's two unarmed skinny little runts, and they've got their guns out and on the ready, and they're calling for backup. It just blows my mind sometimes, how intimidated they can be. They treated us pretty rough—drug us by our wrists with handcuffs on behind our backs and that kind of stuff, but nobody got hurt.

From that day on, when people walked in to pray, the association was made. "You're part of the confrontation." People got arrested, whether they were throwing blood or saying a prayer. That went on for a long period. For a long time, they just gave one-year barments.* For some of us, there was fairly frequent violating of these, but even then, nothing ever happened.

You never know what *will* happen, though. You could be going to jail for six months, and then again you might do it a hundred times and never go for one day. That makes it tough. If you knew the rules, you could say, "Okay am I or am I not going to go through this?" But you don't know. You could be throwing the whole thing away every time you go over there.

At any rate, nothing happened until 1982 when things changed again. They decided to get somebody for the first time. On Ash Wednesday, we had a big ceremony with conventional ashes, but burning IRS forms and draft registrations and army literature. There were about twenty security officers in front of the

---

* A "barment" refers to a "ban and bar letter." This quasi-sentence forbids reentry onto the base and says that such reentry will automatically result in arrest. Many military installations issue these letters for first offenders.

gate, and we all started to walk away. Then I don't know what got into me, but I just decided I was going all the way in that day to pray, and that's all there was to it. I said to everybody, "I'm going back. Does anybody want to join me?" I think ten of us ended up being inside. Then three of us went back in on Holy Saturday and were picked up and told they were going to prosecute.

That trial turned out to be one of the very good public events. Carl Kabat and Larry Rosebaugh came down, and they brought one of the Brandywine Mark 12-As that had been stolen from King of Prussia.* We took the thing into the courtroom, and the federal marshals were going bananas. They called the Pentagon and the White House and the FBI and got complete denial that [the weapon] could be there on Rock Island. This federal marshal told me afterwards, "I'm staring at that thing, I know what it is, and they're saying it's not there." It drove him nuts.

They finally decided they could find us guilty, and that was the longest one for me—ninety days. After appeals, I finally went to jail in '84. In Peoria. Between the trial and going to jail, I had reentered the Arsenal about sixty times, and they never did anything about it.

Ro: You know, I'm thinking. One of the essential Gandhian principles is to commit civil disobedience in a spirit of love for the enemy. It doesn't sound like you love these guys much.

Chuck: Well, actually I know some of them very well. I can't say I have good feelings towards all of them—some of them have beaten the crap out of me— but I wouldn't say I hate any of them. There are some of them that I've had very close . . . I'd almost describe it as a friendship. I can't say my heart has always been pure. It wasn't so much aimed towards them—it was the goal.

Ro: Chuck Trapkus, how about you? Now you were in Rock Island when so many resisters in your group went to prison for the Silo Plowshares action. I remember you telling me you felt lonely and isolated.

Chuck Trapkus (Rock Island, Illinois): Oh, really! I *am* lonely. There's just so few people around now to talk with. At the Midwest Sugar Creek CW gatherings every fall, we share some of that with other folks, and I recognize I'm not the freak I seem to be. When we all get together, we have a lonely hearts radical group, I guess. [Laughs.]

---

* Chuck is referring here to the first of the Plowshares resistance actions, which occurred in the General Electric plant in King of Prussia, Pennsylvania, on September 9, 1980.

Ro: Why aren't you active in the other peace groups, like your buddy Chuck Quilty? The diocesan stuff. Or Pax Christi.

Chuck Trapkus: Well, the more you hang around with moderate folks, the more I think you tend to accommodate them. And that's not necessarily a bad thing if you want to reach people where they are, like Quilty does. But he didn't used to feel that way and when I try to figure out why, I think it's because the crowd around him used to be different. I think you always kind of go with the flow, and I just have a harder time going with the flow that's here right now.

Ro: Why?

Chuck Trapkus: There are some things, I guess, that in my mind do not admit of compromise. Like working at the Rock Island Arsenal and also being a member of Pax Christi.

Ro: Sounds pretty elitist.

Chuck Trapkus: Yeah. That's certainly not a compliment. I'm a . . . I'm not interested at this point, I guess, in forming coalitions or in building movements or that kind of thing. I'm more interested in getting my own soul clear. To me it's a real struggle to maintain my . . . who I am and what I believe. I have to remember that my feelings about a lot of things over the past five years haven't really changed so much, but some of my behavior has.

Ro: Why has the behavior changed?

Chuck Trapkus: Because it's too easy to slip out of patterns when others aren't around to keep you in check. That's the value of community.

Ro: So you're the . . . you're having to do all the calling to faithfulness yourself, more or less?

Chuck Trapkus: Calling myself? Right. Calling myself to faithfulness. That's partly why I guess I yearn for a community again.

Chuck Quilty: I can wholly understand your perspective, Chuck. You came to Rock Island and Davenport when there was more resistance going on than there ever had been. It was really intense for a couple years. On the other hand, I can look back over twenty years and see the ebbs and flows, and I guess my feeling is that there's a time to let that happen and [a time] to reflect about what's gone before. The resistance time will come again.

Chuck Trapkus: The most important thing to me is to let our lives conform to what we believe. And so we first have to be real clear about what we believe and how that fits in with the world around us. Then all the movements and everything else doesn't matter. If I'm the only person praying out at the Arsenal, it's just as important to me as if there's five hundred around me. We shouldn't be concerned about whether the press picks up on it or not or whether people are getting a message. You know, the Catholic Worker appealed to me at the beginning but now I think it pretty much *is* me, not something I can take on and put off. And it's all connected at the Rock Island Arsenal—the nuclear and the conventional weapons and the poison gas and everything are all here. It still sends shudders down my back just to talk about it.

Ro: So you're worried about compromise?

Chuck Trapkus: Yeah. It's so easy to ignore the hard issues of our faith. I don't think this would apply so much if you didn't have to keep bringing God into the picture. It's a way of life that wouldn't make sense if God did not exist, as they say. It's very hard to keep in mind what it is we're about, especially when the community dwindles and you have to fend for yourself.

It's also very hard to live in community. It's very hard to be vulnerable and to open yourself enough, not just to the strangers but, more importantly, to the people you're living with on a regular basis. That involves a lot of risk taking. I mean anyone who's married knows the amount of risk taking that's involved. And then living with the knowledge that at any moment you might be called to act on your conscience in ways that are going to jeopardize everything else, maybe even the relationship.

I remember once we were driving across the Centennial Bridge and saw a train stopped on a siding. It was coming from the Arsenal. All these flatcars loaded down with howitzers. We stopped, of course, and went over to inspect a little closer. (You can get right up to them.) The guns were bound for Thailand. Here they are shipping these things out right under our noses! The train was stopped. What do you do? It's like here you have this opportunity and all of us . . . when it comes right down to it, how many of us are willing to actually put our lives on the line?

So the first thing we do is run and get some bedsheets and make up some banners and run out there and at least *label* the thing. That's a good start, right? It isn't long before the newspapers come by with cameras, and they recognize something is going on and then of course, it's not long before the people who are in charge of the train see this, too, and wonder what's happening.

Just as we're about to take a lunch break, and as a couple people have vowed to actually stand in front of the train when it begins to move, zip, it's gone. At a moment when there's only two of us holding a banner. We like run alongside the thing as best we can until it's out of sight. And we just felt so helpless and so stupid and so worthless and so inconsequential. Of all things and at all times! We . . . we should have been able to do something.

So we wait for the next occasion. But do we really? I dread the next occasion in somewhat the same way as I would dread the phone ringing at the Worker house, knowing that I was either going to have to turn somebody away or have to take somebody in. In either case, it involved a problem for my soul and a problem for my body.

Ro: Now some people would call this great guilt.

Chuck Trapkus: Well, it is. But it's not that guilt doesn't belong, for crying out loud! To be a rich Christian really demands guilt. Like in Ron Sider's book, *Rich Christians in an Age of Hunger.* If we don't feel guilt, something's wrong. Guilt alone won't get you into the eye of the needle. It's just something that will last until you can do something about it.

Fr. Tom Lumpkin (Detroit): We're at a point in our history when it's not enough to protest, but there's still a feeling that civil disobedience is not an appropriate response for people of faith. I don't think that any of the people who are resisting have ever said that it's the *only* response, but we're attempting to communicate that it is *one* response, and an appropriate one. If we look at things historically, any social change movement in our country—from women's voting to civil rights to forming the country itself—has been accomplished through a combination of some legal actions and some civil disobedience actions. We need people working on the legal ways, too, you know, need people writing to Congress, and stuff like that. But no significant social change has ever taken place without some element of civil disobedience.

Ro: What was it like being in jail? Maybe it would be good to hear from a number of you about that.

Tom: I've been in jail probably about a dozen times. Always in jail, not in prison. And . . . I've always found it not easy. In some ways, it's like the old seminary. Probably a person who'd been in the old seminary, or a woman who was in a religious community in the old days, would have it easier in jail than would maybe a younger person. In that the environment is very institutional and very male-dominated, of course. Very hierarchical, very ascetic. All that is very similar to what I knew when I was in the seminary. The difference is that it's noisy, while the seminary was quiet. And the company, the conversation, is much coarser and cruder than in the seminary. And, of course, it's extremely confining. That's probably the worst thing. You never get out.

Sometimes you hear people say, "Well, why would you ever want to go to jail, because you'd be so much more effective outside, working and stuff!" I think that's questionable. Maybe it has to be decided by each individual at certain times in their life, but there's certainly all sorts of opportunities to minister in jail. It's not at all that you're just sitting there waiting to resume your life and do your ministry when you get back.

Ro: Have you ever been afraid you were going to be attacked?

Tom: No, not personally. Bill Kellermann's the only one I know, of all the people who have gone to jail around Detroit. (Some of the guys were trying to be macho with him. He never actually was physically harmed, but there were verbal insinuations.)

For resisters it's even better in prison than in jail 'cause they're put in minimum or medium security prisons. And you do get outside, and can work, and have more access. You have more freedom than you do in jail where you're really just cooped up in a small space. (Thank goodness, because it's a longer term.)

Scott Schaeffer-Duffy (Worcester, Massachusetts): Yes, but as Workers in general, we're in control of our own lives in an incredible way. Even in jail, there's *always* something you can do about it. You don't have to accept anything except God's will.

Like when Dan [Ethier] and I were in jail . . . some minor infraction happened in our cell block, and a guard's notebook was thrown in a toilet. We were in a minimum security part of the jail. The guard overreacted to this little prank by having the phones shut off. On a Saturday night yet. Denying all outside recreation, all kinds of things. Also denying people's visits, which were the next day.

Usually what happens is that the guard kind of turns his back. And you turn somebody over. It doesn't matter if it's the person who really did it. That's the way a lot of prisons that I've seen work. They don't investigate infractions, they punish the whole group and then let violence take its course.

Ro: They let the group punish . . .

Scott: Right. Whether it's the [right] person or not. And usually it's not. It's usually whoever's got the shortest time. That's the good side of it. The worst side of it is if there's somebody unpopular or weak. In this case, there was somebody weak. Men began saying, "He must have done it," and leaning on this person, threatening him, to make him confess to this thing, which would have gotten the guy five to ten days in the hole, you know. There were four of us on the tier in from civil disobedience, and so we talked about different responses. Said, "You shouldn't let them [do this]. We're free. We can do anything we want." Then I suggested that we fast until we had our rights restored. This went over like a lead balloon with the men, but it pointed them in a direction, and they finally decided they'd refuse to work. I didn't realize it until afterward, but nothing upsets a prison worse than that. The whole jail system relies on prison labor. And so eventually they . . . Dan, myself, and another guy, Scott Palmeri, were sentenced to thirty days in lockup for "inciting a riot."

When we went before the captain at the disciplinary board hearing . . . they had kept us for three days stripped to our waists in these really cold cells with no bedding, just a metal bunk and no light. Then they bring you before this board, and you've got no representation even though it's supposed to be a little trial. They read the charges, and they ask you if you have anything to say. Almost before you're done speaking, they find you guilty. So I was standing before this captain, and I said to him, "This is a violation of our rights."

And he says . . . he screams at me, puts his face very close to me and says, "You *have* no rights! You're a prisoner. You're a ward of the state."

"I beg to differ with you. Whether you know it or not, you and I are brothers. We're children of the same God, and God loves me as much as God loves you."

Then I said, "We're going to pray and fast for justice, not only for myself but for this prison and all the men on our tier." The prison was stunned. Never heard anybody say anything like this before, you know. Then Dan and I, in our different parts of the jail, fasted for ten days, and then all the charges were dropped.

You can, you know. Whether you're successful or not isn't the issue. In your will, your state of mind, you don't have to succumb. You can just . . . you can be your own person, and it's fun.

Jeff Dietrich (Los Angeles): Well, going to jail was a very, very important part of my life.* A rite of passage, almost, like shooting rapids or something. I can remember the night I got out. My father came over and brought a case of beer, and we had a party. I heard my dad tell someone he was proud of me. And I started bawling. I guess I realized that my going to jail was a way of saying, "This is really a serious commitment, and I'm willing to risk everything on it." It was totally different from my background, and who my parents are and what my experience was in middle-class American life. So it was a break, a maturation. Becoming a man, in a sense, separate from my parents. So to hear my father say

* Jeff described his experiences in *Reluctant Resister.*

that he was proud of something I did, proud of me going to jail, was a real moving experience. A confirmation of who I was as a person, and the values that I had that were distinct from . . . not just his values, but from his as representative of the culture at large. To have that, and then to have the judge change his mind about the sentence, and let me out, and all that publicity and then the book I wrote about it . . . it was very good, but it was real bad, too. I mean I got a swelled head and, you know, I thought I was really great. Now I try to put it in perspective. I only did two months in jail. I haven't done that much time since then. I continue to be challenged by Plowshares people and feel a call to do more but feel, at this point in our history as a Catholic Worker, that it's not possible for me. So I . . . one doesn't want to rest on one's laurels, and it's probably not the best thing in the world to get one's letters published as a young man.

✦

"And they shall beat their swords into plowshares, and their spears into pruning hooks; nation shall not lift up sword against nation, neither shall they learn war anymore" (Isaiah 2:4).

Art Laffin explains Plowshares actions:

> Recognizing the imminent peril nuclear weapons pose for all life and after a process of spiritual preparation and reflection on the Biblical imperative to "beat swords into plowshares," individuals and communities have symbolically yet concretely disarmed components of U.S. first-strike nuclear weapons . . . Accepting full responsibility for their actions, the Plowshares activists have peacefully awaited arrest following each act . . . As of May 1989, over one hundred individuals had participated in these and related disarmament actions . . . In their trials, many have attempted to show that their actions were morally and legally justified, and that their intent was to protect life, not commit a crime. Those convicted for plowshares disarmament actions have received sentences ranging from suspended sentences to seventeen years in prison.*

Unlike the journalists who covered the Catholic ultraresistance during Vietnam and in the early years of the Plowshares actions, the media today is bored with trespass, property destruction, and prison terms. The activities detailed below now receive little publicity except in the newsletters of the Catholic Left. No one is looking and yet the hammering continues.

---

* Art Laffin, "Plowshares-Disarmament Actions, September 1980–May 1989." Pamphlet available from Plowshares New York, 2763 Webster Avenue, Bronx, NY 10458.

Paul Magno (Washington, D.C.): Our [Plowshares] community had very serious discussions about [different outcomes of our action].* We did a "what if" thing. "Now look here. We're going to Florida, which we understand to be a conservative, maybe reactionary, place where we could face real, real consequences. Ten years in jail. Is it still worth it?" "What if we do this and not a soul hears about it? What if Martin Marietta and the local authorities are completely successful in blacking us out? What if we hammer on these weapons and get arrested and thrown in the jail and tried and sent to prison and not a soul ever hears about us? Will it still be worth it?" "What if we're all given ten-year prison sentences and dropped in solitary?"

Ro: Did you ever "what if" that you wouldn't be caught?

Paul: No. We never even contemplated leaving without taking responsibility for our actions.

Ro: Did you as a group talk about the negative aspects of the jail experience?

Paul: I'm trying to remember. In retrospect, I'm not sure we talked enough about jail.

Ro: What were your prison experiences like?

Paul: Well, we spent several months in local jails, but most of the time in federal prison camp. And it *is* a camp. Jail has bars. Prison has high concrete walls and guard towers. A camp doesn't have any fence, only lines that you're not permitted to cross. You're in mental lockup. You can cross the line knowing that when they track you down, they'll send you to a prison. Or you can not cross the line and follow the rules. It was very interesting for me to make decisions not to cross the lines in order to protect some latitude and some stability.

Ro: Did you think it was more coercive than a prison with guard towers?

Paul: Oh, it is. You police yourself rather than all the responsibility for supervision being on the institution. In one respect, it's less dehumanizing, though. In the sense that you do become more responsible for keeping yourself under the government's . . .

   As I thought about it in the long run, having some responsibility over your own life leaves you a more functional human being. If you go into the dungeon for three years, you become dysfunctional in terms of responsibility for yourself. If

---

* Paul took part in the Pershing Plowshares action in 1984 at Martin Marietta in Orlando, Florida.

you spend three years in a cage having your meals shoved in to you, you can see what . . . that's why people come out of prisons socially dysfunctional. They became basically defective as social human beings. It's a cultivated thing. And [the authorities] don't understand why people are recidivists. You know, jails really lobotomize prisoners.

Ro: Yeah. But by your voluntary obedience, by choosing to cooperate, you're buying into what they want you to be.

Paul: Yeah. You're definitely buying into aspects of it. I had what I felt was a very constructive monastic routine by the time I was six months into Allenwood. I worked every morning. Routine maintenance work—mopping floors, washing windows, sweeping, cleaning the dormitory. I found a job where I only worked half the day, so I'd shoot hoops for two hours all by myself. Or else I'd go into the weight room and do some working out. Then in the evening after supper, I'd read my mail and spend two or three hours doing some correspondence. After nine o'clock count, between nine-thirty and ten-thirty, I'd spend an hour with my political friends in discussion. This went on most nights of the week. A very steady rhythm and a very constructive one from the standpoint of my thinking and my prayer and a balance between physical and intellectual work.

Ro: Umm . . . Hmmm. Do you think you'll do another Plowshares action? Or anything else that will get you another long jail term?

Paul: I don't know how I can exempt myself from that kind of risk. You know, we're from the United States, the most powerful country in the world. We largely run the world. And we're able to continue to run it because we make people suffer, both elsewhere and in the third world sectors of our own country.

I watch the consequence of that every day at the [Zacchaeus] soup kitchen. And it doesn't seem to me that we can make our country change, that we can really break the kind of violence that this society generates in the world, unless we seriously commit ourselves to resisting it. If you want to stand with the poor, you have to stand in their experience. You have to take the ride they've been taking. You go to jail. You get marginalized. You enter into their suffering for a little bit, anyway. I was in jail for a little over a year and a half, and that's a paltry suffering compared to . . . uh, fifty thousand kids starving in a day.

Ro: Have you been in jail since the big [sentence]?

Paul: No. I've been on parole and probation, and once I thought I was going to get arrested, but they didn't. It was when we dug a grave on the Pentagon lawn, dug a hole three feet deep, and put a little cardboard child-size coffin into the ground. There were a bunch of cameras around. We knelt and said a prayer and sang a song. Kept waiting for the police to step into the circle and . . . it never happened. I think the Pentagon Federal Protective Service made a decision not to make bad press for themselves that day.

Resistance is really an ongoing workshop. Something of a contemplative experience. We do resistance for its own value, not for its impact on the workers [at the Pentagon] or its impact on the public, but just for what it does for me—the resister.

Ro: So one does resistance for one's own soul?

Paul: Yeah, I think so. Franciscan pilgrims don't go to Assisi to encounter people or to make a public statement. They go for their own spiritual growth, because they need that experience. One does resistance for one's own soul. To restate your place in the world, and your purpose in the world.

Ro: Do you feel drawn to what movement people call "systemic change?"

Paul: Well, I see that it is very, very important.

Ro: I'm talking about you.

Paul: It really needs to happen.

Ro: You, personally.

Paul: Well, what I get apprehensive about . . . let me put it this way. I'm tempted sometimes to do that, but I get apprehensive that I'd get too far removed from my basically healthy outlook on life if I were to . . . for instance, to take a job in a think tank or a lobbying organization. I try to integrate my approach to politics and my approach to faith and lifestyle by assuming that my faith and lifestyle component is invariable and unquestionable. What I do politically can vary as long as it's reconcilable. I guess I'm sort of biased toward making politics secondary, or at least contingent.

I think as often as it's valuable for people to invest themselves in social change organizations, those people always say that the best inspiration—the most important inspiration—they get is from the people who actually *do* it. People who [collect money] for hunger relief are inspired because Mother Teresa goes from person to person in Calcutta. Washes their wounds and hands them food. Michael Harrington . . . as good a book as *The Other America* is and as large an impact as he had, he'd be the first to say the most important inspiration for him was his experience with the Catholic Worker—with people who are doing it. I'd rather be doing it and learning how to do it more creatively, more faithfully and better, because ultimately I think that will be my best contribution to changing the politics of our society. And I think that's not just true for the service work, but also for the resistance work. That's why I think I most prefer to do faith-based prophetic action rather than political organization, rather than popular consciousness-raising or public education. I'll never say "never," though, because I've seen too many people go through too many changes. I've got another forty or fifty years in front of me, God willing. Who knows where life will go in all that time?

Ro: Marcia, can you talk about your experience in resistance, particularly, I guess, about being separated when you were married?

Marcia Timmel (Washington, D.C.): Sure. Let's see. Actually, it was the day after Paul and I got engaged. I was invited to join a Plowshares community, which I did. We managed to squeeze our wedding in four days after the end of my trial and ten days before my sentencing.* But I can speak of the separation, I think, far more acutely from having been the person on the outside when Paul was incarcerated in Florida. That was a horrible time of life for me. It put a lot of stress on our marriage. Paul was in jail for our first wedding anniversary, and counting the time I was in, we were together about eight months in the first three years of our marriage.

When you go to jail, your life goes on hold and nothing . . . is . . . supposed . . . to change. When Paul came out, he was expecting everything to be exactly the way it was, and I saw it as my responsibility to make that happen for him. (This is where the whole "good wife" syndrome comes in. It was not a whole lot different than Harriet Nelson wanting to have a nice meal for Ozzie. I mean, it's just what's drilled into women. Whatever our husbands want is what we're supposed to deliver.)

Well, when I got back from being in Florida near Paul, I walked into a situation in our community [that had already changed]. I kept feeling that if I could just give a little more and be a little bit more competent, I could fix it up and not let Paul down. Finally, though, there was a point when I told Paul that I just didn't know if I had the strength to hold it together. And that was devastating to him. He said, "You've got to. If you don't, I won't have any home to come home to. If you go somewhere else, it will be your home, but it won't be *our* home."

And I felt, "Great! If this community falls apart, not only has my dream and my community and everything that I've sweated for gone down, I've failed in marriage, too." And it was . . . I don't think that was how he was intending it.

* Marcia took part in the Plowshares Number Four in 1982 at General Dynamics at Groton, Connecticut.

I talked to my spiritual director. "I can't bear it anymore. I'm so tired." I was just a mess. Shaking and crying. He told me I had to take time off. Paul didn't understand at all for a while, but finally he heard how all of this was killing me and he began to see. And we worked it out that time.

Ro: So you think it's easiest to be the one in jail.

Marcia: Before we had children, I definitely would say it was easier inside. Now, when I think about being separated from the kids for longer than a few days, I just take a deep breath. I don't know now which would be more painful.

Ro: Darla, you were the youngest person ever to do a Plowshares action, weren't you? *

Darla Bradley (Davenport, Iowa, and Chicago): Yeah. I was twenty-two when I got arrested.

Ro: Can you kind of trace your motivation there? What made you decide to do it?

Darla: Well, it was kind of circumstance. I happened to be in the right place at the right time. I'd heard about Plowshares [actions] in college, and I thought they were really good, 'cause I really like actions that concretely do what you want to have happen. Also, the idea of taking . . . of defining the law by a higher standard than our government.

Oh, there were so many factors! I don't think you can make a decision like that from just one thing. Part of it was making a life choice and [the Plowshares action] was a real concrete way to do that, I think. Part of it, too . . . oh, I don't know how to say this, but kind of a response on behalf of the [homeless] women I worked with at Ruth's Shelter [in Chicago]. Just seeing the strong connection— or contrast—between the care and protection the weapons system is given ver- sus the care we give to people, you know. It seemed like a closely knit thing, the right thing to do out of the context of what I had been doing at the shelter. And I didn't have any real commitments in my life, so it seemed like a good time.

Ro: How did it feel not to go to jail right away?

Darla: It was kind of like marking time, I guess. You know you have this prison sentence ahead of you, so being out is really awful. We had trouble getting along in community, you know, because of all the pressure and . . . and it was just really hard. It was definitely the hardest time I've ever had in my life.

* Darla was one of the Silo Plowshares, a group of six resisters with ties to the Quad City Catholic Worker community. They entered two Minuteman missile silos in Missouri on Good Friday of 1986, damaging the silo covers and pouring blood on them.

How many times do you say good-bye to somebody? My parents were more upset before I went to prison, but once I got there, they were okay 'cause they realized *I* was okay. They don't share my politics, either.

Ro: But they didn't say, "You're not my daughter" or anything real dramatic?

Darla: No. My sister said that I was killing my parents, though. She was pretty bad. Yeah, she was . . . she was bad. She lives in Dallas, near Fort Worth women's prison. It was like, "Oh, God! Anywhere but Fort Worth!" And then, of course, I was sent to Fort Worth.*

Ro: Did she visit you very much?

Darla: Yeah, she visited a lot, and it was really hard at first because we weren't getting along at all, but she's like very loyal to the family, so we kind of developed a relationship out of that, I guess. I didn't like visits. They were kind of weird.

Ro: Define that.

Darla: I guess I was in some sort of twilight zone between . . . I felt very separated from the outside world. Prison was like its own world. And then there's the world out there. When you go into the visiting room, it's in between.

Ro: What were other bad things about being in prison?

Darla: Probably feeling powerless was what got to me most. You know, realizing that the system is so huge and awful. I think that was probably the biggest shock. I'd always known the system from a position of no power, but I [still] felt I controlled my own life, you know. The way you know that it really affects you is that little things really get to you. I can remember one time Jean [Gump] and I were in county jail.† We'd been sentenced for contempt of court for refusing to answer questions about who drove the cars, et cetera. They kept asking the same questions over and over again during the trial, so we got six counts of contempt and were sentenced to seven days.

On the night we thought we were going to get released—they had said we were going to get released at midnight 'cause that's how they do it—we packed up all our little stuff, you know, and got all ready to go.

We were supposed to go downstairs at ten o'clock and they . . . they kept not taking us. At ten-thirty they began to lock down for the night.

"Go to your cells."

---

* Darla was sentenced to eight years with five years probation and ordered to pay $1,680 restitution.
† Jean was a member of the Silo Plowshares with Darla.

"Why?"

"We're not telling you!" They wouldn't tell us anything, just told us we had to go back [to our cells], and they wouldn't tell us whether we were going to leave or not. Finally, they told us we were going to stay the night. And when we asked why, they said they didn't know, which was a lie.

We had already called someone—Father Dick Wempe from Shalom House in Kansas City—to pick us up. They weren't going to let Jean call Dick to tell him not to come, you know, and he was staying up for us, and so . . . It was like all that stuff really made me upset, just because it was like . . . even basic things like not letting us make a telephone call or not telling us why. Just to be mean. That's when I realized that I wouldn't hold up under torture very well. I'd be a mess in no time.

Ro: Was it basically the same thing then, when you got to prison?

Darla: I think they try to break down everyone at some point or another, [either] right when you get in or right before you're going to get out. New people tend to get a lot of extra duty to make sure they realize who's in charge. Then when people are leaving, it's just kind of a parting shot. Either something happens to them and they get a shot, or they get just something to harass them.

Ro: What do you mean, "get a shot"?

Darla: An incident report. [You've] done something wrong and you might get days or something for it. Who knows? Parole boards are horrible. I hated the parole board. Every three months the whole prison would go into depression, you know, because everyone has these high expectations. You hope for the best. Even though you expect it to be the worst, you're really not thinking it's going to be as bad. It was kind of like when I got sentenced. Even though I knew intellectually [that] I'd get a lot of time, I wasn't ready for it. And the same thing with the parole board. Even if everybody talks like they don't believe it, they really get all built up for getting out and then end up being depressed when they don't.

Ro: So not very many people get parole then?

Darla: No. It's usually not good news, at least the first time.*

Ro: So when you finally got your sentence reduced, you'd decided to pay the money back, right?

Darla: Right. I pay them when the pressure gets on.

---

* Darla was granted parole in June 1987 after her sentence had been reduced to one year and she had agreed to pay restitution.

Ro: Did you have to make any other promises?

Darla: I basically promised not to break the law and not to go on a military installation and to pay the restitution. I had a real hard time when I first got out. Feeling guilty because I'd agreed to all the things. Violated what I thought were absolute principles. I'd think, "Jean [Gump] would never do this" or "Ardeth [Platte] would never do this."* I had some big adjustments, just coming to terms with what I decided. And realizing that whether it was the right or wrong choice didn't really matter. It was the choice I made. And it's done.

Ro: I see. Uh . . . it's been a couple of years now. Looking back on it, would you do it again?

Darla: Oh, I hate that question! I knew it was going to come.

Ro: Well, would you? After you pay the money back, for instance?

Darla: Not in Missouri. Although I'll be in a different space then, I don't know if it's worth the time in Missouri. I . . . I . . . it's still a big question. You know, people are getting up to two years [just for trespassing]. I like Plowshares actions, like the idea of disarming the weapon, like everything about them. I . . . I haven't decided whether the price is too high and whether you can do just as much good in another place or not. That's kind of where I'm still debating, and [that debate] will probably go on for a long time.

I still believe in doing resistance. On a lot of levels, Plowshares are very . . . you're choosing to follow your conscience and your ideology and what you think is right and what you believe in over human beings. Well, it *is* choosing human beings, but in the more abstract way. When I decided to get out of jail, I had to call a lot of things into play to analyze everything. On the one level, there were the effects of violating my conscience and also the conscience of the resistance community to a degree. Because whether you choose to resist the state or cooperate with the state, I think [it] has some sort of ripple effect.

There's also all the human level. Like what if the Davenport house didn't survive, you know? What would the human consequences be, the ripple effect of the house closing? And what about the consequence of my family and [their] knowing what my choices were? If I chose politically to stay in, how could they handle that? And then also in my own life—the idea of eight years with no parole, when you're twenty-three or twenty-four . . . to be thirty when I get out. That blew my mind!

* Darla had been imprisoned with another resister, my friend Sr. Ardeth Platte of Oscoda and Saginaw.

Ro: A whole decade gone.

Darla: To spend my twenties in prison. Yeah. Then all of the mixed feelings I had about what happened after the action and how that affected and flavored the action and the whole idea of the bad human relationships that developed.

I think someone who comes from a more ideological perspective can separate these things better than I do. The more intellectual type would see just a right choice; I saw two wrongs. Could only see a wrong choice of staying in and all the pain and suffering or the wrong choice of getting out and the violation of my conscience and the conscience of the community. I think, though, that even though it was a hard choice, it was the right choice for me.

Ro: Now Tom, you're the only person I've talked to who was involved in property destruction during the Vietnam War and is still doing it twenty years later. What differences do you see? *

Tom Lewis (Worcester, Massachusetts): Well, some things are still the same. Both when I was living at Viva House in Baltimore and now, when I'm living across the street from the Mustard Seed in Worcester and helping out there, I've [heard] arguments about who makes the soup if people go to jail. Politically, or maybe pragmatically, it makes more sense to continue serving the soup, but doing what's morally correct involves a kind of trust that someone will replace you.

But the difference: in my experience, and I can sense this with others, within the Plowshare preparation there's far more discernment and preparation than what we were doing with draft board witnesses in the sixties. In fact, the building of community really becomes more important than the action, so that may be what we're learning, actually. And that may be helpful in the future. 'Cause you certainly do live on the edge when you're preparing for a Plowshares—live on the edge spiritually, psychologically, and physically.

Ro: Are the trials different now?

Tom: Well, I've averaged about one a year. Not much jail time. And I've experienced judges telling us to continue the good work and judges throwing us in jail for trying to quote the bishops on civil disobedience. Trials are always new and different. And the fear never wears off. I personally believe in preparing what you're going to say, and then trusting the Spirit. I had written about three dif-

* For Tom's description of the Baltimore Four and Catonsville Nine actions, see Chapter 1. His Transfiguration East Plowshares action in 1987 resulted in a sentence of six months probation and one hundred hours of community service, one of the lowest sentences ever given for such an action.

ferent sentencing statements for our last . . . for our Plowshares and ended up referring to none of them and just really speaking from the heart. Very much caring about the judge, who was a black woman. I said someday we'll all be joining hands and protesting these weapons together—us and the judge and the prosecutor—but that I knew from experience, from the civil rights movement through the last twenty years, that in order for this to happen, some of us have to go to jail. She really didn't have anything to gain politically by going against the government's recommendation, and I respect her for that. She really . . . it was an act of courage on her part. There was a healing going on in that courtroom.

CHAPTER 10

Paper Cranes and Fighter Planes

Kathleen Rumpf of Syracuse, New York

One of the military personnel said, "You've done a million dollars' damage." And I'm thinking, "Oh, come on! How could we do a million dollars' damage?" But then I remembered they spend four hundred dollars on a hammer.

—Kathleen Rumpf

Kathleen Rumpf: I went to the Catholic Worker in '72. Before that, I lived in the South and campaigned for Nixon. I grew up in a very racist, anti-Semitic family and was even out of the church. Really alienated. But a friend I met while I was working in a nursing home started telling me about the Catholic Worker. She was trying to get me to go back to church, but I wouldn't hear it, you know. And then she gave me some of Dorothy's books. Well, I couldn't even read them. I didn't know what she was talking about. "Social justice? What's that?" I'd never even met a vegetarian or a hippie.

I just wasn't part of that circle, couldn't relate to Dorothy's books, but what my friend told me about visiting the Catholic Worker somehow connected. She told me about all the older folks at Tivoli, and I realized they could use the help. But I still don't know what made me do it. I was raised in a very problematic family—alcoholism and certainly a lot of problems. Guess I was just desperate to get away from Florida!

Now this is very humbling to relate, but in the trunk I took to the Catholic Worker, there was a Zsa Zsa Gabor hairpiece. And a polyester evening gown. I took all that stuff right to the farm with me. When I got there, I found out that Stanley Vishnewski was supposed to have written and told me not to come 'cause there was no room. But he forgot or didn't do it, and I showed up. That was the beginning. I was like a duck out of water, but I could do the nursing, and so I spent the first few months just doing that. And watching everybody. I mean, Tivoli was a crazy place!

About eighty people were living there. A lot of people from the psychiatric . . .

just a lot of different people. I wasn't too afraid, but I'd never been around these people before. I had no idea what half of them were talking about, but I could rave on with the best of them after a few weeks. And then Dorothy was coming in and out.

By little and by little, I started absorbing some of the excitement and was able to understand more. My politics were totally opposite at the time. But the more people I was exposed to and talked to, the more I started turning around. I think Vietnam did it for me. Meeting certain people . . . I remember in particular a doctor who was removing legs from people who'd been in the Tiger Cages. And the cages had been made in the United States.

It was slow, and the more I started understanding, the harder it got. I almost had a breakdown when I realized that a lot of what I'd been taught or raised to believe was a lie. It was really, really hard for me, the whole maturing process, I guess I'd call it now. I lost perspective on life. Nothing mattered anymore. But I stayed at Tivoli and worked, worked there for three or four years. I worked and worked to the point . . . and I got TB, and then I had to take a break. So I left briefly.

Yeah. I could talk about just the good times, but that's . . . that's not the real story. I really loved it there at the Worker, but it was hard, the poverty. Once I got the TB, I had to apply for welfare. And my voluntary poverty . . . I'd lived for several years in *voluntary* poverty and all of a sudden, I *really* had nothing.

It was a real hard time to work through the welfare, a really harsh, very truth-revealing lesson to work through that welfare system. I can remember hitchhiking about nineteen miles into Poughkeepsie, in eight-degree weather. To get some boots. I couldn't really ask for help from the Worker because *everybody* was desperate. Plus I just have a hard time asking for what I need. So I went to the welfare people for boots. And I can remember people pointing and laughing and thinking it was funny that I'm freezing on the road. When I got to town, all I could hear was the Christmas music in the mall. I got to the welfare. No help. They turned me away. I said, "Used boots, anything. I just really need them." It was hard lessons I learned there for a while. Hard but good.

But the philosophy of the Worker . . . When I knew Dorothy, it was toward the end of her life. For many years, I never realized what a great woman she was. To me, she was just good and interesting and a good friend. Somebody really nice and compassionate to talk to.

Ro: Did you sit around the table at Tivoli and talk to her a lot?

Kathleen: Yeah. Yeah. And I'd go on trips with her to see her daughter. I liked going to Vermont to visit Tamar, who I still see on occasion . . . just a really wonderful woman. Those were wonderful times. I was always looking for family. And it's pretty scary to identify Catholic Worker as being your family, but they were.

Ro: Why is it scary?

Kathleen: Because it was so crazy. So many comings and goings and attachments. And then looking at the people who weren't so fortunate as I was, really identifying with them, being afraid, 'cause "there but for the grace of God go I." When I was growing up, my mother used to point to the poor people when we were downtown and tell me, "If you're not a good girl, that's what is going to happen to you." So I was raised to believe that people were poor because they were bad or lazy and that they deserved it. And all of a sudden, I was with them and they were family to me. The abuse they took! It's scary to see people dying on the street and to go to Bellevue Hospital with them.

That led me further and further to the point of activism. I'm awful slow. But once I started . . . I began going in and out from the farm to the city all the time. I was very close with several old people at the farm and as they died, I went more into the city to expose myself to that and to learn and to be near Dorothy.

Ro: Did you "come back to the church," as they say?

Kathleen: I would say that I went through a conversion into a real church. And that real church was the Catholic Worker. What I was raised on was not the real church. Everything was fairy tales—no reality.

So I started going more and more into the city. It was mostly derelicts in the Bowery and then all of a sudden, as our governmental policies changed, the homeless population changed—I mean radically. Mental illness is something I've struggled with all my life. And to see what can happen to people with no support system and nobody who cares, to see mentally ill people in the streets—they're really the most desperate of all. And then it was the elderly, and then it was Vietnam veterans, and then it was this one and that one and it . . . I mean it was very easy to see that anybody could end up homeless. The lines were not so far apart anymore. People were in shock. Homelessness is something that's supposed to happen to somebody else, to derelicts. And all of a sudden these people were homeless and just in total despair because they didn't know how this could ever happen to them. They didn't realize how easy it could be.

Answering the phones and turning people away from the door was heartbreaking, actually heartbreaking. And I was tired a lot, too, you know. There weren't enough hands to do the job. I used to cry myself to sleep every night, but I always had a bed. Always had a bed.

Finally, I was hearing more and more about resistance. I had been arrested at nuclear plants and that was always fun for us. We'd go to Seabrook or Indian Point and get arrested and know that we were going to do a few days in jail. It was really good compared to the reality we were living. We would say it was time to go "on retreat" again.

And we could laugh. You have a jail cell to yourself, and you have time to read. It *was* a retreat, really! But the more I was in the jails, and saw the homeless who were jailed, the more I realized that I had no right to go to jail to rest, that there was an awful lot of work to do in there. I started reading about nuclear weapons and the Berrigans and started educating myself and realizing that the money . . . that the problem was the money spent on wars and weapons.

In 1980, I went to the Pentagon for the first time. Went with a vanload of Catholic Workers, and we were all to be arrested. Well, one by one, everybody backed out. Here I am alone at the Pentagon. This is the evil empire and I'm here. I'm saying, "I can't not do this! I just can't *not* do it." So I went to look for another affinity group. I had done a lot of blocking and simple things at the nuclear plants, but I wanted to do something big and symbolic this time. I went from group to group to group, and there were many.

Finally, I came upon this back room. All these interesting faces in this dark corner, you know. I walked in—a total stranger—and said, "I'm looking to do something symbolic, and I can't find anybody to do it with." They were doing blood and ashes, so I asked to join them. And there was this hesitation. (I had no way of knowing these were all the heavies, the so-called resistance heavies, you know.) They're looking at me and, at that point . . . I don't know if I want this in the book or not, but . . .

Ro: You can take it out if you want.

Kathleen: I was, at that point, over four hundred pounds. And so how people responded to this—you know, me walking in this room and not knowing me— I could really understand their hesitation. But there were a few real good souls who just kind of spoke up right away, and I was able to join.

We had all our actions synchronized. All these wonderful plans. I decided to do ashes. I didn't know what I thought of blood, but I know it's hard for a lot of people, and I . . . God! Blood! [Laughs.] So ashes was an easy choice.

I was very moved by the Vietnam veterans. They vigiled all night long out in the bitter cold. You could see the pain in their faces. And some of them were homeless people from CCNV [Community for Creative Non-Violence]. They spent a very bitter night, too.

First, the veterans did a die-in on the front steps of the Pentagon. Well, some of these guys really know how to die! They really caught my eye. I'm supposed to be on the steps throwing the ashes, and instead I'm watching everybody die.

And then I see the blood go up on the pillars of the Pentagon. (This is before they put the plastic on the pillars to keep the blood from staining.) And it was another conversion for me. I thought, "Oh my God! The blood's already there! We've just refused to see it." I saw it. Meanwhile, I'm holding this bag of ashes, and I'm supposed to be up on the steps doing my thing. But I was really, really moved. The symbol became the reality. The veterans are dying and the blood was going up on the pillars, and I really was knowing where I was.

Well, I finally made it up to the steps. I'm taking ashes and pouring them out of a bag, and this policeman taps me on the shoulder. I look at him, expecting him to drag me away, you know, but he's just pointing at the ground. So I look down, and there at my feet is a veteran who had "died," and I'm throwing the ashes right in his mouth. "Oh God! I can't do anything right!"

When I finally got arrested that time, I told the police that if they weren't nice to me, I'd go limp. I always say that now, and I always seem to get my way.

After that, I decided to move to the Baltimore Catholic Worker. I lived there for two years, so I could be close to Jonah House, close to Washington. Resistance became really, really important to me—that whole tradition within the Catholic Worker.

It was really, really hard with the New York Catholic Worker to . . . when I was going to do the Griffiss Plowshares, I was back at the farm at Marlboro, New York, and I was discussing my need to do a Plowshares witness. People just cringed. At that point, I'd been arrested many, many times and had been also in court many times and listened to some of the Plowshares trials. And I thought, you know, if things weren't so imminent, I would never do this. I'd leave it up to the Dorothy Days, the Dan Berrigans, and those wonderful articulate people who I had so much admiration for. I have many contradictions in my life. I watch war films on TV and have these funny little quirks. So who am I to speak the truth?

But then, I was seeing people literally freeze in the streets. It wasn't so much what's going to happen if the bomb drops because I know we're loved by God. I feel so secure in that, that God will be there for us. The real sin is to not speak out now while children are starving and people are dying in the streets.

So I went into the retreat process, and I discussed the Plowshares thing with different people at the Catholic Worker farm. They were frustrated with me, but I was on a mission, and I knew it. I had spent six months reflecting with Phil Berrigan and Liz McAlister at Jonah House, reflecting on whether I was going to do this or not. So I was in and out of the farm. They never knew when I was going to come and when I was going to go.

And then I was in and out of jail so much. Liz described me in court as a one-woman crime wave. Cute, but . . . And I could really understand the frustration at the Marlboro farm because who was going to care for the land and care for the people? But I certainly knew that I had a mission. Painful. One morning I went up to the fields at Marlboro farm to hoe cabbage. I always especially liked the purple cabbages. I was struggling because I knew the people in New York didn't want me to go to Griffiss Air Force Base. And all of a sudden the whole field turned to blood, and the cabbage heads became heads of Salvadorans. I just dropped my hoe and walked off the field. I knew that I couldn't deny what was going on inside of me, and that I had this mission.

I was really heartbroken to leave everybody, but I think it's almost harder for the people who stay behind and do support, because they feel the same frustrations, but they go on with their everyday faithfulness of putting the soup out and taking care of the farm, while [the Plowshares people] could have some kind of celebrity status. There were a lot of tears. "Please don't go. We need your hands."

And I said, "There are never going to be enough hands. We have to make sacrifices, and maybe your sacrifice is me not being here. And my sacrifice is that I'm going to be in prison."

I really expected life in prison. That's what I was trying to prepare myself for because we were the first ones to go onto a military base, and I knew I couldn't do it without expecting life. And then this problem I have with depression. If I don't find hope, I have to make some. There's no hope if people aren't doing anything. The only hope is if we try. And then there's hope to live in. *Real* hope. A very realistic hope.

What we do is very little, we know. People ask me all the time about effectiveness, and I just don't know. I could go nuts if I asked myself if I'm effective while I'm in a jail cell. I want to be effective. God knows I want to be effective! All of us want to be. But I also have to let go of that. This is a witness that goes beyond being effective, that goes into what I believe we should be doing. Into faithfulness.

So much of this was grounded in the Catholic Worker and in the philosophy that I learned there. Some folks ask me if Dorothy would approve destruction of government property. And when I heard Dan Berrigan's definition of property . . . that in the dictionary property means proper, so property means enhancing to life. Those ovens in Germany were not proper. They were non-property, as he would say. Some property has no right to exist.

I know that Dorothy had many struggles with what the Berrigans did. But in the long run, what I felt from Dorothy was that if people really sincerely believed with all their hearts, she would support them. Even if she had disagreements with them, she would support them as people. There were people at the New York Catholic Worker who were in disagreement with what I did and my philosophy and who I was, and that was particularly hard for me. I shed many a tear over that because I thought myself to be a failure at community. I thought if I were really a good community person, people would be with me, people would understand.

Ro: You talked about property that doesn't deserve to exist. Have you ever thought of doing things that are more than symbolically destructive?

Kathleen: No. No. That's real hard for me 'cause I would like to define myself as a pacifist. I just . . . I don't consider a Plowshares a violent action. See, the whole thing is symbolic.

I was having fun the night before we went into Griffiss and joking around and couldn't really sleep. Excited. I felt ready. I kept convincing myself that I wasn't scared. But once I got over the fence, I couldn't breathe. I mean talk about a bunch of klutzes! Vern Rossman drops his hammer and his goggles and we had to go back over the fence to get them. I'm trying to get everybody into the woods before the security car comes around. Meanwhile alarms are going off, but we never did find out what they were.

It was quite a long walk—over the fence, through a field, then through the woods and over a golf course—to the airplane hangar. There were jets sitting around. When I'd been on the base before, there were people all over the place. (I had been almost caught, actually.) But it was a holiday, and we lucked out. They weren't working on the holiday.

And then the doors opened to the B-52, and we went in and began hammering on those weapons. My little hammer would come back and almost fly in my face without leaving a mark. While I was hammering, I realized that I didn't hate these things. Like my hammer blows were not, "I hate this, I hate this." The ring and the ping of the hammer were like bells proclaiming my love of Christ and my love for the people on this planet. Ringing my love in the witness, you know. It was all symbolic.

I also painted on the plane, "This is our cry, this is our prayer of peace in the world." And the symbols that we brought with us—the many pictures of the children, the indictment that we put on the plane, the blood we poured. I hung paper peace cranes on the different engines. The only place [the FBI lab] found my fingerprints on the whole base was on the peace cranes. They kept calling the cranes paper airplanes.

When we went into the hangar, we never expected all the doors to be open and all the lights to be on. We had already played all these different scenarios out—best case, worst case. We decided we would do twenty minutes of symbolic destruction or other symbols, but just hammering. No more than that.

In reality, we were there for about two and a half hours. All that time, we kept looking and wondering what we do next. We didn't want to do more destruction because we had done our symbols, and hung our art, and done some spray painting, too. We were very happy to be able to complete everything we'd wanted to do, like writing the words on the side and on the hangar floor. Finally, we had to wave them down to arrest us.

Ro: So you ran out of things to do?

Kathleen: Yeah. We phoned the press from SAC [Strategic Air Command] top security lines. Someone interrupted us: "This is a top security line, you know." And in the next breath, he said, "Oh, it's Thanksgiving morning. Go ahead."

We sang and prayed on the tarmac. We held our banners. We tried to wave people down. Went inside to make phone calls. Went in to go to the bathroom. Went up into a B-52 and just looked around.

We were charged with sabotage. Had we been about that, we certainly would have had time to do it. In fact, we've been credited with helping security in the United States. Because now they have changed it . . . tightened it.

When we were finally confronted, after we did get somebody to stop, the police asked us, "How did you get on?" And we said, "Well, who wants to know?" Just making jokes.

They said, "You're going to go off the same way you came on." They usually release us at a Burger King. And they were going to do the same thing that night, take us to the Burger King. And I said, "Well, gee, you might want to check Hangar 101 before you release us."

So they go to the hangar and then they get on the walkie-talkies, and then we had about sixteen or eighteen guys with forty-inch necks, marching double time with M-16 rifles. After we had to wave them down so they could see us, after we told them to check the hangar, then they come in with this formation of guys. Have us kneeling in the sand and the dirt, holding rifles on us. Very ironic.

Sitting on that bus . . . we were on the bus for eight, nine hours, and they wouldn't let us talk, and they had us handcuffed behind our backs, and they were somewhat violent. They were waiting for the FBI to come from Albany, and that was quite a trek. But certainly I could understand where they were coming from. That's a gift I've had, raised as I was. I can really understand people and their fears and what they are raised to believe. So it's easier for me to be patient, but it was a very hard eight hours with my hands behind my back and hearing this constant, "Shut up! Shut up!" We'd say, "Well, we didn't join the military. You did."

Ro: They wouldn't let you talk or sing or pray?

Kathleen: No. They didn't.

Ro: Did you try to pray?

Kathleen: Oh, I never stopped.

Ro: I mean out loud.

Kathleen: No. Because at that point, we were all too scared, I think. They'd taken Karl Smith off the bus and they were kind of punching him. He was talking about the Gospels, and they told him that the Bible didn't exist on Griffiss Air Force Base. They said, "Well, that doesn't exist here. This is a military installation."

I didn't expect so many hours of that. I couldn't be . . . I couldn't feel very funny at that point. I ended up being kicked off the bus and kneeling in the dirt. They kept telling us to shut up, and they wouldn't let us go to the bathroom. Different things. I have arthritis, and it was getting very painful. They kept saying, "If you're not quiet, we're going to put you out in the mud."

It was sleeting and snowing and raining all at once, but after I'd had enough, I stood up. "Well, put me out in the mud." And they did. They took me . . . picked me up by my handcuffs and kind of pushed me off and set me down in the mud outside. I got some relief then 'cause I could move around a little more. And the next thing I knew, Vern Rossman was out there with me. And then Liz McAlister was out there with me. That forced them to deal with us. We had been on the bus for so long. Cars were driving by, and we're out there like prisoners of war, you know. Finally, the FBI arrived and started interrogating us, and we got our bologna sandwiches.

One of the military personnel said, "You've done a million dollars' damage."

And I'm thinking, "Oh, come on! How could we do a million dollars' damage?" But then I remembered they spend four hundred dollars on a hammer. And that was contested all the way through the trial. We had Paul Walker saying we did between twelve and fifteen thousand dollars' worth of damage. One interesting thing—the blood did the most damage. It seeps down and corrodes the inside of the engines.

Ro: Did you use your own blood?

Kathleen: Yeah, we did. We got the sabotage charges about two days later. It was funny, too. I have this thing about Cabbage Patch dolls. Cabbage Patch was [the first item] on national and local news for several nights in a row. And after that, they'd get to the news of the protesters who were caught at Griffiss, which was big news for the area. I heard on the news that we'd been charged with sabotage and were facing twenty-five years in prison, so the next morning I woke up and yelled for Liz and Jackie [Allen] and Clare [Grady]. "Well, only twenty-four more years, three hundred and seventy-two more days to go."

Ro: How long . . . did you stay in jail all the time before the trial?

Kathleen: We got kicked out at three and a half weeks. I was never so surprised in all my life. Here I was expecting life in prison, and we go into the courtroom and the judge brings up bail. Well, we don't pay bail. There are too many people sitting in jail who don't have any resources, and we are in solidarity with them, so we never expected to see the outside, but they released us in the custody of different people. I wasn't prepared for that surprise. There's a courtroom full of people from the community, and the judge was questioning our community ties, saying, "You don't even live here."

I stood up and said, "I live wherever people work for peace and justice. That's my home." I told them I was born in Syracuse and was delighted to be back. So we got released three and a half weeks after the Plowshares, to prepare for trial. I remember so vividly walking out of the courtroom, going down the elevator, and then past the desk. I didn't know which way to go. I couldn't understand that I was let loose. I was waiting for somebody to tell me where I should go next 'cause I had already been somewhat institutionalized.

The bishop from here was very good. He came into the jail to talk with us. We were getting some pretty rough treatment, a lot of strip searches, even after he came. There was a shakedown and some real hard, hard situations, but we were adjusting to that whole jail regime, so I was totally off guard to be out. I didn't want to go back to New York City. Everybody went back to their communities, but I stayed here for the six months before our trial. To prepare—to find an office to use, and to start the support work going.

Liz went back to Jonah House, but I didn't feel I had community anymore. And I had . . . it was still festering for me. I have a deep love for the Catholic Worker but at that point, I felt let down, just like I'm sure they felt let down by me. I was in jail three and a half weeks, and I never heard from anybody. I had a lot of time to sit and feel sorry for myself. But eventually things healed and eventually people accepted our witnesses a little bit better. Even New York.

Ro: So you were the first one to come right from a Catholic Worker community to do a Plowshares action?

Kathleen: Yeah. I wanted to be a voice for the voiceless. I stated in court that I wasn't afraid of the bombs dropping, but that I had come across bodies frozen in the streets, and I was more afraid of not speaking. The people who are dying are real faces and real names to me. A lot of people don't . . . didn't care, including my family. I could talk until I was blue in the face, but some people treated the homeless as if they were invisible. I said, "I'm not here for me. I'm here for the homeless." I talked with the jury about my years at the Catholic Worker. Four people on the jury cried. When I was finished, there was dead silence. And the two prosecutors . . . there was nothing they could come back at me with, so I didn't get cross-examined then.

Oh . . . it would be interesting to ask Ann O'Connor at [Catholic Worker] Unity Kitchen about this. We went there one night for a roundtable discussion. And then while I was in prison doing my sentence, I got a newsletter from Unity Kitchen. And they denounced . . . somewhat denounced our witness and said that we weren't truly doing Christ's work. She said that we didn't proclaim the name of Jesus Christ a lot. I'm sitting in a jail cell, and I get this from the Unity Kitchen. I was really, really hurt. And there hasn't been any healing. People have been hurt by their judgmental nature and their . . . their style of Christianity. So even here at the Catholic Worker, there were problems with the witness. But the only one that really affected me was New York Catholic Worker because that was my family. And I was totally convinced about what I was doing, so I could even deal with that.

My biological family? I have a brother who's full time in the National Guard. He's been training in Panama. Head of intelligence. Another brother who's a millionaire. A twin who married a Vietnam veteran who calls Vietnamese "gooks." My stepfather is a retired officer. My mother is a retired postal worker. And my father just a year and a half ago died of . . . in destitute conditions of alcoholism. Totally destitute. When I got out of prison and I went to visit them, every other word was "nigger" and everything was a conflict. And it was just . . . I had enough. I had spent all those years at the Catholic Worker, and I was very faithful in writing many, many times about what I was experiencing. My mother is a convert and a devout Catholic. And when I was home two years ago, she asked me if the Catholic Worker was like the Moonies. That's the last time I've seen my family.

I think it's fear. People don't *want* to hear, sometimes. And I really wanted my family to hear, really wanted their love and support. But we were very traumatized. So I could always understand why . . . we never had a chance to be family, really, to find any real bonding. Because of the alcoholism and all the violence.

Ro: Yeah, I see. How long was your sentence?

Kathleen: Two years. And I did eighteen months. Before I had only done thirty days here, sixty days there, ten days another time. I'd been locked in the psychiatric ward for non-cooperating. I've done many, many jail times, so I knew what I was going to get into. And then to have only the eighteen months. And it really . . . prison was really valuable. I've heard prisons described as the monasteries of the future.

I didn't . . . I couldn't cooperate. I tried to. Well, first I was medically unassigned. I'd had back surgery and bad arthritis, so I spent a lot of time medically unassigned. (Even though there was no such category, even though there should be.) They kept playing with me, and if I got into trouble with caseworkers, then all of a sudden, they'd assign me to the most horrible places. And I would just walk away from it because I couldn't compromise myself.

They knew I was an artist. And the first place they asked me to work was the decal factory which was making decals for the Strategic Air Command—decals of the eagles clutching the missiles. Also a lot of chemicals and bad ventilation, and I couldn't do it. I said to them, "You know, you might want to reconsider this, considering my charge."

There were times when I said, "I wish I could just do my time like the others." They wouldn't let me teach art or pottery or work in the chapel. Anything creative is stifled. I just couldn't do a lot of the stuff. And I would end up in tears, crying my eyes out, and I'd walk back to the cottage and say, "I'm really in trouble." It was a real temptation to be put in the lockdown, to go in confinement where you're by yourself all the time, instead of being in fourteen- and eighteen-bed dormitories like we were in the beginning. But I wanted to stay with the women. As hard as that was. It was almost a drawing string to go within myself in prison.

Ro: But would that have been good if you have a tendency to depression? To go in the lockdown?

Kathleen: I feel like I would've done real well. Could have still had visits. And more time with books and drawing. It was pretty hard dealing with the caseworkers and all those people who have control over your lives. You're totally defenseless.

They'd ask me a simple question: "How are you adjusting?"

"Well, how do you adjust to injustice?" The words would keep going through my mind, and then I'd just sit there crying, and it was the hardest thing for them. They didn't know what to do with me. They can stand almost anything but seeing somebody have real feelings.

They wanted to make me numb. I'm afraid to get numb inside. Numb is what most of the world is . . . uh, where a lot of the world is. I don't really want to stop crying, but I don't want to overdo it, either.

Ro: You haven't done any Plowshares actions since then?

Kathleen: No. The last witness I did, I went back to Griffiss Air Force Base. The banner is in the living room. "Trust in the Star of Peace, not war in the stars." With a woman crying and reaching up to this big star. And we had a big cross. It was Good Friday. I crossed the line.

It's pretty friendly there now. My first arrest after the Plowshares at Griffiss, the investigators just opened themselves to me when I got onto the base. I talked with them. Two detective types said to me, "We're starting to understand what you folks are about. And we somewhat agree with you. But you shouldn't be getting arrested. It's a waste of time. You can do more on the outside."

When I get arrested now, they save my number. They have numbers from one to ten or twenty, depending on how many are arrested. And I told them I always wanted to be a ten. So when I walk in on the base, they give me my ten.

There are some new people, so every once in a while we get pushed around some. They had me handcuffed behind my back last time. And with my arthritis and the high steps into the bus, I just can't do it without using my hands to boost myself up. These guys were new, and I said, "Most of the time they handcuff me in the front." Well, they wouldn't hear of it. So I'm trying to get on the bus and I can't do it, and this one guy kneels down next to me, this soldier in full uniform. He wants me to step on his leg and then step into the bus.

I said, "You don't understand. I can't do that."

"Oh, come on, come on!" And I started laughing because it flashed in my mind that this was the same position a man would use if he was proposing to you.

And I said, "Really. I can't do this." And they insisted. So I take one step on the guy's leg and he falls over. [Laughs.]

Ro: Oh my God!

Kathleen: So I said, "Listen guys. I'm going to be charged with assault if you don't cut it out. Just undo my hands so I can get on the bus." Which they ended up doing, so I could get on by myself.

This time I really didn't expect to see the prosecutor ask for a maximum sentence. Just for me. Nine months in jail and a thousand-dollar fine. Jerry Berrigan has been arrested more than I have, but I did a Plowshares, you know, and he asked for it just for me.

The last judge I really loved a lot. He's dead now. He died, and we have this new judge, so I didn't know what to expect from him. I went to the old judge's funeral and wake. His wife put her arms around me and told me that I was her husband's favorite defendant. And the new judge . . . he was very bored with us.

He told us in the courtroom that our concerns were irrelevant to him. I think he meant to say "irrelevant to the law."

So I didn't know what was going to happen to me. But I got a personal letter from my prosecutor, who had recommended the max. And he apologized. He said, "If anything, I wish that there were more of you getting arrested. I'm no better than a hypocrite because I don't believe in the policies, and I'm here just to get a paycheck. But I want you to know I'm sorry for recommending that sentence."

Well, I didn't get the [maximum] sentence. And I wrote the judge and said, "You might not know this, but I have a whole collection of unpaid fines. It's probably a couple thousand dollars at this point." He gave me a three-hundred-dollar fine, thirty days in jail suspended, and three months unsupervised probation. I told him I wouldn't cooperate with supervised probation, that I could only guarantee fidelity to God, not to the court. Like the banner I made for the action—"Trust in the Star of Peace."

CHAPTER 11

Workers Who Are Scholars

This is the reality which I have to have before my eyes—the bottom
of the pile. We could call it an epistemological principle. Where do you
want to situate yourself to have the clearest vision? For me, there's
no question—this is the place.

—Meg Hyre

T HE ideas were so much a part of our lives." This refrain echoes throughout the interviews, particularly from those who have lived in the New York
Catholic Worker community. The movement has always attracted people who
want to think—and talk, sometimes endlessly—about the theory behind the
work they do. In fact, this emphasis on ideas may be what demarcates the Worker
from other lay Christian communities. The Peter Maurin ideal—workers who
are also scholars—is easier to talk about than to do, but the Workers we hear
in this chapter seem particularly committed to preserving a balance between
hearts, minds, and bodies.

Meg Hyre came to the Worker in New York for two years and then left to
study at Oxford. This conversation occurred shortly after she had returned
to the United States.

Meg Hyre: The Catholic Worker seemed to be a place where one would be pretty
naked. With no . . . no intermediaries, really, between oneself and the people
one came into contact with. No procedures or whatever. I mean you would really
find out what you had or didn't have. But I had read just enough in the paper—
in the house columns, particularly—to encourage me that they were real people
here, and that they had a life, and you could get it down to that level, so it was
approachable.

The other thing that attracted me to the Worker . . . it was an understanding
of the world, a vision that . . . well, I had never come in contact with anything
remotely like it. Reading the *Worker,* to me it was a very hard kind of approach.
There was a real toughness of analysis and a readiness to take things as they

came. An ability to . . . to embrace reality and not to remain blind for the sake of one's peace. That impressed me very much. And also an honesty about the difficulty of the work here, the failures, the vast imperfections. Plus, the sense of humor completely took me.

So all of those things together really made me *have* to come. I came not knowing if I could spend forty-eight hours even, or flee in an opposite direction. But I came and stayed and then stayed some more and stayed some more.

Ro: Did you have a Roman Catholic background?

Meg: No. I converted to Catholicism when I was seventeen. Had no religious upbringing, although there were some pretty terrible years within fundamentalist churches. For me, entering the church was entering into a place where I could really . . . would not have to disown myself, in a way. I mean intellectually, as an individual. There is within the church a sense of the solitary that I didn't find [anywhere else]. And also the Eucharist, the centrality of the Eucharist. All these things. The longer I'm Catholic, the more reasons there are.

I'm here for the foreseeable future. I came back here from Oxford because . . . well, in some ways I feel I never left. I left because I knew I should take this opportunity to study, but it wasn't out of any desire to leave *here,* even though I felt it probably was time to sort of plunge back into the world and see . . . to see how it added up. In some ways this is a sheltered environment. There are challenges that one doesn't have to meet while one's here, challenges particularly of skepticism or, you know, disinterest.

Ro: Were there tensions when you were at Oxford?

Meg: Oh, tension was the whole . . . if I had to put one word on my time there, it was tension. Because after having been formed by those two years, to go back to a university—a place of such privilege—was extremely hard. And I did not . . . I mean it wasn't my cup of tea.

Ro: How did it feel, then, when you came back here?

Meg: Well, it was coming home. Like I had never left. I decided to pursue philosophy [at Oxford] because I felt I had to take the daily experience of being here and bring it to some kind of analytical level. Philosophy was the tool I needed for that. Thank goodness, the philosophy waited until after I had been here because I never would have extracted as much if I'd come to it more innocently.

In some ways, though, it was much more of a struggle because of the effort to integrate what I knew to be the case from my experience here with what I was being handed, which didn't seem to bear any relation.

Ro: That's what you need to talk about in your writing.

Meg: Yes, you're right.

Ro: Is there anything that's keeping you from writing while you're here?

Meg: Well, you've seen enough of this place and other Catholic Worker houses to know the amount of chaos and the . . . It's very hard to set aside time for reading, let alone for writing. Maybe I'm just making excuses . . . well, I'm not completely. We talk about making scholars into workers and the workers into scholars and trying to find that balance. But to have room for scholarship here is difficult indeed. Partly it's a matter of time and feeling scattered. You're so tired at the end of the day.

But let me tell you, if it's going to happen for me anywhere, it would only be here. Or in a setting such as this, where one is attempting to live a life of poverty. This is the reality which I have to have before my eyes—the bottom of the pile. We could call it an epistemological principle. Where do you want to situate yourself to have the clearest vision? For me, there's no question—this is the place.

When I say writing, that's another word, I guess, for thinking, but for me it's only through writing that things really take form. And the other thing . . . you asked me what I learned [at Oxford]. If I had to put it in a word . . . I think it was Feuerbach who said, "Compassion is before thought." If I came back persuaded of any conviction, it's that. One cannot just *think* oneself into a frame of mind of love or compassion. You're there or you're not, and then you do your thinking from that and by that, so that's prior to any thought, any analysis. And that is the antithesis of the tradition of philosophy that Oxford stands in.

I was so blessed in the teachers I had when I came here—Gary Donatelli, Peggy Scherer, Jane Sammon, Frank Donovan, Kassie Temple. I don't know what to say except that they really guided me. From knowing them and seeing them, I was drawn into a different way of being. Each of us can only really deal [with] what's put in front of us and answer the questions that are put to us in all conscience and integrity. Take one step and the next step. The next step could lead to someplace completely different.

Ro: One of the arguments some people have, particularly people who try to make a human science out of spirit, is that Catholic Workers don't do any good because they don't make changes in the system. How would you answer that?

Meg: Well, I think I . . . thank goodness, I think I have a bit more of an answer to that than I might have had two or three years ago. These days I'd probably throw it back on the other party and say, "Well, what do you mean by changes in the system? Where do those get you? Can't that not add up to just more of the same?"

This [idea of changing the system] gets back to all kinds of progressive assumptions, gets back to a very material way of looking at the world. That changing the environment will automatically impinge on the organism, that you can manipulate things and get automatic results.

I also rejected a scientific . . . a world which would say science is basic. There's a reality to that, but it's not the primary reality. I don't buy the primacy of the material. I know it's going to sound really foolhardy or sentimental to say the only fundamental change is the change of heart. But that *is* the change. You can talk about changing systems all you want, but if there isn't that most basic or radical change, if there isn't a conversion of being, then it doesn't really matter what system you've got. If a group of people is trying to live out that conversion, then within that, you could have any number of different written arrangements. Do you know what I'm saying? It's so hard to talk about these things in a way that's really challenging, in a way that's not almost insipid.

Also, it seems to me one of the pervasive difficulties is that we're at a stage of the game where discourse breaks down. People can't even talk to one another. This is something that I also observed during my time in Oxford, how quickly discussions break down to polarization, so constructive discourse [doesn't happen]. In many ways, I think the task is to find a way to talk to one another, to come into contact with [others who have] diverging standpoints and to be able to engage them. I don't see that happening, and I don't know if it's possible.

Maybe we're in a moment of things breaking down. Sometimes I really believe that. That it's out of our hands. We're talking about a civilization which is really . . . you know, sometimes I say we're living a dying civilization. And one sign of this dying is this inability to talk. Where are we seeing the big breaks? I think the question really is, "Am I willing to tough it out with this vast number of people . . . this whole people of God?" Or do I retreat off into my own little enclave for the sake of my purity of spirit? That's an option I find I can't take. It's the via negativa. If you want to talk about various dead ends, for me, that's one of them.

But in terms of this larger question of fostering change, I've become more patient because I see that it's not going to happen in the short term. If it happens, it's going to happen over the very long haul. And I mean "long haul" in that you've got this people of God, people of faith, who are moving through history on this journey to God. And if that's your perspective, then the United States in the twentieth century, this particular time and place, begins to look like pretty small beer. That does not mean that one lets up on the struggle, stops forging forward.

Ro: But you don't look for results.

Meg: And you don't try to take shortcuts. There's something in me that keeps drawing me back to the thick of it. As frightening as that can be. Because in retreat I'm never comfortable. I can't seem to . . . to try to create a situation for myself where justice and peace prevail when that's manifestly not the case in the world at large. One has to be out there, and I would hope that my journey would be ever more toward the center of it, into the thick of it.

It seems to me that the only way to enter that center is through poverty. Well, let me qualify that. To be able to live out that experience of tension isn't really in poverty, it's in not having anything that you are clasping to yourself, not having anything you can't give up. Material poverty and poverty of the spirit, too.

Now whether I will have the nerve to do that is another question. Whether the grace will be given, whether indeed that is what I am going to be about, I don't know. It could be the case that I'll spend the next five or ten years here, but that in the end . . . I don't know. I don't know whether this is really it and yet as I say, if I'm back [after going to Oxford], it's because I haven't found anything better.

But I do find life here taxing. I'm not certain if that's anything I'd ever want you to put in a book because it's counting costs, I guess.

Ro: I think that's a very important point, though. Too many people have an idealistic view.

Meg: This is not a controlled environment, and I value that very much. One cannot exercise a lot of choice over who one is going to be living with, what the circumstances are going to be, what the tasks are going to be, what is going to be asked of one. I've heard myself say, "If that happens, I absolutely cannot take it." And then, of course, it happens and I take it perfectly well. And that giving up—that always daily giving up—of one's self and one's supposed needs. This is one of those things that takes a toll and one has to be vigilant about. If it's causing actual harm, then it's better to find another place. That's one thing; the second and last thing would be that to act in a way . . . to be able to act in a way that's going to foster change—that's the kind of action the Catholic Worker is about—one absolutely has to be rooted in prayer. One acts out of that. Otherwise, I don't see how one could go the distance or have wisdom, patience, balance, vision, any of those things. Particularly wisdom.

One of the things that I so much admire about Dorothy Day is just this balance in her being. It really amounts to a kind of brilliance, to stay on this even keel of seeing things in their right perspective. That, above all, is what one needs to have, and for me, the only place to find that is in God.

I interviewed Angela Jones and Mark White at the Los Angeles Catholic Worker where they had met as members of the community's summer internship program. We can see this couple as representative of the young people who are making a commitment to the Catholic Worker part of their commitment to each other.

Angela Jones: I started the Catholic Worker in Brisbane, Australia, with three or four other people. In 1982. We had a hospitality house, and we were very much into the Peter Maurin vision of cooperative work and village economy. We made bread and soap as a cooperative and sold it—had a shop called Justice Products where we sold our own stuff and also stuff from other Australian and third world cooperatives. And also prisoners' work, crafts and arts and stuff like that.

Ro: How did you get into this?

Angela: Well, we were influenced by reading the *Catholic Worker* and by books about the Catholic Worker. We were politically involved, originally over things like civil liberties in Queensland and uranium mining in Australia, and so we became interested in the Catholic Worker through their kind of radicalism, and through seeing that as an expression of one's Catholicism. A fitting together. We were trying to say the world can live together in peace. But just try getting together with six other people! You find it's practically impossible. People had different ideas about hospitality, about everything, so we finally decided we needed to leave each other.

Ro: Why did you decide to come to L.A.?

Angela: Well, we had all dreamed of coming to the States. You know, we were the only Catholic Worker in Australia, and it got a little lonely sometimes. We didn't know if we really looked like we were supposed to or anything. I came to the States and really liked it here in Los Angeles, so I decided to stay.

Ro: Mark, how did you get to L.A.?

Mark White: Well, I had just graduated from college, from the University of Tennessee. And I wanted to get out of Tennessee. I'd been a Catholic convert for about a year. I was converted to the Catholic Church in Belgium, while I was studying theology at Louvain. I'd been reading a lot of decentralist stuff and critiques of urbanization and things like that. Becoming interested in Peter Maurin. By the time I graduated, I knew I wanted to do a year of service, but I was fully intending to go to graduate school and study the New Testament, get a Ph.D. in New Testament.

I came out here [to the L.A. Catholic Worker] just intending to do the summer internship program. It was very life-changing for me. It was really the first time I had felt hands-on Christianity, really living out the things I'd read about in the Gospels. And it was really a strong call to me, but it also caused a lot of tension because I was on this very academic path. The Catholic Worker is a path which calls for daily practice of the works of mercy, and I couldn't really figure out how those two could be resolved.

Ro: Is there tension with your folks?

Mark: They think it's bizarre. I remember my mother calling me at nine-thirty one Sunday morning after I had decided to stay. And she's saying things like, "Why are you wasting your life on Skid Row? Why aren't you going to school? What are you doing with your life, anyway?"

"Mom, I'm not trying to *do* anything." I think the Gospel has been too tamed in our culture. People don't do wild and crazy things like go off and live on Skid Row or go to the desert. But maybe it was always like that. Maybe people have always raised an eyebrow. My mother keeps on asking me if I've decided what I'm going to do with my life or if I'm going to do something called "social service." And I really retreat from that idea, that it's something special or something that some Christians are called to do and some Christians aren't. That's not how I understand the Gospel. When Christ was talking about the works of mercy, the beauty of what He was saying is that if you want to be a disciple, you have to do these things. It's not like your career path or something. It's not just a job. It's being faithful and that means a large thing.

The Gospel has been so subverted and so assumed into the culture that our mind just glides over it. That is *so* contrary to what the Gospels are intending! The Parables were intended by Jesus as a subversive strategy. To get people to open their mouths in amazement and to be shocked—shocked into this new level of awareness. Almost like a Zen koan. It doesn't happen now. It's so familiar. But that's how tradition always works, I think.

In fact, it's how the Catholic Worker tradition works, too. You've got this powerful original vision and then, as time wears on, it starts to wear down around the edges and gets more familiar and comfortable. But there's always the possibility it can be revitalized.

It's a peculiar thing. I don't really know all the dynamics of it but . . . in the thirties and early forties, people really thought they were going to change the social order. The Catholic Worker thought the revolution was just minutes away, that it was really a possibility. After the war, it looked like that was not so likely. And then the military-industrial complex got off to a start. Catholic Workers start getting more into resistance as a witness against all the stuff that's going on. Reconstructing the social order started getting put on the back shelf. It's always been the harder thing to do—the farming communes and the cooperatives and stuff like that. So what I see going on now, especially after Dorothy's death, is that the houses are getting . . . they're almost moving toward a kind of respectability.

You know, all the books being written about Dorothy. All these people in Pittsburgh with Thomas Merton plaques on the walls of their condominiums. There's a danger that the tradition will be ossified. Now, I'm not going to be judgmental and say I have the Catholic Worker orthodox party line or anything like that. But you see houses now that are nonprofit, tax-exempt corporations. They've made very pragmatic decisions saying they can serve more people better if they take state money. I really question that, and I would challenge the houses that are doing that.

Ro: But who is to challenge them? In a movement with no hierarchy, a movement rather determined to be anarchist, who is to challenge? Do you just sit and gossip about it?

Mark: No. That's what roundtable discussions are about, supposedly. This process of revitalizing tradition has to be an internal one, done within the communities. Looking at the original message and asking how we can be more faithful, and judging [ourselves] honestly about it.

One thing that we're interested in is combining liberation theology with Catholic Worker. Catholic Worker has traditionally been about serving the poor, and there's a lot of new talk coming out of liberation theology about walking with the poor and empowerment and things like that. So there are lots of questions the movement has to ask itself. Like how does the soup kitchen serve as an empowerment? Can it be empowering? What does empowerment mean? The Catholic Worker hasn't really dealt with that.

The Catholic Worker is a school of living. It's a way of coming into a situation, of being reeducated into a new lifestyle, a new way of living, a new way of being. It's countercultural. I see the Gospels as very countercultural. So the Catholic Worker is a form of reeducation. In that sense, it is like a college or university used to be in the Middle Ages where a professor would gather students around himself (they were all men back then), and they'd just get together and sit around and talk Socrates for hours. The Catholic Worker, in my view, should be kind of like that. You know, people who are living the Gospels seriously, getting down and doing the actions and then reflecting on them.

Ro: Maurin's "The workers shall be scholars and the scholars shall be workers." In actuality, though, I think going to graduate school requires a degree of intensity, a commitment to the intellectual life, that's hard to carry on when you're doing hospitality, when you're working on a soup line. The worker-scholar, scholar-worker thing is great if it works. But how is it going to work?

Mark: Well, I don't know. It's a difficult question. One thing, I think, is that the Catholic Worker was never intended to be a movement of just hospitality houses. Peter and Dorothy's vision was far broader than that. They viewed people who were doing intellectual work as . . . they could be Catholic Workers who didn't live in a house of hospitality. They saw that there's a tension between doing the daily practice of the works of mercy and [the intellectual life]. Peter always was quoting writers and intellectuals and so was Dorothy.

So there is some tension. It's not easy. It requires that you not be overwhelmed by your personalism, that you not bite off too much in terms of service and start neglecting the intellectual roots of the Catholic Worker. You know, Maurin said there was no revolution without a *theory* of revolution. So the two go hand in hand. I think the intellectual has been slighted a little bit in the Catholic Worker.

Angela: Personally, I think intellectual pursuit is as important as being actively involved. I don't know how well that's going to work in a traditional setting, but they should be dependent on one another.

Let's look at a traditional soup kitchen. You're no longer serving the same people. What we have more and more is the permanent underclass, especially the black underclass. Suddenly you're handing out bowls of soup to young black men who have never worked or who will never work again. And that's very difficult. We really have to start doing some serious intellectual work, looking at the state of the economy and the state of the country.

Perhaps handing out a bowl of soup to a young black man is not what we should be doing. Sure it's feeding the hungry, but there's something inside you that goes . . . wrrrench. We really have to look at where this is going and where these people are going, and what's happening with our economy. Catholic Worker communities are being confronted more and more by a whole class of people who are completely excluded from the economic life of this country, who are *never* going to be involved.

Mark: Who are not even necessary. That's a point Marc Ellis is making. He thinks maybe half of this country's population and half the world's population is really nonessential to the running of the economy. So those people are "marked for extermination." He says the twentieth century is an age of holocaust. With the massive growth of the modern technological state, these people can be exterminated. We've seen that in the wars and concentration camps.

Angela: We mightn't get to the point where we're herding people into camps and gassing them, but we certainly are at the point where those people are being hidden and forgotten. They say Peter Maurin and Gandhi and others saw the coming darkness. Marc Ellis would say, "They saw the coming darkness, but none of them guessed how dark it was going to get." And I think that's part of it, that time and history move so quickly that if you stop looking at it for five minutes, the world's changed and you don't know where it went.

Mark: You know, all theories and constructs have to jibe with your fundamental experience. That's what the Catholic Worker is, trying to give middle-class people like myself and Angela experience in seeing the poor and seeing the results of the social system. It just makes you physically ill to own a lot of stuff if you're living on Skid Row, or once you've seen people in forced poverty. There really is no other human response than to embrace simplicity and voluntary poverty.

Ro: And you two met here in Los Angeles. Catholic Worker romances seem to be a Catholic Worker tradition.

Angela: That's right. Somebody said the Catholic Worker is just an alternative dating service. [Laughter.] You know, we were just scrubbing pots together. I mean it's a really romantic atmosphere at the L.A. Worker. Up to your knees in suds, you know, and ordering people around on the line and stuff. Romance just naturally blossomed.

I remember saying, "This is crazy! We can't decide to get married! We don't even know each other very well." And someone said two months at the Catholic Worker would probably equal a year's worth of normal dating. That's true, you know, because you're in and out of each other's pockets like twenty-four hours a day. Just working together all the time and in community together all the time.

We got married in July of '87 and oh, I'm still just learning *so* much! One of the things I have really enjoyed is the great training in nonviolence. When you're talking theoretically about nonviolence in an action, it's one thing, but when you're standing there with a guy who's six foot two, and he's got an iron bar and you don't have anything, and you just stand between him and the guy he's trying to beat over the head . . . that's a very powerful training. Now that's not to say people don't get hurt sometimes. It's just that many times the power of an unarmed person—someone just standing there and not moving—does have a tremendous effect. We learn by the acting what the theory really means.

In the section that follows, written as a roundtable discussion, Workers discuss anarchism, the role of tradition, and what I call concrete theology, the doing of the Gospel.

Chris Montesano (Sheep Ranch, California): People have viewed anarchism as meaning "Nobody can tell *me* what to do!" And there has oftentimes been tremendous chaos in Worker communities as a result. Dorothy and Peter said anarchism is the willingness to take personal responsibility. In order to take personal responsibility, you have to work together with others for the common good.

Ro: I remember Kathe McKenna talking about people using [the concept of] anarchism as an excuse to be sloppy—an excuse to not take responsibility for what's not being done well.

Chris: Yes. And a lot of people in the Worker have used anarchism as an excuse for not getting along with people. So anarchism has been one of the big downfalls of the Worker movement. I think it's also one of its strengths. The way I personally view anarchism is in the tradition of Kropotkin. The basis of anarchism is free association, that I choose out of freedom to associate with others, to come together for the common good, whatever that is.

And I don't see requesting a commitment from someone to be a conflict with that because the commitment we make is open-ended. What we're formalizing is a person's free choice. I wouldn't want to formalize it into vows.

Now I think another issue enters in here. Many young people coming to the Worker are going through their youthful rebellion. I did when I came. Anarchism is a banner under which you can carry out this youthful rebellion. And in your youthful rebellion, you don't want to recognize what I would call legitimate authority. In anarchist thought, there is a legitimate authority, the authority given to an individual when they take the personal responsibility to do what is right, or to do what they deeply feel called to do. For example, someone who deeply feels called to be a nuclear resister . . . you know, to go to a launching pad and beat a missile into a plow. They're operating out of a deep call of personal responsibility, and there's an authority there, a legitimate authority in taking that kind of action. And there's authority, a legitimate authority, in anarchism. You could probably call that authority leadership.

Catherine Morris (Los Angeles): I remember one of Dorothy's illustrations of anarchism. It was so embarrassing, really. See, we were at Tivoli at the time of the Peacemakers Conference, and the place was a mess. Just a mess! Right in the middle of the driveway, there was this huge pond of sewer water. And the toilets were backed up, and I'm not into that kind of stuff. Anyway, Jeff and I decided to clean this bathroom. We hunted around and found a bucket. (Our toilet's always doing strange things, so I know all about gravity flushing. You fill a bucket and pour it down and get rid of all the stuff.) And so when we got back to the bathroom with our bucket and mop and sponge, who's there but Dorothy. I left the bucket, put my sign up, you know, this little directive on how to gravity flush. When we came back, someone had put a swastika on it. The next time someone had ripped it down. And the toilet was in the same condition as when we started on it.

Well, then at the section of the conference when Dorothy was speaking, she started going on and on about the visitors from the L.A. Worker. How we'd come exhausted and wanted to rest and to visit. And what did we do but clean the toilets! "Now that's anarchism! When you see something that needs doing, and you do it, that's anarchism."

Pat Jordan (New York City): Well, Dorothy was not a systematic thinker. For example, I always felt that she never explained her anarchism well at all. She'd often repeat herself. From being around her, you had the sense that it had more to do with St. Paul and the sense of freedom, you know, the freedom that we all need, rather than some sort of lawlessness. A lot of the younger people . . . there was a rough time at Tivoli, and they'd throw this in our face—that they were acting as anarchists. That's not what she had in mind. And yet because of her own radical experience and her great devotion for anarchists who had been such stalwart humanitarians, she wouldn't throw away that term "anarchist."

She meant more a Christian communitarianism, I think. But her certain alliance, her sense of the IWW people and Sacco and Vanzetti and people like that . . . she wasn't averse to . . . she didn't throw out terms to upset people, but she wasn't averse to using terms that might upset people.

Eileen Egan (New York City): Dorothy was always concrete. They would say, "Why don't you put your ideas on peace and war into an organized system?"

She'd answer, "Well, I write as I write."

How can you call yourself a Christian and switch into a way of life in which every work of mercy is reversed? War is that reversed way of life. This is the simplest of theology.

Ro: There are people who say it's too simple to be a theology.

Eileen: Yes, I think they do. But Jesus' theology wasn't above that of the ordinary man. He chose very ordinary men [as his followers], men who didn't have to go to theology books, you know.

Ro: You were talking earlier about how we needed more women theologians. Dorothy's being a woman, I think, helped her to see clearly. She could see that Jesus' message is really just beautifully simple. Hard, but simple. Do you think maybe having women theologians could get us away from some of the cluttered theology that seems to just multiply words?

Eileen: Yes, I do. I do. They call theologians merchants of abstraction. And they are. You can take course after course after course in so-called theology and never hear the message at the heart of Christianity—the message of Jesus which is indiscriminate love. This includes loving the enemy. Now how can you skirt that?

Somebody has said that much of theology consists of getting around the Sermon on the Mount. Dorothy and Peter didn't get around the Sermon on the Mount. They accepted it straight on. Now in order to justify war, you have to get around it. Have to put it somewhere. Put it in a box and lock the box. Dorothy was concrete. When she talked about poverty, she talked about poverty in the concrete.

Ro: But yet people criticize her for this. I hear it sometimes as almost a put-down. As if not being abstract is not quite the right kind . . . is simple thinking.

Eileen: Right, right. Well, I think the closer we get to simple thinking, the better Christians we become. I feel sorry for men. They are so easily fooled. A man will say, "Well, it's a sign of great patriotism and power to lay down your life for your country."

And the woman simply says, "But you're going out to kill. To kill somebody else's son or father." And it's an entirely different approach. One is the abstract—lay down your life for your country. The other is the concrete—you'll be killing a real human being.

John Cooper (Berkeley, California): And I guess that's why I'm with this outfit, actually. I'm learning, through being here, a profound respect for an individual and their feelings—in contrast to ideas, principles, intellectualizations of things. I've gained a strong respect for instincts, intuitions, gut feelings.

That extends to this sort of work in this way: When a person says, "Oh, hell! I really wish I could stop drinking, but I can't," I believe he's telling me the truth. He's not giving me some cock-and-bull story.

When someone says, "Hey, man, I just can't hold a job," I don't think of him as a bum who is just shiftless and idle. He's telling me the truth about something in his life. [Long pause.] I have learned that this sort of belief is not generally shared by people, I'm sorry to say, the growing belief that . . . it's very difficult to put this into words. [Pause]

Ro: Do you trust words?

John: Yes. I think, on the whole, yes. Some people have a hard time of it in life. But the hard time they have lies within them. I say lies within . . . it may derive from an unhappy childhood, an addiction to the bottle, something invisible to an outsider. Hence the outsider generally discounts it. We say, "If I can't see it, it doesn't exist." A person has lost a leg. That I can understand is a limitation. Another person looks hale and hearty. The fact that they had a rough childhood, had a rough adulthood, is not seen by me, and, therefore, it doesn't exist. But it exists very much for the person concerned. It's a major shaper of their lives. I believe it. I credit it. The mere fact that you can't see what shapes a person doesn't mean it doesn't exist. And if they have the goodness occasionally to tell you something about it, you'd better take them seriously.

I face that problem in writing for our Berkeley newsletter. It's very easy, especially when you're writing for our type of audience—generally an ecclesiastic, religious audience—to use the pious phrases. However, that's incomplete. There's always another side to it. To a degree that may be slightly unusual in this type of work, I've tried to give that other side as well.

I wrote once about a furious argument I had with a black woman in the park about refusing her seconds on milk. She said I was refusing her seconds because she was black, and I said it was because we couldn't afford it. We had a steaming argument. It upset me for the rest of the day.

When I came home, I realized that her rage was legitimate. She had got the wrong target. I wasn't discriminating against her because she was black or as she later said, because she was a woman, but I was certainly using my authority, and she resented that. So I wrote about this incident in our newsletter and about that temptation to get some capital out of doing good work. To be the dispenser and also the withholder of food. I had realized, to my shame, that I was actually enjoying that role. That's probably not commonly alluded to in this work.

And finally, I realized that I hadn't quite completed my little essay. It would be pleasant if I could write that subsequently the woman and I became friends. But I couldn't say it. The truth is I don't like her, and that's what I wrote. And there was a furor. People thought it was undignified, and that I shouldn't be talking about the bad side of human nature. Hell! That's the way it happened and that's the way it's got to be written! Whatever one does and whatever one writes, it has to be honest and complete. If you alienate donors, so be it. We are in the hands of God in this work. I'd rather do it the right way and not get very much work done than do it the wrong way and get into megabucks.

Somebody came to my apartment once and looked at all my books with interest, the Russian novelists and so forth, and then cried out, "These are all novels!" I also went to that person's apartment, looked at their books, and cried out deliberately, "Oh, no! They're all religion and psychology!"

I have a general reverence for life as it's lived. Life as it's written about and talked about. The story has a story. It's not a lecture on an aspect of life, even though that's always between the lines in a good story.

Ro: That's why good fiction is true.

John: Good faith, yes! Books on psychology and religion are dishonest because they've taken the essence out of life and are holding some generalization up for inspection. It becomes desiccated very quickly once it's taken out of its cradle. You can write a long essay about religious belief, but you can also write a story about someone dying of cancer crying out in the night. And you have a different view of the same thing, a view which is much more real.

Fr. Tom Lumpkin (Detroit): I think anyone who's been with the Catholic Worker for any number of years would say that the experience of the Catholic Worker on a day-to-day basis certainly humbles you in being glib about using words like "love" and "pacifism." Dorothy speaks about "harsh and dreadful love." I've never been . . . I used to think I was a fairly loving person, a fairly patient person, a fairly peaceful person, until I began to live in a Catholic Worker house, live the day-to-day life, and realized how much hostility and anger toward people I had inside me. I mean, it really, really humbles you to see the poor that you see in a Catholic Worker house. Really stretches you to your ultimate limits of compassion, and patience, and love, and it really helps you to realize how little of all those things you have, you know, and how careful you should be in speaking about such things.

The "Dorothy Says Syndrome," or the direction of the movement now that its founders are gone, has occupied Workers for ten years now.

Jane Sammon (New York City): What does one do in a family when you have people who were sort of looked upon as . . . let's use the words "matriarch" and "patriarch"? How did they get to be that? Probably not because they cracked the whip. Probably because of some sense of goodness and decency and integrity that was demonstrated to others. Constancy, steadfastness . . . you name it. Not that there weren't foibles. But they were truly people of greatness—greatness of stature—and they pass that on to others.

There's invariably going to be the feeling of loss. Whether it's a religious move-ment like the Franciscans or, if you will, a lay movement like the Worker. Or a family. We should not try to . . . whether it's St. Ignatius, or Dorothy, or St. Francis, we can't freeze them into some kind of . . . "Well, that's what they said."

The other thing I have to say is we've got to realize that for some reason, these souls were chosen and given this gift. It doesn't mean that they were gods, but they may have really been given a grace that gave them this kind of wisdom, a wisdom we need to be aware of. For instance, no one will ever convince me that usury is something the Catholic Worker ought to dismiss as irrelevant now that Dorothy and Peter are dead.

I don't think that means, though, that there aren't going to be problems with that. Or that we may use the founding voices and maybe dismiss other good voices who might have things to say, too. Does that make sense?

Jerry Ebner (Milwaukee and other cities): I think in any community, any family, you always have different factions. People use hero figures to support what they're saying. "Well, Dorothy did this." To substantiate their own wills. When Francis of Assisi died, there were splits in the Franciscan order. You had what was called the Observant Movement, people who would do exactly what Francis did. Exactly, you know, to the T. There's a story about Francis putting ashes in his oatmeal once. So you have this crazy group of Franciscans who put ashes in their oatmeal. That isn't what Francis wanted. That isn't what Dorothy wanted. But that's what some people in the Catholic Worker movement do.

Tina Sipula (Bloomington, Illinois): You can pick anything anybody says and say, "Well, this is what they believe in." But it's not their *whole* belief, you know. You can take lines that Dorothy said, but that's not the whole picture.

Catherine: Dorothy made decisions and Dorothy kicked people out. She not only kicked guests out, she kicked people who were connected with the community out. When you go back to [Catholic Worker] literature, it's kind of like rereading Scripture. You have to read Scripture for the time in which you live, take it as metaphor, not literally. So you look at how Dorothy did things, and when she did them, and with whom she did them, and then you look at your own situation and try to discern what you're supposed to be doing to follow that spirit and that philosophy and that openness that she had. She wasn't so open, though, that she didn't call a spade a spade.

Jim Forest (New York City and Alkmaar, Holland): I remember the differences we had [during the sixties], based on things Dorothy had said at one time or another. Different groups or factions would take to this or that aspect of Dorothy. I mean it was a bit funny, really. Like the great butter crisis.

Ro: The butter crisis?

Jim: Yeah. Dorothy, of course, was a great traveler. I'm not sure if it was because she just couldn't bear to come into the New York House, or whether she had other things to do. A little of both, I imagine. But certainly she had lots of other things to do besides baby-sit us.

And while she was away, all kinds of things could happen. She'd come back, and sort it out and then go off for another trip, or go on retreat or something. And the butter . . . see, sometimes we'd get butter, and sometimes other things— goodies, relatively speaking, but not enough for everybody. The practice had been that they would go to "the family," meaning the people who actually were part of the Catholic Worker community. (I'd guess you'd call most of them permanent guests. They'd actually been there much longer than any of the so-called volunteers.)

Well, anyway, Stuart Sandberg and Diana Gannon Feeley decided that the butter should be given to "the line," as it is referred to in the Catholic Worker community. To the anonymous people, largely, who came in just to eat and didn't have a regular place in the community. So you had these . . . these very new, very idealistic kids, basically, deciding what's going to happen with the little edible treasures that came into the community. And it was, of course, outrageous to the people in the family who were suddenly not going to be receiving these eggs or this butter or whatever.

And I remember different people put quotations on the bulletin board to support their position. Quotations from Dorothy. One of them had Dorothy saying that we should roll up in newspapers on the floor to make room for people. Well, nobody in the New York house when I was there ever rolled up in any newspapers. It was very unusual for somebody to even give up their bed, for God's sake! And somebody else had another quotation from Dorothy about how we have to accept our limitations, that not everybody can do everything.

Now these were the polarities which Dorothy lived within. But you couldn't live on just one or the other of these extremes, you had to live within that tension, which we don't like to do. We want to have either the Dorothy Day who rolls up in the newspapers or the one who says it's okay not to roll up in the newspapers. But we don't want the Dorothy Day that has both of these messages because, rationally speaking, they cannot be combined.

In the actual experience of living, though, they have to be combined. You have to live in the tensions. It's not grey, it's . . . it's just flickering black and white. She came back and, of course, made the decision that it was right to continue as things were. The regular household would get the goodies. Dorothy never was trying to mass-produce a certain kind of Christian, or to give the correct list of possessions to people: "This you can have and this you shouldn't have." Rather, she was asking you to keep living with certain questions.

CHAPTER 12

Harvest of Dreams: Catholic Worker Farms

A Roundtable Discussion

> Running a farm is very demanding. People would speak very poetically about following the cycles of life but golly! You're *tyrannized* by the cycles of life!
>
> —*Julian Pleasants*

A RETURN to the land, a living out of Peter Maurin's vision of decentralism, a re-creation of the medieval village with its self-sustained economy based on craft—these are regularly unrealized dreams of many Catholic Workers. As Pat Coy says, "A lot of dead dreams have been harvested on Catholic Worker farms." Nevertheless, there have always been farms, and several of today's rural communities are thriving.* In this chapter, Jim Eder, Bob Tavani, Chris Shepherd, and Ed Forand reminisce about Tivoli. Chris Montesano describes the growing interest in farm and craft, and Sr. Anna Koop of the Denver Catholic Worker discusses the several motivations behind that community's coffin-making attempts. Brian Terrell and Betsy Keenan tell why they moved to isolated Maloy, Iowa, and how they're working to "build a new society in the shell of the old." Jim Levinson of Noonday Farm, a community affiliated with Haley House in Boston, recounts some amusing incidents as academic and clergy types learn the intricacies of farming. Gayle Catinella, who now lives with her husband on Mary Farm in Nebraska, remembers visiting Sandy Adams's farm in the West Virginia Hills. Pioneer Jim O'Gara, former editor of *Commonweal,* concludes the chapter.

The New York community has had farms at several places, but it's the one at Tivoli that stirred the senses. Crazy but beautiful Tivoli, high above the Hudson, with room for everyone—aging alcoholics from the Bowery, Catholic Workers who came up the river for a rest, and "Catholic shirkers" who used and abused the buildings and grounds during the sixties and early seventies.

---

* For a description of three earlier experiments, see Chapter 1.

Jim Eder (Chicago): I remember the first time I came to Tivoli. Came down the road to the river, and the Catholic Worker house was nowhere to be found. Finally I saw there'd been a landslide with all kinds of rocks and a big tree across the driveway, so you couldn't see any buildings. We moved this big tree out and went up a really hard, crummy old road to a building they called the "mansion." It was huge but in great disrepair. Past Maurin House to what they called the "casino," [which was an] old hotel. It looked really dingy.

I met a few people outside, and we started talking. Then we went in for supper, and I was just horrified! The dirt and the cockroaches were . . . you know, I'd never even seen a cockroach before! I thought everybody was crazy, but I ended up staying for two months.

I met Stanley Vishnewski and we became very good friends. So that was a big influence for me. I began to pray the office again, something I'd always loved when I was in the monastery. We said compline every night at Tivoli. When I was there, a hundred and twenty people lived there, twenty so-called Workers and the rest guests.

Bob Tavani (New York City and Minnesota): The New York Catholic Worker was chaotic all the time, but it was a little less chaotic at the farm. Johannah [Marge Hughes's daughter, who was born at Tivoli] told me Tivoli was peaceful in the beginning. Not a chaotic place, but a peaceful place, and a clean place. I think it got carried away by the times. Society went into chaos, and the people who drifted in, myself included, brought the chaos with them and changed the nature of the Worker.

Chris Shepherd visited Tivoli when she was a teenager.

Chris Shepherd (Saginaw, Michigan): The farm was . . . I remember that there were different groups . . . you know, it was community, and yet you felt people were sort of off doing their thing. A few people were doing some writing and there were some conflicts going on, but then everybody came together for dinner and Marge Hughes was my . . . Marge and Andy [Chrushial] were my main people. I spent a lot of time with Marge. She was kind of the mother of the farm. Ran things. Very high-profile person at the time. She made the bread and that was the focus . . . the kitchen and the big dining area. There was a place that was always a little active in that big dining area whether there was a meal going on or not. Marge's bread would be out and peanut butter and jelly and coffee. And music most of the time. Marge presented a real positive outlook in spite of a lot of personal problems she had. She loved me as if . . . and my friend Mona and Andy and I played music, so we always sat around together and played. I think that way we got more attention from Marge. And everybody always wanted attention from Marge. She was sort of the matriarch of Tivoli.

Ed Forand (New York City): Tivoli was just a beautiful place on the Hudson. Gorgeous! Huge! But so open . . . you could wake up in the morning, and there'd be twenty-five people out on the lawn. Lots of them on drugs and shacking up. No way to keep them out. So what are you going to do? You feed them. No way to get rid of them. It was awful! So I hardly ever went up there. Finally Dorothy just had to close it up.

Part of the new generation, Chris and Joan Montesano left San Francisco in 1976 for Sheep Ranch in the High Sierra. Archaeologists have discovered that the farm is on the site of a Northern Miwok village wiped out during the gold rush. According to a Sheep Ranch newsletter, the Miwoks had been there for eight hundred years and "were known for their gentleness and peacefulness." This community supports itself by crafting candles and marketing them by mail order, and is, I believe, the only Worker community where craft is so consciously practiced. Sheep Ranch has sometimes served as a place for retreat and reflection for other Workers.

Chris Montesano: It used to be that those of us on farms were kind of like on the side of the movement, but the direction of farms goes along with everything else. It's all part of one larger movement: the idea of beginning to create a "new society in the shell of the old." I think it's breaking open. More people have been in the movement for a number of years now, and that's giving all the houses a lot more depth. I think the national gatherings have helped, too, have been a really important tool in allowing everyone to hear each other and to sense the importance of what each one is doing.*

It sounds like many houses are interested in starting farms, so it's a very exciting time for me because I've been . . . we've lived on this farm since 1976 and it's an aspect of the movement that we've been trying to foster and create. We work together in our candle making. Decisions are made in common. It's creating a whole different sense in terms of work and then it also addresses [other aspects of] craft. There's a kind of dignity. Making candles in our small candle shop is very . . . uh, prayerful.

Except for the candle making at Sheep Ranch and the weaving Betsy Keenan and Brian Terrell do at Strangers and Guests, craft is another

* Since Dorothy Day's death, there have been several national gatherings—in New Jersey, Milwaukee, Las Vegas, Denver, and Boston.

part of the Worker vision that is rarely realized. Sr. Anna Koop of Denver describes one of the most unusual attempts.

Ro: Could you talk a little bit about your coffin making? What you do and how it works?

Sr. Anna Koop: Well, it doesn't work. We initially thought it might become a cooperative where we would employ homeless people. It started with coffins; we expanded it to children's toys. Tried to sell them at churches and several different places. And found out not only that we aren't good at marketing, but also that we hate it. We're not willing to do it. We had hoped to produce a low-income product, something that would really benefit people who didn't have a lot of money.

The other part of it was really inviting people to become more involved in the burial of their family and friends. Purchasing a pine coffin was the first part of that because they had to figure out how to do things a little non-institutionally, not just turn it all over to the mortuary. And [we hoped] they'd then think about ways they might decorate the coffin or different things they'd like to do with the service, and it would just keep kind of expanding.

We have been able to do some of that at the house. For instance, we had Issie Burns's funeral last Friday at the house and it was just lovely. Wednesday night is prayer night at the Worker, and we had Mass and kind of your Irish wake. You know, just lovely remembrances . . . A lot of women wrote notes to Issie, thank-you notes. She was a wonderful, simple woman. And people read these [at the funeral] and then laid them on the coffin. I mean there was just a kind of at-home-ness with it. And the pine coffin . . . at one point, the mortician was screwing down the lid with a Phillips screwdriver. (I'm sure he's never had to do that before in his life.) I said to someone, "I think one of us should have done that. There's something very good about the finality of screwing down the lid." I've heard of a Native American ritual of hammering the lid on the coffin. Makes a lot of sense.

Now the woodworking . . . it's therapeutic for me. I have to say quite honestly that the shop has offered me a wonderful balance to being at the house.

Ro: Who else works there?

Anna: We have, at different times, hired people who were living at the house to do some work. And that's been good, but it's been spotty, and it doesn't get anybody on their feet because we're not "in production." We don't have orders. At some point this winter, we just got royally ripped off. They stole a lot of our tools that we haven't replaced, and it's been a real time of questioning whether being able to operate it as a business is fantasy. Part of me says, "Okay. Catholic Worker is not supposed to be a business. And if we sell a coffin only once in a while, so what?"

I first met Brian Terrell at the 1987 Dorothy Day Birthday Celebration in Nevada. We laugh about it now: he wears bib overalls and I assumed he'd known farming from childhood. Quite the contrary. He and his wife, Betsy Keenan, lived at both the New York and Davenport houses before buying land in rural Iowa. Two years after the Nevada gathering, I spent an idyllic summer's day resting at their farm, Strangers and Guests. Brian had the day off from his part-time job at a nursing home.

> *For the land belongs to me [says the Lord] and to me you are only strangers and guests.* —Leviticus 25:23

Betsy and Brian grow most of their food and make cheese. They raise goats for milk and meat. They keep bees and grow hops for beer. Betsy has an herb garden, a bed of potatoes, and even the beginnings of an orchard. They've planted grapes, but the vines aren't doing well. Drought threatens this land.

Brian Terrell: A few years ago, even in the movement, people would say, "Well, which Worker house are you supplying with food?" or, "What city house are you affiliated with?" As though there really was no vision of the Catholic Worker farm in itself. The idea for Strangers and Guests grew slowly. More than I did, Betsy had a feeling for the Catholic Worker farm. She really has a green thumb, especially with herbs.

When we told people we were leaving the Davenport Worker and moving to the country, they said, "Oh, we understand. You've got Elijah and Clara now, and you can't do that hospitality stuff anymore." The kids were fine. *I* was the one who was sick and tired. Exhausted. It was good for the kids to be in Davenport and to see other kinds of people and to see suffering people every day. Children are good for those people, too. I know people who have had bad experiences with children in hospitality, but I almost think we need to compensate for taking our kids out of such a good environment. Children also get more wariness and street smarts about strangers when they've been around them.

The farm idea has been one of the most neglected [parts of the movement], partly because most Worker farms have started in the shape of the American family farm. And in most Worker farms, there might be a community instead of a family, but in relation to its neighborhood, it's just another isolated family. That's the biggest challenge—trying to find the contacts with the people who live here, to make the community with the neighbors, not just with ourselves.

Peter Maurin's idea about the land was not that we're all going to be farmers. Peter's vision was of the European medieval village, a small community. In that community are farmers who go out to their fields every day and do that work, but there are also craftspeople and teachers and horseshoers and blacksmiths and millers—all these different gifts and vocations in one place, rather than as now, where no area is self-sufficient.

Betsy Keenan: We're lucky to have Bernadine Pieper here. She's a Sister of Humility with a doctorate in botany, stationed right here at Immaculate Conception in Maloy. Bernadine knows all about what kind of tree to buy and everything. This area is an ecological disaster. And an economic disaster. And a personal disaster for most of the families. There's no way their kids can afford to buy land and stay nearby, so the families are disintegrating. Generations are . . . the farmers who are making money are mostly over sixty, and the young people can't afford to start.

Brian: The average age is fifty-five or something. This county has the highest average age of any county in Iowa, and Iowa beats the whole rest of the United States.

Betsy: Brian's job is in the growth industry—nursing homes. [Laughs.]

Brian: The economy is a shambles. Whole roads have been closed off because no one lives down them anymore. See, the corporations take over the land, and they don't need the houses. Where we are, Travelers Insurance and John Hancock are the culprits.

You know, people may be sentimental about the family farm, but I think most of us believe the capitalist lie that bigger is better. People here grow corn and soybeans. When they get the money for the soybeans, then they buy their food, which is all canned in Michigan or Ohio. The majority of people see farming as a way to make money and not a way to raise food. Or else there are so many chemicals in their soil that they can't raise a garden.

Betsy: We try to be pretty self-sufficient with food and to show our neighbors that they can be, too. They buy all their services from outside, go thirty or forty miles to see a movie or hear a band or get their shoes fixed. We have a weekly sing here at the house where people bring music—instruments, voices, whatever—and have a sociable evening together. It's not really regular yet, but that's our goal.

Brian: The very reason the world looks at this little area and says it's hopeless is the reason we're able to afford to live here. It's empty. Almost any idea will fill a void. We're hoping more people will come to join our community. This part of Iowa is exciting because the shell has crumbled so much and so many basic services aren't being offered. The houses are cheap, so almost anyone can get a house with ten acres.

Ro: Can you talk about the community store you've opened here in Maloy?

Betsy: Sure. We opened in March of '87. Cleo and Regina Lynch bought the building to save it. (It was a former store and dance hall.) Everybody came, and we painted it up and put down new carpeting and some plumbing and lights. We opened it up just as a place to drop in for coffee. Had a food pantry shelf and a borrowing bookshelf. And some people did stop in, but not real regular. It didn't really catch on, I think because we were strangers. But we kept up hours.

In June we started the craft store. The crafters pay a monthly shelf rental and set their own prices. There's no markup; the crafts belong to them until they're sold, and we send them the money at the end of the month. Jim and Mary Peifer-Runyon bought an old rug loom down in Missouri, and we set that up in the store and we weave blue rag rugs from old jeans. And Mary compiled a craft catalogue of the county. She contacted people and got the information all in one place, partly to instill pride, but also to see what skills are available. If people want to exchange or barter or buy supplies cooperatively or learn a new craft, they can look in the catalogue.

Now, because of Regina Lynch (a wonderful woman), we're carrying bulk food—dried fruit and grains and nuts. People are buying the food and traffic is increasing a great deal. We're open five days a week, six hours a day. Regina does a day or two a week and Veronica Ray is now doing two days a week. It's not real busy, but we're doing quite well now. This month we've made two hundred dollars again, mostly selling weaving. (Well, grossed probably two hundred, made a hundred fifty.)

Brian: I don't think there's ever going to be a whole lot of money in this area again. (It never was very wealthy.) People are frustrating themselves, just beating their heads against the wall, dreaming of owning all this *stuff.* The only way people are going to be able to live here is if they decide not to buy into the dominant system.

Ro: If the young people are leaving as fast as they can, who are you going to be able to influence? Are they going to have to come from outside, like you did?

Betsy: Little by little, we do make a difference. We've met some people who are interested in the kind of life we want, and they were here before we came. They're interested in working with what's here, like we are, and in alternative economy—in cooperation and barter. Also, there are some people who, from where I am, look like they'd rather be in suburbia, but when I talk to them, they say, "I wish . . . I'm trying to simplify my life. You encourage me. I'm going to do it. I'm going to do something different."

Brian: The people I work with . . . they're just amazed that we don't have television. They don't think they have a choice. The people who live in town get cable and the people in the country have satellite discs. Poor people. Working on minimum wage.

Ro: How do you react when people say you're being elitist? Living this good, simple life, and the rest of the world has to take all those pressures.

Brian: People don't have to take them.

Betsy: I think if there's any way to get away from . . . from the follies of the world, the deceptions of our system, it's not going to be by living in the trenches. We can't live in the trenches forever. We could do things a lot purer here if we got rid of electricity and stopped buying food from the store and just lived on what we could grow. But people who have done that kind of homesteading stop after a couple of years. Move to California and get a job in insurance.

Brian: [Pause] I'm beginning to think more and more that Christian life can't be lived outside of some kind of community. Not everybody sharing houses and things like that, but if we're going to be Christians, we have to know that we're going . . . we have to have people close to us who are going to bear our burden so we can take risks, even with a growing family. Those risks can be taken, but not by an isolated person. I'm thinking of my own family history. My father died when I was six years old, and my mother was socially, financially, and emotionally isolated with four children. My father dying . . . people die. That's part of life. And as Christians, people being away on missions or going to jail for resistance is part of life, too. For a long run, you know, we really have to develop the kind of community that can sustain and support each other through those times.

I'm not going to stop doing [resistance]. I feel very much the sense of vocation to do these things. I remember once there was a young man from Chicago who said he thought resistance was self-indulgent. He'd only been at the house for some months, and he said, "I love the people at the Catholic Worker house so much that I'd never do anything like you're doing, to risk not being there for them, to risk not meeting their needs."

Ro: Is he still there?

Brian: No. He wasn't even there the next year. No one even knew where he'd gone.

Ro: Isn't it all self-indulgent in the long run?

Betsy: That's what the sociologists would say. You do what you want to do, you know?

Ro: Larry Purcell says the Catholic Worker is for the Workers.

Betsy: It makes it easier to be good. That's the whole point.

> Noonday Farm in Winchendon Springs, Massachusetts, is an offspring of Haley House in Boston. Set in rural Massachusetts, it seemed idyllic to me on a warm and sunny spring day. Lots of children, baby chickens, music and laughter, and intentional decision making. The good life, Catholic Worker style.

Jim Levinson: Even though the farms have been the weak link within the Catholic Worker, every Catholic Worker house thinks, "Well, ours will be different." Since its inception, Haley House had looked at farms and had ideas, and when we got a grant of money specifically earmarked for a farm, we decided to get serious. So we drew a circle on a map with a radius of an hour and a half distance from Boston, and said anything within this circle is fair game.

The first place we looked at was this farm. The owner said it wasn't really available because the tenants were planning to buy it, but he said we could see it, so we drove out. Well! When we found the place, the buildings were all locked up. And there was this *goat* protecting the house! (We call it the attack goat.) Now this wasn't exactly the kind of welcome we expected, but having driven an hour and a half, we wanted to see the place.

Someone managed to get the goat by the horns and tie it up. And even though the house was locked up, we found a way in. Within five minutes we discovered why they didn't want us in here. The whole second floor was a plant for the drying and processing of pot! (No wonder the renter was sure he was going to be able to buy it!) After that, we looked at about twenty other farms, not finding anything that we really liked and always thinking that this first place was really ideal. And then the authorities must have caught up with the tenants because they left suddenly, without even paying the rent. So we were able to get it after all. That was in 1984. We have eighteen acres altogether, but not all of it is under cultivation.

Ro: Do you get your produce into Haley House as you planned?

Jim: Oh, yeah. And we're beginning some serious work with fruit trees and bees. Also, this is our first summer with chickens. And the chickens are making it. We are three families with a total of seven children, and the kids love the chicks, of course.

Ro: And who knew . . . did anybody know anything about farms?

Jim: Not really. Maybe a little gardening experience. We really were rank amateurs, and we made some tremendous mistakes. Incredibly, things grew anyway. One of the classic mistakes was in spreading manure. You know, the truck comes and dumps a load of manure, and you're supposed to get your mud boots on and a wheelbarrow and your shovels and spread it. Well, being city folks, we said to ourselves, "Surely there's a more efficient way to do this." We had a truck with a snow plow, so we decided just to drive the truck out there with the snowplow and smooth it around. So Bill [Beardslee], who's an assistant minister at a nearby Congregational church, gets in the truck and heads for this manure pile. Gets a head of steam on and then, with all the kids watching, he hits the pile. And the truck just sinks right down in the manure! And there was Bill, working frantically with the four-wheel drive! Pushing every control he could see and screaming curses. The neighbor who came to pull Bill out said he "never heard a man of the cloth talk like that!"

For several years, Sandy Adams tried to make a go of a farm in West Hamlin, West Virginia. Folks like Gayle Catinella would vacation there.

Gayle Catinella (Chicago and Wisner, Nebraska): I've never lived that simply before in my life. There was a real romance about the farm in West Virginia. No electricity. No running water. The tax on the land is twenty-five dollars a year, and theoretically, that's the only bill you have to pay. Everything else can be taken care of by the land. But I'm not sure if I'm quite ready to jump into that simple a life. I still have some more letting go to do.

Jim O'Gara was one of the founders of the original Chicago Catholic Worker.

Jim O'Gara (formerly Chicago, now Rockville Center, New York): I have to admit that the farm movement never struck me very forcibly. I had to . . . certainly anybody with any sense could see that there were people living in the slums who would be better off on a plot of land somewhere. But as a long-range solution to the social question, I didn't think that was the direction [we could go].

Someone gave the Chicago Catholic Worker some land in Minnesota and Marty Paul tried to make a go of it. But in spite of all the hard work, the land was so poor that it was almost impossible to make anything grow. And I believe that was true of other places, too. That and the fact that a lot of people in the Catholic Worker didn't know too much about farming.

Of course, the Catholic Worker people who are going to farms are doing something of value, that is they're creating Christian Catholic communities in which they can share values and ideals with other people with similar tastes and background. This seems a very important thing, a very useful thing. Maybe the farm part of it is not going to be very successful, or maybe it's not going to solve the social question. But it *is* going to provide a lot of people with a community environment in which they can flourish and develop. It's a kind of withdrawal from the society whose values they are in constant conflict with. Now is this isolationist?

Ro: Well, *is* it?

Jim: I prefer the idea of permeating society and influencing society. But there are other ways besides my way. In a sense, you need places like that to be reservoirs of values and ideals. Then maybe their children will permeate the society or their example will influence society. We always say we're trying to permeate society. But society doesn't look like we're doing such a wonderful job.

CHAPTER 13

The Mother House, New York

The Catholic Worker movement is so fluid, it needs some stability, and New York will always be the mother house, so to speak. There are people in the movement who are hostile to whatever New York says, but there are also people like me who are interested in hearing New York's journey.

—*David Buer*

DOROTHY Day and Peter Maurin met in New York and started the first house of hospitality there. Two houses make up the New York community on the Lower East Side, St. Joseph and the larger Maryhouse two blocks away. In this section, I've united the voices of people who are still at these houses with those who have moved to other endeavors or other houses. Jane Sammon came to the Catholic Worker in 1972 and remains in New York. Ed Forand lives down the street and has seen many changes in the Worker over the years. Gary Donatelli works at Bailey House, an AIDS hospice. One of the Catholic Worker travelers, he describes differences between the houses. Tom Cornell, a former editor of the paper, has a house and soup kitchen in Waterbury, Connecticut. Jo Roberts came from England to New York in 1988 and stayed.

Jane Sammon: St. Joseph House would uh . . . particularly reflect all that goes on in New York. The uncertainty. And the rather frenetic and chaotic pitch at times. What goes on here, then, is sort of a "surprise by joy," an invitation to the unknown. It shows the need to be really uncompromising in one's reliance on the graciousness of God. It shows we can't get attached to controlling.

You know, Rosalie, we're in a city that has a reputation for arrogance. And here at St. Joseph House, we're in the midst of people who have been victims of that arrogance. The great desire would be to offer people hospitality. On a practical level, the Worker does the works of mercy on a daily basis. So we have a meal five times a week. A simple sort, the stock of the Catholic Worker—soup and bread and tea or coffee. But one wants to serve that meal with hospitality.

Yet we don't wish to be sentimental about the life here, as if there is no sin in the world, in other words. There are moments when you have to say no. Or there's your own sinfulness. Maybe your "no" is based on a whim. It's . . . it's a terrible thing to think that power can be reduced to those who have bread and margarine and those who don't. Or to those who have the potential to close the door on some other person.

On Sunday, I had to tell a whole crowd of fellows . . . you know, it was bitterly cold. The men jump in front of the door for warmth and also because human nature doesn't like to stand on line. So we had a lot of angry souls outside, waiting to get in, and fellows lingering inside because it was warm. Then you just have to say it—to ask them to leave. You know, we can only seat twenty-eight people at one time in our house.

I think we all had to shed some of our coats when we came. Many come as volunteers. With our own opinions, our own ideas, our own thoughts, our own sense of how we can wrap this up very nicely, thank you, by doing it differently. It's often easier for someone new here to see the person at the door, a person who presents the need in such stark fashion, and not realize that some of the people living in the house began by being at that door. And so we might invite someone in on our own, and disrupt an entire life here.

It's partly because we're always at battle with our instincts and our . . . this veneer, if you will (maybe more than a veneer) of individualism. We don't easily trade that in for personal responsibility. What often gets mixed up with the big doctrine of personal responsibility in CW life is not individualism but a sentimentality that says, "Gee! That guy just broke my heart, so I invited him in."

I find many of the fellows who come into the house have had so little, for instance, in terms of another person to speak with. And I don't say I do that necessarily . . . speaking *with* as opposed to *at* a person. But I would say I try to be gracious to the people who come into the house for the meal, for the little bit of time they're going to be here. And maybe, just like families, you know, we're more welcoming towards someone who's just visiting, as it were, than to people we're with all the time. But then, I don't know if that's true because I've known a lot of the men from the street for fifteen, sixteen years.

Ro: Do you know what I like? That you know their names.

Jane: But I've been here so long, Rosalie.

Ro: And you *use* their names. That's important for people.

Jane: Well, some of those folks are so good to me. When I was in the hospital, one of the fellows on the line wrote me a nice note and sent up a little diary.

And then another thing—with some of the guys, it's a matter of just . . . I don't know how you can describe an exchange of life between two persons. Whether the person is on the street or whether the person is in the house. I don't think you can really articulate so many little moments.

Ro: How do you decide who lives in the house?

Jane: Well, I think the big decisions about living in the house come from . . . I think some of it is always a risk, but with the hope . . . "When I was a stranger, you welcomed me." The bottom line is that people aren't going to be able to stay in the house if they're manifesting violent behavior, or if they're destructive in some way. Sometimes it comes out of one's intuitions; other times out of one's sentiments, no doubt. Sometimes it's just . . . you're absolutely certain, because of experience, that this person is in need. And that's it. I think I would say that we're probably less inviting to younger men. There seems to be a kind of bias towards older men whom you might see more easily as victims. In terms of the streets, they're not going to have fast reflexes, like when somebody snatches their shoes at a city shelter.

Ro: I see. You know, you seem happy here. You smile a lot. Your eyes sparkle. Can you say why?

Jane: Well, I think it's the sense that you're not excluded from life here. Life isn't just this bunch of comrades who sit around and read books, and it's not just a bunch of workmates. You are really seeing the cross and the Resurrection. It's truly . . . you see so many people who *give* life. In the most perverse circumstances of their own lives, the greatest senses of deprivation.

Ro: Dorothy said it could be dangerous, that you could be guilty of arrogance, living this life, giving up Beethoven, et cetera.

Jane: Well, you don't give up the Beethoven. That's the important thing. Maurin's whole idea of "culture and cultivation" was to encourage and foster this use of one's mind, this proper disposition, if you will. The proper ordering of one's senses. Beauty certainly comes through our senses. [As Dorothy would say,] "The world will be saved by beauty." You know how much Dorothy loved that idea from Dostoyevsky, and didn't buy the false attitude that poverty should mean devoid of any beauty. I think [not seeing] that can be the danger in the Catholic Worker.

That's another thing that the Worker can teach us—how much beauty there is in the world and how much you long for that when you're in a situation where there *seems* to be so little. At times, we all confuse voluntary poverty with destitution. We're encouraged to take part in the cultural aspects of this great city but not to be arrogant or extravagant about it. It's not as if you tell me you like to play guitar and I say, "Let me break your fingers." If we're not careful, we can get to this extreme point of view that we're not to participate.

If you're at a Worker house, you have to have joy in you. I'm very fond of music, and I really have to hear it, you know, at some moment in my day. I can get it on our little radio there until the roaches invade it. Then it gets very ragged.

Ro: The roaches are inside the radio?

Jane: Oh, they love it! [Laughs.] It's warm in there, so they get out of the cold. And then once they get in there, you can't find stations 'cause they're pushing the dial their way, and you're pushing it your way. A battle of the wills with the roaches!

Early every morning Ed Forand comes in to St. Joseph's to make the coffee.

Ed Forand: I was at the Worker full time for about eight years, and then for the next ten years, I used to go in and do the soup every morning during the week. I wish I could still do it. Wish I had the strength, in a sense. Not only the physical strength but also the psychological strength. But I can't anymore.

Ro: What sort of changes did you see in the people on the line over the years?

Ed: There's a big, big difference. I came into the city in '61. At that time, we had a soup line of maybe a hundred and fifty or so at the most. Mostly alcoholics on the Bowery. Older fellows. White. The Bowery at that time was very heavily traveled. It isn't today. And the line was usually a pretty quiet affair.

We moved over here to First Street twenty years ago, in '68. In the beginning it was pretty much the same, but through the seventies and certainly now through the eighties, it's changed considerably. Mostly I think because of drugs. Now the line is mostly made up of young blacks. And many, many of them are on drugs, so it's a much rougher line. And the young blacks, you know, are . . . it's understandable that they are very bitter and angry. Justifiably so. But it comes out, too, in their actions and in the way they react to you. So it's entirely different from what it was in the early sixties.

Gary Donatelli spent the formative years of his life at the Worker.

Gary Donatelli: Sometimes life at the New York Catholic Worker would just get too crazy, you know, and I'd have had it with the soup line, the community—everything! So I'd just hit the road. Like head out. Satisfy my wanderlust. First, I'd hitchhike to Ohio and visit my family, and then I'd start West. I'd make a point to get to certain houses and make various connections. I'd go to . . . say Detroit, Chicago, Milwaukee, and then the Quad Cities, hitch across the midwest, stop at Seattle and then go down the coast. All the way out and back, a number of times.

I learned an awful lot about the Catholic Worker that I might not have learned living in New York. It gave me a real sense of the diversity within the movement. The kind of hospitality [houses would do] would reflect what was going on and the kind of political activities would be specific to the location, even though certainly reflecting things going on nationally. I probably saw it as less monolithic, and I certainly grew to see that the New York Catholic Worker was not necessarily the ideal Catholic Worker community. St. Joseph House and Maryhouse were rather large and in some ways tradition-bound. I mean it would be like going to Rome to see the ideal Christian community. Or Jerusalem for that matter. Just because Christianity was founded there doesn't mean that's the best example of what's going on.

That's not to say there's not an awful lot of good going on at the New York Catholic Worker, or that there hasn't been. But it was . . . I found it very enlightening to see other communities—communities made up of people who had never met Dorothy and hadn't had Peter Maurin visit. Newer communities as well as older communities. Or younger communities that had connections to previous communities in the same city. Different kinds of continuity.

Ro: Is anybody from New York doing that kind of visiting now?

Gary: No, I don't think so. I always found it real exciting just to see what the other people were doing. Because over and over again I would feel so bound to the [New York] house, bound to the hospitality, bound to the traditions. You know, that had a certain beauty, but it didn't always make sense.

Tom Cornell: The Worker downtown is the flagship. Dorothy always pointed to the failures of the New York house, so to point to its failures now, to think that this is a change, is a mistake. I'm defending the kids downtown. They're putting out the paper, and the paper is quite often really superb. The soup is bad, but it's always been bad, and it's better now than in the old days.

Jo Roberts, a young lawyer from England, is representative of the hundreds of educated young idealists, both from the United States and from other countries, who have found commitment and hope at the "mother house." Some stay for a year or so, some spend a lifetime. I interviewed Jo in 1989; she was still there in 1993, an integral part of life at Maryhouse. In this segment from our conversation, she describes the routine of her day and discusses some of the dilemmas in providing long-term hospitality and responding to a mentally ill woman with only dead-end options.

Before coming to New York, Jo had spent one summer at an international youth work camp in Germany, and another few weeks in India, working with Mother Teresa in Calcutta and New Delhi. After completing her law degree and a postgraduate year, she volunteered for a summer in the United States at the Community for Creative Non-Violence (CCNV) in Washington, D.C.

Jo Roberts: So I almost had a dual career pattern. Sort of carrying on with the traditional career training, but also getting involved in other things. I was very impressed with CCNV, and I was tempted to stay, but it wasn't exactly what I was looking for. So I went back and I passed the exams and carried on working in the law I'd always been attracted to—legal aid work.

Ro: Did you like the practice of law?

Jo: I did very much. But I began to realize that only a small part of me was actually being fulfilled in doing that sort of work. I don't like the way that if you choose a career, you have to shut off [other] sides of your personality. Just timewise, there wasn't time to do much with the other. My mother said, "Well, you could always have a law practice and volunteer in a homeless shelter on a Friday night." No way! I wanted to commit myself to something that's fulfilling in itself, rather than dividing myself up. Then it all came to a head, and I decided to leave for a while and come to the Catholic Worker.

I didn't know about how the houses were set up, and I wrote to New York 'cause that was the one address I had. I thought it was like a clearinghouse for the other houses, thought they'd tell me to go to California or whatever. They said, "Come here."

Ro: You didn't want to go back to Calcutta? What was the experience with Mother Teresa like?

Jo: That was a great eye-opener. I went with a friend, and we both learned an awful lot, and we were very much aware that we got a lot more out of it than we gave, in a sense.

Ro: But you didn't go back, and you didn't go back to CCNV, either. Earlier, you mentioned that CCNV was not faith based when you were with them. Were there any other differences, Jo?

Jo: Well, CCNV has a much higher profile politically, and that appealed to me a lot. I was very impressed with everything they were about, but I just didn't feel in tune with it.

The political thing—if there were more people here [at Maryhouse], I'd like to do a bit more of it. But I also feel that what we're doing is a political statement in itself. The whole concept of a house of hospitality—of really saying, "Yes, I am prepared to take personal responsibility for people, prepared to be my sister or brother's keeper"—that's political. Yes.

Ro: Do you do anything that could be called resistance?

Jo: We did up until Christmas. I've only got a certain amount of time, and so I guess I feel the other things I'm doing are more important.

Ro: What if one of the four of you [who sign the roster for house duties] decided now—tomorrow—that she was called to do something that would take her out of the community and leave you shorthanded?

Jo: If you have brackets, put in "Jo laughs hysterically." Well I . . . what can I say? I mean I wouldn't leave. I'm here. I guess we'd just carry on and pray that somebody would come.

Ro: Would you resent it?

Jo: I wouldn't resent that person leaving because I trust and respect the people here, and I know that they wouldn't do that unless they felt it was something they had to do. But I wouldn't be very happy about it, to be honest. I think then we'd have to seriously think about what the priorities were and whether we . . . if there were three people here, we'd be like on the door every day. And I personally . . . I'd need to have a day off. We'd then have to think about whether we wanted to change the structure of what we were doing and perhaps draw in a bit until we got some more people.

Ro: What's a day in the life of Jo Roberts at Maryhouse?

Jo: There is no [typical] day. We take the house morning or afternoon or evening. Each one of those times is very different. I like taking the house in the morning, but each morning is very different, too.

I come down about seven-thirty. Somebody has already got the coffee going, so I just carry the pot into the dining room and get out the mugs and the cups and the sugar and the bread. And then give out meds. (We have little med envelopes. Usually about seven or eight people have to be given stuff in the morning. And three people need insulin shots.) Then if it's a Monday, it's eggs for breakfast. I feel awful sorry for people because I haven't yet mastered how to do sunny-side up without breaking the eggs.

Ro: So you don't just do a bunch of scrambled eggs.

Jo: No. Individual orders. (Sometimes the scrambled and the sunny-side up don't look too different.) Later I go over to St. Joe's and pick up food for the soup. And then it's making the soup. In between, it's stuff like answering the phone and the door and just getting people things they need. I'm on my feet all the time, which I like.

Ro: Some of the older women at Maryhouse probably aren't able to help much, but is it all just the four of you taking care of people who can't take care of themselves?

Jo: I think about that good old Marx thing: "From each according to their ability, to each according to their needs." It's sort of a sliding scale. Like Margaret sits out there and folds papers. [Except for Jo, the names of the Maryhouse residents in this chapter are pseudonyms.] That's her work, and she's an important part of the mailing of the newspaper. And Pauline goes over to St. Joseph's and chops up vegetables in the afternoon. Other people clean. Most of the ones who don't work aren't able to. All Sarah does is get the butter out, but to me it's really important that she do that, and I think she sees it as important, too. That's her contribution.

If I'm doing the afternoon, it's very busy around just after lunch time. Sometimes it's a bit difficult to get people to leave, especially if it's cold outside. Sometimes it can be just really hectic, and there are no seats. We start lunch at eleven-thirty, so the women who live here can go upstairs before people come in. Because the women who come in are usually younger and can be a bit too loud for some of the people.

Ro: I remember Tim [Lambert] writing about respecting the family that lives here and particularly the older women who have their own places to sit and things like that. This is a home for them. Dealing with the tensions between that and the needs of the street.

Jo: Yes. That's one thing I think about a lot, especially when we're a bit stretched. The responsibilities we have for the people who live here, and the need (which I think is a very real need) to be open to people coming in. They need it and we need it. It's part of what we're about. But I feel there's so much happening in the house with thirty-five people living here. Some people who are living here seem to be carrying a lot of pain with them, and I feel I'm not getting to them. Through [lack of] time or whatever.

Ro: What do you think is the very best way to . . . to be with them?

Jo: I think just hanging out in the dining room and talking to people. That quote of Dorothy's about "we know each other through the breaking of bread." We learn to understand and love each other through that.

Ro: Not rushing around trying to fix up their lives all the time, but just being there.

Jo: Yeah. I think so. I mean there's a lot we just can't do. Yesterday Nancy and I took this woman out to Bellevue. She came in, and she was completely out of it. Really. I thought, "I can't let her out in the street because she's just not capable of looking after herself." So we decided we'd take her up to Bellevue, and that was very distressing.

We called Project Help, and they were closed. (You don't get sick on a Sunday.) So we called Bellevue and talked to the woman on the psych ward. She's saying, "If you bring her up, come into the emergency room and in a few hours, she'll get admitted. And then because we don't have any beds, she's going to have to hang around for a matter of days in the emergency room until she can get proper care." And I just couldn't think of anything more degrading. It's bad enough on the medical ward, but just the total inhumanity of somebody who's completely bewildered and alienated being stuck out in a corridor.

I felt very, very angry that the choice—the only choice she had—was the street or [a chair at Bellevue]. It didn't seem like any choice at all.

Ro: And of course some people would ask why you didn't keep her here.

Jo: Well, we talked about that. And we were painfully aware that we . . . it wasn't a situation we could deal with.

Ro: And what would have happened if she had stayed here?

Jo: She *was* here for a couple of hours. And in that time there was tension in the dining room because she was wandering around, and people . . . people were saying, "What's this woman doing here?" So you start getting this tension in the house. We had to think about how she would fit in with the lives of the people who live here.

Ro: Whom you have already committed yourself to.

Jo: Right. We both felt that realistically there really wasn't anything we could do, so we got a taxi and took her up to Bellevue. She realized when we got out of the taxi that . . . what we were planning to do, and she didn't want to go in.

She had a very open face and big, wide, brown eyes and she kept saying she was a saint and was going to go to heaven. There was a feeling about her of quiet joy. She said to us, "Isn't religion wonderful?" But she said she didn't want to go into Bellevue because the walls would close in. (She'd been there before.)

What could you do? I know you have to make choices for people when they can't make them for themselves, but I feel it's a question of power that you have to be very careful about. Where do you draw the line between them being capable of making decisions and when you make them for them?

Ro: Particularly when she saw that as such a non-free place. So what did you do then?

Jo: She wandered off and we stood and watched her go, and then we ran after her and gave her the food we had brought up for her. I was thinking also that she might be killed. She was totally incapable of protecting herself in any way, and a woman on the street is just *so* vulnerable. But I felt that the best thing possible had happened in a sense because at that moment, she was happy.

Ro: She wouldn't have even had that [moment] much longer if she'd gone into Bellevue.

Jo: Right. And so . . . but again I was stuck with the total [lack of] options.

Ro: Doesn't that lead right back to political change?

Jo: Yes, it does. As we were walking down, I was sounding off about cities and how if this had been in the Middle Ages, she would've been a village idiot type.

Ro: But now we have so many village idiots! And nobody's taking care of them. There's no village.

Jo: Well, real communities can absorb a few people like that. It's in the whole big city scene that you get this tremendous alienation. I seriously thought about going into politics, but now I seem to have moved to the opposite end in that I really believe real change—the sort of change we're talking about—is not just a sort of political revolution, it's a whole . . . it's a "revolution of the heart." And that's not going to come from just having political structures imposed.

I really feel change has got to come from the grass roots. And if you really follow that through, you're talking about individual people. And that individual people matter. So that woman *did* matter. Then, of course, we question what we actually did. But that's a different question from putting the emphasis on the individual or trying to change from the top.

Ro: But how are you going to get these revolutions of the heart?

Jo: The more I think about these things, the more depressed I get. I mean I really can't see any cause for optimism on a secular level, so I guess it's through faith. I think Thomas Merton said, "There's little cause for optimism but much cause for hope." Hope is like faith in the sense that it's a belief in divine providence bringing goodness, although you really can't see any sign that it's going to happen in human terms or in rational terms. You have to take it on trust. But you know, people *do* have these revolutions of the heart.

When I write letters home, I use the word "family." And I'm thinking, "This is just so soupy!" But it's true. The longer I'm here, the more different perceptions I get on what that means. To how we relate to each other. How the whole household, the whole community, relates to each other. You know, the Catholic Worker is deeply infused with the reality of being part of the Mystical Body of Christ. And all of us here, Catholic or not, respond to that in our own different ways.

Ro: You're not Catholic?

Jo: No. I go to St. Mark's Episcopal Church in the Bowery.

Ro: Oh. Does the Catholicism . . . the Roman Catholicism of the house bother you at all?

Jo: No. I've had a lot of familiarity with Catholicism and an awful lot of respect for [Catholics I know] and [for] Catholicism. Although I don't feel that I want to join the church. The basic Catholic thing for me is the Catholic Worker.

Ro: Do you leave the house much?

Jo: Oh, sure! Meg [Hyre] and I are taking classes in metaphysics. That's one thing that's just been tremendous for me. When I started school, I really loved learning—literally *loved* it! I had this great vision of universities where scholars would get together and sit at the feet of these masters. Like the medieval centers of learning. And it's just not like that at all. The students, particularly the people I met during law, were very much there because it was a step on the career ladder. I got very disillusioned. But when I came here, I just rediscovered [my love for learning].

I've been doing a lot of reading. And I've been talking—just talking—with so many people about so many different things. Back in England, I guess I would've been spending a lot more time and money on going out, on the arts. I love opera. It makes me so angry! When you think about Mozart and the way *Figaro* was staged originally. It was cheap and it was for the people, both the rich people up in the boxes and the people who'd paid very little to get in, and who'd be just as enraptured by it as everybody else. Now opera's this elite thing.

That's one thing my parents can't understand, though—this whole voluntary poverty thing. "You love opera, you love theater. How can you reconcile that?" But a friend came over a few weeks ago and she took me up to the Met. If tickets come in donation, I'll go, but I won't spend money on it.

Ro: How long are you planning on staying here, Jo?

Jo: I must say . . . [Pause] I can't really now imagine myself going back now. It seems just something alien. I feel very comfortable and very at home here. That's frightening in a sense—to come to a new country and a new city, and a new community and just really feel this is where I belong.

Since I've been here, I've realized that I [used to live] in the future. Like "I'll do this training to get this qualification, so I can do that training so I can get this job." And I was also thinking that at some point, I was going to take time out and do something I really believed in.

Now I've found I'm living more for the present. And it's leaving me more open to being able to do whatever it is I'm supposed to be doing instead of imposing my own ideas on everything.

Ro: Don't people ask you why you don't do this kind of thing in London?

Jo: Oh, sure. And I have a whole lot of questions about how I feel about Britain at the moment. I think that had something to do with me coming over here. I was just getting so depressed at what was happening in Britain. I can be more objective about America's problems.

But there are other reasons, too. Here there seems to be this whole subculture of people who are dedicating themselves to protesting something or other and who can live that. Over here you have this broad political spectrum. Britain is much more conservative religiously, and it's very difficult to take a stand, I think, and to live in the sort of way it's possible to here. That has something to do with the political climate, but in a broader sense than just what's happening at the moment. I've met so many people in Britain who have the same concerns as me and can't see a way of focusing it. There doesn't seem to be the place for really putting your theoretical ideas into practice.*

Whenever I had an evening with a good friend, we'd just get so depressed. We'd sit there and talk about all these different things that bothered us. Everything from El Salvador to education to housing. And we just couldn't see an end to it. I refused to get despairing or cynical because that just seemed hopeless. And here I feel that I've sort of gone through a doorway and that I'm on a path. I'm on the path.

---

* When Jo returned her transcript, she told me that Judith Dawes and others were starting a Catholic Worker house in Oxford, England.

PART THREE

Living Together

CHAPTER 14

Community

A Roundtable Discussion

Mother Teresa asked me, "How do they manage? Don't they take any . . . don't they make any commitment?" No, they don't. They stay as long as they want and they leave. It goes on year after year on that basis.

—Eileen Egan

W HAT unites Catholic Workers, the work or the community? Who's a part of the community? What kind of commitment should people make? What happens when people leave? Who makes decisions and how? The business of daily living is hard for everyone, particularly for the strong egos attracted to the Catholic Worker movement. In this roundtable, written as if it's occurring at a national gathering of Catholic Workers, I've combined portions of interviews with many Catholic Workers, again giving the city or town of primary affiliation, even if the narrators no longer live there.

Ro: Tina, what's the biggest problem in thinking about Catholic Worker as community?

Tina Sipula (Bloomington, Illinois): People leaving. No doubt about it. It's the whole emotional thing. People come to Clare House, and you get attached to them and love them and become a part of them and it's family and then they're ripped out of your life and you never see them again.

Ro: Guests or Workers?

Tina: Both. If a Worker says, "Well, I'm here for the duration," you put a little more energy into them. But you're kind of hesitant if you know they're going to leave. You invest more and more energy and more and more energy, and then BOOM! They're gone! It's like a kid moving away from home. You have all this investment, and the kid stands up and says, "I'm leaving now." That happens maybe five or six times in a family, but here it happens all the time.

But we see that in the New Testament. They go to a new community and get involved with them and then move on. I think it's the same thing now, the same process. On and on and on. And you have to love enough to let go and keep on going. It doesn't help the hurt a whole lot except to recognize that it *is* all one community. Unless you base yourself in that faith and that loving, you can't keep on. So it's a total growing process. I think that's why Dorothy stayed. I think that's why *I* stay.

Darla Bradley (Davenport, Iowa, and Chicago): I see the problem with Catholic Workers as the community, too. The care they give is better than any social program I've ever seen, because it's a very personal one-on-one relationship. But I think there's just always a lot of stuff [about] how people interact and get along and . . . and part of that is maybe because, you know, there's very few personal rewards, so people get burned out, yet they don't leave until they're *really* burned out.

Fr. Jack Keehan (Chicago): You know, Catholic Workers put aside their own needs and deal with a bunch of often very unpleasant people. Treat them the way we're *supposed* to treat other people. We're able to discipline ourselves into listening to some absolute lunatics and treating them with dignity and respect. Then when we're completely exhausted, one of our co-workers does something to disappoint us, and we berate them like we probably were tempted to do to the lunatic. I see that happen. I've done it myself. I've had it done to me. That displaced anger is one of the perennial problems of the Catholic Worker.

Pat Jordan (New York City and Staten Island): When Kathleen and I were at the Worker, the most remarkable thing was that sense of forgiveness within the community. You would see people do terrible things to one another and yet, because of this unwritten sense of Christian forgiveness, people were able to come back and start again. We saw this happen again and again and again. Dorothy kept repeating "seventy times seven." You have to forgive seventy times seven.

Jim Eder (Chicago): I think the prayer helps, too. When I was living at St. Francis, we had common prayer and house meetings once a week. No matter what. Some people think because you work together all day long, you don't need that, but you do. You need that time to pull away from everything. And then also, the "staff" would go out together once a week, and we couldn't talk about the house. We'd go bowling or go for pizza or to a movie, and we got to know each other as friends. I think that's a good formula, so I kind of kept trying to pass it on.

Gary Donatelli (New York City): The Catholic Worker, over the years, has talked a lot about basic Christian communities. But God forbid that [it] should try to function like a basic Christian community! It doesn't work that way. When I was living [at the New York house], we'd talk about the "invisible hierarchy of Catholic Worker anarchy."

Ro: Hmmm . . . Jim, you lived in the same house as Gary, but later. How do you see decisions as being made in the Catholic Worker?

Jim Kelly (New York City): You know, I asked Jane [Sammon] that very question the first month I was in New York, and we talked about it for a long time. It's a hot topic around here, and I still haven't figured out the answer she gave me. We have meetings—what an ugly word—and decisions are made by consensus, but there's not a real self-conscious approach to that. Nobody says, "Okay, we're going to decide by consensus."

People talk about a certain need in the community and have suggestions on how to address it. It takes a long time to really talk something out, [but the advantage is that] everybody gets to speak his or her own piece and when a decision is made, nobody feels they were ignored or voted down. In some ways, we get the most effective answers 'cause we integrate a lot of different approaches.

The decisions are being made by a group, but still in some sense, we have an inner circle making them because the people who come to that meeting on Sunday nights are people who "take the house" for the most part. So there's a division of the community, really, and it's most clearly seen on Sunday nights. Everything seems to be happening [in New York] by the grace of God, in a very natural but also very unconscious and sometimes clumsy way.

Ro: You know, I wonder who's part of the community anyway. Is it just the people who make the decisions?

Chuck Matthei (New York City): Well, I've got a great story about that. Maybe most people think the CW community is the people whose names appear in the paper, or who you would interview for your book. But I remember one day at the house in New York. Dorothy came up to me chuckling. "Do you want to hear something a little bit amusing? Several of the young people have just come to me and they're very concerned. 'We've just taken a look at everyone's schedule and over the Thanksgiving holiday, everyone is going to be gone.'" And Dorothy said, "Truly, *everyone's* going to be gone?"

There are always simple folks who aren't theorists and scholars, who in fact, do the dishes. Farmer John [Filligar] was one. Arthur [Lacey]. And Smokey Joe. Mad Paul, who used to take the scraps of food and go into the street and pass them out to the pigeons half the night. Mad Paul rarely had a direct, intelligible conversation with anybody. Would mutter to himself and carry on. But Mad Paul and Smokey Joe had more to do with keeping that soup line going, year in and year out, than any of the lovely volunteers who pass through a Worker house.

Kathe McKenna (Boston): At Haley House, we've been working this out for a couple of years, working out who is community and who makes decisions. You see, we technically have a "board of directors" because we have a nonprofit status, unlike most Catholic Workers. We got that early on. For a while, we'd meet once a year or whatever the requirement of our bylaws was, and mostly just deal with big decisions like buying property. But we never had a closed board meeting. A board meeting for a big decision was a meeting of everybody, everybody who lived in the house, everybody who was interested in the issue. We'd come together and we'd work through it for however many meetings it took.

But even that became awkward for some people—too much a mirror of the corporate world. And even though [the board had] never exercised their authority to override something with the day-to-day workers, they technically could. So we said, "Okay. How do we keep the perspective of people who are not involved in the day-to-day stuff but have something very important to offer us? Including more stability than the day-to-day workers who change so frequently. And yet not leave the power in the hands of this group."

So we started a new process. First, we had monthly staff meetings to get business done. Too much business! So we had to have committees. Now we have a finance committee, newsletter committee, speaker series, housing, farm, peace, et cetera, et cetera. All these committees meet and take care of the business and do the work in their areas. At our monthly staff meetings, all these committees share what they're doing and also any decisions that overlap or supersede or any questions that come up about a particular group.

Ro: Do individual committees work by consensus? And the staff meeting, too?

Kathe: The actual method goes like this: One—a proposal is made (with an explanation). Two—clarifying questions are entertained. (This part is adapted from C. T. Butler's *On Conflict and Consensus.*) Three—concerns are voiced. If all concerns are "answered," then we have consensus on the proposal. If a person has a concern that's not answered, he or she can either record it and "step aside," asking the group to take note of the concern, or "block consensus." Blocking consensus can only happen if *everyone* in the group shares the underlying premise on which the concern is based. Then we all agree to work on and "own" that blocking concern. Sometimes this means preliminary work must be done prior to the proposal being accepted, sometimes the proposal is altered or sent back to a committee for work.*

Under this new procedure, instead of having a separate group being the board of directors, one of the committees is the oversight committee—people who aren't involved in any of the daily work of the committees but who've been associated with us for a long time and whom we will call upon to join us when we make a big decision. Because we accept consensus, it doesn't matter whether you're on the oversight committee or on the newsletter committee. You're still one person. And when the whole group sits down to meet for a decision, each person has the same power.

So the oversight committee is not the board of directors. In order to meet the requirement of the state, we have each committee elect or somehow choose a person to be on the board of directors so that the board of directors in fact is a conglomerate of the whole organism. The board of directors as such never meets because when the staff meeting meets every month, the board of directors is meeting in the midst of this body. All the committees are open and anybody can join any committee.

Ro: What if they don't want to join any of them?

Kathe: They don't have to.

Catherine Morris (Los Angeles): Well, I've seen someone who's been in the house for two weeks come to a discussion and say, "Oh, I block consensus on that." And they don't even know what they're talking about.

Charles Walzem (Washington, D.C., and other cities): Well, I see it a little differently, I guess, being one of those people. I think too many meetings, too much worry about consensus, can be tedious.

In ways, I found similarities between monasteries and Worker communities. Both are close-knit. If a monk went away for an afternoon, he'd talk about everything that happened because he didn't want to alienate himself from the others. And I find this to be true in Worker communities also, like St. Francis in Washington. The closeness of the individuals is real and the commitment is on the same

---

* Kathe felt she didn't answer the question completely in the original interview and added this procedure when she returned the transcript.

level. Except in a religious order, there are more trappings, more externals, more rituals. In the Worker, a lot of these things are more open-ended.

Ro: Perhaps these patterns of community are more unconscious and harder for people to learn in a Worker house because they're not spelled out.

Charles: Yes, but I think you can actually confront these things rather than just say, "Well, trust me."

Ro: But do you agree that through consensus, people who are new to the community can, in fact, change [its] direction?

Charles: Oh, I think so. If they're given the proper footing. I think that relies on their point of maturation. Everybody always has the idea that this [new] person is fairly unacquainted with "our" mode. "Doesn't appear to be mature to us. Needs to make a commitment before his opinion will mean anything." You can go on and on.

Ro: I'm hearing you disagree with that.

Charles: Oh, yeah. A new member is an injection of vitality in a way. For some very staid people, that's hard to accept. To draw a parallel, there's almost a corporate structure.

Brian Terrell (New York City, Davenport, Iowa, and Maloy, Iowa): I think it's good to have people coming and going. A community can get stagnant if it's the same bunch of people living together year in and year out. You need new ideas. But when you have the larger part of the community being new people, it gets pretty crazy.

Darla: There's not a real screening process in a Catholic Worker, usually, so it's open for chaos. But we probably *do* have something to learn from the religious orders. [Sister] Ardeth [Platte] would talk about the intensive training [she had from the Dominicans] in putting the other person first. That helps them live in community because it takes away the ego part of it, you know, and thinks of the good of the whole. I don't think that happens with Catholic Workers. A lot of people in Catholic Workers have strong egos. Egos and community don't go together.

Ro: I remember Rio Parfrey telling me that there are too many leaders in the Catholic Worker movement, that they're bumping into each other.

Jane Emerson (San Diego): In my experience, young persons will get together and start a Catholic Worker. They live together. They *do* have a house, but it isn't a community to me. They attract people who help them, but there's always one person who is calling the shots, one person who runs things. And if it doesn't run their way, or if it turns out that there's too much conflict, the thing folds.

Now our San Diego Catholic Worker doesn't live in community and we suffer from that because we frequently have terrible lapses in communication. The right hand doesn't always know what the left hand is doing, which is a very hard thing when you're doing as much as we try to do and have so few people. We just go off and do it. But then, on the other hand, I sometimes wonder if we'd still be together if we lived together.

Ro: Now Don, how do you deal with the ego thing in Milwaukee, where everybody sees you as the leader? Now that you're away from the house more, how is that affecting the community?

Don Timmerman (Milwaukee): Well, I'm still there at least one or two hours a day. But I think [my being away] is a good thing. Because everybody *was* kind of depending on me to do all the decision making. Now it isn't just Don doing it, and that's good. More volunteers are coming because they see that there's something they can do. The volunteers are also on the fringe of society, in a way. We're *all* kind of outcasts coming into the house and watching over the guests. We're friends of the guests who are preparing the meals and answering the doors and the phones.

Ro: Some people talk about CW as their family.

Don: Oh, it is! It is to me, at least. The people at Casa Maria are more my family than my regular family. You know the quote: "I am a two-edged sword and because of Me, the father will leave the mother and the son will leave the father and the mother." That's happened in my life a lot. I've been cut off from people because of this house, because of this work. The movement separates people as well as brings them together.

Sue Frankel-Streit (Washington, D.C.): To a certain extent, I see the Catholic Worker as very self-contained. We live in our own little world. I find that difficult because most of my friends from before are not doing anything like this.

Ro: Do you see those friends much?

Sue: I do. Not much, but I do. When I first came here, I didn't see many people much. One of the difficult things is . . . you make people feel guilty just by what you're doing. You don't even have to say anything. But at the same time, it's my life, and if I don't talk about it, then I don't have a whole lot to say. I think it would be a shame [to lose contact with my old friends], though, because part of the whole idea of community is to spread these ideas. If the world is going to change, your way of doing things has to go further than just the community that you already have.

Ed Forand (New York City): Well, I remember that we had friends from outside. When we were on Chrystie Street in the sixties, we saw more than just the folks in the house. Every Friday night, a whole gang of us, everybody from the Worker plus about twenty other people who came to the meeting, we'd all go to this beer tavern after the meeting. There was a young couple we knew, and a fellow who used to play the guitar. And we'd all drink beer and dance. This went on every Friday night. Week after week after week. This whole gang of us, see? Some from the Catholic Worker and some just interested people. That went on for years. And then all those people left and then, you know . . . it just sort of petered out for me.

I've often thought—and it's like a fantasy, I guess—maybe we should . . . if almost everybody who had come to the Worker and been able to stay had formed some kind of big community around the neighborhood. Even the ones who got married. [Michael] Harrington and . . . and somebody else would be a journalist and somebody else a doctor and what have you.

But golly! All the older people I knew have died. *Dozens!* Dozens of them! And all the young people . . . hundreds of young people have left. The older people— a lot of them you get to love just like your brothers and sisters. And the younger people, likewise. And after a while it's . . . I loved the people around the Worker, see? All the old-timers and the young people. But so many died or left. And after a while, it just takes . . . it takes a lot out of your own heart.

Bill Griffin (New York City): If you're a single person, you need to feel, you know, that you're taking care of something, as most people in the normal way would, with a family. This [has been] the human model for thousands of years. And the kind of community [we have in New York] is in a sense a larger family, and you make your contribution and you have a sense of belonging. The belonging is important, but you want to belong to something valid, you know, something that points to something valuable. So in the middle of our nationwide crisis of homelessness, to be taking part in the work here . . . helping to keep going what I think is a good model of a small, well-run, humane, and respectful community for people who have been through the experience of homelessness, is a revolutionary act. And an important act. That act of revolution helps to keep a community going. That's how I make sense of it. And then it allows me to . . . it's a marginal position in society. The people [you were talking about, Ed] who I met at the

Worker, who had lived this life—[they] give me the courage to continue with the life for now.

I wish, you know, it was a friendlier community. I mean people who are in difficult situations aren't necessarily the politest people or the kindest people or the most noncomplaining group of people. It's a broken community, and I wish it were more welcoming, so that the younger volunteers who come with all this energy would maybe be attracted more. Our community has a lot of rough edges because people have had a lot of rough deals in life. It's not an easy place. And it's . . . you kind of wish life weren't as harsh for so many people.

Brian: I've seen a sad thing in some Worker houses where spiritual development or community development are seen as selfish, as a luxury. So when we moved together to the country, to Maloy, we didn't want to get so taken up with activities that we ignored each other. We try to build a good strong community life together. In a sense, that's made it harder because we're not letting [relationship problems] go. In the history of Worker houses, things bother people and they're too busy or too scared, so they shove it down. Just won't deal with it. And things get so bad that somebody finally has to leave. That's really a hard way to live. But it's also hard to bring up something that's bothering you. That can be frightening as well.

Chris Montesano (Sheep Ranch, California): I would also say there's been a dimension lacking in the Worker movement generally, and that's the area of human feelings. In many Worker communities, the emotional level is ignored or not dealt with, and that sometimes creates unhealthy situations. Good schools of psychology—Carl Jung and others—have validated the legitimacy of feeling in people's lives. I think whoever negates that is using their attitude as a block. They're not wanting to let other people into their lives and that's ultimately harmful to the movement. We need to form deep personal bonds with our co-workers. Now you need to have . . . a certain amount of human distance that is necessary and good, but too much distancing isn't healthy.

Ro: What about the people who just rub you the wrong way?

Chris: That definitely happens in community. And the only way that I know how to deal with that is prayer. I find that there's no other vehicle for love and acceptance, and usually it's . . . I mean there are personality conflicts, no question. What do you think, dear?

Joan Montesano (Sheep Ranch, California): Well, it's like, "Gee, I like these Catholic Workers, but I sure wouldn't want to live with them all the time!" [Laughter.] But then I *have* lived with lots of them for long periods of time.

I think some people are really pretty basically incompatible. And if you get two real strong leader types in a group, it probably won't work. On the other hand, I've never been one to be interested in following a guru type, so I'm real careful about not getting into that kind of thing. No matter how painful community is, I'd rather thrash it out than to just have a leader with a set way and all these other people behaving like children.

And in terms of incompatibility, well, I lived with Beth [Dondlinger-Whatford] for years and had a hard time really liking her, and now I just love her dearly. She's just about my closest friend. Part of that was living through and working through and loving on a day-to-day basis. Finally coming to understand, to *stand under* where she is, where she's come from and to love all those crazy parts of her just like she loves all those crazy parts of me. So I think it's possible to live through those conflicts, to work through and to pray through and laugh and cry through them. I think it's also possible that some people just cannot exist in the same close community.

Chris: There *are* some occasions, some people, with whom it won't work. But first you really have to make the effort to love. At one point in our history, we used to have what we called "feelings meetings." Basically a time when we could get together as a community and if someone was deeply disturbed about something, they could share it. With this kind of meeting, we tended to have fewer outbursts in the community, fewer times where someone would just sort of fall apart and you would have a big conflict erupt.

We used to have a saying. "Did someone leave with blood on the floor?" Or does someone leave with a recognition and support that their path is different? That's something we've really worked on. You know, sometimes when people leave, they have to put down the place they're leaving. It's the way to justify their decision.

And here's another thing. Out at Sheep Ranch, we're actually moving in the direction of requesting commitments of long-term people. Initially when someone first comes, we do several weeks. And if the several weeks work out fine, then we talk about a month. If the month works out, then we talk about six months, and then eventually longer commitments. And that's kind of . . . I know L.A. is doing that kind of thing, too. I think people are requesting commitment.

It's not . . . I would say these ideas are coming from those of us who have been here over the long haul. Joan and I are here for a long time with God's grace. We're asking for this [commitment] so we can handle things better. I don't know whether it's necessarily right, but it's one of the ways we can survive.

Ro: Teka, can you tell us about Karen House? It seems to be a very intentional community. Do people take part in some sort of joining ceremony, make a formal commitment?

Teka Childress (St. Louis): Yes. It's not a big legal thing, but there's a definite line. It's clear to everyone who's part of our community and who's not. In a sense everyone is, even people who only come to Mass with us and stuff, but we're fairly structured in our intentional community. People who are a part of our community agree to take on the responsibility of running the house, and everyone who's part of the community comes to the weekly meeting at which we make decisions by consensus. Every other week we have a part of community meeting called "Tradition" where we talk about some issue that's relevant to the Catholic Worker, either some Catholic Worker reading or something current in the paper, or a political issue that somebody brings us, something that's somehow related to Catholic Worker tradition. And we have discussions [on these issues].

Pat Coy (St. Louis): We have other inbuilt mechanisms to build community, too. Every Wednesday night, we're together for dinner, prayer, and a meeting. On Tuesday night we have liturgy and on Sunday night we have our community time, "ordinary time" together. And we go away for all-day meetings every other month. These days are times of prayer, recreation, business meetings, and community-building activities.

We value community life [in St. Louis]. We work on it. We're careful about the size of the community and who becomes a part of the community. We share economics. Some of us have jobs outside in the capitalist economy. Others of us work, you know, more full time in the house or for social change, and we pool those economic resources to allow people to choose the kind of work that's most meaningful for them. Oftentimes people get penalized for making those kinds of choices in the capitalist economy, but by being a community that's willing to share finances and cars and that sort of thing, we're able to do that.

Ro: Now when I visited Milwaukee, Don, I noticed that your house seems to have an ebb and flow. Everybody doesn't feel they have to make huge commitments.

Don: Right. We never . . . very few people put guilt trips on other people. I mean a person can live here on third floor and still not spend a lot of time in the house. We don't want people here who don't want to be. That's the big thing. Because if they don't want to be here, they're going to be rude to the guests. You have to enjoy being here. Otherwise it's not going to go, not going to continue.

Catherine: All that enjoyment . . . sometimes, I've felt, over the years, that the community gets so focused on itself and has such a good time together that it sort of misses what it's really supposed to be doing. It still goes on—the kitchen goes on, the community goes on—but what's really happening is we're entertaining ourselves.

I can remember one time at our house in L.A. It was just driving me crazy that everybody got so into sports. Everyone was just constantly going off to play basketball and volleyball and this and that and the other thing. I thought it was really weird. It seemed like we didn't want the work to be getting in the way of our scheduled events.

Ro: Would you have felt that way if somebody got into a really heavy reading program?

Catherine: Well, I . . . you know, like Jeff reads much of the night, but you don't find him sitting around reading novels in the middle of the day. I *have* been annoyed when people . . . when I'm working my ass off and someone is sitting there reading a novel.

Ro: Okay, but what if it were, you know, the latest economic analysis or one of Dorothy's books?

Catherine: Well, I think it's important to read in general and important to read about the movement and all, but I think it's also important to know that you're sitting on your haunches when someone else is doing your work. I guess I think our use of time sometimes needs analysis. If we're getting ready for a demonstration, and there are eight things that need doing and only two days left, and someone decides to go off to a concert, I think they're maybe missing the whole picture. But then, of course, there's lots of good times and times when having fun is good to do. Like this last summer with something I thought was a really stupid idea at first.

Ro: What was that?

Catherine: Well, Jeff decided we should have a prom. He likes theme parties. The prom . . . it was a thrift shop prom. About a hundred and fifty people came. We sent out invitations and mentioned it in our newspaper and people came in prom clothes. We decorated the hall at the USC Newman Center just like a prom with the revolving ball thing and the streamers and the aluminum foil stars catching the lights and all that stuff. A band and dresses and tuxes and cummerbunds. The whole thing.

I thought it just sounded so stupid, but everyone wanted to do it, so I did what I usually do—you know, all the organizing, getting everything there and all that kind of stuff. Got my friend, Pat Carter, to help. Everyone had a *wonderful* time! Everyone thought it was a great idea and it just worked.

Nevada [the national gathering of Catholic Workers sponsored by the Los Angeles house] was the same way. We didn't know really quite what we were doing. We thought of this great idea and printed it in the paper. People started responding, and we didn't even know what it was going to be. But "by little and by little," it fell into place. And then suddenly we were heading out there to Nevada, and we had never seen the school [where the gathering was held]. And then it just came together. Those are the best times for me.

Some of our Masses are the best of times. Sometimes at Christmas. We serve this incredible meal at the kitchen—ham and hash browns and scrambled eggs and fresh fruit cocktail and coffee cake and bread to make sandwiches 'cause there is so much ham. And candy canes and just everyone loves it. Sometimes it just comes off without a hitch, and we have a Mass at the end for the volunteers and go away feeling great.

Sometimes it's just little things that weren't planned. Sitting up in the community room and laughing at ourselves and laughing at our guests and at everything that's happened.

Joan: I remember that Dorothy wrote about the community coming together around the work. She didn't talk about intentional community the way they talk about it today. When we were in San Francisco, the work was the main thing and if you're not there for the work, get out. That appealed to me because in religious life, I felt the community existed for its own good. For instance, we had to stop functioning at certain times. No one could enter the convent after such and such hour of the night, and you didn't expect people to call you after nine-thirty and all that sort of stuff. What were we protecting ourselves from, or what were we doing? It felt kind of inbred.

I liked that aspect of the Worker, that we were out there for others. But we were having some problems at the house in San Francisco, and one of the people in the house said, "If we can't meet the needs of the Workers here, then it's not going to work, either." At the time we didn't really see it that way, but in the long view they were right. There's got to be a balance.

Larry Purcell (Redwood City, California): We see the work as the cement. We try to work like mad together and have that work overflow into some prayer. And yes, we do have a lot in common with monks. Monks pray like mad and hope that the prayer flows into the work. We kind of reverse that. So in our ten years of existence in Redwood City, we really haven't tried to have the Workers do everything together—work together, play together, pray together, live intensely together. We work together, and we do some praying together. We also take a month off every year to rest. Once a year, we go away to a monastery together . . . the whole group of Catholic Workers. On a traditional retreat. Very, very Catholic. We go to Redwoods Monastery in Whitethorn, California, which has a wonderful group of Trappistine women.

Dick Dieter (Alderson, West Virginia): Most Catholic Worker houses, I think, are just trying to figure out how to get to tomorrow and not how to take care of an institution called the Catholic Worker. It's different from a religious community too, in that a religious community builds and preserves more than the local house, which is all the Catholic Worker ever was concerned about. There's nobody really concerned about preserving the Catholic Worker movement. Well, I guess that's probably not [entirely] true. And religious communities have to think financially in terms of the far future—their buildings, their schools, their hospitals, whatever. They really have a lot sunk into an institution.

Maggie Louden (Alderson, West Virginia): I don't know if my prime goal when we were living as Catholic Workers was creating community. I believe it's important in community to *work* at community, but I really feel . . . Orsay, the theologian, used to say that there are basically two kinds of communities. One is an apostolic community and it exists to carry on the apostolate. Therefore, the work is the most important and the community supports that. And then there is a community which is more contemplative, where it's the community that's important. I really felt that the Catholic Worker was the former. But everybody has a need for companionship. Community's the way it's expressed and that's important, too.

Dick: The exciting thing about the Catholic Worker was that it gave us an outlet to really work, but to do it with other people who had similar minds. That was beautiful! That was . . . to try and do it alone would have been impossible.

Ro: What made you decide to identify with the Catholic Worker [when you were establishing the prison visiting ministry at Alderson]?

Dick: I think we felt like we were isolated somewhat, way down in the West Virginia hills. First of all, we *were* [isolated] geographically, but then you think in terms of how [you want to be] connected to a bigger movement. And the Catholic Worker was clearly the closest thing that we could associate with. We didn't feel we always lived up to the poverty of the Catholic Worker movement, for example, because the rural area is not like the inner city. It was beautiful there. And Catholic Worker people wanted to identify the house that way. "Can we include you in this directory?"

Ro: That larger CW community does seem to be important to everyone. Even though there's no abbot—or abbess—to keep it together, the national reunions seem to do that in some ways. Now Joe, you've been to several reunions. Can you talk a bit about them?

Joe Zarrella (Tell City, Indiana): Oh, I love going. Love meeting the people, hearing what they're doing and, you know, exchanging ideas with them. It sometimes gets kind of lonely being way down in Tell City and taking positions where people don't necessarily agree with you all the time. So a reunion is always a sense of renewal.

Fr. Richard McSorley (Washington, D.C.): One thing the Catholic Worker movement offers: if you get somebody from the Catholic Worker in California to come to your house to help, you know pretty well the kind of person you're getting. You know their values. And one of the joys of being with a group at a national gathering is to feel you're with people who understand you and whom you understand without hardly knowing their names. You don't have that in a parish.

Jeff Dietrich (Los Angeles): I guess the best way to describe it is communion of saints. You know, you hear that term all the time but in the Catholic Worker you really have a sense of it. The communion of saints is right here in this house. It's with the Catholic Worker community, and it's with the people who live here, and it's with the people down on the streets and in the soup kitchen. In some way, in both a mystical way and a real pragmatic way, you're united with them in the here and now.

You're also united in this tradition that goes all the way back to Jesus and Moses and the Passover. Everything seems to come together for me in our Passover celebration when we break matzo together and feel so united with our history. The Eucharist extends that tradition from Jesus back five, ten thousand years to Moses and to the Promised Land and to all of the prophets. This feeling that you're a part of that tradition and that you're choosing to be. It isn't some kind of rigid, narrow ritual. It's a celebration!

I remember one year. At one point during the Passover ceremony we had readings from the Bible and from St. Francis and from Dorothy and Daniel Berrigan and then someone read this piece from my book.* And I just . . . I was so

---

* The book is *Reluctant Resister.*

overcome at hearing my own words read back to me in this context that . . . that I'm a part of that. It . . . it does obviously move me.

Karl Meyer (Chicago): Yes, the communion of saints. I believe that we are . . . we *can* be in communion with Gandhi and Jesus and Joan of Arc and the other people that we admire in history. As Oscar Romero said, "If they kill me, I will rise again in the Salvadoran people. I will live in them."

The saints live in us, too, maybe more than other people do. Maybe that's what saints are—people whose vitality was such that it carries on in the memory of the coming generation and we appeal to them. They are still living, moving us. A. J. Muste, Dorothy Day, Ammon Hennacy—they are still very alive to me because of what I learned from them.

And then the Eucharist, the idea of the breaking of bread. "They knew Him in the breaking of the bread." The idea of the breaking of bread is in the last page of Dorothy Day's *The Long Loneliness*, that very, very beautiful passage in which Dorothy speaks about community.

"We can't love God unless we love each other. And to love we must know each other. We know Him in the breaking of bread and we know each other in the breaking of bread. And we are not alone anymore."

CHAPTER 15

Families in the Worker

What do you do when the cries of the poor are louder than the cries of your own kids?

—Kathy Shuh-Ries

COUPLES meet, marry, and sometimes divorce through the Worker. In this chapter, Workers of all ages discuss their courtships, weddings, and family lives, including the economics of raising a family in community.

Paul Magno and Marcia Timmel are active resisters who left Dorothy Day House in Washington, D.C., to begin the Olive Branch Catholic Worker.

Marcia Timmel: I had reached a point in my life where I wasn't really even dating seriously, simply because I was committed to going to jail periodically. Also, I wanted to live in the slums and live in shelters with homeless people, and how could you ask anyone to share that sort of life with you? I guess I saw myself sort of as a lay nun.

In fact, I think that mind-set might have made it easier to get to know Paul. We weren't constantly sizing each other up, thinking, "What sort of spouse material is this?" I helped at St. Francis over the Christmas holiday, and we really got to know each other through the work, which may be the healthiest way to avoid the really sick stuff that the culture has instilled in us about dating and romance. In the end, it occurred to me that I might find someone to share this kind of life with, but it was watching how the children were being raised at Jonah House that gave me the nerve to think that I could even *consider* parenting.*

I saw that it was possible for people to come together in the midst of all this craziness and to choose to live differently. To say they're not going to do it per-

* Phil Berrigan and Liz McAlister are the models here. While it does not call itself a Catholic Worker community, their Jonah House is an intentional faith and resistance community with close ties to the Worker.

fectly but are going to keep trying anyway. I think what we've tried to create here, and definitely what they create at Jonah House and what I think the Catholic Worker is all about, is this understanding that we're *all* family. We are all sisters and brothers.

Ro: But Dorothy and other people have said it's too hard to raise children when you're doing hospitality, particularly with people who might be mentally ill.

Marcia: I can understand that. And there might have been a time when there was some hope of isolating children. I don't know if that was healthy or not. Today, if I were raising my daughter anyplace in Washington, D.C. (assuming that I had gone any route except getting myself up to the fifty thousand dollars a year which would enable me to isolate myself out in the suburbs), she'd be exposed to drug pushers in her elementary school. Exposed to child molesters, confronted with . . .

The sort of life that I think Dorothy would have liked for Tamar, and that she encouraged Catholic Workers in an earlier age to try to provide for their children, doesn't exist in America today. I don't know if it ever existed. But to the extent that this fairy-tale ideal of the good life for children is aspired to, what we end up raising is a generation of very self-absorbed citizens. Not necessarily selfish, but self-absorbed. Who even do their giving in a self-centered way. "How am I being affirmed by this? How is my giving gratifying me?" I'm almost at a loss for words to describe it . . . Shallow. Living in a vacuum. Numbed.

I don't see that you can raise children in a traditional nuclear family environment. In this day and age, it would mean mom and dad going to work because the only way we could afford that fancy house in the suburbs would be with both of us working. And that means day care, which means that your children are being raised with someone else's values being instilled in them rather than yours. And having so little contact with your kids! I don't think that's the life Dorothy envisioned for families, either.

I look at intentional communities now as the place of refuge, as the healthiest possible place. All the better if you're raising your kids with direct contact with the poor, but in the sense that we look at them as our peers, not as underlings that we're going to minister to in a sort of subservient way. Ideally, what you're doing when you're living in an intentional community that is also a shelter is providing an alternative culture—an alternative environment of healing for a lot of kids who have been marginalized. And it's a lot easier to raise your own family in a shelter where you're offering hospitality to other families. I think probably the biggest reservation I had about leaving Dorothy Day House was taking Sarah out of that environment.

Ro: But I've listened to families who have decided not to raise their children in community. One reason they gave was that the values they were trying to live out as a family weren't always the values of the families they were serving. Did that go into your decision to leave Dorothy Day House?

Paul Magno: That wasn't a deciding factor. If you're doing family hospitality, you shouldn't feel yourself above living in community with those families—living as a family. If the service you're providing and the kind of life you're offering in the house is something you think is reasonable and tolerable for them, but you somehow don't think it's reasonable and tolerable for your family, that's something of a double standard. And I wouldn't . . . although, there are some real culture gaps . . .

Ro: Like violence and trying to raise nonviolent kids.

Paul: Sure. There would be features of life in families coming into the house that we'd be concerned about. For instance, we don't have a television here [at Olive Branch].

Marcia: The kids [at Dorothy Day House] have never seen a lion, have never seen an elephant. Don't have the slightest idea what a giraffe is unless they've seen a cartoon on TV. Until we take them to the zoo. In Dorothy's age, the majority of the homeless were men, not children. In the United States today, the majority of homeless people are children. That's mind-blowing! I think Dorothy would realize how important it is to have models of stable, healthy, loving family life for these marginalized families who have suffered so much violence.

Two years after this interview, on All Saints Day 1991, Marcia wrote the following:

> The reality of the violence around us has forced us to teach our children tough lessons: *never* touch a needle on the ground; *always* drop to the floor or ground when you hear gunfire. Then two weeks ago we experienced an episode that has left me with no alternative but to move. As we were coming into the house on M Street from a wedding, a free-ranging gunfight broke out on the street. Our two daughters, Sarah and Ariel, had to lie on their stomachs on the living room floor, for fear a stray bullet would come through the window. They were safe; unfortunately a little boy who lives around the corner was caught in the crossfire.

Unlike the neighborhood boy, Marcia had a choice. She and the girls moved to a safer neighborhood.

✦

Terry Bennett-Cauchon and her husband Leo founded a house in San Diego which served primarily women and children. At the time of the interview, Terry was living in her own apartment and they were sharing child care.

Terry Bennett-Cauchon: When Leo and I first decided that we were going to get married, it was as much a decision to be Catholic Workers for life as it was to be married for life. I don't think that either of us [would stay] with the Catholic Worker for life separately.

Ro: What are the differences between living in community with someone and living in community when you're married?

Terry: Oh, there's a big difference! When you're single and living in community, it's who you are as a person that reflects on community and reflects on each person that you deal with. But as soon as you become a couple, whether you're married or not, there seems to be a new dynamic of you relating to the community as a couple as well as the community relating to you like that. They have a hard time separating you, and you relate to the community in terms of how they're reacting to your spouse or your boyfriend.

I've spent a lot of time trying to get the community to understand Leo and Leo to understand the community. It's just much more complicated in dealing with a couple. Leo is a very strong personality, and he often communicates in ways that are unique, and he's really hard-nosed about a lot of things. And sometimes he would not be able to make that bridge between where people are and where he wants them to be. And [for me] to try and get *him* to hear *them* and then to turn around and get them to understand where he's coming from—that was a real strong dynamic in community. That was real difficult. It really complicated things from being a single person.

Ro: What about taking care of the children?

Terry: Leo *is* a feminist, and he's very, very involved in the raising of the children except for this past few months where he's had to work out of the Worker for money. And he's really good about house cleaning and all that kind of stuff, so that nitty-gritty work isn't something that falls totally on my hands just because I'm a woman.

But there's another dynamic: Leo's very work-oriented. He's a workaholic, which most Workers tend to be, especially the male ones. So the burden often falls that he's busy, and I end up with the kids all the time. He thinks in terms of work values, and he doesn't focus as much on community and the values that I think are more feminine. I'm very relationship-oriented. The relationship ends up being the last thing on the agenda. We're supposed to "feed off what was in the past and wait for the future." That's a Leo line.

When I first started this work, my relationships with the guests were very, very . . . they developed to be close. I'd feel good about the guests, and they could suck me dry. They could need and need and need, and it didn't burn me out, you know. I had plenty to give, but after a while, if you're not feeding yourself, and you're not feeding your relationships, there's nothing to replenish that.

Leo's always joking that we don't recruit Workers, we grow them. We have four children, you know. But there's a reality in that, too. Although the work that we do here is much more complicated because we have children, it's also easier. They're a real resource in themselves. The children who come here are stressed out. Their lives have been jumbled up for so long, they don't know where they're going. They're very insecure, but here they deal with kids who are rooted. They spend a lot of time playing with my kids and working out their lives and they calm down.

It's really interesting. [Our older boys] are only seven and six but they know that their lives are partially taking care of other kids. They talk sometimes: "When the kids come here, they're so angry, Mom."

"Well, what will you do?"

"We play with them, see, and then they calm down."

The hardest part for me is living in poverty. I had no problem with that when we lived as community at the San Jose Catholic Worker. I had a strong relationship in the community, and I lived right there on the streets with the people and felt their poverty. It's much more difficult as a family when my kids are affected. I'm basically their oppressor if I'm forcing them to live a life of poverty that isn't natural. They know they don't have to live this way. It's *our* choice, not theirs. And so I'm always trying to walk a thin line. I think I've kind of erred on the side of living a little too well for a Catholic Worker. I'm not totally comfortable with what I have. I don't want to enforce a strict extreme poverty upon my children and have them grow up and resent it and reject it and go live lives of conspicuous consumption when they leave here. I'm really afraid of that. I've talked to different people who say that's exactly what happened to them. I think at times I *do* pamper them too much because I was deprived as a child. It's a hard balance for me. The hardest thing.

Lynn Klein and her fiancé (now husband), Bob Lassalle, of the Oakland Catholic Worker traveled throughout the United States in the summer of 1990, meeting Worker families and talking to them about raising families in community.

Lynn Lassalle-Klein: I believe there's a *gift* of voluntary poverty. Some people really desire it, desire that desert experience with God, that real extreme. The danger is if it's spiritualized as something "higher" or better. And of course, it changes when we talk about having a family.

Bob Lassalle-Klein: The Catholic Worker movement is basically a movement of middle-class solidarity; none of us are living like the poor of Latin America, Africa, or even East Oakland, where our house is. Some, of course, are living more so than others. That's where the questions come in and we need some humility about that. None of us . . . I haven't met anybody in the Catholic Worker movement who looks like a really, really poor person, a person who's destined to die before their time, to die for economic reasons.

But the question is, "How much do you want to push that?" In the Worker movement, there's a whole range of options. I think we're clear about what we want to do. At our age . . . I mean I'm thirty-eight and Lynn is thirty-two, and we're clear that we want to do solidarity. We're also clear that being poor is very hard. Gutierrez, the theologian, talks about making the option for the poor in three ways: being *for* the poor, being *with* the poor, and being *like* the poor. It's a movement of solidarity, solidarity of one class to another. In terms of living *como el pobre* or "like the poor," we're basically making practical accommodations because, for us, the important things is to stay. For instance, we're not under the illusion that we have to condemn our kids to a substandard education in the Oakland public schools (which are in receivership) because we have to be *like* the poor. That's something we decided to be practical about.

And then there's health insurance. Lots of Catholic Workers don't have it. We don't have it in Oakland, either. But what I see here is a boycott of the insurance industry, not living as the poor. Almost every single Worker house we've visited has solved the problem of insurance. Either they have a clinic or they have personal connections. Or they're religious and their order pays for it. Or the diocese. We've met almost nobody who always uses—really uses—the services that the poor use. So it's a boycott of the insurance industry. Let's call it what it is.

Ro: Some people barter to get the health services, or work them off.

Bob: Exactly. My point here is that this is revelatory of a bigger picture, which is that we're essentially middle-class people with connections.

While Dorothy didn't encourage young married couples to do hospitality in the early days, Lou and Justine Murphy in Detroit raised their children in St. Martha's, a house that welcomed families. I interviewed them a year before they died. Here is what Justine remembered about raising a family. Because the Detroit community had a farm not too far from the city, their children were able to spend summers in the country.

Justine Murphy: It was a wonderful break for the family after being cooped up in the city and living with other families. To really get away and be out in the woods and to join the 4-H and all those good things. The children loved that.

Ro: Now you had six children and you all lived in St. Martha's House.

Justine: Yes. At first it was a concern to us. How would the children be affected by this very intimate association with poverty? When they were very young, it just added up to a lot of . . . a lot more work for me in organizing the house and seeing that the work got done. Looking after my own family. Looking after other people's children at times. But we never went without the necessities of milk and juice and, you know, an adequate diet for our children.

Ro: What about raising children in a house with people who had problems, tensions, possibilities of violence?

Justine: We were spared from any serious problems of violence. I'm certain that had that been a real issue in our lives, we would have had to change things a bit.

Ro: What about mental illness?

Justine: We had some, but they were the controllable type. For example, I recall this one woman who had lost her baby. She was very much affected by that, and she'd go in our children's bedroom when there was no one there, go into the closet and just fondle the little dresses and things that our daughter had. We were concerned about that. And I remember we had a family dog that the children loved, and it stayed up in their room. So we had that sense . . .

Ro: What were the advantages of raising your children in a house of hospitality?

Justine: I think it gives them a choice. And we did hope and pray to God that they would be influenced by our concept of what real religious spirit is. To love one's fellow man. And that was the thing that I suppose we were attempting to get across. And sometimes it came across in rather strange ways, you know.

For instance, at Christmastime we had many, many family friends who were very, very good to our children in the sense of presenting gifts. Because there was not money for us to go out and buy gifts and that sort of thing. I remember someone gave Maureen a doll with a little suitcase with clothes and everything. She was just thrilled with it!

It was always our custom that when any one of us got something—a really lovely, lovely gift—we were to share it. So the children agreed that each one would choose one of their gifts to give to a poor family in the area. (At that time, there were many, many very poor families that had nothing for Christmas.) I'll always remember when Maureen decided to give this doll. I was kind of heartbroken. She was giving her most favorite. It was beautiful.

The work was not easy. We had our own family, and we might have laundry from thirty people who lived with us. The physical work was . . . was extraordinary.

Ro: Well, people say you can tell why they call it the Catholic *Worker.*

Justine: Yeah. It *is* harder than raising a family. I mean I can look back now in the comparative ease of my retirement and remember how demanding it was. Not just the ordinary everyday work, but the calls that would come in at three or four in the morning from the police division and so on. But I do think that the Lord does give you the strength you need. He absolutely does! I can recall at one point where I'd sleep only about four hours a night and still feel physically able to do what had to be done.

But the question remains . . . here we are forty years later, and if you were to ask me if this was a success, I would say I don't know.

Ro: How does anyone know?

Justine: Yeah. How do I know about myself, even? It seems at each phase of our life there is a slightly different emphasis. I think of those years of raising the family as the *doing* years and certainly, you know, you did things. You were convinced that they were the good works of God. Then in your later years, you sit back and you wonder. Doing, then being. So don't ever ask me: "Hey, do you feel that you did the right thing?" We did what we knew was necessary at the time. Every moment, every day, every year.

Tom and Monica Cornell met at the Worker in New York in 1963. They moved into their own apartment after their marriage, but have always done hospitality of some sort. Currently, they live in Waterbury, Connecticut, and care for adolescents at Guadalupe House in addition to doing soup kitchen work. Tom was ordained a deacon shortly after we talked.

Monica Cornell: We had our reception at the Worker. And oh, there was a lovely transformation of the second-floor room, the one used for mailing out the paper. A very energetic, organized kind of woman who was volunteering at the Worker—Clare Bee—decided she would get crepe paper and white tablecloths. It was quite astounding! Most of the Worker social events are no-frills or at least low-frills, but this was amazing. She had little finger sandwiches, you know, tea sandwiches. And they had gotten a cake, a real wedding cake. (It might have been donated.) We figured the wedding cost ninety-six dollars. I can't remember if that included the seventeen-dollar dress. (We splurged. My parents bought the dress at Arnold Constable—a seventeen-dollar dress.) I was very practical. Didn't want to get anything that I wouldn't use again. I still fit into it, too, and I'm thinking I'll wear it when Tom is ordained deacon next month.

Tom Cornell: It's been good. Been good. A lot of red diaper babies sell real estate.* My daughter is organizing anti-apartheid demonstrations at Smith College. She identifies herself as a Catholic Worker. She wrote a marvelous extended essay . . . well, a lot of it was about the tension between her and me as she grew up, and how she began to understand what it was about. Extremely powerful. Her professor gave her an "A" and sent us a hundred dollars. Deirdre is very like me in some ways. Her spirituality came out in the essay—her identification with the church, her identification with the Catholic Worker, her identification with the struggle, if you can call it that, her recognition of the price that's been paid. [Pause] We've paid the price.

Our son Tommy is different—the coolest person I've ever met. Nothing fazes him, and he's been that way since he was the smallest child, climbing his way over a guy's body in the Bowery. He sees it all. He is deeply spiritual. Very sensitive. Very faithful.

Ro: Is it hard for him to be little Tom?

Tom: Probably. Sure. Harder for him than for Deirdre. Being male. Having the same name. So he runs [the afternoon] soup kitchen with a minimum of supervision from me. Which is nice for me, too. He's capable of doing it. I insist, though, that any changes go through me. I bring recommendations to the [Council of Churches] committee, and there is a chain of command, as it were. But I give him as much free space as I can.

He's a terrible public speaker from a technical point of view, but he's powerfully effective. The first time out, he brought back a thousand dollars. He gets up to that microphone, talks right into it, hesitatingly. He's got a fine vocabulary. He is a . . . he could become a writer. He always hits hard on the spiritual aspects of the work. I mean here he is with all that hair, a red bandanna on his head. People say, "There's the hippie. Looks like walkin' 1968. But I wish my kid could be like that. My kid's a walkin' hard-on! Doesn't have a thought in his

---

* "Red diaper babies" are children of Communist Party members.

head." A lot of Catholic Worker families have had success in keeping their kids, in transmitting . . . much more so than Old Left families, or our Quaker friends.

Ro: Why?

Tom: I don't know. But I'm just very grateful. We must have done something right. Monica . . . Monica has a genius for raising kids.

Pat and Kathleen Jordan also met and married at the New York Worker.

Pat Jordan: When we . . . finally asked each other to be married, we . . . I guess it was the next day, we went to the Worker to tell Dorothy we had decided to get married. And her response was, "I never thought he'd ask."

A number of times over the years that Kathleen and I had known each other, [Dorothy] had said, "Don't get married unless it's really compelling." She had seen so many marriages around the Catholic Worker not work out. But Dorothy was very indirect, often, in her advice.

Kathleen Jordan: She'd often tell you a story. And you'd wonder if she was ever going to get to the point. And then all of a sudden—wham! I certainly found that very often. And maybe that's why it took us longer to make this decision. We met in '69 and we were engaged in the summer of '72 and married that September. When you read some of Dorothy's writings, though . . . I mean there certainly were a lot of . . . almost tragic situations. And I think she was trying to discourage a romantic notion of both marriage and celibacy.

Ro: Did she encourage you to leave the Worker then after you were married?

Kathleen: Oh, not at all. She was the opposite. I mean we were very close to her by then, and it was very hard for us that we were leaving. At one time she actually asked, in an indirect way, if we would stay. And then she immediately stepped back and just sort of fell against me, and I was patting her on the back. Then she straightened up and said, "Don't pity me." I felt she was really saying something to herself, but she certainly was saying something to me, also. So it was very hard to part.

Kathy Shuh-Ries and her former husband, Leo, married and had their two boys while at Casa Maria in Milwaukee.

Kathy Shuh-Ries: I grew up in a very large chaotic family. There were fifteen of us. A lot of chaos, a lot of noise, a lot of commotion. The Catholic Worker house is like that. Always somebody acting up. Always somebody needing help or needing cooperation with projects. We learned how to work hard at very early ages and also learned to share anything we had. Those were things that went with me to the Catholic Worker house.

But I grew up a survivor, and I don't want my kids to be just survivors. It's a hard place to be, just almost recycles the issues for another generation. Prior to this year, we always lived in very, very poor neighborhoods. Central city. I noticed that our children were beginning to become real racists. They were becoming more violent. One summer we had four turtles killed in front of them. They were tired of having their bikes pulled out from under them. Children breaking their toys. They were beginning to have this anger, so we moved here, where it's a lot quieter.

Ro: What about raising children in the community itself?

Kathy: We saw both positive and negative with that. The positive was that the kids belonged to a larger community. The hard part was that as those community members moved in and out of their lives, they experienced a lot of loss at an early age. The other part is . . . what do you do when the cries of the poor are louder than the cries of your own kids? Do you listen to the person who has no food to eat, who's standing at the door and needs that extra half-hour when you were going to take your kids to a park? What do you do? You tend to put your own kids off more. Tend to be less available. Tend to be gone to meetings all the time and your family, your wife, your kids get put on a back burner. Then it becomes just as harsh for them as for the people who are walking in off the street. It can be very harsh. So I think the couples and families that do make it build in some safeguards.

The good part is the children have more role models. They also see more situations that have not been good, the situations that have failed. They see where they could end up. It's bittersweet. It's a mixture. And there are no guarantees, but there are no guarantees when you're outside the Worker movement, either.

Where we live now is a very working-class neighborhood. Most of the people on the block work, or one person works, and there is much more emphasis on family. Actually, there is more community than I have experienced living in inner-city neighborhoods. We were all struggling so hard to survive and to eke out a living there that we didn't have time to be family or to be joyous. It was just survival.

Patti McKee was a single Worker living in the Des Moines house when we talked.

Patti Mckee: Right now, I think it's partly because we're a little short-staffed, but we get so caught up in doing all the work that sometimes there's not enough time to really do a lot of constructive things with the kids. And so they end up being out on their own, getting into things that a lot of the other poor in the neighborhood get into, things that are eventually going to get them into trouble.

It . . . it's really hard sometimes. [One thing] I got very frustrated with was that the person who had the house ended up watching the kids. You're busy enough answering the phone and cooking the meal and all this kind of stuff, and it's really hard. Especially when the kid's a two-year-old. You blink your eyes and they're halfway down the street. I think we run into other things, too. Like the parent will leave and not tell anyone exactly where they're going, and just assume that we know they're going to be back. But what if something happens to the child in the meantime?

> The following voices are from the Noonday Farm community in Winchendon Springs, Massachusetts. David Specht is married to Claire Pearson and they have young children; Louise Cochran and Jim Levinson's children are a bit older. Jim speaks first of being a part of the Boston community.

Jim Levinson: There were people coming to eat at Haley House [when we were there] who were so wounded or so angry that I had no access to them, no matter what I would try. But Noah did. I'd bring Noah down and he would bring light into the eyes of these people. It was remarkable. One person told us that seeing Noah kept her alive.

Ro: But I think, Jim, that many young parents worry about the violence in people who don't always have control. Did you ever have any experiences where you felt your children were in danger?

Jim: Never with the kids. Plenty of times myself, but never with the kids. There's something just remarkably disarming about kids. Really disarming. The one problem we had was trying to keep people from giving Noah junk food, particularly the older folks.

Ro: Louise, what about your children's spiritual life?

Louise Cochran: Right now, we pray with them every day. And they live in what's essentially a Christian community. They celebrate Advent, they celebrate Passover, they celebrate Hanukkah, they celebrate Christmas, they go to the High Holy Day services.

But we do take them to Jewish Sunday School. So it will be interesting to see which path they choose. In my own life, I know the Christian path is right for me. But I can't say, you know, that the others are wrong. I believe that every path leads to what Christians call God.

My children are little, but I hope that what I feel is philosophically true now will be emotionally true as they grow up. That as long as they have a relationship with God and are people of faith and treat other people kindly and respectfully out of that context, I don't care how they worship.

I mean on Pentecost, Jimmy was in Sri Lanka . . . God knows what he was doing, but the children and I were at the Peace Pagoda which is run by our friends, the Buddhists. Noah was helping to decorate the booth that was constructed for the celebration of the Lord Buddha's birthday. And I was overcome with a sense of gratitude. When somebody says to him, "Those Buddhists! They're such heathen. Worship idols," he'll say, "No. Some of my best friends are Buddhists."

Ro: And their formal education?

Louise: The children have been going to the local public school, but we've decided to send them to the Waldorf School in the fall.

Ro: How does that square with the intentional simplicity?

Louise: Well, it probably doesn't. But inconsistency is, after all, the spice of life. We feel that it's just too difficult for the children to try and fit in to the local ethos.

Ro: Which is?

Louise: Well, it's materialistic. It's very unspiritual. And patriotic in the worst sense of the word. Meaning that it's dogmatic and it's . . . I don't know. Parochial, in the sense of limited, I guess. This is a lower-middle-class town. A lot of prejudice, and I think dogmatic thinking about what's been passed down.

For instance, Noah said to me the other day . . . one of his favorite things to eat is the *samosas* from India. We brought him one from the Indian restaurant in Worcester and I said I'd stick it in his lunchbox. He said, "I'm never taking one of those to school again. The kids laughed at me."

Ro: Now he's growing up in this alternative lifestyle. He'll be going to a Waldorf school. He'll probably go to a good college. But what if he wants to go to Merrimac Community College and be a beautician?

Louise: Well, that would be hard for me. Yeah.

David Specht: The folks in town here wonder about us. For instance, once a contractor was working on the front of our porch. He was here for the better part of a week and sort of asked little questions around the edges. And the last day he was here, it was rainy and we invited him inside for coffee. We're sitting around the table.

"Mind if I ask you a question?"

"No, go ahead."

"Are any of you married or anything like that?" [Laughter.]

Claire Pearson: Living up here in community on a farm is so much fun! It's particularly fun to be around David so much and not to be a nine-to-five couple anymore.

David: Yeah, it's good, real good, to be together and to have the families together. But one thing we wrestle with right now is three families who have three different sets of parenting styles. We draw different parameters for our kids. Different bedtimes, different . . . you know, all that kind of stuff. How do we work that out?

Ro: And how do you and Haley House folks handle the plentitude? The grants, the largesse. Haley House has . . . is it a million dollars? (I was looking at the literature.) Over a million dollars worth of real estate. It doesn't seem to be Catholic Worker simplicity.

Jim: That's right. None of this is owned by any of us, including the vehicles, and we try to think of it as stewardship. We feel grateful to have it. We want to be good caretakers and use it in a way that people through history, along that golden thread, would have used it. And we . . . being in community and being conscious of that notion of stewardship, we try to keep each other really honest about that.

Ro: What if you want to buy a book? You have money to buy the books you want, don't you?

Jim: Well, you know, that's one of the tricky things. There aren't that many models yet for a community of families that's based on consensus decision making rather than being hierarchical. It's really tricky. We've been trying to do economic sharing and that's a particularly challenging experiment.

A central question is, how do we live according to the vision of Dorothy Day and at the same time live in a situation that she really didn't envision? Also, Dorothy was always complaining that people would never stay too long. We want to be able to do it for the long haul. There are no good models for that, so we have to evolve one. We started by giving ourselves ten dollars a month in spending money. Now we find that it may be necessary to give ourselves a little bit extra to draw on for Christmas shopping, for summer vacations, for stuff like that. Not much. But enough so that it doesn't feel like perpetual deprivation and sacrifice. There's a place for deprivation and sacrifice, and we all experience that, but with kids and families, we wanted the pot to have *some* water in it in the sense of when the pot is totally empty, it burns at the bottom. So we're evolving, continually experimenting. The three families at Noonday Farm are committed for the long haul.

Rò: Does anyone work outside?

Jim: We all work outside part time. Particularly in the non-farming months. Whatever [income] comes in just goes into the common pot. I do a little consulting. Of course doing so little, I can be very selective. But it feels very different because I feel so grounded in this life. I can be engaged but also detached in a way that I could never have been [in the old life.]*

Louise has been doing chaplaincy at a nursing home. Lisa [Mahar] operates a nursery school. Bill [Beardslee] is a minister. David edits a journal called *Centering* at the Center for the Ministry of the Laity; Claire works at a local art museum. Jack Seery, our spiritual director, said the challenge may be to try and *not* earn to our full capacity.

David: Before we started, we had a lot of sit-downs with the household. Wrote out questions and concerns that we wanted to explore together. We were just all wanting most of the basic stuff at the same time. A worship life that was structured. More intentionality around our economics. But that's been a rough transition for us. We discovered how attached we are to control over our own money. You know, we miss that. It's really different signing over your paycheck.

Claire and Scott Schaeffer-Duffy have a small Catholic Worker in Worcester, Massachusetts. Their community is deeply influenced by the Franciscan tradition. When we talked, they were expecting their second child at any moment; they now have three children.

Claire Schaeffer-Duffy: In a lot of ways right now, Justin's childhood is somewhat similar to my own. He's the only white in all the children on the block, and when [I grew up] in India, it was mostly Indian children who lived around us. The beauty of children is they don't have categories. The challenge, though, is that the children next door are poor. We feel so conscious of it. If they compare their situation to Justin's, it's . . . that's inspiration for us to keep it simple.

Compared to India, ours is a very disproportionate way of life. Very, very disproportionate, I think. People pursue so many unnecessary things. You see how these children survive on this street. They're happy with a lot less than what

---

* Jim had done some university teaching and consulting as well as working for the State Department, with posts in India, Bangladesh, and the Philippines.

the baby magazines tell you you've got to have for children in order for them to become healthy adults. (It can drive you crazy if you listen to all of that.)

But I just feel education is so important. I was raised in an environment where it was really stressed, and it's a wealth I want to give to Justin. It's a power and a . . . when I say power, I don't mean to wield over other people, but I want him to think for himself. There's a possibility Justin can go to a Montessori school next year completely free, because the woman [who administers it] is a very good friend. I mean I can't beat that anywhere, but I sometimes feel guilty about it.

I tend to think he'll go to a public school in first grade. Or to a school that has really a sliding scale or something where we can barter—exchange labor for letting him come. You know, our poverty is kind of that way. Many doors are open to us, and I feel like they're real blessings. I hope we don't waste them. Because it's not the poverty our neighbors have. It's just . . . it's so different if you're black.

Ro: It's so different if you choose it.

Claire: Yes. It's very different if you choose it. But the odds are just so hard for somebody who is black. I mean I love living in a black community. This is the second time that we have. In D.C. we were the only whites there, too. I just think more and more whites should do it if they have any prejudices.

The children next door—we try to encourage them and kind of share some of the good fortune that we have in terms of . . . like we sit out on the steps together and read, and the three girls and I went down to get library cards. They're very good readers. I just think it's such a tragedy to waste a child, not to let a child really learn.

You know, the children really change your circumference of movement for a while. But they also . . . they enlarge your heart. I think it would be very interesting for women in the Catholic Worker to talk about the reality of their husbands going to jail. Also poverty. I think there's a different perception of voluntary poverty for women than for men. And it would be . . . I think there often . . . there's sometimes some tension over it.

Ro: Are you thinking of women alone or women as mothers?

Claire: I'm thinking, I guess, primarily of women as mothers. Having a child is perhaps the most dramatic life change for a woman. And maybe I'm just saying that because I'm about to have another one, but several women have said that nothing changed them more radically and quickly than having a child.

Ro: All of a sudden you have another person. And you have her forever.

Claire: Right. I think as women, we have to talk about your love for your child, your own child. It's very, very strong and very deep. I feel sometimes it's . . . and myself I have to watch this. It's a tension. It can become . . . I don't want to say an excuse, but it will maybe become a *reason* why women won't step out in situations of risk. That's a very natural response because you know that if you take a risk for yourself, you also jeopardize your child. And if something happens to you, indirectly that child is going to be affected. Or very directly. The younger the child is, the stronger a woman knows this. I think men know it, too, but not to the same degree.

But sometimes we can become almost obsessed with our own child and forget, you know, that there are other mothers and other children whose life needs to be just as rich. I think it would be useful for mothers to sort of look at the energy that comes from maternal love, which is a very good and positive thing, and let it really flourish collectively.

Ro: To help those mothers who are maybe at risk when you're not?

Claire: Yes. You know, not to let our children become a reason for not being involved in the world. I don't know. I'm scared to say this because I really struggle with it myself. Part of me just wants to be very nesting and domestic and only take care of my children in a peaceful, serene way.

And yet . . . I just wish that the whole world was set up like that, so that all parents could spend their life raising and enjoying their children. But then the other part of me—there's just like a nagging voice sometimes that says, "Yes, but what about [the other] person's child?" This is a luxury that I have here as an American woman—to be able to do this without enormous anxiety or fear. I don't know. I'm really not coherent on this.

Ro: No, I think you're doing very well.

Claire: Sometimes it's hard for women in the Catholic Worker. Especially after they have children. They're [no longer] who they were when they came into the movement, when they had greater freedom. They often don't get support, maybe, from other people or even sometimes from their husbands. Or if the house is predominantly single people or many men or maybe even single women, they don't understand. They haven't experienced that degree of psychological and physical change. So you can feel a little bit lonely, you know, or even guilty that you're not doing more, that you are . . . that your world has sort of shrunk.

Scott Schaeffer-Duffy: Voluntary poverty has to be really held close to the heart and reformed again and again. Because the tendency in any community espousing it is to move into directions of greater wealth and acquisition. "We can do more if we have more." I believe that was the death knell for the Franciscans. They were given property to use for the poor. Because the use was good, how could they turn it down? Before you knew it, these institutions were large and needed to be maintained, and they began to live for the institutions rather than the other way around.

I'm a firm believer in taking nothing for the journey and living as close to the edge as you can. I think the Worker needs to continually remind itself of that, especially as it grows in age and respectability amongst people who would be benefactors. It takes a lot of discipline to receive a hundred thousand dollars and to pay your two or three hundred dollars of immediate needs and give the rest away. But it takes that kind of discipline to protect the movement. Wealth somehow feeds on itself. It's a danger in and of itself. The more you get used to the regular money, the less you're dependent on God, and the less God is a more powerful reality than the presence of the money.

And we have to go to that table of the Lord—even go door to door—more often than many other communities. Our house, St. Francis and Therese CW, is still not paid for. But God is still moving mountains and parting the sea. We can't be—to use a little profanity—we can't be too worried about the fly shit of the world. So the house is not insured and we don't have health insurance, either. None of these things.

Community economics is one of the problems families face; separation because of resistance activities is another.

Chuck Quilty: Dorothy chewed us up one side and down the other for being involved in resistance and hospitality and being married. I've always disagreed with her, and I've brought up the subject with a whole lot of people, including guys who have done heavy jail time. We all come up with the same answer: She was wrong, you know, but at the same time, she was calling a spade a spade and . . .

Ro: Look at the results. [Chuck is recently divorced.]

Chuck: Yeah. You can't deny it. I don't think she was really right, though. There's a deeper issue. The most thought-provoking thing I've seen on it is an article by Jim Douglass, "Marriage and Celibacy." The point he was making, I think, is that when most people get married, they're basically into what he calls a "bungalow marriage"—raising their kids and getting two cars in the garage and the nice little bungalow. And if somebody within one of those marriages starts taking the Gospel seriously, there's going to be a problem.

I don't want to reduce everything that happens in every marriage to that, even my own, but I think that's a large part of it. Let's face it. We all mature at different rates. (I mean even if you leave the radical politics and everything out of it, people still change at different rates and grow at different rates.) That's always a source of conflict, and it's obviously even more intensive and seems more drastic when you're talking about divorcing yourself from the values that your culture's all about.

We ended up fighting to save our marriage, fighting for twenty-four years. Some times were real happy and others were full of conflict. It was when I was on trial or when I lost a job again that the conflict came up. You know, I don't want to reduce it to that—we had other problems, too, and probably never learned to communicate as well as we should have . . . I've seen a daughter die and my dad die, and I think divorce is probably the most painful thing I've ever dealth with. And yet I wouldn't change it. I saw it coming—predicted what was going to happen—and I finally said, "We've gone through this before. It's time for me to let her go."

I mean that's the only loving thing to do, you know; I don't feel I was wrong about that. It hurts, but . . . what Jim Douglass was doing with the celibacy thing was [saying] that people who are going to be joining any kind of nonviolent resistance to the evils in our society are going to have to recognize the large periods of celibacy within their marriages. But I think it really does make a difference when people enter into it *knowing* the shape their life's [going to take], *knowing* they've got some kind of radical commitment to social change and outreach to the poor. Knowing that's in the equation has got to make a difference!

Tom Lewis's first marriage was one of the casualties of this radical commitment.

Tom Lewis: I was married between the Catonsville trial and the time that we were to go to jail. I married a beautiful woman who was actually working with the Catonsville Defense Committee. That's where I met her. And we had a beautiful wedding in New York with many friends. Quite simply, the marriage did not survive the three-year prison sentence.

The woman I was married to started to understand herself as a lesbian woman during the time that I was in prison. We both talked about that, and both suffered with that. For me, personally, it was giving up the sense of power. Even though I was in jail, I certainly had a sense that I could demand that the marriage stay together.

Ro: Particularly because you were in jail?

Tom: "How could you do this to me?" et cetera. I refused to do that, so for me it was really a beginning of learning to give up power, a power that I had as a male in our culture. But giving it up meant that the marriage did not in fact last prison. We met once after I was out of prison and really have not seen each other again. [Since the interview, Tom has married again.]

Chris and Joan Montesano live with their three children at Sheep Ranch, California.

Chris Montesano: I remember my days in New York with Dorothy. We would talk for hours. I had just broken up with a woman who I was engaged to. Dorothy was very tender to me. She said, "You need to pray." And she said, "Of all the pain that I see in the houses over the years, the whole issue of falling in love is where there's the most pain. If you can offer that up, you can do a lot of good with it." Rosalie, you asked me if I thought Dorothy romanticized marriage. No, I don't think so. She knew that marriage is a struggle and did not really idolize it at all.

Ro: Joan, what about couples with children? Can they make it in the Worker?

Joan Montesano: Well . . . not without a lot of work. And probably a pulling back for periods of time when the children need more. I worked in the laundry with this nun once when I was in the convent, and she used to say, "Give it what it needs. Don't iron something that doesn't need ironing." That's become sort of a guide to life. If you have a kid who needs a lot more attention, you're going to have to give that kid a lot more attention.

For instance, the other day, Pete said, "Mom, I think you are the world's best mother, but you *are* a little busy." If you're doing heavy hospitality, it's real tough to give enough time to the kids. You just can't cut yourself up into too many pieces.

One problem with the children is the older they get, the more the recycled stuff doesn't meet their needs. For instance, Maria, the thirteen-year-old girl, is into nice trousers and Levi jackets and things like that. The kids need some things that look like the other kids. The kids would like it if we had more money, there's no doubt about that. They're always telling me to enter contests, but we never win. We don't have that kind of luck, but we laugh and say we're lucky about the main things. We have a family. We love each other. We're essentially healthy. We have food, we have clothing, we have shelter, we live in a wonderful place, and we have terrific friends, so we have . . . we're lucky in all of those things.

There's so much to balance in community life and in a family and within a relationship between husband and wife and hospitality and personal space. There's a lot to juggle. I think we need to watch that we're not getting too off-balance. Because if we are, you know, the mess is going to land on the kids.

✦

The very notion of marriage, it seems to me, requires a belief in miracles on some level. There is no sane, logical, compelling, defensible reason why human beings should vow themselves to a mutual lifelong fidelity, knowing the various ways human beings change, the various ways needs increase and diminish. At the same time, we have this assurance in our faith that it can be done. And is, in fact, something that must be done in order for two people to stay truthful to the convenant. It doesn't make any sense on a secular level at all, and yet it has been shown to work. And that's not just true of marriage, it's true of vows people take and it's true of witnesses people make.

—Mike Garvey

CHAPTER 16

Catholic Worker Kids

> Kids by and large are very materialistic, you know, which is what
> the culture is all about. But deep down in their hearts, they want
> somebody to stand up and show them how to toss all this shit out the
> window and *be* something.
>
> —*Chuck Quilty*

I WAS able to interview several young people who grew up in Catholic Worker houses: Kate Walsh of Baltimore, the late Kenna Lee Meyer of Des Moines, Becky Delany of Sacramento, and Joachim Zwick of Houston. Chris Shepherd, the daughter of Saginaw friends, talked about what she remembers from her Catholic Worker childhood.

Kate Walsh and I met after a Friday night "clarification of thought" in New York City. Then a sophomore at Fordham University, she's the only daughter of Brendan Walsh and Willa Bickham of Viva House in Baltimore.

Ro: Kate, what can you remember from when you were a little girl and living at Viva House?

Kate Walsh: I don't remember too much of the early days, like back when there were fifteen or twenty people living in the house. My first memories are when I was about six years old and went into first grade. I think you remember a lot of things from your school [years]. And I can remember telling all the kids, you know, that I had . . . that my parents ran a soup kitchen, and that we had poor people come into our house. And they all laughed. I can remember them just thinking I was crazy. They thought I was making up stories 'cause I'd go on and on.

"We live with a bunch of people, and only two of them are related to me." No one could really understand what I was talking about. So it was really . . . well, it wasn't hard in the grammar school, but in high school, things changed a little bit. Because you want to fit in with everyone, and you really can't if you're a Catholic Worker kid. After school, people would hang around and be involved in a lot of different things, a lot of different clubs. And I'd do that, too, but then I'd go home to work in the soup kitchen. When I was a freshman, I didn't tell anyone about the soup kitchen.

Ro: So you had this hidden life?

Kate: Yes. I didn't really tell people about it. Then my sophomore year, I just decided I couldn't hide it. And by junior year, I started really getting involved in Viva House. Worked at the soup kitchen and got other students to be involved and brought them there. I'd take days off of school to go to demonstrations. Then the teachers would want to know why, and a lot of times they'd make me explain to the class why I was absent. It'd provoke a lot of big discussions. Once we had a big demonstration outside of City Hall in Baltimore. I think it was for more adequate housing, for better housing. We were going to spend the night outside in the cold because we wanted to see what it was like to be outside. I came in the next morning so tired, and the teacher made me explain what it was. And all the kids just . . . no one seemed to ever understand what I was doing.

Ro: Think back particularly to your friends in grade school. Do they remember any of that now?

Kate: Oh, yeah! I'm still in contact with a lot of my friends from grammar school, and it's funny, because their parents could never figure out what I was doing, and they weren't too sure if they should let their kids come over to the house. But as soon as they did, they weren't so afraid anymore. I guess the unknown is what you're so afraid of. Maybe they thought that with all these poor people there, their daughter or son might get hurt or something, but as soon as the kids came over, they'd get involved.

That was mainly in high school. We were running the shelter, and we'd have a group of students come over once a month to bring a meal and stay and eat with the people. That was definitely an experience.

I've always worked a lot with the campus ministry offices, [even in high school]. I work at Campus Ministry now at Fordham. [Otherwise] it would be just too hard to get people interested. "Hi, do you want to work at my Catholic Worker?" No one would really understand.

Ro: Were your friends [this campus ministry type]?

Kate: Well, some were like that, doing some kind of community service work, but I always liked to have friends who aren't very much like me, too. It makes life more interesting, I think. So I have a lot of friends, I guess, who come from pretty middle-class backgrounds.

Ro: Did you have friends who were really into clothes? Designer jeans and things like that?

Kate: That's really funny. Yeah. In high school I was, too. From the end of my freshman year, I guess, to the middle of my junior year, I was really, really into clothes.

Oh, it was awful in my house! I was driving my mom and dad crazy, I think. They wouldn't give me money to buy clothes because they didn't think that I should . . . you know, that I needed them. So I got a job and used all the money I made for clothes. Worked at a restaurant. But it was a different kind of restaurant. One of the people who had worked at our house was a Jesuit Volunteer, and she got me the job. It was kind of a radical place.

Ro: But you spent the money being un-radical.

Kate: I still spent all the money . . . yes, right. I bought all the clothes, and I went to all the mixers. I guess that was my rebellion.

Ro: Okay, what did your mom do when you started being different from the way she raised you?

Kate: She . . . both my parents just let me do what I needed to do. My mom says I've gone through every stage very well, and that I really did my rebellion well. But they'd always let me do what I needed to . . . I mean if it got out of hand, you know, then they probably wouldn't, but they let me try out a lot of different things.

They are very open. I mean they didn't push me, didn't say I should live the simplistic life, that I shouldn't buy all these clothes, that I should just think about political things or work at the soup kitchen. It was always up to me and what I wanted to do. Freshman through junior year was a really hard time. I'm glad I'm not in that anymore.

Ro: What kind of school did you go to?

Kate: It was an all-girls Catholic high school. Very, very traditional, very strict. Pretty bad. Freshman and sophomore year, I liked it. And then junior year, I started to analyze it a little bit more, and so I ran for secretary of the whole school. I won, and I thought that I could make a lot of changes.

My mom and dad never said, "No, no, you'll never be able to change anything." They let me go ahead and fall on my face, which I did. I learned. Tried to do all these great things in school and didn't get anything accomplished, really.

Ro: But you said earlier that some of the teachers would want you to talk [about your life] in class? Was it the [school] administration [that resisted]?

Kate: The administration didn't want to have anything to do with it. For instance, when I was in high school, I was in the National Honor Society. And then I got arrested. Well, I was brought in to the Honor Society. They "wanted to ask me a couple of questions." Said that my behavior wasn't . . . I wasn't giving a good example of what a person in the National Honor Society should be doing. And then they kicked me out. In the beginning of my senior year. People always ask why I didn't protest. "That was terrible! They were only kicking you out because you had gotten arrested." But I didn't think it was worth it. I didn't really want to be part of this group. It was very elite.

Ro: What sort of young women did your high school want to educate?

Kate: Well, they wanted women who were going to be secretaries or whatever and then get married and raise a family. Our guidance counselor pushed everyone to go to this one small community college. You know, the college isn't so bad, but she actually told me I'd never get into Fordham, that my grades weren't good enough.

Well, I decided . . . you know, I was really worried at first, but I thought, "Hey, I'll try it anyway!" And I got in. When I came up to tell her, she made me bring in my acceptance letter before she believed me. Only a really small percentage go out of state to school.

Ro: So as a school, it's sort of limiting.

Kate: Yeah. But it's the cheapest private high school in Baltimore. If I went to a . . . if I had gone to a public school, it would've been kind of like going to babysitting. I mean I wouldn't have learned anything.

Ro: Did you study Latin?

Kate: Yes. I took two years of Latin, but it wasn't required. Most of the graduates go to a business school, or a two-year secretary school.

Ro: Was there a more elite Catholic girls' school in Baltimore, an expensive one?

Kate: Oh, yeah. Ours was called the Institute of Notre Dame. And pretty far out in the suburbs there's one called Notre Dame Prep. Everyone gets [the two] confused. Ours is called "the school in the alley" and theirs is "the school in the valley." Same religious order. School Sisters of Notre Dame. I was always taught by them until now when I have the Jesuits.

Ro: And do these upper class kids "in the valley" have more options given to them?

Kate: It's probably more of the liberal background. They have to do so many hours community service, and they're more . . . at least sports-wise, they have more things to do. I mean we had no . . . we have a very small gym, and we had no track, no field, no anything. We had no swimming pool.

Ro: So they put more money into that school.

Kate: Exactly. [Ours was] definitely a working-class, middle-class school.

Ro: When you first went to Fordham, did you meet very many kids with your kind of background?

Kate: Not with my background. I found a really good peace and justice community, though. There's a group on campus called Pax Christi. And oh, that was great! I couldn't believe it. I had gone through high school where I couldn't find any friends who were really interested in the whole political aspect. I mean I could get people to come to work at the soup kitchen but not to go to a demonstration. (Well, I had one friend who did, but besides that, none really.) And so coming to Fordham . . . oh! I was just so relieved to find some people I could relate with. I have a really good friend right now who I'm going to live with next year, and her parents were really involved in the RCP [Revolutionary Communist Party], so she understands a lot. We can understand each other's background, and it's great.

This year I live in a house of eighteen people, and they all do different types of community service. It's good to get into discussions with them. It's a house of hospitality in some ways, but not resistance.

I think getting into Fordham, I had an advantage by being a Catholic Worker. When I went in for my interview, they wanted to know how I'd been influenced and why I came to Fordham. I just described the whole thing of growing up in a Catholic Worker, and the person interviewing me was really interested. I think that definitely worked in my favor. It doesn't usually work in your favor to grow up in a Catholic Worker.

Ro: Why not?

Kate: Well, people don't even know what a Catholic Worker is most of the time.

Ro: How do you explain it, then?

Kate: Oh, I say that I grew up in a different place than they probably did. And that I lived in soup kitchens my whole life. They say, "Well, what's that?" And I tell them it's a Catholic Worker, and then they want to know what that is. So I say, "Well, a house of hospitality. We invite people from our own neighborhood to come in and have a meal. But it's also a house of resistance, so we do a lot of demonstrating and protesting. My parents and I have been arrested."

They always want to know how we can support ourselves. Then I tell them my mom is a nurse and my dad is a teacher, and they take turns getting salaries, and that it's run on private donations. They always seem to be really interested in how we can actually live there.

Ro: Do you find that right away they start to talk about money or the lack of it?

Kate: Yeah. They always . . . I haven't really met too many people who didn't ask me how we funded ourselves. They can't believe that we don't take government money or why we don't. Or that it really works. They don't really understand that there are so many Catholic Workers all throughout the United States, that we're not the only one. And whenever I tell them about Dorothy Day, they always think I'm saying Doris Day. [Laughter.] But it was great last semester when we were having our Viva House twentieth anniversary party. About eleven people from my house [at Fordham] came down to Baltimore with me. When you can actually see something, you can get a better idea of what . . . you know, where I'm coming from.

Ro: What are you studying? What do you want to do?

Kate: I'm majoring in political science. Either political science or political philosophy. (I still haven't decided. I could be in college forever unless I do.) I'm going to definitely minor in Spanish.

I think . . . I don't want to say what I definitely am going to do. Because I have a million ideas. One of them is to teach, and I think I'd like to teach in grammar school after I get out. But I've also talked to my mom and dad a little bit about taking over their Catholic Worker and having them go and travel for a while. One day, I'd like to have a Catholic Worker myself. The Spanish minor would be good for that, and it's great for being in the Bronx, too. I worked in the South Bronx last semester, and I was really able to use Spanish a lot. There's a pretty big group of Hispanic people who go to Fordham, but they're all commuters. There are very few Hispanic . . . they're all treated as commuters. You don't associate with commuters. There are a lot of jokes about commuters.

Ro: Does commuters translate as Hispanic?

Kate: Right. Or black. [At Fordham] because they got a scholarship, not because they could afford it.

Ro: What does this make you think about your church?

Kate: Wow! I don't really go along with a lot of things that the institutional church says. I mean I . . . we try to have our own kind of church within Pax Christi here on campus, I guess. We have Masses of our own. And I really like having that at Viva House. Pax Christi is thinking of having a woman celebrate Mass. That would be a really big thing for the Jesuits because they're so traditional and so strict.

Ro: Who says your Masses?

Kate: There's a priest on campus, this guy, Father [Alfred] Hennelly, who's like a . . . he teaches a lot of liberation theology classes. He's so busy that he can't come to all of our meetings, but whenever we *do* have Mass, he says it.

Ro: Have you talked to him about this feminist liturgy business?

Kate: With him? [Pause] No, we haven't really.

Ro: Most people say if you have a woman celebrate Mass, you just don't have a Catholic Mass.

Kate: Yeah.

Ro: What did your dad think about this?

Kate: My dad . . . I think as the years have gone on, they've gotten away from the whole institutional church. I think he'd definitely be for women saying Mass. But I don't think most people on our campus [would]. It would be a really big action if we were to do that.

Ro: Speaking of actions, do you . . . does your Pax Christi group do very many resistance actions? Anything where you can be arrested?

Kate: Oh, yeah. We just went down for Ash Wednesday to Riverside Research Institute in Manhattan. They do a lot of research for Star Wars—SDI. I think there were maybe five Pax Christi students, and we joined about fifteen other people and just sat outside the front door of Riverside. And they arrested us. But it's no big deal. That was the easiest arrest I've ever had.

Ro: You've never been sentenced, have you?

Kate: No. They'd usually let me go 'cause I was so young.

Ro: But you're not really so young anymore. [Laughter.]

Kate: No kidding! I was scared after I turned eighteen. I was arrested three times before I was eighteen. The second time, they brought me into court, into juvenile court. The judge said that I had to write an essay on why I had done this action, you know, why it was so wrong. And I said that I wasn't going to write the essay because I hadn't done anything wrong.

He got really angry. "Well, you can just do so many hours of community service!"

I said, "I live in a soup kitchen. I do community service every day. What more do you want from me?" And he got even more angry and just threw the case out of his court and said he was going to send me another summons, and I'd have to go to court again. But nothing ever happened. And then this last arrest at Riverside on Ash Wednesday—it was like getting a parking ticket. I mean it was no big deal.

Ro: Now you talked about liberation theology and the class in peace and justice. Is the curriculum giving you things that you want to study?

Kate: Yeah. Fordham is pretty . . . I mean they're not in any way progressive, but they are compared to other schools. They're *worlds* apart from my high school, but even from talking to other students at other colleges . . . Fordham has a whole Peace and Justice Studies program now. You can minor in it, and soon they're going to try and make it into a major. I think that's a really big step. There are a few good teachers who can influence some of the classes, but the administration is getting more and more conservative. They want to make Fordham into an Ivy League school.

Ro: Do you think [that reflects] one of the tensions in the Jesuits themselves?

Kate: Yeah. I definitely think so. The Jesuits are supposed to take this vow of poverty and, you know, they don't look too poor to me. I think that's a reason why a lot of the Jesuit scholastics have left. And Pax Christi on campus is seen as this radical kind of group—crazy left-wing communist, sort of.

Ro: Yeah. [Pause] Okay, we've been talking about everything sunny. There's got to be . . . like in everybody's life, there's got to be stuff that isn't so neat, that you wish had been different about your growing up.

Kate: Gosh. I really can't think of very many things. I mean I'm sure things have gone wrong, but nothing really affected me so much that I wish it hadn't gone that way. [Pause] Well, one thing I really wish is that my parents had more kids. Because I don't like saying I'm an only child. No one understands that. They think if you're an only kid, you must get everything you want, and you must have anything that you could possibly want materially.

And I don't know how to explain that having a Catholic Worker is like having two or three other kids because, you know, my mom and dad don't make a lot of money. And even if they do, they wouldn't put it into me. They would give it . . . I mean they value education, so they would put money into that, but they wouldn't give me other things materially. And it's hard because they give a lot of attention to Viva House, and I guess people don't really see that. They think it would all be directed to me. People don't understand how much time [a Catholic Worker house] can take up or how much . . . you know, money or effort.

Ro: Did you ever feel . . . I mean, it's hard to remember when you were little, but particularly in the early years and when your parents were really involved in the trials of the Baltimore Four and the Catonsville Nine, did you ever feel left out?

Kate: No. There were so many people at the house that I never felt neglected.

Ro: So you were never sort of wandering around alone while the grownups were doing other things?

Kate: No, never! Never. I never felt that way. I always felt there was someone to play with or take care of me. And there were other kids in the house, too.

Plus a big thing growing up in my early years was the [family] who lived next door. That was really a big thing. I was always over there. It was really different. I remember one thing I'll never forget—how every Christmas these six kids got more toys than I did, and it was just me. And they were on welfare and everything. I could never figure it out.

Ro: I think your mom told me that they took the gate down so you could go back and forth.

Kate: Right. I was always over there.

Kate's mother, Willa Bickham, remembers: "The best parenting came from our neighbors next door, Appalachian folks who had six children and all the love and more than they needed. So they shared it with our daughter. We were, of course, in our days of crazy eating with tables on the floor and pillows and heavy, heavy vegetarian. Lots of tofu and all that kind of stuff. Five-year-olds you can't fool, so Kate would go next door to eat—to eat people food."

Kate: I was just . . . I was just like one of their kids. And that's another reason I never felt like an only kid. I was like just one of their kids.

Ro: But then they moved away.

Kate: They moved away . . . I'm trying to think. 'Cause we moved out of the house when we started the shelter, and it was just around that time that they moved, too. That was really hard, but then I was getting ready to go into high school, and things were going to change anyway. So that's what happened. I didn't have any choice.

Ro: Do you ever think about going into the convent?

Kate: That's really funny. When I was little I thought of doing that, but not anymore. I'd really like to have like six kids. And that wouldn't really work if you were a nun. [Laughs.] I always used to tell my mom that I was going to have six kids, but I wasn't going to get married or anything.

And she said, "Well, you better talk to the person you want to have these kids with first." I definitely think I'd rather have had more brothers and sisters, but I know my mom and dad couldn't . . . they didn't think they could handle more. So that's just life. I'd like to have lots of kids, as many kids as I could have and still run a Catholic Worker. And my mom and dad said that they'd help me out if I really wanted to do something like that.

Ro: I'm seeing that a lot of the young couples [in the Catholic Worker] are having smaller houses.

Kate: Yeah. Oh, really? Oh, wow!

Ro: Doing it with and for fewer people. For instance, not soup line every day. Maybe just three days a week. In other words, not trying to do everything really big all the time.

Kate: And do they have lots of kids?

Ro: Well, like the Parfreys [in Santa Ana] have two or three, maybe three by now.

Kate: Oh, wow! I'd like to visit more Catholic Worker houses.

Ro: That would be great! Did you spend much time at Jonah House [when you were small]?

Kate: Yeah. I can remember going over there for a lot of meetings. My whole childhood I just remember meeting after meeting. I think that's why I hate meetings now.

Ro: What would you do while your folks were making these big plans?

Kate: Well, there were other kids to play with over at Jonah House after Phil and Liz had Frieda and Jerry.

Ro: But they're younger than you are.

Kate: Yeah, but I still played with them. The meetings were kind of late at night, so I remember I'd just . . . I'd sit there and listen to what was going on, and then I'd get bored and fall asleep by nine or nine-thirty.

Ro: What sort of problems can you see with Catholic Worker theory? Or I should say *can* you see any problem?

Kate: Geez, I don't know. I think it depends on each Catholic Worker, what they're doing. I mean . . . I think some Catholic Workers do too much of either the hospitality or resistance. I think there has to be a really good blend of the two. You know, I wouldn't want us to just be running a soup kitchen. 'Cause that's not what the Catholic Worker is all about. I see a lot of Catholic Workers who aren't doing any resistance at all, and I don't think that's good.

Ro: I'm wondering. Do people ever say you're just being elitist? You know, sort of trying to live so pure and everything.

Kate: No. Well, at least not the way I've grown up. It didn't seem like that. Just that you choose to live a little more simply. You didn't judge the way other people live, but that it was what was best for you. You realized that sometimes, you know, you didn't want to live that way, and you'd go out and buy some extravagant thing.

Ro: Do you ever think about going to Europe?

Kate: I did! I have. See, one really neat thing about the Catholic Worker is all the different people you can meet. Once this family from the Netherlands came over . . . I think it was about three years ago. They had a daughter and son, and they were just traveling around, and the father was a photographer. He took pictures of the people in third world countries, and he wanted to see what poverty was like in the United States, so they came over and took pictures of people at Viva House, and we got to be really good friends with them, and they wound up staying with us.

I wrote to the daughter for a whole year, and she said, "Why don't you come to the Netherlands? You'll have free room and board if you come." So I worked and I worked and I worked and I worked. My mom and dad helped me out a lot, and I got a lot of graduation money, and I went backpacking through Europe for about six weeks.

It was just great! I mean I felt so reenergized when I came back. And I had learned so many things! We traveled from the Netherlands down through Austria, and then Italy and France and then back up. It was just great. Really simple. We had a tent, and we just . . . we camped out everywhere. We didn't really get to eat that much, but we got to see a lot. And when I came home and told my parents about it, they were just so excited and they think that we should all go over there together, you know.

A few years after I met them, Kate and Willa and Brendan were able to travel to Ireland and to work in solidarity with people in the Northern six counties.

Ro: Uh, Kate, if you were interviewing yourself, what sort of questions would you ask? What should we talk about that we haven't talked about?

Kate: Let's see. I think one of the questions would be "Who are the different kinds of people I've met at Viva House?" And I remember when we had the soup kitchen . . . I remember the guys who came into the soup kitchen, especially these two guys. Whenever it was my birthday or Christmas, they'd always save up their pennies or whatever and they'd give them to me, you know, just because I was a little kid and always running around.

Now when I think about that, I think, "God! What a great . . ." I mean I can't believe they did that. I'm sure they needed that money so much, and for them to give it to me . . . what a thing! I can't believe that sometimes.

I also remember some of the women from when we had the shelter. It was really weird at first 'cause I wasn't used to having people live at my house, you know, and I didn't really know what bag ladies were like. Most of the people who came into the soup kitchen were men, homeless men, but with women, it's a little different.

I remember one of them—Edith. I still keep in contact with her. Edith is from Czechoslovakia, and she just chain-smokes all the time. I remember when she first came to the house and how much help my dad gave her to find housing and all this kind of stuff. It's really nice to see her now. 'Cause she always wants to see me so much.

Ro: I would imagine a lot of them think of you as their child, too. "Othermothers," I call them.

Kate: Yeah, I remember a lot of people being pregnant, and I think one or two babies were born at the house. That was really neat. Actually, the one I remember the most, though, is the first woman who came to the shelter. This woman's nickname was Rebo. And she was . . . I'm not really sure what was . . . she had some kind of mental problem. But if she looked at a phone book, she could memorize it—pages and pages of people's names and numbers.

I also remember some of the volunteers. For three years, we had Jesuit Volunteers. It was kind of neat to have some people who were a little bit younger coming to work at the house. We still keep in contact with most of them, and that's really nice.

Ro: When you go home for vacations, do some of your friends from Fordham come?

Kate: Yeah. Let's see. Amy, this friend who I'm going to be living with next year, she's come down with me. And then there were the people who came down for the twentieth anniversary. Which was great! Just so much fun! My boyfriend Joe comes home with me a lot, too. And last semester two guys from Fordham were living and working there. So even if I can't be there to work, I can at least send other people to work.

My parents are always interested in what my friends are doing, and they always welcome them into the house. That's really different than most of my friends' parents, who sometimes don't even know what's going on in their own son or daughter's life. And they're not really interested in it, either. My mom and dad always get to be friends with my friends. I usually don't think of them as being my parents, I think of them as being my friends.

Kenna Lee Meyer was ten years old when we talked, a bright and skinny kid with beautiful long red hair. She has since died as a result of a tragic accident. I include this excerpt as a memorial to her blithe spirit.

Ro: Kenna, what do you do at the Des Moines Catholic Worker?

Kenna Lee Meyer: Well, there's a million things I do. I help kids, mainly with the crafts. So if the guests' kids are interested, when they leave, they have a lot of skills in crocheting or knitting. They usually catch on pretty easy.

Ro: Are the kids usually sad when they come?

Kenna: Well, no. Because they . . . as my mom said, they feel more secure about coming here because of us, and we know the neighborhood really well. We take them to the park . . . uh, *I'll* take them to the park, and they'll feel secure because we know just what to do if a fight breaks out or something.

Ro: So you kind of show them around and stuff.

Kenna: Right. A lot of wildflowers grow like in the back alleys, so we go out and pick those.

Ro: What do you personally like about living in a Catholic Worker house?

Kenna: You're helping people. That's about the only thing. The boy who's here now: he's had a brain tumor and has a lot of problems. He's all Indian, and he wishes that he was growing up like an Indian. And I kind of make it so . . . I teach him stuff about Indians.

Ro: What don't you like?

Kenna: The city. And some of the people that come in. Some of them are weird. Some are bizarre. Some of them I have problems with because they try to be my friends . . . like this one lady who did not know a single word in English. But I tried to make friends with her and teach her how to sew and stuff. Of course, I'm teaching her how to speak English, too.

Ro: That's neat! Where did you live before you came to the Worker house?

Kenna: Well, I used to come here with my mom every Thursday, and we'd make pot holders. And Christmas and Thanksgiving we'd help . . . At Christmas, they all came over to our house, and we made candy canes and fudge, and we had a big party. We lived in a cabin out in the sticks over in Dallas County. Lived in the woods, and we had to walk a quarter of a mile to the mailbox. Go across the wooods and over a little footbridge and climb these steep hills in spring.

Ro: So do you like living in the city?

Kenna: Well, in fact I don't. Because I'm not a person you'd want to call a city person. Now I'd be happier if the city was more spread out, and the houses weren't so crammed together.

Ro: How did you learn how to do all your crafts?

Kenna: Well, my mom and myself . . . I figured out how to crochet myself. I had my own book, but that didn't help me any 'cause I didn't know how to read then. So I just got a crochet hook one day and just kind of went along with my mom. She taught me how to knit, though. [Shades of Dorothy!]

Chris and Dan Delany started the L.A. Catholic Worker and a soup kitchen in Pasadena in 1970. Later, as Dan says, they "left the L.A. Worker to Jeff Dietrich and kind of floundered around for a while" before coming back to Catholic Worker life and starting hospitality to visitors of prisoners at Folsom. After ten years, they tired of the routine of serving as a generous motel and when I interviewed them, were completing plans to turn the Worker house into Hope House, a residence for AIDS victims. I was delighted to also interview their twelve-year-old daughter, Becky.

Ro: Becky, you're a Catholic Worker kid. [She giggles.] What do you think of when I say that?

Becky Delany: I don't know. I just . . . that's what I've always been.

Ro: What do you know about the Catholic Worker?

Becky: Not too much, really. I just know that it's an organization my parents were in around the sixties and seventies in Los Angeles. And then they came up here and started their own. I know they help people. It's not any one thing. They don't deal with any set thing like child abuse or anything. They can help in whatever area they want, you know.

Ro: Do people ever say anything to you like your dad said, that your dad and mom were crazy for going to jail and demonstrating and everything?

Becky: No. Usually, my friends . . . when they do find out my parents used to go to jail and everything, I just tell them they do it because they want to and because that's what they believe in. Their parents go to work because they want to and they have to. And that's just like what my parents do.

Ro: That really makes sense. What do you personally think when your parents . . .

Becky: I think they're two of the most unselfish people I know. Because I've never really seen them do anything, you know, totally for themselves. It's strange because all my friends' parents, you know, they're adding on to their house, or they're getting promotions and making more money. And my parents are just doing things for other people. Some of my friends think that's a little strange. But it's not like they don't accept it.

Ro: Did you . . . how did you feel when they were working with prison visitors?

Becky: Well, we moved here when I was about two, and they started that when I was about three or four. So I've just always been used to the idea. It wasn't weird to me at all. As soon . . . as long as I can remember, the house has always been used for other people. We've never used it for ourselves. (The Delanys live in back of the large house they use for Worker activities.)

Ro: Now you won't be able to talk about the fact that it's now used as an AIDS residence, right?

Becky: Yeah. It's confidential. And that's kind of okay with me because my friends would really freak out. "Oh, my gosh! I don't want to go over there anymore." So [the secrecy] is okay with me. If they ask, I just tell them it's a residence for sick people. It's not like I'm trying to cover it up. At first I was a little freaked out, but now I'm not ashamed of it.

Ro: You talked to your folks and studied it and stuff.

Becky: Yeah. It's amazing how ignorant people are about the whole AIDS thing. You know? When they first told me about it, I was eleven, and I was real ignorant about it, too. But after I learned, I thought, "Why not!"

Ro: I see that as what a Catholic Worker does . . . you know, look around and see what needs to be done almost before anybody else does. Dorothy Day wrote against the nuclear bomb right after Hiroshima, not ten years later.

Becky: Yeah.

Ro: Now the house is supposed to be confidential, but what if people find out and your friends say they're not going to come over here anymore?

Becky: Well, then I say, "Fine!" My friends wouldn't really do that. They're not really my friends if they do.

Ro: Do you want to be a Catholic Worker when you grow up?

Becky: Hmm . . . I don't know. I mean I'm twelve and most twelve-year-olds I know are like me, me, me, me. So I don't know right now. All sorts of things are floating through my mind—what I want to do, you know. I want to be a psychologist. I know that.

Ro: Do you see a contradiction between the two?

Becky: Not really because they're [both] helping people. I want to help people because when they're really distressed, they need someone to talk to. Sometimes kids my age don't have anyone to talk to. I know kids at school that are involved with a lot of stuff like drugs. I know people in my class who are pregnant, and I'm only in the eighth grade. Whoa!! And I ask some of the people I know who were starting drugs, "Why do you do drugs?"

"I don't know. It's just something to do." Because they go home, and there's nobody there. So I want to be someone somebody can talk to.

I met Joachim Zwick at the Denver Catholic Worker reunion. His parents are Mark and Louise Zwick, two tireless Workers who manage a huge house in Houston. At the time we talked, Joachim was a sophomore at Notre Dame. He has since transferred to the University of Houston, where he is majoring in viola.

Ro: Have you ever wished your folks were like other people's folks?

Joachim Zwick: Yeah. Oh, definitely, especially in middle school and like during the first couple years of high school. If we hadn't moved from California, my dad would still be a regular social worker. You know, he'd be making pretty good money right now. I used to think about that. Dream about that, I guess you might say. But now not at all.

Ro: Did you ever feel neglected?

Joachim: No. Well, we didn't live at the Worker. Still don't. You know, I'd come home and one of my parents would cook dinner, and they'd be around for a while. I never really felt neglected at all; the big problem I had was adjusting at school. Middle school was just really rough. There was obviously a certain way you had to dress to be popular and a certain attitude you had to have.

The group I hung around with through middle school and high school were kind of the outcasts—the nerds, I guess you could say. I didn't mind being . . . I mean I don't mind that at all. They were different. Tended to accept people on their merits more than the others did.

In high school, I guess I made a serious effort to try to break away from the Catholic Worker ideals, except for the just war theory. I always wanted to be a conscientious objector.

Ro: Did you register?

Joachim: I registered, yeah. But I have a file with letters from my high school teachers and stuff saying that [these are my views]. If you don't have a file, it's hard to get CO [status].

Ro: So if there is a draft, you'll have your file all set.

Joachim: Right. I went to an all-boys high school in one of the richest areas of Houston. Ironically, the Catholic Worker is just beyond the school, so I walked to school every day. The other guys were driving up in their new BMWs and $150 shoes and stuff.

I'd read about all the arguments for Catholic Worker and all, but when you have thirty people all telling you the same thing, and you're sitting there trying to defend yourself, it's very difficult. One on one, it's pretty simple, but I only had that opportunity once or twice. I was kind of uncomfortable with [not being] the same. You needed to get close to people to be comfortable and relax.

So I really tried to fit in more. Dressed better, got involved in things, the whole bit. And it . . . nothing really happened. Everything was just the same until senior year. I think it took that long for people to start accepting me and what I had to say.

Ro: So you were kind of lonely.

Joachim: I wasn't the last year. Got elected to the presidency of our service organization. (It wasn't so much service, though. We parked cars for Mother's Club and for the symphony, things like that.)

And I was in the honors program. There was a nerd group in the honors class, and I was in that. I definitely . . . I was lonely quite a bit, but I made some pretty good friends in my senior year in high school, had some good friends for the first time since we moved [from California to El Salvador and then to Houston]. I'm really enjoying college. Lots of friends. You can always find people you can relate to there.

Ro: What's important [about the Catholic Worker] to you, Joachim?

Joachim: Well, the experience of . . . relating to the guests and hearing their stories. You know, we hear horror stories of people walking from Nicaragua to Houston or something. Or how the coyotes treat people. They kidnap people and hold them for ransom and rape the women. Stories like that certainly opened me up to an awareness that some other people don't have. They see Hispanics as thieves or real lazy.

I was very, very sensitive when I first went to middle school. When I tried to adapt myself in high school, I think I lost a lot of sensitivity. It's just now coming back.

One thing living in the Catholic Worker taught me was . . . I did learn self-reliance. I like to do things for myself. I get annoyed when people insist on doing them for me. I like to be myself and just watch people sometimes.

Bill and Mary Shepherd moved from Midland to inner-city Saginaw in the late sixties, when some of their children were already teenagers. Years later I interviewed their daughter, Chris, who here remembers the Worker influence during her teen years.

Chris Shepherd: Well, I remember . . . my parents talked about Catholic Action a lot. Went to the Cursillos.* I think I was in fourth grade when it started, and I remember them being real . . . It was exciting. There was something exciting going on, and they were real stimulated by this and were reevaluating their philosophical outlook.

I remember different books started coming into the house. In fact, I remember seeing *Loaves and Fishes,* Dorothy Day's book. I must have been in fifth or sixth grade, so I was too young to read it, I guess. There was an excitement in the house. Different people were coming over and ideas were being discussed and there was a lot of talk about racial issues and helping people and working with poor people. Somehow this was connected with the Catholic Worker, but that was just part of it.

We were living in a predominantly all-white . . . I don't know if there were any black people then in Midland at all. My parents got more and more committed to social change. Then they decided to move to Saginaw and live in the inner city. At that time, they'd already started this place in Saginaw for alcoholic men.

Ro: St. Alexius House.

Chris: Yes. They'd drive over there from Midland on the weekends. By the time we moved to Saginaw, that was pretty much defunct.

I was thirteen. It was both traumatic and exciting. And dramatic just because I was thirteen. I was in seventh grade, with all my white friends, and we were having fun acting like seventh graders. All of a sudden, we're moving to Saginaw, and we're going to live in an inner-city neighborhood. Well, when you're in seventh grade, you're into what's cool—you know, what's the cool jacket to wear and how you wear your hair and be in the cool group. So I started going through a shift over the summer, started separating myself from my friends. And sort of, I guess, starting to think we were special. That's the way I dealt with it. But also feeling a lot of inner conflict because my friends distanced themselves from me. They thought we were weird, frankly.

I was moving to a world I didn't really understand, a world where I would be an outsider. I was going from an "in" group in seventh grade to being completely cast out. Not to sound melodramatic, but there was that sense to it. I enrolled in eighth grade at Sacred Heart School. I was one of the few white kids, and a lot of the kids treated me funny, you know.

I remember having fights at school and things like that, really having to learn

---

* The Cursillo, or "little course in Christianity," was an evangelical experience with a social action orientation.

to deal with people who were very different from me. There was always two sides to it. On the one hand, it was a tremendous growth experience for me to deal with this world. And on the other hand, there was a lot of loneliness and alienation. I remember, then, going to St. Joseph's High in ninth grade. Things were real exciting in the neighborhood. Other people living in the neighborhood were involved in the Catholic Worker ideas, and there was a sense of community around a purpose.

I remember finally starting to read more. I was really taken by *Loaves and Fishes*. The Vietnam War was going on, a world peace vigil was going on, people were sitting in at the draft board and being taken to jail. I was very young, but I did it one day. I remember sitting in at the draft board. I was reading my copy of Dorothy Day's book as I sat there. It was just so . . . so congruent.

We had a friend who was a priest and he was going through some sort of crisis in his life. He was real depressed with the constraints of being a priest, so he'd come to our house and we'd sit around and sing. Pretty soon, he decided he was going to go live at the Catholic Worker. Left his parish and moved up to Tivoli in New York. I'd always said I wanted to go to the Catholic Worker, and my friend Mona [List] did, too. So the next summer, he picked us up and we went out to the Catholic Worker. We split the time between Tivoli, in upstate New York, and First Street in the city.

Mona stayed across the street. Dorothy had rented some apartments . . . oh, those God-awful buildings, you know, where the bathtub's in the kitchen. They were just terrible and they cost a . . . I mean I thought they were incredibly expensive for what you got. I stayed in the actual First Street building where there was the soup line. On the second floor was a real small dormitory—I mean *small!* And I had a bed in there. Dorothy was on the same floor. She had her little office and her little room there. So I spent some time with her.

I was seventeen. Going into twelfth grade. She was . . . my memories are more like little snapshots. I remember I was scared to death to meet her because I had built her up so much—put her on a pedestal. I told our friend I was nervous, and he said, "She's just a regular old lady." And in some ways, that was true. She *was* just a regular old lady. When you talked to her, it was like she was almost gazing out the window and telling you stories—telling memories. She was a little bit self-absorbed, which was interesting. I never would have thought Dorothy Day self-absorbed. Of course, she wasn't completely like that. She'd get up every morning and go to church, and she was always disappointed that the young people weren't more traditional. You know, this was in the sixties. People were rebelling. Her grandchildren were swimming nude in the Hudson River. She was just trying to deal with all that, I think.

New York was pretty chaotic, and I'd never been . . . I mean I'd only lived in Saginaw and Midland. Now what did I know about New York? I couldn't . . . I was stunned. There were no trees. Someone said, "Oh, go look at our patio." So I went out back, and there were a couple of funky tables and this little stick tree. But it was like intriguing to me, too. Depressing but in a romantic way. I was seventeen years old, and it was sort of cool.

Pat and Mary Murray, Peninsula, Ohio. *Photo by Mary Farrell*

"And it's still going on." *Dorothy Day, Postscript to* The Long Loneliness

St. Francis House, Detroit, ca. 1945. The St. Francis statue on the table is now in Day House, the present Catholic Worker in Detroit. St. Francis founder Lou Murphy is standing in front of the window on the left. Diocesan priests are serving the guests. *Courtesy Marquette University Archives*

"The fact is that one person has to come to others for food because he doesn't have any money, because he doesn't have a job, because he drinks heavily. He has that right." *John Cooper*

Nina Polcyn (Moore) at Maryfarm in Easton, Pennsylvania, in the 1940s. *Courtesy Marquette University Archives*

"There's a saying that St. Teresa saw this "T" written in heaven. Well, I saw this "CW" written in heaven. The *Catholic Worker* spoke to me." *Nina Polcyn Moore*

Getting the paper out, ca. 1934. Dorothy Weston in foreground; Frank O'Donnell sitting under blackboard; Dorothy Day on right. The message on the wall reads: "Counsel of St. Ambrose: No duty is more urgent than that of returning thanks." *Photo by Henry Beck, courtesy Marquette University Archives*

Jeannette Noel, Maryhouse, 1983.
Jeannette is queen of the computer
file for the *Catholic Worker*. *Photo by
Tina Sipula, courtesy Marquette
University Archives*

Dorothy Day with friends at Tivoli. *Black Star Photo by Bob Fitch*
"She had an enormous capacity for friendship." *Mary Lathrop*

Ammon Hennacy on the porch of Joe Hill House in Salt Lake City. The sign on the door reads, "Don't bother the neighbors." *Courtesy Special Collections, University of Utah Library, Salt Lake City, Utah* "One of our Notre Dame friends who came to hear Ammon was a gung-ho marine. And Ammon . . . well, Ammon was a gung-ho anti-marine!" *Julian Pleasants*

Peter Maurin at Maryfarm in Easton, Pennsylvania, July 1941. *Courtesy Marquette University Archives* Scholars must be workers.

Tina Sipula giving out groceries at Clare House, Bloomington, Illinois.
Photo by Mary Farrell
"We operate a food pantry out of the house. And that was a long, long saga, with the city trying to close us down 'cause they didn't want lines of poor people on Washington Street." *Tina Sipula*

Ray Clark serving soup at Hospitality Kitchen, Los Angeles Catholic Worker, 1976. Clark is now a priest in the diocese of Owensboro, Kentucky. *Courtesy Marquette University Archives*
"I rather like the idea of the works speaking on their own." *John Cooper*

Demonstration by Casa Maria Catholic Worker in Milwaukee during a Lenten fast undertaken by the community in 1968. The back of the picture reads, "Michael Cullen gives a public reading of the Passion of Jesus Christ." *Courtesy Marquette University Archives*

"Pacifism has to do with honesty to the moment." *Pat Coy*

Demonstration sponsored by Mobilization for Survival and Casa Maria Catholic Worker in Milwaukee, December 28, 1979, Feast of the Holy Innocents. Don Timmerman wearing sign. *Courtesy Marquette University Archives*
"Change is not going to come from the top." *Sue Frankel-Streit*

A Friday night meeting for clarification of thought at Casa Maria Catholic Worker in Milwaukee. *Courtesy Marquette University Archives*
"The ideas were so much a part of our lives." *Gary Donatelli*

"Smokey Joe" Motyka. This photo was found in Day's photo album with the following caption: "Smokey Joe—former Marine who pursued General Sandino in Nicaragua in 1928 while I worked for Anti-Imperialist League helping Sandino." *Courtesy Marquette University Archives*

"But Smokey Joe had more to do with keeping that soup line going, year in and year out, than any of the lovely volunteers who pass through a Worker house." *Chuck Matthei*

Robert Marino in the backyard of St. Francis House, Chicago. *Photo by Carolyn Prieb*

"If men really throw themselves into the work, they definitely become more . . . they're looked down upon sometimes [by the world outside] because they do these kinds of women stuff, so they become more in tune with the oppression of women." *Maggie Louden*

The Cornell family of Guadalupe House, Waterbury, Connecticut. Tom Cornell, Jr., Monica Cornell, Tom Cornell, Sr., Deirdre Cornell, Susan Stanczyk. *Photo by Mary Farrell*

"A marriage or a family that is not somehow arranged to welcome the stranger is not a real secure marriage, anyway." *Mike Garvey*

Fr. Frank Cordaro, Des Moines, Iowa. *Courtesy Marquette University Archives*
"Won the best legs contest in college. Two years straight." *Angela Cordaro*

Virginia Druhe, St. Louis Catholic
Worker. *Photo by Mary Farrell*
"I remember feeling that I knew
silence very well, and [knew] how
varied silence is." *Virginia Druhe*

David Stein, St.
Francis House,
Chicago. *Photo by
Carolyn Prieb*
   "Life is a seemingly
endless series of
irritating distractions
from woodcarving."
David Stein

Kathe McKenna, Haley House, Boston. *Photo by Mary Farrell*
"For me, it doesn't really matter whether you're doing standby actions or a sink full of dishes. What matters is what's happening on a deeper level." *Kathe McKenna*

A Catholic Worker guest serving coffee on the street. Las Vegas Catholic Worker, 1987. *Courtesy Marquette University Archives*
"What I must do about this person who is walking up and down the street is to try and feed him with grace and dignity." *John Cooper*

Clare House, Bloomington, Illinois. *Photo by Tina Sipula, courtesy Marquette University Archives*

"Everybody told us to stay small. We really wanted to make it nice." *Rio Parfrey*

PART FOUR

Doing the Work

CHAPTER 17

Miracles at Martin's

Martin de Porres in San Francisco

> This building was originally an auto body repair shop. The space in front was basically a five-thousand-foot concrete slab, but we've made it into a garden, a restful, peaceful area for folks to wait in.
>
> —*Carole Arett*

POTRERO Street, San Francisco. People use the word "miracle" a lot here. Along with the hundreds of supporters and volunteers and guests, three very different people made up the Worker family at "Martin's" when I visited. I was able to interview two of them, Carole Arett and Charlie.

Carole Arett: We usually say we're Catholic Worker with a small *c* here, primarily because most of the volunteers aren't Catholic. We don't ask questions of our guests, and we don't ask questions of our volunteers. If they believe in our goals and philosophy and are willing to do the work, we welcome them, whether they're Catholic or Zen Buddhist or Methodist. Insofar as Catholic is concerned, we might not be Catholic Worker. Insofar as trying to live the Catholic Worker philosophy of taking personal responsibility for the poor and for the people who cross our paths . . . I think we do that. If that makes us Catholic Worker or doesn't make us Catholic Worker, I don't know and I don't really care.

We try to reduce as many barriers as we can, and the guests . . . I think that the guests here generally feel this is their home. You don't build barriers in your kitchen at home, so we designed our kitchen without barriers.

Because we have the yard area, we're able to open the gate before we actually start serving. We serve breakfast from six o'clock to seven-thirty in the morning, and we open the gate at four-thirty, so the guests can come and rest. They're off the street. Nobody asks them to move along. A lot of people like to get out of the streets before people start coming to work, so no one will interfere with them.

At the beginning of the month, we probably serve at least a thousand meals a day and towards the end of the month probably sixteen to eighteen hundred. Three days a week, we serve one meal. The other four days we serve breakfast and lunch. We let people take food with them, too. Our basic lunch meal is soup and bread. Volunteers bring jars and the guests can take bread and soup for their evening meal.

Ro: Do you have overnight guests?

Carole: This is a very stressful place. You never know what's going to happen. We have a lot of people who are mentally ill, people who are physically ill, people with drug and alcohol problems. Constant crises. And you can only . . . you have to have some time to process these things if you're going to be able to start out again the next day and really offer hospitality. So, at least at the present time, we don't feel that we have the time, energy, resources . . . whatever, to be able to have people sleep here. That's not to say that we won't be able to do it in the future. But right now, we figure we've bitten off as much as we can handle.

One of the things that San Francisco has in housing for the homeless is called "Hot Line." People stand in line and get a ticket for an appointment. Then the next day they stand in line again and get a hotel room for three nights or something like that. Well, we hear a lot of complaints from our guests about the problems with this system. So to find out for ourselves, a couple of people went through it. Went with some of our other guests. Stood in line, did the whole routine, stayed in the hotel overnight, and then contacted someone at the mayor's office afterward and said they'd like to talk to them about it. Said they thought the system was very inefficient and demeaning. So that's one of the things we did.

Ro: Tell me about the move from the old soup kitchen, from the original Martin's.

Carole: We lost our lease on Twenty-third and Bryant, so we had to move. When we tried to rent a place, we found that no one would give us a lease because we had no assets.

Ro: Was it because the landlords didn't want their property used as a soup kitchen?

Carole: Well, we didn't say we were a soup kitchen. We said we were a restaurant. Because, in effect, we are. As far as meeting health codes . . . whatever, we are a restaurant—a restaurant with no money changing hands. But anyway, we couldn't get a lease, so we finally decided that the only possibility was to buy.

We had no idea how we'd finance it, though. After better than six months of looking at properties, one of our guests told us about this place. In the beginning [of our search], when we found a piece of property that cost $187,000 or something, we shuddered and said, "No way! We couldn't even begin to raise that kind of money!" But when we found this place and the price was $625,000, we didn't even hesitate! Because we knew this was it! We figured if we were supposed to be here, it would work out, somehow or other. And if not . . . well, we would start someplace else again.

This whole area has become gentrified, so when the developers and big property owners found out we were moving in here, of course they raised a lot of fuss with the planning commission. (I think the term they used was that we were in their "path of progress.") So we had to go through a hearing and all these things. They hired attorneys and investigators, and actually formed a group called the Potrero Hill Boosters. Held meetings and everything to figure out how to keep us from opening.

We had a lot of controversy, which was very difficult for us because we had always maintained a very low profile. Newspapers and radio and TV stations wanted to interview us, and we've always shunned those kinds of things. One policy we were really firm on was no pictures of our guests. We felt that was infringing on their privacy and it was also undignified.

So anyway, at the planning commission hearing, the attorneys [for the opposition] gave their speeches and questioned people and everything. Our guests, of course, knew that all this was going on. It was a difficult time for them, too. They felt very insecure and afraid, and we had to continually reassure them. They really wanted to help us, though, so we told them they were welcome to come to the planning commission hearing. They could use part of our allotted time if they wanted to speak.

Friends kept telling us, "You can't do this! You don't even have an attorney."

"We don't hire people to chop onions for us, and we don't hire people to speak for us. We'll speak for ourselves."

Actually, I think our guests used as much time as our supporters did. About 150 of them came to the hearing. People were just totally overwhelmed! Anyway, we were successful, I guess, and the planning commission agreed to let us operate a soup kitchen here. We agreed to certain conditions, but not to others, and they let some go. We said that we were interested in keeping this neighborhood a pleasant place. Didn't want it to be a garbage-strewn area. (In fact, that was the way we found it when we moved in here, and we were the ones who cleaned it up.)

But those were some of the things they used against us. Most of them were fears. The people in the neighborhood were afraid because we were an unknown. A lot of the things they'd written and said about us were lies, I think. For instance, they said they'd never had homeless people in this area, and we knew that people had been sleeping in their doorways for years. But I think they really *didn't* know it. They didn't want to see these people, and so they really didn't.

Just the way they acted at the planning commission hearing—you could see them cringe and get really uptight with our guests because they don't see these people as people. I think it helped some of them to see us together at the planning commission, though. When the head of the commission gave us the approval, we were all hugging and kissing, you know.

The neighborhood people said, "What is this? You're *touching* these people?" They'd always tried to avoid them. One woman I remember . . . she was going to cut through a row to get out the door. She happened to look down and see that all the people sitting in that row were guests of Martin's, so she turned and walked clear around the end of the room. She wouldn't even walk past them!

I think generally we have good relations with our neighbors now. One is still very surly, but I understand he's never happy with any neighbor. He calls with complaints about a coffee stain on his sidewalk or whatever. We try to go out of our way to communicate with him and to be reasonable but . . . Excuse me. [Carole answers the phone and responds to a question about someone's mail.]

Ro: Do you act as a mail service?

Carole: Not formally. Informally, yes. Some people need an address for SSI disability or something. Until they get the money, they can't afford to rent a place and don't have an address, so they use this one. If it got too large-scale, one volunteer would probably have to just handle mail. We've talked about that, in fact.

We have lots of wonderful volunteers. One volunteer lives in subsidized housing, and she collects things from other people who live there. Like she collects the jars, washes them, wraps them individually in newspaper and puts scotch tape on so we know it's clean. And she knows that one of the things guests really need are shoes. So when the thrift store on Mission Street has a sale on shoes, she buys shoes and brings them over here. She has a twin sister, and they will be eighty-three years old on December eleventh. Really a sweetheart—just keeps going all the time!

Up until the time that we had to buy the building, we always said Martin's subsisted on the widow's mite. You know, lots of little ladies like this Mrs. Meyers. After we got the publicity, someone said, "Well, I suppose you're looking for somebody to buy the building for you."

We said, "Absolutely not!" The price of the building was $625,000. That didn't include the $125,000 it cost to earthquake-proof it, and the renovations, and everything else. We said we'd like to find six hundred people willing to each donate a thousand dollars.

Well, it was surprising. A number of people *did* send us checks for a thousand dollars, people who had never heard of us before, but liked what we were doing. I don't know. I think part of it . . . we talked about this many times afterwards, and I think they figured we were a bunch of losers. Everybody kind of reached for the underdog. It was like they were sort of betting on us and hoping that we would succeed. Willing to take a thousand-dollar risk that we could do it.

When we first talked to foundations, it was much like getting credit. If you don't need money, the banks want to lend it to you. If you need money, they're not interested. Foundations also . . . in the beginning, I think they didn't trust us . . . weren't sure we were going to be around. Even though we *had* been around for fifteen, sixteen years, they didn't know whether or not we were going to make it with a project of this size.

When we got the money for the down payment in a period of a couple of months (and it was something like $210,000), they said, "Well, wait a minute! Maybe these people will make it." Then people kind of jumped on the bandwagon. But it wasn't really that easy. One of our volunteers, Steven, has done a great deal of work in contacting foundations and filling out all the petty forms. He's willing to do that. If Steven hadn't been here, I don't know who would have done it.

That's one of the miracles of Martin's, too. Whenever there's a need, there seems to be somebody who can do what needs to be done. Somebody just shows up who has the skill or the connection—knows somebody, whatever. That's why I guess we can go on faith. We know that it's always worked before.

I mean there are times when there's very little bread at the beginning of the day. Sometimes we get a little impatient and someone runs out to buy bread and before that person gets back, somebody else had brought in a load, and then we have bread coming out of our ears. It takes patience and faith. There's a lot of faith here . . . like we continually give everything away. People say, "Wouldn't it be wiser to hold some back for a rainy day?"

"No. The more you give, the more comes in."

So we try to be sort of instruments—turning things over, whether it's money or food or clothes or whatever it is.

We try to keep the personalism. We're working on the garden. We have artwork out there, mostly contributed by guests, so it's a pleasant place for people to just sit or read. Sometimes a newcomer asks if it's all right if he falls asleep on the bench and we say, "Fine! We'll wake you up when it's time for us to close." They can sleep or read or just sit there in the sun.

Several of our guests are actually buried in our garden, or their ashes are buried there. As a matter of fact, we had the memorial service here for the last guest who was buried—Michael. He was a regular at Martin's for a number of years. He died in the streets, and we made arrangements with the coroner's office. We contacted members of his family and they weren't able to deal with it, and so we had a memorial service and a burial here and invited guests and volunteers to come and participate. It was very nice, and the guests appreciated it. I think it made them feel a little bit more secure knowing that when something happens to them, there'll be somebody who cares. And knowing that when we say we care, we care forever. And also it's good for the guests to be able to deal with their grief, just like anyone else. Michael's friends can come here and pay their respects.

We want it to be hospitable. I think the definition of hospitality is that you create a space for people to be themselves. Different individuals come to Martin's looking for different things, and we hope that we're able to provide that for them. Like one of the things that's different about Martin's is that some people need to vent anger or frustration, and in other soup kitchens if they raise their voice or something, they're asked to leave and sometimes asked not to come back. We like to have as much latitude as possible here. Sometimes people are very angry and want to scream. As long as we keep it somewhat under control and it doesn't disturb all the other guests, we allow that to happen.

Ro: Do you have much problem with physical violence?

Carole: No. I don't think so. I mean occasionally there is some disturbance, but compared to other places, no. I think it's primarily because we have a relationship with these people. They're not strangers, they're part of our family. They feel at home here, and people don't destroy their own homes.

Ro: Do you have a policy about calling the police?

Carole: There's no point in having policy 'cause you have to change it all the time. So we don't make policies, but we rarely call the police. Each situation is unique. Some people might act out some aggressive behavior, and somebody else knows that all they need is a hug or a pat on the shoulder. Or to be called by name. Different things work for different people. Anytime that I'm the first one into that kind of a situation, I never have any idea what I'm going to do. All I know is that something has to be done before somebody gets hurt. What I say or do, my presence, is . . . something that comes from the Spirit, I guess. I don't plan it, it just happens.

I think at Martin's we have only two policies—no drinking and no violence.

That doesn't mean that people don't occasionally come in and try to get by with drinking, or that people won't sometimes display some violent behavior. When we see that, we just try to contain it. We don't tell that person they can't ever come back again. Most times we don't even put them out for that day. If we can get them a bowl of soup and sit there and talk to them, sometimes that works. If that doesn't work, we may walk outside with them, walk down to the park and sit down with them for awhile. You have to be flexible.

A lot of our guests end up in hospitals, and someone goes to visit with them. We call the hospital and try to talk to the doctors, find out what the person's condition is, so they know someone is concerned. Sometimes we run down there and let the nurses know that we're not leaving until that person gets some kind of medication or something. Things happen faster that way. Sometimes people are left alone in a room with nobody paying much attention to them, so we're there at mealtimes to feed them. Sometimes they don't understand what's wrong with them, or what their treatment is, or what their alternatives are as far as treatment, so we talk to the doctors. And sometimes I think homeless people are used as experiments for medical stuff, so we ask what the treatment's going to do for the patient.

Martin's is . . . it's very personal for a lot of people. This is the only home they have. Even if they aren't here, this is still home base. People who are in the hospital call us and say, "I'm feeling better" or "Today is a rough day. I'm really depressed." We're the only ones they have.

Lots of guests don't even eat with us. They come because they have some dignity here. We're their friends. People like to visit their friends, so they come to visit. It's like a private club for the homeless. We even have a wonderful guest— John—who used to play in nightclubs and restaurants, and now plays background music during our lunch. A couple of people have said it isn't seemly for a soup kitchen to have a piano player, but most people like it.

You know, there's a very, very fine line between guests and volunteers at Martin's. A lot of the guests are kind of crazy, but a lot of the volunteers are kind of crazy, too. As a matter of fact, maybe some of the volunteers are crazier! I always think of myself of being basically a fairly average, normal, conservative-from-the-Midwest kind of person, and then all of a sudden I listen to myself talking to you and I realize I'm not.

Ro: Carole, how did Martin's find you?

Carole: I had gone to St. Stephen's . . . a parish that was involved with Martin's. At the time, I managed a coffee and donut shop, and the owner of the donut shop used to throw the day-old donuts away. So instead of throwing them away,

I started bringing them down to Martin's. The guests would see me coming and holler, "Here comes the donut lady!"

Finally, the donut lady started working like three days a week at Martin's and then they asked me to move in as caretaker. I lived in the old Martin's for a year, and then moved here during renovations. One of our volunteers had an old trailer, and I lived in the trailer for something like six months. We hauled it inside the building when it had no roof. We had to replace the roof and then when the rains came, we had things that couldn't get wet, and I'd be up covering things with plastic. We had no electricity and it was very exciting, believe me!

The cat lived through the whole thing with me. Cats are not usually very adaptable, but this cat managed to adapt to a lot of confusion. Pandora is as much a part of Martin's as anybody else, I guess.

You know, it's not always easy to find a place where there are no limits, where you can give everything you have to give. I guess that's what I found at Martin's. What in effect happened is my realities changed. This became the real world. When I would go to the donut shop, for instance, and talk about what happened here at Martin's, people would say I was being very unrealistic. But as far as I am concerned, this *is* the real world.

Ro: And your relationship to the Catholic Church?

Carole: It was through the Catholic Church that I started my journey on the path. I haven't found any reason to take another path, but you know, if aliens had arrived from outer space while the pope was visiting San Francisco, they'd think that the main topic of concern for the Catholic Church was sex. That's all the newspaper and media people were talking about! They weren't talking about spiritual issues at all.

When I was younger, I was an "exemplary Catholic" in that I met all the . . . When I look back on it now, I was like a Pharisee. I lived the letter of the law. I wouldn't give an inch on anything. Actually, I ended up being very judgmental, very un-Christian. Now when I'm able to let go of the rules and the laws and try to live the Christian principles, it's much easier. I try every day to lead a loving Christian life. And I'm not so concerned how that falls between rules or laws. I'm trying to be open to whatever love there is and what I'm able to do.

✦

Charlie: I'd be really happy if you'd just call me Charlie. Very few people know my last name 'cause I rarely use it. In fact, some newspaper once made a point of saying, "prefers to be known as *just* Charlie." So that became a running joke around here. "Oh, it's 'just Charlie!' "

Ro: Well, how did you get to Martin's, Charlie?

Charlie: I'd been involved in different things—political work. Really involved in the collective movement here in San Francisco. In starting a community food store and then a collective cafe, sort of a cultural center where people who were working in social change could come together in a social atmosphere. Trying to become kind of a networking place for people. But I hadn't done anything for several years. That last experience was really painful from sort of a . . . It ended with me having to go through a lot of emotional . . . It wasn't just the personal. It was a hard lesson politically and spiritually for me, that experience. So I was a little shy about getting passionately involved with anything else. And I hadn't really thrown myself into anything since '81.

I was doing free-lance carpentry, so basically I had control of my life, my schedule, and I live very inexpensively because I care more about what I do with my time than how much money I make.

I used to bring outdated milk down here . . . I guess it was in 1984. The place felt really nice. The old Martin's was very small. And it was just good. One day I finally said, "Okay, I'm going to make the big leap." I decided I'd work one day a week for the lunch crew, which starts roughly at eight o'clock in the morning with preparations and runs to about three-thirty or four o'clock for cleanup. I decided that would be the highest priority of my life, and anybody who wanted me to do carpentry for them would know I was never available on Thursdays. (Enough people appreciated my carpentry so that I was able to do that.) So I started working on a Thursday crew.

One of the things I liked about it initially was how . . . well, I guess I could use a word that has a lot of connotations—the word "anarchist." It fits. I've considered myself an anarchist for many years, at least ten, thinking of the word politically. I liked the way things were run here. It seemed very autonomous. Each day's shift seemed to have almost total power over what they did. There wasn't a bureaucracy and they didn't have meetings. Okay, another reason I started working here is 'cause I saw it as a perfect situation in that I could do something useful, but I didn't have any responsibility. In all these projects I get involved with, I always end up over my head or having more responsibility than I want.

"This is great! I have someone else to tell me what to do. I'll just chop onions and do something that's useful." And for the first year and a half, that's in fact what the situation was. Then very quickly, you know, we had the eviction, and we had to find a new place, which ended up being here. The building was enormously expensive, needed total renovation, and I just had, you know, I . . . that's where I was. I mean I was in that place at that time. I could have said I really didn't want to do it, but . . . it just felt like that's why I was here, to be involved in taking on a lot of the responsibility at that time.

For the last year and a half, when the construction was going on to renovate the building, I concentrated on playing—and I use that term very emphatically—*playing* general contractor and basically overseeing the general contracting. I did it. I usually didn't know what I was doing, and I was way over my head ninety percent of the time, but I did it. Essentially it happens through . . . I don't know. I was actually surrendering myself to a higher power at that point.

It's a real double bind in my life. A chronic situation when I have a lot of responsibility. See, when I was in the collective movement, I had an ideal, that everybody take equal responsibility. I no longer feel that way. I feel that everybody needs to push themselves on how much responsibility they take, but what I used to do was get in a situation where I would resent that not everybody was taking equal responsibility. Now I realize that everybody has different abilities and talents and skills. And one of those talents is the ability to take responsibility.

You know, somebody calls on the phone and wants you to make some kind of major decision. I realize there's no such thing as a *right* decision. It's just . . . you make the best decision you can. You just make it. Other people don't have the same ability to do that. There's a certain level where I don't care. I'm willing to back up anything I do, but I know that some of those decisions are going to be wrong, and I don't worry about them.

See, I distinguish between leadership and authority. Authority I see as a much more arbitrary thing. It's not necessarily based on wisdom or talent. You were born into money, you were born into power, you know, and so you have this arbitrary power over other people, and have the ability to exploit other people, and so on and so forth. Whereas leadership and wisdom are more of a natural . . . it's putting everything into place where they're most useful to the common good. And that's a constantly dynamic situation. Constantly changing. Somebody who at one point is only good at taking instructions may, at another point, be in a situation where they can take on the responsibility. But at any given time, there's a certain order that seems to work best.

And, you know, the obvious question is who decides who's in charge. Actually, I don't think it's a decision. When a situation is working, you just know you're in some kind of harmony, and when it's not, you know it's not.

Ro: What do you do when you're not in harmony?

Charlie: You try and look into yourself as much as possible. I try and see in what way I'm contributing to things being out of harmony and try to bring myself much more into harmony. This seems to have an effect on other people and their ability to be in harmony. Rather than, you know, seeing someone else as fucked up. You've got to straighten yourself out.

When this [eviction] crisis happened, it was really necessary that certain people move into positions of leadership or whatever you'd call it. It had a lot to do with faith and spirit. It was . . . I was one of a few people here who thought that it was possible for us to move.

We were being evicted. Everybody hated the poor and the homeless. Nobody was going to rent to us. We had no money to find another place, to renovate it and to continue feeding people as we had been doing. Some people had to really believe very strongly that it could happen, so the people who were a little less sure would at least go along with it. All it took were a few people to really believe strongly enough. It's not that there weren't times when we were hit with the impossibility of it all.

"You can't do this! You're out of your mind! Do you think you're going to raise six hundred thousand dollars, a million dollars, to buy the building, to renovate it, do all these different . . . why, it's impossible!"

But there were enough of us who just said, "Maybe we're crazy and maybe we'll fail, but we're going to do it, anyway."

I think that's what made it happen. I mean it was the faith. And that's where, in terms of leadership, I felt I *did* believe it was possible. I believe anything is possible.

Ro: So the faithful became the leaders?

Charlie: On some level, yeah. And also took on a lot of the actual responsible work. In other words, I did the contracting. Barbara [Collier] did a lot of the fund-raising. She's very good at talking to people and separating them from their money. They just melt. They find their hearts in a way that they have never found them before, and the money just seems like a detail at that point. People who came prepared to give ten thousand dollars all of a sudden say, "Oh, no, that's not enough. I'll go back to my board of directors. I'm sure we're looking at twenty-five thousand." And that's happened.

My belief that anything is possible goes back about fifteen years. That was the first time I really got involved in doing anything outside of living my own sort of narrow life. I started seeing myself being committed to the greater need, the greater good, of the human family and found different ways of doing that. In the sixties, there was this belief that utopia was going to arrive within five years certainly, maybe six at the outside. There was a real belief that the world, in fact, was going to completely change, to change from one of violence and greed to one of love and plenty. It was very painful to realize that first, it didn't happen, and second, it's not going to happen. Not in my lifetime, not in this lifetime, not in this incarnation. And yet it doesn't matter.

So the reasons that I do things have nothing to do with an end goal, but I did have to go through that [period] where I thought we were going to reach that end. And when I realized we wouldn't, it was extremely painful. I've seen a lot of people who were involved in political work completely give up, become completely cynical. In fact, not only did we not come closer to those goals, but sometimes it seems we were further away from them. I was involved in antinuclear work. Got arrested four times and was involved in a lot of other demonstrations, too. But in the late seventies, I became more interested in creating positive alternatives than in doing a lot of opposition.

I totally support that both [opposition and alternatives] need to happen simultaneously. But there wasn't enough positive. People need to be involved in creative alternatives that give immediate satisfaction, like serving food to somebody who's hungry. It keeps you going spiritually. Whereas, if you're constantly beating your head against the wall trying to stop nuclear weapons, when in fact, they just keep getting bigger, it seems like you can only end up in despair. Unless you have some part of your life involved in positive alternatives.

Ro: That sounds so much like the other Catholic Workers I've talked to. So why do you seem so determined to stay away from anything that says Catholic Worker?

Charlie: Like call myself a Catholic Worker? I've never called myself anything except anarchist, and I try not to call myself that. As far as Catholic Worker books go, I've liked most of the stuff by Peter Maurin. I probably used to be a lot more like Maurin in the sense that I thought that I could sit down and come up with a blueprint for utopia, for the future society. I no longer believe that. I believe it's much more a spiritual path, just surrendering yourself to what you're called on to do. The more we surrender ourselves, the more the natural order will just emerge.

It's sort of like sculpture. You chip away at the pieces and eventually the sculpture, which is already there, just emerges. I know the limits of my own evolution. I know where I . . . well, I *don't* know where I am. But I know that I have a long way to go, and it's just not possible for me to come up with a blueprint for the ultimate. So I'm much more dubious than I used to be about any kind of master plan or anybody who thinks they have a master plan.

I guess I think there's both hope and faith. Everybody talks about hope . . . this may be just my own semantic difference, but hope has to do with a goal in life and change. You lose hope when you see that things aren't getting better. Whereas faith is much more of that surrender. It doesn't have anything to do with end results. You're doing it because that's what you're supposed to be doing. You don't even know why necessarily. Which might be where the love comes in.

CHAPTER 18

Snapshots
Larry Purcell of Redwood City, California

This is Gina. Gina was five when she came here. The first sandwich Ronnie ever gave her, she growled, ripped it in half with her mouth, and threw it all over the living room. Ronnie grabbed her arm and said, "If you ever do that again, you won't eat in this house."

One night we were watching TV, and the word "cocaine" came on. Gina said, "I know that word." I said, "Yeah? What is it?" She said, "Well, you line it up with a little sharp thing like this, and you take a straw and you suck it up."

—Larry Purcell

I T's dusk when I find the address Larry has given me, a comfortable home in the hills above San Francisco Bay. Larry's wife, Ronnie, and their new baby are playing in the kitchen. He's planned my visit and doesn't waste any time, but sits me down in a comfortable chair and begins.

Larry Purcell: I grew up in a family of nine children. Had seven sisters and a brother, really close to each other. Very wealthy. (I learned to drive a Cadillac limousine when I was sixteen.) While we had everything you'd ever imagine, my parents were very clear that they put people first and that relationships were the most important thing.

I was ordained a priest in 1970 and was a diocesan priest for ten years. Worked in a huge parish. After about three years, I became convinced that people were not the number-one priority in parish life, that the rules and the buildings seemed to dominate. So I left parish ministry and swore to myself I wouldn't do that again. It took me four years to find another way to be a priest. During those four years, I learned that you can live simply and live a very rich life.

I tried community organizing, Saul Alinsky style, which basically teaches you to beat the system at its own game. Not nearly enough. I tried the peace movement. Good, but not enough either. Then I went to San Jose, to the Catholic Worker house there, and lived with Peter Miron-Conk. Most of what I know about the Catholic Worker came from Peter, who is a very strong personality and a high-quality person.

I lived at the San Jose Catholic Worker for six months. It was very rough. We slept about 20 street people a night and fed about 120 a day. Prior to going down there, I had pictured Catholic Workers as chopping onions all day, and I thought I could do better things than that. But being in San Jose, I found I *loved* working with the poor, loved working out of the principles of the Gospel, loved the voluntary poverty.

Voluntary poverty is a misnomer, though. I have about twenty-one years of schooling, a graduate degree, and so forth. You can't really be poor with the kind of flexibility an education gives you. Anyway, after working with Peter, even though it was good, I didn't see how it intervened in the cycle of poverty.

When I came back here, I studied a lot of different places in San Mateo County [looking for the right place to start a Catholic Worker]. That was where I had worked as a priest, so I knew a lot of people. It's a big county, suburban and middle class. Blue-collar and white-collar workers mixed together. Relatively conservative. I wanted to locate here because I believe the political power of the future lies in suburbia. Also, the need for alternative ways of life is very high in suburbia. Where there's just house after house after house and block after block. You can't even tell one city from the other.

I decided on Redwood City specifically because the land was relatively cheaper than other places, and supportive people lived here. After being a volunteer at the local juvenile jail and sending out a lot of feelers, I landed on the idea of opening a house for troubled teenagers. That was in '77.

I had nothing—only a motorcycle and a job at two hundred dollars a month, working two days a week. I wrote a letter to two hundred friends, and in a month they sent me seven thousand dollars.

So I got serious. I didn't want to rent. Had seen enough newsletters from Catholic Worker houses that said they only had thirty days to raise forty thousand dollars or they'd be evicted, or something like that. I always thought that was kind of blackmailing their supporters. So I decided I'd try to buy a place but not take more than two years to pay it off. Make a hefty down payment.

I had the seven thousand dollars. Had no idea what a house cost. I called up six realtors, none of whom I'd met. Five of them volunteered their services, took me all over town to find a house. And two women came to help me, right after I got the seven thousand, two nuns that I'd known very well. That's when

I knew it would work. One, Joan Murphy, had been a real leader in the diocese. A very powerful woman who had decided in 1970 that power was not the way of the Gospel and left being Mother General of the Presentation Sisters. She and I were close friends until she died. The other nun taught me in the second grade— Mary Jane Floyd, another Presentation Sister.

So there were three of us. Not knowing what the hell we were doing, we sent out two more letters. In a three-month period, the three newsletters raised twenty-one thousand dollars, so we made a down payment on the house. Then the new archbishop, John Quinn, came in and lent us the other forty thousand to pay off the house.

We started having teenagers come and live with us. It was a three-bedroom house at the time. The nuns lived in one room, and two boys and two girls lived in the other two bedrooms, and I slept in the living room. We learned over experience that four teenagers is the most we can have and still approximate a family environment. So they live with us. No one gets paid. No one gets charged. We don't accept foundation grant money. We don't apply for tax exempt nonprofit status. The teenagers come to our home . . . and it's often the first time in ages that someone is working with them who's not being paid. Social workers, probation officers, foster parents, counselors, lawyers—everyone does it for a living.

We get some from the court system, we get some through social services, we get some from hospitals, and we get some directly from their families or the streets. The majority now come directly from their families. The only teenagers we don't deal with are schizophrenics and teenagers who've been assaulted by other people. Only because we aren't equipped to handle it.

There's very little difference between a teenager who's been arrested and one who hasn't. The [ones who haven't] just haven't been caught, that's all. Many of the kids in jail aren't in for very serious things. It's mostly a breakdown in the family. They're the victims, just like the street alcoholics. There's nothing, I mean *nothing*, in this county for teenagers unless they get arrested. And then what's for them is jail or a probation system that sets them up in foster families. Which is like a permanent blind date.

We have someone living at the house all the time. Try to line it up one teenager to one adult. We try to meet all the needs—economic, educational, psychological, legal. And so we have lawyers, psychiatrists, dentists, doctors, counselors— you name it—who work with these kids a lot. If they need glasses, we can get them glasses. Whatever they need. It's just extraordinary, the support system we have. In fact, our biggest challenge is staying simple.

As the teenagers leave our home, lots of them move into their own apartments, and we stay as their family. If their real family is completely gone, I become their parent. We've got three in college now, and others who visit regularly. Steven, Kim, Danny, Barbara—maybe about twenty. They generally show up when things are either very good or very bad. Trauma time or exciting time.

Ronnie, the woman who has since become my wife, worked full time with the teenagers for four years. We've had some very rough teenagers. Had a couple go to prison, one for attempted murder. And after one of the teenagers threatened to kill her, she decided she wanted to open a house for smaller children, children under seven. Went through all the procedures to apply to be a foster parent. To do it at no charge.

She worked for two years to save money to build this house, raised thirty thousand dollars in two years. That bought this lot. And that was cheap! The cheapest lot down in Redwood City was fifty thousand. Half this size and down by the railroad track. We organized craftsmen, and they built this place. All the labor was donated and most of the material. This house was built for forty thousand dollars! I don't ask plumbers to paint; I ask plumbers to plumb. (I think that's a mistake Christians often make. They ask people to do things they're not skilled at, and wonder why they don't like it or don't do a good job. So a parish will ask a plumber to teach [religious education]. Dumb!) It took us a year to plan the house and a year to build it. It's for children under six.

Let me show you some pictures of our children. [We begin to look at a photograph album.] Here's Gina, the first child we ever had. Gina was five. Gina was arrested for shoplifting. She'd been slept with by her father, her stepfather, and her mother's secret lover. Her six-year-old sister had been permanently removed from the mother. A three-year-old brother was removed with a broken leg and Gina was finally taken, also. Gina and her little brother were placed in the same emergency foster care, and she kept sexually assaulting him. The social workers knew this house was opening, so they asked Ronnie if she would take this child and isolate her. Not take other children. She said she would.

So Gina came here. The first sandwich Ronnie ever gave her, she growled, ripped it in half with her mouth, and threw it all over the living room. Ronnie grabbed her arm and said, "If you ever do that again, you won't eat in this house."

One night we were watching TV, and the word "cocaine" came on. Gina said, "I know that word."

I said, "Yeah? What is it?"

She said, "Well, you line it up with a little sharp thing like this, and you take a straw and you suck it up."

"I know what drunk is. Drunk is when mommy's boyfriend drinks too much beer, and his head goes like this. But Larry, he's not asleep. Mommy and I have to drag him to bed."

Gina would stop on the sidewalk and go pee. Ronnie said, "What are you? A dog?"

She'd say, "My mommy does that." She was like a puppy that had never been trained. She was thought to be borderline retarded. She'd walk up to teenage boys at the other house and unbuckle their belts. The first time I ever kissed her, she asked me if I wanted a hickey. And Gina was five.

She had clearly been raped. Sexually molested. But she was like a Cadillac that had been driven into a wall. Not retarded at all. In fact, she was extremely bright, even though she couldn't read. Didn't know the difference between numbers and letters. She didn't know what the word "beside" was, and so she flunked all the intelligence tests.

One day we're driving down Highway 280. Now she's only five, remember! She says, "I used to live around here."

We're miles away. I thought she was kidding, so I said, "Show me." So she zipped this way and that way and there it was. San José Avenue. Where she used to live.

Then she said, "Do you want to see where Sal lives?" (He's the guy who molested her.) As we drive up to Sal's house, she slides lower and lower in the seat, screaming, "Don't let him get me!!"

Ronnie tells her, "Don't worry. We're not going to let him get you." So we get his address. Gina shows us his van, and we get his license number, and we report him to the city police. Nothing was ever done.

After three months of this child being in our home, her social worker wanted to return her to the mother. That was the county's solution to this problem. Well, Ronnie fought for this child, and Gina ended up living with her for nine months. She's now been adopted.

We're an emergency crisis foster home. These children have been removed forcibly from the home, either by the police or by a social worker. And they usually come here without having gone anywhere else. Before they go into long-term foster care, they have to go through a court proceeding. And then after a court proceeding, there's a placement period while the social workers look for an appropriate family. It's supposed to be thirty days. But it's usually three months. It could go on for a year. It just goes on and on.

[Showing another picture.] Here's another classic example of how people are not important. His name is Matthew. Four years old. Lived with his daddy who worked nights, so he locked Matthew in the bedroom. If the kid wet his bed, he got beaten up in the morning. Matthew couldn't talk. We had to teach him. He was so sick that he couldn't be in a foster family. They figured if we couldn't handle him, nobody could.

These children go through dramatic changes in a one-to-one loving environment. I mean the power of love is miraculous. Matthew started talking. It turned out he had an ear problem. Two weeks after he was here, it was diagnosed and he was operated on. He'd been in the county system three months.

Here's a newborn, two days old. The mother was insane. She thought she was pregnant with a rat and wanted to kill it. She was . . . well, she had been drugged to keep her from going schizophrenic. She was on Haldol. The child was born asleep and really didn't wake up for a couple of weeks. It took us an hour to feed it an ounce of milk.

Here's another newborn, another Gina. She was born with cocaine in her system. Cocaine is the most dangerous drug for infants, the most dangerous drug for mothers to take during pregnancy. There's a lot of sudden crib death with children of cocaine users.

[Turning pages.] This child was bitten by the mother's boyfriend. This child's . . . the back of his head was completely flat. He'd never been lifted and turned over, just left in his playpen all the time. He had no leg power at all, so we bought a bouncy chair. When a child's feet touch the ground, they get excited. In two weeks, he could crawl.

These children have tremendous resilience, unbelievable resilience. This one was filthy when he came. They lived in a van. The mother, this child, and a dog. The social worker said she didn't want to touch him. Ronnie threw out all his clothes. They were just . . . it was a pig sty.

We just had our own baby, seven months ago, so we haven't had a child since then. Now we're going to classes to prepare ourselves to take AIDS babies. They're looking for families to care for these infants until they die, and we're preparing ourselves to possibly do this. If the child tests positive for AIDS at nine to twelve months, they want you to take the child until it dies. They want you to take the child forever.

Unless you have questions about what I've said, I want to go into what I think about Catholic Workers. First of all, I think most county jobs—social workers, probation officers, any kind of job that works with the poor—are basically systems to employ people. Now I don't feel too bad about that because I think most Catholic Worker houses are kind of the same thing. They're primarily places for the Catholic Workers, for those who choose to be there. Somewhat like monasteries. Places for people who look at the world around them and say, "This is not for me. There's got to be a better way than this."

If Catholic Worker houses are for the adults who run them, you have to do everything you can to protect those adults. Not from the hurt or the pain that's contracted from hard work, but from insanity, from stupidity, from unhealthy stuff.

Ro: From their own stupidity or from the stupidity of the system?

Larry: From their own stupidity. You have to learn to say no. You have to learn what you're good at and do that instead of something else. If you're good at working with street alcoholics, that's great, but if you're not, you'd better look for another area.

Catholic Worker houses are for the Workers who live in them, and I think it's important to be clear about that. But hopefully, the Workers need to be close to the poor. So they're not just sitting around doing nothing. Or using the poor.

You try to set up an environment that makes sense out of everyday life in the Gospels. And it's not making sense out of everyday life in the Gospels if you can't be a good lover. If you can't develop and hold on to dear relationships. If you can't relax. If there isn't a quality of joy.

Ro: Larry, do you still see yourself as a pastor?

Larry: Well, I don't . . . I have no desire to distinguish between life and work. I like life and work to be one. I work at the Catholic Worker house for teenagers. I don't see much difference in what I'm doing now and what I was doing as a priest, if that's what you're asking.

I'm the boss of the Catholic Worker houses. I'd just as soon it weren't that way, but my experience is that people who are here the longest are usually the ones who are running it. And whatever you do to try to avoid that, such as have consensus, which we do, you still have the expectations of the supporters. They know the people best who have been there the longest. "Oh, this is Larry's house."

I see Ronnie and me being here for a long time, barring death or some kind of crisis where our support system could really collapse. I guess I think if you have good workers and good work, the money will take care of itself. I'm not sure that's true, but that's what I think.

The first time I was publicly arrested here in town, it was front-page stuff in the local paper. With a picture. I thought that would slice our income in half. But there was no noticeable change. When I resigned from the priesthood, I thought that would slice our income in half. Again, no noticeable change.

Talking about going to jail reminded me to say something. I think it's very, very, very critical for Catholic Workers, in addition to feeding, clothing, and sheltering the poor, to ask the question, "How come so many are so poor in the wealthiest country in the world?"

It's very clear that the children, both the teenagers and the infants, are not the priority of the government. There just isn't enough money for them, although there's plenty of money for the military. So I think it's important, in terms of both the history and the future of the Catholic Worker, that there be some addressing of the structural sickness in the society. It's not just a minor sickness. It's a fatal sickness.

In the beginning, my primary way of addressing that was resisting nuclear weapons. Then for a couple of years, we did Sanctuary work [with Central American political refugees]. In the last two or three years, Ronnie and I have been working on loving one another, getting married, having the baby.

I am just now at the point where I'm looking for another way to address the social, political structure of this country—a structure I think is very damaging. So I really . . . I see the Catholic Worker in Redwood City and across the country as really having three works. Working with the poor—feeding, clothing, and sheltering them. Working with their support people—offering them an alternative way to live. And challenging the structures that make up this society.

Ro: How do you challenge the structures? Only by symbolic actions?

Larry: Well, symbolic actions are certainly part of it. It's kind of like going to Mass. You know, you don't expect Mass to make everybody one, to unite everyone, the first time you go, or the first twenty times you go. The Mass is a symbolic action, and nonviolent civil disobedience is a symbolic action. I don't think it's enough to go from arrest to arrest to arrest. These folks who are getting the long prison terms . . . I have tremendous reverence for them. I mean I'm not going to do it, but I bow to them for being willing to pay the price.

Larry has spent as long as seven months in jail over a thirteen-month period and estimates he's been arrested about twenty-five times.

Larry: My life in jail is very mild. One of the funny things to me was that the razor blades we used in jail are sharper than the ones I use at home. The food is . . . I love the food in jail. I'm not at all intimidated by the inmates. The guards are awful, though. I consider the guards dangerous. Ignorant and inciting. I was the president of the inmate council when I was in for a while once, and I really felt one of my jobs was to protect the inmates from the guards.

Ro: I'd like to ask you one last question. You've grown up like a lot of other wealthy people. What made you different? I mean you said at the beginning that your parents put relationships first. And frankly, Larry, a lot of other rich people say that, too.

Larry: I don't know, but it wasn't something I did. I feel like I've been . . . whatever I am, I was made that way by the people who love me. And I feel that God has been part of all that.

To be healthy you have to have three things. (Some people would say this is spiritual, I just call it healthy.) You've got to have good work. Meaning something that makes sense to you, that's creative and challenging and uses your talents. You have to have a few dear relationships. And the relationships in the working part of it have to be going in a direction that you believe in, toward some kind of vision. It could be spiritual. It could be political or humanitarian. It doesn't matter what it is, but if someone has those three components in the fabric of what they are about, they'll be fine. Unfortunately, most of us don't have all three simultaneously. If we get two out of three, we're doing pretty well.

The need to live this way comes from inside me. I'm very clear that this is good for me. I don't think everybody should be a monk and I don't think everybody should be a Catholic Worker, but if you find something that resonates with the strands deep within you, do it.

CHAPTER 19

The Logic of Grace

Davenport, Iowa

> When the kids are grown up to be plumbers and electricians and can
> support me in the manner to which I am accustomed, I'd love to run
> a soup line. I would sit with the guys and just shoot the shit. Not
> because it's heroic but because that's where the most fun happens.
> —*Margaret Quigley Garvey*

MIDWEST Workers tell lots of Margaret Quigley stories. She began the Davenport Worker and now lives in South Bend with her two boys and her husband, Mike Garvey, who writes for Information Services at Notre Dame.

Mike Garvey: When I married Margaret, my parents said, "We got rid of the Edsel." But it was not really a big departure for me to go to the Worker 'cause my father ran a Catholic bookstore—Templegate—and he was part of that whole intellectual Catholic stuff. Used to get stacks of the *Catholic Worker.* No, going to the Catholic Worker was probably a lot healthier than some other things I did.

It always used to crack me up when people would talk about us. And of course it was enjoyable when they would praise you for this incredibly rigorous Franciscan life. Living among the poor. But we had it made! It was a very nice life. And it was so much more interesting than anything else that you could do.

But you know . . . some of the most violent and fucked-up people I've ever met in my life were members of the Catholic Worker movement, and I'm sure that sentence is going to get extricated from your book. Those particular people weren't enjoying it, or they were enjoying it in a pretty perverse way.

Ro: That's the Jansenistic thing, the stuff I got pumped into me when I was little. You know, that "joy in suffering" bit. It's not holy if it doesn't hurt.

Mike: Yeah, enjoying being holy. Or being in a position from which they could judge other people. The power over bourgeois folks. We all fall into that, I guess. I remember . . . I think it was Sonny [Frank] Cordaro. Chuck Quilty, Sonny, and I were leafleting down at the post office on tax day or something. Some nice little old lady comes up and said, "I don't like nuclear war, and it's terrible what's happening in our country. What can I do to help?"

We're being so Christlike, you know. A bunch of whacked-out hippies passing out leaflets. But Sonny said, "Kill the aggressor in yourself!"

Jesus Christ! Here's this little old lady who's . . . she's probably more holy than anybody we've run into in all our lives. Certainly more holy than any of us. And he says, "Kill the oppressor in yourself!"

Margaret Quigley Garvey: All those people in the sixties were nuts when you think about it. Weren't they crazy? Sonny Cordaro! Michael Cullen! Now there's a piece of work! Michael Cullen was nuts. But there had to be something. Mike Cullen talks, Chuck Quilty hears it, Chuck Quilty quits his job at the Rock Island Arsenal and starts Omega House. Good old Margaret Quigley spends a weekend at Omega (eats toast the whole weekend, not knowing they're eating real dinners downstairs) and decides this is what she was meant to do. I used to go to Omega House on weekends when I was in college and met all these Zulus from Evanston—Johnny Baranski and those people who were doing the draft board actions.

Mike: Margaret so desperately wanted to hurl herself.

Margaret: I didn't want to go to prison, though.

Mike: All you've got to do is go to prison once, and you don't want to go there again.

Margaret: Prison doesn't appeal to me. Not at all. Rachelle Linner has the best line. She said, "In the olden days, we used to get plenary indulgences. Now we get prison sentences." Going to prison shouldn't be easy.

Mike: It's pharisaical. They already have their reward. You know, they're in the paper. Everybody sees them get arrested. It's great. Now to be fair—some of the Plowshares groups who've been in for incredibly long, horrifying sentences and then go back to do it again—I can't deny there's something terribly admirable about that. But I still have difficulties. I guess I just don't see the wisdom in it.

Ro: In a way it's a guarantee, like the indulgences, a guarantee of heaven. But so is being a Catholic Worker, isn't it?

Mike: That's the whole business with being a Christian. Trying to figure out a guarantee.

Margaret: It shouldn't come this easily if it's really a spiritual act. You shouldn't go on a retreat for two days and say, "Oh, my God! I'm enlightened!" and then go out and commit yourself. The people who did civil disobedience back when it wasn't trendy spent lots of time praying and thinking about it. We need to invent some new, creative ways to make a sign about what we're doing. It shouldn't be just climbing over the fence and going "do-dah."

That was the beautiful thing about what happened in Catonsville and with other draft board actions. They were innovative signs. Now it's just an arrest thing. I don't want to sound corny, but there isn't any liturgical sign that goes with it.

I think the Catholic Worker needs some quiet time. We resurrected the whole Catholic Worker retreat thing when we got our farm outside of Davenport. When I was there, it was never really a directed retreat. It may be now.

Ro: I'm hearing you calling for more spirituality.

Margaret: Everybody who's been through the Catholic Worker lives a very active life. Whether it's something like we're doing, you know, being grandparents to the South Bend house, or helping in a soup line or doing something else—it seems to me that we need time for reflection or quiet time with God.

We always had that at the Catholic Worker. I don't know. I laugh now and say [being at the Davenport Worker] was a piece of cake because if you were totally exhausted, there was always the community who could keep the house going and you could get away. And I really think that's the case in most houses now. Unless there's only one staff person or no volunteers. And that's pretty unheard of.

Ro: As a mother, I think it would be neat to have somebody "take house" sometime without my telling them to do it.

Margaret: You know, I visited the house in New York, and I thought our house was cooler than it was. I loved the flavor of our house. It was maybe a Midwestern . . . a different form of hospitality. The first time I met Dorothy . . . a funny story. Our house had been running for maybe a year or so. And Rachelle [Linner] came to visit. She told us Dorothy Day was speaking at De Paul University in Chicago.

"You have to meet her. She's getting old and . . ."

This Rachelle is a very special lady, so I said, "All right. We'll take a day off. We'll drive to Chicago and hear Dorothy and drive back that night." So we did it. We made it for the last two minutes of the talk. I think I heard Dorothy say, "And thank you so much for inviting me and God bless you all."

Rachelle literally pushed me down the aisle and up to Dorothy. There were these priests on either side of her, putting her jacket on and it was just . . . "Oh, my God! What am I doing here?"

"Dorothy, I want you to meet Margaret Quigley."

Dorothy turns to me. "Oh, so this is who you are!"

And I'm thinking, "This is Dorothy Day, the saint! My God, she probably knows I threw somebody out of the house the other night."

She said, "Where is your newspaper?"

And I said, "Well, Dorothy, we don't have one."

"Well, what do you do with your time, then?" And at this, the priests whisked her away.

I thought, "You horse's ass!"

I wrote her this just scathing letter and said, "Who do you think you are? I'm sleeping with fifteen men a night. Answering the door all night long, and you're asking me what I'm doing with my time! A newspaper is the last thing I think of." And then, of course, I started a newspaper.

Ro: Of course! [Laughter.] You know, I've heard lots of stories about the Davenport house. What ones can you tell?

Margaret: Gosh! Some of those old toots! I remember one from the first days we were open. This insane man came in. Sullivan. We had the phone in the dining room and I heard him from upstairs. He said, "Hello. Detective Sullivan here. Yeah, they're running a whorehouse. The fat one's upstairs getting laid and the other one's always down here answering the phone." So this was our introduction to the Davenport Police Department. Sullivan hit the bricks.

I think there's a lot of drama about hospitality. I did the dramatic stuff for a long time. For seven years. Loved every minute of it, but I wouldn't have the energy now to do what I did then. The first year, we would have fifty people a night sleeping on the floor. And then after a lot of violence (and we had a lot of violence), we cut back. One of our staff was beaten up with a railroad tie. And we all agreed that we couldn't let people keep coming in droves.

Mike: The rules in that house kind of came out of the guys themselves.

Margaret: They really did. See, I didn't know Dorothy then. I didn't know anybody in the Worker except Chuck Quilty. I'd read *Loaves and Fishes* and all those other books, and I thought, "Well, you're supposed to let each guest come in as Christ." So we did.

Mike: What would you do with Christ if Christ came in drunk and making racist comments? You'd kick him out, too. Remember the guy who used to fake epileptic seizures? He'd come in drunk and cause fights and stuff. We'd say, "Pearl, you've got to go!"

Immediately, the eyes would fall back, and he'd start shaking like a house afire. One day, Bert had him by the arms and I had him by the feet, and we're dragging him out of the house, and I'm calling over my shoulder, "Get the crutches! Get his Goddamn crutches!" Just as some bunch of Franciscans are coming in. And they were all horrified.

"Oh, just don't pay any attention to him. It's just Pearl."

Margaret: Oh, God!! When we opened, we had an enormous number of people living with us and a lot of people who would come just for dinners. But that was the time when they first closed all the institutions, so the people were out on the street. Then we cut back, and we seemed to acquire three or four kind of family members who lived with us till they died.

Mike: Yeah, the guy with the trains. He lived with us until he died, and John Cook did, too. On his dresser mirror, there was a little index card on which he had written, "Catholic people" and our number.

Margaret: See, we bought Peter Maurin House because we had about five men who had been with us a long, long time, and we wanted a house so more permanent folks could have their own rooms. (The main Davenport house is not much bigger than where we're living now.) But it didn't work at all. All the guys who lived in Peter Maurin ended up going on toots, so we turned it into a family house.

In that whole period though, how many people croaked? We had about four people die all at once. But there was a whole transition. We wanted to have these old farts live with us for the rest of their lives, and then they would go out on benders and . . . Hey, remember the steaks? That was the *best* time! [Bob] Chaps had come as a student volunteer for the summer. He kept writing to his old neighbor, Tom Crotty.

"You can't believe what this is like. This is the pits. These guys—they've got nothing. Their feet have these huge sores, and you can see them through their shoes. And they all have lice, and I have to delouse them! It's insane!"

So Tom comes to see for himself. The day he came, someone's freezer broke and they donated seventy-five sirloin steaks. Seventy-five steaks! So when the guys came for lunch, we told them they couldn't get dinner unless they dressed formally. It was summer, and we set up grills and ate outside. Carnival time.

Baked potatoes and sirloin steak and a tossed salad for dinner. "How would you like your steak?" Candles on the tables. Just beautiful! And this is the day Tom arrives at the Catholic Worker. He stayed for three years waiting for another sirloin steak.

✦

Here are some of the Margaret stories I heard:

Tina Sipula: I heard this great story about when Mother Teresa came to the Davenport house. And there was this old guy who was living there in a rocking chair. His name was Ben, I think. He was real crotchety. Had this cat, and he was into his cat and his blanket and his rocking chair and that was it. He was like eighty thousand years old, you know.

So Margaret kept saying, "Mamma Tess is coming. Now you behave! Mamma Tess is coming!"

So Mamma Tess shows up, and she's got a little scarf around her head, a little babushka, you know, and she says, "Hello Ben, how are you?"

And he looks at her and says, "Mamma Tess, get the fuck outta my face!"

Ro: Oh, I know another cute story about Margaret. (I forget who told me this.) Anyway, someone asked Margaret if Christ lived in the [Catholic Worker] house. And she said, "Yes, and he doesn't flush."

Tina: And here's one: Sargent Shriver came to visit while he was campaigning. FBI agents all over the place. He's walking around the house throwing his weight around. "Tell me, Margaret, what do the poor need more then anything else?"

"Teeth!"

Charles Walzem: That Margaret Garvey. She was special all right! In some Catholic Worker houses, you have people who are willing to care for just one person and Margaret did a whole lot of that. She bathed those old guys, she clothed them, she fed them in their beds if they were dying. Margaret was extraordinary. Her vitality, her . . . just her whole sense of loving the poor. It was there.

She was strong, too. She'd have solitary vigils in front of the Federal Building, just by herself. Form an opinion about something and stick to that opinion. Unswervingly. Which was, I think, a real blessing for her 'cause it also showed in her compassion to the individual. She could stick with the hard cases.

✦

Margaret: Those old guys! Other than that steak time, we always had casseroles 'cause none of them had teeth!

Mike: Well, teeth were the one thing you didn't get by praying. I wonder why folks are so reluctant to talk about miracles. You know, no kind of with-it Catholic likes to be caught believing . . .

Margaret: Well, maybe that's because with-it Catholics have never been low down in gully dirt.

Mike: Yeah, that could be. But then how do you distinguish between . . . I mean, there are folks in El Salvador who believe that if their kid doesn't get ashes on Ash Wednesday, he's going to burn in hell if he dies.

Margaret: Well, there's a differnce between that and miracles. Miracles are when you pray to someone for a specific favor. There are lots of miracles at the Catholic Worker. Believe me, I'm a victim of one of them. My St. Joseph's statue is still in the kitchen. One of the guests gave it to me when we first started. We didn't have a stove then, just a hot plate. And the day the hot plate blew, somebody phoned in with a six-burner stove. Other times when we would have *no* money at all, we always put notes under St. Joseph's statue.

Mike: But that's superstition, too.

Margaret: Michael Garvey, when we were starting the Catholic Worker here in South Bend, I went to the library at Notre Dame and opened the book where Dorothy Day's name was and slid a petition in there and said, "Dear Dorothy, if this house is meant to start, please help us." It's just something that you do.

Ro: Most people won't talk about the signs. They just say, "Oh well, it just happened."

Mike: Nothing just *happens.*

Margaret: Another thing about the Catholic Worker miracles is the whole aspect of faith. "O ye of little faith." And I don't want to sound like a charismaniac, but those things never happen until the people think they're not going to make it. It never happens until they lose faith and then see the faith of other people. Many a time when we had nothing, all of a sudden a check for two hundred dollars would come in.

Mike: It would be exactly what you needed at the time you needed it. Let me tell one folklore story. You can do with it what you will. Brian Terrell told us that a bunch of folks who'd been at the Catholic Worker a lot when Dorothy was

there, and especially the younger people, went out to McSorley's the night before [Dorothy's] funeral. And I guess most of them got really, really smashed.
Not just tipsy but like stomping on tables. Fraternity party type. And nobody
was hung over the next morning. Nobody! They were all ready for the funeral.
And somebody said it was a miracle. I love to think that was true. You'd have
trouble getting it through the Vatican, though. The first Dorothy miracle.

Ro: Well, it *was* an instance of getting what you need when you need it.

Mike: I'll never forget . . . it was the only time Jerry Falwell ever said anything
that I thought was neat. He was being interviewed on the McNeil-Lehrer Report, and he was asked, "Don't you think it's sort of bizarre, Mr. Falwell, that
in this entire galaxy, all these little specks floating through time and space, that
God would choose to descend upon this one speck and the Maker of the entire
universe would suddenly be revealed and manifested?"

Falwell said, "Yes, it is bizarre! I think it's the most astonishing thing that could
ever possibly happen." It is, in fact, an astonishing thing. Looked at from that
point of view, why should we be so shy about miracles?

Ro: Well, maybe it's because we feel that the charismatics . . .

Margaret: Put a hex on it.

Mike: Well, none of us want to be caught worshiping the blood of St. Januarius
as it liquefies in Naples. Miracles are very tricky stuff.

Ro: I feel more comfortable with the word grace.

Mike: I guess I'm more comfortable—although I guess the idea is not to get
comfortable with anything—I find more compelling the notion that there is a logic
of grace which is not the same as the logic of the world. For instance, the very
notion of marriage, it seems to me, requires a belief in miracles on some level.
It doesn't make any sense on a secular level at all, and yet it works. It has been
shown to work. And that's not just true of marriage, it's true of vows that people
take, and it's true of witnesses that people make.

Ro: Why did you leave the Davenport house?

Mike: 'Cause I married her. I guess we kind of figured that with us married,
there'd be a community inside the community, and that would be kind of weird.
We see ourselves as grandparents to the South Bend Worker, though, and that's
worked out real well.

But we couldn't live there. Let me show you why. When the South Bend
house first opened, I remember being down there one day with our boys, Michael

Francis and Joseph Benedict, when they were six and five. There was a typical Catholic Worker scene. As a grown-up, it was sad, but adults can deal with it. A beat-up car pulled up in front. A woman who'd been staying there had gone out that afternoon, and I mean she had hit every bar in South Bend. Had been smoking dope and taking pills and just, you know, completely out to lunch. Real, real drunk. Screaming at the people in the car. Every obscenity you can imagine.

I was there with the kids. Joseph's eyes were the size of saucers and Michael Francis was peeing his pants. They're thinking, "Look at that lady! She's all goofed-up and she's scary-sounding, and she's saying these crazy things and she just fell down in front of the car!" I'm all for maintaining even an illusory childhood as long as you can. When they're grown-ups and want to get into something like that, that's great, but I would not want to hit them over the head with it. It's rough enough being a kid without it.

Ro: Do you think you might go back and do hospitality when the kids are older?

Mike: I haven't slammed the door on it as a possibility, but until you mentioned it right now, I hadn't really thought of it. Maybe we will.

Margaret: I think that's one of the biggest flaws of the Catholic Worker in general. People look at hospitality as being a house where you have fourteen transient men and shopping bag ladies sleeping in the living room. I think that the needs are so overwhelming right now that aside from the model Dorothy set up, smaller models are certainly valuable. And different models. For different kinds of people. I don't think that we'd ever be a traditional Catholic Worker.

Mike: A marriage or a family that is not somehow arranged to welcome the stranger is not a real secure marriage anyway. A kid growing up in a family that is entirely closed off from that kind of contact is an abused kid. And knows it. He knows something is wrong with his family if there is this closing off from the outside. But I would never live like we did in Davenport with kids.

Margaret: When Michael's dead and I'm still alive and the kids are grown up to be plumbers and electricians with no degrees in anything and can support me in the manner to which I am accustomed, I'd love to run a soup line. I would sit with the guys and just shoot the shit. Not because it's heroic but because that's where the most fun happens. Sitting around and drinking coffee till four in the afternoon with people who have led incredibly wonderful lives. Well, some of them have been real crappy lives, but you just sit and you talk about it, and you laugh, and you tell jokes, and you read newspapers together and . . . I'd love to do that.

"Hey, you gotta interview Chaps!" they'd tell me in the Midwest Worker communities. Bob Chaps's stories are legendary, especially his tales of the crazy times in the Davenport and Chicago St. Francis houses. He's now married and living in a Detroit suburb.

Ro: I hear you're the number-one Avis salesman in Detroit.

Bob Chaps: Yeah, I guess I am. I've been here for ten years, and I'm a national account manager, so I handle all the major accounts—General Motors, Dow Chemical, UNISIS, Upjohn, Whirlpool—all the Fortune 500 companies. I sell corporate rates to accountants. Not a hard-sell sort of thing. I like it, and it's challenging. When I lived at the Worker in Chicago, I worked for Avis, too.

Ro: That's kind of unusual, isn't it?

Bob: Yeah, it is. You know, when I first graduated from college, I was very judgmental. (My folks couldn't stand me. I don't think any of my friends could either.) But when I started working for Avis, I . . . I started to find out other people's stories. Everyone has a cross or a tragedy in their life, and I was stupid not to realize that. I'd be real critical of someone, saying how selfish they were, and then I'd find out they spent a lot of time with a mentally handicapped sibling and . . . I put my foot in my mouth so many times that I finally realized that everyone is pretty much trying to do their best.

I had a degree in marketing and I started in sales. Just hated it. Talk about a transition! From the Catholic Worker to sales—it was just very, very difficult for me. But I had a great boss. Really a great guy, a great friend. After three weeks I said to him . . . "Maybe we made a mistake. I can't do this. It's just not me."

He said, "Just give it a try." Which was the nicest thing, you know. If he had said, "You're not trying hard enough," or "You need to change your value system," I would have left right then. But he asked me to give it a try and that I could do. So I did it. And I like it.

When I was doing Catholic Worker in Iowa, I was a maintenance man. I always worked. The Catholic Worker takes a lot of energy, and [working outside] allowed me to bring energy to the Worker. Maybe it's similar to parenting. If you parent full time, it's hard to bring energy to it.

Ro: What was the best thing about being in Davenport?

Bob: Well, one thing was that [Margaret] Quigley was always drawing new people, and people in the extended community were bringing down meals and were very visible. We had a lot of help, a really good operation. Maybe part of it is that Quigley's hospitality was not just for the guests, it was for everyone.

It was for me who wanted to go there for the holidays or anybody who wanted to come.

Ro: Or someone from the suburbs who wants to bring in a casserole.

Bob: Exactly. We weren't judging a person. We weren't saying, "Geez, you can bring in your casserole, but we don't like the way you dress."

Ro: Who were some of the characters you remember from Davenport?

Bob: Oh, we had 'em. We had 'em! A funny thing, though. You see people helping the elderly in movies, and the elderly are always nice people. But some of the people we were with, they were cranks. Cranks! Not easy to get along with. They were alone for a reason. Because they had pushed everybody else out of their lives.

Like the old vet who was living in the house in Davenport when we moved in. George. Real eccentric. Poor as a church mouse, you know, and wore one of those undershirts with the straps. Very thin, and just a real crank . . . a very cranky man. He never cleaned. Thick dust all over everything. I think he used to feed the cat and not himself. And he was crazy about trains. His drawers were full of train cars. Beautiful! Drawers and drawers and drawers full. Track on the floor. He just really loved trains.

Ro: Can you talk about how you came to the Davenport Worker?

Bob: Oh, yeah. When I was in college, I was a pretty normal kid. Didn't go to Mass. Drank a lot of beer and had a ball. Met Margaret Quigley and some other Catholic Workers just by accident, through Father Jack Real. Liked what I saw, so I started coming on my holidays—Christmas and Easter. I was tired of going home and seeing my friends and getting drunk for four or five days and then coming back to school.

Finally, I was graduating. Quigley said, "How would you like to come for the summer?" I planned to stay three months. Stayed for two years.

Father Jack Real had introduced me to the Worker. His philosophy was to break one rule every day. That was the way he could stay being a priest—to break a rule. He taught us to find the niche where the fun is. That was our approach in Davenport—to have fun. And we did. I had just a ball. Margaret Quigley and Frank Cordaro . . . just too much to take!

The Davenport house was right by the railroad tracks. People would jump off the cars. When I first came, most of our guests were alcoholics, with lots of hobos. When I left in '77, it was probably fifty-fifty, half alcoholic and half mentally ill. When the state institutions started to let people out, the change was very, very evident. We used to pray for an alcoholic. "Dear Lord, don't send us another crazy." It was hard and frightening because you just didn't know what was going to happen with someone who was mentally ill. We were very open in the way we lived. We didn't have any security or anything like that.

Yes, Margaret was very funny and very strong when it came to hospitality. But I'll always remember. One day she came into my room and she was just sobbing. (I never know what to do with anyone when they're hysterical.) All Margaret could say is, "It just keeps going. It just keeps going. The men never . . . get . . . better. It will never change. Never, never, never!" So she had this casual side to her, but . . .

Ro: Well, crying doesn't mean you stop.

Bob: No, you don't stop. But it's not an idealistic sort of thing with her.

Ro: Everybody says that Margaret had this . . . this touch. She loved these old guys.

Bob: Yeah, she did. You know what else she did, though? She considered the house to be ours. So we wouldn't allow people to violate us or the property. If someone spilled something on the floor, we weren't happy about it. It wasn't an institution, it was our home.

Ro: Um . . . hmmm . . . Did you ever do any resistance?

Bob: Never anything that I'd go to jail for. But we used to picket. That's hard. People swear at you and give you the finger. They yell at you and everything. In Davenport, we'd say what we really felt about things. I hate picketing. You're confronting people and you're challenging people. I mean . . . if you like it, there's something wrong because it's not fun.

Ro: Yeah. Can we get back to this Avis thing?

Bob: Sure. One thing . . . I always had a brand-new car [because of Avis] and when I lived in downtown Detroit, I had very little ever done to my car. I think that was because people knew who I was, and there was a respect for the fact that I lived in the neighborhood.

Ro: You were one of them.

Bob: Yeah. I lived [close to] Day House, the Detroit Worker. On Trumbull and Butternut. There's a lot of single parents [in the neighborhood] and I loved to be involved with the neighborhood kids. We'd play sports. And you know what? I think me wearing a suit to work every day was important to the people. It was saying that I was there because I wanted to be. There wasn't the "suits" and the "not suits."

In the neighborhood where we lived in Detroit, no one gets out of there who isn't an addict or a prostitute. They don't see an alternative, don't see anyone with a life outside of the neighborhood, don't see people getting up and going to work at eight-thirty in the morning. I think that the inner city and the soup kitchens are changing again. [First it was] the change from alcoholics to the mentally ill. Now you see more younger people.

Ro: Now you and Jimmy [Sweeney] used to have folks staying with you in your apartment [on Trumbull]. But you can't do that kind of thing out here in the 'burbs, can you?

Bob: Not very easily. You'd have to be pretty selective. Uh . . . No, you can't. And we don't. There are different types of hospitality, though. For instance, Deb McEvoy has never lived at the Catholic Worker in Detroit, but she's always been a part of the community and she opens her house up to everybody. Everyone goes to Deb McEvoy when they want to talk or, you know, just to visit. Not too different than the hospitality provided at a Catholic Worker house.

Ro: Do you miss that living out here [in the suburbs]?

Bob: Sure. This isn't much of a neighborhood here. The only time you see the neighbors is when they cut their grass. I miss the neighborhood downtown. It was a real neighborhood even if it was broken.

Ro: Do you think [living at a Worker house] ruins folks for this kind of quiet suburban life?

Bob: No, I don't think it does. Not many people can take a Worker for a lifetime. And I don't think that's bad. Maybe that's why some people are afraid of it. They feel they have to commit themselves to a lifetime. That's too much to ask.

Ro: One last question, Chaps. Why did you do it? Come to the Worker, I mean.

Bob: Why was I at the Catholic Worker? [Long pause.] A couple of . . . I think it probably made my faith make sense. It made the Gospel make sense to me, the crucifixion story. That and I liked it. That has to be said in the same sentence. It was a great way to live.

CHAPTER 20

A Family Affair

The Cordaros of Des Moines

> All this education I got. Tom and Frank were my teachers. I became
> the pupil, and I was very open, very open.
>
> —*Angela Cordaro*

A NGELA Cordaro and her sons Tom and Fr. Frank—a warm Italian family,
generous with their words, generous with their lives. Although each was
interviewed separately, I've combined their words into a single conversation.

Angela Cordaro: I never in my wildest, wildest, wildest dreams ever thought
Frank would be ordained. He was a jock on campus. Won the best legs contest
two years straight. Such a ham, oh my God! He went to University of Northern
Iowa, and got his degree in coaching, of course. Wanted to be like his Dad. A
very frank and open boy.

Fr. Frank Cordaro: My father was the athletic director at the all-boys Catholic
high school in my home town, and I lettered in four major sports. Eight different letters. President of the student body, president of my class, a big man on
campus.

  Basically, there are two types of deviants in high school: the juvenile delin-
quents, the ones everyone can pick out—guys who smoke and cheat and leave
school—and the other deviants, the ones who've got the system beat. They belong to all the clubs, and they're officers, so they run the school and can get out
of all the classes they want. That's what I was. I was a "go to the head of the
class," play-the-system kind of guy. Of course when your dad's the A.D., it's not
hard to rise up in the ranks.

  I was a real Neanderthal. The Vietnam War was going on. I would have fought
there easily, all the way through college. (I went to college between 1969 and
1973. For Iowa, the sixties happened in the early seventies.) I was on a campus
that was not radical at all, but for two of the four years there, spring term tests

were called off because of the antiwar movement across the country. It was a unique time to go to college, but I was just on the fringe. I got elected president of a fraternity because I was one of the few sober and non-drugged-out people in the whole group. Just really oddball folks—no political conscience whatsoever. However, I was very much involved in the Newman Center, going to daily Mass, which was odd for my jock image and my fraternity image.

I'd been dealing with this damn priesthood idea since way back.* You know, you go to Catholic schools and . . . but I wasn't the one. My brother Joe was. He went to Loras, but when my dad died, Joe moved back in to Des Moines to be with the family, and I got to go to college because I got a football scholarship. And then Joe got married, but I still wasn't the best shot for priesthood. If you want to pick a guy with more perceived priestly qualities, it would be Tommy. Temperament-wise, anyway.

It's real . . . I never fell in love with the cheerleaders. So I decided, "What the heck!" I didn't feel like I wanted to work after I graduated, so I went in to see Bishop Dingman. Great man!

I hemmed and hawed and said maybe I'd like to, but I didn't know. And of course if you've got a B.A. in anything and the right plumbing on the outside, the door's open. Bishop Dingman got me into Aquinas Institute in Dubuque, the Dominican Studium. I had a great three years.

Spent my first summer in the South Bronx, at a black and Puerto Rican parish, and I finally began to question the assumed realities that most kids like me are brought up to believe. You know, the cold warrior stuff. America the best. Being in the Bronx just kind of concretized the whole thing. And also, while in college and in seminary, I was five years as a charismatic, which is very vital. It allowed me to read the scriptures for the first time. I never, never did that as a Catholic. Now I read those Gospels as stories and let them speak to me. And the other thing [the charismatic movement did] was personalize my faith in Christ. To claim Christ personally.

Ro: Why do some people move out of that inward spirituality into application, and some people just stay there for years, happy as a clam?

Frank: Beats me. For me, to stay there would have been terribly stifling. I didn't need the constant stroking. The issue was this—was being a Catholic going to be important or just peripheral? I could be a cultural Catholic like a lot of my relatives and the people back home, which is all right. These are good people. But I

* *Angela:* He told me once he would have liked to become a priest earlier, but he'd flunked Latin. And then we went into the Vatican II and he didn't need it anymore.

wanted to know whether it was going to be real. And the charismatic movement made it central to me that Christ and my faith was going to be real.

Given that, what do I do with it? I went to seminary thinking I might want to become a priest. When I spent that summer in the South Bronx, in a black and Puerto Rican parish, that just changed my whole life. I came to the conclusion that if the only poor people in the world existed in the Bronx, there were too many. And because I'm a Gospel person, I'm going to spend the rest of my life trying to address those issues.

The other thing I learned in the Bronx is that I ain't black, and there ain't nothing I can do about it. I'm white, I'm middle class, I'm educated, I'm from the Midwest, I'm a Catholic, and I'm a male. A white male. Where can I stand with some integrity and be a Gospel person in this country with all those things going against me?

We have what they call a January month during the seminary. We can go do whatever we want. I lined up a month with Bishop Dingman. My bishop. Just the two of us. I lived at his house. I drove him around. I did some work for him. We studied the scriptures, and I read William Miller's *Harsh and Dreadful Love*. Boy, the Catholic Worker movement was speaking to me! So that summer, I went to the Worker in Davenport. I visited Margaret Quigley who started the Worker there, and God! I fell in love with the movement. Spent the summer there. God, I had a great time! Margaret was a great woman, the first woman my age that I really respected and looked up to. She was just a very good woman. Good spirituality. Good sense of the Catholic Worker. Lots of fun. A great love in her for the men that she worked with. She was . . . she was good.

That summer was the first time I experienced a space where a white middle-class educated Catholic Midwesterner could be critical of society. Critique it from a Gospel perspective and be supported in this critique. Not in an abstract way but through a learned encounter with the poor.

Angela: One day, after three years of seminary, Frank says to me: "Ma, I'm going to start a Catholic Worker in Des Moines."

I wanted a priest. I didn't care about no Catholic Worker house, you know. So I said, "Listen!" I said, "Let somebody else do that. God wants you to be a priest."

"Mom, I'm seriously thinking about it."

"Well, I'm going to pray that you don't think."

When he decided for sure, I said to him, "If you make a Worker house in Des Moines, make it for women and children and families." And he did. I told him if he didn't, the women on the street, you make prostitutes out of them, right?

There were two guys as co-hosts—Frank and this Joe DaVia. It was funny. These two men there with the women and children. The first thing everyone thought was that these two guys were gay. Of course, after you know Frank, that's the furthest thing from your mind.

As Reagan came more and more into his regime, there were more and more people on the street. More and more kinds of people would come to the Worker house to eat, come to get food. Young married couples with two or three kids, out of a job, very clean, just . . . and they'd have a house or maybe even be working, but didn't have enough money to carry them over. It just broke my heart.

It was a good arrangement. I'd babysit that house. We'd have great Masses on Friday night. It was a good thing. The poor and everything, you know. After about two years, after [Frank] got the house established, he got into his peace and justice. I remember on Good Friday, Frank would carry the big wooden cross right through town, you know, and parade down to the cathedral. God bless that Bishop Dingman! He never told him once not to do it.

I look back now on all the things that Frank did downtown—marched in the streets, carried signs. Every time a politician came, all our presidents and senators and people with the political backgrounds—they were there. Senator Grassley is our Republican senator, and Frank would go one-on-one with him, challenge him.

Frank would throw things at him about the military and all that waste, and Grassley would say, "Well, I'm not informed in that." Or "I haven't learned too much about that." I was there, too. I can remember. All this education I got. Tom and Frank were my teachers. I became the pupil, and I was very open, very open.

People will say, "You don't pay taxes. What have you got to say for the country? Go to Russia!"

We've been called everything from . . . you name it and we've been called. Or they'll say, "I don't want to hear about it. I'm happy. I'm content. Don't tell me about all that stuff."

Sometimes we wonder if Dad would approve, but the only way people will hear you is to do something crazy. I can remember the first time they arrested Frank. People came to me and said, "George would turn in his grave." (George is my husband.) I thought, "God, that's a terrible thing to say!"

I'd say, "Listen! George is up there telling him what to do." No one said that to me again. And I do believe he is. I . . . we had great discussions when Frank first started this. Our family had to adjust to all of that, and it was good.

Ro: Now, if you hadn't been a widow, would you be this involved?

Angela: If I hadn't been a widow, I don't know if Frank would have been a Catholic Worker. You know, I love my boys very much. They're all doing what I think God wants them to do and all are true to themselves. The Lord's been very good to me. I had a rough time when my husband first died. I had . . . I have six children, okay? We were two people, and then I became a one person. It was very, very hard for me to adjust. I'd say, "Why me, Lord?"

The charismatic movement helped us really a lot, but the people are so inward. I don't go there anymore. I don't . . . I don't dislike them, you know, but that just isn't my cup of tea. There's such a big world out there.

Frank: If Dad hadn't died, I don't think I would have gotten into this stuff at all. I think I probably would have went on to be a coach. A great coach. Dad was the most important person in my life. Died on Easter Sunday morning of my senior year. My father was a great man, but his dying did more for our family than anything he ever did. Because with his passing away, we came together much closer, and my mother just blossomed into a full human being. Took on lots of responsibility. We just celebrated the twentieth anniversary of Dad's death and had a family Mass. Still very powerful stuff. Wherever I get my strength, it's got to be [from] my family background.

[I realized this] especially after [being with] the Worker. You spend any time at a Catholic Worker . . . I'm blown away by the abuse and the drug abuse, and the other cultural things that are just tearing away at our guests. But as amazingly high as it is in the guests, I realize it's [present] also in the people [who] come to work with us. Many of the people who come to the Worker, either as Workers or guests, are victims of violence. Especially women. I learned vicariously that most people begin their adult life insecure, without a good self-image. And I'd been gifted with lots of breaks. Lots of love. Lots of people caring about me. Lots of attention. Lots of people saying, "You're gifted! You've got things going for you." So for better or for worse, I don't have that . . . I didn't go into becoming an adult with a major problem dealing with self-image and self-esteem.

Anyway, when I got back from New York, I did my internship at a campus ministry in Iowa City and fell in love with a woman. That spring I told Bishop Dingman that I didn't think I was ready for the priesthood, and I didn't think the priesthood was ready for the type of ministry that I envisioned. [I told him] I'd like to help start a Catholic Worker [in Des Moines].

Ro: Did you tell him about the woman?

Frank: Oh, yeah. He knew her. Jacquee. I met her in Iowa City when I was doing my internship. And we had a lot of things in common, but we just didn't get along well in a regular normal way. Perhaps one of the strongest things we had is that we both have a call to a ministry of the church and priesthood. Anyway, Joe DaVia and I, we started the Des Moines Catholic Worker on August 23, 1976. It was a great life. I spent seven years there, more or less. Spent about ten months jail time in those seven years. For different acts of civil disobedience. I did eight months at Leavenworth once, and it was then that I really decided to deal with the priesthood thing again. It had been plaguing me all this time.

Angela: Bishop Dingman was nearing seventy, and Frank thought he'd probably be the only bishop to ordain him, so he went for it. The bishop sent Frank up to St. John's. Very wealthy [college]—they had ROTC on the campus, and he'd picket that. He got the seminarians all stewed up. It was a gorgeous, gorgeous setting for a college, on a little island peninsula.

Ro: Ivory tower?

Angela: Oh, yeah. They had a boarding high school and a college and a seminary. They treated the seminarians like . . . well, they called them "princes of the church." Princes of the church! I didn't like that. Not really, not coming from where I was coming. There were some priests, though, who were very active in the peace movement, very supportive, but more of them not.

Frank: It's easy to play a Catholic campus—a college which has the consciousness ought to know the problem. St. John's was vulnerable because it's so far off where it was in the thirties when Dorothy Day and Peter Maurin used to go there.

I mean these Benedictines have bellied up to corporate military America. They no longer . . . the whole spirit of St. Benedict is to live in harmony off the land, and [have] the discipline. These people [at St. John's] don't grow their own food anymore. They hire it out. They hire out people to clean for them. They hire out people to [do] maintenance for them. It's a rich boy's club. They are literally putting the spirit of St. Benedict at the disposal of upper-middle-class kids from Minneapolis. They rely more on their portfolio than subsistence living. The one good thing I can say about the Benedictines is they didn't stop my ordination, and they could have.

I was really in a cultural shock up there after seven years in a Catholic Worker, you know. I told the bishop, "This is crazy! Why are you sending me there?"

"I want to see if you can survive in the institutional church."

"Bishop, why don't you just put me in a parish? Why did you send me to a seminary?"

And he looked at me and said, "Why do you think they make seminaries?"

"Oh, Bishop! I don't think I'm going to like this test."

"That's what makes it a good test, Frank."

Next to my own father, Dingman is the most influential male in my life. He was my best priest model, too. He's a great bishop.* Bishop Bullock, the new bishop, I would call C-plus. A good man. Certainly not one of the more Neanderthal bishops that have recently been appointed. He's probably left of center. It's unfortunate, though, that he followed Bishop Dingman. 'Cause compared to Bishop Dingman, he comes off looking very concerned about authority. Very concerned about control. Very concerned about boundaries and stuff like that.

Ro: How do you live with this church of ours?

Frank: Uh . . . very uncomfortably. The guy who gives me a language I can work with right now is Matthew Fox. I've grown to have a great deal of respect for him. He's pointed out that the church is a dysfunctioning organization, very much like a dysfunctioning family. And it's tragic by design at this point; there's a design flaw in our church that it's not embracing women as it should. In a sense, the hierarchy is by design—I'm not talking about any personalities here, just the design—the hierarchy is like the alcoholic father.

Ro: Aren't you participating in the enabling by being a priest?

Frank: Yes, I am. We all buy into it. It's the church of all of us. The thing about this language of a dysfunctioning family is that it *is* family. It's my family. It's my dysfunctioning family. I don't leave family. The important role for everybody who's in a dysfunctioning family is to act like an adult and stop being an enabler. So that's the challenge of being in the church today. To be an adult.

Ro: How do you decide whether you're playing into it, being an enabler?

Frank: It's not easy. Right now I'm in very intensive dialogue with a new bishop. I'm a priest so I'm . . . I'm in the club. That means [the bishop's] really concerned about me. My priesthood by definition is an extension of his bishopric, and he's responsible for me. So he's in a very difficult [position].

Ro: You are, too.

Frank: Yes. I have said that to him. I told him that the relationship I had with Bishop Dingman was a celebration. "But with you, we disagree on major things.

---

* Bishop Dingman suffered a stroke April 7, 1986, and died February 1, 1992. Later in 1992, Fr. Frank invited resisters to an action at SAC headquarter, asking them to "do for Bishop Dingman what he couldn't do himself—cross the line for a more peaceful world."

I don't think that's bad 'cause if I can make it with you, that means I can make it with the mainline church."

At one point, I asked Bishop Dingman, "Don't you get angry about all the limitations of the church and the mistakes of the church?"

And he said, "Anger is negative. If you get angry enough, you'll eventually hate and leave." He said the proper attitude to have when the church makes mistakes is to *grieve* for the church. To be pained by your church that's doing the wrong thing. And I agree. I'm in grief over my church's inability to really address the major issues of the time. These days, we seem like we're entrenching and going backwards. It's silly, even tragic, this consolidating and holding on to powers and structures that are antiques. Dinosaurs!

Angela: You know what really bothers me? God love 'em, a lot of the priests in Des Moines today, their insight is so down the narrow path. You know, there are a few, but just . . . they get up there and they talk with tongue in both cheeks. They talk about justice, about clothing the poor, about this and that, but they never practice what they preach. It's very discouraging. If I had a lot of guts, maybe . . . I'm more outspoken today then I ever was in all my life 'cause I don't have to hold a job. (I work for Manpower now and can work whenever I want to.) If I had the guts . . . when they start talking about that, I would get up right out of that pew and walk right down that main aisle and right around in front of him and walk all the way out.

Frank: I challenge the church from the pulpit. Yeah, I do. A lot of people had trouble with my homilies in the beginning. "Too much social justice. Too much political rhetoric."

I said to Bishop Bullock, "Well, you know, I might be. I might be abusing the pulpit. I might be going too far to that side. But Bishop, how many of the guys do you call in for saying *nothing* about peace and justice? I may well have made mistakes and will continue to make mistakes, but our folks are so used to hearing nothing that if they hear anything, they think it's too much."

We're a mission diocese, and we're short of priests. I told the Bishop, "Let me try and find another priest from outside of our priest pool who will come to Iowa, and we can yoke our priesthood into one pastoral position. And at any given time, one of us would be there."

"Well, what makes you think there's anybody out there?"

"If I exist, somebody else might exist."

I am in these difficult moments with my bishop right now, but they're really good moments as far as dialogue. Amazing discussions! I asked to cross the line this August. He asked me not to do it, and I told him I wouldn't out of love and deference to him. And then he said, "Well, let's add obedience, too." He said obedience in the broadest sense means listening and that "this time we're going to try to listen to each other."

When I went to jail the last time, this man gave me one of his pectoral crosses. I told him, "I'm not going to take this to jail. They'd rip it off. But I'll give it to my mother to hold." I mean he's doing the best he can. But I think he's beginning to realize how vastly different we are. At one point in our discussion, he asked me what I meant by jail being kind of a redemptive suffering.

Like Larry Morlan, the guy who I did time with at Marion [Federal Prison], is doing six years. No one seems to know he's there, and it's very lonely. And I gave him as an example. These guys are paying the price, doing the spiritual groundwork that needs to be done for the conversion to come.

He said, "I like that. I understand that redemptive suffering." Then he said, "But redemptive suffering comes in all different sizes and places. What if I were to ask you to spend the next five years in Logan and not do any civil disobedience? That would be redemptive suffering, too, and I would know it. You would lift that up to the Lord to let the Lord use it, and you would be in obedience with the bishop."

I looked at him. "Bishop, if you ask me to do that, I don't think I could. Because I don't trust your vision on the bomb."

"What?"

"Whenever you talk about the consistent life ethic, and you use the nuclear weapons issues, you say we've got to 'stem the excess of nuclear weapons.' Bishop, as far as I'm concerned, every nuclear weapon is an immoral redundancy."

And when Bishop [Thomas] Gumbleton came to Omaha and crossed the line at SAC [Strategic Air Command at Offutt Air Force Base], clearly by your behavior, regardless of what you said, you saw what we were doing out there as detrimental to the church.

Angela: The editor of our *Catholic Mirror* came on that two-day retreat when Bishop Gumbleton [was here]. She took pictures and wrote up the articles and everything and then couldn't publish it. The bishop told her not to.

Ro: So they don't want Frank's influence to spread?

Angela: Well, there were other priests, too—five of them.

Frank: I said to Bishop Bullock, "One priest came in to ask you if he could cross and you told him he couldn't. Bishop, clearly you saw [your actions] as damage control." He was kind of uncomfortable with that 'cause I named it so well. I said to him, "The church and bishops are willing to risk a lot for abortion, to risk a lot on homosexuality and birth control, but you won't do a darn thing for the arms race.

"You're willing to use your bishopric to change the laws in this country. You're even willing to risk your own nonprofit status in your struggle. You want to see all federal funding taken from abortion, and you want to make abortion a criminal act. But what do you do for the arms race? Nothing. You're not seeking to take all federal funding away from nuclear weapon production. You're not seeking legislation to make possession of a nuclear weapon a criminal offense.

"The church by and large has blessed and supported the nuclear establishment from the beginning. Catholic nuclear physicists put together the bomb. Catholics are on those production lines. Catholics are in those missile silos, ready to use a weapon on a moment's notice. You just don't have the same commitment. It's not consistent."

Ro: Frank, are you going to do a Plowshares [resistance] action?

Frank: I'm certainly open to it. But let's be . . . I'm not ready to sit in jail for a number of years, and that could happen. At this point, I've been doing this thing at SAC. It's my . . . you grow where you're planted. Everybody's got a piece of the Pentagon almost in their backyard. At SAC, we're talking about the main command post for the land and air components of our strategic nuclear weapons—the total workbook on how to go to nuclear war at any given moment, at any given time, at any given level. And the guys who are working there are updating war plans that include first-strike nuclear war, plans that believe if we go to war, we go to win. Which are completely contrary to the conditions that the bishops put forth for the moral acceptability of deterrence.

Over twelve years of jail time have been served by people in the last ten years, just for crossing the line at the Omaha SAC. You couldn't get a more abstract, more pristine civil act. Draw a line and put your body across it. That's the statement. No blood. No ashes. No property.

Angela: I tell him, "Frank, he's short of priests. How can you say you'll go do a demonstration just to satisfy yourself? When he may need you?" I just hope eventually Frank will mellow and know where his needs are.

Frank: See, Bullock's worried because I don't stop. I'm not going to stop recruiting other priests. I tell him, "Bishop, this is puny. This isn't even a beginning. I'm embarrassed that this is all I do."

But I understand his position and I want to respect it. 'Cause we *are* different. Let's admit it. Now what relationship can we have and coexist? It's not easy. [Pause] It's not easy at all.

Ro: It seems to me that being a priest really forces you into a lot of contradictions. How do you deal with that?

Frank: I just know that when I dig deep enough, the contradictions disappear and [I see] the many gifts that the church has been for me. One of my prayers before I got ordained to the diaconate was, "Dear God, keep my faith safe and keep my love for the church safe." They're not the same things. If I had to pick one or the other, I hope I'd pick my faith. But as long as I still have a deep love for the church and my family, I'm going to keep both, my faith and my love for the church.

Because there's more good than bad. The biggest strain I have on my ministry is the pull between pastoral work and resistance work. I think most people say about me, "You're difficult, but the church needs people like you. Let's take the risk." I hope my bishop continues to embrace that sort of mentality.

Ro: You don't like being in crowds, do you?

Frank: Well, I'd like to be in a crowd at the [SAC] base someday. Instead of 250,000 people showing up for an open house to watch these weapons play games in the air, I'd like to occupy the base with that many people. That's the kind of crowd I'm looking forward to. It's not like I wouldn't want to be in a crowd. There just aren't a lot of crowds where I'm at.

If we really wanted to stop the arms race, we could do it. What we're missing is the political will. The spiritual will. We're not going to *think* our way to the [end of the] arms race. We're going to *act* our way out of it through nonviolent direct action.

Ro: When some people talk to me about nonviolence, they say it's exactly your sort of confrontational spirit, I guess, that's violent. That nonviolence means being accepting of everything.

Frank: Oh, then those people have never read the Gospels—Matthew, Mark, Luke, or John. I mean those people are living in . . . that whole idea of having an absolutely clean heart before you act, that's weird. I don't understand people like that. I mean fine and well, but you'll never leave your house. You'll never leave the pot. I'm sorry.

When I act, I act as a broken person. I also know that a significant amount of the violence that I'm addressing on the outside is [also] in me. It's a catharsis thing, an exorcism. I got to do it. It's trying to get rid of the violence in me as I address the violence on the outside. And we make mistakes. Lots of them.

Ro: Speaking of mistakes, lots of people say you've got the funniest resistance stories in the Worker. Like the ashes at the White House. And that time you saw your teacher at the Pentagon. Can you tell those for the book?

Frank: Oh, sure! They are kind of famous, I guess. Well, here goes. [Pause] It's November 1979. I'm not a priest yet. Jimmy Carter's pushing the SALT II treaty, and I somehow get my name on a list to go to D.C. To listen to a pep talk on this treaty and have some wine and cheese with the president. I got an invitation to go to the White House! What a surprise, huh? First of all, I had already done blood spilling at the Pentagon. I'd been arrested at Rocky Flats. My orientation was pretty well established.

They told us to send in our social security numbers to get a security clearance, which I did. Again, to my surprise, I got the clearance. I begged the money to fly out there. Spent the night at Jonah House with Liz McAlister and Phil Berrigan, trying to figure out what I should do if I got into the White House. We settled on ashes. I'd try to get an opportunity to use the ashes and say what I could. So I got some ashes out of their fireplace, put them in a plastic bag, and tucked it down inside my pants and went on down to the White House.

That's quite a trip from Baltimore into D.C. Right through some of the meanest neighborhoods in the world. And then within a few blocks of the White House, everything turns into an open museum. Everything's clean. Everything's white marble. Monuments. All white.

I was the first person in my family ever to be invited to the White House. So I'm going through these major struggles and tensions. "God, what do I do?" Here I am invited, and at the same time I got a bag of ashes in my pants, and I'm going to try to say something to the president.

We went into the basement of the White House, which is no basement at all. It's a major mansion. And my God! Everything in there was an original. One room had all these gold plates. When Reagan came into office, I remember Nancy says they needed a new china set 'cause theirs had been eaten off of. I'm like, "Hell! You've got all these gold plates right in your basement! They're not rented. Take *them!*"

Finally, they asked us to come upstairs, and I tried to jockey myself to make sure I got a good seat. I took third row center aisle, maybe fifteen feet away from the president's podium.

I'm very nervous, of course, 'cause I know what I'm going to do. And I'm sitting there and looking around and in comes Bishop Thomas Gumbleton. The only bishop in the country who wrote against the treaty, not because it gave the Russians too much but because it allowed for the development and employment of first-strike nuclear weapons. When I saw him, I just felt such confirmation. But I'm just so nervous, so I get up and go see the bishop. Tap him on the shoulder. I lean over real close to him and I say, "Bishop, would you say a prayer for me?"

"Why, yes. I will." The poor bishop. He looks at me like, "Why is this crazy man bothering me?"

I think the president's going to be the first one to speak, but he's not. First there's a guy named Ziggy Brzezinski. Carter's answer to Henry Kissinger. (Someone who speaks funny on his cabinet.) Ziggy goes on for about forty-five minutes talking about why they need the SALT II treaty. Mooning would have been an appropriate gesture for the baloney that was coming from him, but of course you don't moon the national security chief in the White House.

Then this other guy gets up, and he's a Texan. Former chief of staff. Military person, but in a tie and suit. He was real funny. He has this Texan drawl, and the gist of his statement is, "President Carter, *he* don't trust the Russians. Mr. Brzezinski, *he* don't trust the Russians. I want you to know, *I* don't trust the Russians. You can't talk about security and trust in the same sentence."

And I'm thinking, "What more do we need? If we don't have trust as a component of security, we're bankrupt." Appropriately, I should have stood up and wrenched my clothes and yelled, "Blasphemy and idolatry!" But of course you don't do that in the White House. Certainly not to some big Texan who doesn't mean much.

Finally a woman said, "Ladies and gentlemen, the President of the United States!" And at this point, I start seeing more of what I was feeling than necessarily what might have been really happening. Because as soon as she said that, everybody got up and I got up with them. And I started hearing music in my mind like "da da dada" . . . the presidential march.

Then all these camera lights . . . bleep, bleep, bleep, bleep. Intensive TV lights. Now this party was not a news story. But any time the president goes up public, all three major networks are covering. That's why they could catch someone like Jerry Ford eating a tamale with a wrapper on it or coming out of an airplane and bumping his head. If you had a camera on you all the time, they'd be catching you with your finger up your nose. The intensity of the media around this man is amazing.

Well, not only did I think I was hearing music, but everything went into slow motion. 'Cause when you're in a tense moment, it's like *Bonnie and Clyde*. You know, that last scene where they were killed . . . Everybody's clapping, and in my mind I'm clapping real slow, and I'm standing up and I'm watching Jimmy Carter come up the center aisle. Not only is everything going slow but I'm so nervous that I literally . . . everything in my life is going through my head. "Hey! This is the White House. I'm with the president of the United States. Three major networks are covering this. Maybe he's right, and maybe I'm wrong."

"My God! This is it! Maybe I shouldn't do this." My life goes through my mind, and I literally bilocate, get out of my body. I look at myself and I say, "Frank, are you sure you know what you're doing? Here you are at the White House. These are the chandeliers. This is the president of the United States. These are the senators and representatives. Maybe you're making a mistake about your critique of the SALT II treaty."

Then in my own mind, I went into what I call "willful doing." "I'm an actor. This is a play. I've got a certain role to play. The president has a certain role to play. We'll just play it out."

So I'm clapping and I'm watching the president get up to his podium. I unbutton my pants 'cause the ashes are underneath, you know. And then everyone's sitting down. At this moment, I know I have to hit the center aisle. So I get up and grab the ashes out of my pants. I take a step out of my seat towards the podium. My back is to the crowd. I've got a hand in my pants. If you saw it from the back, you'd see a man who's hunched down and taking a step in front of the president, so it looks like he's going to pull out a weapon.

Now I'm an Italian American, but this was nine days into the Iranian crisis and if you look real quick, I could look like an Iranian. So I took that step towards the president, and the whole crowd just stopped. Their hearts stopped. If you wanted to, you could have picked up the hearts and put them in baskets. I took a step, and I immediately turned around 'cause I did not want to personally confront the president, but just stand in front of him. Then a number of things happened simultaneously. The crowd, who just a moment ago was catching their breath and wondering what was going to happen, saw that I was an opportunist to the full extent and started to boo me and scream at me. "Sit down, ya' bum!"

Which is interesting. All these people were dressed to the hilt, and they were in the White House and they were trying to act very, very, suave and debonair. But it sounded like a baseball game: "Sit down!" "Get that guy out of here!"

My voice is kind of high normally, but I'm nervous, so it's even higher. [In a high-pitched tone] "Friends! SALT II is a lie, and Jimmy Carter's lying to us. These ashes represent the dead from first strike."

I take the ashes out. Now they've been in my pants all morning, so by the time I got them out, the moisture was condensed into the bag, and they come out like clumps of clay, you know. "These ashes—and I'm looking at them [hits himself on the head]—*boing, boing*—"these ashes represent . . ." Everybody's laughing.

And then to add injury to insult, my pants . . . I never had time to button them up, so when I started to shake the ashes, my pants started to come down. I had to stick my butt out like this to make sure they wouldn't fall down. [Here the reader must visualize the Cordaro gyrations that accompany this story.]

Then, quick as can be, this secret service guy comes and grabs me by the arm. "There, there young man. You're all right. Just come on out here." Like I was some kind of loony.

Of course, no one heard me. No one heard a word I said, but it was all on the TV. It picked up everything, and later on, a woman from Iowa got up and said, "Mr. President. I like that young man from Iowa whom you had dragged out of here. We're concerned how anyone in the peace movement can support a treaty that allows for first-strike weapons." So the media people got ahold of her right away and got my name, where I'm from, the statement I was making.

First, the secret police wanted to know if I was crazy. Secondly, they wanted to know if I had planned to do any harm to the president. Thirdly, they found out my record . . .

Ro: Didn't they want to find out what that clumpy mass in your pants was?

Frank: Oh, yeah. Then they realized, "What the hell!" They said they just wanted to keep me out of the media 'cause I had already made a . . . and they didn't want to press any charges 'cause I was an invited guest. About all I did was to be rude. Rudeness is not necessarily an illegal act. The enforcements are saying to themselves, "How in the hell did we let this guy through in the first place?"

One of the last comments the secret service guy says was, "Well, I guess you know this means you'll never get invited to the White House again."

That night it made all three major networks. Walter Cronkite mentioned my name, and it was all on the front pages . . . it was a front page picture in the *Washington Post,* the *New York Times,* and papers all over the country. The prophet Isaiah never got that kind of exposure. 'Course when I went back to the Jonah House people, they're all saying, "Wow, man! You could have got shot."

"Wait a minute! Liz and Phil didn't say anything about being shot!"

Ro: What other crazy things have happened to you?

Frank: Well, a couple things. When I first got arrested at the Pentagon in '77, I did a blood spilling. Just before, when I was at a pillar on the steps, holding one of the signs, I ran into my eighth grade teacher. He came out of the Pentagon door. We were spelling out DEATH, and I had the "E." I had a bottle of blood in my bib overalls, trying to figure out how best to get it on a pillar. There were cops all over the place, and everybody was real tense. Of course I was thinking of myself. It was the first time I did CD, and the first time I ever got to see the Jonah House people, and again, I was questioning if I really know what I'm doing.

"My God! Here I am from the Midwest. These guys, they don't know me. I don't know them. And now I'm going to do this blood spilling." I began to have lots of second thoughts. And out of the door of the VIP entrance to the Pentagon comes Mr. Amadao, my eighth grade teacher. He's in the air force.

"Coach Amadao!"

"Cordaro!" He comes back up the steps to talk to me. You should have seen the Pentagon cops. They were really taken in by this—two guys from Iowa meeting on the Pentagon steps: one's in the air force, one's a demonstrator; one's a former teacher, one had been the student.

We talked for a few minutes. He asked me three distinct times if I really knew what I was doing. He didn't say I was dumb, he didn't say I was stupid, he just wanted to know. And I could say with a great deal of conviction that yeah, I did. But I'm thinking to myself, "Gee, coach." I mean, it's one thing to spill blood on the Pentagon pillars. It's another thing to do it in front of your eighth grade teacher.

Luckily, the guy he was with said, "Lieutenant Amadao, your car is waiting." And he shook hands and left.

Then we all let go of our signs and did the blood spilling on the pillars. No sooner did I get the blood on the pillars than my hands were handcuffed, and I was under that canopy. We were screaming out, "The Pentagon is the temple of death! The Pentagon is the temple of death!" And the sound would reverberate up those large pillars. Then out of nowhere comes these storm troopers, maybe seventy strong. Blue jumper suits. Big American flag. Large clubs. Complete helmets. All of them black except for two—one kind of chubby white guy and one white woman. (At the Pentagon, if you're pushing a drum, if you got a broom, if you're doing any dirty work, or if you're low man on the totem pole, you're black. And if you're wearing a tie, you're white.)

We're still screaming, "The Pentagon is the temple of death!" They take us to a bus. These two big black guys were my partners, and as soon as they got on the bus, they took their helmets off and sat down and said, "We're real glad you guys keep comin' here because these people are nuts. And they *will* use nuclear weapons. You're just right on!"

Every time I went to Washington, something unique would happen. Sometimes you have to use gimmicks to get things across. I've fallen into that.

Ro: Resistance as theater.

Frank: It's good liturgy, and it's good theater. And it should be entertaining.

That's another thing: if you're going to say a harsh message, I think you ought to be entertaining. Actually, I think if you're going to stand in front of any group of people, you ought to be entertaining.

We've done several things at SAC. The first thing we ever did was to climb over the fence and say a rosary on an active air field. No one came and got us, so we said the whole rosary, the whole fifteen decades. They never did come, so we said, "What the hell!" and climbed back over the fence.

One time . . . God, when was it? In December of 1980, we edited the sign at out there. SAC's international motto was "Peace is our profession," which of course is a lie. They had a big billboard at that time out in front of the base. A hundred of us showed up for a prayer service. Ten of us crossed out the word "peace" and put the word "war" in its place and doused the sign with blood. All the TV channels were there. They only arrested three of us. They missed the priest. They missed the two nuns, and picked the socialist and two crazy-looking Catholic Workers, and I was one of them.

They say not everybody can do civil disobedience [or] be Catholic Workers. And I say, "That's right. I'm not looking for everybody. If one percent of the Roman Catholics in this country become Catholic Worker types and resistance people . . . just *one* percent! One percent of fifty million Roman Catholics in this country is five hundred thousand. Imagine a half a million Roman Catholics— crazy Catholic Worker types—gunking up the legal system. Out there on the streets. And the rest of the church supporting them.

Ro: Do you miss the Catholic Worker? Do you miss living in a house?

Frank: Oh, I miss it bad.

Frank's brother Tom was the first Cordaro I met. He now works for the national office of Pax Christi.

Tom Cordaro: I was born on August 29, 1954, to Angela and George Cordaro. Had an Italian upbringing, living in the south end of Des Moines, which is predominantly Italian. A group with a strong sense of family and extended family, also, since all of my neighbors were relatives. My father died at forty-six, and this had a profound effect on our family. It drew us together. One by one, we began to take our faith more seriously. Then when Frank encountered the Worker house in Davenport, it had a profound effect on him, that he shared, or at least tried to share, with the family.

I felt that it was very good, and it seemed to make ample sense, just logical sense. Such an obvious kind of behaving. Unfortunately, in those early days, Frank was pretty heavy into condemning our middle-class value system and all of that, you know, like most people are when they get turned on by a new idea. At that time, I was still in college and had been doing a lot of student organizing, mostly in the charismatic renewal format. The charismatic renewal provided a place for me to develop my leadership qualities, my speaking abilities, and organizing skills. At that point, I went to Ann Arbor, Michigan, for a summer with the Word of God Community.

One instance that really made me think happened when I was placed on a street evangelizing team. I was nervous. "I'm a Catholic. We don't do those sorts of things." But I wanted to be as open as possible to the experience, so I went out and began to share my faith with people. I found out that people were receptive if you weren't belligerent, and that they were hungry to hear and to talk about their own faith experiences. Unfortunately, I made the mistake of beginning to reach out to street people and to evangelize them.

Well, I bumped into a Native American who had a bum leg and his motorcycle had been stolen and, you know, he had no place to stay and nothing to eat. It seemed natural to me, after sharing the word of God with him, to invite him home with me. I was living in one of the community homes at the time with, I think, seven other men who were part of the Word of God Community. I brought this fellow home and, my goodness, it was like . . . everyone was shocked that I would do such a horrendous thing! And I was shocked that they were shocked. I remember in particular that I was asked to sleep in front of this guy's door to make sure he didn't sneak out in the middle of the night and steal things from the house. Like a watchdog. To say that Jesus Christ is Lord to me means that He is actually the ruling reality of my life. And whereas that was true in charismatic renewal for their spiritual and social existence, it didn't seem they were bringing that into their political or economic existence.

At the same time, because of my brother Frank and the civil disobedience he'd been doing, I began to really feel that the arms race needed to be addressed, that it certainly was an issue. So in 1978, I began publishing a newspaper called *The Voice of the Prophet,* which was an ecumenical Christian newspaper for students on campus, to help them and expose them to the social issues of the day. We had a publication of five thousand, and we were on over a hundred different campuses across the country. That was in my third year as campus minister at Iowa State. Also, at that point, I began to feel a real pull to the Catholic Worker.

At the same time, I was afraid to do more. In particular, I began to realize that my possessions had control over me. They possessed me—I didn't posses them. I was afraid—afraid of being ripped off mostly. I was unfree, a slave to my things.

Well, one evening after having a few drinks and getting ready to go out with friends, I got a call from the church that there was a transient that needed some help. Of course initially I said, "Why me, Lord? I don't need this kind of thing now." But on the impulse of the Spirit, I said, "Send him over."

After hanging up, I went around, and in a kind of ritualistic way, said "Good-bye stereo," and "Good-bye TV." And my microwave and . . . I went through this kind of ritualistic cleansing of myself from these things. Then the man came to the door. His name was Francis, and I really do think that was providential.

"Francis, the refrigerator is over there, and you help yourself. The couch is here. Here are some pillows and your blankets. I'm going to be gone for the evening, so you just make yourself welcome, and I'll see you in the morning."

And when I walked out and pulled the door behind me, I had an incredible, exhilarating sense of freedom. That, to me, was a real turning point in my conversion experience. You see, once you taste that kind of liberation, you want more of it. So shortly after that, I sold all my things and opened up a hospitality house in Ames, along with two students—Jamie Barmettler and Chris Murphy— the Loaves and Fishes Hospitality House and Peace and Justice Center.

We set up hospitality. And began to learn the lesson that "love in action is a harsh and dreadful thing compared to love in dreams." I began to understand that while it was easy for me to let go of my things, and of my space, I was still holding very tightly to my privacy. While it was easy to let transients and homeless people into my house, it was a lot harder to let them into my life. I was afraid that if I did, they'd consume me with their need, and that I would just not be able to handle it.

Well, what I learned through that experience was that the poor are prophets. They tell us just who we are, in very plain ways. And I always say, "If you think you are a loving and warm individual, go to a hospitality house and learn the truth about yourself. Just see how far that cuddly love gets you."

Always, always a struggle. Always a humbling experience. To make room in your heart, not just your home. That was always very tough for me. I was never very good at it, but that didn't excuse me from doing it. I thought that I was always doing very, very meager hospitality, but I learned a lot.

Before doing hospitality work, I was pretty much of a judgmental person. Expecting people to shape up and fly right. It was only after seeing the brokenness of the world that I was able to turn and accept the brokenness in [friends and relatives].

Naturally, the course of personalism flowed into the political scene in the form of civil disobedience. It was just so natural. If there is evil, you say no. With your own body, you take personal responsibility for what's going on.

I remember the very first action I did was with some Catholic Workers from

Davenport and Des Moines at the Rock Island Arsenal. It was during Armed Services Day, and we were to walk onto the island where the arsenal is and go to the museum. Some of the folks were going to unfurl a banner, and I was going to read scripture about love and war.

Well, it was like "mission impossible." We were all kind of covert, sneaking onto the base and walking around in this museum, waiting for a big crowd to come so that we would do our action. Waiting and waiting. (I bet we probably only waited five minutes, but it seemed like five hours.) Finally, we did it. And I sprang open my Bible. "Brothers and sisters, listen to me." My goodness! Everyone turned around and listened. I began to read the scripture, and all the time I'm thinking about our plans. We had thought, "One or two sentences, that's all we'll have time for before they leap on us and drag us away."

Well, I read the whole passage and nobody was doing anything. So I flipped through the Bible and read another passage. Nothing was happening, and I'm running out of material, so I'm forced to do this kind of extemporaneous sermon. All the time I'm saying to myself, "Please someone, come and take me away." Well, we were finally taken away. We weren't even given ban and bar letters, just driven off the base and dropped off.

That was my very first experience. Since then, I've been arrested many times. I don't know how many, anymore. And have done some jail time. I have also left Ames. I was trying to do full-time campus ministry, do the house, and do peace and justice work at the same time, and I found that I wasn't doing justice to any of them. The resistance pushed up on my agenda to being number one, so I began full-time organizing for campaigns of nonviolent civil disobedience at the SAC base.

Ro: Have you ever had anything happen in prison that you were afraid of?

Tom: I've had frightening experiences, but most of them were not from prisoners. They were from the system. For instance, they have this thing the prisoners call the merry-go-round. It's a kind of floating Siberia in the federal system. For disciplinary reasons or at the whim of any official, people are put on what they call disciplinary transfers. That means they're in a lockdown situation and moved from place to place to place.

It has the effect of making you disappear. When you get to the new place, you may not have the ability or the right to make a phone call, to contact your support people on the outside. And when you do finally get a stamp to mail a letter, you may be moved again before your people get a letter back to you. It's a way of keeping prisoners in this kind of no-man's-land.

In fact, the last time I was in the federal system, I started in Omaha, Nebraska.

My destination was Sandstone, Minnesota. I was sent down to Leavenworth, Kansas. From Leavenworth I was to travel to Terre Haute, Indiana. From Indiana I was to be sent to Chicago. No, from Indiana I think I was going to go up to Michigan and then down to Chicago, and from Chicago finally to Sandstone. This was on a fifty-five day sentence. No way I could reach my destination during that time! You know these movements aren't quick—you could be in transit for months and months.

I think they're very frightened of people like us. At Leavenworth, some guy in the suit-and-tie department of the administration said to me, "We know you're a troublemaker. We got word on you." That carries with you all the way through.

But I've already seen the worst. The merry-go-round is the worst, but, as a matter of fact, in my case, it turned out much for the better for me and for the movement. The one letter I was able to get out was to my mother. I told her what was happening to me, and she got that letter to Tom Fox at the *National Catholic Reporter.* He organized the whole damn country! They were swamped with letters, just overwhelmed by all the letters, and got so frightened that when I got to Terre Haute, they decided to put me in a camp. Because of mom's initiative. A lot of the public would never have known about this floating Siberia except for her.

Angela: I myself am very ashamed of my country. I'm ashamed. I . . . you know this flag deal that Bush is pushing out here . . . I can remember parades where the hair on my arms would stand up straight when my flag went by. I haven't . . . I haven't had that feeling for a long, long time.

CHAPTER 21

Inner City Solitude

Virginia Druhe of St. Louis

> When I was living in solitude, I'd hear a lot about other people doing
> it. In a lot of religious communities, there are people tucked away
> here and there . . . Many, many motherhouses, it turns out, have a
> trailer on the back forty or something.
>
> *—Virginia Druhe*

VIRGINIA and I talked in the kitchen of Ella Dixon House, the smallest of
the Catholic Worker houses in St. Louis. Virginia sorted beans for dinner,
moving them rhythmically with her fingers as she had done daily when she lived
in Nicaragua. As a member of the long-term Witness for Peace delegation there,
she lived in a small village when she wasn't leading visiting groups on fact-finding
tours of this war-torn land. She was one of those kidnapped by the contras on the
river between Nicaragua and Costa Rica. Although she frequently visits Nicaragua, she has chosen to stay in North America. Virginia explains: "We have to live
out our own struggle rather than to only take on theirs . . . Also, the part of
me that would be contemplative—that part of me has been too formed by North
America. Although it feels like I'm cutting away all the husk and only saving the
dried-up corn, one place has to be . . . I have to be more here than there."

Virginia Druhe: The Worker in St. Louis was started by eight women and was a
house for women. We didn't have a man join the community for . . . I don't know
how long it was. It was a result of the reality of life in the church in this country,
and who's willing to do what. In the justice movement, there are far more women
than men, and that was especially true fifteen years ago.

We were all feminists by . . . not by ideology but by experience. And we believed . . . we decided early on that community would be important to us, and
that we would make all decisions by consensus, so there was just nothing in us
that leaned toward giving over any of our power or authority to anyone else. And

that's a lot of what feminism is about, I think. Women doing that. Doing it until the men come and join us.

Actually, being at the Worker the first couple of years was a real love-hate sort of experience. It was all I had hoped it would be and it wasn't, both at the same time. Most days I found myself thinking I couldn't possibly live like that another day, and I also couldn't possibly live anyplace else. For a long time that was a big conflict, but I stayed. Why? Because life was so much . . . so much richer there than I had ever known it to be.

None of us [at Karen House] had any experience in being a shelter for women. We didn't know about drugs, and we didn't know about welfare, and we didn't know about violence in the house. We had to learn all of that stuff. We were also very different people among ourselves. It was very difficult to form community. (In many ways we didn't.) It was very painful, and we tried different decisions about how to handle guests and how to run the house while we had all these conflicts going on among ourselves.

It was all really horrible, and at the same time, Eucharist was more exciting than it'd ever been for me in all my life. And also, knowing the guests and knowing all the people who came to help out was just more exciting than life had ever been. So it was impossible to give it up, but equally impossible to live it through. I remember I was sick a lot that first winter. I was down in bed sick three different times, something that's never happened before or since.

We had seventy guests, seventy people living in a house that was built for maybe twenty-five. The noise was terrible! That was a lot of it, and the overcrowding led to a lot of stress on us and the guests and therefore a lot more violence. It was really not a peaceful place.

The guests would often offer to double up in their rooms, you know, so a lot of the momentum toward keeping the house very full was their willingness to do that. We'd sometimes let two families live in a room together, and then afterward see it wasn't a good decision. We learned it all by doing it wrong, I'd say. We were probably open a year and a half before we agreed very firmly to any limit.

I think . . . the first decision was that there were certain particular individuals that we could not have in the house, that we couldn't handle. They were too dangerous, too destructive. So that was the first big limit, and it was very difficult. It was a family, and the mother was psychotic. We had them sleeping in a room with four single women, and they were constantly setting each other off. I guess we just beat our heads against the wall until we finally conceded the wall was there.

So we said we were going to close down in order to do some painting and repairing on the house and just sort of catch our breath for a couple of weeks.

What happened was that we ended up with fifteen in the house even after we "closed down."

Ro: So closing meant you got down to a manageable number.

Virginia: Right. And I remember being aware of how different the relationships between us and the guests were during that time. That's when it really became clear for me, when I remember beginning to argue seriously for having more like twenty-five guests in the house instead of sixty. For me, those early years were an experience—the feast and the famine, the guts and the glory. Very extreme.

Ro: How long did you live in community before you decided to be the "first Catholic Worker hermit?" [For over a year, Virginia lived alone in a small room in Cass House, a very large CW community operating at that time in St. Louis.]

Virginia: Well, four years, I guess. It was a gradual process. What happened was that after Karen House had been open about two years, I was absolutely conceding defeat. I just couldn't do it anymore, mostly because of my own stupidity about how to be a Worker, you know. I just couldn't put up with it anymore, and I moved that summer out to a little cabin in the woods with another woman. We had no electricity, no running water. It was really beautiful, a little makeshift cabin in the woods with a creek down at the base of the hill. We lived there for four months, and I really wasn't sure that I'd come back to the Worker.

In fact, I was pretty sure that I wouldn't, but in the course of that summer, nothing else presented itself as being very compelling, so I went back. But telling everyone it was only to be part time. So I started, as a discipline to myself, to leave the house one day a week, to leave in the morning and not come back till night. Started doing whatever I wanted all day long every Tuesday. The community was tremendously supportive, and always has been. I did that all of one winter, and then decided to spend three days a week that way instead of going to the woods all summer.

By that time we had Cass House, but it wasn't open entirely as a shelter yet.* I would often go over there to a spare room and stay two or three days—do my laundry, pray, read, rest, think, take a bike ride, go to Mass—just that sort of stuff. And the more time I gave to prayer, the more my appetite for prayer grew.

One day I was sitting in the chapel praying, sitting with the big marble altars

---

* Cass House started in 1979. A large and elegant (but ultimately unworkable) old mansion, it served as home to many guests and Workers before the community sold it to a Baptist congregation for one dollar.

and all that. It's amazing—just like a church. I looked up at this little window that leads to a room on the second floor. And all of a sudden I felt myself thinking, "I could *live* in that room. Nobody uses it. It's quiet. It's beautiful. It looks out on the trees." And I was so excited by the idea that I made a major decision.

I really think it was a fruit of a thirty-day retreat I'd made earlier. I guess I'd been thinking that if I could spend thirty days in solitude and silence and still not be sated, that was significant. Really right for me. So I talked to the community about it, and I talked to the man who directed me on the retreat, and I talked to my spiritual director here, and everyone agreed that it was a reasonable thing to try. Which was very important to me, all of that support. And the people at Cass House were delighted to have me. You know, I think there are many religious who don't get the support of community that I got. And it was wonderful. I was very, very happy living that way.

Ro: Now, did you live in silence?

Virginia: For six days a week. On Thursdays, I'd work in the morning at Karen House and in the afternoon at Cass House, and I'd go see my family every two or three weeks. And then if anyone came to my room, I would see them there. Those were sort of my ground rules. I started doing . . . people started asking me to do spiritual direction during that time.

After about two and a half years of living that way, I was feeling pretty sure that I was nearing the end of the time [of solitude] that I needed. I was praying three hours a day during those years, and I started feeling certain that I could sustain the prayer without the solitude, which was sort of the issue to me.

It really was a gradual going in and a gradual coming back out. I started doing more speaking on nonviolence and feminism. You know, you sort of fall into those things. A sanctuary [for Central American refugees] opened, and I started doing [Spanish] translating and working with them more. Worked with neighborhood housing and helped to start a land trust in the neighborhood—you know, things like that. I started doing more because I felt that I could. And I wanted to.

Ro: Earlier, you said there is a burgeoning monastic movement, a movement towards solitude, in the United States. Could you tell me what you know about it?

Virginia: I know that when I was living in solitude, I'd hear a lot about other people doing it. In a lot of religious communities, there are people tucked away here and there . . . Many, many motherhouses, it turns out, have a trailer on the back forty or something.

Ro: Those would be mostly suburban or rural environments, not in the middle of a house of hospitality.

Virginia: That's right. But then Cass House was an extraordinary house. The space really allowed for separation. Although being in the house was very important to me. I could hear soup line. I could hear if there was a fight in the house. I could hear the kids outside playing. And it was very important to me to have that proximity. I've found that there are lay hermits and lay people trying to live in solitude and earn their living at the same time in a number of places. Two city women—one in San Francisco and one in Chicago. The one in Chicago supports herself by cleaning office buildings for two or three nights a week, and she lives in this little apartment in a sort of boarding house.

Ro: What was it like, really, to be so alone and to pray so much?

Virginia: It's so hard to say. It's sort of . . . this is an image, an analogy, and I don't know if everyone would take it the way I mean it, but it's sort of like having a love affair, you know. How do you sum it up? It was just . . . Nicaragua's the same way. It's so hard to sum up something inside you and total the experience. But I learned to hear, to hear on a level that wasn't possible while I was being reactive—to hear myself and to hear other people and to hear the inner life.

Ro: I remember from my brief experience with silence, which was two or three seven-day retreats, not even a thirty-day one, that it sort of heightens perceptions, you know. Heightens all your senses almost, which also happens with a love affair. Well, I think it *is* a love affair.

Virginia: I remember feeling like I knew silence very well and knew how varied silence is—that there are just lots of kinds of silences.

Ro: Now, you've never joined a traditional religious order. (I'm sure people ask you about that all the time.)

Virginia: No, I haven't.

Ro: Have you ever missed the permanence of family?

Virginia: Sure. Sure. Although . . . that was much more an issue in the first years. This community is such a wonderful place to come back to, where I knew people understand what I've been through. So I think, "What more can I ask than what this community has been for me, consistently, for ten years."

Ro: And the work? Some people say the soup line and hospitality model is only perpetuating the problem.

Virginia: I think that's a fair criticism of . . . it's a fair critique of the Worker, that it's only a band-aid. It's something we should always be guarding against because the tendency is very much there. And yet that way of being with the poor, without a specific empowering project, is what in liberation theology is called "accompanying the poor." Walking with them. It's an incredibly powerful experience, and it's the only way, I think, to start being with the poor. It's being with them on their terms. Walking where they're going without you being in charge. I don't think the Worker is brilliant at that, but we do it somewhat, and it's such a central part of conversion. And it empowers the people you walk with. Or can.

Ro: And you?

Virginia: Yes, yes. There's genius, you know, in Dorothy, in what she put together as a way of life. There's real genius or holiness in it that gives life all around, and that's wonderful. And the being with the poor—simply, constantly, basically, poorly. When I was on trial one time for civil disobedience, the prosecutor got a little pompous and said, "Well, what would you do if someone just came into your living room one day and sat down and wouldn't leave?"

I laughed. I said, "That happens pretty often, really. We wait. We talk to them. We find out what they want. We explain to them what we have." But to be . . . that commitment to nonviolence and to always trying to put yourself in the other person's shoes. Those sorts of contacts are the wonderful part, I think, of the life in the Worker. And not letting go of the love of the church, the commitment to the long tradition of the church.

And the joy of it. There is a liberation in being known by, and accepted by, and sometimes even loved by, people who are in very difficult times in their lives. The simple conversations that can happen in being with those people are such a grace. For instance, the young man who lives here [in Little House] with us has had a difficult life, as difficult as anyone. Last year when I was first home from Nicaragua, I said . . . oh, it was a beautiful day and I said, "Why can't it be like this every day?"

He said, "It would be like a picture postcard. It wouldn't be real."

And I thought, "Well, shut me up!" There's a wisdom and a courage and generosity in people like him that's . . . that's really liberating.

So much of what is called important in this society just isn't. It's such a relief to be away from it, you know, and to be in this funny little neighborhood where no one thinks anything happens. It's very good to walk these streets and have Reverend Burke say hello and Dean come up and talk about someone's garden. It's so healthy, being with hidden forgotten people in hidden forgotten places.

CHAPTER 22

Uptown

St. Francis of Assisi in Chicago

One day Terry [Gates] said, "God's telling me that we should start a soup kitchen." And I said, "Well, then you and God can start a soup kitchen. Because we can't! We can't even keep the doors open at St. Francis."

—Jim Eder

At St. Francis House, the focus has always been shaped by individuals. When Denise Plunkett was there, the Catholic Worker house was a soft touch for poor Latin Americans. When Mark Miller moved in, he began working with Laotian refugees, the Hmong particularly. As one person comes and another leaves, you can see the house shift focus. Some folks have a hard time living with that. They'll cling to an idealized picture of how it was at this time or that time—usually the time they were there. In the long run, you know, the Catholic Worker doesn't give enough shelter to make a dent. But what it does, and does well, is to treat people with dignity.

—Fr. Jack Keehan

UPTOWN. The only neighborhood in Chicago Saul Alinsky said could never be organized. Uptown. Flashed on the nighttime news during the seventies as the national home of arson for profit. Ethnically diverse and constantly changing Uptown, or "Poor World," as Fr. Mike Rochford called it, "where rich people come to play out their fantasies on the poor." Catholic Workers have been in Uptown since 1974, living in a warm and ramshackle house of hospitality named after St. Francis of Assisi. An equally strong presence is the Soup Kitchen a half-block down Kenmore Street at St. Thomas of Canterbury Church, Catholic Worker–initiated and still "directed" in a sense by Worker Jim Eder.

Fr. Jack Keehan (former associate pastor at St. Thomas): A lot of people come to Uptown to change it, and they never learn from anyone else's mistakes. As

Jim Eder once said, "Every wave thinks it's the first one to hit the beach." A few lead a Marxist revolution. You can try that one out. If you believe in some sort of primitive Christian community, you can play that one out. If you believe in . . . Pick your poison. You can do it in Uptown. And I would say that the average person who comes to Uptown tries one of these things and lasts about six months.

On the other hand, some people stay for a long time. Some get chewed up and burned out; some don't. I'm sure it takes a toll on all of them. And one of the things I saw is that those people who are most patient and most loving are the ones who suffer the least burnout.

Jim Eder: Now Lenny Cszewski, Jerry Cherno, and Kris Pierie started the house. Then a couple months later, Lenny went in the hospital, so Kris asked me if I could come and stay during the night. I said I would, and she told me I could have Lenny's bed. So I came in and I was sitting on the bed.

"What's Lenny in the hospital for?"

"Oh, we think he has TB."

I remember looking at her and thinking, "You want me to sleep in this bed of a guy you think . . . What kind of nut are you? What am I getting myself into?"

But then I said to myself, "All right, God! This is your bag. I'm doing this for you, and if I get TB, well, that's your problem, not mine."

I stayed there until Lenny got out of the hospital, and then I would come up on Saturdays and fix windows. The neighborhood was a lot rougher than it is now. When we kicked people out, they'd always kick the windows in, so for a couple years that was my Saturday duty—replacing windows.

Let me try to give you a picture of the neighborhood when we first moved in. It was in the process of being burnt down. In fact, all those lots [you see] across the street from the Worker had houses on them. One was a whorehouse, and you'd hear all kinds of things all night long. We had black fellows staying with us, and the white supremacists in the neighborhood would write threatening notes and paint swastikas on the house. And tell us, "We know you've got a nigger in there! Get him out or we'll burn you down." Stuff like that. Yeah, this is pretty easy duty now, compared to what it was.

Back then, the whites would always walk on the south side of the street, and the blacks would walk on the north side of the street, and the Orientals would use the alley. And we kind of broke that down, I think, because we didn't adhere to it. Of course, the demography of the neighborhood has changed so much. It was heavily Appalachian then. Where that Jesus the Answer Church is—kitty corner from the Worker—there was a hillbilly bar. Our entertainment on Friday and Saturday nights was to sit on the porch and watch the fights roll out of the bar. We never went in there. I'd always go to the bars up Lincoln Avenue, in the German neighborhood.

The bars in Uptown were funny, too. You'd think you'd have white bars, black . . . and Spanish bars, but the ethnic groups were so tight that you'd have Alabamian bars, Kentucky bars, Cuban bars, Puerto Rican bars. Blacks were a rarity twelve years ago.

Denise Plunkett: Next door to the Worker was an apartment for poor people. They torched it. Torched a child . . . two kids, I think, burned to death in there. Screaming for help and [no one could] get at them. The whole side of St. Francis House is still all dark, scorched from this fire. Anyway, even after the fire, the poor lived in that building. With no utilities, no water, no heat or electricity, nothing. They ran an electric cord from the Worker across this little space into a window so they could have a light.

Then there were the mentally ill. When the health code was liberalized, I think between forty and sixty percent of the patients in mental hospitals in Illinois were released. The vast majority relocated in high-rise buildings. So a lot of mental patients live in the neighborhood, and many of them become the homeless. They don't like the halfway houses, don't like to be considered a number. They kind of wander away and oftentimes they come to the Catholic Worker.

But thanks be to God, Henry Nicolella and Mike Sullivan came to the house in 1978 from Syracuse. Like angels from heaven! They were absolutely wonderful. Henry had the biggest heart on earth, and Mike is one of the funniest people who's ever lived in the neighborhood. The poor absolutely loved these two people.

They just . . . I don't think they ever turned anybody away. The scene at the house got crazier and crazier as it got more and more crowded. In the winter of '78 and '79, there were maybe thirty-five people living at the Worker, and it's only a four-bedroom house. The whole attic was filled with people sleeping on the floor. The basement . . . they had mats or cots or just simply blankets around the furnace. Five people slept in the living room. Mike brought a big black dog with him, and so it was really kind of a crazy time, but I don't think Henry could ever turn anybody away.

After a while Bob Chaps moved in with them. He was like Mike, just hilarious. It was so much fun to go and visit there, to be associated with it. And then Jim Holland showed up. I think he probably slept on the floor in the attic at first. Jim was just an unbelievably talented, a really wonderful person and a lot of fun. Played a guitar and had lived in Appalachia as a seminarian, so he knew all these mountain songs, which he'd sing by the hour. So during Jim's stretch, the whole thing was upbeat. Of course, there were problems off and on, but anybody coming to the neighborhood would come over to the house because it was a lot of fun. Those years were really wonderful times. People seeking shelter also had a good time and provided a good time.

In that whole period of time, three or four years anyway, we never thought, for instance, that we couldn't leave because we were in charge of the house. We didn't look at it that way. When we went out for a good time, sometimes we went with ourselves—the staff. Sometimes people from the house came with us. There was no thought as to who was running the show. The people in the house ran the house. The offered hospitality to the other homeless in the neighborhood if there were empty beds. It was always obvious, though, who was really in charge because they had the keys to the front door.

But where else on earth would you have blacks, whites, Central American refugees, unwed mothers, everybody else living happily under one roof? Cooking together. Cleaning up together. Having a good time together. It was a lot of fun. It . . . it sure was.

Jim: Oh, have we got stories! For instance, there was William. One of our big victories was getting William to keep his pants on. William was so out of it that he didn't really remember to keep his pants up, and he would often not wear belts, and his pants would come down at various times. We spent weeks and weeks on this, had these house meetings on how to keep William's pants on. Finally, Denise thought of bib overalls. Perfecto!!

Then there was . . . uh . . . Margaret, who was . . . she had two kids, Zing and Zong, who were periodically taken away from her. She used to hang around, and she would often take her clothes off. We didn't quite know what to do with that. Anyway, Father Roy [Bourgeois] was living with us, the Maryknoll priest. He had the gift to touch just about anybody. Margaret would scream at me, but she'd talk to him in a real civil way. I remember him saying, "Well, Margaret, if we're going to keep on with this conversation, you're going to have to put some clothes on." So she would.

One good story I remember was about this crazy guy . . . this crazy Indian named Saul. Always drunk and ranting and raving about white folks. Kris Pierie was living at the house. She came over one day and said, "Jim, you've just got to get rid of Saul. I just can't take him anymore. I just can't!"

I thought, "Geez, this guy's even bigger than I am!" But it was just . . . he was being so obnoxious, he had to go. So I went down there, and I started talking. He grabbed me and started screaming at me, "You killed my ancestors! You took my dignity!"

And I'm thinking, "True! True!" It *was* true, and I'm feeling all this sympathy for him, but also thinking how I was going to get him out of here so he didn't kill me. Finally, I said, "Well look, Saul. If it was up to me, I'd let you stay. But Kris has just had it up to . . . she's just fed up with you, and she's going to make my life miserable if I don't get you out of here."

And he looked at me and he said, "Okay, chief. I understand. When the squaw gets upset, that's hell." He turned around and walked out.

When I first moved into the house, all the street guys . . . well, not all of them but a lot of them, decided not to fight. They really got the pecking order in line. I couldn't understand that 'cause I wasn't going to fight them. But it was really almost an animal thing. I really don't get in fights regularly, and if I do, I just grab a guy and hold him down with my weight, just kind of pacify him. But really, when you think of the people and the situations that we deal with, violence is almost nonexistent.

Did you ever hear about Jimmy Hughes? I always think of Jimmy as an example of what people will do for freedom. Jimmy was a painter, I guess, and had fallen off a ladder and fractured his skull, and he had kind of a concave hole in his head. A dent. Looked like somebody had hit him with a hammer. He was disabled, but he got good checks—three or four hundred dollars, something like that. And it was always gone within a day 'cause he'd get rolled.

Jimmy drank copious amounts of coffee. He was really a thorn in Mark Miller's side because he would hang around the Worker for the free coffee. Mark slept in the living room, and he'd see Jimmy Hughes late at night, asking him for a cup of coffee. And he'd wake up in the morning and Jimmy would be standing there asking for a cup of coffee. I've seen Jimmy drink thirty, forty cups of coffee in an hour.

He got shanghaied, though. Uptown Ministry found out he had a brother who was a priest and lived in New Jersey, so Mark Miller and Tim Roemer decided to take him out there. Then, of course, he didn't want to go, so we used Sister Jerome to lure him into the car. He'd do anything for her. He'd write us these letters from wherever he was. "Dear Brothers and Sisters in Christ. How goes the struggle against evil?" You never know. I mean he could hardly talk, but he would write beautiful letters.

And I remember a meeting for a St. Francis support group, right at the beginning, around December of '74. We were introducing ourselves. You know, "I'm Father Blaze and I'm into poverty," and "I'm Sister What's-her-name."

Well, they came to Jimmy Delgado. He was at the house before it opened, and he's been there ever since. So he says, "My name's James Donald Delgado, and I'm in banking and real estate. The problem is I have 350 million dollars, but the bishop's got it all tied up, and I can't get my hands on it. So I'm bugging the cardinal." Jim was treated like a member of the family, not like he was totally off in left field, which he was, really. He wasn't shunned. He wasn't told to shut up. You just sort of learned to deal with him. That's what I like about the Worker— we don't shove people off. It's our family, and if you want to be part of it, you have to deal with the problems.

Mark Miller: I remember when I first had to turn someone away from St. Francis House. It was real hard because you knew that there was literally nowhere else to go, that they'd ride the trains all night or something like that. It was hard.

Sometimes there was literally no more room inside the door, though. On days when it was below zero, we would literally fill up the house. You couldn't walk from one room to another. Everyone in the whole place had to shift so that one person could go to the bathroom. You kind of become callous and say, "Well, I do what I can do." Or, "We do what we can do, and this is what we can do."

Ro: Does this crowding increase the violence?

Mark: I think it depends, if you will, on the relationship of hosts and hostesses to guests. If it's one-on-one and there's a thousand people, it may not be a problem. But if there's one host and a hundred guests, it's crowded even if the space is as big as Soldiers Field.

Ro: Have you ever been in a place that's one-on-one?

Mark: Well, yes I have. Here in our apartment it's two-on-one.*

Hauled into Housing Court

Denise: The one week that I was by myself as staff at St. Francis, I got a call at work. The city housing inspectors had just left the house. I almost died! About a day later, we got this notice from the Department of Inspection, citing all kinds of violations. I was in a complete panic. Took off work, went to City Hall, tried to track down who put us in housing court. It's all confidential. You can't find out who did it.

That was the beginning. It dragged on for years. Mark Miller was a lawyer, so that was real good. He could at least talk their language right back to them. But people in the neighborhood really rallied around and came to our support and would go to court and be a visible show of strength with us. We'd have large numbers in court.

---

* Living with Mark and his wife at that time was an older woman. She has since been able to move into her own apartment.

It was a big drag. We had to take out all the mattresses we put on the attic floor. It had to look like nobody ever slept there and so forth during those days.

This handful of owners had a block club type of thing and they were pushing to sweep the poor out. The Worker was there years before these yuppies with attaché cases wanted to move in. And then they want us out to keep from blighting *their* neighborhood. That was the neighborhood they chose to put themselves in. So it's a strange scene, but more and more buildings in this neighborhood are being rehabbed and sandblasted and so on.

I asked Mark what he'd tell other communities that had to deal with housing court under similar circumstances.

Mark: Well, I guess I'd tell them to talk it out. Don't give in. Believe in what you're doing and fight them. They might put you in jail, but they probably won't. In the end, a judgment against you is just a piece of paper. And I can say that as a lawyer. A judgment is just a piece of paper and nothing . . . The law is designed to produce certain types of behavior. More specifically, courtrooms are designed to intimidate people. Those in the know intimidate those who don't know, and that's all very much a part of the legal system. But so what? You know what you know, too. Don't be buffaloed. Don't be precipitant. Don't let them panic you.

Elaborate defenses normally are technical legal defenses and you play right into the . . . you become a part of the very thing that you started out protesting against. And when you rely on legal . . . uh . . . finesse, technical or substantive, you're shifting attention away from the moral basis of what you did. Law and morality are not the same.

Soup Kitchen

Jim: I really didn't have a thing to do with it. The people who started it were Terry [Gates] and Denise Plunkett and Bill O'Brien, a Jesuit who lived at the house, and Tom Florek, a Jesuit scholastic, and a couple of others. It just sort of grew and grew and grew and grew, and I really wasn't much a part of it at first.

Starting the kitchen was really, really a blessing, and I had been totally against it. Odd, though . . . most everybody else is long gone and I'm still here because of the Soup Kitchen. I'm known as the director now, and I often wonder about that. What would I be if I wasn't? It's almost like an honorary position.

Soup Kitchen was really the big thing for developing the do-gooder community [in Uptown]. See, most of the people who came to St. Francis House were mentally ill, so if somebody came in to help, you had to go through this long list of what to do and not do and what to watch out for. Like Willy. On some days,

William was Che Guevara. Some days he was Zapata, and some days he was Castro. You had to find out what his current name was because if you called him the wrong name, he'd fly off the handle. It was really intimidating for new people who came to help.

Well, the Soup Kitchen gave an entry for them. People could come to work there and, at first, they would just hang back and dry dishes and not deal with people. Then they could slowly work in. The next step was to move into the house for a while. That happened to any number of people. Now we have people [living] all up and down the street.

Denise: Soup Kitchen started small. We cooked enough food for sixty people, expecting twenty. Absolutely nobody came and Tom Florek went out on the streets and dragged in six people. Well, everybody was served with serving dishes as their personal dish, and people took food home. The next week those six all came back, and they brought a few friends with them.

Within a couple of months, there probably were sixty people and just kind of overnight the sixty increased to a couple of hundred. At first, we were all able to get to know each other and the people coming to eat helped do the dishes and sweep the floor and wipe the tables off afterwards. When they came back with their friends, they'd sometimes come bringing a little bag of lentils, a bag of pinto beans. One fellow brought a used plastic pitcher so that we could pour coffee. They would help us prepare the food, too, chop the vegetables or what have you. At first, if it weren't for the people needing the food, there wouldn't have been a Soup Kitchen because they did as much as the people, say, whose idea it was, basically. And that was kind of the tone of Soup Kitchen for a long time. It was very equal. Even after the crowds got bigger, we all still sat down together and spent a lot of time talking with the people. Really knew them well. That part was really fun.

But something happened. The media caught on and stories were written. Seminaries, colleges, and so on started asking if they could bring people down. Could a confirmation class come? Could the youth group come? The Center for Creative Spirituality would bring groups either to serve or to entertain. And everybody . . . we got way too many volunteers. That was a very hard time.

The saddest part was that a choice needed to be made. And we let these suburban teenage kids come and experience the fun of being at a soup kitchen. So they could see that being with the poor is not a dismal scene, and that they're like you and me. They have families. They get sick. Some are fun. Some are crabby. Old people, young people, little children . . . everybody.

But I remember the poor people feeling kind of edged out of the little jobs that made them feel less "served." The good thing that has happened is that many of these kids [from outside of Uptown] have been really molded at Soup Kitchen. They are opting to be with the poor, so that's good, so now we have a whole neighborhood of young, educated "do-gooders," as they're called around here.

Fr. Jack: You have to see these people working day in and day out with poor people to appreciate it. Everybody comes to Soup Kitchen to see real live poor people. Jim Eder used to sit them all down beforehand and say, "Look, the purpose of this is not to see how many dishes of beans and rice you can deliver to the tables in how much time. The purpose of this is to talk to people. Treat them like friends. If somebody wants to talk to you, talk to them. Somebody else will deliver the beans and rice. We're doing this because these are our brothers and sisters. And we're not here as disciplinarians. We're not here as somebody different from them." Although we couldn't really do it, we always thought it was far better that the visitors should eat at Soup Kitchen than work at Soup Kitchen. But after it was all over and all the do-gooders and their little flocks had gone home, there was Kathy Kelly with her toilet brush going into the men's washroom to scrub it down.

Sometimes it's hard to tell who's a guest and who's staff at St. Francis. The Soup Kitchen originally was that way. You couldn't tell who dug down in their pockets and got the twenty-five dollars together to put on a spaghetti dinner and who came because they needed the meal. They'd all eat together and talk together. Some of them actually looked a lot alike. If you go to the Soup Kitchen now, right away you know who's who just by the clothes they wear and the age and everything else. There's another difference, too. When they started, six people could run Soup Kitchen. Six people *still* could. But when you have thirty and forty people showing up to help at Soup Kitchen, obviously the atmosphere's going to be very different. Especially if it's their first time and they're scared of all these people.

Mark: With respect to the Soup Kitchen, I would say the best contribution I ever made toward making it a more peaceful place was when I was kind of a supporter from afar. I kept hearing about the problems with all the fighting and so forth. Since it's held in the basement of the church, I simply suggested that, if no one was opposed, what I would do was to vigil . . . go up and be with the Blessed Sacrament from the time they started their meal preparation till the last person had left. And I did that for several months. Other people from Soup Kitchen began to do it and came up and took turns, and as far as I know, they're still doing that. I think that the violence there has lessened as a result.

It starts with prayer. And that's not to suggest that if you pray, there won't be any problems. But I don't know—there's a truth there. I think a prayerful community is going to be more peaceful. I think if a peaceful atmosphere can be created and nurtured, people who come into that are going to be more peaceful. Because of the air they breathe, if you will.

I also think a personal relationship with people reduces violence. In a practical way, in a way that we can live out, that's the most important thing—establishing personal relationships with people. All of us, I think, tend to be less violent if we have a sound relationship with someone else. We're not going to deliberately hurt that someone. Or if we do, often there can be a reconciliation.

You know, violence is a large word, and I suppose I should be specific about what I mean. I kind of learned from my mentors, from Workers who had been there before. In those days, the standard definition was, you can yell and be verbally violent (not that it was encouraged, of course) but if you hit somebody, you were gone. That was the general rule. If you engaged in physical violence, you would be asked to leave. Depending on the individual and the nature of what they had done, they might be welcomed back the next day or they might be . . . be unwelcome indefinitely. The way I dealt with violence perpetrated by other people [in the house] was a little bit different than the way I dealt with violence perpetrated by myself. I never kicked myself out of the house.

Ro: What did you do about the verbal violence?

Mark: Well, you can always ask people to be quiet. Ask them what's wrong. A lot of it is circumstantial. It's one thing for a person to be verbally violent to another specific person. It's quite a different matter if you have someone who's acting out and screaming obscenities to whoever may wander into range. With that, you ask them to shut up. If they don't, you ask them to take a walk or whatever. I don't have general rules, but I always reacted to the specific situation and the specific person.

Fr. Jack: People get healed at Soup Kitchen. And at St. Francis, particularly. It takes . . . it's a slow process. Once a nun came for a summer, and she did what anybody does when they're new at the Catholic Worker house—she began to clean. (When you don't know what else to do, you clean house.) And again, the goodness of the person showed through enough that by the end of the summer, several people were helping her. If some folks ever hear this, they're going to let out a . . . they're going to blister the paint on the wall. But some people changed dramatically that summer.

Denise: You know, in Uptown, it's really amazing how the differences are so reduced. The differences between, say, the do-gooders who go there to help and the people coming in need. I think that the needs are just as strong among those who choose to help out. They need to fulfill themselves. They need to be included in a community, to be part of a group, to be . . . to share in a family kind of setting. All of those needs are common for all humankind. And we find it all in Uptown.*

* Denise continues to live in the neighborhood and to work at St. Thomas Church.

CHAPTER 23

Light and Shadow
David Stein of Chicago

> Lest I come across as a complete rationalist and atheist, I do believe
> in God, and I do practice Judaism in my own way. I define Judaism
> as the repudiation of idolatry, period. This society makes an idol of
> money, status, power, clout, military supremacy, luxury, fashion—
> many, many things. To live in a place like the Catholic Worker is to
> renounce those idols.
>
> —*David Stein*

David Stein: I came from New York City, lived there until I was in my early
twenties. Started hitchhiking around the country and doing a lot of searching and
just sort of ended up in Chicago.

Ro: Why Chicago?

David: Nothing in particular. It's just where I ended up. I was just so lost, and
I didn't fit in anywhere. I had this idea that by means of geographical travel, I'd
find something, but I never did. Maybe some people do.

I lost my wanderlust, finally. At some point I came to the decision that the way
to make your life mean something is to simply make your stand somewhere. To
say, "Okay, here I am. I'm going to build something here." Chicago happened to
be where I was when I arrived at that understanding, so Chicago it's been. Not
that I think Chicago is such great shakes, but it's as good a place as any.

I'm attracted to big cities, even though I hate what the city is. The concentration of power and wealth, it's . . . If you go downtown to where all the skyscrapers
are, there's just this unbelievable crushing oppression and despair and crassness
and greed. I hate it. I stay because it's my adversary. I get up in the morning and
I do battle with it, and to leave would be like retreating from the field. If you want
to change things—and I do want to change the state of affairs that concentrates
all this power and wealth and technology in the cities and transforms them into

places of such surpassing ugliness and decadence—if you want to fight that, you go where it is.

Ro: I've heard that you live under the viaduct.

David: Well, I did. For quite a while, I lived on the street. I'd drop by St. Francis House every few days and wash my clothes and rest up and get some human companionship. While I was on the street, I was for the most part completely solitary. I'd stay here at St. Francis until the solitude started to seem appealing again, and then I'd go back downtown.

I left the street, though, and I feel a certain amount of shame and defeat over that. I guess I got hooked on the house. Or hooked *into* the house. I became more involved here and came to feel that I owed it to the house to stay. I didn't feel right about leaving Gayle [Catinella] and Steve [Soucy] in the lurch at that point.

Actually, I've lived at this house three different times, not counting all the times I dropped in while I was on the street. The first couple of times, I was here as a guest, not a Worker. But even then, I was more involved than most guests in what was going on here. I had a background in the Catholic Worker movement, so I knew what the house was about, which most of the guests never quite figure out. And I hung out with the Workers. I had a great deal in common with the Workers, and so I was perceived as one of them, even though I wasn't. (I didn't go to the meetings, and I didn't really have to do the dirty work, like telling folks they had to move out. You have to do that sometimes, and they want to know why, and you've got to tell them.)

That seemed pretty idyllic. I had all of the benefits of community and could contribute to the community. You know, work around the house—do what I could to try to make the Workers' lives a little easier, offer a shoulder to people who needed somebody to talk to—but that was all. Finally one day, I got invited to one of the staff meetings, or the Junta, as we affectionately call it here. The next thing I knew, my happy days were over.

Ro: Do you see living on the street as sort of selfish?

David: No. I don't think it's any more selfish than a lot of things. Well, that's not much of a statement. But . . . no, I don't think it's selfish. I don't think everybody has to do any one thing. There's plenty of room in the world for people to be vagabond wood-carvers. Maybe there are corporate presidents who should be vagabond wood-carvers.

Ro: Do you think about going back on the street again?

David: Oh, yeah, all the time. I'm always discontented. When I'm living in community, I think about how great it would be to be on the street and be free and be able to wander around and find stuff in dumpsters and be able to spend eight hours carving wood and not be interrupted by phone calls or people problems or anything. I crave that.

But when I'm on the street, I'll often start to feel lonely and want to live in community and have all that warmth and companionship. So I always have something to complain about. Maybe the oscillating arrangement of going back and forth was the best of all possible worlds. I'm able to do good by being a Worker here at the house. I'm also able to do a lot of good by living on the street. You don't have a lot of responsibility on the street. You have to endure certain hardships, but that doesn't necessarily do anything for anybody else.

I really was doing a lot of good while I was living on the street. I was constantly going up and down the alleys and scavenging things. I'd find food in dumpsters. Find clothing. Find all kinds of things that people would throw out, and I'd distribute them. For example, I found lots of stuff for the kitchen here at St. Francis, found it in a dumpster in back of this gay bar downtown. They threw out all of their kitchen equipment. I found pepper mills and four big mixing bowls and a big gallon can of Kikkoman soy sauce, so I loaded all of that stuff on my back and carried it up here. When I was on the street, I was able to be a one-man war against the wastefulness of this society.

I also got a tremendous amount of wood carving done. I'd just sit . . . sometimes I'd get up in the morning and just sit and start carving and by the time I was done, the sun would be going down, and I would have finished something, which I rarely have the time to do now.

And I was able to do a little bit of educating. I remember I spoke to this group of young church people, young Protestant people who were going to go into some kind of ministry or something. There was this all-day seminar on homelessness with different speakers from different agencies. I was the last speaker, and I talked about why you should choose to be homeless. Completely blew people's minds. And afterwards this young guy came up to me—he was studying to be a Baptist minister, of all things—and said, "I'd really like to meet you downtown sometime, and you can show me some aspects of your world."

So I met him down at the Water Tower, and the first stop was this bakery dumpster. They throw out all of their day-old bread every evening. There'd usually be a whole garbage bag just full of perfectly good stuff—nowhere near stale. You know, it wasn't like you had to dig through all kinds of funky garbage to get it. So I dragged him out in back of this bakery and opened the lid of the dumpster.

Voila! Just like pulling a rabbit out of the hat! I pulled out this bag of bread, and he was completely stunned! I took a couple of loaves to take back to my lair, and handed him a loaf of bread, and we left the rest for the next street person. 'Cause other people were hip to that dumpster, too. The guy took the loaf of bread out of my hands as if he were holding this sacred relic, the Holy Grail, the philosopher's stone.

The wastefulness of this society, I think, is one of our best-kept secrets. When I tell people I get food out of dumpsters, it's like saying I swallow live rats or something. They refuse to believe that perfectly good food is there for the taking until they see it with their own eyes. That can be a beginning of a whole shift in perspective.

I've thought about this a lot 'cause I had a lot of time to think when I was downtown. I think of it as some . . . as a light and shadow thing. For most people in society, the world of light is . . . let's say in the context of downtown, the world of light is the offices, the stores, the shops, the sidewalks, the public places—the places one has access to if one has money and social rank and a job and all of that. That's the world of light in which you dwell. And the world of shadow is the alleys, the dumpsters, the viaducts, the railroad tracks, the riverbanks—those cracks and crevices where most respectable people, people who have officially sanctioned roles in society, never have any reason to go and never think of going.

When you live on the street, all of that is reversed. The light becomes shadow and the shadow becomes light. The shadow world of the alleys and dumpsters and viaducts and . . . and the train tracks and the weeds next to the river and the canals and the places underneath the bridges—that was the world where I felt most free. Those are the kinds of places I'm attracted to. I'll look for those desolate places. I'll seek out those cracks. I'm drawn to them and feel comfortable there. And meanwhile the world of the offices, the stores, the shopping malls—all of the places that are light to people who have societal credentials and positions of respectability and status in society—all of that is my shadow world.

For me to walk into Marshall Fields department store would be as eerie and unnatural and troublesome as it would be for the average socialite or business person to frequent the alleys and dumpsters. But I relish the opportunity to show someone from the light world a little of the shadow world. To help them to see, to let them peer into those cracks and spaces.

Ro: When you were on the streets, where was your . . . your lair?

David: I lived underneath the viaduct at Chicago Avenue and Halsted Street. An old guy named John has lived there for years but not many other people. I'm sure he's still there. (Well, I don't know where he is tonight 'cause it's below zero out, but when I go down there in the spring, I'll see him.) Other people would pass through, would stay under there for a while, and then go on.

Ro: Did you cook there?

David: No, I never did. I didn't want to mess up a good thing by having smoke to attract the fire department. I was pretty good at finding food that didn't need to be cooked. Like I'd go to the Pizza Hut's dumpster. They sell what they call the Personal Pan Pizza. It's this little round pizza, and their selling point is that they can get it to you in two or three minutes or whatever. Well, they do that by making up a whole bunch ahead and keeping them warm under these lights. The downtown Pizza Hut gets hundreds of people over lunch hour, so they make a lot of these little pizzas. If they sell a thousand and have to throw out fifty, that's nothing to them.

So sometimes when I would go into their dumpster, there'd be twenty or thirty or even fifty pizzas, depending on how many people had beaten me to the dumpster. They throw it out in a little cardboard box and everything—nothing dirty or unsanitary about it. I'd just pig out on cold pizza. Now Pizza Hut has since put up a locked gate that prevents access to their dumpster, and a lot of other places have started doing that. They'll build a gate or put a padlock on the dumpster. All of the new supermarkets now have compactors where they smash all the food that they throw away.

Ro: To hide the waste?

David: To keep people . . . to keep people from getting a free meal, I suppose. I don't know. I don't even want to speculate on the psychology. But one of the reasons . . . one of the factors that contributed to my moving in off the street was that I felt I was being starved out of downtown Chicago. More and more places started coming up with barriers to keep people from eating what's being thrown away, so I needed to spend more and more of my time simply foraging for food. Yeah. It just became harder to survive.

Ro: Did you interact with the other street people much?

David: Well, I didn't see myself as having some kind of ministry to homeless people or anything. If I was carving and somebody came along, you know, I'd say hello and introduce myself, and if they wanted to interact, I'd interact. I more or less treated them as I'd treat any stranger that I encountered. I didn't go out of my way to embrace them and bring light into their lives or anything.

Ro: How did you get interested in wood carving?

David: Well, I used to mess around with all kinds of art. When I was in my teens, I was a lot more creative than I am now. I finally took up wood carving when I was just out of high school. I was so messed up that I didn't . . . I guess I was searching, but I didn't know where to search or how to search or how not to fall flat on my face while searching. Or even if there was anything to be found.

I just started carving, and I guess . . . maybe one reason why I stuck with it, as opposed to other types of art, is because in my youth I was very frequently homeless and destitute. Not by any type of choice . . . well, you see, I feel the idea of choice is much more subtle or complicated than most people think. Lots of grey areas.

You don't have some people with absolute free choice and others with no choice at all. Everybody has varying *degrees* of choice. There are people living at CW houses or living on the street or . . . living wherever, who theoretically have other options they could take, but they feel those options don't work for them, so they don't consider them to be options. And in a way, they "have to" be where they are. The street person too proud to go on welfare, the Catholic Worker revolted by a conventional lifestyle—in a sense they have made a choice and in another sense, they are doing what they *must* do.

In Catholic Worker houses, there may be a very fine line between those who have "chosen" to be there and those who "have to" be there. The degree of choice isn't really the central issue. It's what you do with the circumstances you're in, what you make out of what you're given. Do you feel like you're stuck where you are? So is everybody else! Make something out of it!

Well! But at any rate I . . . I also was homeless in New York for various stints. I used to sleep on the Staten Island ferry and on the steps of Federal Hall on Wall Street, et cetera. I found that wood carving is the perfect art form for the vagabond in that the raw material can be found anywhere and costs nothing. The basic tools are inexpensive and portable, and you can work anywhere—outdoors, under a bridge, in the woods, on the beach. You can work on the street corner if you don't mind being stared at. It's absolutely ideal. It can be practiced anywhere and for nothing. So my art, I think, evolved as a response to the kind of conditions I was living in.

I feel if I teach someone the basics of wood carving, I'm giving them a craft they'll be able to carry with them, no matter what happens. Short of having their arms amputated or losing their sight, they'll always be able to practice this wherever they go. So I feel like I'm giving them . . . I don't want to use the word "empower" because it's such a cliché. Like "empower" is right up there with "affirm" and "nurture."

Ro: And "community?"

David: Yeah. Than you, that was so affirming. I really resonate with what you're saying. So without using the word "empower," okay, I'm giving them . . . uh, something they'll always have. Lately a few people around St. Francis have started taking an interest in it, and that gratifies me.

Ro: You mentioned that people say you should grow up and get down to business. Now you're thirty, David, and that used to be the dividing age. Do you feel like you're thirty?

David: I feel it, but I can't accept it. It blows my mind sometimes. In places like this, the years fly by. You can be twenty-three and then be thirty before you even know it.

Ro: You can live this kind of life for years and not be measured by progressions, by . . . you know, having children, getting promotions . . .

David: Yeah. I think that has a lot to do with it. There's not the pressure here to achieve material goals. You know, why on earth would you measure your personal worth in terms of how much money you make or how many vacation homes you have or how many scholarly theses you've published?

Ro: Do you miss having kids?

David: Well, sometimes I am beset by doubts. You know, shouldn't I have a home and a family and all of that? I don't know how much of that is coming from me and how much are the values of the larger society seeping through and affecting me. I mean we're not completely cut off here, not completely isolated from the world. Maybe that's part of my "grass is always greener" syndrome. But I'd be discontented with that life, too, and nostalgic for the Catholic Worker. You know, this is not an idyllic existence and these are . . . these are not questions that we've completely solved and dispensed with.

Ro: What about people who are married in the Catholic Worker? Does it work?

David: I've seen it work. If it didn't, that wouldn't say much for the Catholic Worker movement. If it were only something that could exist on a monastic model, then I don't think it would have much to offer to most people. It just needs to catch on. I don't think anybody's going to pick up a copy of the Catholic

Worker newsletter and have an instant blinding conversion. Or an unblinding conversion, I guess it would be. But I think it can raise questions in their minds, and if they've already got questions, it can maybe help them realize that somebody else is asking those questions, too, or that somebody thinks they've got some answers.

You know, if there's anything that I don't like about the Catholic Worker, it's the word "Catholic." I think the name drives away more people than it attracts and confuses more people than it enlightens. Probably about ninety-nine percent of the people who see the Catholic Worker sign in front of this house assume that it's run by the Catholic archdiocese, that it's part of the Catholic Church. I spend half of my time explaining that we're not. They'll say, "Well, I go to Mass every Sunday."

And I'll say, "Well that's nice. I don't 'cause I'm not a Catholic." It blows their minds. I spend a lot of my time explaining to everyone how I can be at the Catholic Worker if I'm not Catholic. Or how this can be the *Catholic* Worker if it's not under the direct jurisdiction of the parish priest, Cardinal Bernardin, and the pope.

I don't see the Catholic Worker as having the remotest thing to do with being Catholic. I justify the Catholic Worker on logical and rational terms. On terms having to do with distribution of wealth. Having to do with environmentalism. Having to do with the elevation of human dignity. The Catholic Worker makes so much sense to me on all of those levels that I don't see a religious justification as necessary.

I know that a lot of people in the Catholic Worker are real staunch Catholics, and if you ask them anything about the Catholic Worker, they'll talk about Christ telling us to do this and that and the Gospel saying such and such. "Inasmuch as you did this for the least of my brethren, you did it for Me" and all of that. That's fine. Although I'm not a Christian, I don't have any beef with Christianity. I just don't need to have some leap of faith to account for something which, for me, is eminently logical and sane, as opposed to the ways that we're taught to live and to think, ways I consider completely chaotic and demented.

Lest I come across as a complete rationalist and atheist, I do believe in God, and I do practice Judaism in my own way. I didn't come to this way of life through Judaism, but I think it's helped me to understand and to formulate my Judaism.

Ro: What . . . how do you do that?

David: I define Judaism as the repudiation of idolatry, period. This society makes an idol of money, status, power, clout, military supremacy, luxury, fashion—

many, many things. To live in a place like the Catholic Worker is to renounce those idols. I think it would be great if a Jewish community wanted to live this way. It certainly befits Judaism just as well as it does Catholicism.

I'd do away with the name "Catholic Worker." Just have the individual houses be called St. Francis House or Dorothy Day House or Ammon Hennacy House or Mother Jones House or Henry David Thoreau House.

Ro: But what about the connections between houses?

David: Well, it might be good for the movement as a whole to retain its identity. These houses are not just isolated entities. They have a common tradition and a common bond, and this gives us great strength and great permanence. And that's the best argument I've ever heard for the opposite point of view, for calling every house a Catholic Worker. I just wish there were a way to retain that bond and that tradition without having a name that's guaranteed to mislead ninety-nine percent of the people.

Ro: You know, you finally mentioned Dorothy Day for the first time. Catholicism was very important to Dorothy and Peter. Why haven't you mentioned them?

David: Because I'm real sick of hearing about Dorothy. and reading about Dorothy. There's too many damn books about Dorothy Day. Too many posters of Dorothy Day. That icon the Claretians put out makes me want to lose my dinner. Getting back to idolatry, I think there's a real danger of making an idol out of Dorothy Day in the same way that a lot of so-called Christians have made an idol out of Jesus. As long as you genuflect before the image of the saint, as long as you pay lip service to this superhuman, heroic figure, then you don't have to worry about the way you're living. You don't have to be personally very uneasy about your own actions. It becomes an easy way out.

I admire what she started, and I have found much of value in what she's written, but there's too much religiosity for my taste. You know, the idea about the homeless person who comes to the door being Christ, so you must welcome him. Okay, fine! That works as long as you can continue welcoming him, but what happens when it's time to throw him out? He comes in drunk or he cusses you out or takes a swing at you or steals your typewriter or whatever. It comes time to put him out the door, and there you are putting Christ out. Maybe my theological understanding is missing, but if every person is Christ, you can't deal with them as the human beings they really are. So when Joe or Fred or Jane comes through the door, I treat them as they are. In this society, we've got so far to go to recognize people's humanity that to be talking about their divinity is rather putting the cart before the horse.

I admire Dorothy Day and Peter Maurin and I thank God that they started the Catholic Worker. I don't know how many times I've listened to someone give a rap to a bunch of students about the Catholic Worker, They'll start out, "Well, in 1933 a woman named Dorothy Day met a man named Peter Maurin and they . . ." Who cares? Let's talk about cottage industries and why being a wood-carver or being a . . . or why planting a garden might be a better idea than buying a new computer. Or talk about the old woman who got evicted because the rent went up because the building is being turned into condominiums for young stockbrokers. That's better than all that airy spirituality.

Ro: But how did you find the Catholic Worker?

David: Well, somewhere in my wanderings, I ran into people who ran soup kitchens and clothing rooms and shelters and hospitality houses. That was something I had no knowledge of, although I knew it intuitively, knew in my gut, that there was something terribly, terribly wrong with the status quo. I've never been able to be molded into any of the roles that have been decided for me. Hence my wanderings and my vagabondage. But until the Catholic Worker, I had never known that there was anybody else who felt that way, or any movements or groups of people devoted to looking for radical alternatives. It was a revelation to me, just a tremendous breakthrough and turning point. And from that point on, those were the only places where I fit in or could be myself and feel natural.

You know, I've been asked many times how I ended up in the Catholic Worker, and I sometimes feel there's a question behind the question. It's like, "How did you turn out to be so weird?" So maybe it's, "How did I end up at the Catholic Worker as opposed to working for a corporation or a university or the government?"

Well, I feel the Catholic Worker way of life is a natural and sane and rational and realistic and sensible and utterly pragmatic way to live. I don't think we're doing some foolish leap of faith, and I get rather annoyed when people say things like, "Well, we're fools for Christ. And even though this doesn't make sense in the world's terms, we do it anyway because we have so much faith." That's bullshit!

This way of life makes perfect sense! It's completely sane. I think working on the ninety-fourth floor of the Sears Tower, punching buttons on a computer for eight hours a day, and driving home in a traffic jam on a twelve-lane expressway . . . that's the insanity and the foolishness. It's utterly unrealistic and unpragmatic. When I'm asked about the Catholic Worker, I feel like turning the question upside down and saying, "How have you *not* ended up at a place like the Catholic Worker? How have you avoided arriving at this self-evident truth?"

Once again, the light and shadow. In an insane world, a sane place like this is going to appear insane. Allow me a quote . . . G. K. Chesterton said, "The only way to see the world is to stand on your head. For the world is upside down." That's why I'm here. Because this makes sense. I'm prepared to argue the sanity and rationality of the Catholic Worker at the drop of a hat. Particularly with anybody who says either, "When are you going to grow up and get serious?" or, "We're within the system to change the system." That path is broad. People who aren't willing to work within the system, people who blaze their own path off the beaten track . . . those people are so comparatively rare that we need all we can get. I always urge people to drop out of the system. Most of them aren't going to, and that's fine, but the few that will are infinitely precious.

CHAPTER 24

Laughter and Learning

Angelus House in Toronto

I'd never really met a poor person. I thought they were all old men who drank too much and wore dirty, long coats. I thought this was going to be a miserable life, but that it was the right thing to do, any-way. You just didn't have any choice. Once you saw it, you couldn't go back and say, "Well, I've decided to do something else instead." That wouldn't be a moral option. But I was wrong. I mean I've never *had* so much fun!

—Lauren Griffin

W HEN I interviewed her in 1987, Willa Bickham, who founded Baltimore's Viva House with her husband, Brendan Walsh, told me: "Last week, a young married couple came to ask how we started the house and how it was to raise a family at the Catholic Worker. They were doing the same thing we did on our honeymoon, trying to think through things and see if they could really do it. You see the whole cycle being repeated." In this narrative, the couple who visited Willa and Brendan describe their early years with Angelus House, one of several Canadian communities. They've since moved to Cobalt in northern Ontario.

Charlie Angus: I was nineteen and playing in a band. That was all I ever wanted to do: that was my dream. We were really politically active, organizing teenagers, mostly in the punk movement. Lauren had just left a radical feminist collective on the prairies and had come to Toronto. I met her, and we fell in love. (Well, we were roommates, and then we fell in love.) We were having this sort of long search for what we should do, because I was beginning to become much more committed to Catholicism.

Ro: Was that a childhood orientation?

Charlie: Yeah. I always figured I'd end . . . I was terrified I was going to be a priest. My biggest fear. I figured I better have as much fun as I could before . . . Well, moving in with Lauren, starting to read the Berrigans and Thomas Merton—it was really opening up a new world. But there seemed to be something else. Both of us were trying to define what this something else was, but we had no way of putting any name or any kind of vision to it.

I was in a bookstore one day, and I saw *Loaves and Fishes: The Story of the Catholic Worker Movement.* I came home, and I was jumping up and down and saying, "Lauren, this is the best book I've ever seen!" It just blew me away. Right away I thought, "This is it. This is the real radicalism of the Gospel."

Lauren Griffin: I came from Edmonton, in Alberta. Had been working in the women's crisis movement for about five years, and was in university. Was going to be a lawyer.

Charlie: Would you take that off the tape, please? [Laughter.]

Lauren: I'd just finished my first year of law school and decided that I didn't want to be a lawyer anymore. Continued to work in the women's movement, but became increasingly disillusioned with [its] long-term vision, because it lacked a moral base. It had a really strong political base and a political vision, and there was a lot of compassion and caring there, but the issue of morality was a real taboo. There was a real reaction against traditional morality—against family, against a lot of the things that I had been raised with.

So off I went to Toronto to go back to school. Got an M.A. in moral education at the Ontario Institute for Studies in Education. By the time I'd finished, I realized that I didn't want to be an academic. What became apparent was that people there had good ideas, but they weren't willing to risk anything by living with the people they were writing about. And that for me was a real problem. It [all] came together in the Worker. Although it terrified me.

And I was terrified of poor people. I'd never really met a poor person. I thought they were all old men who drank too much and wore dirty, long coats. I thought this was going to be a miserable life, but that it was the right thing to do, anyway. You just didn't have any choice. Once you saw it, you couldn't go back and say, "Well, I've decided to do something else instead." That wouldn't be a moral option.

But I was wrong. I mean I've never *had* so much fun! But at the time, I was really panic-stricken. Because I really liked nice things. I had a really nice cottage. Lots of privacy. Lots of order.

Ro: Did you come from a Catholic background?

Lauren: Oh, yes.

Ro: And did you leave that during the feminist phase or just sort of put it on the back burner?

Lauren: No. I went to church every Sunday. Said my novenas and my rosary and just didn't deal with it. Didn't deal with the fact that there was a conflict.

Charlie: I mean, I wasn't a male chauvinist pig. (I'm a loud-mouth reactionary. Everyone knows that.) But the sort of really intense hatred of the Christian vision [in the feminist books] just blew me away.

It took us, I guess, about three more years of reading, of getting our nerve up, of learning to live simply. Like giving up eating meat. And not buying clothes. Giving away a lot of my records. But it took Lauren to get us going. I would always say, "Well, when we have the house" or "When we're Catholic Workers." And Lauren finally said, "Charlie, there's no *when*. You either are or . . . it's not that you don't get on the road. You're *on* the road!"

Lauren: At first the ideas of the Worker really scared me, and Charlie loved them. It was the ideas that really appealed to him, and it could have stayed that way forever.

Charlie: I remember going to meet Mary Mullins, a name I remembered from reading the *Catholic Worker*. And thinking, you know, "What if she's some crazy old hippie who wants to move in with us?" What a goof I was! We knocked on the door, and I remember looking in the mirror. I'd just got a brush cut and was wearing my leather jacket. I thought, "Why did I wear that? She's going to think we're just punks."

Well, Mary answered the door. She's an older woman from Atlanta, Georgia. Real tall and big. "Oh, honey, come on in! Sit down. You just have yourself a beer now, honey."

She had this American beer that I'd never seen before. And then she gave us this talk about what the Worker would be. She said, "You know, y'all are gonna get your house and people are gonna call you to go to this meetin' and they're going to want you to represent this group or that. Just don't go! You've got a house to feed, and you've got to play cards with the boys, and you've got to go bowling with them. You don't got to go to no meetin's!"

Then she said, "When you get that house, honey, you're gonna have so much fun, you're just gonna die!"

After we left, I said to Lauren, "I don't care if Mary Mullins never speaks to us again. I'll open a house [with a good feeling, just] knowing she's in the same city." That was it! That was what we wanted. We didn't want a life of . . . we expected it'd be really hard and miserable and all that, but we also wanted that sort of excitement.

Lauren: The passion.

Charlie: Yeah. That anarchistic love of life. That it didn't matter what the hell happened. Then we were looking for community, and that's where we got Sandy. If you saw Sandy, it would all make sense.

Ro: Did Sandy come for community or as a guest?

Charlie: He came . . .

Lauren: He came as an angel of the Lord, Sandy did. See, he can't talk properly because he doesn't hear properly. He's a loser, a classic loser, but throughout the four years we've known him, he's been the one who has taught us the most and hauled us up on the carpet when we needed to be. Constantly.

I mean he's no joy to live with, that's for sure. Sandy's parents had put him in this program for the mentally retarded, and he's *not* mentally retarded. He hated it. Every day he'd say, "I can't stand living here." But we didn't want to deal with the fact that we might have to live with Sandy. We wanted one of our *friends* to have community with.

Charlie: We were thinking . . . well, we could let Sandy live with us, but we couldn't run a Catholic Worker house if we had a guy like him in the house. You know, how would he cope with strangers? Like a family would say, I guess: "Well, we'd like to offer hospitality, but we can't because we have children."

Lauren: Eventually we realized that we were being schmucks, so he moved in with us. He's neither a Worker or a guest, he's something else altogether.

Charlie: Our primary responsibility has been to make a world that's safe for Sandy. So the model we've gone towards [in the house] is family. At first, we'd try and be egalitarian, and say . . . for instance, this woman named Kelly lived with us. Kelly was really shy, a real "Little Flower" type. She did a lot of the sort of work that nobody else [wanted to do], and didn't . . . she wasn't that outspoken. But we tried to insist that Kelly would have as much authority in the house as we did, to sort of try and balance it out.

And community doesn't work that way. By us saying, "Kelly is in charge when we leave," we were saying to Terry, who was a street guy, and Donald, who was an alcoholic, that *they* didn't have a say. And it was their home as much as it was Kelly's. So now we try to be family. Everyone has a role. But there's nobody who runs . . . like Lauren and I are considered sort of the parents, and the guys are like uncles or . . . and they help in the running of the hospitality, too, because they're given that kind of authority.

Lauren: Some nights it's like all our kids come home. They come to use the laundry and get some advice. But they give to us, too. It's sort of funny to see ourselves as getting older and older.

Charlie: Yeah, it is. Again, when we started, we had no battle plan, so things arose as they arose. We were such a mess ourselves. The men—the alcoholics— gave us the help in dealing with other alcoholics. We didn't know what alcoholism was, and we were way over our heads. We got in with child abuse and . . . and violence, too. Finally, we realized that we had been wimps because we were frightened to stand up to people. We thought if *we* were nice, then everybody'd be nice. So the cunning ones tore the community apart. Knew that we didn't have the chutzpah to stand up to them. The weaker ones got trampled.

The first few times, it was really awful. I remember the night Dan was ter- rorizing his son in the kitchen. Stalking him. The kid was screaming, and I came running downstairs. That should never have happened. It should never have got- ten to that stage. But it did because we didn't have . . . I think part of it was we didn't have the knowledge, or the sense to be able to go on our intuition and tell when trouble was coming.

Lauren: Also, I think that there's a real kind of knee-jerk response to treat the poor with kid gloves. And they seem to demand it, too. You know, either you think they have nothing to offer, or you think you have to give them the world. Instead of just having a normal relationship with them. Like Dan mythologized himself, and we mythologized his pain and his anguish and his hard times, too. You get overwhelmed by people's misfortunes when you've had none yourself, and it's hard to sort of say, "Screw this! Shake it off, buddy!"

Charlie: We always prayed that an older person would come, [to help us] and no old person ever did. So there were some bad scenes, and we began to realize that we couldn't keep going with the strain of having a crisis every single day.

Ro: What about all those Catholics who were giving you the go-ahead? All those Jesuits and others. Where were they?

Charlie: They were supportive, but they weren't there when stuff was happen- ing. It's a whole different world. We couldn't really talk to them about Frank O'Leary sitting outside our door every night and calling Lauren a whore. And then torturing the cat. Or about someone like Dan who comes home on acid and terrorizes his children.

Lauren: We also weren't very good at asking for help.

Charlie: We thought we were too young to have to make all these decisions. But then we realized—hell! People younger than us have been through a lot worse. So finally I started to act like a middle-aged father. (Well, I started to act like *her* father. Not my dad. My house was a zoo.) And she started to act like a middle-aged mother.

Suddenly things changed. Well, not suddenly. But we . . . it didn't work with all of us trying to collectively deal with authority. You know, it was a joke. When shit would hit the fan, community would disappear, and Lauren and I would be stuck at the door, facing this drunk. And we'd be so upset at the rest of our community for doing that to us. Then we realized that was our lot. Authority, we realized, is not so much a power trip as having to be the one to deal with the shit. And also to sort of balance the community—to try and find the strengths of the people who volunteer. And so we began to discern and to learn to really trust our instincts. Intuition is rarely wrong. We started to pick things up because we had to.

Ro: How many people usually live here?

Charlie: We've slept fourteen.

Lauren: Which is too many. Between seven and ten is nice. Again, it depends on . . . you know, if you only have one person who will clean the toilet, then six is too many.

Who do we have? It seems to be cyclical. There was a time when we had mostly prisoners. A time we had mostly alcoholic men. A time we had families. It comes and goes, but we're sort of an open house.

Ro: Do you have some house rules?

Charlie: Yeah. We started with no rules because we thought Dorothy Day didn't have any rules. Of course, we were so blind. [Laughter.] There was never any drugs allowed. Then the first rule was no drinking in the house. Before that, people drank in the house.

Ro: So now you two can't drink in the house, either?

Charlie: Well, right now there are just three of us who can. In the beginning, I thought [allowing] beer was a sense of trust. Alcohol was our nemesis for about two years—our battle. A constant battle with alcoholism. Every single day.

Lauren: For a while we had our own stash, something I think happens in a lot of [CW] houses.

Charlie: I had my bottle of whiskey.

Lauren: And then we realized that was really lousy. First of all, they all knew. I mean an alcoholic knows within ten miles if someone's drinking. But also, we'd all sneak up to somebody's room and drink, and that was a really divisive and kind of arrogant thing to do, I think.

There were the four of us: Kelly, Julie, Charlie, and I. We were all really good friends, so there would be evenings where we'd all go out to the local country and western bar. And there were men in the house who drank at that bar, but we'd never go with them because they were alcoholics, and it would be a *mess*. But they all knew we were going, and it always felt crummy.

Charlie: When Sandy came in drunk, he got in. When Donald came home drunk, he didn't. Laws are there to be broken. Because it's the person. Sometimes you've got to be really hard line with somebody; other times, that's the worst thing you can do.

Ro: That happens in families, too.

Charlie: Yeah. That happens in families. You have to say, "Well Donald, you could go out drinking with us, but you come home and throw up all over the floor and cut yourself with a tin can and almost bleed to death. So you can't, that's all."

One problem, I think, in the Catholic Worker, is the tendency to see yourself as working on behalf of the poor. To see yourself as an activist, a troubleshooter. You count up how many times you've been in an emergency ward and how many times you've been robbed. Your old-soldier stories become a "red badge of courage."

So we've been really moving towards breaking down our own understanding of ourselves as radicals, and trying to be like our grandparents were—working people who welcome in people when they need to sleep. They were poor. They had a big family. Men would come off the railways and sleep [in their house]. And they made do with what they had. We had to relearn the skills that our grandparents took for granted. And what we . . . I think what the Left has lost is the natural community that went with . . . say, baking bread or the women doing the dishes in the kitchen, you know, which we think is a really sort of oppressive thing.

You get together over a shared job. It doesn't have to be a "dignified" job. I mean, cleaning out the backyard isn't a dignified job but when everybody does it, there's something amazing about it. We learned that as we rediscovered these skills that our grandparents took for granted. And here we thought we were on the cutting edge of something new. Now I call Lauren the Grandmere.

We began to move into the neighborhood, to move into the parish, to be just a couple in the parish who are Catholic Workers. The Catholic Worker is now as accepted as the Legion of Mary. And people in the neighborhood welcomed us, not as Catholic Workers or activists but as just another working family. And now we're sort of just common people.

That was really hard for us because when you're young and arrogant, you don't want to be common people. You want to be sort of dangerous young radicals. Part of it, also, was having to work. I mean we had to pay the bills here. And we both decided . . . Lauren was writing curriculum for the Jesuit Center, stuff on the Guatemalan refugees. We began to be really influenced by the Little Brothers of Jesus who are our neighbors across the road—their whole understanding of manual labor. A Nazareth experience, they call it.

So Lauren quit her job and became a housepainter. We tried to work at the same kind of things that most of the men [in the neighborhood did]. We'd like to be able to say to couples, you know, "Families can do this. Hospitality belongs in the family."

Ro: Lauren, I noticed that your newspaper, the *Angelus,* says "the Canadian Catholic Worker." Do you see yourself as being a parent house in a way?

Lauren: No, I think it's more that we're trying to redefine the Catholic Worker in a Canadian context, [and we see the paper] as a large part of our mandate.

Charlie: Our paper goes out to people who have no connection at all with the Catholic Worker movement. Or with the ideas. The old folks of the church—we give them the *Angelus,* and they give us holy medals. In a sense, we give them a bit of the Gospel they wouldn't normally see, and they give us a bit that we wouldn't normally see. So it works out.

We print a paper that an average person could read, and that's . . . I guess that's our focus if you want to call us a parent house. Not for the sense of centralizing anything, but we go wherever we can to try and tell people the joys of quitting the rat race, the joys of living the Catholic Worker vision.

We've spoken to thousands of students in three years. When we first started speaking, we'd tell stories and, you know, sort of do a little Charlie-and-Lauren show. It was fun, and the kids really liked it, and we had kids coming over to the house from the schools, you know, to help out, and kids [doing] food drives and dances and walk-a-thons and stuff like that. We were sort of big entertainment and word was spreading. We were a good draw.

Then we realized we weren't doing the truth. That we weren't there to entertain them. We weren't there to make us look like exciting and fun people. Instead, we were there to say, "Look! We're not very special people. What we do is what any of you can do." I always say this to the Italian school. The Italian schools are all up in the suburbs, and they have filthy-rich kids driving Mercedes Benzes to school.

Lauren: Like *literally.*

Charlie: They drive their own Corvettes, and they've got gold watches. They're from immigrant families that have done real well. I love it—I get up in front of four hundred Italian students, and I say, "I'm here today to tell you to quit school. Not to go for a big career. Sell your car and come and live with the poor." And you hear this groan. They think I'm insane. I say, "Now that you're convinced I'm a lunatic, I'll show you why." The response is amazing!

Ro: Do they still come down?

Charlie: Yeah.

Lauren: Not as much. Not as much, for sure.

Charlie: A lot of students . . . there's an incredible cynicism among them. They don't believe in the system, but they just figure it's what's going to happen.

Ro: They believe they can't get along without it.

Charlie: Yeah, that's it. For someone to challenge it, and to do it with joy . . . yeah, it's amazing. Some kids, well, one kid . . . we spoke on Good Friday two years ago at St. Catherine's. This sixteen-year-old boy came up and said, "Okay, let's do it!"

Just like that. He said, "My mom has a business career planned for me. She's got bonds put in my name. But I read this book on St. Francis, and I've heard you guys talk and I want to know where to go *now!*"

Lauren: Well, of course, we panicked.

Charlie: We panicked. "Well, we were just kidding about quitting school." We said that he had to educate himself, to start reading. Gave him a list—you know, Chesterton and Gill and . . . I wrote him about a year later and told him I remembered him.

Ro: You ought to call him.

Charlie: Well, I reminded him not to get caught up in other stuff.

Ro: I bet he's lonely up there.

Charlie: Yes. He phoned me right afterwards, and he said, "Thanks for the letter. It really came at a good time." He never did come down. But he's seventeen, and I figure seeds are planted. I'll call him again in a year and maybe when he's twenty-one, he'll come down.

Lauren: One thing we've really worked on is having good relations in the parish. You know, going . . . we used to go a lot to weekday Mass. We go to Sunday Mass, and Charlie reads. So our worship hasn't become a form of elitism. Sometimes we go to this Portuguese Mass and can't understand a word, but there's this sense of something really sacred that I never got at Mass up in the suburbs.

Charlie: I think the greatest tragedy in the church is that we identify our religion, or our religious tastes, with those who agree with us. All these small communities that get together and worship together, and just thank God they have all they want right there. This sort of yuppie middle-age religion is . . . we all want a God that reflects us.

Ro: Do you have Mass here?

Charlie: We have Mass here . . . well, we were having it every Tuesday. Any of the old Legion of Mary ladies could drop by or any of the young anarchists. One priest came for about a year. He'd been stationed in China, so he had a really Oriental presence, and his Masses were really beautiful.

Lauren: When things get really crazy and you don't feel like praying, you begin to feel like you're doing this on your own. That's when your community really falls apart. We finally realized that you always have to be in touch with the fact that someone—that God—is working through you. We say morning prayer and evening prayer together. Night prayer is usually a reflection.

Charlie: You know, what you often mistake for spirituality is just adrenalin. And adrenalin burns out. Sometimes things were so bad, there wasn't anything you could do *but* pray. And sometimes we'd be so scared shitless that we'd have to do something really simple like saying the rosary. I mean I had no real background in saying the rosary. I can never make up my mind whether I hate it or not.

Lauren: Well, it's probably the prayer that our grandmothers and their grandmothers would have said when they were scared, too. There's something really amazing about working the bead that people have worked before. I come from the classic Irish Catholic background where the mother is . . . in a kind of bizarre way, she's a real center and a real rock. You pray to Mary, and she goes to the Father. And also that whole notion of the mother and the mother making things safe.

There was an Irishman in the house who . . . the only kind of communication we could have with him was to pray the rosary together. That awoke familiar memories in both of us. (When I was young, I prayed novenas to the Blessed Virgin. On trips, we prayed the rosary for safety. Very traditional.)

Charlie: The only thing we had in common with Martin was the rosary. He was just so full of rage. I mean he's a man clinically possessed. When things were really bad, we'd say to Martin: "Say the rosary." And he would lead.

Oh, let me tell you this one! Trudy, the leader of Madonna House, gave us the prayer of St. Michael, the Archangel of Exorcism.* It was the ancient church prayer of exorcism. I said to Lauren, "Here take this. This is your kind of stuff." Oh, my God! Well, we've used it once!

Ro: Oh, tell me about it!

Charlie: Okay. We had a Guatemalan refugee who held the house hostage all night. Threatened to kill everyone. And we weren't here. (It was our first anniversary and we were away celebrating at my sister's apartment.) Phoned the next morning, and the house was a mess. People were terrified. They'd been up all night with a maniac. And two of the guys in the house . . . their solution was to take to drinking. Anyway, we waited from noon till about eight o'clock at night, not knowing when he'd come home.

I said, "Well, when he comes I'll explain to him that he's violated the rules of community." Everyone just laughed at me and said he'd rip me apart. They said they'd never seen anything like it, and these guys had been around, you know. So we were panicking.

When crisis erupts, things are happening, and you respond, and the Holy Spirit is there, and you're not afraid. But when you wait and don't know, you become a quivering wreck.

Finally he came and tried to get in. He was two days drunk and insane like it was like Vietnam. (I guess it was Vietnam syndrome. I mean he'd probably seen one too many killings in Guatemala.) He would kill anything. We had to call the police, but then I didn't want them to take him away. They were saying, "Hey boy! You got papers? Boy!"

I thought, "Oh, gee! This is sickening!" I figured I'd calm him down and he'd realize [where he was]. So I was saying, "Gabriel, we're your friends. We're your friends. Why would you want to hurt us?"

As soon as Gabriel saw the cop leave, he said to Lauren, "I want to fucking

---

* Madonna House is a Catholic secular institute founded by Catherine de Hueck.

kill you." Finally, we had to call again and the police came back and took him away. And, of course, fifteen minutes later they phoned and said they were letting him out.

"We've got no grounds to hold him."

One of the guys in the house said, "If you don't want him held, they'll hold him, but if you want him held, no way." Gabby phoned a minute later and said, "I'm coming over."

We thought we were dead. We turned all the lights out, just had one candle lit by the phone, so we could call the police again.

And it was funny. None of the men in the house left. Nobody . . . like anybody could have left at any time, but nobody did. Anyway, we got right down on the ground and started to say the rosary. What else could we do? You know, I was *so* scared. And as soon as we . . . and as soon as we finished the rosary, I began to be a little less frightened because I realized that God was there, and that what would happen, would happen.

Then I said to Lauren, "Quick! Get that prayer [of exorcism]." We said the prayer of exorcism at the front door, and we anointed all the windows with holy water. And then Martha Miller and Robbie Gamble phoned to wish us happy anniversary and heard that we were going to die and came over with a bottle of wine. And we all sat on the floor and waited for Gabriel.

We waited for fifteen minutes. We waited twenty minutes. And finally people went to bed, but Lauren and I slept on the floor in the front room. It was the scariest night of my life. We thought he'd come through the window, so we wanted to be where we could grab the phone. I couldn't believe it when morning came. I was never so glad to see daylight! I just couldn't believe it—we were still here.

And then we looked out the window, and he was standing outside. He must have walked around the house all night, but he hadn't come in. Someone might say, "Well, maybe he calmed down. Maybe he realized . . ." But he'd been in a murderous rage for two straight days. I don't think he'd calm down in fifteen minutes. We had said this prayer, and the prayer forbid the evil from entering the house.

Lauren: It worked.

Charlie: We haven't said the prayer since. We figured we're not going to push it.

Ro: Oh, Charlie, that is the neatest story! [Pause] Uh . . . what about money for the house? Didn't you tell me you're a drywaller?

Charlie: Well, I'd been washing dishes. In the band, we had to take jobs we could quit at any time if we had to go on the road. I began to see a real Christian beauty in it. Like I took the worst job in the restaurant and loved it, took a real pride in it. And I was content to do that [when we started the house] too, because I got food from the restaurant, and I could go to work and just blow off steam when things were really pressurized here.

Then we decided if we wanted to be doing this when we were seventy, we had to start learning skills. One, so we could be more self-sufficient. But another [reason was] so that we could maybe start to do things in a smaller community. I mean a dishwasher can only do so much.

So I had the opportunity to . . . well, I phoned up this friend who was a carpenter, the last of the Vietnam expatriates, and asked if I could work with him. He really took me under his wing and insisted that I learn everything I needed to know within three months because he was moving back to the States.

Lauren: That's not what happened. [Laughter.]

Charlie: It is.

Lauren: No, no. Just because I think it's important: What happened is that I was working part time with Philip, learning to be a carpenter. And then Charlie started doing a little bit with him, too. And then it became clear that Philip was leaving, and if both of us kept on with him, we'd learn diddly squat.

Also, Philip, I think, saw more potential in Charlie. But we also decided that Charlie should do it because it was more . . . I think because the role made sense for him in terms of the dynamics of the house. It made more sense for us to be in more traditional roles. I didn't mean to interrupt, but we need to make it clear that we were consciously making that choice.

Charlie: For world history, okay! Well, just before Philip left for the States, we got this job working for Sandy, this crazy old Italian construction worker who made a fortune in construction and retired, but then hated it. He hired Phil and me to come up and do work for him, so he could yell at us and feed us red wine all day. One day, Sandy says to me, "So Charlie, what are you going to do when Philip leaves?"

"I don't know. I guess I'll be unemployed."

As an Italian workman, the fact that I'd be unemployed with a wife was just too much for him. So he said, "You come up when this job is done. I got work for you."

So I'd come up every day on the bus. It'd take me an hour and a half to get there, and he'd pick me up in his pickup truck and the whole way [to the job] he'd be yelling at me for not having my license. "What kind of good-for-nothing husband are you?" "Your poor, poor wife!" "What a dummy!" Then, out of the blue, a woman phoned me and asked me to renovate her house. Totally out of the blue.

Ro: So now you're able to have work when you need the money?

Charlie: That's what we've done for the last year. I took that job on, and then I had to find someone to go with me, so I found my friend Jason, who is a good Catholic Worker, and trained him exactly the way Philip trained me. We have a sliding scale. If we work for rich people, we charge them the going rate. Twelve bucks an hour. And we don't . . .

Lauren: That's a little below the going rate.

Charlie: Yeah. I mean it could be twenty bucks an hour. But twelve bucks an hour is . . . but for like middle-class people or working people, it's anywhere from seven dollars an hour on up, which is really cheap.

Ro: Do you pay income tax?

Charlie: No. That's the other thing. We didn't want to have anything more to do with paying income tax. Again, Canada . . . six percent goes to the military, so it's more a question of just the total basic grotesqueness of this system— the squandering of money in Canada on big corporations and on conservative functions. We've decided we're not going to do it anymore.

Ro: What about usury? Do you put your money in a bank?

Charlie: No. We took our money out of the banks, and we belong to Bread and Roses Credit Union. It's a local alternative credit union that offers a non-interest account.

Lauren: The interest accounts are called "bread accounts" and the non-interest ones are "roses accounts."

Ro: Neat. Tell me about your work with the union movement.

Lauren: Well, in Canada unionism is a lot more of an issue than it is in the States.

Charlie: There's a real last-ditch fight. People really feel under the gun and feel if something isn't done, especially in light of free trade and increasing Americanization, we'll go the way of the States, which will be the breaking of the union.

We noticed something when we first went [to a Worker gathering] in Milwaukee. This is a guess, but a basic difference between America and Canada is we don't have a war economy here. So for us [resistance to militarism] seems much further away. (I mean the Canadian Army has always been a joke. The biggest budget is for uniforms.)

[We were involved in] the Canada Postal strike, which was the major strike here recently. This whole neighborhood was . . . there were police battle cordons like in South Korea. They took over the streets. Because the big postal plant [is near here]. Again, we were trying to make a presence, trying to bring a Christian vision to labor at this time. We came up with fiddles and cookies, came, you know, as neighborhood people. People have questioned if a Christian presence should be out on picket lines because of the violence. That's all nice and well, but working people are out there and violence occurs. At the postal strike, we bring a loving presence, and there are ways of defusing violence.

Ro: What sort of connections do you have with the Catholic Left in Toronto?

Charlie: They know us. We know . . . with some, it's really strong. And other parts, it's really not at all. I think we sort of sidestep a lot of their issues. We're here to live the Gospel and not argue about the church.

Lauren: We're not so much challenging church hierarchy as [challenging] average Christians. I think our interest is more in getting lay people to realize that you can wait forever for the church hierarchy to live the Gospel. For instance, women's ordination is not a burning issue for us.

I think, also, the Catholic Left in Toronto is older. We came in on the tail end of the generation that isn't interested in the church at all. And so in terms of that, we address a really different group of people. That separates us a lot from the Catholic Left in terms of the way they operate, which is meetings and briefings and lobby . . . like the Jesuit Center for Social Faith and Justice does great work, but it's on a whole different scale than anything that young people are really into. So again, it's partly an age thing.

Charlie: Yeah. Maybe it's just sort of the practical anarchism that Dorothy Day . . . she could live with the dichotomies in the church. We were invited to be speakers at this big gathering on the laity and the church. I think a lot of the Catholic Left thought we were reactionaries or something because we were saying, "Why argue about who's going to be pope? Let's just live the Gospel."

To me it's simple. Sure, there are big, burning issues, but for us . . . well, there are times when we *do* speak out. For instance, we crashed Cardinal Carter's seventy-fifth anniversary banquet.

Ro: Oh, that sounds like a story! Tell it.

Charlie: Well, I guess we caused a big stink. But we did it in a very respectful tone. We prayed about it a long time beforehand and came as brothers and sisters. In a loving manner.

Lauren: It was a fund-raiser for local charities. The cream of the crop were invited to wine and dine with the cardinal.

Charlie: Two hundred dollars a plate.

Lauren: And each parish had to buy ten tickets. For most couples, that's like a week's salary. You know, it's outrageous! The whole drawing card is that you get lavished all this attention. Our point was addressing people who were sort of beguiled by the wealth and [telling them] that if you want to help the poor, you eat *with* them and *like* them.

Charlie: But some people would've paid just because they thought it was a real honor to represent their parish.

Ro: Encouraging elitism.

Lauren: We got as dressed up as we could. We quietly went. Gave out a little pamphlet that described our position. You know, asked people to reconsider and then left.

Charlie: That's not exactly how it was. [Much laughter.] She's trying to soft-pedal it.

Lauren: No. That's what we did.

Charlie: What we did was . . . The prime minister was there. The governor general of Canada was there. The biggest and the richest heads of corporations . . . all the Tory money in Canada were there.

Ro: Did all the local people have to pay, or did the parishes buy the tickets?

Lauren: I imagine some of them paid and some of them needed help.

Charlie: So we were really outraged. We talked about crashing it. Talked about protesting. Talked about playing guitars outside. We talked about kneeling outside and saying the rosary. Finally, we decided to crash it. We shook down our parish priest for information, to find out, you know, the setup of the hall and where they took the tickets. We said to him, "Look Father, if you don't give us information, we're going to go down there with signs saying "St. Joseph Catholic Worker." (That's the name of our parish.)

"Okay, but when you see me at the dinner, pretend you don't know me."

"Fair enough."

Then he told us they didn't have a person taking tickets 'cause it was too fancy. So we could just walk in. I borrowed a suit and Lauren and Kelly dressed up.

I mean, it was a joke . . . like Kelly was real working-poor background. And Kelly's idea of dressing up is like . . . well, they managed to get in. I guess people thought they were nuns.

We took a cab the last little way, so we'd look like the rest of the people coming in cars. But we were too early, so then we had to kill time. Finally we went in. Went up the stairs and there were RCMP [Royal Canadian Mounted Police] and Secret Service agents everywhere because the prime minister was there. They were looking for troublemakers or dangerous radical types. At one point I had RCMP on either side of me. Sort of protecting me from someone, I don't know who.

We finally thought, "Okay, this is it." I started to give my pamphlets out. And I'd say, "Good evening, ma'am, good evening, sir." (I'd worked in a restaurant. I knew how to talk.) And so people were taking the pamphlets.

Lauren: I think they thought we were giving out the programs for the evening.

Charlie: I was waiting to get hit, just waiting for some woman to start beating me with her purse. These were like the richest people I've ever seen. I mean this was high . . . this was old Toronto money.

Lauren: There were three thousand people there.

Charlie: Yeah. And so . . . but people started to take them in droves. We went through like six hundred . . .

Lauren: Seven hundred.

Charlie: Seven hundred pamphlets in fifteen minutes. If we'd stood outside, nobody would've taken them.

Ro: So who told you to leave?

Charlie: Nobody. After we passed out seven hundred, we said, "Let's get the hell out of here." After we got down the stairs, apparently this priest came running out saying, "There's a bunch of loonies here. Giving out stuff on poverty." But a lot of priests read the letters and stood right beside it and were just roaring with laughter. We expected hell. But we just laughed so hard. We got rid of seven hundred pamphlets. People took them.

Lauren: And read them.

Charlie: It said, "Greetings in Christ." They thought it was from the cardinal or something, so they read it. We just waited . . . I thought we were going to get dragged down to the chancery office.

Ro: You had your name on it and everything?

Charlie: Oh, yeah. We took full responsibility for it. Our new archbishop is apparently real right wing. All the Catholic Left are terrified of him.

Ro: Look who appointed him.

Charlie: Yeah. He's from Albania, this guy. So anyway we expected the worst, and Kelly did get in a lot of shit at work. She worked at one of the archdiocese shelters—the AIDS hospice—and they sent her home without pay one day and stuff like that. But we got phone calls from people saying . . . like a nun in Saskatchewan said we restored her faith in the church. We went to visit my aunts in a convent in Cape Breton, and they said they were so glad when they read it, and their nun friends who were at the affair were upset at the way the banquet was held. They were reading our pamphlet out loud, loud enough to be heard from the head table. These are like seventy-year-old nuns.

Initially, the chancery probably got . . . people were really mad from what I hear. If the chancery told us to come down, we would have. You know, I think it's the same thing that Dorothy Day faced. If the chancery says to us . . . but nobody's said anything yet. (Maybe they don't know we exist. I don't know.) If they said what we wrote about the church is wrong from the position of faith, we'd listen to them, and if they were right, then they're right.

We were very careful to be respectful. And when the cameras came up the stairs, we kept our mouths shut. Because we weren't there to do a publicity stunt. We were there to talk to our brothers and sisters who were wealthy. And we felt that it was really important to establish that so that the chancery couldn't say we were media-hungry. They never said nothing. I can't believe it! [Laughs.] The greatest gift of the Holy Spirit is laughter. And this is a house of laughter. We always think we're sort of the first and the last in people's lives, and when we realize we aren't, it's a real freedom.

Lauren: Speaking of freedom, we're going to be moving from Toronto, I think. I think we'll go north. A lot of the guys who come to the house are from small towns that have just been killed by the bigger cities and by big corporations. The whole story.

A big part of the reason we started in the Catholic Worker was the vision of something better, a society that was better. And that it wasn't going to happen down the road, it was going to happen if you *made* it happen. Our desire is to live the new society in the way that Peter Maurin visioned it. Within a Canadian framework. In either a smaller town or just outside a small town.

Charlie: We thought it might be a useful witness to . . . to make it possible for them to stay in the towns they love and not have to come to a city like Toronto. You know, we all have dreams of where we want to live. In the north, which is real working-class mining . . . rough . . . there's a rawness in the air.

Ro: What you're saying sounds romantic.

Charlie: Oh, yeah.

Lauren: Although I think . . . you start off saying, "Well, this is what I like and this is where I want to go." But in the end, you go where you're told to go by God.

Charlie: One town that really excited us used to have fifty thousand people and three hundred mines, and now there are sixteen hundred people; it's a dying, burned-out mining community. It would be an amazing witness. What would we do? We might start running a local theater or open up a bingo parlor or . . . we asked at each town. What would we do here? You know, what kind of witness needs are here? Maybe it needs a Saturday night barn dance.

CHAPTER 25

Unity and Diversity

Syracuse Communities

All people need are bread and miracles.

—*Dostoyevsky*

SYRACUSE, New York, had several different Worker houses when I visited in 1988. I stopped at three of them: Dorothy Day House, a restricted shelter for abused women, Unity Kitchen, the most conservative and Catholic of the Catholic Worker communities, and Unity Acres, a farm for older alcoholic men in nearby Orwell. While none of these could be called typical—a "typical Catholic Worker" is a contradiction in terms—they demonstrate the tremendous diversity in theory and practice found even within one community. (Note: Dorothy Day House was not listed in the May 1992 list of houses published by the *Catholic Worker,* but I include it here as representative of communities in the movement run for and by women.)

Dorothy Day House

Pat Sher: We have to go back, probably to 1979, when a Sister of St. Joseph— Sister Lee Connolly—was the director of the Urban Ministry Board, a group of inner-city churches here in Syracuse. She believed, as many of us did, that the plight of homeless women and children was being completely overlooked. So the Urban Ministry came up with three thousand dollars to start a three-month pilot project. It began in January of 1980, and I was one of the original volunteers.

This pilot project was called Dorothy's Place after Dorothy Day. And then they hired a coordinator for a thousand dollars a month! She was a very, very nice lady. Unfortunately, she didn't have a lot of expertise in the type of homeless that I knew we'd be serving. At that time we were at the crest of the wave of deinstitutionalization, and all those mentally ill people were simply pouring onto the streets. We were turning most of them away from the house, and that bothered me a great deal. I'd been receiving the *Catholic Worker* for years and following Dorothy Day, and I held her in very high esteem. Which I still do today. And so I found myself more . . . I was there more and more. And fewer and fewer people were being turned away because I used my expertise as a psychiatric nurse. So women who were epileptics, women who were schizophrenic, women who were manic-depressive, women who had obvious emotional problems, were no longer turned away.

But then the money ran out. Three of us were . . . uh, responded to Dorothy Day's name, and we kept saying, "What are we all arguing about? Why can't we just take up a collection and pay the rent?"

"Oh no! We have to get money to hire a coordinator." And this and that.

I said, "No. You're not listening. Is this Catholic Worker or is it not? If it is, let's take up a collection." I felt deep inside of me that this was really it, what God was leading me to. I'd always been searching. Had done so many things. Seeing women huddled in doorways and seeing them coming through the door raped and beaten and brutalized . . . and the mentally ill especially, the women who were victimized. I felt I had been getting ready for this all my life, so I jumped at it.

The executive director of Catholic Charities found us this house. When we saw it, we were so excited! But it was an absolute disaster when we got inside. Filthy! You had to sandblast the toilets to get them clean. But it was if . . . you know, if we put in an order, we couldn't have got anything so perfect. We wanted something small because we really believe we can touch each person that way, and we firmly believe that people need more than bread alone. And more than just shelter. If they leave this house with hope and a sense that there is a place, a sanctuary somewhere, where there's love and where they're totally accepted for who they are . . . And we've managed to keep that and maintain that.

It's a very quiet, peaceful place. I truly believe that we *do* greet Christ. Each one is Christ. So we want to make it as nice as we possibly can. As clean as it can possibly be. The nicest food served on a plate that doesn't have a crack in it. Each year we get nicer furniture. It's homey. And why not? They deserve it. You would do it for Christ. If I ever hear anyone say, "That will do," I'll say, "Do for who? Do for what?"

We don't believe in putting people corner to corner. We leave room for them to cry. To sit and talk quietly. And it's very therapeutic for the women who have long-term psychiatric problems.

And all the volunteers, all our people, all our Workers . . . The house is in a scary area. We're right in the thick of it, you know, and some people hesitate. But the people who *do* come and stay, they're wonderful! So wonderful! They make a commitment. And we are a real community.

Ro: Now you call this Dorothy Day House. Didn't she say she didn't want houses named after her?

Pat: Well, that's a sure sign of humility and only makes her more saintly. She didn't want to be [regarded as a saint], but I say, "How can one know God's plan for us?"

"I'm sorry Dorothy, my love. Don't deny us because we need you." If it wasn't for Dorothy Day and the example of her own life . . . Years ago I was active in my parish. A multiple person, doing three or four things at once and getting no sense of . . . I just wasn't feeling fulfilled. I didn't feel I was really, really giving. And she showed me the way.

Quite frankly, I couldn't live with lice like she did. We get someone with lice in the house and boy! Wham, bam! Here comes the Kwell! I can't relate to saints like St. Rose of Lima, either. What she did to make herself ugly and unacceptable—ugh!

Ro: The bedrooms are all named after saints, aren't they? Who named them?

Pat: The original core group did. Each one had her own favorite, of course. My favorite was Mary Magdalene. I was outnumbered for St. Joan of Arc. She was just too much of a warrior saint for my tastes, but the younger women were raging feminists and they outnumbered me.

Ro: And St. Dinsma?

Pat: St. Dinsma lives and thrives in this house. St. Dinsma, who was murdered by her father. She's prayed to, yes, she is. And of course St. Monica, who was an abused woman for fourteen years. And St. Elizabeth because we get a lot of middle-aged women here. We've watched them as they reach out to the younger women. In my vision of St. Elizabeth, I see her at the visitation reaching out to little Mary.

We have Mass every second Thursday. I wish it was more heavily attended. It's not. But it's . . . we need to have Mass in this house. Every woman in the house comes, no matter what. We don't ask people if they're Catholic. Whether I'm theologically correct or not, I don't know. I cannot see a compassionate Christ turning anybody away from His table. That's my theory. Right or wrong, I have to carry it with me.

We have a wonderful house priest who recognizes . . . who feels the same way, has the same philosophy, and he explains the Mass to everybody. And then offers them the host. If they feel they'd like to take Jesus . . . he explains what we believe, and leaves it up to the people. If we have children, they are just so part of everything. He keeps hosts aside for them that are not consecrated. We have Kool-aid and Father blesses it.

It's very close, very intimate. We've had many volunteers say this experience has brought them back into the church. The kiss of peace here means something. When we hold each other, and they say, "Oh, you are so good to me," we say, "Why shouldn't we be?" Because we are as one. We are standing side by side. Because we are all broken. I am broken. Everyone here is. There's that sense of unity and solidarity with women. That's what promotes this hope; the little glimmer suddenly lights in each one.

Ro: It's a "safe house," isn't it? In other words, the address is never published?

Pat: It's never published. And it's never photographed from the outside.

Ro: Do many of the women have addiction problems?

Pat: We're seeing more and more of it. I would have to say about sixty-five percent are cocaine related. Either the husband is addicted or the wife, or both of them are. And the brutality is absolutely in extreme.

Ro: What about rules?

Pat: Well, we didn't come in here with a set of rules. Just the basic ones: No alcohol. No weapons. No drugs. No violence. No male acquaintances to come to the door. But over a period of nine months, uh . . . we learned by experience. For instance, we almost had a fire, so now you can't smoke upstairs. We made rules as we went along, but we still only have a page of rules.

We want it to be a sanctuary away from the madness outside. We don't have a television. I won't let one in this house. I won't bring the violence here. This is one place they can come and find tranquility and sisterhood and community and love.

We don't want to take people who are violent. We can't deal with them. We have volunteers here at night who haven't got the experience. And who wants to be having the police here every five minutes?

Ro: Do you have to call the police sometimes?

Pat: Unfortunately, yes. When someone has become psychotic and is a danger to themselves and to the rest of the house. And when someone is very violent, they obviously should not be here. As Stanley Vishnewski once said, "There's always room for one more. But it's not you." They obviously need help. And of course the only way to get them involuntarily committed for treatment is to call the police. It's not something that we like to do, believe me. But we have to think of the children and the other women and the welfare of this person when her mind is like a salad and she can't distinguish what is right from wrong or everything is too unreal.

Dorothy Day said you should do as much as you possibly can and when you can't do any more, then it's time for the state. The state has to take some responsibility. Then we gladly take them back, you know, when the episode is over.

Ro: I noticed a box that says, "The Grace of God box." What's in that box?

Pat: There are a few people that we just can't take because they're a danger to themselves and to the house. Like someone who will turn on all the [gas] jets. Someone who is extremely violent. Someone who steals everything in sight. I know we're supposed to give everything plus the coat on our back. But if we have no food to give people when they come in, you know, we're not much use, are we? It's generally for very good reasons. But these are people that we can't have here. And . . . and their names are in that box. If a volunteer is on duty and gets a phone call, she looks in that box. You know, if we want to keep the environment . . . we can't save the world. We can only do a little bit.

We want to give quality to the people that we have here. Especially children. We have to be mindful of the children. Because they are coming from trauma, coming from situations that . . . it would boggle our minds. They don't need to see or hear an abusive woman screaming and cursing and yelling, and we certainly don't need for someone to go into the kitchen and light a cigarette and blow the bloody house up, now do we? So these are the kinds of people that are in the "Grace of God" box. There are about seventy, which isn't bad over eight years.

Ro: Do you have a limit on how long the women can stay?

Pat: The brochure says approximately twenty days. Years ago, that's all it took to get someone hooked up to services and a place to live. Now with the housing situation, it's catastrophic. And so the length of stay could be anywhere, thirty-five days or even longer. We had one woman with seven children [who stayed] fifty-five days. We had an AIDS victim for three months. We take people according to their crisis situation, and we work with the problem. It's not "Okay, twenty days, up and out on the street you go." There are compromises made all the time. We throw the rule book out the window. "Well, let's try this."

Many times you get up to a point with people, though. See, it's so nice here. They settle in. It's like home, so they don't feel they have to make too much of an effort because everybody's so nice. But then the time comes. "Well, listen, what have you done [about changing your situation]? Because we're turning away people."

Department of Social Services will not issue vouchers for single women. Not even for a bed. They'll give money for an apartment but not furniture 'cause they want [the women] to try to get it free first. So we go out and we collect things.

We'll take anything as long as it's not over three hundred and fifty pounds and needs food. Linens . . . anything, and we store it. Because the women come here in what they stand up in, and when they resettle, they need just about everything. God has always been so generous. We're not rich. But we've never been at a point where we have to say we can't go on. We always have just enough, just enough to keep us straight.

Ro: Who goes out to talk to groups to get the furniture and raise money?

Pat: Well, Rita Gormley does some of it, but they lean on me pretty heavily. It's like being a conductor, you know. I must say I like to do it, though, and if I'm talking about the Gospel message, I can honestly say it's not me doing it. I always say a little prayer on my way to a talk. I say, "Please, Holy Spirit, take over for me because I'm doing it for You and I want to do it right."

At first it was very frightening to me. My voice would quiver and shake. I used to write everything down and read from a paper. This went on for about six months. I just kept praying. Like St. Terese, I pray and expect it's going to happen. So gradually I began to [talk] off the top of my head. I'm a fairly avid reader and I remember anything to do with the homeless—statistics—I know what's happening nationally. The numbers and the horror stories. I've got a hundred of them.

My opening speech is, "I didn't come here to spread good news. And if I send you home depressed, I apologize beforehand. It's a very depressing subject. But it's a subject, by God, that you're going to hear about! You *must* hear it!"

Ro: Do you ever have children here who sometimes have to be . . . their mothers can't take care of them, and they have to become wards of the court?

Pat: Oh, yes. Yes. It's never done arbitrarily. It's . . . we see two sides here. We see a person who cannot cope with her own life, and we see a little victim who cannot speak out for themselves. We've seen some pretty gross negligence, and it's our duty for both people. It's not done in a vindictive way, and it's not done arbitrarily. Unfortunately, we don't get the results many times that we hope for.

Ro: You mean from the system?

Pat: Through the system. Many times we see a situation walk out that door and all we can do is hit our knees. We've seen some pretty bad things here. We probably saved a child from being killed upstairs. The mother just . . . she was a very big woman, and she just threw herself on top of this child. We could hear the muffled screaming, and we ran up and pulled her off this little girl. It's kind of scary. It *is* scary.

You know, I believe to be a Catholic Worker you must be an advocate. You must be a voice, a voice [against] injustice, a voice against war. I see all this money spent on the military as clearly a violation of the rights of millions of people, the right to have a roof over their head and to be able to have work so that they can put food on the table for their family.

I see this as just as serious and just as terrible as the nuclear question. When I go and get arrested for civil disobedience, I'm going for the homeless. I'm saying, "How dare you spend trillions of dollars on these weapons of destruction when our people are living on the street and suffering and dying and children are being victimized and brutalized because you insist on spending money for arms."

If you had known me twenty years ago, you'd never have dreamed that I'd be able to . . . the telephone terrified me. I never liked to pick up the telephone because somebody would say hello, and I'd have to say hello back, and I'd have to carry on a conversation. This is a fire that's not me. It's coming from somewhere else. Now I think being arrested is nothing. It really isn't. It's very easy to do. They're very nice to you. Just frisk you a little bit. Take your picture.

Ro: But they're not always nice to you, Pat.

Pat: Oh, one gentleman . . . I must admit . . . a great big tall air force person pushed me up against the wall, and he handcuffed my . . . he handcuffed me very, very rough. And my friend Peggy who is about eighty-five pounds—he just looked at her and went, "Nah." I must look like a real criminal. [Laughter.] Anyway, he threw me in the back of a . . . he was very, extremely rough. I said, "Why are you so angry at me?"

I know why he was angry. Because I was holding a sign accusing the government of all kinds of atrocities, which are true. He was copying it down, writing furiously word for word. And the more he wrote, the angrier he'd get. If there's a next time, and there surely will be, I'm going to have my wits about me. I'm just going to make a big holy pest of myself.

Unity Kitchen

Ro: Was it in '79, Ann, that you began to get . . . to become more defined?

Ann O'Connor: That's a good way to say it. In 1979 we began a very lengthy and deep process of discernment: Who are we and what is God's will for us? What is our vocation as Christians and as Catholics? Where do we go? What are we doing, and why are we doing it?

Ro: What was the catalyst for that?

Ann: Well, it was kind of strange. Dr. Wolfensberger, Wolf Wolfensberger from Syracuse University, asked us if Unity Kitchen would consider having one of his teams evaluate us as a human service under the PASS program (Program Analysis of Service Systems). Wolfensberger had a reputation around town as a "normalizer" of human services. How could anyone ever normalize us in any way? We all got a big kick out of it. But we could get two free courses at the university if we accepted the evaluation. "What the heck! It's going to be a joke, but at least we'll get two free courses."

Are you with me still? So in comes Wolfensberger's evaluation team. Spent a week or two with us in terms of talking and being there and observing. And then many months in preparing their report. Of course, when we finally got the report from the evaluation team, it was disastrous! My feelings over the years had been that there was no other way to serve poor people. There [were] things that I wasn't comfortable with, and lots of things I had doubts about, but I didn't know of any other way. Anyway, when the report came through and pointed out what we were doing to these human beings, it was like a breath of fresh air.

Up until 1979, we were a big soup kitchen, giving out food and clothes and all that. Two meals a day and a shelter at night. We had thirty-five beds upstairs, and we slept maybe sixty-five. Distributed clothes for men and went to court and did all these things. Typical Catholic Worker, I guess.

One of the solutions [the report suggested] was to close down the Kitchen. That it was *so* bad and we were doing so much damage to the poor people in *so* many ways. But one of the praises was the commitment of the workers and the hard work. They saw that our ideals were still fresh. Everyone was there from a highly idealistic perspective and motivation. Another thing they liked was the tremendous amount of self-sacrifice.

What they criticized was the devaluing and dehumanizing situation—context and environment and service and *everything*. It was dirty, and it was crowded and it was noisy and violent and impersonal.

Peter King (Ann's husband): Let me add that the institute Wolf Wolfensberger has is called the Human Training Institute. They train human service workers to be agents of change in the institutional environment and in society as a whole. They were very much the agents of change for us, or at least the agents of reflection. One of the things they kept asking us, over and over again in the interviews, was what our decision-making process was. And we didn't *have* a decision-making process. Of course, their concern was how would we implement change if we didn't have a decision-making process?

Ro: In their analysis, did they tell you what your hidden decision-making process was? I mean there always is one.

Ann: It was pretty obvious to us. We just let things happen.

Peter: Yeah. We'd make a decision, and it wouldn't be comprehensive enough, so we'd make another decision to shore it up. Then we'd make another decision to veto the former two and come up with another one. Very helter-skelter. Catholic Worker anarchy, maybe.

Ann: Not real anarchism. Even though we didn't have a decision-making process, they felt that, given some of the good points of the Catholic Worker hospitality and personalism and history, given the fact that we were young and we had ideals and a sense of a willingness to suffer for them, they thought that *maybe,* you know, something good could come from the work.

In the spring of '78, there's a key event I should mention because it always stays in mind. We had spent a whole afternoon talking about the problem of large numbers. Wolf said, "Well, now, when all you people get together and pray, I suggest that you begin to pray that God would reveal His will for you."

I looked at Wolf. "We don't pray together."

And Wolf almost fainted. "What are we talking about? What are we spending all this time on? This is where you must begin. This is it!" And he threw his arms up.

He said, "Can you draw some people together who will pray together about the Kitchen? People who are involved as volunteers, as workers, just anybody who cares about what happens to the Kitchen, or is willing to pray with you and has faith as a Christian? Can you do that?" So that was the beginning of our Christian discernment.

It's very clear now that Wolf Wolfensberger was instrumental in the changes in the Kitchen, even though he wasn't really a member of that original evaluation team. (They just submitted drafts to him as project director.) In the spring of '79, we began to meet. By July we were down to Peter and a guy named Ron Jaworski and Harry Murray as workers. And of course myself—I was doing a lot of the background stuff, the newsletters and all [the] organizing of food volunteers and drivers and so on. The discernment was going on within what we began to call the base community. We were also working on a document for an articulation of our identity and of our vocation. And that document, that articulation to ourselves and to the world, took four years.

The original document came out on the fiftieth anniversary of the Catholic Worker movement. The ten members read sections of the Declaration at Mass on Sunday, May first, 1983. We've made two revisions, always additions, since the first one, one in 1985 and one in 1987.

Ro: What do you call the document?

Ann: Declaration of Faith and Principles of Unity Kitchen Community of the Catholic Worker. A little history on the base community: In the beginning, we decided we wanted to grow organically. The first meeting was four people. At every meeting, we'd invite a few more, and that group grew to at least thirty active people. Over the years, we've invited eighty or ninety people. Some came and stayed a while and left, some said no, and some came and stayed a long time. As the discussion deepened and the issues became more profound, there was an attrition rate.

Our decision-making process was to reach consensus. Everyone in the group had to agree. After long discussions and painful times—tears and everything—the group was finally . . . then everyone would agree and that would be it. A long difficult process.

Ro: Did some of the people leave because they didn't want to take the time for the process or because they could see that their ideas would never be a consensus?

Ann: Or they just couldn't agree with the direction we were evolving in. I think more Catholic Workers than you realize have tried to draw up statements of some sort. Since 1983 when we first published ours, we've seen quite a bit of it. We see the real weaknesses in them and the good attempts, you know, and the goodwill involved, but they're not able to come to grips with the real issues, so they just sort of fade away. The Declaration for us has been very, very important and continues to be in so many ways. It guides us in so many things.

Ro: Now do you ask people to subscribe to it when they join you, or how does that work?

Ann: For hospitallers—Peter and myself and Mary, the full-time people who've made the work [their lives]—we would ask for a real identification with the Declaration.* Volunteers: they get it. They know who we are and what we believe. And even though they can't subscribe (maybe because they're not Catholics, you know), if they can accept the hospitality, for example, as servers, and can live with us being who we are, fine. Base community members definitely have to be able to identify with it.

* In transcript review, Ann and Peter suggested substituting "some form of support for" for the original words "a real identification with."

Ro: What's the difference between hospitallers and base community members?

Ann: The base community members are people who have longtime or serious commitments to the Kitchen. They have families, they have jobs, but they identify with the Kitchen. So the Declaration gives all of us a real sense of stability and continuity.

Peter: Let me clarify something here. A new member of the Unity Kitchen base community would not have the background or the benefit of six, seven years of discernment. So that person, while identifying in substance, could work their way into some of the more difficult concepts handled in the Declaration. I wouldn't expect them to be able to go out in public and teach on the Declaration, for instance, after being a Unity Kitchen base community member for only a month.

Ro: How do people join the base community?

Ann: They are invited.

Ro: Can they petition for membership?

Ann: Sure. I don't know if that's happened lately, but I have no problem with that.

Peter: Hospitallers are not automatically members of the base community. They, too, have to be invited. Even if they've accepted the Declaration in substance. There is a loose trial period. Even if a hospitaller were here, let's say two or three years, they would not automatically be a base community member. Nor do they automatically share in the decision-making process that would define policies or take on a new witness or sponsor a new event.

Ann: The unity of life position is a very important stance within the Kitchen community. Let's say that person is working through a lot, is really trying to sort it out. Maybe there's even a movement towards a real antiabortion position, but it's not really clear yet. Well, that person would not really be able to make it in this community. Would not be accepted or invited to be a member if they hadn't really come to a clear position. And they might never.

Peter: This discussion may seem very alien to Catholic Worker practices. But we've seen people who come to Catholic Workers with let's say a one- or two-year commitment and make very serious decisions that could change the direction of a house for years to come. They make these changes and then they leave. Who lives with the decision?

People who are not what we used to call full-time Workers but who attend Mass regularly at the Kitchen or have been supporters for five or ten years have a much better feel for the spirit of Unity Kitchen Community than a person who might come full time for one or two years.

Ro: What's the main difficulty that people might have with the Declaration of Faith?

Ann: I think there are three or four. Our identification as Catholics in submission to our local bishop and in submission to the teaching authority of the church is a real hurdle, particularly for Catholics.

Another is the unity of life position. You know, we speak strongly against abortion and euthanasia and capital punishment and war and all kinds of oppression—the whole death-making system at work in our nation.

There's our teaching of the doctrine of the Fall. People have a hard time understanding that all institutions or structures are fallen and are therefore under some degree of demonic control.* And our position about unholy alliances. As Christians proclaiming the sovereignty of Jesus Christ over all life, we try to be very clear in our public witness about that. To get involved in a public witness that includes those who might be very strong, let's say, against capital punishment . . . we would be comfortable with being with them because they're against capital punishment, but maybe they've been publicly notorious for their pro-abortion. We'd call any involvement with them an unholy alliance. Because it weakens our clarity, and it would weaken our witness in terms of the unity of life.

It's very important to us that these issues are not isolated. If anyone speaks for the sacredness of life on one level but then is incoherent or contradicts it in another level, we couldn't really align ourselves with them. A lot of the Catholic Workers might say, "Well, we're against abortion . . . well, most of us are, but some of us aren't, so we can't deal with it. We're not going to really try to get involved in that issue."

Ro: Where do you get the money to keep going?

Ann: Donations. It's mostly individuals now. We're losing the church. We've lost support over the years—personal support and financial support and individuals coming in, too—as our witness became clearer and clearer, and we became more articulate and bolder about it, really. Especially about the unity of life or the demonic forces at work in our culture and in our institutions. Lately, we've taken a stance about [General Electric], which is a big sacred cow here. Every time

---

* In transcript review, Ann and Peter requested that the phrase "including the CW movement" be added to modify "people" in this sentence.

we take a stance like this and a public witness, people either leave physically and don't volunteer anymore or withdraw their financial support.

Ro: What do you do to witness politically?

Ann: We get right down in the marketplace and leaflet. We've also done preaching in front of the cathedral on a Peace Pentecost event promoted by Sojourners, and we've done lots of leafleting on different occasions on different issues. And our newsletters . . . it really amazes me that this little mimeographed newsletter that we send around can cause such a to-do. You know, it's as if it's the *New York Times!*

Ro: I remember reading in one of your newsletters that you had an outdoor stations of the cross.

Ann: We do that every year. It's very political. I mean we're speaking to very clear issues, and they're all connected in the statement that we make and the publicity.

Peter: We've lost two co-sponsors, Jail Ministry, which is some kind of a closet Catholic Worker in Syracuse, and Syracuse Pax Christi. We lost them because of our need to witness in public to the unity and sanctity of life and the indivisibilty of death.

Ann: Particularly abortion.

Peter: Particularly on abortion. Going to Planned Parenthood was controversial. Since then, we ask those who are going to present the meditations for a specific station to be able to assent to the unity of life position.* So that cuts down on who can be a presenter, too. Most everybody who does a station is someone we know and have had discussions with over the years. We invite them. It's important, as I mentioned, that the stations have real integrity, so to have someone do a station on one life issue but on the other hand really be pro-war or pro–capital punishment would be incoherent for us.

When this GE issue began last January, the diocesan response to it was very negative. No particular person publicly, but people who called gave us heck about it and wanted to close the Kitchen and all that. We want the bishop to be able to claim us as part of his flock, want the bishop to be protective of us as a shepherd because we submit ourselves to his teaching authority. Perhaps the bishop

---

* Peter and Ann changed the last seven words, which said "identify in substance with the Declaration" on the tape.

didn't feel too protective of us because one of our stations this year was at the chancery. Taking the church to task about its usurious wealth.

Ro: Is your group dwindling because of the purity of your purpose?

Ann: Well, hospitallers stay about the same in terms of the numbers. The base community is down to four or five members now. Numbers are not a problem. We've lost a few volunteers, too. And I think money . . . we've been in a money squeeze now for a while.

Peter: We've been described as an island that's getting smaller and smaller.

Ann: But when you lose one person, we often gain another. So it's hard to say.

Peter: I think we'll go down to a certain level. Then we'll start coming up again.

Ann: Maybe at that level, we'll sink. [Laughter.]

Peter: Well, that would be all right, wouldn't it?

Ann: That would be all right.

Ro: What about your relationship with the larger Catholic Worker community?

Ann: There's a real sense of being alone here. We love it when Catholic Workers come through and visit and share stories and tell us what's going on here and there and the other place. You can't tell what's going on in the Catholic Worker house by their newsletters and newspapers unless you become astute at reading between the lines. I wish there was a Catholic Worker or Workers who would just travel.

Ro: What do you see as the marks of the Catholic Worker?

Ann: The Catholic Worker, by its very name, is *Catholic.* Okay, that's first. It's submissive to the teaching authority of the church. It's Catholic worship, not some of the vague stuff. (That's very Dorothy Day and Peter Maurin.)

Then I would believe there should be a unity of life stance. The overarching issue of the day in this country is the sacredness of *all* human life. Not just peace and not just abortion. The overarching issue is the sanctity and unity of *all* human life. The Catholic Worker, I think, somehow has got to resolve that and identify with that, or they're not going to continue.

There has to be real personalistic hospitality. Not these big, massive, impersonal efforts that devalue the poor. Also, we used to feel that the work was everything, and if you had community, that was a good by-product of the movement. Now we think differently: There has to be community, an explicit Christian community, and the work comes out of that. What would be predominant would be prayer and discernment of God's will for the community.

Ro: Peter, what's your central focus?

Peter: Well, I like to think of myself as living a life. People are goal oriented, success oriented. And to "live a life" means you're quality oriented. There's a wonderful thought in Thich Nhat Hanh's *Be Here Now.* As a young novice in a Buddhist order, one of the first criteria in his novitiate was to learn how to make and serve a cup of tea. I think that's what we're learning how to do. We're learning how to present Christian hospitality to the poor, and we're feeling wonderfully the sanctifying effects of that.

Ann: There's one more thought I'd like to add. I think my experience is unique. Most Catholic Workers see themselves as serving upon the poor, serving upon the wounded or the marginal. But my experience as a handicapped person is that I'm served upon as much as, if not more than, the poor. I'm very much served upon, not only by my community and Peter and Mary and all those in the base community, but by our guests. That's really a very important part of my life. Simple things like people at the table helping me with serving food to myself and helping me with the tasks that I have in the Kitchen and community. The roles are constantly reversed.

> After this conversation, which took place at Hesed House, where the hospitallers live, Ann and Peter took me to Unity Kitchen, where I was their guest for dinner. Then Ann and I finished the interview outside under a shade tree, while Peter and Mary, the other hospitaller, finished up the kitchen work.

Ann: We began what we call lavish hospitality for the poor. It was hard, but we cut the number of guests down to twenty-four, mostly the old men in the streets who are so vulnerable, the ones who fall through the so-called cracks. When someone dies or leaves town, we add someone from our special guest list.

Ro: It didn't look as if there were twenty-four when we were eating tonight.

Ann: It is . . . it was down tonight. It's unpredictable. (I guess it is with soup kitchens, too.) You never know. Some nights you know, it's really a full register.

Ro: You planned your surroundings to be so special. How did you fund that? And can you describe them?

Ann: We sent out a letter of appeal. I spoke to churches and we got some money that way. The space used to be a printing shop. When we moved in, it was really grimy and oily, and the floors were a mess and the walls were dingy and covered with pasted-on calendars. So we stripped everything, just gutted the whole place. Everything that you see in the Kitchen, which is so beautiful, is what we've done—a large, spacious dining area; bright yellow paint; beautiful pictures and posters. In the front when you first walk in, there's a nice lounge with beautiful carpeting and rockers and tables and lots of good literature and magazines.

Ro: When do the guests use that area?

Ann: We have a five-thirty dinner, so guests can begin to arrive about four-thirty. There's always ice water in the lounge before dinner. And they can stay afterwards as long as we're here, but I'd say the greater number leave shortly after dinner.

When you come in, there's a real sense of space, which poor people don't usually have. They are usually crowded and crazy. The dining area is well laid out with really beautiful tables that we designed specially out of light woods— oak and ash. Six tables that sit six each with matching chairs. They were given to us by the Bruderhof.

Ro: Where do you get your flowers?

Ann: We have a connection with a flower wholesaler. One guest who used to get so crazy went out the other day and picked a beautiful bouquet of wildflowers and brought them to the Kitchen because the ones on the tables had wilted from the heat. He said to me that night, "I'm a divorced man. One of the reasons for my divorce is we didn't have enough flowers."

Ro: And the food?

Ann: All our food is donated. A food volunteer makes a commitment to bring in seven dollars worth of X kind of food once a month. You know, like . . . the minimum is seven dollars worth of let's say pork chops. I lay out the food list, and we send it out every four months. We also have some nice connections with caterers, so we very often get beautiful food from them. Friends who work in some of the school cafeterias sometimes shuffle stuff our way if it piles up on them or something. Food comes in various ways like that, but we know what's coming, so we can plan.

I want to say something else about our guests: Some people think we have a select few—the elite of street people or whatever. But I'd say half of our register are the same guests who used to be aggressive and very often violent in the old place.

Ro: Hmm. Do you still have problems with violence?

Ann: Well, when you're working with wounded people, there's always that potential. And you have it with . . . sometimes volunteers get angry. Now the man who ate with you tonight goes to the night shelter and acts out every night, practically, in really aggressive ways.

Ro: He was so courtly with you, I thought.

Ann: He's wonderful. But he has a lot of rage, you know, and every now and then it will come up. The potential violence here is so much different and so much more manageable and so rare. That's a proof that if you treat people with respect and expect them to respond, it's automatic—it just happens.

Most of our guests are very concerned about retaining peace in the Kitchen. They're greeted at the door with the peace of Christ. If anybody is really aggressive at the door, really acting badly, we invite them not to come in. Because they can't accept the peace of Christ. But I can't remember when one our registered guests came to the door drunk, and we had to say no. They just don't come. There's really a lot of respect for the place. You give a reciprocal respect towards people and you receive it back. And they're very concerned that other guests regard [the Kitchen] in the same way.

It's really amazing. You know, when we began the changes, people would tell us that we couldn't have glass dinner plates and glass glasses. (Everything used to be plastic.) "Because you know how they throw things around, and they don't know how to eat and nobody's going to pass food at the table." As soon as we began the family-style dinner, all these beautiful manners emerged.

I love to see a reversal of roles in hospitality when the guests respond to somebody new. They really try to make them feel welcome, you know, and keep an eye out for them.

Ro: I was entertained by them. I felt that. And I liked the clean look with the fresh flowers and different napkin colors and the light furniture. Sort of Scandinavian.

Ann: Yes, everything matches, every little thing. We had the silverware monogrammed especially for UK, and it's still all there. In the old days, we couldn't even have salt and pepper on the tables because people would throw them at each other.

Ro: Now the Kitchen is very efficiently organized. Is Peter sort of the efficiency expert?

Ann: No. I think we've just evolved into a way of doing things that seems to be the best for us.

Ro: I'm going to have to say good-bye now, but have you any "famous last words," anything else we ought to talk about?

Ann: Well, I think the Catholic Worker ideal is Catholicism. Real authentic Catholicism. The vocation is to be a prophetic witness to the church—to the church and to the world, but really our primary witness is to the church. Calling the church back to its true vocation so that it can call the world back to submitting itself to Christ.

Unity Acres in Orwell

Fr. Ray McVey: We borrowed money to get the house [in town]. Just on collar power. (I had no salary, but of course, the banker didn't know that.) Kate [Stanton] was too busy to be very involved in the house in the very beginning. But after . . . oh, I guess about three or four months, there was . . . no bills were being paid. If any money came in, I used it for the immediate needs in the neighborhood. A group of women went down to a bank and took out a loan to pay off all these bills. And I've never handled money since.

Ro: And has that sort of evolved on you, Kate?

Kate Stanton: Yes. I got things going, and I'm still doing it. Twenty-two years.

Ro: Twenty-two years.

Kate: Well, I took a break once. Went into the city for seven months. But I had to come back.

Ro: Now, even when you had the house in town, were you mostly doing hospitality for men?

Fr. McVey: Yeah. I started just by walking the neighborhood. The first man who came was a heroin addict. Right on his heels were . . . it was filled. We had three tiers of bunks. Wall-to-wall people. That was the idea: just hospitality, no rehab. And also to feel the pain . . . just to be one with them. That's all. And then we realized that it was just inhuman to live like that, that there was no way the men could be whole. I knew this place out here existed. It was an old tuberculosis sanitarium and it was empty. Finally, we were able to get it. The whole thing cost seven thousand dollars plus two thousand in taxes. Seven buildings and 135 acres.

Kate: I went to the New York house and told Dorothy what our plans were. "You go back and tell him he's crazy. It'll never work."

Fr. McVey: She said, "It would be the act of a fool. Don't you dare do it!"

Kate: The first time she came up, she says, "Kate," she says, "Every time I've thought of what I said to you, I've wanted to bite my tongue."

Fr. McVey: [Laughs.] We came up with just five men. I announced it in the house and told them we were moving in a week. Only five dared risk the country. In a very short time, we got up to 180 men. Whoever comes, we welcome.

We haven't tried to do anything in depth. Just offer hospitality and try to encourage community. The men are marvelous, they really are. To have this many people without fights. I've always considered that the minor—or maybe major—miracle of Unity Acres. That there are no fights. If there are, the man has to leave for good. He knows that.

Ro: But you have some rules.

Kate: Two. No drinking and no violence.

Fr. McVey: If they drink while they're here, they have to leave for thirty days.

Ro: You know, when I walked in today, everybody greeted me. I didn't feel any demarcations. Do you think the physical space you have here helps with the nonviolence?

Fr. McVey: Yes.

Ro: You can walk away. You can walk off into the woods. Or up the hill to the cemetery.

Fr. McVey: In every building there's a common room, a room where you can just have space. In those early years, we had wall-to-wall beds everywhere and a lot more tension. Now there's more space, and a man can really be alone if he wants to. There's a coffee room that's open from early morning—five, six o'clock—to eleven o'clock at night. They can have community there if they want to. There are only two dorm areas; everything else is one, two, or three beds in a room. They can have a refrigerator in their own room. They can put in a TV. Anything but heavy appliances. They smoke wherever they want to. That's another minor miracle. Or a major one because the smoking habits aren't good. We've only had one bad fire, and no one was hurt, thank God.

Now most of the men get SSI, social security, or veterans' [payments]. In the early days, the few that had checks could buy anything they wanted, buy themselves stuff at check time. And then we reached the point of saying, you know, that we really had to encourage them to be responsible, so we'd ask them for half. But then it was really quite possible with just a little bit of help maybe, for us to be almost independent.

Kate handles the finances. It's her worry, not mine, but I went away and prayed about it and came back with this real elaborate thing. That we will give all the men's donations to third world poverty, to poverty beyond us, to unfunded causes. I thought, "Kate will never buy this. I'll never convince her!" But she said, "Great idea!"

Kate: The amount of money we were getting, it . . . it kind of bothered me, and I had never mentioned it to him.

Fr. McVey: We were too independent. And independence is not . . . has never been a goal of the Gospel. [Giving the money away] frees you up to live by faith. Then we had to get this point across to the men. We had a big meeting and said, "We may go hungry." ('Cause we really thought it would be difficult.) "But this is the way it's going to be." There was an immediate response. And we've never really struggled or had . . . we've had to ask [for donations] a few times but very seldom.

Kate: The poor are helping the poor. The men still keep some of their money. And then the men who don't get any checks get a dollar and a half a day from the men who do get checks, so they have a little something to spend. (There's a little canteen where they can buy things. A cheeseburger. Some pop.)

For a long time, we gave the extra money to Hope Wallis who wanted to start a Catholic Worker–based co-op, a working co-op. That reached the point when it should be on its own, so the latest thing is a parish house of hospitality. The men who should be receiving the benefit are the ones who are helping. We now have a parish house of hospitality in De Witt, which is a suburb of Syracuse.

There is some opposition, some formal parish opposition. The people are saying, "Well, it's not our problem." But it *is* their problem. You [bring it up] in the parish council—a parish house of hospitality—and it will never go. But we're confident that in time and with the good will of . . . There's a man who is just giving his all. He left everything and is living there. And he's calling in people. Like ten days out of the month he's got covered now with families making meals and bringing them to the house. It will come from the people and not from the parish council.

Ro: Some people say that men who have lived on the street and have lived in tense situations for so long . . . when you put them in the middle of noplace, they just can't take it. Can't take the quiet. Do you have much of that?

Fr. McVey: Yes, we have some of that. Of course. But some will change. We can see the growth of many, many people who have been sober now for maybe four or five years.

Ro: Is your population getting older?

Kate: Oh, it is indeed.

Fr. McVey: We've buried seventy men up on the hill. We have a huge medical problem, especially with these veterans. And that's one of the roles of the hospitality house [in De Witt]. The men can stay there and get good hospitality and kind of a break from here. And then they'll run them to the clinic. It's kind of a connector or link. The men don't want to go into nursing homes. So this, too, could be a role of the hospitality house. It's too bad Unity Acres has to exist so far away from the city because the involvement [of volunteers] isn't great.

Kate: Almost nil.

Fr. McVey: A Methodist couple came years ago. He came in a dream. He had just retired, and he had a dream one night. And he woke up and he said to his wife, "I've got to go to that Unity Acres." The dream was of a lonely man on a hillside.

Kate: They were a beautiful couple.

Fr. McVey: Yes. They gave day and night for twelve years. She died suddenly, and he's eighty now. He was over last night. One of the big problems is society's neglect of older men. We've struggled with that for years. We don't have a big volunteer group here. Getting people to appointments and all this sort of thing is hard. The men generally care for each other, but the rooms get awful dirty. Personal bathing and just, you know . . . so that's our . . .

Ro: What about folks to talk to people?

Fr. McVey: Oh, you'll have to meet Carol Guthrie. That's all she does. All day. She sits and talks. All day long. That would drive me crazy.

Ro: You're a plumber, a fixer . . .

Kate: When you can make him sit down, it's very unusual. I'm certainly enjoying [talking like] this today. We live in the same building, and outside of Mass, I probably see Father ten minutes in a whole day.

Fr. McVey: So many chores that need to be done, you know. To just sit and talk . . . or if anybody mentioned the word counseling formally, I'd shake. If it just happens within a lifestyle, okay, but Carol does this and it's good.

Ro: Oh, that's great! Father, what's the biggest disappointment you've had with Unity Acres?

Fr. McVey: Biggest disappointment?

Ro: I keep trying to get you to say something negative. [Laughter.]

Fr. McVey: Biggest disappointment? I really don't think in terms of disappointment. One of the big ones, I guess, has been the slowness of parish houses of hospitality to emerge. It's really the role of the church. Faithfulness in families is a lost concept today.

Kate: The men have such a fear of having to leave here.

Fr. McVey: So we try to be faithful to them.

When I left, Fr. McVey was sitting in the canteen feeding lunch to Bob, a former guest who now lives in a nursing home but who comes home to Unity Acres one day a week.

CHAPTER 26

Across the Country

> To start a house, all you have to do is get a house and live in it, and put up a sign and you have a Catholic Worker going. There are no formalities. But that's the easy part—getting started.
>
> —*Fr. Richard McSorley*

Barbara Blaine: I still think you can only feel what a Catholic Worker is by being there. I remember one time Gary and I traveled to about thirteen or fourteen different Worker houses in a period of a few weeks. Every house is different, and yet there's something the same, too. Every house is chaotic in certain ways. Every house seems to have roaches.

Gary Olivero: The first word you choose is "chaos" and the second is "bugs." Now we're getting to the essence of the Catholic Worker!

THIS chapter examines what some might call "ongoing accidents," or how individual Catholic Worker communities adapt the social vision that is the Worker to meet the circumstances of time and place. As I collected the interviews, I visited about half of the over 130 Catholic Worker houses currently in operation. (No one ever gets a really accurate list but the *Catholic Worker* often provides an update; I've included the 1992 list as Appendix B.) The houses described in the following pages represent only a few of the many configurations. There really are as many different kinds of Worker houses as there are houses.

San Jose, California

Peter Miron-Conk: I visited like six or eight Catholic Worker houses and got a pretty good feeling for what was going on. Said, "Yeah, this is for me. This is what I want to do." Came back to California after the summer. I guess I was somewhat in awe of the Catholic Workers. (I still am.) So I wasn't really going to call myself a Catholic Worker house. I was just going to do hospitality and stuff. I got a lot of encouragement from people, but nobody offered to help or anything, so I thought maybe it wasn't such a great idea after all.

Finally, one day in January a friend of mine said, "If you just keep talking about it, it's never going to happen. Let's just do it." So we went down to St. James Park where a lot of homeless and needy hang out, and we started serving them food. We'd show up in my old Volkswagen with food in the back. About fifty, sixty, people a day would come and eat. At the time, I really didn't know who the homeless were. And I certainly didn't love them. So being in the park was an opportunity for me to find out who people were and to learn about them and care about them. It was really personal. No institution at all. When you move into a house, it's immediately seen as an organization. Eventually, I *did* rent a house in downtown San Jose, though, 'cause we kept getting hassled by the health department for serving outside.

We didn't have much money. Coffee was the single most expensive item that we used, and that started to rub me the wrong way, so a group of us had a little education about ourselves and coffee. It was really pretty clear that coffee was just a commercial cash crop and had absolutely no food value, so we decided not to buy coffee or serve it unless it was donated.

We also said if we weren't going to serve coffee to the people on the street, then we wouldn't drink it ourselves. So we had a coffee-free house. I haven't had a cup of coffee since 1974. I think we were somewhat arrogant and self-righteous and not aware of how many other compromises we were making just by living, but still we . . . we were trying to make important decisions and to do things that were right for people. And certainly, in terms of what we gave to the community, the economic cost was really minimal.

We served meals seven days a week. We also did a lot of bizarre stuff. Social Services learned that if they couldn't resolve a problem, they could call the Catholic Worker because we could do whatever we wanted. We did anything—move old ladies and so forth. We had a sixty-five-year-old psychotic, an undocumented man from Mexico, who refused to sleep inside. Who would urinate all over himself and hallucinate seriously. Well, he lived with us for four months 'cause nobody else would deal with him. Finally, they were able to get his papers straightened out, so he could go into a nursing home.

At that point, I was pretty self-righteous about the fact that I lived in voluntary poverty, and didn't get paid and worked long hours and gave everything away— all that sort of stuff. Some of which was received appropriately . . . uh, a lot of it was received appropriately. In other words, people saw me as somebody who was trying to come to grips with some really difficult situations. Maybe a little bit arrogantly, but that's one of my weaknesses. Of course, some people just didn't see it at all.

It gets kind of crazy because at that point I didn't wear shoes—hadn't worn shoes for ten, twelve years. On . . . on the positive side, it was a willingness to try to do without and to live simply. On the negative side, there was a certain amount of ego invested in this. But I don't know anybody who lived any simpler . . . We sometimes got in discussions or disputes with other Catholic Workers in terms of simplicity of lifestyle. Again, that was my pushing things to an extreme, but the more it looks like a nonprofit agency, the less I think it's Catholic Worker.

We mostly supported ourselves through part-time jobs. Like I learned to do tile and aluminum construction. I'd work off and on—plan it, you know. Some people wanted to be in the community and work like half-time jobs, and we said they couldn't. I have to admit . . . I mean I set the tone for [the house]. If you're going to be here, you're going to be here.

We didn't need very much money. You know, we could pay our expenses for the community on two, three hundred dollars a month. Anything donated would go immediately to purchase food. At the height, the most money we ever spent was about twelve thousand a year. Serving two hundred people a day, twice a day, and hospitality with six to ten people. Then we had the women's shelter with ten to fifteen women a day. All for twelve thousand dollars a year.

Peter married Norma Miron and they had children.

Peter: Children were the first thing in my life that were more important than Catholic Worker ideals. Suddenly, rather than just doing what I thought was right or best for the world in terms of being on a mission, here was a human being who had needs and could ask things of me. What I thought was best for me now became second-most important and what was best for them became primarily important. And living in community was hard, with people making decisions about what we should or shouldn't do with our children.

We lived in a zoo there—crazy people all the time. This is not the best way or the healthiest way to raise children. It's okay for us as adults to live in this environment. To choose that. We are who we are. But not children. So I think there's been a lot of hurt Catholic Worker children throughout the years. That was a big part of why we chose to live as a family. That lifestyle also included more privacy and being able to have control over our . . . how we raised our children. Not living in such chaos. So we closed the men's house and found Sisters Monica May and Caroline Sanchez, Sisters of Notre Dame, to take over the women's house, Casa de Clara.

Later I talked to Sr. Monica and Sr. Caroline.

Sr. Monica May: Peter was a wonderful, charismatic fellow. At the Second Street house, there got to be more and more women with children joining the lines of the men, and it was rough down there. You kind of had to whistle a happy tune going down to serve because you'd walk through a lot of . . . there was violence very often. There was a lot of alcoholism, and it wasn't a good place for the women and children to be. I think that's what prompted Peter and Norma to start this house for families. We were able to come in and continue the good thing that he had started, but we couldn't have started it the way Peter did.

Our house is a real safe place. It's a home—where we live—and other people share it with us. Here our sisters can meet people they'd never meet on the street. It's two separate worlds, but here it's a real easy place for people to be who they are and just be okay with each other. A lot of our sisters have come here, and it has been kind of that bridge. It takes away some of the fears of the other—whether it's mentally ill or street people or real poor or alcoholic or whatever. It's different when they're sharing a home with you.

Ro: What's the hardest thing about what you do here?

Sr. Caroline Sanchez: For me personally, it's working with people who are mentally ill. The unpredicatability and the not knowing, really, what's the best thing to help them.

Ro: Do you find that the mentally ill sometimes disrupt other residents?

Sr. Caroline: Sometimes, but not terribly often.

Ro: Maybe that's one of the reasons it's good to be small.

Sr. Caroline: Yes, I think so. And also, this is one of the advantages of having people leave the house during the day. They don't get on each other's nerves.

Sr. Monica: We serve breakfast and provide food for lunches. We serve the evening meal four nights a week. The other three it's available at Loaves and Fishes, which is close by.

Ro: Who does the beautiful garden with the roses and all?

Sr. Monica: Sister Anne does the gardening. She has a wonderful green thumb, and she's . . . we usually have beautiful flowers and vegetables.

Ro: You were telling me earlier about a visitor who came through once and said something about not being a true Catholic Worker house because there were rugs on the floor.

Sr. Caroline: We try not to overcrowd the house, to provide not only a clean place but also a dignified place. To bring some beauty and order into people's lives when they're under a great deal of stress and are just going through some very difficult times.

Joe Zarrella told me, "Oh, that Los Angeles Catholic Worker is something else! They're like the Benedictines, who start another house after they grow bigger than ten people. That's what the Los Angeles Catholic Worker is doing—sending out missionaries, if you will!" Here are stories from two of these missionaries, Julia Occhiogrosso, who went to Las Vegas, and Rio Parfrey, who went with her husband, Jonathan, and their small children to Santa Ana in Orange County, California.

Las Vegas, Nevada

You know, there's a spiritual malaise—a spiritual poverty—that's so deep in Las Vegas. It's a good place for Catholic Workers. So biblical, out in the desert and with all that Roman imagery.   —Mark White

Julia Occhiogrosso: In Los Angeles, we finally clarified what we valued of the Catholic Worker vision through looking at the history and the tradition of Peter and Dorothy. It implied more and more radicalness. As a community, we had grown pretty large and we were losing a sense of identity as a Catholic Worker. We had become comfortable and established. We had enough money, more than enough money. The conflict in the community challenged us, and a lot of people left, but we finally became somewhat of a cohesive group, and decided we couldn't grow in the same way that we had grown before, as an L.A. Catholic Worker. We needed to grow out and start other communities. Even if it meant that we had to sacrifice relationships. We miss each other and there is a sense of loss at times, but we really believe that's a part of radical vision.

I'd been out to the Nevada Nuclear Test Site on my own during Lent. And in 1985, I made a ten-day retreat there and had a lot of time alone in the desert. It was very moving to confront the power of the Test Site and at the same time confront my own powerlessness and recognize the vulnerability that the desert forces upon you. I came back to the L.A. Worker really on fire about how we should be involved in witnessing up there. I grew quite persistent.

It took some time. Finally, people began to see the necessity of resistance at the Test Site as part of the L.A. Worker. Then we had a retreat to find a direction for the community and decided that we would open a house in Las Vegas and a house in Orange County the following year. This was . . . there were only eight of us, and this was a total act of faith. We had to be willing to go out as messengers, to be willing to let go and detach ourselves and move out into the world. And certainly that's what being "on the edge" is about. If you're not on the edge, then you're not aware of how totally dependent on God you are.

Then Rick Chun came by. He was the first, a very beautiful, wonderful man. I had found the house here and began fixing it up. I felt it was so important for Rick and me to be clear about our shared values, our Worker values, so we didn't have different ideas of the Catholic Worker. So the first thing we did after the house blessing in Las Vegas was to sit down together to look at the beliefs and values of the Catholic Worker. Through this discernment process, we came up with three basic areas that we wanted to focus on—community, resistance or prophetic witness, and service.

In the area of community, we planned an open house. Then we had some round-table discussions and decided that we were going to have Wednesday evening Mass, a liturgy, and that when we said "community," we were looking towards the local Las Vegas community.

In the area of service, we decided we were going to have guests in the house, and that we were going to go out on the street, too. We started by serving ice water on D Street in the summertime. Now we serve coffee and donuts. Every day there's at least one outside volunteer. We give out blankets and clothes, take people to the hospital. We also started the newsletter, a quarterly newsletter called *Manna in the Wilderness.* And then on Thursday evening, we serve a meal out of St. James Church to about 125 people.

Orange County, California

Rio Parfrey: Everybody told us to start small. "Slowly, slowly, take your time." So that's what we've done, and we think it's good. We're open to the public on Tuesdays, Wednesdays, Thursdays, and Sundays. On Tuesday we serve snacks, and we let people take showers in our converted garage area. We have a bathroom back there and a nice sitting room. They can take naps on the couches or just hang out with their friends for pretty much the whole day, from nine until three o'clock.

Ro: What about drinking?

Rio: If they drank, we just wouldn't tolerate it. We're monitoring. We're around. And then on Wednesdays and Thursdays, we open also from nine to three, and we serve a formal sit-down meal, a luncheon meal, at eleven o'clock. We serve approximately thirty-five people, as many as will fit in our dining room. We set the table with tablecloths, cloth napkins, china, glasses. No plastic. We really wanted to make it nice. We try to serve different foods, not just soup and bread but a salad and bread and always another cooked vegetable, a main protein dish (either beans or meat) and then some kind of a starch (either potatoes or rice), and a dessert. A real full, full meal.

A couple volunteers really love to cook, and they make their specialties. Like today, our friend Robbie made onion biscuits, which were very good. One day, Ann O'Hare made lasagna for everybody, and that was the best meal we've ever had.

Ro: What happens when the thirty-sixth person comes?

Rio: Well, usually the room is full by ten o'clock, and someone stands outside and tells the folks who come later that we're sorry, but we already have enough people for our meal. "Will you please come back tomorrow?" Even in L.A., we weren't able to serve everyone. We would serve a thousand people and then the thousand and first person would come.

We're a home, and we have extra rooms, and we like to share them with people we know who need a place to stay. We have eleven bedrooms here, and we'll take any combination of people: families, a couple, single men, single women, and let them stay as long as they want to. People are pretty much on their own and out of the house during the day. There are certain things you just have to take into consideration when you are a family. And we have small children, you know. Like we can't take severely mentally ill people or battered women, because the husband will be coming and being violent.

We usually take referrals and don't like to take people just straight off the street unless we've seen them at our lunch tables, although we have asked specific people if we thought we could help them. "Would you like to stay with us?" A lot of times they say no.

And the guests . . . I think it's hard for a lot of people who come to us to accept that we're not a shelter. It's hard for them to think, "I have to be myself around you. I can't lie to you. I have to be responsible to you guys because you're treating me like a responsible human being, so I have to be one." If they can't handle it, they have to leave. That's all I can say.

We're asking people to be responsible, and a lot of these people just can't because they haven't done it for so long. They have to have everything done for them, and that really makes me sad. But it's neat to see people come with that mind-set and then grow into responsibility and become more relaxed and able to share themselves. You know, people do open up sometimes, but it's hard to be vulnerable when you've been stepped on so many times. You have to have your hard shell on and not tell anyone anything, and not tell people the truth because you're so scared that if they know the truth, they'll reject you. We tell people not to lie to us.

Waterbury, Connecticut

Tom and Monica Cornell met and married at the New York Worker. A former editor of the *Catholic Worker,* Tom held a variety of positions in peace-oriented organizations before moving with Monica and their two children, Deirdre and Tom, into the large convent of St. Thomas Church in Waterbury and beginning Guadalupe House, a Catholic Worker community that provides hospitality to troubled male teens. They also manage the Council of Churches' two soup kitchens.

Tom Cornell: An old friend in the peace movement told me about this job [running the soup kitchens for the Council of Churches], told me about the trouble they were having, like the heroin addict who was stealing everything. The salary was fifteen thousand dollars a year, but I came.

They didn't quite know what they were doing when they let us move in to what's now Guadalupe House. The pastors said, "Look, we've got this empty convent. It's vulnerable to kids and vandalism and stuff. Why don't you move in? Temporarily, while you're looking for something else." After about eight months, they said, "Tom, what's your idea of temporary?"

"It's until you throw us out, George." One of the scandals of the church in the current age is that we have a lot of property that's underutilized. It's a very interesting relationship we have as Catholic Workers with the parish and with the diocese. Peter Maurin's original idea was that every parish should have a house of hospitality. Over the years, some Catholic Worker houses have had a tangible relationship with a diocese. For instance, Lou Murphy's original house in Detroit was owned by the diocese, but this is the first time that I know of that there's been such an intimate connection between a parish and the Catholic Worker.

We moved to Waterbury in September of 1982. In 1984, I joined the diaconate program. That, I suppose, put a different light on things. If I'm a cleric assigned to this parish, it's more obvious that there's a link between the parish and what goes on here [at Guadalupe House]. But the day-to-day operations are our responsibility. We don't have a parish council meeting and ask if we're going to kick out one of the boys.

Ro: Do you do any clarification of thought here in Waterbury?

Monica Cornell: Yeah. We've done some very interesting discussion groups. At the first meeting, some of us talked about . . . we called it "Dorothy Day Remembered." Just sort of informal recollections.

Ro: Passing on the traditions.

Monica: Yeah. And Bishop Rosazza gave his first talk here after the economics pastoral was released. We've had Plowshares people, antinuke people. We've had a priest who is working in Nicaragua. We've had slides of a visit to the Soviet Union. We've had a session on abuse of women. Our discussion groups, by the way, have included Robert Ellsberg's wonderful book, *By Little and By Little*. We did two sessions on that. Silone's *Bread and Wine*. And a bunch of us did *The Brothers Karamazov*. For Bishop Rosazza, there were fifty people. That was the largest group we ever had. It's very hard in Waterbury to draw people out.

Tom: I'm salaried by the Waterbury Area Council of Churches to run the soup kitches, to feed 270 people a day, seven days a week. A committee is responsible for meeting our budget, which is about eighty-two thousand a year. Now this frees me. I don't have to beg for the maintenance of this house. I can maintain this house on my own salary. And it takes the entire salary. There is no discretionary income here. When I need something like a set of tires, I call up a friend. Most often it's the auxiliary bishop who scratches it up.

The archbishop now trusts me; he didn't when I first came. He asked me to [help] reestablish the Justic and Peace Commission. We now have a CO registry, which means that the archdiocese officially has taken a stand that it will be of assistance to a potential conscientious objector. That's very important. We've addressed the question of Central America, pretty much in line with what the bishops have done, but that's radical for here. Gone a little farther perhaps, on specific issues. And then we hold conferences that are sometimes extraordinarily good. I'm known in the city. It's almost . . . I draw attention. I don't know why. But since I was a boy . . . if I went on a date, it was in the papers.

Ro: But you're not drawing national attention anymore?

Tom: No.

Ro: And you're not writing much, like you did earlier.

Tom: No. I do have a chapter coming out in a book the Thomas More Association is publishing on the beatitudes. It's about thirty pages, just kind of a recap of my glorious career up to this point. And what blessedness has been derived from it. [Pauses.] The blessedness is really in the kids.

We're different here [at Guadalupe House] from any house that's ever existed.

My own personal vocation, Monica's vocation, the kids' vocations, are different from anybody else, but we identify the source of our vocation in the Catholic Worker movement. We want to be in harmony with it, want to be able to project it into the future.

Chicago, Illinois: St. Catherine of Genoa

In 1989, I spoke to Al Mascia and Anne Crowell from one of the newest communities, one with a specifically defined mission.

Ro: Al, which came first, the Catholic Worker idea or serving the needy from the HIV-positive population?

Al Mascia: Well, it's a chicken-and-egg question, but I'd say the need surfaced first. And then as we considered how to address the need, it seemed immediately apparent that it should be the Catholic Worker because of the Catholic Worker tradition of working with the most disenfranchised, most marginal population. People with AIDS oftentimes really suffer from a lack of personal contact. They've been alienated and ostracized from family, friends and society because of the fear of contagion. So it seemed appropriate to use the Catholic Worker model with its emphasis on personalism. St. Catherine's is a transitional house with the goal being independent living, maybe in a shared accommodation with other people.

Ro: Why did you name the house after St. Catherine?

Al: Well, we think she fits. St. Catherine of Genoa was a little-known but very exciting sixteenth-century lay woman who worked with the major health issue of her day, the bubonic plague, and was able to be both a hospital administrator and a mystic. She also worked primarily with the destitute, as we do.

Ro: How do you get your support?

Al: Mark and Louise [Zwick] at the Houston Catholic Worker helped us at first and we've been getting little grants, but it's a real ongoing problem. We stay away from any money that would attempt to tell us how to do hospitality work or would want to turn us into an emergency shelter.*

Anne Crowell: The homeless community is very difficult to outreach, very difficult for change to occur in, and yet we're seeing more and more infections there.

---

* When he returned the transcript in 1992, Al commented: "This is not the case anymore. We don't apply for grants, and we refused to renew our nonprofit status."

Ro: Probably because there is no community.

Al: Right. And then all the concomitant issues of substance abuse, chemical dependency, alcoholism, mental illness. There's just so much grief! Prostitution makes it even more difficult to work with that population as far as HIV is concerned. We have to have more connection with agencies than other Worker houses, and we also make more . . . more concessions, practices at variance with some Catholic Worker traditions.

Ro: More rules?

Al: Yes. We need a lot more structure.

Anne: We're constantly maintaining a mission and ministry status, but sometimes it's hard to keep our balance.

Ro: In other words, you don't want to be case managers.

Al: Right. That's not what we want to be. Many of us were and we chose not to continue in that.

Ro: Now part of the personalism of the Catholic Worker is that one lives with the poor and one accepts the life of the poor, so you blur the line between people called staff and the others. How can you do that?

Al: I think there are . . . I wouldn't call them barriers, but there certainly are distances. You can try to blur the lines, but the reality is we can never be . . . just as we can never be the poor. We can never be what we're not, not physically. And to spend a lot of time and energy striving for that impossible goal is to detract from what *can* be done. On the other hand, we respect people, so we're able to say, "I don't know how you feel because it's not my experience. But I'm willing to listen to it and hear you and learn something about it."

Ro: What other differences are there between your house and a more mainstream Catholic Worker house?

Anne: The nutrition is very important, of course. You know, three square meals a day and good snacks. Many are on intensive medication—AZT and other things. A lot of them don't have good appetites and they have real fragile digestive systems, so we can't use food out of dumpsters like some houses do.

Ro: Would the Catholic Worker chaos model work at your house?

Al: Our guests bring their own brand of chaos with them. In fact, they're at our house because chaos has overwhelmed them. Maybe they were chronically homeless, and now they've got a terminal illness on top of that. So we feel that for their sake, we've got to model as best we can some kind of order in their lives. Without doing violence to our own selves. You don't want the refuge from the storm to *be* the storm.

We feel the same way about the notion of voluntary poverty. We all mostly ascribe to that, but we also feel that because the people who come to us are chronically—perpetually—uncomfortable because of their illness, we won't impose the trappings of poverty upon them as well. It'd be un-Christian to make anyone already so uncomfortable feel even more so just for us to express our principles. So we spent money on good mattresses and comfortable chairs and things like that.

Ro: What about the addiction problems?

Al: It's hard. If we discover anyone using in the house, they must leave. And this is based on the advice of substance abuse professionals. But we try to deal with every person on an individual basis.

Ro: Al, any "famous last words?"

Al: Well, I guess just that this is do-able. We're not saints, we're just a bunch of lay people who came together to respond to a rather big problem. And we did it.

Washington, D.C.

For years, Richard McSorley, S.J., has been a prophetic witness to his order, to the Georgetown University community, and to the entire Washington, D.C., area. Here he describes how he started St. Francis House. Polly Mahoney, who with her husband, John, is a current St. Francis householder, illustrates "harsh and dreadful love," and two men who worked in that community give their observations. Paul Magno, who has been a member of two Washington communities—Dorothy Day House and the Olive Branch—gives us an overview of the Worker in Washington.

Fr. Richard McSorley: I started the Catholic Worker in Washington, D.C., in about 1980. We used a building owned by a Lutheran church. There were just three of us—a married couple and myself. Some folks wanted to call it something else, not the Catholic Worker. I said, "Well, you're foolish to start anything with another name because with the name "Catholic Worker," you have a philosophy of life, a theology of life, a background. You have an acceptance by parishes and by ecumenical Christians across the board. If you start something else, you have to start your own tradition and build it all up and explain it and overcome people's doubts. That's all been done with the Catholic Worker. It has proved itself." Pretty soon, they put the "Catholic Worker" in it.

But it's a continuing struggle to get the staff, to get people who are committed [to living] without salaries, people who are going to stay faithful to the ideals. If they aren't, nobody tells them to quit. They just die off themselves.

It's transitional work. Staff usually turns over about fifty, seventy percent every year. Within three or four years, there's a new staff. We've tried to allow for that in the [Washington] Catholic Workers. In two of our houses, the ownership of property is in the hands of a board of directors. So if the staff leaves, it doesn't cause a problem about ownership. And this also does away with an owner living in the house who asserts importance because they have the ownership. It also solves possible conflicts of people wanting to change the nature of the house. People who used to be staff are on the board. Dorothy might not have done it that way herself, but she wouldn't complain about it.

Polly Mahoney: Jesus asked us to love one another. And I don't love people well at a distance. Love to me is something that you have to grow in, and usually you go through a time when it's difficult. You have to get to know the person and their faults.

I knew if I was going to be serving the Lord, I wanted that kind of a situation. So when we agreed to take over St. Francis House, I asked Father McSorley if we could have an open-ended hospitality, allowing people to remain as long as they needed to. And that was granted, and now St. Francis is somewhere between a shelter and a transitional house.

Our goal is to create a home environment, to be good brothers and sisters who encourage folks in trouble to do what they need to do. And to be firm if they won't live up to their commitments. That's it. The goals vary. And as you get to know the people, the needs become apparent. The first goal they articulate might be "I want to get a job and get on my feet." Then you discover that the person has a drinking problem, so the community will meet with them, confront them with their behavior or with the indications, and ask them if they're willing to deal with them. At that point, the goal can change to going to AA and doing therapy. We're willing to retain them as guests as long as they follow the community rules and as long as they're taking some responsibility for their lives.

Ro: What if they fall off the wagon or stay out all night? What if they disobey the rules?

Polly: Then we meet with them and give them a serious warning. We usually have several meetings when someone is not adhering because we're trying to call them forth. But if it becomes clear that we're not going to succeed, then we say good-bye. And that's hard. But it is, in our opinion, part of life.

We have . . . I'll give you one instance. I always go back [to this] because it's hard every time you do it. It's hard either because they make you feel guilty or because you just feel bad, period.

We had a woman here who had an alcohol problem. We had met with her. We had talked with her. She had agreed to go to AA, but she was doing it just to maintain a place to stay and wasn't doing it seriously, so it wasn't working out. Finally she came home drunk again, and we met her at the door and we said we were sorry but she should pack her things. She left. And came back an hour later, saying she had been raped.

We said we'd drive her to the hospital or we'd take her to the rape crisis center, but we would not give her shelter. We knew that it was all alcohol-induced. We didn't know whether she had been raped or not. But that even if she had been, the root cause of that was her alcoholism. And what we were saying to her was, "We'll take you to a place where you can begin to deal with the whole nine yards." Because if we took her to Rape Crisis, they would have put her in detox, and she knew that.

She wouldn't go. And then we said, "Then we will not in any way support you, even to offer a blanket." It was a rainy, cold night. One of the community members spent an hour trying to help her do something constructive. She refused. But she spent the night on the front porch. It was cold. It was rainy. In the morning she was gone.

The community was feeling very, very badly. It was really very hard to do. We're a small house and you can't live with someone and not get to know them. About three days later, she called. She said, "Okay. I want to go to a treatment center." The "no" to somebody can be hard, but it's a positive "yes" to something else. We have to trust . . . and that's where your faith comes in. Trust that something is going to happen.

I talked to Charles Walzem when we were both visiting the L.A. Catholic Worker. One of the "floating" Workers, he recalls the St. Francis style of hospitality.

Charles Walzem: St. Francis House is closed from nine o'clock in the morning until four o'clock in the afternoon.

Ro: So what do the people at the house do? Do they work someplace?

Charles: No. Most of them are incapable of working.

Ro: Where do they go?

Charles: They just wander. But let me tell you a story about the hospitality at St. Francis. One day a priest with AIDS came and was requesting help. He was recommended warmly by priests at Trinity Church in Georgetown. He'd been turned down by everyone, including his diocese in Houston. Had come to Washington hoping for some sort of help, some compassion. Polly and John Mahoney, who are the householders, agreed.

Now St. Francis House has a unique system with their long-term hospitality. They actually interview folks and make written records on whether a person is accepted or not. It's a group decision. Usually there's a period of discernment, generally in the same evening as the interview. Perhaps a person is sent to the chapel to decide whether . . . to pray if they are so inclined. At the end of the moment of discernment, the person is either accepted into the community, or asked to give it more thought.

Ro: And the records are kept?

Charles: Oh, yes. It's probably one of the more unusual, organized attempts at cataloguing. After that priest was accepted, I went to visit a couple times. I was surprised at how the other guests had accepted him. It was so easy for them to take him in.

Brother Michael Leahy spent a year working with the Mahoneys before returning to a monastery in Indiana. He died in 1992.

Michael Leahy: I hope to be of service here. Of course, it's entirely different from the contemplative life. A lot of interaction. Some tension. Some joy. Lots of emotion. Some work. But overall I think what I'm doing here is important. I think what John and Polly [Mahoney] are doing here is important. It's a beacon for this community. It's a type of holistic approach to the problem of poverty, feeding and clothing these people but also doing counseling.

✦

Paul Magno: I see two tracks of the Catholic Worker's development in Washington. One of them travels from Father Dick McSorley and St. Francis House to Day House to Olive Branch Community, and the second one is what I call the Mike Kerwan branch. Michael operated, or initiated (he doesn't like to claim to be the operator), two hospitality houses over on Fourth Street. At one point, that community dissolved and he considered seminary, so he turned those houses over to homeless families. Free. Later on, he and the archbishop parted ways over whether he could be a seminarian and operate a hospitality house at the same time, and he subsequently initiated some houses along T Street—the Llewellyn Scott House and the Mary Harris House. He also bought several tracts of land, primarily in West Virginia, and he operates a couple of Catholic Worker farms there.*

Ro: What do you see as the difference between the two branches?

Paul: Well, there are some philosophical differences, but I don't think they explain why there are two different trends in development. Michael's parents were great friends of Dorothy Day. He was sent to New York for Dorothy's version of a finishing school when he was in his late teens or early twenties. Came back to Washington and started going to school and encountering homeless people and taking them in. So it's a very serious devotion to Dorothy's memory and vision and to the Catholic Worker movement that has led him to run these houses. I think he's a little less structured than Marcia and I have tended [to be] in approaching hospitality. But it works.

Ro: In other words, it may be personality.

Paul: He's charmed volumes and volumes and volumes of money out of his supporters, which is why he can pay for three tracts of farmland in West Virginia. Over the years, he's bought four different buildings in Washington and paid for them, essentially. So that's quite amazing. And when he wasn't paying for hospitality houses in Washington, and I was in jail and Dorothy Day House was in a financial crunch, he came by and left several hundred dollars.

Ro: He doesn't do much resistance, does he?

Paul: No, because he is very singlehandedly facilitating all of this stuff. He shuttles back and forth between T Street and West Virginia. Really pours his heart and soul very intensely into taking care of the people he's become family with. In some ways, I really admire him and think he does better than we do. He intensely pursues living in community with the poor people that he meets and really deals with them as peers.

Ro: Rather than living in community with people who are just like he is.

Paul: Yeah. And that's a real special thing, a real challenging thing. So many of us are reluctant to look on the poor as our peers. And that's something to remember—to value.

Ro: Yes . . . yes. Can you tell me about how you decided to begin Olive Branch?

* I interviewed Mike Kerwan the day my brother-in-law, Fr. John W. Troester, died. In the ensuing confusion, the tape was lost—the only one to disappear. I'm sorry, because Mike's voice belongs in the book.

Paul: Sure. When I came home from prison in Florida, the only person who was still at Dorothy Day House who had been there when I left was Marcia, so I was really dealing with a whole new batch of people. It was difficult. I came into a process that wasn't mine. I didn't own it anymore. After a little more than a year, we decided to [start this community]. We left Dorothy Day House because we were . . . uh . . . faced with a number of things. We were feeling that we wanted to devote more attention to resistance than we had been. We realized that our daughter, Sarah, was getting bigger, and the more she grows, the more responsibility she is, obviously. You can just tuck a newborn baby under your arm, but a one-year-old takes a lot more work. So there was a concern for the ability to do everything we wanted to do. In the context of that, we ran into some real differences of opinion about the direction Dorothy Day community ought to go, some philosophical and community questions that were difficult and protracted and not really solvable. And we said to ourselves, "Well, we can either stay here and live in these contradictions and be aggravated and frustrated, or we can identify the elements of our vision and go someplace else and live that and hopefully be more at peace with ourselves." That's what we decided to do.

Ro: I've heard people say you can't have a Catholic Worker house if you're not doing live-in hospitality. How do you answer that?

Paul: Well, I'm not sure I . . . I'm pretty sure I don't agree. Obviously, we're here [at Olive Branch] doing this, so we justify it. The point is to do service, to be involved in the works of mercy. [Zacchaeus] soup kitchen is a work of mercy. For that matter, so is confronting warmakers. People used to call it a spiritual work of mercy—rebuking the sinner and/or instructing the ignorant.

I miss not living in community with the poor in a day-in, day-out basis. That's a choice we made in order to be able to work at . . . well, partly in order to have a little sane space for our family. It gets a little frantic and hairy over at Dorothy Day House sometimes, what Yolanda, a child of one of the guests, calls "circus-y." So to take a little pressure off our family and our marriage, to give ourselves something of a haven where we can do some reflection, where we can do industrious resistance work, where we can do a little scholarship, we started the Olive Branch.

Those are features of the Catholic Worker movement which have been valued insistently over the last fifty-five years. You can't have everything, so we've chosen what we want to live most. Sometimes it gets comical, actually. People ask me about hospitality and personalism . . . well, Mike Kerwan is doing it best because he's really living in community with the poor and taking it seriously. The rest of us are a little paternalistic, unfortunately. But at the same time, Mike tells people, "Paul and Marcia are really doing what Dorothy Day was doing in the first place. They have an apartment, and they have a vision, and they do some things, and that's how the Catholic Worker started. It wasn't always just hospitality houses."

Alderson, West Virginia

Dick Dieter and Maggie Louden had a special ministry—serving families who came to visit inmates at the federal prison for women in Alderson, West Virginia.

Maggie Louden: We kept the house open twenty-four hours a day. One of us was always on call. That hasn't always happened since. And I can understand the need [to get away] because it can be very draining. But I think it was that Catholic Worker philosophy that says if you have a service, you can't say, "Not today."

Something else [we did] and I think it comes out of the Catholic Worker model: The local town needed someone to rejuvenate the weekly Meals on Wheels. No one was taking it on, so Dick basically rejuvenated it. And then we did a food pantry, too. Finally the police began to see us [and realized] they could bring someone anytime. There was a lot more interaction with the community than I had originally thought.

Dick Dieter: It was inevitable. We were not back-to-the-landers who lived in the hollers and away. We were right in town, just a block from the train station. In fact, we got the train to stop there again, which the town deeply appreciated. It was this great old train station. And we worked and worked and demonstrated up in D.C. and finally got the train to stop in Alderson. We wanted it for the visitors, but the town people could also get on and go places. They loved this train. Trains have a real place in rural communities.

They weren't wild about these Catholic radicals coming into their town. That we heard quite clearly. But eventually . . . People are people. We had a kid in the schools. And there was a flood and we had a big eighteen-room house on a hill, away from the flood. We offered that. The pastors, you know, they had great, uh . . . goodwill, but they didn't know what to do if somebody was homeless. They certainly weren't going to put them up in *their* homes.

Maggie: Even if it was a member of their own church. People think rural people often respond to each other's needs. But they're very . . . they're very individualistic. And they have a real sense of space. I remember one of the parishioners saying to me that she felt guilty in a way 'cause they really haven't been supportive of us, and yet when they had a need, that's where they turned. So it became . . . yeah, I think we really did [interact with the community].

I think that was important because you shouldn't just take out of an area or use an area. You really should . . . you have responsibilities to that area even if its needs are different from what you're perceiving. I think there has to be that openness to their needs, not what *we* want to do. Also, I think we made Catholicism a little more palatable to the people there.

We also worked with the state prison, although we hadn't originally planned on that. It was just ten miles away from the federal prison. The new warden there asked us to come out and let the prisoners know about this house. They had the most outrageous visiting situation! Maybe two hours on a Saturday and two hours on a Sunday. And most of the prisoners come from the northern area, the city areas, the east and the west, not the area where we lived. So they never got visitors because [it was too hard] for their people to come down five hours for two hours visiting and then another five hours going back.

So we got involved with that prison, too, and I started working with a social worker there who wanted a group for abused women. (Some of the prisoners were abused spouses who had murdered their husbands.) Dick began a GED program, and a few of the women got their GED, and that had never ever happened before.

Dick: Anybody who works with prisoners in a sympathetic way opens himself to the potential of problems—to abuse by the prisoners or abuse by the prison, which is not open to people working with prisoners in a sympathetic way. Part of our reason for going down to Alderson was not just the visitors but the prisoners themselves. We wanted to have a direct relationship with them. They were the street people, so to speak, of that area—the most needy. And you have to work through the closed doors of the prison to get to them. We'd visit people who requested our visits. But you had to get on a visitors' list, and the prison would sometimes make [it] very hard. Later on, an opportunity opened up to work through the chaplain's office, to visit some people who maybe wanted to talk a little bit more. I volunteered for that, and it was in that context that I got a request to visit the prisoner Sara Jane Moore. She was infamous because of having tried to assassinate President Ford. Through this volunteer program, I went through the chaplain's office and was given a private room. In fact, I saw the whole thing as serving in a role similar to a chaplain.

Ro: A confidential counseling relationship.

Dick: Yes, absolutely! A very confidential thing. And that's the way I went into it. Anyway, one day I met with Sara Jane Moore and that very evening, she escaped! Just went over the fence. (It's not that hard to escape from Alderson.) Sara Jane not only escaped, but came to the Alderson Hospitality House. Maggie and I weren't even there that evening. She was recaptured within a couple hours, but the next morning the head of [prison] security came knocking on our door, along with the press, the FBI, and one of the associate wardens. Everybody wanted to know what we had talked about when we had met the morning before, and had I helped or had the house helped in some way?

We were probably a little more open and forthcoming than we needed to be. The basic rule is never even to talk to people like that, but we invited them in. We were perhaps naive. I told them, "In terms of any conversations I have had with her, that's confidential, and I'll keep it confidential."

"Well, if you don't tell us, you'll have to tell a grand jury."

Ro: Did they in fact subpoena you?

Dick: Sure enough, yes. Grand jury subpoenas, which we fought every step of the way. Some lawyers who were friends of ours agreed to do what they could to defend us. We were barred from the prison, and I told the people who were pursuing this that I was not going to talk. That was scary, 'cause there's a twofold problem: you can be jailed for not testifying, and then you can also be convicted on what you say or what anybody else says.

Ro: Did you ever have to testify?

Dick: No. It really was touch and go, but I didn't have to, in the end. I felt I had the confidentiality of . . . it was kind of a clerical confidentiality.

Ro: A professional confidentiality, certainly.

Dick: Which they told me is not recognized. Even clerical confidentiality is not recognized.

Maggie: We did talk with Bishop Sullivan and also with the canon lawyer who's at Notre Dame, now, I think. McCormick, the Jesuit. He basically told us that there just really isn't [any recognized confidentiality] unless you're a priest. And that the court system was doing its best to circumvent even that. Even ministers' confidentiality is not recognized.

Ro: Did this Sara Moore business harm the house?

Dick: Yeah. It certainly hurt it in the sense that we were not allowed to visit any more. We had to have other people around just to drive people up. Eventually we just ignored their order, and they did, too, after the grand jury thing was dropped.

Ro: Why did they drop it?

Dick: Two reasons. One was we decided to make it a very public case. Rachelle Linner, for example, did an article in the *Catholic Worker.* There was stuff in some of the local papers, and it was starting to be picked up.

Maggie: We had a campaign going. We were writing letters to the warden . . .

Dick: They knew they were going to be dealing with a very public group.

Maggie: And I think they also knew there wasn't much to go on.

Dick: It was vindictive towards us. It would have been an interesting battle, though, and we were ready to take it on even if our lawyers felt that we would lose, that we really didn't have any precedent.

Maggie: One of the motions we wanted to bring was a wiretap motion. We questioned whether there wasn't wiretapping on our phone. There definitely was on the prison phone. And the judge was interesting. He told the defense lawyers there were no wiretaps because he had to sign [the requests]. And the lawyer—whose office itself was tapped and she had proof of that—said, "We're not talking about *legal* wiretaps." And so the judge granted the motion and said that the government had to put forth their information. Gave them thirty days to comply, and then the government requested a thirty-day continuance after that. The grand jury died during that time, and they chose not to continue it. My feeling is there probably were illegal wiretaps.

Ro: And they didn't want that to come out.

Dick: Right. Once that motion was put in, they started asking for delays. I think they might have feared the publicity would reveal the wiretap.

Ro: They were able to get to you, and, of course, to convict Sara Jane Moore, without jeopardizing their system for finding out stuff.

Dick: Yeah. They made sure I couldn't visit anymore. I was even banned . . . "banned from the prison" is the way they put it. We had already had a somewhat confrontational relationship with the prison, and this gave them a chance to separate us.

I think in the long run it hurt the reputation of the house a little bit. The prisoners, of course, are most concerned about their own survival. That's what they've got to be concerned about. They didn't want to have their family tainted by staying at a house that was in trouble. So that hurt for a while, and it made it hard for us personally to do the mission that we wanted to do. The community didn't come down on us, though, except for the people who worked at the prison.

Maggie: But the community also didn't come forth. And that was another thing.

Ro: They see the prison as economically important to Alderson, don't they?

Maggie: And I think the prison saw the house conceptually as something which was part of the [prison] abolitionist movement. Which it was.

Ro: Why did you decide to move on?

Maggie: Well, there was Simone, our daughter. She was already in the third grade, and the teachers had said they felt the school was very limiting for her and really held her back. She is a very bright person. Not that there aren't bright people in rural areas, but there's a difference in articulation. Some kids come to school [not even knowing] how to speak.

The teachers also told me that, from kindergarten on, the role models in terms of women and men were very, very stratified. Dating starts very, very young, and a lot of . . . the girls either get married right out of high school or before.

Dick: Also, one of the factors was that we didn't have that direct relationship with prisoners anymore. And we had hoped that there would be more dimensions to the work there than were possible. It was such an isolated town. To be involved politically, you had to make the trip to D.C. We were there eight years and learned to slow down and garden and chop wood and work with wood stoves and local people and things like that. But our roots were in a city.

Dick has recently completed his law degree at Georgetown University and is working for the Death Penalty Information Project.

Phoenix, Arizona

Fr. Mike Baxter was a product of the late sixties, listening to idealistic young teachers in high school, studying Marx in college. He entered the Holy Cross order in 1978. Mike and another Holy Cross priest, Fr. John Fitzgerald, started a house of hospitality "in the Catholic Worker tradition" in Phoenix, Arizona, in 1984. "Fitz" has since started another house in Oakland, California; Mike is now a doctoral student in theology at Duke University. Worker Mary Ann Phelps provides specific details.

Fr. Mike Baxter: We're never very certain to what extent we belong to the movement. But that's the wrong question to ask. There's no sign-up sheet, no requisites. And yet, in spite of that vagueness, there's this tradition, this resilient web of beliefs and practices.

I'm convinced of the ideal of the Worker. I'm not convinced that I, as a Holy

Cross priest, and our house, as Andre House of Hospitality, fit the bill. Because a lot of the things that we do in Phoenix seem to be different than some other Catholic Worker houses.

One of the differences: In Holy Cross, it's traditional that we get a hundred dollars a month for personal expenses. That's a lot for Catholic Worker standards, but that's what we get. The lay people in the community get the same, and they're covered on our health plan, too, which is also not "Catholic Worker," what with precarity and all that. Some of the mores that we have as religious can be sustained in mixed communities like this. Lay people are really cleaving to some of the practices that traditionally come out of the religious life. For instance, we have compline after our soup kitchen now, and people love it.

We're really a mixed bag. There's a brother, a seminarian, a priest, and five lay people—men and women. And as a community, we open our houses to people who need to stay there, people on the streets of Phoenix. Really, the people who brought me to the Catholic Worker were lay people—Michael and Margaret Garvey, whom I dearly love. Through their stories of the Davenport Catholic Worker, which Margaret started in 1974, I learned a lot of what it takes to practice the works of mercy and to be people who live out the Catholic Worker ideal—never taking it too seriously, but never forgetting God's demands of us, either. Sitting around Garvey's dining room table on the weekend and drinking cheap red wine until three in the morning—that's where I learned about the Catholic Worker.

Ro: Do you see the Catholic Worker community in Phoenix as your flock?

Mike: Well, I don't want to be embarrassed about being a priest and ministering to the people I live with. I feel obliged to put forth a vision for the community because I helped to create it, and because I think I understand it. For example, why do we put the thousands and thousands of dollars that it takes to keep a soup kitchen going into a non-interest-bearing checking account? Now I have a pretty clear idea why, and if that makes me out to be the shepherd of the flock, fine. But it's really just trying to hold fast to a worthy tradition.

Mary Ann Phelps: Andre House was started in December of 1984. On Christmas Eve, I believe, they started . . . they threw all their turkey bones in a big pot and cooked it all up, and the people who were there at the house went down to the outdoor shelter and sang Christmas carols and served their first soup line to about maybe a hundred people. So that was the beginning. We now have a men's and a women's house, and a plot of land right beside it with a garden and chickens.

Ro: Chickens?

Mary Ann: Five blocks from the state capitol.

Ro: Oh! You have your Catholic Worker farm!

Mary Ann: I take care of the chickens. They were a birthday present a year ago. They lay five or six eggs a day.

Ro: That's really something! What kinds of guests do you have?

Mary Ann: Most of our guests tend to be younger people, I would say. Boy, a lot of them are alcoholics and a lot of them . . . well, I wouldn't say chronically mentally ill, but they've been on the street or have been in really rough situations and just need a place to stabilize for a while. I think, for the men, the average length of stay is usually two or three months. We don't really have a cut-off time as far as length of stay. The women tend to cling a little longer than the men do.

We've kind of set it up on a three-strike system, so when they have broken the rules three times, they're gone. The rules have to do with either not coming in at night, or coming home intoxicated, or something like that. "No violence" is one of our rules, and the guests really seem to abide by it. It's more of a problem in the women's house. I've found them to be more emotional than the men and more easily hurt.

Ro: How do you say "no" when you don't have room?

Mary Ann: I usually try and be really kind and also find another place for them to go. Even if they're intoxicated. Because I feel like there's some reason I can't perceive why they're in the situation they're in. And so just to treat them with the most compassion I can. It's difficult, sometimes. It really is.

Ro: Do you help them to make decisions about their lives or . . .

Mary Ann: We spend a lot of time talking to them 'cause they all seem to really have a need for that. As far as job placement, we don't do that at all. But a lot of conversation, especially with the women.

Ro: What do you think is the biggest problem in doing that kind of hospitality?

Mary Ann: Trying to do too much, to take on too much. At times it just seems overwhelming. It's exciting, but there aren't enough hours in the day. So it's a good thing to . . . to really love doing the work. It's not a job, it's a lifestyle.

You know, our soup line is really different than most soup lines in the country because of our location. We set up tables outside at the outdoor shelter. That way we serve more people and neighbors can come from the surrounding area.

It's the city's outdoor shelter, and then there's the men's and women's indoor shelter right beside it.

Ro: So people actually sleep outside?

Mary Ann: Right. They have tents set up all the way around the fence and then some ramadas for the elderly people to sleep under. They're open on the outside, and it's back by the railroad tracks and the cemetery, so it's not a real becoming place. We serve between five and six hundred people six nights a week.

Ro: How do you get the food?

Mary Ann: There's a grocery store in town that donates twice a week and then a big produce supplier gives us two truckloads a week, so that's real good. And then we have individuals. One man stops at four grocery stores on his way into town in the morning and picks up bread and brings it by on his way to work.

Ro: What does your family think about your lifestyle?

Mary Ann: My father sort of thinks I've taken up with the Moonies or something. He doesn't understand why, so I try to tell him how much of what they've taught me really brought me to this point. They are not offended by it at all, but I don't think they understand it too well, either. But . . . anyway.

I guess if I was going to say anything else about the house, it would just be that I get the most satisfaction from working with the people who come to live with us and just getting to know them and seeing how different each of them are and how much they're really to be treasured as people. They are good people and they all have stories to tell and that just really delights me.

Houston, Texas

Mark Zwick: We're very practical beings, I guess. The Catholic Worker [model] allows you to be very practical. We started out renting a big room in an old, old building, you know, with one toilet and one sink. It grew gradually. We began to distribute food to anybody and at any time. We were just helping people. One was a blind man who got shot in the eyes; we still help him ten years later. He's undocumented so he can't get any aid. We started with food and clothing. People just discovered us. The Catholic paper wrote about us. (They've done that all along—the *Catholic Herald.*)

Then our place burned down on July 7, 1982. So that was a very decisive time. Ironically, we were all over the press. I mean Houston's major channels all had . . . the major papers wrote this up. So the support came. The trust began. We raised $40,000 to put a down payment on a $110,000 building.

Refugees were the issue, so there was a lot of publicity. For several years, though, we didn't talk to the press because we were dealing . . . technically, we were breaking the law because we were housing undocumented people. But somehow or other, the parishes adopted us. Providentially. Some nuns helped us. Then in 1985, we had another fire.

Ro: That second complex?

Mark: Yeah. The two main buildings burned. [They were] paid for, so '85 was another watershed year. It was hard, but we were able to raise money to start building a new building. Concrete block and steel. That was sort of the theme, that it wouldn't burn down.

So all this while we're growing. More people coming for food. More refugees. So we built a very large building—twelve thousand square feet with twenty-one bedrooms upstairs for women and children. Downstairs we house anywhere from fifty to one hundred men, close to that. That building was built and paid for within a year.

Ro: Let me get this straight. All this time, you're really working outside the law. And yet people with quite a bit of power are supporting you financially. Would you say they were protecting you in a way? Keeping the immigration authorities from coming down?

Mark: I think the threat is there. If they arrest us, the bishop would speak up for us.

Ro: The religious orders?

Mark: The biggest religious women's community would be behind us. The pastors of the richest parishes, at least several, would be behind us.

Ro: "Don't mess with the Zwicks?"

Mark: Well, I never said that. But somehow or other, we got our roots into the community, not just the Catholic community. The big Presbyterian churches helped us build the building. Somehow I think the Catholic Worker philosophy of voluntary poverty . . . they can't figure it out. We keep in touch with Catholic Worker people, to think through what is Catholic Worker. We're always thinking about that. Being Catholic Worker probably helps us the most because we don't compete with people. We're not saying, "You're the bad guys." We know who's good and bad and who's lazy and who's not working and all that in other agencies.

You always know that. But the Worker philosophy is "just do it." Not a lot of bull, basically. The diocese probably loves the relationship. If we do good work, they can say, "Look at what Catholics are doing!" If we do bad work, they can say, "They don't belong to us."

Louise Zwick: That trust . . . well, it comes from years of knowing that refugees are accepted without question at Casa Juan Diego. The men don't stay very long, just two weeks. There are always more pouring through. But it's amazing what you can do in two weeks in terms of getting oriented to the United States, finding some work. It gives time for their families to send them money. A location to get some mail. They start here but they move on.

But what I started to say was in terms of the trust. For example, we're given so many clothes that a whole room fills up with clothes every week. And every week that whole room is given away. People really like the fact that they're given away immediately and not stored somewhere.

Ro: I'm not sure, but I think you're the biggest Catholic Worker as far as quantity of housing and meals and different services. Because of that, do you have lots of rules?

Mark: We hark back to our mental health experience, and we make a contract when they come. "These are the rules. You have fifteen days. No drinking . . . you can't get drunk. You can't bother the women." Then we talk always about the importance of work and jobs. We die to get jobs. Parishes, again, are cooperative. We put announcements in various bulletins. We write on the fence around the building. The picture of Romero says "Come and get workers." People think this is defying the law, but we never even think about defying the law. These people need jobs and we go that way.

But back to the rules. The rules are there basically to protect them. When they're there to protect us, then we've made a mistake. That's what agencies do. All agencies' rules generally are to protect the staff. That means the people become the enemy.

A staff member here has responsibility for twelve guys. He's got to come up with the plan for those twelve guys. I work with all the staff, but I'll take twelve or twenty myself because I meet with all the men a lot, at least every week with all of them. So rules are important. But I think more important is the contract. To let people know where they stand and that kind of thing. Rules can get out of hand.

Ro: Now it sounds as if there's a different system for the women.

Louise: That's true. Especially for women with children. They may stay a very long time. We have seven apartments . . . Our battered women have no resources. We can't get them in government job training. If they have some children who are born here, they can get a little bit of welfare (Texas is forty-eight out of fifty in how low its welfare payments are), but many children come from other countries. We have families who have been with us three, four years.

Mark: We make a commitment to any battered woman who comes in to us, Spanish speaking, usually undocumented. We say, "You do not have to return to that man. We will take care of you." And we mean that.

Louise: When some of these families have gotten settled and know us, they come back to the main house as cooks. Because we've found that we need to have Latin American food if our people are going to be comfortable eating it. And they're very helpful.

In fact, our Worker community includes four Central American couples who came as refugees and are now part of the community. Plus other Latin native speakers who come as volunteers. The Spanish-speaking staff at Casa Juan Diego has the same responsibilities, if not more responsibility, than the Anglo staff.

Mark: There's no distinction . . . we don't even allow people to think about white people as being in charge here.

Ro: But they *have* to think of you as white people being in charge.

Mark: Well, we certainly try to inhibit that. Like we all meet together, you know, we all make decisions. There may be that danger, yes.

Louise: I guess what you may be verbalizing is, say, a young person comes to work with the Catholic Worker for the first time. They may be interested in Central America, they might come with that mind-set, and we're very conscious of that new person not feeling that the Central Americans might be second rate. As a matter of fact, on the day-to-day practical interface with guests, the Central American couples have a lot of wisdom to offer us.

Ro: Well, part of the philosophy is to erase the distinction. Knowing that we all need help. But the reality is that the people who are most likely to be white, who are most likely to be the Workers, are better educated and more sophisticated. I don't know whether sophisticated is the right word, but just look at where the children of Catholic Workers go to college, for instance, compared to where the children of working-class people go.

Louise: You know, we have a bias in our country that poor people are not sophisticated, are uneducated, don't have much conversation. But what we discovered when we lived in El Salvador was that even though people in Latin America are very poor and suffer greatly, they are tremendously cultured. They have a sophistication and a culture that we don't expect to find among our poor here in the United States. It's a profound culture. In terms of values and how they view things and a faith attitude, they may be more cultured than the Anglos who come out of the University of Notre Dame.

Ro: But what happens when the refugees hit American pop culture? Television culture?

Mark: Very often it's tragic. They think these are the proper values because the people who have money have these values. So there's a danger. The worst danger is they are separated from their roots. The culture of TV and radio does not identify with fidelity to your spouse and does not identify with commitment and does not identify with generosity. It's almost the opposite. So it is a problem. We obviously speak openly about this in our . . .

Louise: In our liturgies and talks with the people. We have a liturgy . . . well, we have three times a week liturgy, but the main celebration is a Wednesday evening. We sing the songs from Latin America, and sometimes we don't have a priest and those are very rewarding evenings. We have the liturgy of the Word and we have a dialogue.

Ro: As some of them have done in Latin America.

Louise: Exactly. So they are very used to that. And we explore some of these issues and talk with people and they have a lot to contribute and share.

Mark: We talk about materialism. And about fidelity to their family values if they are separated from their spouses. We talk about how we all serve the poor. We expect them to serve the poor. We expect them to start Casa Juan Diegos in New York because there ain't any in New York, and there ain't any in Miami, and there ain't any in Washington, and there ain't any in Los Angeles where we've sent thousands of people.

Ro: What about the gender values? "I have to be a big man."

Mark: Yeah. Well, just looking at our couples, every one of those women are strong, independent people.

Louise: And all the men know how to cook. We really think the macho thing is a bit overplayed in the press.

Mark: Right. Every one of the men works in the kitchen.

Ro: So you don't see the separation that the pop culture would tend to say is there.

Louise: Well, it's there. But it's also there in the United States. We don't see that it's a whole lot worse among the Latin American couples.

Ro: How do you get the other volunteers?

Mark: Well, our work is attractive. It's like going to Central America. Sort of like a postgraduate year serving the poor. They're all from different . . . some are Buddhist and some are ex-Catholics and some are Protestants who are more Catholic than the Catholics and some are Jewish. It's an interesting mixture, but what brings them together, hopefully, are the Catholic Worker values. We say the only thing we don't argue about are Catholic Worker values. If we can figure out what they are. [Laughter.]

Ro: Do you ask them for a definite time commitment?

Mark: Well, we're now saying nine months, but often it's a year or a year and a half. And we're . . . I don't know if other Catholic Workers do this, but we're listed in *International Liaison* and volunteer books and that kind of thing. That's a big help.

Louise: Did you know that we have a house in Mexico, in Matamoros? Casa Juan Diego Matamoros.

Mark: It's seven hours drive from us. Just across into Mexico. Now it's a silly thing to do because we've got enough to do. In fact the bishop of Brownsville . . . Louise, remember when it started? He said you had "ants in your pants." But it gives us a chance to get away together because we drive down alone in the car. We can talk to each other. We can have a night together peacefully and go out to dinner. And on the other hand, we can visit this house. We also have an extension of our program in Southwest Houston. You know, there [were] no medical services in all of Southwest Houston for the poor, so that's developed as a big medical center.

Ro: How do you get the doctors?

Mark: It's all volunteer. We collaborate with Baylor University and also University of Texas. University of Texas medical students really run the clinic in Southwest Houston. Officially here at Casa Juan Diego, Baylor has a practicum, but in South Houston, the first- and second-year students are just doing it on their own.

Ro: Can you talk about the "Year of Jubilee" that I read about in your paper?

Mark: Well, it happened this way. Someone gave us a fifteen-hundred-dollar gift certificate for Foley's, the big department store. You know, for fifteen hundred dollars you'd walk out with a little bag full. Not much. The idea dawned on us that if ten families didn't buy clothes for a year, we might be able to buy an inexpensive house for the poor. We have a separate Jubilee Fund. One woman sent us a thousand dollars.

It did work some, and we did purchase a youth shelter. It's to be a longer-term house for Central American youth. [But the Jubilee idea] didn't really grow as much as we would have liked.

Ro: It attacks this whole TV culture *so* directly. And so simply.

Mark: The most response we got for the Jubilee fund was presenting it to a big parish. The church allows us to talk at Masses. It's not so much that we raise money through that, but we plant the seeds about the house, and they subscribe to the paper. There might be five hundred subscriptions to the paper [from one of these talks].

Ro: Who does all this paperwork? It's got to be . . . there's a lot of money coming in and a lot of money going out.

Mark: Yeah. Well, it's a lot of work. I mean we work even too much for being workaholics. But we have a lot of help. We have the four couples and five single people plus four more coming, God willing. And for our paper, there's a permanent support group of four other couples. They've been with us almost from the beginning and they own Casa Juan Diego with us.

One couple does the paper and keeps track of the addresses with a computer. We print close to twenty thousand papers a month. They pay the bills, and they also mail the paper. After the guests help them label it, they get it mailed out. A CPA does the thing for the general revenue. That's one couple. The other couple . . . she's a psychotherapist. I am, also, so that gives us some security in being able to recognize problems. The therapist does a group every week; she's also Hispanic. Another couple does the paste-up for the paper. They're both lawyers if we need lawyers. Louise and I write the articles. We made a decision early on that our paper would not be a radical sheet, but be to reach the Catholics of Houston. Not just the already convinced. We write for the guy who's an accountant for some oil company.

Louise: It's a bilingual paper, you know. And it's not always the same [in the Spanish and English versions].

Ro: There's got to be somebody in Houston who would just as soon you moved back down to El Salvador.

Mark: Well, our neighbors. The business people in our neighborhood would like to arrest me.

Louise: Because there are so many men around on the street and so much activity around the house.

Mark: One man said it's a plot of the pope to bring all these Catholics up here. [Laughter.] Little does he know they are all evangelicals nowadays, all fundamentalists. Yeah, the neighbors aren't too happy.

And in the early days in the Sanctuary movement, we used to get some criticism about "just" housing people, as opposed to getting publicity and changing the structure. We've always felt we should do both. Catholic Worker values have helped us survive the Sanctuary movement, as a matter of fact. Because you *must* house the poor. You *must* serve them.

Louise: We send people all over the United States, help them go. Their families send money or we help them go. We never used to worry about their safety on those trips, but now they're being picked up and deported, so we kind of study the routes and the time of day. We say, "Leave at four o'clock in the afternoon or leave at ten o'clock, and you'll get out of this area." Buses are very cheap and we can get a twenty-five percent discount 'cause we're Catholic. See, it pays to be Catholic. [Laughs.] We save thousands of dollars, just thousands, by that.

Ro: What do you worry about the most?

Mark: Where do we lose our sleep? We lose our sleep over a pregnant mother who's fourteen years old in her head. A mentally ill woman gave birth just a few months ago in our house. She had been denying she was pregnant. Just miraculously, you know, she didn't get to that baby before we did. One of our staff picked the baby up, cut the cord, slapped him on the fanny. And fortunately we were having a clarification of thought at our house, which we do once a month with some other couples. There were two nurses in that group, and they helped tie up everything, along with the fire department. But I think we worry about medical problems. We worry about violence and medical problems more than anything.

Louise: Our biggest worry is staying on top of things. We have so many people. I mean it's not just like we have one family, and we're all buddies together. We especially worry about the women. We tell them, "If any man bothers you, let us know immediately." [We're] the management—that's an awful word to use. But being in charge . . . responsible. We say our titles are "Los Señores de la Culpa."

Mark: We learned a lot over the years. Presently no man is allowed upstairs. Speaking from the voice of experience. Hard-learned experience. The last two Christmas Eves, some people have gotten very drunk. Just being able to survive that with no one getting hurt, you know, is sort of miraculous.

Ro: Do the guests help each other in that regard? Do they police each other?

Mark: Well, yeah. If someone's fighting, they would intervene. We don't have a lot of fights, and we don't have a lot of drunks. But it's always a problem when it does happen.

Louise: There are good guests who would help out.

Mark: Remember, Louise, the person who came into the library . . .

Louise: Said he had nowhere to stay. He was from Colombia.

Mark: It was a very primitive place, that first house. Anyhow, someone threw a pair of women's panties in his face, and those were fighting words. He opened up his suitcase and took out a knife and started swinging. Cut a guy's ear. But the other guests intervened.

I guess part of holiness is sticking with it. Being close to the work, even though it's a pain, even though it's painful sometimes, and you're tired and headachy. The idea of doing it the next day, you know, is an act of the will. Somehow that's related to holiness. Trying to do what God wants you to do. I think of Dorothy, and that seems to be the way that she would respond. You know, no glorious visions but just some sense of satisfaction that you're doing what you're supposed to be doing, even though you're tired and grouchy.

Ro: Can you think of any happy times?

Mark: Yeah. I guess we *are* neglecting the joyful times.

Louise: Our work is very hopeful and joyful because of the population we work with. A sixteen-year-old comes with no education, doesn't speak English, what kind of future does that person have in our sense of future? But by comparison with the population at some other Catholic Workers, people who are burned-out schizophrenics and alcoholics, there's tremendous hope.

Mark: "All you do is house people," they say. I think of all kinds of smart things to say, but I don't. That's our joy.

Louise: We're a check-cashing, we're a travel agency. We're a post office. All these things. One of our Central American couples recently put a sign on the window, "The post office closes at six P.M." They'd knock at the window at eleven o'clock at night. "Do I have any mail?"

We distribute food once a week, not just to the refugees who live in our house but to anyone who's hungry. Because then we can maintain people in their own homes and with families. That's *so* important. We don't give fancy foods. It's very simple . . . rice and beans. Flour, bread, and milk. But the fact that we don't just serve the "deserving poor" got us in trouble with the food bank in Houston.

Mark: Yeah, they cut us off because we didn't investigate people. "How much do you make? How many people live in your house?" But we just keep relating to the food bank, you know, and, they're gradually forgetting they cut us off. See, if you make the minimum wage, all your money goes into utilities and rent. Rent for apartments is higher in poor neighborhoods than it is in the suburbs. So we're working with the people who live on the margin.

We provide in the neighborhood of four hundred thousand meals a year with three hundred in-house meals a day, plus the people who come for food. Let's see. More joy . . . Finding jobs for people is very joyful. So the joy would come in meeting the needs. I think that's crucial. That joy would be more ours, I guess, than the people working with the typical Catholic Worker population. Our population has a future. They're young, they're hopeful. We might have 100 or 150 people in any one day to feed and clothe. But it's a population that can work, you know, that's in touch with reality and has some culture. And you can joke and laugh about things with them. That's a key to the joy, maybe.

You know, the biggest joy is when you catch somebody who's refused to pay these guys. And you catch them good, right in front of the big boss. Sometimes these guys work for two weeks and they don't get paid. A subcontractor will do this, so you find the boss and tell him this rat did not pay these guys. And the guy is very upset and pays them immediately. Well, that's joy. That's pure joy because you've got three hundred bucks for these guys. That's like three thousand dollars. Or even more fun is when you go to River Oaks (that's the ritzy section) and you knock on the door. "This guy wasn't paid for helping build this brick wall. And we want him paid immediately."

"Oh, that's terrible. My wife loves the pope."

"I don't care who she loves, just pay these people!" That's joy!

In September of 1992, Casa Juan Diego announced that its main building would house women only, with hospitality for men continuing a block away.

Bloomington, Illinois

Tina Sipula: In true Worker fashion, a call came in from Omaha, from a woman who was running a house out there by herself and needed help. She was desperate. Joe Kelly said he'd send me. Pay my airfare. So I went. I walked in and Beth [Daddio] walked out. She was real tired. And it was inner city with all black people. Some of them were prostitutes. Some of them were murderers, as we found out later, and the police came and were looking for them. But it was intriguing to me. It was exciting. It was . . . at no point did I feel frightened. I felt very safe, and it was like . . . it was a calling. I came home and Joe Kelly picked me up from the plane.

"Well?" he asked.

"This is it."

Ro: How long did you stay in Omaha?

Tina: One week. Beth asked me to come back. "No. I need to do this here. I need to do my own thing." I found out that Bloomington needed a shelter for women, particularly abused women. "This is what's needed, so it's going to happen." Based upon what I'd read and what my faith said, I knew it would. I didn't know how. I was maybe twenty-two. Had this extremely idealistic, wonderful, romantic attitude. Was afraid of nothing. Invincible. Could do anything. Joe told me to come and talk with some of the townspeople who came to the Newman Center. We started meeting in November of 1977. It just snowballed. One of the women in the group called up a realtor. "We need a house."

"Let's talk about it," he says. We started working on it, and he gave it to us. And it just . . .

Ro: He *gave* you the house?

Tina: He gave it to us rent-free with a four-year contract. Understanding that we were not tax exempt, that it would just be a freebie on his part. We had to bring it up to code and that took six months. I moved in in June of '78 and in

December we opened. Lots of extended community folks helped out and brought stuff and all that. But I was living here full time.

Ro: Who did the work?

Tina: I did a lot of it. People would come in and teach me. "This is how you sweat-solder copper tubing and put in hot water lines." I worked maybe sixteen hours a day hard labor.

Ro: Plumbing and drywalling and all of that stuff?

Tina: Yes. Oh, I've got great stories! We call it Clare House. I knew I wanted it to be a woman's name because it would be a house for women. And there were too many Mary houses.

Ro: But not *Saint* Clare.

Tina: No. Once you "saint" something, you really distance it from the people. Anyway, a year after the second contract with the realtor guy, we had the big fire here. In June of '81. And on Good Friday of the next year, he called up and said, "I can't do it anymore, can't afford to give you the house."

We thought we were going to lose the house. And then we said, "We're going to fight because our blood is in the walls." We put out an appeal to the whole country. All the Worker houses. Wrote a personal letter to everybody who'd given us fifty dollars or more, and we raised thirty-five thousand dollars in nine weeks! Gave it to him in cash, in hundred-dollar bills. All laid out on the table. He had to come here to get it. "There it is. Give us the deed to the house."

Ro: Oh, that's a story!

Tina: Yeah! The stories *are* the Worker!

Ro: Oh yes! Can we back up to your first guest and how that felt?

Tina: Oh, God! I was so naive! Her name was Suzy Houston. She had six children, and the oldest was fifteen. And it was horrible. *Terrible!* I hadn't figured out any kind of guidelines, any kind of rules. I was going to be a totally open Catholic Worker, and they were going to come and I was going to take care of them.

They literally destroyed the house. They ripped doors off by swinging on the towel hooks. They ripped the sideboards off our Honduras mahogany table. They broke the furnace. It was in the middle of winter, and I woke up to thirty degrees in the house. I mean this all happened within the first couple of days. I cried and cried. "What am I doing. What *am* I doing?" But it got better. It got easier. And I started to relax and make rules and became a lot more firm and grew up real fast.

Ro: Have you ever had much community living with you?

Tina: Yes. Several times we've had four or five community people here, and it's been wonderful. In the beginning there were always really young people coming from the universities. And then something happened in society and with the universities, and we had nobody from the universities. All of our volunteers were retired or elderly. Now it's swinging back. We're getting university people now that we haven't had for maybe six years.

We're a very small house compared to most houses. We don't put anybody on the couch or on the floors. People are integrated into the family of the house. They're doing dishes with us. We're watching television together. We're eating together, we're crying together, we're laughing together. We're going for walks together and swimming together. If you make it a flophouse, it doesn't work that way.

Ro: How long do the guests usually stay?

Tina: We tell them two weeks. In the beginning, all I took were abused women. I ran into some real, real dangerous situations. Men coming to the doors with guns. And talking to them and talking with them and doing a whole nonviolence thing with them. They're screaming and yelling at me and pointing the gun at me, and I'm bringing them down emotionally. Being very empathetic with them. "How are you doing?" And "How long has she been gone?" And "This must be really hard on you." Getting them into a nonviolent phase and having them trust me. All the time the woman is standing behind the door shivering. That went on for years.

Lately, it's mostly women who have been evicted. There's a real growing population in our country—women and children who are becoming homeless who never were before. The "new homeless." Or the "near homeless," as the sociologists call them. They've been traveling around and living with relatives and friends, and they reach a point when they run out of options. They're right there on the edge. They've lived from check to check and something happens. A kid gets sick or the car breaks down or . . . it just throws them. The other population would be people traveling, looking for work. A couple of years ago people were coming from all over the country to work at the new Diamond Star auto plant that opened here. They literally packed up their whole lives in little tiny, beat-up trucks or automobiles. We had a family of eight that drove here from South Carolina in a Pinto. He worked as a mechanic in an old garage. And it was pathetic. They had nothing. Nothing.

Ro: Was he eventually able to find something?

Tina: Roofing houses. Raking leaves and roofing houses.

Ro: What do you do besides being a home for families?

Tina: We operate a food pantry out of the house. We had a hard time for a while, with the city trying to close us down 'cause they didn't want lines of poor people on Washington Street.

Ro: This is a "nice neighborhood."

Tina: Very nice neighborhood.

Ro: Why did you pick a "nice" neighborhood?

Tina: It wasn't my pick. The house was here. Now it's one of the nicest houses in the neighborhood. We do food pantry twice a week on Wednesdays and Fridays. We give away whatever's donated to us. Then we operate a soup kitchen downtown and serve about sixty-five for lunch twice a week. We have a core group of about ten people [who volunteer], most of them retired, widows and widowers who are alone. They've become a family.

Ro: Do the same people who volunteer for you also provide money?

Tina: Some of them do. Some of them on a weekly basis. Some bring in vegetables from their gardens or go around to other people's gardens. Some bring in blankets. Some who help hand out groceries see that there isn't much of one thing, so next week they'll bring in groceries.

And nine times out of ten . . . no, it's almost ten times out of ten, these are people who are very, very poor themselves and have known extreme poverty in growing up and been through the depression and live very simply. When we had to buy the house, most of the money came in five- and ten-dollar checks.

Ro: Tell me the saga about the city trying to close down your food pantry.

Tina: Okay. I battled with them for six months. A strong, hard battle. They said that we were "operating a business without mercantile exchange." That meant we were giving away free food.

Ro: That's against the law?

Tina: That's against the law. A man came in with a clipboard and told me I was disobeying the law. See, the city doesn't want to recognize that there are poor. I was told that. Our town is growing, and becoming a very affluent city. It's becoming both more and more affluent and more and more poor.

I knew I was involved in an incredible battle, so I called every media in the area and they came out and filmed people lined up on our street. It was a commercial district—a gas station, law offices, a place that does car lube jobs, a fast-food joint on the corner. What we were doing was a real service. And the media appealed to the reality of the poor being here and being very orderly and . . . and that's why we won.

The town as a whole was [and is] real supportive. I used organizational skills based on Saul Alinsky, which I studied. I contacted every church in town. Asked them to write letters to the editor every day of the week, to space them out. And then I asked them to write letters to the city council and the zoning board and the planning commission and space those all out. They were getting so many every day. And then I asked them to contact their social justice organizations and have them call the mayor and the city council. That went on for six months.

I called in the media. When we met in the city council chambers, the television camera crews were there from three different towns. And the radio stations. And the newspapers. We had a real slick lawyer who volunteered his time. We were ready to go, and they backed down. Said they weren't going to vote. We said we wanted them to, and they said no. "We've decided there's nothing in the zoning code that fits food pantry, so we'll rewrite the whole code for you."

That was the beginning. We thought it would be easy, but it was real icky from there on. They made it real difficult for us. So we just kept doing it. I put out a petition, and we had six thousand signatures, and we sent it around town and presented it at every meeting. Lots of organizing.

Ro: Did you like that organizing?

Tina: It was a lot of work. I knew exactly what to do. It was like something over my shoulder said, "Do this do this do this." So I did it, but it was a lot of work.

Ro: But you won finally?

Tina: Yeah. Oh, sure. I knew from the beginning we would.

Ro: Did this help other shelters?

Tina: Yeah. It helped the whole problem of the homelessness. And we got lots and lots of media. Every day there was an article in the paper. It helped us a lot, too.

Ro: People say this is the Hilton of the Catholic Workers. And it really is a beautiful house, with all the pretty furniture and beautiful plants. Where did it all come from?

Tina: Ninety percent is donated. The other ten percent is something I buy to make it more of a home. The first thing Stanley [Vishnewski] told me was to put oil paintings on the walls.

The difference between our house and other Catholic Worker houses is that I'm here. It's my home. Lots of people have been involved in this house from the beginning who know I'm not going anywhere. They know they're giving [money] to a place but also giving it to the people here.

I think a number of people have reached a different level of suffering *with* people. It has nothing to do with eating oatmeal three times a day. It comes with being with people till they become intertwined in your guts and you're bleeding with them. That's what we do. We bleed with them. We laugh with them. We grow with them. We become one with them. That's "being the body of." That's what we do. It has nothing to do with the physical things that surround you; they help ease the suffering and I have no qualms about that. I'm here for the duration. And for the bleeding time, too.

People need wings. My philosophy is to be with people to their most extreme potential. And to my own. That's giving wings and loving. If you recognize the wings that are involved in flying with yourself and with other people, great heights can be reached in loving and growth.

A person can walk in who's all shriveled up in a ball and if you look at them and love them a little bit, they start to unfold. And then if you can see who they can be and treat them that way, they'll *become* that way. You can see it happen! It's exciting! It's wonderful.

Boston, Massachusetts

Kathe McKenna and I spent a morning together on the second floor of Haley House, a fixture in Boston's South End since the sixties. Sounds of soup kitchen and street sirens below. This house, and its changing missions, could stand for others that have survived more than two decades of change. We pick up the narrative as Kathe describes purchasing a rooming house.

Kathe McKenna: What happened was . . . we were watching all these rooming houses die in this neighborhood. And that had a tremendous effect on the homeless. It started with the men. When we first opened, if you were sober for a couple of days, you could get a room. Anywhere. And often for less than fifteen dollars a week! Well, as the number of rooms decreased, it affected the alcoholic and the transient population first. They became permanently homeless.

Then it began to affect the borderline people. Some were semi-retarded who could work as dishwashers or maids, whatever, and keep a room. All of a sudden, those marginal people became homeless. And the mentally ill. And the women. A lot of the women were on the edge, but for years they'd been able to survive in a room or in some kind of cheap housing. With the housing shortage, they ended up on the streets.

So anyway, along came David Manzo, just graduating from [Boston College] and wanting to do something. Dave is an "operator," a *wonderful* operator. And he wanted to really get this place to the fullness of what it could be. He hadn't been involved much with the Catholic Worker, more in the encounter movement and other stuff. And he was just a real dynamo.

That was the first time there'd been a wave of young people coming as a group and making a serious commitment. Haley House really became a home again and it was great! With this new energy, the first thing was an elderly program in the evening. We knew all these folks who lived in rooms around here, and they were especially shut off from each other in the winter. At least in the summer, they could sit on the stoops and chat. So we began serving meals to the elderly in the evenings, which is a big part of what we do now. And David and the new group also started the clarification of thought series on Friday nights.

We also began to search for a rooming house because we became very acutely aware that these were disappearing before our eyes. Again, in the Catholic Worker tradition, we can't stop capitalism from plodding on, but we can get one rooming house.

Dave got together with one of the Jesuits who was running the [Boston] Marathon. They put out a flyer saying, "You can't save the world, but you can save one rooming house." Then Dave Gill ran the marathon and asked people to donate for the down payment. And we got enough money. Exactly.

The rooming house idea caught people's minds. It was making the connection, and people were beginning to see what the dollars invested in gentrification were doing to individual lives. Now Pine Street [Inn] is doing that on a very large scale. They have a whole trust which works on permanent housing. Anyway, the rooming house got purchased and it's for elderly, like the folks who lived there when we bought it. Then there are two units for folks who manage it and who set the tone.

Another house, John Leary House, got started in 1983. It's housing for low-income families—women and their children and their friends. Lots of violence, lots of difficulty figuring out what we're doing there. "Is this just low-income housing or are we trying to help these people at some other level?" Some of that is still being sorted out. One thing that happened somewhat deliberately—we needed more stability in John Leary. So more of our "fellow travelers," as I call them, moved in to act as house mothers or fathers or something. At the rooming house, it's mostly elderly folks. The trauma is much easier to deal with. Whereas at John Leary, the trauma is more severe. Drug addicts. Family violence. All kinds of issues. So now two families live there in their own apartments, and there is outreach to more stable low-income families.

Here's another thing. The people who purchased and began John Leary House made some contacts with a foundation. And [the foundation] came through with some very big bucks for us. They bought John Leary House and then gave it to us so the original buyer could be reimbursed and move on. The foundation also really wanted to see John Leary House get some stability, and thought being more integrated into Haley House would help.

Ro: Now does this foundation have any sort of continuing input?

Kathe: Well, they're not a local group, so they don't want to do stuff on a continuing basis. But in fact, they got us a van. They paid off the mortgage on the farm. And they gave us some other money as a matching grant to spark local contacts.

Ro: What about the Catholic Worker idea of being "on the edge?"

Kathe: Well, we are in a way. We're certainly better off than we've ever been before. That happens just with longevity. More people know about you, so you've got a firmer base.

Ro: And when you own your own buildings, you're not as afraid of the real estate developers or the wrecking ball.

Kathe: Exactly. But now we've got these buildings, and we have to keep them up, and that's very expensive. So what we're finding at this point is that we *are* on the edge after all. For instance, we haven't been able to afford insurance. We've started to dip into the foundations as a resource, and we're using some of those inroads to take care of brick and mortar issues—windows, roofs, new wiring, things like that.

Ro: Your buildings look pretty good on the outside.

Kathe: True. This building hasn't been painted for ten years, though. The problems are more internal. Fire issues and leakage and stuff like that. This building is actually in pretty good shape. The rooming house and John Leary aren't.

Ro: The same concerns middle-class home owners have.

Kathe: Exactly. What we did with the insurance . . . it's kind of a unique situation. Because of the gentrification and the values in this area, we could never afford one hundred percent insurance. We always got what they call co-insurance, so if we had a serious loss, we wouldn't be paid the full value, but we felt we'd get enough to start again somewhere.

Finally, we said, "Why are we giving the insurance companies all this money just for that?" Because of the present real estate values, if this building burns to the ground, the land itself is worth about what we'd get from co-insurance. So we said, "To hell with the insurance. If we have a total loss, we'll sell it off and move on."

Ro: Have you ever felt you'll want to leave this neighborhood because it's too nice?

Kathe: We considered it for a while. One, it would mean selling everything. And that would mean speculation. It would be doing exactly what we've criticized other people for over the last twenty years. That's number one. Number two, in Boston the few neighborhoods that we could move to are going through the same process, just fifteen years behind this one. So wherever we move, we'd simply face the same thing. We'd end up in the same place, but we wouldn't have the community ties that we have here. It took us twenty years to win some people over.

Also, for a number of years, we've concentrated on building community in the house. Getting people to live here so we could get the work done and keep our spirits up and be a family and all that kind of thing. Let's face it, grappling with Dorothy's "long loneliness." What we found was that we have been more successful at it in the last five to seven years because we now have an enormous diversity to offer people.

Before, you had to quit work and move in. That only answers the needs for a few people and for a short time, usually. But the different number of options has kept new people longer. It has also produced a larger community which shares the work. People have outside jobs, so they do one shift a week or one a month instead of one a day. The same amount of work gets done. In fact, *more* work gets done. It's just split up among a larger group of people.

Ro: Kathe, what do you enjoy the most?

Kathe: Oh, all of it. I mean I . . . it's a joke around here that I go to more committee meetings than anybody else. I love process. I love encouraging and being part of Haley House's development. Watching it grow from a one-family operation to an extended operation to . . . and then trying to make sure that as we grow, we realize where we are. I love to think of how we do what we do and why we do it. And I love all the different kinds of communities, large and small, that we've experimented with. The friendships have been marvelous.

Ro: Any nostalgia for the old days?

Kathe: Oh, absolutely not. The good old days were wonderful. I loved it. But those were the good old days.

Ro: What do you see for the future?

Kathe: Anything is possible. In the early days, when I was much more an ideologue, you know, everything was black and white and red all over. The only criterion was if it was the most radical thing to do, the most politically correct. I remember a meeting with Phil Berrigan and Mike Cullen and a couple of other folks in a hideaway up in New Hampshire. We were planning . . . we wanted to set up an underground railroad to get people out of the country who were going to be involved in more strenuous resistance. And I remember having absolutely no patience with Phil and Michael and others who wanted to do standby actions. A part of me was saying we needed to have people who are willing to hit and run. "It's great what you're doing, but we need ten thousand times more." There was just a tremendous impatience and emphasis on results. For the hard hit.

But I think as time has gone on, I've seen enough changes (both good and bad) that there's more involvement in the how and why. For me, it doesn't really matter whether you're doing standby actions or a sink full of dishes. What matters is what's happening on a deeper level.

Ro: You haven't mentioned the word "Jesus" once.

Kathe: Oh, but I *did* that . . . I mean that was the big deal when I was at YCS. [Kathe had been a staffer at Young Christian Students after graduating from college.] That's all we did. God-talk all the time.

Ro: Did you reject that?

Kathe: Yeah. Had it up to here.

Ro: Do you think of yourself as Catholic?

Kathe: Oh, no. Not for a long time. I'm attracted to Buddhism, and it's meaningful to me. Catholicism is meaningful to me. I certainly go to liturgies, I mean Masses. I love rituals. One of our friends just joined the Orthodox Church, and I *love* that liturgy.

Ro: One last question. Why did you call it Haley House?

Kathe: Well, we named it after Leo Haley. Kind of an up-and-coming Catholic young man of the year. Very involved in the Catholic Interracial Council, but not too much involved with us. We were really more on the radical fringe, you know, involved with SDS [Students for a Democratic Society], with the Black Panthers, with people on the fringe. Leo Haley was ideologically very sympathetic, but his goal was to use the system to make changes. A wonderful guy.

And Leo died very tragically. He was on his way home one night from one of his multitude of meetings, and he stopped to help some guys by the side of the road. Well, they pulled a gun and started a night of absolute horror. He died the next day. They finally let him go, but took his identification and threatened his family, so Leo went to a friend's house to talk it out. There was this tremendous dilemma: He didn't want to prosecute them because he really didn't think prison did anything for anybody, but on the other hand, he didn't want this to happen to anyone else. He also had this big Mass happening the next day, and he was very traumatized during the night. He had been born with a congenital heart problem and had a fatal heart attack going to Mass that evening.

Obviously, as young people always are, death was not part of our understanding of reality. When Leo died, it really hit us hard. Leo . . . there was something about what Leo did when no one was looking, when no one would have known, and when no one would have faulted him for bypassing those guys. So a part of us said, "This is really what it's all about. It isn't . . . it doesn't matter whether you wear a suit and are head of the Catholic Interracial Council or whether you think you're a dynamite radical on the fringes. What matters is how you live your life when those choices are given to you. What you're going to risk." That's what Leo's power is for me. And I've had a great time. It's been good.

Spinning a Web

NINA Polcyn Moore once characterized the Catholic Worker network as a spiderweb. I've been thinking about her metaphor for five years now. Spiderwebs are both strong and fragile, often attached precariously to a structure, but quite capable of fulfilling their task if no one disturbs them. They can stretch over large areas and often exist in out-of-the-way places. When they're bright with dew in the morning sun, spiderwebs are beautiful, but they're hard to see unless the light is right and are downright scary if your hand touches one in the dark. It's hard to describe the difference between one part of a web and another, but each intersection is both distinct from and unified with the whole. Yes, the Catholic Worker is spiderwebby.

PART FIVE

The _Catholic_ Worker

CHAPTER 27

Spirituality

A Roundtable Discussion

One has to admit that, in communities of any form, "Praise the Lord" has always worked.

—*Chuck Quilty*

You know, what we often mistake for spirituality is just adrenalin. And adrenalin burns out. Sometimes things were so bad, there wasn't anything we could do *but* pray. And sometimes we'd be so scared shitless that we'd have to do something really simple like saying the rosary.

—*Charlie Angus*

For myself, I'm a little bit leery about too much overt religiosity. I think it's a pain in the ass. I rather like the idea of the works speaking on their own.

—*John Cooper*

I N this conversation, I'm putting together the "things of God" that don't fit into church as institution. Calling. Commitment. Meditation. Prayer. I grew up in the privacy of the fifties and thus share my generation's reticence. In that era, it wasn't considered polite to ask about a person's prayer life; therefore, most of the speakers in this chapter brought the subject up themselves. Perhaps that's why you'll find both a more contemplative and a more ecumenical spirit here than may be present in the movement as a whole.*

Included in this roundtable are Jim Forest, lay protégé of Thomas Merton, now living in Holland and a convert to the Russian Orthodox Church; Larry Ray-Keil of Seattle's Family Kitchen, an ecumenical community with meditation as a spiritual practice; Louise Cochran of Noonday Farm in Massachusetts, a former student at Harvard Divinity School and a convert to Catholicism; Holy Cross priest Mike Baxter, now a doctoral candidate at Duke University; and Fr. Tom

* For further reading, see Daniel DeDomizio, "The Prophetic Spirituality of the Catholic Worker," in Coy, *A Revolution of the Heart.*

Lumpkin of Detroit's Day House. As in all the roundtable chapters, I've occasionally paraphrased portions of a conversation or inserted a transition to show that the dialogues that occurred during our individual interviews are part of an ongoing conversation about the Catholic Worker.

Jim Forest (New York City and Alkmaar, Holland): People talk about their coming out of the closet as gay people, but I think most of us are far more embarrassed to come out of the closet as spiritual people. As praying people. As believing people. That's far more embarrassing than anything else we can think of, so out of tune with so much around us. It's what I mean, though, when I say we need to experience the Catholic Worker as a commitment.

Have you ever noticed? When you're leafleting, say on a street corner, the response will almost always depend on what the first and second person in a particular group do. You know, they come along in bunches and if the first people take a pamphlet, the rest of them usually will, too. Now these are a bunch of strangers. Absolutely no connection with each other, but their response still depends on whoever happens to be in front.

We're basically social beings, very much connected to each other. Our behavior, too, is connected. What we do, even spontaneously and with complete strangers, has to do with this truth about ourselves. So to make the analogy to the spiritual life, we're living in a time where the leaders in front of every bunch of people are not believing persons, not getting down on their knees in any sense of the word.

To be a believing person is to be exceptional in our world. We're in a post-Christian era. (Thomas Merton suggested this in a little book of his that was never published, "Peace in the Post-Christian Era.") That's where we live, and we might as well own up to that reality, and acknowledge that Christian activity and Christian belief are not normal. It's not even normal among Christians, not to say among everybody else. As a result, we're constantly trying to conform ourselves to the people at the front of the crowd, so that our religious activities aren't too ridiculous and too embarrassing and too isolating.

The amazing thing about Dorothy Day is that she simply wasn't impressed by that crowd psychology at all. She worked through that and found the place where she would be free to be a believer. When you're with one of those people, it hits you pretty hard.

Fr. Mike Baxter (Durham, North Carolina): Well, the Zen guys say, "If you see the Buddha on the road, kill it." If you think you've made it, you haven't. You stand in the same place before God, day after day after day, and you just try to offer to God the most faithful witness you can, the most faithful response for that day. And that's it. We have nothing to offer but that.

It doesn't matter if you're ready to step over the line at the Test Site and get arrested, or if you're changing diapers, or if you're going to visit your sick father in a nursing home, or if you're trying to be a decent kid. Just do what you're doing, as Dorothy said.

The point is that we really need to be freed from our own self-consciousness, our self-centeredness, our concern with ourselves. And the way to forget ourselves is to get involved in something outside of ourselves.

The desert fathers talked and wrote about the demons that attack us. All these demons play into our self-absorption, as Cassian says, whether they're the demons of listlessness or despondency or lust or whatever. There's the demon of acedia, the noonday devil. Where you sit in your room and wonder what it would be like if you weren't in your room. Looking at the greener grass. What we're called to do is to say no to all that, to say, "Hey, I'm going to make a conscious decision to live for others, and I'm going to start now. And if I flop in two minutes, okay! On the third minute, I'm going to keep it up." It really comes down to that moment-by-moment stuff.

Dorothy quoted Francis de Sales. Something to the effect that "every moment comes to us pregnant with the will of God. We can either respond to the moment or not, before it goes plunging off into eternity." But the wonderful, promising thing is that there are always more moments. *Every* new moment is an opportunity to respond.

Here's what I think: We need to live out the vow of poverty with our feet. Not with our thoughts, not with our intentions, not with our prayers, not with our time, but with our feet. We need to live with and among people who are poor, to try in a disturbingly vicarious and perhaps even phony way to live among the poor.

I say phony 'cause we're educated and we're white and we're male and so on. It's important that we say, "Okay, given all that, we're going to do what we can from where we are." The response boils down to the concrete. I try to be faithful to the gift of the day. (Of course I fall from that regularly, within minutes after waking up.) You never reach the point where you feel humble enough to be worthy of the reign of God. You can't say you want to be happy and that's the reason you're doing things. You just have to be faithful and forget yourself. Then you realize that you're dependent on God and that it will all work out in the end because He'll see that it does.

You know, it used to drive Dorothy Day crazy when people would give that band-aid analogy. Part of it may have been because many of the people who were criticizing weren't themselves doing anything concrete for the poor. But also, there was just this incredible lack of faith—no faith that handing this person a piece of bread would have any eternal meaning.

Larry Ray-Keil (Seattle): Well, what we do to address that . . . every week we try to take a "Mindfulness Day." That's a day, or at least a half a day, where each person as an individual doesn't work at the Family Kitchen, or do any other of the business things we do. Instead they stay pretty much alone and do reflection or meditation in any way they see fit. It doesn't always work out that we can take this time, but at least we have it as a goal.

The makeup of our house [in Seattle] has always been real ecumenical. Catholics and Quakers and Lutherans and Episcopalians and atheists. I think you'll find this in most Catholic Worker houses. Many people are very bitter against some of the social structures of the church and the awful things that it does institutionally, but they want to do the work.

The spiritual practice for almost all of us here is meditation. Eight or nine years ago, we started doing these contemplative retreats with the monks at Our Lady of Guadalupe outside of Portland, and we'd get priests who also had Zen training. Gradually, then, we left some of the Catholic stuff and started doing just meditation, which is a form of prayer that can be used with any kind of religious beliefs. It's not . . . I don't think we've quit being Catholic. It's just that we don't pray in the traditional Catholic way.

And always our house has had a strong feminist element. We tried not to have . . . to always rely on a priest. We didn't want to be dependent on a hierarchy that we didn't believe in, so we'd do our own liturgies. Actually, meditation as a way of prayer fits in really well with that, anyway, and it's nonverbal, so you don't . . . you get out of a lot of problems with words that can have so many different meanings and connotations. You know, words all have a cultural history and usually that history is sexist and . . . carries all that baggage. It's just easier all around to do without that.

Louise Cochran (Winchendon Springs, Massachusetts): We have an ecumenical community at Noonday Farm, too. Some of the group are Protestant ministers and [my husband] Jimmy is Jewish and I've become a Roman Catholic. My father was a Presbyterian minister and he always talked a lot about ecumenism, but sometimes I'm surprised at how truly ecumenical I am, how easily I'm able to talk about the intersections of the various religions.

The Bible speaks to me—there's no question about that. But for me, where religion happens is not in a church setting on Sunday morning. It's in the context of my daily life. And I think that the Hindu and the Buddhists in Asia have much more of a sense of the integration of religion with the rest of life than we do in the Western world. I have grown to have a great respect for that.

After Jim and I were married and we went to live in Bangladesh, out of curiosity I spent six weeks in a Tibetan monastery in Nepal. It was a meditation course given for Westerners, so there were teachings and then long periods of meditation. It was the first time I had experienced silence, experienced fasting and intense concentrated meditation, as well as what I saw as authentic spiritual teachings. That was a real turning point for me in my spiritual journey.

When I reentered Harvard Divinity School, I began to look for that kind of experience here in the West. It took me a long time to find it. I looked in the Tibetan community, and I looked in the Christian community, and finally I found the Catholic Worker. I think the thing that really attracted me to the Worker is that it's religion and life all mixed up together. A life of the spirit.

Ro: Well, theoretically, anyway. Maybe it's possible at Noonday Farm, which is much less busy than many urban houses. But with the frantic life in some of the hospitality houses, how can you do it?

Louise: You can't. That's why we're at the farm. We just couldn't make it living at the soup kitchen with a family. It was just tearing all of us apart.

Ro: How do you find time to develop the life of the spirit here?

Louise: Well, every month I go away for two or three days. And twice a year I go away for an eight-day retreat.

Ro: Do you have a spiritual director?

Louise: I do. It's Father Jack Seery and he's connected with Haley House. Jimmy and I actually see him together for direction, and we like that very much because we're able to share that dimension of each other's interior lives. Which we don't always have time to do otherwise. It was especially helpful to us at a time in our marriage when things were really rough. We could come together with Jack, and it was a safe space, a familiar space. I joined the Catholic Church during the Easter vigil at Haley House. Jack Seery was officiating, and Jimmy sang the *Exulte.* I know that I never would have [become] a Catholic if I hadn't come through the left door of the Catholic Worker.

We came to Haley House during my last semester at Harvard. And I realized that . . . I mean I was on the track, moving right along towards ordination. And I realized that I couldn't do Haley House and a church at the same time. It would just tear me apart. With Jack Seery's help, I realized I wanted Haley House. And then it was only a year later that I realized that I . . . that the Roman Catholic

Church, with the depth of its spiritual traditions, was my spiritual home. The sacraments are very important to me, as are the things that the Catholic Church offers to everyone, lay and religious alike, in terms of developing and nurturing a personal relationship with God. I think that's what I was always yearning for and never found in my own Protestant tradition.

Ro: But Noonday Farm isn't particularly a sacramental community, is it?

Louise: We have sacraments together once a week. And I go as often as I can for daily Mass at the Carmelite Retreat House in Peterborough.

Ro: What about women in the church?

Louise: You know, for some reason it's not a big deal for me. I've been able to find ways of preaching . . . I'm invited to preach at the little Protestant church here in town every summer. When I'm working at the nursing home, I lead services [there] twice a month. So I'm able to lead worship and preach and do the things I want to do.

You see, I lived out my disappointment with institutions in the Protestant church. It's perfectly clear to me that every institution is human, and so it's flawed. I'm really sorry that the Roman Catholic Church doesn't allow women [to be ordained] because I know some very gifted women who would be wonderful priests. Much better than I.

Ro: But you don't worry about it much.

Louise: No. I do feel I'm on my way to becoming a spiritual director. My real love in life is talking to people about their journeys toward God. It's the most interesting part of my own life, and it's just astounding to me—the different ways God works in different lives.

I believe that every path leads to what Christians call God. I have this image in my mind of all the religious traditions being like spokes on a wheel that lead to the one center. Different paths are right for different people. But there are barriers on the different paths, also, and some people can't get past them, so they try another path.

Ro: How do you know when you're on the right path?

Louise: Because you sail ahead. So, you see, I can't disparage any religion. I just know that this is the right one for me. On Pentecost, Jimmy was in Sri Lanka and the children and I were at the Peace Pagoda which is run by our friends, the Buddhists. And I was just overcome with a sense of gratitude for the richness of all the religious traditions we're able to share.

Ro: Hm . . . hmmm. Now Dorothy said it was a dangerous life. How are you dealing with that?

Louise: Well, living here has not led me to pride. Humility, maybe, but not pride. So I feel a lot of gratitude because there have been really rough times, both in the community at Haley House and in the community here. I think probably the roughest patch of my whole life has been here. The pull was between . . . among the different parts of myself. It was here [at the farm] that I really came to understand that I didn't know my own needs. That I was always trying to please other people.

Ro: [This realization] could have happened anywhere, couldn't it?

Louise: Yeah, but it happened in a *great* way at the farm. I mean it just couldn't have been more clear. It slapped me in the face. I think it would have had to happen for me in community, not living as a nuclear family.

Ro: So what did you do then?

Louise: First, we moved into a larger space. And I began to really take notice of what my own needs are. Now I combine a Buddhist practice for the development of loving kindness with the ideal of what a Christian would say is learning to love as Jesus loved. It's called the Metta meditation. I pray, "May I be free from anxiety. May I be free from trying to please others. May I know my own needs." And I receive those gifts.

I also believe that God can work in any situation. I mean there we were in Bangladesh with a tax-free salary that was higher than any salary I'd ever been able to imagine, in the poorest country in the world, living this luxurious life with servants and all of that stuff. And God led us out of that into this.

People change. I've seen people leave the FBI, leave the CIA. I just pray that I'll have the . . . I pray to Mary sometimes, pray for the capacity of waiting and pondering and . . . hoping.

Ro: Oh, yes. [Pause] One of the things I wonder about is what kinds of experiences make some people change while other people have the same kinds of experiences and don't change. Tom, why do some people hear some things and not others?

Fr. Tom Lumpkin (Detroit): I really have no idea. I think it's the mystery of vocation. Why, for instance, just in the area of peacemaking, do some people feel a calling to civil disobedience and others feel a calling to work in legal ways? I don't know if you can really say.

Ro: How do you know when God is calling to you to do a particular thing?

Tom: Well, you probably never know for sure, but there are some general "rules" for discerning. First of all, some way an idea comes into your mind that this or that might be a possible thing. You pray about it, certainly. Talk to other people, people you respect as having a certain amount of holy wisdom, if you will. And then if it's possible, you try it out tentatively. Also, I think even more basically, there's something to say about God's call in some way corresponding to the particular gifts you've been given. Like I don't feel I'm a very good organizer. And one of the things that attracts me about civil disobedience, you know, is that I can kind of do my own thing. I'd just get boggled trying to work in a congressional race, or something like that. It's a question of particular gifts and talents.

Mike: Everyone is called to vocation, not just priests and members of religious communities. Before Vatican II, we had a layer-cake model of church where people in religious life were the ones called to the counsels of perfection, the theological virtues and all that. They were supposed to be the really holy ones. Lay people were holy but one step removed from the mandates of the Gospel. They weren't supposed to live out the counsels of perfection, but to apply faith to the "real world." That's what I mean by the Gospel once removed. Usually it was conceived as some form of natural law ethics for lay people. The priests and sisters and brothers had the theological virtues of faith, hope, and charity. The lay people handled the natural virtues—justice, fortitude, temperance . . . what's the other one?

Ro: It's been a long time. I do remember feeling sort of second class.

Mike: Oh, prudence. The queen of the virtues. Well, Vatican II said, "Listen! Everyone is called to holiness." *Everyone!* Not just priests and those in the religious life. Well, Dorothy had been saying that all along!

The Catholic Worker movement has traditionally been a lay movement, but my vision of the church includes this call to *all* of us—to live all mixed up in a community with lay people and clergy and men and women and brothers and sisters in religious life, all living together. I feel as called to the values of the Catholic Worker, as called to the Gospel, as called to live out the beatitudes— just as called as the next person. I feel called to that as a priest. In fact, in some ways, I feel more disposed to that because . . . well, frankly because I'm celibate. Because I think it's hard to do hospitality when you're married with kids.

The beatitudes are for everyone. You try to do them where you are. For me, that seems to lay the groundwork for rationally integrating the works of mercy into our lives, no matter what our "state of life" is. And as a religious, therefore,

I feel like the Catholic Worker movement sharpens my role. As a celibate, I am unmarriageable in order to avail myself, not in a better way, but in a *particular* way, to the reign of God and all that it entails.

Do you know where the line is? Not between clergy and laity, as if the religious are called to holiness and the laity aren't. It's between church and society. That's where the line is—clergy and laity together as church in the midst of the world. Our original call is to build a new society within a shell of the old. The way we do that is by providing an alternative to the ways of the world, even as we transform it. So for me, there's a real confluence between the witness of the Catholic Worker movement and the original witness of religious communities. Starting with St. Benedict and even before. They were always countercultural. The monasteries were seen in many ways as a kind of ark. Culture and dignity and learning and faithfulness were carried by religious communities throughout the medieval era—carried like in a womb. The Gospel was alive in the midst of these communities of people who tried to live out their life together, to love God with all their strength and soul and mind and heart, and to love each other as themselves.

That's what St. Benedict's Rule is all about. That's what the Catholic Worker is all about. To preserve the moral and intellectual life, to have spaces for grace, to have communities where the Gospel is lived out in all its concreteness and dreadful directness, in all the frightening demands it puts upon us to forsake ourselves and be at the service of others. Maybe the Catholic Worker movement can do that preserving in this particular era in America. I think it does, in fact.

You know, the Catholic Worker is not a liberal movement. It's a radical movement, and there's a sharp difference. Liberals say, "Hey! The homeless aren't being fed. Let's march on the city hall." Radicals say, "The homeless aren't being fed. Let's feed them." Radical is very conservative. Getting down to the basics means *I've* got to do it. *We've* got to do it. We've all got to make this thing concrete in our lives. And that's all we have to give—our lives. Any authentic reformation in the church is not something new. Like Peter Maurin said, it's so old it seems like new. The prophets didn't say, "Hey, let's try something new here!" The prophets said, "Let's return to the heart of the law." We say, "Let's return to the heart of the Gospel, to the beatitudes. Let's really live this life as the early Christians did."

Let's live the kind of cultural life that doesn't pinch incense to Caesar but says we're different. We're going to give an ethics for Christ the King, not an ethics for the empire. It's November spirituality. Every November first, we listen to the beatitudes and we reflect on the feast of All Saints, and we know that we're all called to be saints in the Kingdom.

CHAPTER 28

The Worker and the Church
A Roundtable Discussion

I don't think any of us knew how nip and tuck it had been sometimes with Dorothy and the chancery, how hard it had been for her to keep the paper going as an up-front Catholic publication called the *Catholic Worker*. Not "Christian Worker" or "Jesus Says," but <u>Catholic</u> <u>Worker</u>.

—Jim Forest

I feel kind of caught really right now 'cause it's like the church versus the modern world, and I don't like either of them. So I guess the Catholic Worker is really where I belong.

—Ellen Rehg

THE *Catholic* Worker. The Catholic *Worker*. The catholic worker. From the beginnings of the movement, when the word "Worker" was pejoratively associated with communism, the combination of "Catholic" and "Worker" has been problematic. Today, we worry about "Catholic." Most don't think of it as small *c*, although there are many in the movement who aren't Roman Catholics and many more who live uneasily with their church, as I do. In this roundtable, priests and lay people struggle with what it means to be both Catholic and Catholic Worker.

Fr. Frank Cordaro (Des Moines, Iowa): To me, the church is continuously making a fool of itself. That's sad. It takes away from the power it has to speak. Power to me isn't the power of place, the power of institution. The real power is the power of truth, and the church's real power is when it is speaking truth.

We're talking about my family here, something I love. For two thousand years, we've done everything. Been the good guys. Been the bad guys. Been the good and bad guys at the same time. Our age challenges us to new forms. I believe the Catholic Worker is developing a new spiritual movement within the larger church. A radical one. One that . . . not one that breaks off but one that is on the porch. Like St. Francis. St. Benedict. The Dominicans. That's what the Worker is, but it won't be canonical in the same sense 'cause as we develop and grow in this church of ours, we have to let go of these antiquated structures of hierarchy and dominance and control. If we're going to get rid of war, I believe we have to get rid of this kind of structure of dominance within our church.

Gary Donatelli (New York City): Well, I see the Catholic Worker, or at least the New York houses, as siding with . . . I would say the hierarchy. That's why I appreciate it when Dan [Berrigan] says, "Welcome to the lower-archy." I'd much rather be with the lower-archy than the hierarchy.

Ro: And Father Berrigan talks about being with the outsider. AIDS victims and gays are the outsiders now.

Gary: Right. It's unfortunate the Catholic Worker has decided to stay so doctrinally close to the Catholic Church. If you look at [CW] history, I would say it leaves you with the outsider. Not just the outsider of an economic community, but also the outsider of an ecclesiastical community. But when we as a community of gay people are told that we can't use any church building from the archdiocese of New York, that we can't go to church as a community, as Dignity . . . At this point in my life, ortho-practice—right acting—has sort of drawn me away from orthodoxy, or right [thinking].

Ro: You've been thinking a lot about this, haven't you, Gary? You wouldn't be using those words if you hadn't thought a lot about it.

Gary: Well, I've spent so much of my life so deeply involved with the church. You know, I gave it my all, and ended up getting screwed.

Ro: Bill, how do you see the Catholic Worker in relationship to the church?

Bill Griffin (New York City): I see the Catholic Worker as *part* of the Catholic Church. I don't see it in relationship or in competition. There is no question that the wealth of the Catholic Church . . . the spirituality of the desert fathers and the Gospels are a repository of human wisdom that we're all in great need of in our crazy society. Harkening back to values that are in our past [and] that are inside of us. If we can dig below all the overlay of superficial culture, [we can] find our true selves. So the Gospels and the religious practices are a discipline that promises to open up the way to finding a person's true self. I'm grateful to the Catholic Church for being there. We don't have to reinvent the wheel.

Steve Soucy (Chicago and Orland, Maine): The Catholic Church is my heritage, too, and I agree that you have to kind of come out of your own roots and your own experience. Not that it's impossible to switch courses in the stream but just that it's a heritage that has a lot of power for me. And a lot of truth.

I have no problems whatsoever respecting people from other heritages, or no particular heritage, but who are people striving towards some kind of truth that they can pull from their own experience. I view the teaching of Christ as having been meant to be inclusive rather than exclusive. And it seems whenever they set up a religion, the first thing they figure out is who they're going to exclude.

It's hard for me to reconcile some of the behaviors and the actions that have been done in the name of Christ. I think it's hard for anybody. And yet the church is very human and so it's the church of sinners. I kind of just have to let go of that because, I mean, that's history. To the extent that I myself can change, it doesn't have to be that way for me. I don't have to choose to exclude people from . . . from well, from my love. It gets into a much broader area of how you practice your religion. And for me [the Catholic Worker] is just a very down-to-earth way of putting your mind where your mouth is when it comes to Christian faith.

Ro: Do you see these conflicts in how people look at the word "church" as a real problem in the movement?

Steve: Well, I don't know. The problem in the movement . . . I mean first you have to decide who's a part of the movement, and then you have to decide who thinks it's a problem, and then, you know, if you want to analyze it that way, sure it could be a problem. But it's not just the movement's problem. It's the church's problem. My concept of church has just grown a lot in the last three years. I still sometimes use the term to refer to the leaders or the visible church—you know, the building down the street and the men in black clothes who live there, or the hierarchy or whatever. But I think I've changed some of that thinking to include everybody else who claims to be of God.

Pat Coy (St. Louis): We have to remember, I think, that the Catholic Worker movement has had a tremendous influence on the U.S. Catholic Church. In a couple of ways. First, many people have found a spiritual home in the Worker for a time, and then gone on to be active in church circles or other kinds of professional activities that still have to do with working out their salvation in the modern world. Taking everything seriously and being contributors to the dynamic of the Catholic Church in the United States. Over time, that has sort of seeped into the bone and marrow of the U.S. church.

Marc Ellis (Maryknoll Seminary): Well, I see that the Catholic Worker made its intellectual and cultural and political contribution to the Catholic Church in the thirties. And then again in the sixties and early seventies. It will never again be a major force in the same way; the movement that informs the North American church (or that part of it that wants to be informed) is liberation theology. That's where the cutting edge is.

But that theology is not far from the Catholic Worker. Politically, the Catholic Worker has maintained much [of] what Maurin and Day said, particularly the personalist understanding. Which is a stance that liberation theology is in sympathy with but moves away from 'cause they're very much in the structural level.

Ro: It seems to me that Catholic Workers are looking at our own third world, the third world within the borders of the United States.

Marc: Exactly. That's why I don't want to make a big point about who's on the "cutting edge." The two critical parts [of] Catholic thought today, [are] critique of church—internal church—and structural critique of society. These things the Catholic Worker has always had, but in a different [historical] framework. They haven't made the transition. The New York house has had grave discussions about how critical one can be of the church. Is that a part of Catholic Worker history? Actually, it's very much a part of it. Peter Maurin was greatly critical of the church.

Kassie Temple (New York City): I've heard other people say that, say that the Catholic Worker has not raised questions about church teachings. But it has always raised questions about activities within the church, practices that seem to be not living up to the teachings that the church has given. I think there's a certain amount of confusion between the teachings of the church and the practices that may not live up to the teachings. For instance, the issue of tax-exempt status does not seem to me to be a church teaching one way or the other. So challenging the church on that, as we did in the editorial a while ago, calling the church to not accept certain privileges, should perhaps be seen as a challenge to the church but would not be a challenge to church teaching.

Eileen Egan (New York City): To me, it's important that what we do not imperil the future of the Worker. Now there are people in the Worker who have their own agenda, an agenda which differs from that of the church in general. And to be true to the church and to Dorothy's fidelity to the church—that's the one thing that bothers me sometimes. Nothing has happened, but disagreements raise their heads all the time. And I think we just have to pray that the future of the Worker won't be imperiled by something like that.

That's what would imperil it. Because Dorothy was teaching a little-known doctrine of the church, global pacifism, and stressing something that is not generally stressed, which is simplicity of life and the daily practice of the works of mercy and hospitality. Peter's "cult, culture, and cultivation." They were accepted because she was *totally, irrevocably,* faithful to the teachings of the Catholic Church. If she had deviated in one iota, the movement would have died. Because there were so many enemies, enemies who honestly felt the Catholic Worker was a danger to the church. I think some of the young people may not understand how frail the Catholic Worker is in that respect. In order to carry a very old message, a message of peace and nonviolence, we have to be absolutely above suspicion, you know. Do you know what I'm trying to say?

The church I knew growing up in Wales was beleaguered from without; now it's beleaguered from within. It's good to criticize the church. The way Dorothy criticized the church was with love, and you felt that. But there is a lot of very trenchant, unloving criticism now.

Pat: Well, we all remember Michael Harrington's famous quote: "I went to the Catholic Worker because it was as far to the left as I could go and still stay in the church." Harrington said that in the early fifties, and most Workers today would still agree that it's [the only way] we can stay in the church, a church that many of us love but see every day, as Dorothy said, as the cross. Because of the way women are treated, because of the way gay people are treated. The people in the Vatican say they're afraid of liberation theology's association with Marxism. But I think they're afraid of liberation theology's theology, liberation theology's model of church.

Ro: Father, how do *you* see the Worker as relating to the church as a whole?

Fr. Richard McSorley (Washington, D.C.): I go back to Dorothy, just as Eileen did. Dorothy was affecting both the structure of the church in society and the structure of society itself. War and peace, racial justice, economic justice—these things which are now looked on by many personalist Catholics as politics, she saw as faith. She wanted people to see the peace movement, the racial justice movement, as coming from faith, alive with faith.

Before she died, I asked her: "Do you think it's necessary for Catholic Worker houses to publicly express and live out their affiliation with the Catholic faith?" And she said, "Absolutely!" And the proof of that is that those that don't do it, don't continue. In Washington, we're listed in the Catholic directory as a miscellaneous operation of the diocese. And that gives us the right to tax exemption if we want it and also to some other tax privileges. So we rate as a religious community, not as a shelter. I think that's more what the Catholic Worker is. It's a religious community with no jurisdictional or organic ties to the church. The only way we're to be Catholic Worker is that our lives show it. There are no documents, and that's very appealing to a lot of Catholics, especially those who want independence from religious structures but still want that commitment to the church.

Ro: Sometimes, though, I see the Catholic Worker as a sort of safety valve for the church. If one isn't comfortable in a traditional parish, there's always something like the Catholic Worker which will keep the traditional parish from changing, from becoming Gospel. You know, "If you want the Gospel route, go to the Worker. If you want to stay a regular capitalist American and contribute to the collection basket, stay at St. Hedwigs."

Fr. McSorley: Well, Dorothy would never have accepted that division. In Washington, we purposely don't have any Mass on Sunday, so that everybody in the Worker belongs to the parish they're living in. A parish can find a great support in the Worker house. But you don't have in a parish what the Catholic Worker offers in community. And because it's transitional work, it has a lot of alumni and [others] who consider themselves associated with the Worker, even though they've maybe never lived there. That's another part of the genius—you can be a supporter of the Worker as much or as little as you want. You don't even have to be Catholic.

Ro: Now what would Dorothy think about all the dissension in the church today?

Fr. McSorley: Since Dorothy's time, there's been an increasing division in the church between . . . you might call it the far right and the far left. But more in the Gospel terms, those who see religion as a personal religion, a religion related to God without any social aspect to it, and then Catholics who work for justice and peace and very often leave out the personal and also don't do much personal prayer. That division is widening by misinformation from one group against the other. Dorothy brought it all together; the Catholic Worker brings it together. It's very much a personalist religion because you deal with the person. And through that person, you affect the whole social structure.

Ro: But would she like all the discussion by the feminists, for instance?

Fr. McSorley: It's interesting. I went up to see her about a year before she died. With another priest and a nun. We had tea and spent about three hours together. She was very serene and seemed to realize that time was short. We asked her all kinds of controversial questions, and there was no sign at all of any . . . that they were controversial. She had been on record as saying that she wasn't in favor of women priests. But this time she said, "I don't think that it will go on [the same way] forever. We will have women priests. Probably the first step will be married priests. And then when women are closer to the altar by being associated with priests, married to them, then the culture will be ready for women priests."

Chris Delany (Sacramento, California): I think the Catholic Worker lifestyle will be the religious life of the future. All the religious communities are dying out and I don't think that's by chance; I think it's part of God's plan. Small communities will supplant them, not necessarily the Catholic Worker, but that type of community, one that lives the Gospel and resists the forces of evil and cares for the poor.

Margaret Quigley Garvey (South Bend, Indiana): Actually, the Catholic Worker is pretty legitimate now in most places.

Ro: Is that good?

Mike Garvey (South Bend, Indiana): There's no shame in being legitimate as far as the church is concerned. A lot of the distinctions we make between the institutional church and the "parallel lay church" . . . they're crazy, anyway. The church is Dorothy Day and Frank Cordaro and Mr. Ranahan and his trains . . .

Margaret: It's the charismaniacs . . .

Mike: And every kook in Christendom, including all of us. And Pope John Paul II and Cardinal Ratzinger and Hans Küng. It's "Here comes everybody!"

CHAPTER 29

The Controversy over Homosexuality

Historically the real staunch support of the Worker has been gay men and lesbian women. As Catholics, they've had no other community; the Worker was open to them.

—*Chris Montesano*

What do they call it in Italy? Pelvic theology. I call it the Mason-Dixon line of the Roman Catholic Church. Everything below the belt we see crystal clear. We hold everybody to accountability. Everything above the belt is anybody's ballpark. We'll rationalize everything, even thermonuclear war.

—*Fr. Frank Cordaro*

I've always thought the church was operating on not very good information.

—*Richard Cleaver*

THE issue of homosexuality is the most disturbing conflict within the Catholic Worker, according to many of the 208 people I interviewed. Because of the intimate nature of some of these conversations and because one of the concerns is that there has been little careful discussion of this issue, I've compiled these interviews as separate conversations, not as a roundtable discussion.*

Chris Montesano was active in the San Francisco Catholic Worker and also spent time in New York.

Chris Montesano: Dorothy wouldn't talk about the issue of homosexuality directly, but when I was in New York—and I think this can go in the book because it's history—they started the Good Soup Co-op in San Francisco, and we'd gotten this little pamphlet from them. I came into the office and was raving about it.

---

* There have been some forums on this subject; David Buer described a fruitful discussion at St. Francis in Chicago, and there may have been others.

Angry. I said, "These gay men are taking advantage of the movement, exploiting it for their own purposes, blah, blah, blah."

Dorothy looked at me very coldly and said in a very stern voice, "*Someone* has to minister to gay people."

At that point, I left the room. Now I realize that every other man in that room was gay. Every other man in that room. And Dorothy knew it. She chided me because she'd realized I'd hurt those men deeply.

Dorothy would not open up the issue to discussion because she felt it was too volatile. She was clear that her stand was traditional church. I don't agree with that, but that was clearly her stand. I think Dorothy definitely loved many gay people and loved them very well. In terms of what she did to me, I'm glad she did it. I mean she had to. In a certain sense, she was taking a stand to support them and to love them in a nonpublic way. That's history and it's important and it's a memory I hold dear.

In San Francisco at the time, we held the traditional view of the church. What finally broke through to us was when one member of the community came to us and said, "You don't know what you're doing to me by taking the traditional church stance." He said, "I was born gay. From the day I first had consciousness, I knew I was different from other children. What you're saying to me is . . . you are allowing me no other choice but to remain celibate for my whole life. I can't take that choice."

You know I . . . it was a personal one-to-one confrontation and statement about who he was, and that just . . . when we took it back to prayer, we realized we couldn't continue to take that kind of stand and be present to that person. And, in fact, he is the godfather of one of our children.

Also, some lesbian relationships started up in the community and again we were confronted. We just felt that there was no way we could remain in love and force people out of our community. So the position we eventually moved to was that we can't make any statement of judgment about other people's lives, about people who are gay or lesbian. The only thing we can do is love.

I made a statement like that at the Fiftieth Anniversary CW Conference [in New Jersey]. I said that we have in our midst a group of people who have been in great pain and that I feel the movement has not acknowledged that pain—the pain of our gay brothers and sisters—and that it is time to open ourselves up to this issue and try to live with the Gospel, which is love.

Ro: People talk so much about Dorothy's adherence to tradition. Maybe some people are taking the conservative stand because they think they're being faithful to Dorothy's vision.

Chris: And I actually think they are *not* being faithful. To be faithful to Dorothy's vision is to love. But there hasn't been that love, unfortunately, in some places.

Gary Donatelli spent the formative years of his life at the New York Worker, although he was one of the "travelers," often leaving the hectic Lower East Side for the Midwest of his youth or the West Coast, where he had special friends in Chris and Joan Montesano. Gary now works on the staff of Bailey House, which was the first hospice in New York for homeless AIDS patients.

Ro: Do you still consider yourself a Catholic?

Gary Donatelli: Oh, I guess. What does that mean? I don't know. You know, it's . . . sometimes I do, sometimes I don't.

Ro: Did you ever get involved with Dignity? [Dignity is a Catholic activist support group for homosexuals.]

Gary: Not a whole lot. You know, I guess I don't like being ghettoized. Although I would occasionally go to Dignity, and I found a certain amount of strength there, you know, which was very good. Worshiping as a community. But I was never real tight with Dignity. It's a crazy world out there. People are dropping like flies from AIDS, and I have more important things to do than to picket the cardinal. You know, for the life of me, I can't understand what he's doing or what Cardinal Ratzinger is doing or most of the time what the Holy Father is doing.

In a lot of ways, I'm beyond the pain they caused me growing up. Probably deep down inside, I don't think the Catholic Church should be allowed to get their hands on children. I think it's a dangerous institution. But, you know, I'm not going to press that. I have more important things to do. The cardinal doesn't want to listen to anything I have to say. And he said that much.

Sometimes I think gay people are really nuts for even bothering to try to be a presence within the church. I need to change myself. It's not me telling the other guy what to do. It's me figuring out what to do and doing it myself. That's what Peter Maurin meant. Dorothy would point out that no one knows what effect we're having. I figure anything we're able to do that's good—that's encouraging, that gives people strength to live well—anything we do is helpful. I don't imagine I'm going to see a revolution. In this country or within the church. All I can do is try to love the people I work with, the people I run across, wherever that is. Whether it's the folks who are still at the New York Catholic Worker . . .

Ro: Is that hard?

Gary: It ain't easy. I think they might have made a few mistakes, major mistakes, that have affected my life. I suppose in some ways I still mourn over it. You know, it's not easy. I probably avoid talking a lot about the Catholic Worker just because it's . . . you know, it's not something I really care to talk about. Because it was a real hard time. Although I thank God that I'm doing what I'm doing [working at Bailey House], as thankful as I am for the time that I spent at the Catholic Worker.

Ro: Do you want to talk about that time, about the big divorce?

Gary: Well, see I missed a part of it. I was at the Catholic Worker farm in Sheep Ranch when the ball started rolling or when it picked up momentum. (It had probably been rolling before then. It has probably been rolling since before Dorothy died.) Sure, I'll talk about it.

Ro: Hasn't it been there from the beginning?

Gary: Oh, from the beginning. You know, I could run down a whole list of gay Catholic Workers who were there from day one, but I won't. Folks who got left behind. Folks who were very hurt by it all. Folks who just kept quiet and persevered while not being appreciated or not being accepted as whole people. That's real painful history, one that probably should be written sometime.

Let's see. I think I started getting letters, from Peggy Scherer and from Ernesto de la Vega, telling me things were happening. Part of it had to do with Ernesto becoming one of the editors and some controversy over [his] writing an article that was published in [the *National Catholic Reporter*]. An article that was, I guess, critical of the Catholic Church's teaching on sexuality. Some of the editors felt that someone who publicly questioned the magisterium on Catholic teaching couldn't be an editor of the *Catholic Worker.*

I'm out in California thinking, "Now wait a minute! I never heard this before. This isn't something Dorothy talked about." And then I started thinking about all these people I knew who were gay and who had quietly given their lives to the movement. And . . . oh, it made me really angry! And also because like over several years prior to this happening at the Worker, I was coming to a sense of myself. And then before I returned to New York, I found that the editors had made this decision—that someone who is an editor could not publicly question the church.

I was one of the editors. A group of us had been singled out the previous year as the folks that were . . . you know, where the buck stopped. I guess there had been some discussion the previous two years about who was in charge of this newspaper. Or who was responsible for it. And so there was a group, a small collective within a larger collective of the New York community.

Ro: So your name was on the masthead.

Gary: Yes, yes. The editors were Frank [Donovan], Jane [Sammon], Kassie [Temple], Tim [Lambert], Peggy, and myself. There might have been more. So I was sort of surprised that they came to this decision [about always going along with the magisterium] without consulting me. And actually none . . . well, Peggy wrote me about it, but none of the other editors did. When I came home, I said I couldn't remain as an editor if they didn't reconsider. They were in the midst of these sort of dreadful weekly meetings, large group meetings discussing all this stuff.

Ro: So other people attended those large meetings?

Gary: Yeah. You'd have people . . . people who were active in the community. People who worked on the soup line. People who were marginally involved with the community. It was my decision that I couldn't be on the list of editors any longer. It was just . . . I couldn't go along with this sort of attitude.

Ro: And did you leave the community then?

Gary: Well, over the previous year, I'd been trying to figure out what I should do. You know, it was real clear that in some very important ways, the Catholic Worker was not a supportive community for me.

Ro: For you as a gay man?

Gary: Yeah. It was difficult to conceive of intimately throwing my lot in with a group of people who were throwing their lot in with the magisterium. Who needs it? Life's too difficult and life's too short. There are other people out there who don't think I'm an abomination, who don't think I have an intrinsic inclination toward evil.

I didn't fault the Catholic Worker for not taking on AIDS as a cause. And yet more and more, I myself felt that was what I wanted to be doing. It gave me a sense of the importance of every individual human being. It magnified the Catholic Church's teaching on . . . you know, just the whole sense of the Mystical Body and that everybody is part of it and everybody is infinitely valuable. Peter Maurin's personalist vision and Dorothy's interpretation of that. And then the way that was passed on to me, not so much directly by Dorothy but by the people who I worked with at the Worker.

Ro: Before all the discussions, before Ernesto's *NCR* article and everything, had you told people at the Worker that you were gay?

Gary: It probably gradually surfaced over a number of years before that. For most people. I don't think it was a surprise to anybody. It wasn't like, "Oh, my gosh, Gary! I didn't know."

Ro: Do you think the fact that you left might make it harder for other gays in the movement?

Gary: I think it probably would make it more difficult for gay people at the New York Catholic Worker. I would never tell a gay person that they should go there. I might not discourage them, but I would never encourage them. It's not a very receptive place.

One thing that I really fault the editors for is not writing about it in the paper. It's their paper. You know, the traveling I did was real important. It always gave me a certain perspective on the New York Worker, and I knew that just because we did it a certain way didn't mean it *had* to be done that way. Because this community functioned in this mysterious sort of way, with decisions made without anybody knowing about them. I realized that I didn't want to fight this hard to belong to this group of people. I could do other things. And I could still walk in and do the soup line. I could still be acquaintances or even friends with some of these people. But I couldn't live in community with them.

You know, I probably came out of what happened at the Worker with a deep sadness. I think people like Peggy and Ernesto came out a little more burnt to a crisp. Maybe it's just that I have a different temperament. When I came back, I realized it was a losing battle. It wasn't worth fighting for.

It was my life for so many years, though, for so many years. And my dad was real upset with all this happening. Because he felt it was some security for me since I wasn't going to get married and have a family. He hated my going to the Catholic Worker at first, but once I got here, you know, he warmed up to the idea. It gave him some reassurance because he knew that I had people around who cared for me, loved me, and all that good stuff.

Peggy Scherer tells her story of the pain of separation. (This interview took place on August 7, 1988.) When we talked, she was working at Bailey House with Gary. She has since moved to Washington, D.C.

Peggy Scherer: I want to say that, right now, I find it very hard to talk about the Catholic Worker with any enthusiasm. The events in the last two years have burned me deeply. At other points [in my life], I have described things differently.

Now there's just so much sadness around my whole Worker experience . . . for twelve and a half years, it was my life, and I thought it would continue. And the fact that I feel I had to leave in order to follow my conscience hurt me very, very deeply. For those reasons, I don't think a lot about the Worker.

As someone said, my departure was like going through a very messy divorce. With time, I'm sure things will change. They've already gotten easier. I've gotten very, very involved in other things, especially this last year.

Ro: Well, I remember you once said, "You can take the girl out of the Worker, but you can't take the Worker out of the girl."

Peggy: And I've been amazed at how hurt I feel. I guess when I said that, I was still convinced that things just had to work out. They didn't.

Ro: When you left, did you go right to Bailey House?

Peggy: No, I didn't. I did almost nothing for close to a year. I was . . . even my departure was spread out over months. It was rather agonizing.

To backtrack to the beginning: In February of 1985, I submitted an article for the paper. At the time, I had no idea things would unfold as they did, but part of me really felt we needed a community discussion [on homosexuality in the church]. Sometimes a written piece can be a vehicle for discussion or help to guide it.

Eight months later, that article went in the paper in a totally different form. It was published after four rewrites, each of which was done through a consensus process with about twenty to twenty-five people, three or four days of recollection, ta-da, ta-da, ta-da. Innumerable large and small group discussions. I've never had so many one-to-one, heart-to-heart discussions in my life. Then a couple of other articles were published.

Many of us were kind of excited and felt we were really grappling with a very difficult issue. It was difficult for everybody, because even those who were gay or lesbian in the community didn't agree with each other on many things, much less people who were straight. People were everywhere [on the issue]. The thinking didn't follow lines of sexual preference. (It still doesn't, and that's fine.) But it was a very vibrant discussion with openness and sharing back and forth, and that all seemed good.

A few months later, a writer submitted an article which mentioned that women should be ordained, and there was a lot of flack about that. It was never published. Eventually some people said that they felt nothing should ever be written in the paper that at all disagreed with the church, even if it was an expression of personal difference. I deeply disagree with that.

To challenge the church per se in doctrine and to talk about the pain were very different things. People had been hurt by people in the church. Early on, the Worker had talked about racism in the church and anti-Semitism and had put forth pacifism at a time when no one in the church wanted to hear that, and I didn't see a huge difference.

It eventually became very clear what I had to do, and I could not do what I felt pulled to do, staying at the Worker. I needed to leave to do that. It was very difficult and very painful because I didn't feel then that it should have been necessary. On the other hand, I don't regret leaving. Life does go on.

A very basic problem was there was no real resolution on the question of authority—who had the authority to make decisions, who is the community. There was just a lot of confusion. Because it wasn't clear how decisions were made and by whom, making a decision, especially about a very difficult topic, became next to impossible.

Early on, I had suggested having mediators—facilitators—and some other people were interested, too. That was rejected. I really felt, and still feel, that if we had some outside people who we trusted . . . We were all too close to the problem, and someone from outside could have helped to frame the questions and guide the discussions. We just kind of jumped here and there.

Ro: Well, that's a pretty modern idea. Let's face it, that wouldn't have happened when Dorothy was here. She would have thought it was sort of a crazy idea to ask somebody.

Peggy: She probably would have. But again, Dorothy died. I feel that some people, at least, want to act as if Dorothy is the ongoing authority. In my mind, that means they never do anything Dorothy didn't do, which means they're not responding to anything that's happening now. That I find very restricting. I feel that with prayer and reflection and making errors—Dorothy was humble enough to know that she would make mistakes, too—the potential is there for the people to go ahead. And for people to exercise leadership and acknowledge that they exercise leadership.

Dorothy was where she was. I certainly feel strongly that Dorothy and Peter didn't found the Worker just to preserve their views. It was a vehicle for them to become more faithful to God in an active way, and they would hope that for us, as I understand it. That's why I feel that, even though one must look to the founders, there's a time and a place and a way where you move beyond that.

Dorothy didn't set a plan in place. And my departure didn't end people asking questions. Dorothy directed things with an iron hand. In the first years after her death, things went along. There were a number of us who had been around during her life, and we just continued on. But, as would happen with any order or any group, at some point after the death of the founder, things change. And you have to deal with it, whether you choose to or not. The questions of authority, and who has it, and what kind of decisions they make—that was underlying everything.

It can be argued that the Worker was never intended to be a community or a democracy. As I understood [Dorothy], the work comes first, and community might form around it. But even if you don't use the word "community," it seems to me that if [everything you're about] talks of treating every human being with respect, you must also treat the people you live and work with respectfully. Otherwise, I think there's a measure of hypocrisy when you talk about nonviolence everywhere else in the world but don't do respectful, courteous things to the people you live with.

Ro: Um . . . hmmm. It seems to me there have always been issues of homosexuality in the Worker. And maybe they've never been dealt with in the same way as in traditional orders, which I'm guessing probably directly asked homosexuals to leave.

Peggy: Yeah. It's not new. There's another person at Bailey House who was around the Worker for fifteen or twenty years and who left because, among other things, he was not welcome as a gay man. It's not new. He left a long time ago. But it's hard, and a lot of the hurt is because the people at the Worker have been welcoming to so many [other] people who were rejected. That was the whole point of the Worker.

In some houses, I know people can be much more open; in other houses, there are tensions. Certainly there have been tensions since the very beginning. No one knows what proportion of the total population is gay, but I found a rather high percentage of people in the Worker who were gay and lesbian. As I've found in other service works. So I'd say, yes, some people have found a home.

[At Bailey House], people are openly gay and lesbian, and are fully respected and embraced, not just tolerated. That doesn't happen at the New York Worker because of the church's teaching and because of people's understanding of the church's teaching . . . or interpretation or application. If someone has hesitations about a person's sexuality, I don't feel they can be fully embraced. And so the atmosphere at Bailey House would not exist at the New York Worker without some very basic changes. Not to say that things that happen at the Worker are bad, but there is a difference.

As a straight person who has become much more sensitized, I hear more and more life stories of people who have suffered a great deal from the time they were very small. Homosexuality is called unnatural by some people, yet there are hundreds and hundreds of people that I know personally for whom it is natural. Just as heterosexuality is natural to other people. Now, I certainly won't deny that people of whatever sexual preference abuse sex. If you live in New York in the 1980s, and you see certain things, you can get appalled, but if you go to Forty-second Street and see heterosexual sex, you can get appalled, too.

You know, I rarely do any long-range planning, but at some point, I might be interested in doing work with people with AIDS in a community setting. I wouldn't call it Catholic Worker.

Ro: Why wouldn't you?

Peggy: Let's just stop here. Because it's something that might never happen. When it happens, *if* it happens, I might think differently. At this point, I don't want to be associated with the Catholic Worker. Okay? I'm not going to get into the whys. If I would do it, I'd call it something else. Perhaps because in part I would want to be sensitive to all those gay men and lesbian women who've been so hurt by the Catholic Church. I would not use a name which would make them even *think* they wouldn't be welcome.

As a gay friend pointed out to me, it's probably the feminine aspect of homosexuality that upsets them as much as anything. So you'll probably see them ordaining married men and ordaining gay priests long before they ordain any women.

The authority problem in the church is really what all of this is about. Authority in and of itself has no value. Authority only has value when it's helping to further the mission of the church, which is to carry out Jesus' teachings. And the constant, chronic problem throughout history was that people get stuck on the structure itself and the authority itself, as opposed to what the authority is supposed to help further.

[The controversy that resulted in my leaving was over] homosexuality and homosexuality in the church—the lines of the official church teaching which basically says that we accept people who are homosexuals, but we don't accept homosexuality. Which in my mind is a totally contradictory statement. You can't have it both ways. But I don't think many people in the church live up to even *that* teaching. Many gay people have been treated with great disrespect as human beings.

My Central American experiences have helped me in my understanding of the church, and how often what you think of as church is actually a cultural manifestation, one of the trappings and not part of the basic structure. For instance, you had to have Mass a lot in the pre-Vatican church, and now we know that isn't so. Certain things couldn't happen then. They were incredibly adamant. Now of course they can.

I'm glad I've had some different experiences, being brought up in the fifties and sixties in the "before church" and then living in post–Vatican II. I'm glad to see the differences and to see that there still is church—church before and after. God is still very much in the church. There's a lot we don't know, and we don't gain as much as we think we do by thinking we have it all under control. We don't. And we continue to grow.

Later I talked to Bill Griffin, who came to the Worker after the Vietnam War and is still associated with the New York house.

Bill Griffin: Rosalie, while the tape was off, you brought up the issue of homosexuality and gay rights. Do you want my opinions about that or . . .

Ro: Are they real issues?

Bill: Yes, they are real issues. In terms of human realities, in terms of causing human suffering, yes, they are. But you have to be more specific about your question.

Ro: Okay. Do you see that this issue of suffering, the suffering of homosexuals within the church because they feel so disenfranchised, is something the CW should have—"position" isn't the word because I don't see Catholic Workers as having a position—but is it something that should be discussed?

Bill: Yes. It is. And it has been. As I've said before, the Catholic Church is a very big institution. Some people would characterize it as not being very compassionate towards homosexuals, and that's true. But there are other parts of the Catholic Church that have been *very* compassionate towards homosexuals. The . . . I can't pretend to be any expert. I don't know what . . .

Ro: Where should the Worker be on this?

Bill: Where should the Worker be? This is a complex question. The Worker is . . . it's not a political party. It's a gathering, a group of people sharing common activities around the works of mercy—feeding the hungry, clothing the naked. The practical. Through these corporal and spiritual works of mercy which we try to practice, we hope to grow ourselves and we hope to help our society grow and help our world to grow. These differences among people like homosexuality are discussed on one level, and the Worker is functioning on another level, I think. It's not a superior or inferior level, just another level.

David Buer lived for a number of years at the St. Francis Catholic Worker in Chicago and then with Sandy Adams at a struggling CW farm in Hamlin, West Virginia. He is now a Franciscan novice in Santa Barbara, California.

David Buer: Sexuality is a very important issue in community life. If that's not paid attention to, it will destroy community. The Catholic Church's official teaching in the area of homosexuality is accepting of the individual but not affirming of the action. And that represents my position pretty well. Sandy Adams and I . . . Sandy has written publicly about his homosexuality. We had the whole year [while I was in West Virginia] to discuss the issue, and it was good. But I think it's very intense. In some houses, it's been a very divisive issue, but I think the healthy thing to do is to continue discussing it. I think Peter Maurin would want the Catholic Worker movement to continue discussing it in an open and honest way.

It's certainly not just in the Catholic Worker movement. It's in the larger Catholic Church, larger Christian church. Also, it's beyond homosexuality. It also has to do with active heterosexuality in a particular house. And I think . . . I might be called conservative or whatever, but I have a strong sense that God will not bless that. You know, if we're not being faithful to our own state in life, that takes some blessings away. That's the best way I can . . . it's an awkward way of describing it. We can fall from what we really believe in and have a weak moment or whatever, and that's one thing, but it's another thing to say, "No, I don't think this is sin. I don't think this is wrong."

It's important to accept a person. If a person is oriented that way, to accept them as that person. But the act itself is a sin. And therefore God will . . . it will affect blessings that can come to that particular community. And it will disrupt the community. I think the same is true of heterosexuality when it's outside the marriage bond. If you have people who aren't committed to monogamy, it leads to destructive things.

Ro: So what do you do? Do you ask these people to leave?

David: No. I think the houses will just die. If you have a core community, the people who've been there the longest, been committed the longest, have to make those decisions. And if they are active homosexuals, well, they're the ones who have the say, and if you can't . . . well, they can tell the other people to leave. But then I think the house will die.

Ro: Are you going to stay celibate?

David: I feel called to a celibate lifestyle. I feel called to the Franciscan brotherhood.

Ro: And you have to be accepted, too.

David: Exactly. Exactly. Because there can be hostilities to those of us who [have] chosen the celibate way of life. I've certainly felt that. Sometimes homosexuals can be persecutors, too.

Jonathan Kirkendall is a young Catholic convert whom I met at Dorothy Day House in Washington, D.C.

Jonathan Kirkendall: Being gay is just so strange. I want to say, "My sexuality is just a part of my life, an important part, but only one part of me. There's also the spiritual side." And, of course, part of my life is just like everyone else. For instance, tonight a friend is coming over. Just like any other member of the community, I'm having a friend over. But in a way it's different, because this friend is another gay man. Now he's just a friend, like my straight friends, but because we share a common history, the friendship has a different flavor and affects me on a deeper level, or on another level at least.

Ro: Um . . . hmm. What about being gay in the church?

Jonathan: Well, that's very hard. And it's something I didn't even consider when I first became Catholic.

Ro: Was it easy to be gay and Baptist?

Jonathan: No. It isn't easy being gay and human! I've experienced a lot of pain and a lot of grief over this, a lot of alienation and a lot of inner turmoil. I can't just say it's a part of my life and that I have no problems with it. I'm standing in front of the altar the other day, and I think, "Damn! I can't even go to my church to be consoled. For everything else, I can. There are ears among the bishops for peacemaking. But to tell them I'm gay and lonely . . . I can't go to my church with that."

But then that raises the issue . . . what is the church? The church is not the institution. I can go to my community here. When we have Mass, or when we're just talking, that's my church. And so in a sense I *can* go to my church. But . . . it's a complicated thing, and I haven't quite worked it all through.

When Jonathan sent his transcript back, he added this long postscript about a retreat he attended at Kirkridge titled, "Gay, Lesbian, and Christian." He writes:

I've grown to understand that in order to move to the margins, one must first be willing to listen to the experiences of those on the margins: "I'm a man in love with another man." Then you have to *trust* those experiences: "We who are heterosexual believe that your relationships are as real, as deep, bring as much joy, fulfillment, and pain as our own relationships." Then you must *act* on the experiences of the marginalized: "We will march with you, attend Dignity with you, et cetera."

I came back from Kirkridge, sat down with my community, and said, "I've had enough. When we had South African refugees living here, we began a weekly vigil in fron of the S.A. embassy. Well, you have another oppressed minority here, and I want some support."

Not only did they agree, they were downright eager. It's been wonderful. They've been willing to do the listening, the trusting, the acting, willing to do it one hundred percent!! You know, at first, when I told my community, I know Margaret [Howells] had problems with it. She admits that one of the reasons she did is 'cause she's a psychiatric nurse, and the only gay people she'd seen are people with really severe problems. But she said to me, "I just have to remember that I see a lot of unhappily married people in the psych hospital, too, but that doesn't mean marriage is a bad thing."

Ro: What about being gay in the Catholic Worker?

Jonathan: My understanding is that the New York Catholic Worker has . . . takes a very dim view of active gays, and that hurts. They call them "A&P gays." Active and practicing. Someone in my community said, "I can't believe that's going on in the Catholic Worker!" And someone who had moved out of the New York house said, "It's not. It's going on in one house."

I think if I had the chance to tell them how hurt . . . I don't think they realize. You know, the church is wrong about this. One of my Baptist friends said to me, "When you first told me that you were gay, I thought 'Well, that's all right as long as he doesn't act on it.'" But then she said, "You know, you're such a loving person. It would be wrong for you not to go through life loving someone."

I know what it is to be marginalized. Yet I'm kind of in a unique position because I'm a white man. Therefore, I'm automatically put in the center, and I can let people know or not that I'm gay. It's a complicated issue.

One of my earliest interviews was with Larry Ray-Keil of the Family Kitchen in Seattle. When we talked, he was also working on a help line for the AIDS Project.

Larry Ray-Keil: How are things now with the Worker? Well, I see some real good from not having a leader like Dorothy, but of course one can also say it's bad. You don't have anybody to rely on to make . . . for instance, what is the position on gay Catholic Workers? Because Dorothy always stated a position and people knew it. Now that influence isn't there.

Personally, my problem with the Worker these days has a lot to do with the institutional church and the recent ruling on homosexuality. A lot of the staff where I work are gay, and I was really pained when the papal announcement came out so strongly against people who are homosexual. So the hierarchy is very much involved in my feelings about the Catholic Worker. I really feel that the church has . . . is not on the right track on this. I'm distancing myself even more from the traditional church because of the stand on homosexuality.

Perhaps we need to define more specifically what a Catholic Worker is. The communion of saints does work and sustain us, but so much of what was termed Catholic is no longer operable for me. How can I ask my gay friends to accept a church that doesn't accept them? I miss the community of worship in a way, but I can't honestly accept the doctrine of beliefs which are called Roman Catholic. I guess the pronouncement on gays was the straw that broke.

Richard Cleaver lived at the Worker in New York before returning to his native Iowa and the Des Moines CW. He now works for the American Friends Service Committee in Ann Arbor, Michigan.

Richard Cleaver: I remember the first time it ever came up in any [Catholic Worker] paper, as far as I know. It was in Seattle. Maybe as early as January of '77. All the newsletters would come into the [New York] house, and they'd always get put out and everybody would leaf through them. This one from Seattle had been shoved underneath a heap of old mail in one of the drawers in the desk so that nobody would see it.

The gay and lesbian thing has been really tough in New York, you know. It's never all that tough in the Midwest. It's kind of funny—New York sophisticates and us Midwestern hicks out here . . . but I think most of us never found it a very difficult leap to make.

Ro: What makes it so painful in New York?

Richard: Well, it may have to do with the fact that Dorothy was not at all open to change on this subject. And people there are much more attached to her memory than a lot of other people. I think there are people who feel that it would be an affront to Dorothy to go against what were undoubtedly her wishes in this question. She was very traditional in questions of sexual morality.

Ro: Yes. But yet she had to know that many of the people that she loved and worked with were gay.

Richard: Right. Part of that is that it's easy in personal relationships to . . . it's a lot easier in personal relationships to deal with an individual's character as a whole, even the parts about it that you might not like, than it is [on a] theoretical plane. To use an analogy—when I was a kid growing up in a small town in Iowa, one of the high school teachers—one of the most beloved high school teachers—was a man who was living with another man, more or less openly. Everybody knew it and everybody thought he was a great guy. They knew his total personality and they knew a lot about him besides the fact that he was gay.

Now if a poll taker came into town and asked those same people, "Should homosexuals be allowed to teach in the public schools?" they would probably say no. And they wouldn't see any contradiction between those two things. I think Dorothy was able to keep those contradictions.

There are people in the controversy in New York whom I'm very close to and who always knew me as a gay man and didn't seem to be particularly freaked out about that, but who take exactly the opposite position in this circumstance. I'm not the only person in that position. I think that's another reason why it's personally painful for a lot of people. They feel their own friends have betrayed them. I'm far enough away from it that I don't have that feeling quite so strongly.

I knew and was comfortable with the fact that I was gay before I was at all religiously inclined. In that sense, I came in with my eyes open. The funny thing is that I'm probably a lot more celibate than a lot of priests. I think there's a gift of celibacy, and I don't think it should be attached to the priesthood, either.

Ro: [It's] a gift for heterosexuals as well as for homosexuals.

Richard: Right. Right. I think it's very damaging to most gay people to have to divide themselves in ways that straight people are never asked to do. When people talk about "practicing homosexuals," I always say, "I practice a little bit every day." Everybody's sexuality is present in every relationship. It's what makes relationships relationships on some level.

Ro: Maybe I get more angry at the church than you do because you embraced it and I was embraced. [Richard was a convert.]

Richard: Well, you can't have everything. There is no perfect denominational home. As I said before, coming to the Worker felt like coming home. But like with your biological family, you take the rough with the smooth. I get it from the other side, too. A lot of lesbian and gay activists say I cooperated with the oppressor by becoming Catholic.

Ro: Do you think the split in the New York community over this issue has weakened the leadership they traditionally had?

Richard: I doubt it. It's been very painful for some people. And I think there are a couple of people whose loss is significant—Peggy Scherer, for example. But we've had such a long history of people coming and going . . . this may be not the occasion that one would hope for, but there are always departures. Things keep going anyway.

Ro: What about relationships between the New York house and other communities?

Richard: I think those were already becoming more tenuous. Probably from when Dorothy was no longer able to travel from house to house.

At St. Elizabeth's in Chicago, Barbara Blaine and the late Gary Olivero and I had a far-ranging discussion about sexuality and the church.

Ro: Gary, what about gays in the Catholic Worker?

Gary Olivero: I don't see the Catholic Worker as having an institutional rejection of gay people. Dorothy would feed, clothe, and love the homosexual. She'd respond personally and that's what the Catholic Worker is—that feeling response. "Love is the solution."

The church, as an institution, can only have an *intellectual* response. The bad side of the institutional church, to begin with, is the lack of ecumenism, a problem John XXIII tried to change. That sense of arrogance. When people read Dorothy Day, that sense of arrogance somehow comes through—that sense of planting herself there in the rock of the church. I think those struggles continue in individual houses and within individual people, struggles between the more radical, noninstitutional, seemingly unreligious, unspiritual people in the Catholic Worker as opposed to the traditional, very spiritual people.

Ro: Catholic with a capital *C*?

Gary: Yeah, that connection. Party line, you know. But Dorothy said, "There is no party line in the Catholic Worker." It's not the Daily Worker, and it's not the Catholic Charities. Or the Catholic Church.

Ro: What if CWs lead a life the institutional church thinks is sinful?

Gary: Well, who doesn't? Supposedly we're all sinners. We all say that but at the same time, we chuckle and wink and pretend that we're not, rather than own up to our own sins.

Barbara Blaine: Well, it's one thing to say, "I'm a sinner because, you know, I get stubborn with people or I'm not nice to somebody or I'm . . ." I can legitimately feel bad about that. It's another thing to say, like the institutional church would say, I'm a sinner because I engage in homosexual activities.

Gary: Why is it another thing?

Barbara: I was going to explain that. Because this person who's engaging in homosexual activities is saying, "I'm not sinning by doing this." Whereas we all say it's wrong to be selfish or to hoard something. I'm not saying it's right for me to be selfish, I'm saying that's my weakness. But people who are gay *celebrate* being gay. And the church is saying . . .

Gary: Okay. But American society celebrates being selfish. Celebrates greed and accumulation. It's no different. The individual homosexual, you know, doesn't celebrate the idea of promiscuity—what we would find as sinful sexuality, as painful sexuality and problem sexuality.

Barbara: No. But no one, no one, no one would *say* that greed is not a sin. Would they? People don't go around saying greed is not a sin.

Gary: I don't know. Go talk to Lee Iacocca. No homosexual would say out loud that promiscuity isn't a sin, either. No more than a heterosexual would. I'm saying there isn't any difference between that and society's attitude towards greed. Our society relishes . . . it's built on greed. It *is* greed.

Barbara: I disagree with you in that sense. In the Catholic Worker we . . . we espouse a lot of the values of the church. We have a tradition and history of basically spreading the teaching of the Catholic Church. Okay? Would you agree with that? The church is saying that homosexuality is a sin, and there are people in the Catholic Worker movement who are saying it's not a sin. Whether they're homosexual or not. They're just saying that it's not a sin to be homosexual.

Gary: Yeah.

Barbara: And that's at odds with Catholic Church teaching. What I'm saying is that people in the Catholic Worker—not all people, but a small group of people in the Catholic Worker—say homosexuality is fine. That it's life. And beautiful. Something to be celebrated. But the church says it's a sin.

Gary: Well, wait one second. Let's get off the . . . the one we agree on is greed. Let's go to pacifism. Now there are people in the Catholic Worker movement who wouldn't say pacifism is okay. And there are Catholic Workers who would say the violence of the military is a sin. Okay? The church doesn't, though. So we're back to the institution. We're back with homosexuality. The church says it's wrong. Catholic Worker says it's not . . . or some people in the Catholic Worker say it's not.

Ro: Here's another one. Some people don't see abortion as being part of the pacifist question.

Gary: Who? Well, I agree it hasn't been brought up much. It's not discussed much.

Ro: Some [Worker communities] have made antiabortion their guiding light, and some just don't seem to go for it.

Gary: Those are the nitty-gritty issues. That's what we need to be talking about. Not what makes us the same but those differences. Again, if you go beyond the idea of judging somebody else, you realize that you can hold these ideas and still have your sense of being with each other. It's not the work that makes us the same. It's the call to faithfulness.

Ro: Can you respect Catholic Workers who accept the Catholic Church's official teaching on homosexuality?

Gary: Sure. We're connected to the institution. We call ourselves the *Catholic* Worker. So the struggle is in feeling the pain of the victim. I would use the word "victim" in that conflict between the institutional church and the individual as homosexual.

Barbara: I would, too, but I imagine that people who [go along with the institution] don't see homosexuals as the victims. The Catholic Worker offers sanctuary, in a sense. We offer a space for Workers. We should be able to offer a space for people who have been victimized by the institution, too.

Fr. Bernie Gilgun has long been the guiding light for the Mustard Seed Catholic Worker in Worcester, Massachusetts.

Ro: Father, how do you feel about some of the controversies in the church, controversies that are affecting Catholic Workers particularly. For instance, how do you feel about [Sandy Adams] at the farm in Hamlin, West Virginia, writing in the May 1988 listing of Catholic Worker houses that they're "storming heaven for more recognition of gay, lesbian, and women's rights in the Catholic Worker movement."

Fr. Bernie Gilgun: [Long pause.] I think it's hard to put in words the real dynamic of what's going on in the church and particularly in the Catholic Worker movement. I don't know much about electricity, but I know it's a vibration, and I know that this vibration is a very healthy thing. I know, on the one hand, that there is no way out of it—chastity in our tradition is a virtue. For the married, for the unmarried, for the gays and the lesbians, for the young and the old.

You can't really please God unless you strive to be chaste. Like all the other virtues. We want to know with all the saints what is the will of God—what is good, what is pleasing, what is perfect. And with His grace, we can come to know that. That's what the church is all about. Not sexual indulgence. That must be avoided at all costs. Don't idealize the real—strive to realize the ideal.

On the other hand, I, for example, am gay. And I understand now the teaching of the church. If it is not done publicly or in contempt . . . that is to say, if it is done by those who love and fail only out of human weakness. It is a hard saying, but as we learn in the Catholic Worker, this profound truth that Dorothy so suffered from—love comes with sacrifice. Two gays cannot make love. God is love. Two gays can share love. And I have found that great fulfillment in the Catholic Worker movement, which I might not have been able to work out so easily in the diocese.

A tough struggle. A tough struggle. But an ideal that is attainable. To know what is good and what is pleasing and what is perfect. Ah . . . that's what it's all about.

CHAPTER 30

Abortion

What reason not to abort can I give this mother whose first child had two toes chewed off by rats? How can I tell her that her second child is able to look forward to a life that would be better than death? You tell me!

—Marcia Timmel

The Catholic Church opposes nuclear weapons but doesn't excommunicate the weapons producers. And it opposes capital punishment but doesn't excommunicate the executioners and the judges and wardens. But it opposes abortion and excommunicates women who have abortions.

—Sr. Char Madigan

T HE teachings on nonviolence accepted by most Catholic Workers would appear to proscribe abortion and the death penalty as well as war; however, few of the narrators addressed either abortion or the death penalty. One exception was Unity Kitchen in Syracuse, known throughout the movement for its consistent pro-life stance.

Marcia Timmel of Washington, D.C., was another striking exception.

Ro: Marcia, How did you come to the Catholic Worker?

Marcia Timmel: Actually, I came into the Catholic Worker through the pro-life movement. I . . . I had an abortion in 1973. And had a bad two years, finding out that what the counselors told me just wasn't true. After two years of post-abortion counseling, I was still a basket case. I finally reached a crisis one night and came within a hair's breadth of killing myself. Ironically, that brought me back into the Catholic Church. The only way I can describe it—I've never had adequate language for it—is that I had a . . . a sense of Christ intervening, a Christ I'd been trying to deny even existed. It was scary, because the guilt of the abortion was just destroying me, and I was sure that Christ was present in that room with me. He was there to punish me and yet, at the same time, this presence was saying, "I love you. Come back!" Finally, after wavering the whole night, I got out the yellow pages and found a Catholic church about three blocks away.

I went there, to six A.M. Mass, and it was a first Friday. I'd had a strong devotion to the Sacred Heart when I was a little kid. The priest that morning chose to preach on Christ's promises to Margaret Mary Alocoque, how anyone who'd ever been devoted to the Sacred Heart would never die out of grace, how sinners would find the grace of repentance. It was just everything I needed to hear.

I went to confession. The priest was filled with enough grace to recognize that I was a person really on the brink, not just of going in or coming out of the church but of going in or coming out of life. And he assured me that, yes, even this God could forgive, and if I was there that morning, it must mean that God loved me very much and wanted . . . And I always smile when I think about this, because of the stereotype of the way the church is supposed to guilt-trip women who have had abortions. In retrospect, the church was a lot more helpful than other institutions.

I mean this priest was very antiabortion. He wasn't a modern priest at all. Very conservative, straight-line. Basically he told me, "Yes, you did a horrible thing. You killed your daughter. And nothing you will ever be able to do can make up for it. You can spend the rest of your whole life trying, and you're never going to make up for it."

But then he said, "You know what? That's exactly why Jesus came. He knew that every single person in this world would do something that they could never make up for, and He came to do that for you."

That was exactly what I needed to hear. The counselors had kept on telling me, "Look, you're a good person. Don't think about it. Just forget it." It was much more healing to have someone not deny what I had done but acknowledge it. Acknowledge it in all of its horror. Help me to grieve over it. To say, "You were a mother and this was your child and your child is dead. And yes, it was your fault. And of course you feel terrible! Of course you need to cry! Of course you need to be angry!"

All the stuff that Kubler-Ross talks about in dealing with death and dying certainly could be applied to women recovering from an abortion. My experience is that most women who get counseling are counseled to stay in the denial stage, which is the worst possible place to stay in terms of any real inner healing.

The priest encouraged me to work with kids, not to punish myself by cutting myself off. I learned, finally, to acknowledge that I really did love children and that I wasn't such a beast that I couldn't be around them. After a lot of other stuff [including a stint as Professor of Communications at Morehead State University], I joined the Jesuit Volunteer Corps. They had one placement that really interested me—as an executive director for Pregnancy Care in Akron, Ohio.

At that point, I still wasn't talking very openly about my abortion, but I told them my background and asked them if they thought this would impede my being of value to other women. They said, "God, no! If there is anyone who can speak to women who are in the process of making the decision, it's someone who has been there." And that was important for me to hear. That even out of what really is the greatest tragedy of my life, some specific good could come.

I took the job with a lot of trepidation, though, and was very uncertain what emotions it was going to bring up. And certainly during the course of the two years when I was rebuilding that program and training other volunteers, I really had to speak quite openly at public gatherings. I didn't want to do it in the sort of paternalistic way of so many people in the pro-life movement. "Oh these poor girls!" It can be a very condescending thing. And I found that the only way that I could really reach out and explain what it was like and why women choose to have abortions, without betraying the confidentiality of the women I was working with, was to share my story.

This is important to me. So much of the pro-life movement has made a mistake by being judgmental and so sort of biased in their approaches. So whenever you're working for pro-life, you're carrying all that baggage with you. Some pregnant women who are considering abortions go ahead and have abortions, and some of them choose not to and have beautiful children. And the ones who have abortions, I grieve for. If there is anything I can do to help them from being a repeat, I'll do it. I always encourage women to come back to me, even if they choose abortion. "I won't condemn you, but you're going to need someone."

The way I look at it, two lives are physically at risk to some degree in every abortion. Even if both lives aren't terminated immediately, there is a real good chance that down the line, the mother's life is going to go down the tubes. If not actually physically, in other ways. Our culture sometimes outrageously punishes women who carry on with the pregnancy, punishes them for getting pregnant, or for letting the world know they're pregnant. Or punishes them economically, and that's most heartbreaking for women who already have children.

This used to kill me in Akron. The women . . . one woman had a two-year-old who was missing a couple of his toes. Rats had chewed them off. Another woman's first child had died of a brain concussion when it fell out of the dresser drawer where it was sleeping. And so I changed our agency so that it was not merely doing pregnancy support. If we said we were supporting the pregnancy, that meant that once the child was there, it was our responsibility, too. And if that meant we had to beg, borrow, or steal to get the baby furniture they needed for safety, to get them into decent living environments, to get . . . I became an advocate.

I had a gradual awakening. Part of the process was saying, "Why didn't I know people were suffering like this?" I found myself quickly becoming quite liberal and probably beginning to pass beyond the pale of liberal, even at that point. That was threatening to the more traditional right-to-life elements I was working with.

On the other hand, I was living in a convent with several women religious who were all out working with the poor and invested with a spiritual and social lifestyle that made sense to me. I really respected them, and most of them felt abortion should be an option. So I was feeling very displaced. Wondering if I was the only person in the world who saw consistency between wanting to save the lives of unborn children and preventing the exploitation of women.

I've never met an American-born woman who was having an abortion because she wanted to show she had control over her body. They all feel that if they have this child, their husband—boyfriend, parents, you name it—is going to totally reject them, which is a very real probability. I try to deal with the abortion issue by making sure women have some real choices.

At first the agency was looking to political and social welfare channels to meet the needs. These were totally inadequate, so I'd come to board meetings [of the agency]. "Okay, you don't see it as our responsibility to take care of children after they are born. What reason not to abort can I give this mother whose first child had two toes chewed off by rats? How can I tell her that her second child is able to look forward to a life that would be better than death? You tell me!"

And the right-to-lifers had to begin struggling with it. They were expecting me to have all the answers, and all I had was prayer and what I was getting from the women. I would go to Mass, and it seemed the readings would be "Feed the hungry, shelter the homeless . . ." You know, it seemed very affirming of the realizations I was coming to in the day-to-day stories of the women I met. So I was feeling isolated. Until I saw some literature from a group called Pro-Lifers for Survival—a few articles by Juli Loesch and a reprint of an article by Dan Berrigan on why he was against abortion. Suddenly, there was just this enormous sense of relief. Here was another group that saw the real violence being done to my women and my babies as a pro-life stand.

Fr. Frank Cordaro was a founder of the Des Moines Catholic Worker.

Ro: Why aren't there more Catholic Workers active in the abortion issue?

Fr. Frank Cordaro: It's a tough issue. It's a tough issue. But I think the Catholic Worker has a unique thing to offer in the whole dialogue. Because the abortion issue shows how the institutional church has bought into the whole idea that you can legislate Gospel values. That you can use the law to bring about . . . to force people. You don't legislate these kind of values, you live them by example.

Ro: Has the Catholic Worker done a particularly good job in that?

Frank: No. We don't do a particularly good job at very much of what we do. But . . . but we're where we need to be if we're going to ask the right questions. Whether we come up with good answers is not . . . in this culture, we need to know the questions. And the Catholic Worker is that critical space where white middle-class educated Catholic Americans can stand.

The Catholic Worker's anarchistic position ought to tell us right off the bat that we don't want to make the possession of a nuclear weapon a criminal act, but to get rid of the weapons. And I don't want to make an abortionist criminal; I want to get rid of the need for abortion.

You know, reasonable people and good people are choosing abortion in this culture. That means we live in a most unreasonable culture, a sick and wicked culture. Any time a woman wants to kill, we'll make it a criminal act. Any time a man wants to kill via the state, we'll bless it and support it. So male violence is tolerated, accepted, and embraced in the church. Female violence is not. Again, it's the double standard.

Sr. Char Madigan is one of the founders of St. Joseph's in Minneapolis, a house that provides hospitality for women from abusive situations "in the Catholic Worker tradition."

Sr. Char Madigan: You know, I'm changing about abortion. I find myself . . . I can't be with the pro-life people, and I can't be totally with . . . I can't be in the "always or never camp" anymore on anything. And that's getting away from Catholic Worker stuff, but it's . . . I think these issues need a national debate, both inside the Worker and in the church as a whole. All CW houses are not the same on abortion.

At St. Joe's, we gather for what we call clarification of thought once a month. To tell you the truth, some people in our community would be very pro-life and others very pro-choice. For the sake of not tearing ourself apart over that issue, and so we could still keep running the house, I would suspect that we wouldn't come out too strongly on either side.

Our point is that the Catholic Church opposes nuclear weapons but doesn't excommunicate the weapons producers. And it opposes capital punishment, but doesn't excommunicate the executioners and the judges and wardens. But it opposes abortion and excommunicates women who have abortions. [You shouldn't] be stoned to death after you've gone through that anguish. But I would say that there are people [in our house who] do not want to put this in the newsletter.

I also asked Sr. Anna Koop, a Sister of Loretto, what she thought about the abortion issue.

Sr. Anna Koop (Denver): I . . . well, that's probably another one. I guess it's just not closed for me at all. I mean I . . . I will never say wholesalely that I believe in abortion. And I never will say wholesalely that I don't. Because I believe there are situations in which abortion is appropriate. I probably come down closer to a pro-choice position.

Ro: Is the Worker confronting any of this stuff?

Anna: You don't see a lot about it in the [New York paper]. That's intriguing because the Worker has certainly been willing to confront the church [in the past]. A reporter from [the *National Catholic Reporter*] asked us once if it were possible for the Catholic Worker movement to take a position on current issues. And we all concluded that we couldn't. There's no mechanism, no vehicle for taking a stance as a movement. Because of the anarchism, I guess.

Ro: And if there were?

Anna: Well, if there were, wouldn't we be grappling with things like AIDS and homosexuality?

Ro: Your order can take a position, can't it?

Anna: That's right. We have a mechanism for doing it. But I'm not by any means saying [the Catholic Worker] should do that. Because there's a real beauty in the anarchism, a wonderful beauty in the fact that somebody can open a door to a house and say, "I'm a Catholic Worker." And not have to wade through any kind of bureaucracy.

Ro: And not have to say, "I am pro-choice" or, "I am pro-life."

Anna: Or say, "This is the position." That's probably what holds a lot of people together. They might just kiss it goodbye if they had to decide whether they were for something or against something in order to be a part of the movement.

CHAPTER 31

Feminism, the Worker, and the Church

A Roundtable Discussion

This is a house of men in many ways; the man-woman thing is such a dimension of the struggle here. Some days, for me to go down and answer that door, to work on that [soup] line, is . . . it can be very painful. The threat is very seldom spoken, but I feel my vulnerability as a woman here. Constantly.

—Meg Hyre

Many CW communities have been torn apart in the last few years by trying to decide what it all means. What does it mean to call yourself a Catholic Worker? To call yourself a Catholic? What to believe about what the church teaches in areas of peace, war, abortion, capital punishment, euthanasia, premarital sex, birth control? Other areas . . . gay rights, gay sexuality, lay rights in the church. These areas—especially the gay and lesbian issues, the abortion issue in particular, the women's issues—have torn communities apart. And people have left bitterly.

—Pat Coy

Ro: As a feminist, how do you live with this church of ours?

Sr. Jan Cebula: Oh, gosh! Don't ask me that question. On the edge. Yes, on the edge.

ABORTION. Homosexuality. Feminism. These issues, all relating in some way to sexuality, have caused painful conflict, not only within these imperfectly united states, but also within the Catholic Church, still so Roman, and, predictably, within the Catholic Worker, influenced as it is by both church and culture. Some Roman Catholics see any divergence from the orthodox position that abortion and homosexuality are inherently sinful as arising directly from the feminist movement; most Catholic Workers believe the connections aren't that simple. In this roundtable, participants discuss the role of women in the Worker, the church, and the world and give a description of a feminist liturgy celebrated at the Las Vegas national gathering.

Sr. Char Madigan (Minneapolis): I think we're all haunted. What is haunting me, what got me here to St. Joseph House [a house that gives hospitality exclusively to women and children], is the passion and rage and the anger about women and domination. That just has turned me into a flaming radical feminist.

Stridency has been part of my past. I had a real stage of outrage, but you can't be mad too long. The outrage led me to oppose dominating systems, and then led me to get to know the verbal domination that was inside me and controlling my life. Especially the workaholism and the whole idea of trying to make other people behave in a way I thought was right for them. It's similar to one country trying to make other countries behave. Or men trying to make women behave. So it's been a real growing experience for me to learn the practice of nonviolence. I see it also as not thinking I am the right answer or *have* the right answer.

As a feminist Catholic, I think the dogmas of the church aren't really what Jesus was about. He was more about stories than dogmas. So our attempts to dogmatize either for or against some of these issues . . . and of making everybody feel guilty and ashamed, I don't think He had that in mind.

[The house in Minneapolis] has been, in a way, quite feminist. After the first fire, a director came in who was just enraged that we would be supportive of gay and lesbian things. (We had published something by a woman who'd heard Jesse Jackson speak at a gay-lesbian rally.) Well, the board said to her, "But that's what this house is about. We accept . . . we don't condemn people because of race, creed, sexual preference." But I know that all houses are not the same on that.

In fact, that's what I love about the Catholic Worker. Dorothy and Peter, you know, tell us that the poor are ambassadors of God and how dare you judge who are the worthy and unworthy poor? Or the worthy and unworthy Catholic Workers? So I suppose I'm just weary of blaming the victim or dividing people up between givers and receivers. The church has really perpetuated the myth of domination and the submission of woman, that woman is not only subordinate but evil, kind of. And this, of course, is the basis for domestic violence, the problem our houses sees most. For women to get out of the battering situation, not only does the man have to stop battering, but we have to start believing our sexuality is not only not evil, but holy. Divine.

Women have been hurt by religion. So I've tried to . . . for instance, we say grace before meals, but we don't have an official Catholic line. But what we haven't done is the more empowering kind of stuff. I have the dream of wanting to do that somehow. We really just do the band-aid stuff here. Blotting up the messes doesn't help change the systems. And talking about what the Bible really meant is a far cry from putting food on the table and a roof over your head and getting a guy to stop raping you. Although the clarification of thought about feminist issues is wonderful for me, it's more scholarly, perhaps, or middle class, and the women don't have time for it when they're in a crisis, as those who come to us invariably are.

Ro: Yes. I see. Uh . . . Joan, the growth of feminism may have coincided with the first years of your Catholic Worker involvement. Can you talk about that relationship, if there is one?

Joan Montesano (Sheep Ranch, California): That's a real interesting question. Some of the women at the house in San Francisco, particularly the lesbian women, were feminists, and I didn't identify myself as a feminist at that time. I probably do now, but I don't take on labels very readily, you know. I mean, I don't even say I'm a pacifist, and yet I believe in pacifism. If I'm pressed, I'd say . . . definitely if I'm pressed, I'd say I was a feminist because I tend towards those goals. But I don't like to say something when I feel I'm so far from the image. And the other thing is that I don't necessarily go right down the line with what I consider feminism.

In the early years, it was probably similar to any sort of new growth in a person. When you're first becoming aware of something, you're just not ready to say yes. I probably was pretty antithetical to feminism, in a way. Coming from a pretty self-centered point of view which was . . . well, nobody really ever imposed anything on me. I've always been a pretty independent woman and made my own decisions. You know, "What's the problem?" It's the same sort of thing as, "I'm white and nobody ever pushed me around, so how come blacks are having trouble?" As time went on, though, I became more aware of the . . . of feminist struggles.

The funny thing about the Worker is that a lot of the really strong people in the houses are men. Just look at California. People think about Jeff Dietrich and Dan Delany and Larry Purcell and Chris [Montesano], and I'm not sure that they think about Catherine Morris and Chris Delany and Ronnie [Purcell] or me. I'm thinking, "All these loud-mouth men." [Laughs.] And you know, it's . . . I don't know.

Now as far as my husband Chris, in terms of being caregiver, he's a very nurturing person. He's the one who would bathe men and be the first to offer a bowl of soup. He's also a nurturing father to the children. I mean he certainly changed as many diapers as I did, and all of that. I don't know about the other California guys, Dan Delany or Jeff or Larry. Well, Larry's a very nurturing person, too.

Dorothy always deferred to Peter in terms of the vision, but it was Dorothy who kept the whole show together over the years and expanded upon the vision. She's the one people identify with the movement.

The feminism thing is hard. I don't know how to answer that. I'm the oldest person and the longest connected with the Women's Crisis Line in San Andreas. It was a very feminist group when it started, and I felt a lot of kinship with those women except for the issue of abortion. Most of the people now are not super-feminist, but a lot of them are pro-abortion. And they know how I feel about that, I think. But I'm basically . . . I'm sure I'm feminist. I just don't go around holding a sign.

Let me just say one last thing about feminism. Some years back someone said to me, "If you're a feminist, you believe that the underlying cause of the world's ills is sexism." And I said, "Hmmm. I don't think I believe that." I don't know what the underlying cause of the world's ills is, but I think it's more selfishness or something.

Ro: Maggie, what do you have to say about women in the Catholic Worker?

Maggie Louden (Alderson, West Virginia): Women are really one of the most violated people in the Catholic Church. Yet sometimes women take on a new dimension in Catholic Worker houses. Sometimes with great pain because there are often very traditional Catholics in the houses. Part of it is because a lot of the work in a Catholic Worker house is traditional women's work—cleaning up after sick people, feeding people, helping a drunk. Often this is seen as women's work, yet *everyone* does it in a Catholic Worker house. So I think that adds a dimension of respect for women.

Women sometimes become a little more understanding of men in this process. And men, if they really throw themselves into the work, definitely become more . . . they're looked down upon sometimes [by the world outside] because they do this women stuff, so they become more in tune with the oppression of women.

Ellen Rehg (St. Louis): Maggie, you said women were violated by the church. I still have to work out a lot of what I think about this, but I know the process men in the church use to arrive at a decision is flawed. So that flaws what's coming out of it. Take sexuality, for example. I understand the need for standards and values, but . . . how do you determine the standard? And who does it? If you don't have any women [involved] in the process of deciding what the theory about women is going to be, it's already severely compromised, to say the least.

Darla Bradley (Davenport, Iowa, and Chicago): I'd like to be able to [have] a women's Catholic Worker.

Ro: There are several women-oriented ones—like Dorothy Day House in Syracuse and St. Joseph's in Minneapolis that Char just spoke about. They're usually pretty feminist because they [have] women guests and often deal directly with domestic violence. But as Char pointed out, they may put on band-aids more than they empower. They don't seem as political as you seem to be.*

Darla: Yeah, that's probably true. But actually I see the issue of [homeless] women as more political than [homeless] men. It's like one more level of oppression.

Dorothy was the strong person in her house, and I think the Catholic Worker allows for sexism because of that. They say the people who were the patriarch and the matriarch didn't deal with the issue.

Ro: Well, do you think having a strong leader in a house, even if it's a woman, is a feminist model?

Darla: No, it's not. It's actually a more male model, [and] there could be a dictatorship, either way. I think that's what Char meant when she talked about learning the practice of nonviolence, of not thinking her way was the only way.

Ro: What would your women's Catholic Worker look like?

Darla: I guess human beings would take precedence over ideology and set structural perspectives.

Ro: How would that work out?

Darla: I . . . I don't know, but my sense, at least, is that it quits being correct ways of *thinking* and is more, "This is what I'm feeling." It's a real different way of looking at things, a more human perspective. With the men, it was always their ideology or their philosophy.

Ro: Yes, I see. Uh, Claire, in what ways do you consider yourself a feminist?

Claire Schaeffer-Duffy (Worcester, Massachusetts): Well . . . [Long pause.] I've been messing with that one because I just recently did an article on abortion [for our newspaper]. Which is a sort of breach with my . . . my feminist inclination.

I guess I consider myself a feminist in the sense that I think it's very, very important to praise and applaud what women do and to recognize the differences between men and women and that the differences are good. I'm very grateful to my feminist friends. I'm thinking of one in particular who really encouraged

* When we met, Darla was working for the Pledge of Resistance. She was the youngest person to be imprisoned for a Plowshares resistance action.

women to love other women, which I don't think we're taught. We're taught to distrust one another. And I think men are also taught to distrust one another and to compete with each other.

So *that* idea of feminism—to really love women and encourage women to love each other, I consider a strong part of myself. And also recognizing that there are things that women in the Worker deal with very, very differently from men. For example, voluntary poverty. The way men deal with it is not necessarily the only way, just because it's the dominant way. It seems valid for people who are equally engaged in the matter to look at how poverty affects them. I think there's just a difference, you know, in the way women perceive voluntary poverty. Like Darla said, men might be more ideological about it and women might be more into how not having something makes their children *feel,* for example.

I do have some differences, I guess, with the feminist movement as it's defined politically. I don't support abortion. It's sometimes assumed, if you're in feminist circles, that you do or that you don't challenge it. I'm moving more to a place of really challenging that as being something to applaud for women. Nothing inside me agrees with abortion. Also (and this is more my anarchist tendencies), I'm not a proponent of the ERA. But that's basically because I see changes through other means than the law.

I don't know too many of the other feminist platforms. I think I have less anger towards men than I used to have, which is good. My feminist awakening awakened some anger towards men, of course, like so many other women. But I seem to be going somewhat past that and actually looking at the hurdles that *men* have to overcome. Some of them are very, very difficult, you know, and very . . . I also feel quite grateful to be a woman. I didn't used to feel that way.

Everything for me usually fits in the context of my faith, which is Christian faith. And I guess that would separate me from some feminists who feel that it's inherently sexist. I know there's a lot of sexism in the church, but there's enough that's true and good to keep me there.

Ro: Anna, how do you take up the challenge of being a woman in the church?

Sr. Anna Koop (Denver): Unfortunately, I think the route I've taken is to avoid the institutional church in some ways. I guess I'm not very willing to utilize a lot of my energy in calling the institutional church to task. Sometimes I feel sorry about that. I mean I *am* Catholic, and it just isn't where I've chosen to place myself.

Wednesday night prayer at our Denver Worker has traditionally been Mass at the house, but I've gotten to the point where I'm no longer willing to chase after a priest to come and say Mass. We do our own prayer when there isn't a priest there. And feel very comfortable with that.

I wouldn't exactly say feminism permeates the Worker movement. Dorothy was an incredibly traditional Catholic, and maybe we need more distance from Dorothy for it to flower. I don't know. I don't know. Also, there's the Worker's focus on the oppression of the poor. I know that's the [reason] I kind of haven't leapt into feminism. Because I feel it's not as classist an issue. Does that make sense? We're privileged and the poor aren't.

Ro: Yes. We are privileged. [Pause] Gary, how did *you* come to be a feminist?

Gary Olivero (Chicago): Well, the radical readings in college gave me an open mind. It was obvious that feminist readings were part of a justice battle, and I could feel their pain. It wasn't a matter of saying something was right or wrong. It's sort of like the people we work with. You don't judge them as being right or wrong, as worthy or the unworthy poor. Their pain and need is so obvious that I need to respond. It's the same with radical reading, where people are describing situations of pain. Most people react intellectually when they read. The Worker says to me that we need to get away from that intellectual reaction. If you see somebody in need, either in person or in books, you respond. We're all hurt in some way, all a bit distorted from reality. That's why we need to listen to each other's pain rather than have that intellectual response. There's no need to be afraid of the anger, either. Real anger is a freeing movement and empowering in itself—a catharsis.

Ro: Have you done any reading on goddess spirituality?

Gary: Oh, yes! It's the basis for a lot of this. See, the patriarchal flow of society deprived us of any knowledge of the goddess for centuries. So now the word "goddess" is contrasted with the word "God," and we set up this competition, this dualism.

Barbara Blaine (Chicago): That's what turned a lot of people off to the feminist liturgy at the national gathering in Milwaukee. So much of the Catholic Worker is built on patriarchal worship. Or at least connected to the institutional, patriarchal church. And so at the liturgy in Milwaukee, where there was the sense of worship of the goddess, people said it was pagan, that we weren't worshiping God because we were worshiping goddess. I think it was a total lack of understanding.

Gary: In their eyes, the real God is this father figure. If it comes to us any other way, we can't identify it.

Ro: Well, if they think about it at all, doesn't everyone have to see that God has no gender, that God is both father and mother? Even the most fundamental fundamentalist has to see that God has no sex.

Gary: Well, neither does the goddess!

Ro: Touché! But the feminist liturgies I've attended have been just as exclusive as a Roman Catholic Mass.

Gary: In what way? What made it exclusive? Just because men weren't there?

Ro: Well, they were definitely about goddess with a gender, usually in the form of a fertility goddess. I saw them as very exclusive, predicated on being "other" and proud of it.

Gary: My understanding would be that, given that it was an all-women gathering, why not celebrate that? Specifically. How many times have you been able to celebrate that in your life? Why can't women want to form exclusive things? That's almost a reactionary excuse, to say they're doing the same thing as the patriarchy does. No, they're *not* doing the same thing. Women need to respond, need to let rage out, and need to build the connections that haven't been allowed. That seems understandable and real and important to me. I suppose it could be an exclusive thing eventually, though. I mean obviously there's a danger.

Barbara: The feminist liturgies that we had in both Catholic Worker national gatherings [Milwaukee in 1986 and Las Vegas in 1987] weren't at all like the one you described, Rosalie.

What draws me into the desire to pray with women is the need for healing. At the Las Vegas liturgy, people broke into pairs and talked to each other about how we needed healing from someone or something hurting us, or from the pain we've caused to someone else. We shared that with one other person, and then we symbolically washed each other with water. Then we each said a prayer for our partner, praying for the healing that the person needed. It was just real powerful. Then there's such a worship of money in Vegas that we also wanted to speak to that in the liturgy, so we burned a dollar bill. It seemed really radical. In fact, we had this big discussion. Someone suggested inviting everybody to throw a dollar bill into this fire. You know, you could easily burn forty or fifty dollars that way. That was too much! We decided we only needed the symbol, so one bill was enough.

In burning the dollar bill, we were praying to be released from the bondage that the dollar has over so many people's lives. In Las Vegas it's all so magnified. People lose *everything!* And then in terms of women—the women who are prostitutes there, you know—and the drugs and alcohol and everything. All the gambling halls are filled with women prancing around, basically in underwear. The sense of objectification. So we were praying for a release from the bondage that the dollar holds over Las Vegas.

Then we lit a new fire and lit a candle from the burning flame to symbolize the new life of freedom that we share. And people shared reflections and prayers. Anyone could light a smaller candle from that candle. It was really neat.

We didn't want to exclude men in any way. One of the criticisms we had about the other liturgy [the "official" one planned for the Las Vegas gathering] was that we as women would feel kind of left out, so we didn't want to turn around and have a liturgy that would make men feel left out. But the very nature of gathering and sharing your stories is real feminine, and something men find difficult to do.

Gary: You know, when we use the word liturgy, we think of Mass. So when you talk about feminist liturgy, you think of feminist Mass.

Barbara: A liturgy isn't always a Mass. It's a gathering of people to worship together.

Gary: I know, but in people's minds, it means Mass.

Barbara: Not in my mind.

Gary: Okay, but we're talking about what people perceive. Should we be doing things like we've always done them? Or just change what we've always done on the outside to make it appealing? Do the people in Las Vegas change what's happening at Mass so Barbara Blaine doesn't feel oppressed? Or do we change what is Mass?

Barbara: Or do you always have to have an alternative?

Gary: That's the heart of the question. The male liturgy has failed because it has oppressed. So some people think of being alternative to it, and some of being protective. How do we take another step beyond? This is where people struggle. Is acting in opposition to something acting from your heart?

Ro: Well, maybe opposition is a stage you have to go through to find your heart.

Barbara: Maybe. I think it's a state that we're in. I would like to think that we as Catholic Workers, as members of this movement, can pray together, can all feel connected in worship. The way the "official" liturgy had been planned for the Las Vegas gathering, that connection didn't seem possible for a number of people. We wanted a liturgy that would include everyone. If the [feminist] one we developed was the only liturgy, that would have been exclusive, too. Because other people feel that they have to have a Mass. That's a part of our movement, also.

Terry Bennett-Cauchon (San Diego): Let me interrupt here. It's really all because of Barbara that both liturgies worked out so well. See, Barbara and I were talking about how it was really obvious that the whole weekend was dominated by males, and that they were using very exclusive language—"God the Father, God the Son." Then she said, "What the Catholic Worker really needs is to sit down and talk about sexism in the Catholic Worker." So we went up to Jeff [Dietrich, one of the organizers of the gathering], and we said we'd like to do a workshop on women in the Worker. He was kind of taken aback because all the workshops had been planned, but we found a space to squeeze it in, and it worked out okay. It was a really open forum and Barb divided us into small groups and handled it really well. There were about fifty to sixty people, most of them women, with five or six men, maybe.

The groups came up with a committee to ask the people who had planned the Mass to make some basic changes like inclusive language, which they did, and women eucharistic ministers, which they did not do. They promised to, but didn't. The Mass ended up to be really nice because they invited everyone up onto the altar and that was exciting. It just represented so well who we are as Catholic Workers who have "stepped out of the pews." We've been called to our life just as much as if we were priests.

Ro: Tina, were you involved in the feminist liturgy at the early conference, the one in Milwaukee?

Tina Sipula (Bloomington, Illinois): Yes.

Ro: What did you think of it? I heard some people walked out.

Tina: I found it wonderful and offensive at the same time. Wonderful for the women, but *not once* was it inclusive of men. I found that very offensive. There are men out there who really desire to become feminists and who are sensitive and wonderful and want to change the world. Unless we reach out to them, we're as bad as the chauvinists.

At the Sugar Creek Midwest retreat last year, the community asked me to preside over the Eucharist. Which was shocking to me. I don't know why they asked me to do that.

Ro: Did you?

Tina: Yes. I took a long walk and sat on the earth and did some meditation and came back to the group very slowly, and they were all waiting. And it was very humbling. It was one of those things where I was really called by the community, and I didn't even know it was going on until it happened. It was wonderful.

Epilogue

Claire Schaeffer-Duffy: I'll never forget Barbara. Barbara was a very well-educated young black woman. I think she'd actually gone to Harvard and had a breakdown at some point. (We never knew anybody's exact story at Mary Harris House.) She was most interested in our politics, most aware of activities in the community. But one time, she started to get very agitated. And she wasn't . . . I didn't know [it] at the time, but I guess she hadn't been taking her medication. (I was so young I didn't even know what medications were.)

Anyway, she left the house one night. And it was . . . her anger towards me was building. I was one of the targets. She said, "I'll be back at ten if I'm not in jail for hurting some white bitch." Well, she didn't come back till about three that morning. I was sleeping downstairs on the couch, and she turned the light on in the kitchen and started to cook something. (I had kind of increased the rules and one of them was that you couldn't go in the kitchen and cook at three o'clock in the morning. People slept right in the next room, and they couldn't sleep with all that racket.) I went in to tell her to turn the light out, and she shoved me against the window.

She was very angry. I began walking slowly towards the phone to call the police. (Which we did a lot. I don't know if that was moral or not but, anyway, we did.) But I didn't get to the phone because she pushed me down on the couch and started to hit me in the head. The other woman sleeping in the front room went for the phone, and she was threatened, too, so the phone was kind of left dangling, which was a really awful sensation.

Barbara picked up a chair and threatened to hit me over the head. "Death would be too good for you. I just ought to fuck you up."

Scott had told me, "If you're ever being beaten, cover your head." So I put my head down and covered it with my arm. Then she put the chair down and started to talk about all kinds of things, about all her grievances with me. For *two hours!* And some of it was legitimate. "What do you think you can prove, coming to the ghetto and putting on a facade of poverty and trying to be like us? You can *never* be like us. You can never experience what we experience." And she told me some of her experiences. They were awful. She was active in the civil rights struggle, and her life had been threatened because of her politics. One story was that somebody had jimmied with her brakes. Well, she went on and on for two hours. It was hellish.

Of course everybody was trying to work with her, trying to calm her down, particularly one of the other guests who had been close to her. That woman was an example of a needful person who really rose to an incredible stature when *she* was needed. She was the one person Barbara could trust at that moment and finally they both left the house together.

I left that afternoon. Well, thank God I did because she came back with a kitchen knife. Went upstairs and was still ranting away. These poor women—all of them on the street, you know—it would be understandable if they'd fight back or act excitedly, but they were tremendous. They just talked very calmly to her. "Now, Barbara, you don't want to do that. You don't want to hurt anybody." They didn't do anything to provoke her, which was the smartest thing.

When I came back that Sunday, I saw the TV screen that she'd smashed with a bottle. She was later committed to the hospital but then released, and I always had this fear of running into her 'cause we were never able to . . . to reconcile that encounter.

Now this happened . . . oh, it must have been in '83 or so. In January of '85, we're married and moved to Worcester, and who do I see but Barbara on the street of Worcester! There she was on the steps of the library. It was like something out of Dostoyevsky. I practically had a heart attack, but she was very calm. And the exchange was good. She asked me what I was doing and I told her, and she kind of tittered.

"Well, have you gone to law school like your father wanted?" And I said I hadn't, but I was able to honestly say I had thought about some of the things she'd said that night and that there was truth in them. And there was. I mean it was a harsh message, but it was true. I could never be like her, and it's fake to attempt it. I had to realize that much of what I was doing was pretense compared to what the women I lived with were going through.

So we had this one encounter, and then I was getting close to delivery with Justin, and I saw her again in the library. She was happy that I was pregnant. It was a May night, and she asked me how things were going. And I said, "Well, it's all right. I've got some contractions, but I don't think it's genuine labor. And I've had some swelling."

Of course, when you're pregnant everybody tells you the worst-case scenario. I don't know why they do that but people do, you know. Now this woman is very, very bright, and she said dramatically, "You'd better watch out for that swelling. It could be toxemia. That's the one thing where you can deliver a healthy baby and the mother can die." Just like that.

So I went home that night, and I was somewhat agitated by this message. I had nightmares, and some of them were around what she was saying and around her. Then I woke up very early in the morning, and these little contractions were happening regularly, so I called the hospital.

They said, "Well, it's probably nothing, but come on in." Now my pregnancy had gone very well, and I was going to walk a couple of miles and clean house that day, which I'd been doing all along. But instead we went to the hospital. And they said right away, "You can't leave! Your blood pressure is up. Everything is off!"

I *did* have pre-eclampsia, which is toxemia. And I would have had no idea—absolutely none—that anything was wrong if it hadn't been for Barbara. The worst thing you can do in that condition is to stay on your feet, so they kept me on bed rest until I delivered. And everything was okay, thank God!

Most people never experience an angel warning them the way my angel warned me. Fortunately, I was able to see Barbara after Justin was born, and I told her that I'd always be indebted to her. Barbara saved my life.

Persons Interviewed

The names below reflect the signatures on interview agreements. The names preceded by an asterisk are included in the text. Complete transcripts of all interviews have been deposited in the Catholic Worker Archives, Marquette University, Milwaukee, Wisconsin.

*Charlie Angus (husband of Lauren
   Griffin)
*Carole Arett
*Fr. Michael (Mike) Baxter
 Fr. Robert Begin
 Leo Bennett-Cauchon
*Terry Bennett-Cauchon
*Ade Bethune
*Willa Bickham
*Barbara Blaine
 Luke Bobbitt (son of Wendy Bobbitt)
 Wendy Bobbitt
*Darla Bradley
 George Brannon (deceased)
*Br. David Buer
*Patricia (Patty) Burns
 Anne L. Carter
 Bolen J. Carter (deceased)
 Marcia Cartwright
*Gayle Catinella
*Sr. Janice (Jan) Cebula
*Bob Chaps
*Teka Childress
 Paula Civiok
*Richard Cleaver
*Louise Cochran (wife of Jim Levinson)
*Dennis J. Coday

 Karl E. Coffin
*John Cooper
*Angela L. Cordaro
*Fr. Frank Cordaro
*Tom Cordaro
*Monica R. Cornell
*Thomas C. (Tom) Cornell
 Judy Corrigan
 William H. Corrigan
*John C. Cort
*Patrick G. (Pat) Coy
*Anne Crowell
 Michael D. Cullen
 Annette (Nettie) Cullen
 Ralph Delaney (deceased)
*Becky Delany (daughter of Dan and
   Chris Delany)
*Chris Delany
*Dan Delany
*Richard C. (Dick) Dieter (husband of
   Maggie Louden)
*Robert Jefferson (Jeff) Dietrich
   (husband of Catherine Morris)
*Donna Domiziano
*Gary Donatelli
*Virginia Druhe
 Mary Durnin

*Jerry Ebner
*James (Jim) Eder
*Eileen Egan
*Marc H. Ellis
*Robert Ellsberg
*Jane R. Emerson
*Charles (Charlie) Engelstein
Lucille Evans
*Dr. Arthur G. Falls
*Edgar (Ed) Forand
*Jim Forest
*Susan J. Frankel (Sue Frankel-Streit)
Lloyd Friedrich
Richard Gariepy
*Margaret Q. (Quigley) Garvey
*Michael O. (Mike) Garvey
*Dorothy Gauchat
*Fr. Bernard E. (Bernie) Gilgun
Brigette M. Goulet
Marlys A. Graettinger
*Linda Greenwald
*William (Bill) Griffin
*Lauren Griffin (wife of Charlie Angus)
Dagmar Grove
*Michael Harrington (deceased)
*Sr. Ruth Heaney, O.S.B.
Judith A. Hewitt
Lorine Hewson
Marilyn Hood
Mike Humphrey
*Margaret A. (Meg) Hyre
*Bob Imholt
*Angela Jones (wife of Mark White)
*Kathleen D. Jordan
*Patrick (Pat) Jordan
*Fr. John J. (Jack) Keehan
*Betsy Keenan (wife of Brian Terrell)
*James J. (Jim) Kelly
*Peter King (husband of Ann O'Connor)
*Jonathan Kirkendall
Heike Kirsten

*Sr. Anna Koop
Cindy Kurfman
David Kurfman
*Marilyn J. Klein (Lynn Lassalle-Klein)
*Robert A. Lassalle (Bob
Lassalle-Klein)
*Mary Lathrop
*Br. Michael P. Leahy (deceased)
Matthew Lee
Joe Lehner
*Jim Levinson (husband of Louise
Cochran)
*Tom Lewis
Jeffrey A. Leys
*Margaret Ann (Maggie) Louden (wife
of Dick Dieter)
*Fr. Thomas (Tom) Lumpkin
*Debbie McQuade
*Fr. Richard R. McSorley
*Fr. Raymond (Ray) McVey
*Sr. Char Madigan
John Magee
*Dr. Margaret Magee
*Paul J. Magno, Jr.
*John Mahoney
*Pauline B. (Polly) Mahoney
*Judith Malina
*Ed Marciniak
*Daniel Marshall
*Al Mascia
*Charles L. (Chuck) Matthei
*Sr. Monica May, S.N.D.
*Patti McKee
*Kathleen (Kathe) McKenna
*Karl Meyer
*Kenna Lee Meyer (deceased)
*Mary Kay Meyer
*Mark A. Miller
*Peter J. Miron-Conk
*Chris Montesano
*Joan Montesano

*Nina Polcyn Moore
*Catherine Morris (wife of Jeff Dietrich)
*Justine R. Murphy (deceased)
Louis J. (Lou) Murphy (deceased)
*Mary K. Murray
*Patrick (Pat) Murray
*Jeannette Noel
*Julia Occhiogrosso
*Ann O'Connor (wife of Peter King)
Cynthia O'Connor
*James (Jim) O'Gara
*Joan F. O'Gara
Patricia (Pat) Oliss
*Gary Olivero (deceased)
Hazen Ordway (deceased)
*Rio Betz Parfrey
Rochelle M. Parnes
Gertrude Paul
*Martin (Marty) Paul
*Claire A. Pearson (wife of David
Specht)
Kay M. Peters (wife of Larry
Ray-Keil)
*Mary Ann Phelps
*Utah Phillips
*Julian R. Pleasants
*Mary Jane Pleasants
*Denise Plunkett
*Lawrence P. (Larry) Purcell
*Charles J. (Chuck) Quilty
*Larry Ray-Keil (husband of Kay
Peters)
*Ellen Rehg
*Jo Roberts
*Mary Teresa (Terry) Rogers
*Kathleen Rumpf
*Jane Sammon
*Sr. Caroline Sanchez, S.N.D.
*Claire Schaeffer-Duffy
*Scott Schaeffer-Duffy
*Peggy Scherer

*Mary Aileen Schmeil
Joseph A. Schuster
Norman Searah
Bill Shepherd
Mary Shepherd
*Christine (Chris) Shepherd (daughter
of Bill and Mary Shepherd)
*Patricia (Pat) Sher
Steve F. Sheridan
Karen Shields
*Kathy Shuh-Ries
*Tina Sipula
*Stephen (Steve) Soucy
*David Specht (husband of Claire
Pearson)
Stephen Stachelek
*Kate Stanton
*David Stein
Anne Marie Stokes
*Robert H. (Bob) Tavani
*Katherine (Kassie) Temple
*Brian Terrell (husband of Betsy
Keenan)
Helen J. Tichy
*Marcia A. Timmel
*Don Timmerman
*Chuck Trapkus
Chuck Tuptka
Frank Wolfarth Walsh
*Kate Walsh (daughter of Willa Bickham
and Brendan Walsh)
*Charles C. Walzem
*Florence A. Weinfurter
*Mary West
*Mark White (husband of Angela Jones)
*John Williams
Laura A. Winton
Bettina Wortman
Janet C. Zajac
*Mary Alice (Alice) Zarrella
*Joe Zarrella

Albert Zook
*Joachim H. Zwick (son of Louise and Mark Zwick)

*Louise Zwick
*Mark L. Zwick
Spike Zywicki

Houses of Hospitality

Arizona

Andre House of Hospitality
PO Box 2014
Phoenix, AZ 85001

Casa Maria
401 E. 26th St.
Tucson, AZ 85713

California

Los Angeles Catholic Worker
    Community
Ammon Hennacy House
632 N. Brittania St.
Los Angeles, CA 90033

Hospitality Kitchen
821 E. 6th St.
PO Box 21471
Los Angeles, CA 90033

Oakland Catholic Worker
4848 E. 14th St.
Oakland, CA 94601

Bethany House of Hospitality
PO Box 5427
Oakland, CA 94605

Andre House
5912 Genda St.
Oakland, CA 94608

Elizabeth House
1505 Everett
Oakland, CA 94530

Redwood City Catholic Worker House
545 Cassia St.
PO Box 513
Redwood City, CA 94063

Sacramento Catholic Worker
619 12th St.
Sacramento, CA 95814

Franciscan Workers of Junipero Serra
715 Jefferson St.
Salinas, CA 93905

San Diego Catholic Worker
3159 Imperial Ave.
PO Box 127244
San Diego, CA 92104

Martin de Porres House of Hospitality
225 Potrero Ave.
San Francisco, CA 94103

Casa de Clara
318 N. 6th St.
San Jose, CA 95112

Immanuel House of Hospitality
311 S. Main St.
Santa Ana, CA 92701

This list was updated in December 1992 from the list that appeared in the May 1992 *Catholic Worker.* Some of these communities, while not actually Catholic Workers, have chosen to affiliate themselves with the movement.

Santa Rosa Catholic Worker
PO Box 3364
Santa Rosa, CA 95402

Catholic Worker Farm
PO Box 53
Sheep Ranch, CA 95250

Colorado

Denver Catholic Worker
2420 Welton St.
Denver, CO 80205

Connecticut

Thomas Merton House
43 Madison Ave.
Bridgeport, CT 06604

Dorothy Day Hospitality House
11 Spring St.
PO Box 922
Danbury, CT 06813

St. Vincent de Paul Place
617 Main St.
PO Box 398
Middletown, CT 06457

New Covenant House of Hospitality
PO Box 10883
Stamford, CT 06904

Guadalupe House
79 Beacon St.
Waterbury, CT 06704

Washington, D.C.

St. Francis Catholic Worker
1115 6th St. NW
Washington, DC 20001

Llewellyn Scott House of Hospitality
1305 T St. NW
Washington, DC 20009

Mary Harris Catholic Worker
939 T St. NW
Washington, DC 20001

Dorothy Day Catholic Worker
503 Rock Creek Church Rd. NW
Washington, DC 20010

Olive Branch Community
1006 M St. NW
Washington, DC 20001

Florida

St. Francis House of Hospitality
PO Box 533954
Orlando, FL 32853

Georgia

The Open Door Community
910 Ponce de Leon Ave. NE
Atlanta, GA 30306

Illinois

Clare House of Hospitality
703 East Washington St.
Bloomington, IL 61701

St. Jude Catholic Worker House
317 S. Randolph St.
PO Box 1612
Champaign, IL 61820

St. Elizabeth Catholic Worker
8025 S. Honore
Chicago, IL 60620

St. Catherine of Genoa Catholic Worker
842 E. 65th St.
PO Box 377585
Chicago, IL 60637

Peace House
1460 W. Carmen
Chicago, IL 60640

St. Francis of Assisi House of
Hospitality
4652 N. Kenmore
Chicago, IL 60640

Su Casa Catholic Worker
5045 S. Laflin St.
Chicago, IL 60609

Peoria Catholic Worker
225 S. Saratoga St.
Peoria, IL 61605

Dorothy Day Catholic Worker
901 20th St.
Rock Island, IL 61201

Indiana

House of Bread and Peace
516 Adams Ave.
PO Box 2455
Evansville, IN 47713

Holy Family Catholic Worker
502 N. Notre Dame Ave.
South Bend, IN 46617

Harvest House of Hospitality
437 Main St.
Tell City, IN 47586

Iowa

St. John of the Cross Catholic
Worker House
1027 5th Ave. SE
Cedar Rapids, IA 52403

Des Moines Catholic Worker
PO Box 4551
Des Moines, IA 50306

Casa Canción de Maria Catholic Worker
382 E. 21st St.
Dubuque, IA 52001

Strangers and Guests Catholic Worker
Community
PO Box 264
Maloy, IA 50852

St. Francis Catholic Worker
PO Box 1533
Waterloo, IA 50704

Kansas

Emmaus House
802 N. 5th St.
Garden City, KS 67846

Shalom Catholic Worker House
2100 N. 13th St.
Kansas City, KS 66104

Maine

H.O.M.E. (Homeworkers Organized for
More Employment)
Orland, ME 04472

Maryland

Baltimore Catholic Worker
Viva House
26 S. Mount St.
Baltimore, MD 21223

Massachusetts

Haley House
23 Dartmouth St.
Boston, MA 02116

Noonday Farm
PO Box 71
Winchendon Springs, MA 01477

St. Francis and St. Therese Catholic
Worker
52 Mason St.
Worcester, MA 01610

The Mustard Seed
PO Box 2592
Worcester, MA 01613

Michigan

Detroit Catholic Worker Community
Day House
2640 Trumbull Ave.
Detroit, MI 48216

Loaves and Fishes Hospitality House
1718 Presque Isle Ave.
Marquette, MI 49855

Minnesota

Loaves and Fishes Catholic Worker
1712 Jefferson St.
Duluth, MN 55812

Hannah House
1705 Jefferson
Duluth, MN 55812

St. Joseph House
2101 Portland Ave. South
Minneapolis, MN 55404

Dorothy Day House of Hospitality
714 8th St. South
Moorhead, MN 56560

Dorothy Day Hospitality House
703 SW 1st St.
Rochester, MN 55902

Dorothy Day Center
183 Old 6th St.
St. Paul, MN 55102

Winona Catholic Worker
251 E. Wabasha St.
Winona, MN 55987

Missouri

St. Francis House
901 Rangeline
Columbia, MO 65201

Z. Lois Bryant House
913 Rangeline
Columbia, MO 65201

Loaves and Fishes Soup Kitchen
306 Park Ave.
Columbia, MO 65201

Holy Family House
908 E. 31st St.
Kansas City, MO 64109

St. Louis Catholic Worker Community
Karen House
1840 Hogan St.
St. Louis, MO 63106

The Little House
(a.k.a. Ella Dixon House)
1538 N. 17th St.
St. Louis, MO 63106

Nebraska

Dorothy Day Catholic Worker
801 N. 20th
PO Box 31022
Omaha, NE 68131

Mary Farm
RR #2 Box 78
Wisner, NE 68791

Nevada

Las Vegas Catholic Worker
St. John the Baptist House
500 W. Van Buren
Las Vegas, NV 89106

New Jersey

Leavenhouse
644 State St.
Camden, NJ 08102

Corpus Christi Ministries
D'Agosta House
89 Summit Ave.
PO Box 16057
Journal Square Station
Jersey City, NJ 07306

New York

Zacchaeus House
89 Pine St.
Binghamton, NY 13901

Peter Maurin Farm
Rt. 1 Box 80
Lattintown Rd.
Marlboro, NY 12542

Maryhouse
55 E. 3rd St.
New York, NY 10003

St. Joseph House
36 E. 1st St.
New York, NY 10003

Sisters of the Good Shepherd
Cor Maria
251 W. 14th St.
New York, NY 10011

Catholic Worker of Niagara Falls
931 Niagara Ave.
Niagara Falls, NY 14305

Unity Acres
Rt. 2 Box 153
Orwell, NY 13426

St. Joseph's House of Hospitality
402 South Ave.
PO Box 1062
Rochester, NY 14603

Bethany House
169 St. Bridget's Dr.
Rochester, NY 14605

Unity Kitchen Community of the
  Catholic Worker
385 W. Onondaga St.
PO Box 650
Syracuse, NY 13202

Hesed House
167 Palmer Ave.
Syracuse, NY 13204

Catholic Worker on Wheels
124 Wadsworth St.
Syracuse, NY 13203

Slocum House
208 Slocum Ave.
Syracuse, NY 13204

Casa de la Paz
63 Jamaica Ave.
Wyandanch, LI, NY 11798

North Carolina

St. Martin de Porres Catholic Worker
6615 Old Stage Rd.
Raleigh, NC 27603

Ohio

Dorothy Day House
Xavier University
Cincinnati, OH 45207

St. Francis/St. Joseph Catholic Worker
1437 Walnut St.
Cincinnati, OH 45210

Dorothy Day Diner
528 E. 13th St.
PO Box 10105
Cincinnati, OH 45210

St. Herman's Monastery and House of
Hospitality
PO Box 6448
Cleveland, OH 44101

St. Francis Catholic Worker
877 E. 150th St.
Cleveland, OH 44110

Whitman House
3601 Whitman Ave.
Cleveland, OH 44113

Catholic Worker Storefront
4241 Lorain Ave.
Cleveland, OH 44113

Casa San José
2040 W. 41st St.
Cleveland, OH 44113

Elizabeth House
1703 W. 32nd
Cleveland, OH 44113

Micah House
153 Martin Ave.
Columbus, OH 43222

Joe's Place
281 Keenan Rd.
Peninsula, OH 44264

Pennsylvania

Sr. Peter Claver House
430 W. Jefferson St.
Philadelphia, PA 19122

Jubilee Soup Kitchen
PO Box 42251
Pittsburgh, PA 15203

Thomas Merton Center
Ministry for Justice and Peace
5125 Penn Ave.
Pittsburgh, PA 15224

Duncan and Porter House
1332 Sheffield St.
Pittsburgh, PA 15233

Rhode Island

Advent House
191 Linwood Ave.
PO Box 3099
Providence, RI 02907

Texas

Austin Catholic Worker
Mary House
PO Box 684185
Austin, TX 78768

Jonah House
1011 Hutchins Rd.
Dallas, TX 75203

Casa Juan Diego
PO Box 70113
Houston, TX 77270

San Antonio Catholic Worker
622 E. Nolan St.
San Antonio, TX 78202

Tabor Community
2718 Monterey
San Antonio, TX 78207

Virginia

Norfolk Catholic Worker
Sadako Sasaki House of Hospitality
1321 W. 38th St.
Norfolk, VA 23508

Freedom House
302 W. Canal St.
PO Box 12144
Richmond, VA 23241

Washington

Bethlehem Farm
508 Coal Creek Road
Chehalis, WA 98532

Bread and Roses Catholic Worker
1320 E. 8th Ave. SE
PO Box 2699
Olympia, WA 98507

The Family Kitchen
331 17th Ave. East
Seattle, WA 98112

Suquamish Catholic Worker
PO Box 793
Suquamish, WA 98392

Tacoma Catholic Worker
Guadalupe House
1417 S. G St.
Tacoma, WA 98405

West Virginia

Tyra Dunn Catholic Worker Farm
HC 73, Box 49-A
Alderson, WV 24910

John Filligar Catholic Worker Farm
Route 7 Box 48-F
Alderson, WV 24910

Alderson Hospitality House
203 High St.
PO Box 579
Alderson, WV 24910

Wisconsin

Anathoth Community Farm
2423 Round Lake Road
Luck, WI 54853

Casa Maria
1131 N. 21st St.
PO Box 05206
Milwaukee, WI 53205

Catholic Worker Archives
Memorial Library
Marquette University
1415 W. Wisconsin Ave.
Milwaukee, WI 53233

Rising Sun Gardens
Rt. 1 Box 1110
Soldiers Grove, WI 54655

Mary House
3559 Co. Highway G
Wisconsin Dells, WI 53965

Australia

West End Catholic Worker
269 Boundary St.
PO Box 187
West End, Brisbane
4101 Queensland, Australia

Canada

Zacchaeus House
186 Mutual St.
Toronto, Ontario, M5B 2B3, Canada

Benedict Labre House
308 Young St.
Montreal, PQ, H3C 2G2, Canada

St. Lawrence House of Hospitality
220 Hughson St.
North Hamilton, Ontario, L8L 4M3,
Canada

Uncle Louie's Catholic Worker
#6 1017 22nd St.
West Saskatoon, Saskatchewan, S7M
0S2, Canada

England

St. Francis House
9 Minster Road
Oxford, OX4 1LX, England

Germany

Dortmund Catholic Worker
An der Palmweide 114
46 Dortmund 50, Germany

Netherlands

Jeanette Nöel Catholic Worker Huis
Köningshoef 340
1104 EN Amsterdam, Netherlands

1992 Aims and Means of the Catholic Worker Movement

The aim of the Catholic Worker movement is to live in accordance with the justice and charity of Jesus Christ. Our sources are the Hebrew and Greek Scriptures as handed down in the teachings of the Roman Catholic Church, with our inspiration coming from the lives of the saints, "men and women outstanding in holiness, living witnesses to Your unchanging love." (Eucharistic Prayer)

This aim requires us to begin living in a different way. We recall the words of our founders, Dorothy Day who said, "God meant things to be much easier than we have made them," and Peter Maurin who wanted to build a society "where it is easier for people to be good."

When we examine our society, which is generally called capitalist (because of its methods of producing and controlling wealth) and is bourgeois (because of prevailing concern for acquisition and material interests, and its emphasis on respectability and mediocrity) we find it far from God's justice.

In economics, private and state capitalism bring about an unjust distribution of the wealth, for the profit motive guides decisions. Those in power live off the sweat of another's brow, while those without power are robbed of a just return for their work. Usury (the charging of interest above administrative costs) is a major contributor to the wrong-doing intrinsic to this system. We note especially how the world debt crisis leads poor countries into greater deprivation and a dependency from which there is no foreseeable escape. Here at home, the number of hungry and homeless and unemployed people rises in the midst of increasing affluence.

In labor, human need is no longer the reason for human work. Instead, the unbridled expansion of technology, necessary to capitalism and viewed as "progress," holds sway. Jobs are concentrated in productivity and administration for a "high-tech," war-related, consumer society of disposable goods, so that laborers

This document is reprinted as it appears in the May 1992 *Catholic Worker.*

are trapped in work that does not contribute to human welfare. Furthermore, as jobs become more specialized, many people are excluded from meaningful work or are alienated from the products of their labor. Even in farming, agribusiness has replaced agriculture, and, in all areas, moral restraints are run over roughshod, and a disregard for the laws of nature now threatens the very planet.

In politics, the state functions to control and regulate life. Its power has burgeoned hand in hand with growth in technology, so that military, scientific and corporate interests get the highest priority when concrete political policies are formulated. Because of the sheer size of institutions, we tend towards government by bureaucracy; that is, government by nobody. Bureaucracy, in all areas of life, is not only impersonal, but also makes accountability, and, therefore, an effective political forum for redressing grievances, next to impossible.

In morals, relations between people are corrupted by distorted images of the human person. Class, race and sex often determine personal worth and position within society, leading to structures that foster oppression. Capitalism further divides society by pitting owners against workers in perpetual conflict over wealth and its control. Those who do not "produce" are abandoned, and left, at best, to be "processed" through institutions. Spiritual destitution is rampant, manifested in isolation, madness, promiscuity and violence.

The arms race stands as a clear sign of the direction and spirit of our age. It has extended the domain of destruction and the fear of annihilation, and denies the basic right to life. There is a direct connection between the arms race and destitution. "The arms race is an utterly treacherous trap for humanity, and one which injures the poor to an intolerable degree." (Vatican II)

In contrast to what we see around us, as well as within ourselves, stands St. Thomas Aquinas' doctrine of the Common Good, a vision of a society where the good of each member is bound to the good of the whole in the service of God.

To this end, we advocate:

Personalism, a philosophy which regards the freedom and dignity of each person as the basis, focus and goal of all metaphysics and morals. In following such wisdom, we move away from a self-centered individualism toward the good of the other. This is to be done by taking personal responsibility for changing conditions, rather than looking to the state or other institutions to provide impersonal "charity." We pray for a Church renewed by this philosophy and for a time when all those who feel excluded from participation are welcomed with love, drawn by the gentle personalism Peter Maurin taught.

A decentralized society in contrast to the present bigness of government, industry, education, health care and agriculture. We encourage efforts such as family farms, rural and urban land trusts, worker ownership and management of small factories, homesteading projects, food, housing and other cooperatives—any effort in which money can once more become merely a medium of exchange, and human beings are no longer commodities.

A *"green revolution,"* so that it is possible to rediscover the proper meaning of our labor and our true bonds with the land; a distributist communitarianism, self-sufficient through farming, crafting and appropriate technology; a radically new society where people will rely on the fruits of their own soil and labor; associations of mutuality, and a sense of fairness to resolve conflicts.

We believe this needed personal and social transformation should be pursued by the means Jesus revealed in His sacrificial love. With Christ as our Exemplar, by prayer and communion with His Body and Blood, we strive for the practices of:

Nonviolence. "Blessed are the peacemakers, for they shall be called children of God." (Matt. 5:9) Only through nonviolent action can a personalist revolution come about, one in which one evil will not be replaced simply by another. Thus, we oppose the deliberate taking of human life for any reason, and see every oppression as blasphemy. Jesus taught us to take suffering upon ourselves rather than inflict it upon others, and He calls us to fight against violence with the spiritual weapons of prayer, fasting and noncooperation with evil. Refusal to pay taxes for war, to register for conscription, to comply with any unjust legislation; participation in nonviolent strikes and boycotts, protests or vigils; withdrawal of support for dominant systems, corporate funding or usurious practices are all excellent means to establish peace.

The works of mercy (as found in Matt. 25:31–46) are at the heart of the Gospel and they are clear mandates for our response to "the least of our brothers and sisters." Houses of hospitality are centers for learning to do the acts of love, so that the poor can receive what is, in justice, theirs: the second coat in our closet, the spare room in our home, a place at our table. Anything beyond what we immediately need belongs to those who go without.

Manual labor in a society that rejects it as undignified and inferior. "Besides inducing cooperation, besides overcoming barriers and establishing the spirit of sister- and brotherhood (besides just getting things done), manual labor enables us to use our body as well as our hands, our minds." (Dorothy Day) The Benedictine motto *"Ora et Labora"* reminds us that the work of human hands is a gift for the edification of the world and the glory of God.

Voluntary poverty. "The mystery of poverty is that by sharing in it, making ourselves poor in giving to others, we increase our knowledge and belief in love." (Dorothy Day) By embracing voluntary poverty, that is, by casting our lot freely with those whose impoverishment is not a choice, we would ask for the grace to abandon ourselves to the love of God. It would put us on the path to incarnate the Church's "preferential option for the poor."

We must be prepared to accept seeming failure with these aims, for sacrifice and suffering are part of the Christian life. Success, as the world determines it, is not the final criterion for judgment. The most important thing is the love of Jesus Christ and how to live His truth.

Select Bibliography

Coles, Robert. *The Call of Stories: Teaching and the Moral Imagination.* Boston: Houghton Mifflin, 1989.

————. *Dorothy Day: A Radical Devotion.* Reading, Mass.: Addison-Wesley, 1987.

Coles, Robert, and Jon Erikson. *A Spectacle Unto the World: The Catholic Worker Movement.* New York: Viking, 1973.

Coy, Patrick, ed. *A Revolution of the Heart: Essays on the Catholic Worker.* Philadelphia: Temple University Press, 1988.

Day, Dorothy. *Loaves and Fishes.* New York: Harper & Row, 1963.

————. *The Long Loneliness.* New York: Harper & Row, 1952.

Dietrich, Jeff. *Reluctant Resister.* Greensboro, N.C.: Unicorn Press, 1983.

Ellis, Marc. *Peter Maurin: Prophet in the Twentieth Century.* New York: Paulist Press, 1981.

————. *A Year at the Catholic Worker.* New York: Paulist Press, 1978.

Ellsberg, Robert, ed. *By Little and By Little: The Selected Writings of Dorothy Day.* New York: Alfred A. Knopf, 1983. Reprinted as *Dorothy Day: Selected Writings.* Maryknoll, New York, Orbis Books, 1992.

Forest, Jim. *Love Is the Measure.* New York: Paulist Press, 1986.

Frisch, Michael. *Shared Authority.* Buffalo: State University of New York Press, 1990.

Gray, Francine du Plessix. *Divine Disobedience: Profiles in Catholic Radicalism.* New York: Random House, 1969.

Harrington, Michael. *The Other America: Poverty in the United States.* Baltimore: Penguin, 1977.

Hennacy, Ammon. *The Book of Ammon.* N.p.: Hennacy, 1965.

Klejment, Anne, and Alice Klejment. *Dorothy Day and the Catholic Worker: A Bibliography and Index.* New York: Garland Press, 1985.

McNeal, Patricia. *The American Catholic Peace Movement, 1928–1972.* New York: Arno, 1978.

————. *Harder than War: Catholic Peacemaking in Twentieth-Century America.* New Brunswick, N.J.: Rutgers University Press, 1992.

Maurin, Peter. *Easy Essays.* Chicago: Franciscan Herald Press, 1977.

Miller, William D. *Dorothy Day: A Biography.* San Francisco: Harper & Row, 1982.

————. *A Harsh and Dreadful Love: Dorothy Day and the Catholic Worker Movement.* New York: Liveright, 1972.

Murray, Harry. *Do Not Neglect Hospitality: The Catholic Worker and the Homeless.* Philadelphia: Temple University Press, 1990.

Piehl, Mel. *Breaking Bread: The Catholic Worker and the Origin of Catholic Radicalism in America.* Philadelphia: Temple University Press, 1982.

Roberts, Nancy L. *Dorothy Day and the "Catholic Worker."* Albany: State University of New York Press, 1984.

Terkel, Studs. *Hard Times: An Oral History of the Great Depression.* New York: Pantheon, 1986.

Zahn, Gordon C. *Another Part of the War: The Camp Simon Story.* Amherst: University of Massachusetts Press, 1979.

Index